Modern Hotel Operations Management

Michael N. Chibili (Ed.)

Authors:
Latifa Benhadda
Shane de Bruyn
Michael N. Chibili
Conrad Lashley
Saskia Penninga
Bill Rowson

Noordhoff Uitgevers Groningen/Houten

Design (cover and inside matter): G2K, Groningen, The Netherlands
Cover illustration: Getty Images, Londen, UK

If you have any comments or queries about this or any other publication, please
contact Noordhoff Uitgevers BV, Afdeling Hoger Onderwijs, Antwoordnummer 13, 9700
VB Groningen, The Netherlands, e-mail: info@noordhoff.nl

0 / 16

Printed in Canada
ISBN 978-90-01-87890-0
NUR 801

Foreword

Hotel operations are chiefly concerned with providing accommodation, food and drink services. This requires managers to have a good understanding of room, restaurant and kitchen operations. In some hotels, these core services are augmented with leisure and fitness facilities, or with conference and banqueting services that attract additional guests and revenue. In some cases, the customer experience requires employees having a direct interface with customers. These 'front-of-house' operations involve services produced in the presence of customers. Reception, restaurant, bar, and concierge services are all examples of settings where hotel employees and their activities are on display. Staff performance has an immediate impact on customer experience, and can thereby influence levels of customer satisfaction and dissatisfaction. In other cases, services are produced 'back-of-house'; customers rarely see the production processes involved taking place. Kitchen services and laundry are the most obvious examples: customers do not usually see the food being cooked, or items being laundered. Housekeeping and room cleaning represent something of an 'in-between world' as guests are not typically present when the room attendant services the room. The hotel room is 'front-of-house' because it is where guests 'consume' the accommodation service, but it does have a 'back-of-house' dimension since the guest is not present when the room is being serviced for next night's sleep. These various services and settings found in hotel exploitation mean that a hotel manager's work is complex and requires a familiarity with a range of operational skills.

While the aspects of 'front-of-house' and 'back-of-house' feature in most hotels, the service levels and intensity of customer contact varies across hotel service types and brands. The size and complexity of the food, drinks and accommodations offered to guests range from simple and quite limited, e.g. budget brands, to more complex and elaborate, e.g. luxury hotels. Budget brands have been a growing phenomenon in recent decades. Their key focus has been providing dependable accommodation including *en-suite* facilities, but with limited additional services. Self check-in is a feature of some groups, while vending machines or food services limited to a simple buffet style breakfast are common in other establishments of this nature. These simpler services require low staffing levels and, in some cases, routine unskilled labour. Luxury hotels typically offer a more personalised service, à la carte restaurants, cocktail bars and accommodation with dedicated butlers and servants, all requiring the employment of highly skilled and trained personnel. Therefore, a manager's particular tasks will be a function of the hotel's service level and brand offered to clients. Essentially, however, a hotel manager's role is concerned with the same arrays of issues: managing the delivery of food, beverage and accommodation services; ensuring service quality standards match guest expectations; managing the employees who produce these services; and cost minimisation, income generation, and profit maximisation.

These operational dimensions of the hotel manager's role, however, are just one branch of the managerial skill set needed. First and foremost, a hotel is a business; it needs to operate within commercial boundaries, minimise costs, increase revenue and maximise profits. That being said, there are some unusual features of the hotel business in that its services are perishable and intangible. Additionally, they cannot easily be stockpiled during off-peak hours, to be used when demand increases. Hotels have to be managed in such a way as to ensure maximum revenue every day. Demand patterns are often difficult to predict and are influenced by forces beyond a manager's control; yet any room not sold on a specific day is an opportunity lost forever. The parallel with passenger planes is clear, and like managers of airline organisations, hotel managers are concerned with levels of occupancy and revenue management. The ideal position, where every room is sold at the official room rate, is rarely achieved; a hotel manager is typically concerned with maximising revenue on any one day. Price discounting and forward selling to accommodation agents are two techniques used, but there is no magic formula. Hence, hotel managers are making judgments day by day to maximise the average revenue per room. Edited by Michael N. Chibili, the chapters are authored or co-authored as shown in this foreword.

The Hospitality Industry – Past, Present and Future – Michael N. Chibili provides an oversight of the hotel sector's history and traditions. This chapter shows that providing accommodation from a home base is a by-product of travel. As people began trading goods across increasing distances, there was a need for accommodation at regular points along the journey; these origins have shaped much of the industry's features still used today. Hotel locations are often at a point of destination or along travel routes. The chapter discusses these origins with current trends and developments in hotel provision.

Rating Systems and the Structure of the Hospitality Industry – Michael N. Chibili explores the issue of hotel rating systems. Hotel ratings, or rankings, provide potential visitors with an idea of what a hotel offers in terms of facilities or services. This is particularly valuable for travellers who are planning trips to unfamiliar destinations. Rating systems help meet customer security needs as they help guests develop an understanding of what to expect. That being said, there are a number of different systems across the globe and definitions of what constitutes a particular star ranking are not universally agreed upon.

Hotel Management – Viewed from Above – Michael N. Chibili discusses typical hotel structures where the general manager is supported by a team running the immediate operational departments, such as food and beverage or rooms departments. In larger hotels, there is likely to be a number of other supporting departments; human resource management, accounting, revenue management, reservations, and the like. Larger hotels may contain several tiers between frontline service staff and the general manager. This in turn creates problems for communication and necessitates the creation of a culture dedicated to the aims and objectives of the hotel.

The Rooms Department – Saskia Penninga and Michael N. Chibili explore the specific operational issues associated with providing guests with accommodation. The precise nature of service standards covering both tangible and intangible aspects of the accommodation experiences enjoyed by guests differ between hotel types and brands, though there are some similarities. Servicing of rooms every day, preparing for new guests, re-servicing rooms for existing guests; are all common features regardless of hotel ranking or pricing. In addition, cleaning public spaces is typically the responsibility of this department.

The Food and Beverage Department – Shane de Bruyn and Michael N. Chibili highlight the importance of food beverage operations within a hotel manager's remit. Providing food and beverages in hotels can be an important source of revenue and can also reinforce the hospitable nature of a brand. It is, however, a difficult service to control because of skill sets needed and potential wastage created by food that remains unsold. Some budget hotel chains have met this challenge by removing, or at least minimising, the food services offered to guests. In other cases, menus have been structured around a simple, one-step process, ensuring that training needn't be advanced beyond simple skills.

Hospitality Human Resource Management – Dr. Bill Rowson discusses the processes whereby employees are recruited, trained, appraised and rewarded for their efforts. The involvement of employees in delivering hotel services is not always treated with the significance required. Apart from during immediate interactions of frontline employees with customers, suitably trained staff members have the potential to create a genuine competitive advantage through an expression of hospitability, making sure guests feel genuinely welcome.

Marketing for the Hospitality Industry – Dr. Bill Rowson explores marketing within the delivery of hospitality services. Central to marketing is a clear understanding of the customer profiles of guests a hotel wishes to attract. Apart from the demographic profiles of the guests, there needs to be a clear understanding of the reasons guests use the hotel. On the basis of this information, hotels can send messages targeting those most likely to be interested in both the message and the service on offer. Accommodation pricing and promotional offers are key to ensuring hotels have the maximum attainable average revenue per room.

Financial Control and the Accounting Department – Michael N. Chibili highlights the key importance of cost control and revenue generation in assisting the general manager to generate profits. Additionally, the processes whereby guest bills are produced and processed are important factors. Given the issues discussed earlier, the Finance department assists in providing appropriate information needed by the manager to make pricing and occupancy decisions. Low prices may ensure higher occupancy levels, but there may be a point where a few empty rooms help maintain higher level room rates for those that are sold.

Facility Engineering and Maintenance – Michael N. Chibili explores the processes that are key in ensuring guests have facilities that operate in the way they expect. The failure of these tangible aspects of the guest experience can be a major source of dissatisfaction. In some instances, broken or malfunctioning facilities cause dissatisfaction, but a level of building and accommodation décor also helps create a general impression of the quality of the hotel. The refurbishment of rooms needs to be carefully planned, because this will require rooms being taken out of use, thereby making them unavailable for sale to guests.

Managing Safety and Security Issues – Michael N. Chibili emphasises that safety and security are at the core of guest concerns. Their decision to choose to stay in a known brand hotel is frequently an expression of a desire to be secure when away from their home base. On the other hand, hotels are by their nature points of social engagement where individuals meet with others. A hotel represents both a place of comfort and of neutrality. Managing these tensions is a key issue; an overly secure system of access may create an impression of inhospitality, but an open access policy may cause a risk of potential abuse by terrorists or others bent on doing harm to guests.

Managing Hospitality Services – Professor Conrad Lashley highlights the factors that present all service providers with dilemmas that have to be managed. The intangible nature of the service experienced, the heterogeneity of the service encountered, and the emotional dimensions of the service encountered mean that techniques of mass production employed in manufacturing are not available to hotel managers. Guest themselves are frequently driven by contradictory needs – selecting brands in order to know and recognise the service offering, but also wanting to be treated as individuals. The emergence of hotel brands has produced benefits by enabling focus on identified needs, but also presents hotel organisations with the problem of having to deliver to brand standards across all units and across geographic and cultural boundaries.

Conceiving Hospitality Processes – Michael N. Chibili explores the process through which hotels deliver the accommodation, dining and drinking experiences to guests. In some budget brands, the service encountered has been reduced to a minimum, and even in more up-market hotels there is widespread use of self-service buffets and self-check-in/out. In other cases, menus have been designed around dishes that require one-step cooking; this ensures the skills required can be learnt quickly, thereby making the use of more numerous, low-skilled, and cheaper labour forces feasible.

Designing Hospitality Processes – Michael N. Chibili explores customer touch points between the hotel facilities and staff, which contribute to guest and supplier experiences. These touch points can be designed to enhance greater sensitivity to the needs of the guest or supplier. A thorough examination of each touch point can help enable more effective relationships between the parties concerned.

Delivering Hospitality Services – Professor Conrad Lashley discusses the key importance of customer satisfaction in delivering repeat business, building repute and generating new customers. At heart, this requires hotels to deliver what they say they will. Frontline employees are at the centre of the processes that ensure customer satisfaction. Making sure employees are aware of the brand standards and are trained with skills appropriate to meet them is important. In these circumstances, labour retention is crucial; a stable workforce is more likely to develop personal bonds with guests.

Managing Change in the Hospitality Industry – Latifa Benhadda and Michael N. Chibili demonstrate that managing change is crucial in a dynamic trading situation. The need to review operational practices, services on offer, and guest expectations in this ever-changing environment is vital if a hotel is to maintain a competitive position. At the same time, change can be seen as threatening, difficult, something to be resisted. A hotel manager has to create an atmosphere and culture that encourage change and innovation. They must embrace an innovative climate of excitement about change, recognising that frontline employees are the most aware of these changes and developments.

Managing Quality in the Hospitality Industry – Michael N. Chibili highlights that managing quality ensures that customers obtain the service experience they expect. Central to this is the need to establish a clear definition of service standards being offered and presented to guests. As such, service quality management requires an approach that monitors the services delivered to guests, identifying and correcting points of service breakdown when they occur.

January 2016

Dr. Craig Thompson, FIH, FHEA
Head of School, Stenden Hotel Management School,
Leeuwarden, the Netherlands

Acknowledgements

For Lebongwo, Njingu, Afiandem, and Anja. Always in the confidence that their lights will shine more and more brightly.

This book is the product of an initial two–month review of two Amsterdam hotels (the NH Grand Hotel Krasnapolsky and the Mövenpick Hotel Amsterdam City Centre) in 2011. That was when my school – the Stenden Hotel Management School, Leeuwarden, the Netherlands, permitted me to use the months of September and October to study all aspects of hotel operations from the inside. Having originally come from the banking sector, and having taught finance-related content to students at the school since 2003, back then I had no real-life knowledge of the hotel business – apart from its financial and accounting components. With the school's agreement and the collaboration of the two hotels, the two months I spent allowed me to a have good insight into the day-to-day operations of hotels from behind the scenes of their beautiful frontages and front offices. My eternal gratitude goes to the former Head of School, of Stenden Hotel Management School, Mr. Sjoerd van der Galiën, for granting me leave of absence and supporting me with the time required to transfer my insights into a textbook for students when I returned with more than 40 hours of tape recordings (which were eventually transcribed into more than 800 pages of text), and lots of other digital documents, coupled with a fervent desire to write a book on the subject of hotel operations.

I hereby wish to thank the authors of the various chapters who contributed their rich mixtures of interests, talents, expertise, ideas, opinions, research, and thoughts towards the creation of this book. I am particularly pleased that they could devote the time they did (which, at times, was truthfully forced on them) to contribute to this project. I hope we will always stay friends despite the pressure that I have put you under. I am grateful to Noordhoff Publishers' Ageeth Bergsma (who started the process), Petra Prescher and Ada Bolhuis (who finished things off) for making this book a reality. I am equally indebted to Jan-Willem Tjooitink for all his discerning comments and editorial support. To Lionel Tchoungui and Sylvester Ngoh Njana, I thank their eagle-eyed abilities to pick out the most tiny of errors. For all his background support and belief in me, I am forever grateful to Klaas-Wybo van der Hoek, Vice President of the Board of Directors, Stenden University of Applied Sciences.

I also wish to acknowledge the following hospitality industry professionals (ranging from runners to general managers, but names arranged alphabetically based on their first names), who provided me with their time and support. I do beg pardon for any names I may have omitted.

The Netherlands, Zaandam: Inntel Hotels Amsterdam Zaandam

From my time at NH Grand Hotel Krasnapolsky, Amsterdam: Alex Jost; Antonio Opromola; Ayfer Karakas; Bert Nijkamp; Caroline van Hogendorp; Celestine Daniels; Chaïra Joel; Danielle Stam; Erik Steijling; Fieke Aarden; Floris de Wit; Gerben Feberwee; Glenn Wells; Harol Soto; Heinz Imhof; Herman Klok; Jamal Ouaziz; Jan Schramowski; Jochem de Lange; Jolanda Kamies; Jorrit Hussaarts; Katja Mayer; Mariëtte van Ess; Marije Peereboom; Marije Veenhoven; Marzenna Dabrowska; Melissa Tandjoeng; Minke de Leeuw den Bouter; Mohamed Achetib; Nanda Herling; Nicole Davits; Patrick van Vliet; Patrick Wolffenbuttel; Ramon van Geilswijk; Richard Kommers; Rebecca Sousa de Andrade Passos; Ronald Voorintholt; Rudy Haringhuizen; Sabine Overdijk; Sjirk Groenevelt; Thijs Leurs; Wouter van Dienst; and Yvonne Handigman-Mulder.

From my time at Mövenpick Hotel Amsterdam City Centre, Amsterdam: Albert Rouwendal; Bart van Ruler; Bibi Oerlemans-Engel; Brian op 't Veld; Cem G. Gokpinar; Chris Greven; Christophe Karkan; Christopher Lesiak; Daniel Kaan; Danielle Gerritsen; David Kort; Desmond Hertogs; Dirje van Laar; Dirk Dubbers; Eric Bakker; Hans de Vries; Jane Añonuevo; Jasper van Os; Jeanette Agterberg; Joanna Kessler; John Verhagen; Joyce Berkvens; Kevin Williams; Koen van den Berge; Laila Larjani; Linda Barnhoorn; Lisette Schaefer; Marcel Verhoef; Marco de Wildt; Mariska Denkers; Marjolein de Vries; Mark Okhuijsen; Martine Beket; Maurice Ros; Maya Kalloe; Mirjam Hopman; Myriam Hollevoet; Nynke Offringa; Paulo Kruk; Pedro Wisman; Radu Botta; Remko de Vos; Richard Vis; Rutger van der Kreek van Loon; Sabine Koene; Saskia Dijkstra; Sylvia Abeyie; Tessa de Jong; Tim Holman; Trevor Gunathilake; and Vera Kanninga.

Special thanks are also extended to Alex Kaminski of Hampshire Hotel – Oranje, Leeuwarden; Mohamed Allabari of Blycolin; Susanne Detroy of Protel Hotel Software GmbH; Leonardo Beadoy, Rita Härtwig and Wilco de Weerd of Micros-Fidelio GmbH; and Sandra van Lokven of Van Hessen BV.

This book would not have seen the light without the advice, counsel, suggestions, and support I received from the team of managers, lecturers, students and support staff of Stenden University of Applied Sciences, Leeuwarden. From Stenden University Library, Alie Mud, who ensured that I received all the documents I needed during the book development process at all times. From Stenden Hotel Management School: Dr. Craig Thompson; Prue Nairn; Wichard Zwaal; Frans Swint; Phuong Dao; David Kooijker; Kitty Schagen; David Casey; Leo Dekker; and Joke Tasma. Special thanks are extended to my office mates Radu Mihailescu; Dr. Marte Rinck de Boer; and Anne Keizer, who spent the last three years hearing nothing of value from me that did not in some way relate to this book. Dr. Wouter Hensens, GM of Stenden University South Africa deserves special mention for the assistance he provided me with. From the Stenden Hotel, I would like to extend my appreciation to Victoria Snouck Hurgronje; Patricia Wewer; Marijke de Beer; and Anita van der Meer. The students who helped in the process include Lilian van der Ham; Jeroen Schot; Tristan Post; Merel van Vliet; and Erik Beentjes.

My wife, Cocotte Balela-Chibili, provided me with the encouragement, support, and understanding that I needed during this process, especially when I had to forgo our holiday plans and other fun activities in order to work on the book.

Michael N. Chibili
January 2016

Table of contents

© Noordhoff Uitgevers bv

Effective learning

These blue words mark important topics of the theory.

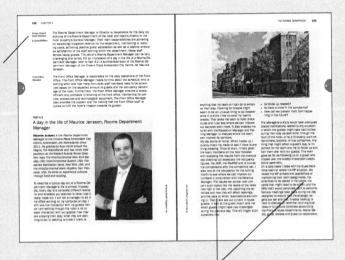

Questions and assignments for reflection offers challenging questions to debate with fellow student in or outside the class room.

Articles from web and newspapers provide a view of real application within the hospitality industry of the concepts.

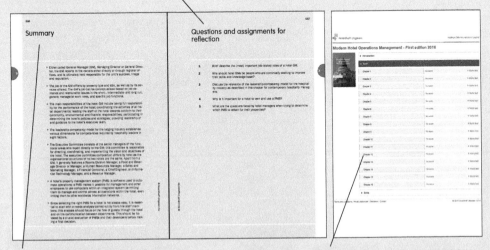

A summary supports self study by presenting an overview over important topics of the chapter.

The website provides additional materials for both students and lecturers. The online self-test is a study tool with feedback and study tips to help you test your knowledge and prepare for assignments.

1

The Hospitality Industry – Past, Present and Future

M. N. Chibili

1.1 Introduction

The history of the hospitality industry is closely linked to that of civilisation. It is a history that has evolved as major civilisations appeared and developed. Facilities offering hospitality to travellers and guests have existed across centuries; they have evolved in their offerings by constantly adapting to the wishes of their most important stakeholders. This chapter introduces the hospitality industry from the perspective of its evolution over time and covers its origins as far back as ancient times through its transformations during centuries of pre- and post-industrial revolution, eventually ending with a look at what the future holds for the industry.

1.2 History of the Hospitality Industry

The hospitality industry, which belongs to the larger business group called the travel and tourism industry, is found within the services sector. The hospitality industry, which, according to the United Nation's World Tourism Organisation, will be the world's largest industry by 2020, generally includes the service organisations that cater to people's needs for food, drinks, and accommodations, as well as recreation, travel and entertainment. To be able to better understand the complex world of the hospitality industry, it is necessary to trace its origins, which began in the early days of human civilisation, and to see how it has evolved to the present day.

Services sector

1.2.1 The Origins of the Hospitality Industry

There is evidence of the existence of the hospitality industry dating back far into ancient times. Such evidence can be traced back to around 4000 BC, and owes much to the Sumerians with their invention of writing (cuneiform), money, and the wheel. All these inventions permitted people to be able to move from place to place for pleasure, and be able to pay for any services

Inventions

United Kingdom, London: The Russell Hotel

received. Prior to these inventions, nomadic peoples travelled as a way of life, seeking out any conveniences from place to place. In those days, people travelled either on foot or on animals and as such could not cover great distances in a day. Upon nightfall, they would seek convenient places that could provide them with such basic necessities as water, food, fuel, and shelter. When they travelled in groups for safety purposes, these groups were called caravans. Figure 1.1 is an illustration of a combined caravan of horses and camels.

Convenient places

FIGURE 1.1 A caravan of horses and camels approaches Aleppo from the Mediterranean coast in the late seventeenth century, from Cornelis Le Bruyn, Voyage to the Levant (1702)

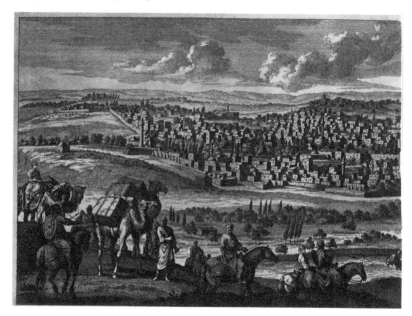

The distance that could be covered in a day depended on the mode of transport travellers were using. At points where they had to stop, lodging facilities tended to appear. These would have been known by different names in various parts of the world. Some examples include *ryokan* in Japan, *dharamshala* in India, *pousadas* in Portugal, *hospitia* in Italy, *hôtel* in France, inn in Europe as a whole, and *relay houses* in China.

Further evidence of the existence of the hospitality industry can be derived from the Code of Hammurabi, which was established around 1780 BC. As shown in the translation in the fragment in Figure 1.2, the code also included rules for tavern-keepers and inn-keepers on various issues.

Code of Hammurabi

Hammurabi was the ruler of Babylon from 1792 BC to 1750 BC. The Code of Hammurabi (which meant 'The Code henceforward') was discovered by modern archaeologists in 1901. This nearly complete example of the Code is carved into a black diorite stele in the shape of a huge index finger 2.25 metres tall. The Code is inscribed in the Akkadian language using cuneiform

FIGURE 1.2 Translated fragment from the Code of Hammurabi (Source: www.constitution.org)

108	If a tavern-keeper (feminine) does not accept corn according to gross weight in payment of drink, but takes money, and the price of the drink is less than that of the corn, she shall be convicted and thrown into the water.
109	If conspirators meet in the house of a tavern-keeper, and these conspirators are not captured and delivered to the court, the tavern-keeper shall be put to death.
110	If a 'sister of a god' open a tavern, or enter a tavern to drink, then shall this woman be burned to death.
111	If an inn-keeper furnish sixty ka of isakani-drink to ... she shall receive fifty ka of corn at the harvest.

Black diorite stele with the Code of Hammurabi

script carved into the diorite stele. It is currently on display in the Louvre Museum in Paris, France.

1.2.2   Evolution of the Hospitality Industry through Time

As indicated in the previous section, the history of the hospitality industry is closely linked to the civilisations of the past. This section draws its inspiration from Levy-Bonvin's (2013) article entitled Hotels: A brief history, as published in www.hospitalitynet.org. The Greeks developed thermal baths in villages designed for rest and recuperation, while the Romans developed an extensive network of roads throughout their empire. This extensive network of roads created the need for lodging facilities for travellers, which later culminated in the construction of mansions that catered to the needs of those travelling on imperial duty. The Romans also constructed thermal baths across their empire, which span across most of Europe and the Middle East.

Civilisations

Before the Industrial Revolution

Prior to the Industrial Revolution (which covered the period from 1750 to 1850), important hospitality industry-related events included the following:

- The construction of extensive networks of roads and lodging facilities by the Romans. They built some 10,000 inns stocked with food and beverages 25 miles apart, to aid their officials as they travelled across the Roman Empire.
- The appearance of caravanserais as resting places for caravans along the various routes of the Silk Road between Europe and Asia. An example of a caravanserai is that of Qalat el-Mudiq in Syria, shown in Figure 1.3.

Silk Road

FIGURE 1.3 The caravanserai in Qalat el-Mudiq, Syria

- Monasteries and abbeys became establishments that offered resting places for travellers on a regular basis.
- Relay houses were set up in China and Mongolia for travellers and couriers.
- *Ryokans* appeared during the Nara period (c. 700 AD) in Japan; some of them have survived to date, such as the *Nisiyama Onsen Keinkan* in Yamanashi, which was built around 705 AD, and has been owned and operated by more than 52 different owners, or the *Hoshi Ryokan* in Ishikawa, which was built around 718 AD, and has been owned and operated by the same family for 46 generations.
- In Europe, many inns appeared. These were relatively small and simple operations, basically fulfilling the housing needs of travellers by providing them with a spare room at a price. Some of these inns have remained famous to date, such as:
  - The Angel Inn in Grantham, Lincolnshire, United Kingdom, which was opened in 1203 and is regarded as the oldest surviving English inn. It was built as a hostel for the Brotherhood of the Knights Templar, and is today called the Best Western Angel and Royal Hotel.
  - The *Auberge Cour Saint George* in Ghent, Belgium, which was opened in 1228, and is now called the Hotel Best Western Cour St. Georges.
  - The *Auberge Des Trois Rois* in Basel, which was opened in 1681 as lodging for the gentry, and is now called the Grand Hotel Les Trois Rois.

Laws

- Both in France and in England, laws were established which required hotels to keep a register of their visitors. Thermal spas were also constructed in both Karlovy Vary (Carlsbad) and Marienbad in what is now the Czech Republic.
- During the 1500s, the first travellers' guide books were published in France. Signs began to be used to identify those establishments that had something special to offer travellers.
- During the 1600s, stagecoaches that used a regular timetable began operating in England. This greatly changed the way people travelled, and also influenced the need to house them at their journey's end. The roads became safer and new junction points were created, which eventually led to the founding of new towns.
- By the mid-1600s, clubs and lodges had become widespread across Europe and America.

From the Industrial Revolution till 1899

The period of the Industrial Revolution had a very significant influence on the history of the hospitality industry. This period was characterised by rapid changes in economic and technological development. The manufacturing and transport sectors saw very significant developments, and their effect on the hospitality industry was a proliferation of the construction of hotels everywhere in Europe and America. These hotels were needed to cater to the needs of the rising establishment of managerial and middle classes taking care of new companies, as well as a growing demand for both leisure and business travel. These classes had the necessary wealth to be able to move conveniently from place to place. Some developments of note in the hospitality industry during this period were:

Significant developments

Luxurious amenities

- The appearance of a new style of hotel that provided luxurious amenities in very opulent surroundings similar to the royal palaces. These hotels were constructed to accommodate a very mobile aristocracy, as well as wealthy industrialists.

- The appearance of the Grand Tour, which was originally about privileged young Englishmen who spent their gap years on an extended tour of Continental Europe. Possibly, the best known of these youngsters was James Boswell, who kept an elaborate journal of his travels and experiences. The first major guidebook for the Grand Tour was published in 1749 by Thomas Nugent. Though the Grand Tour was primarily associated with British nobility and wealthy established gentry, similar trips were made by wealthy young men from Northern European countries. From the second half of the 18th century onward, some American and other overseas youths joined in; participants began to include more members of the middle classes now that rail and steamship travel made the journey less cumbersome. Figure 1.4 is a map of Europe showing the Mozart family's Grand Tour of Europe.

Grand Tour

1

FIGURE 1.4 The Mozart family's Grand Tour of Europe

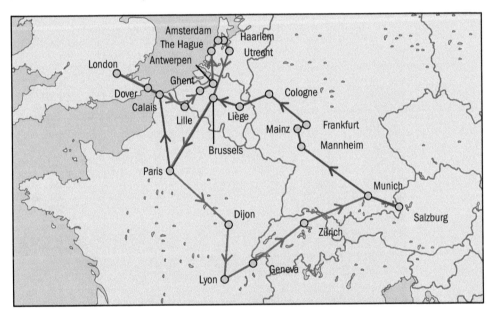

There was a slow decline in the number of highway inns for stage coaches due to the expansion of rail networks and a boom in holiday resorts offering either health benefits (by mineral spas) or cooler temperatures (by mountains and oceans).

Some hotels of note that appeared during this period include:
- The City Hotel opened in New York City in 1794. It is said that this was the first building in America specifically built for the purpose of being a hotel. With its 73 rooms, it was considered to be a very large property in a city with approximately 30,000 inhabitants. The City Hotel also provided meeting rooms and eventually became the social heart of the city. It was the largest hotel in New York until 1813, and stayed operational till 1849.

City Hotel

- Giuseppe Dal Niel rented the second floor of the Palazzo Dandolo in Venice, Italy and turned it into a hotel in 1822. Within two years, thanks to his commercial success, he was able to purchase the whole palace and spent a lot of money on a radical but accurate restoration of the palace, now called the Hotel Danieli.

Hotel Danieli

Innovative features

- The Tremont House (also called Tremont Hotel) was built in Boston, USA in 1829, and was designed by Isaiah Rogers. It was a four-story, granite-faced, neoclassical building with 170 rooms, and had many innovative features for the hospitality industry, such as indoor plumbing, in-room water pitchers, shared indoor toilets and baths, a reception area, guestrooms with locks, free soap and bellboys. It set the standards for luxury and became a model for many hotels that were built during that period. It was also the first hotel to serve French cuisine in the USA. A painting by William James Bennett (1787 – 1844) of the Tremont House, which stayed in operation till around 1895, is shown in Figure 1.5.

Tremont House

FIGURE 1.5 Painting of the Tremont House by W. J. Bennett (1787–1844)

Holt's Hotel

- The Holt's Hotel was built in New York in 1833 and had a hundred-foot dining room with twenty-foot tall ceiling, twenty-five parlours, and one hundred and sixty-five rooms. The proprietor, Stephen Holt, introduced a steam-powered lift, which was a wonderful idea but was too expensive. The Holt's Hotel was declared bankrupt in 1835.

Park Hotel

- The Astor House was built by John Jacob Astor and transformed into the Park Hotel by designer Isaiah Rogers (of Tremont House fame) in 1836. It had 309 rooms in 6 stories, featuring new gas lighting and bathing/toilet facilities on each floor. It became unable to compete with other new hotels by the 1870s, and was eventually transformed and redeveloped into office blocks.

Hotel des Anglais

- The Hotel des Anglais was opened in the early 1840s in Cairo, Egypt; it was renamed Shepheard's Hotel after its owner Samuel Shepheard in

© Noordhoff Uitgevers bv

1860. It was the leading hotel in Cairo and was one of the most celebrated hotels in that part of the world from the middle of the 19th century to 1952, when it was destroyed in a fire during the riots leading to the July 23 Revolution in Egypt.

- The Great Eastern Hotel (originally the Auckland Hotel) was built in Calcutta (currently called Kolkata), India in 1841. Founded by David Wilson, it was extremely elite, and was considered India's first 5-star hotel. Over time its fame and performance dwindled until it became insolvent in 1975. It was reopened after extensive renovations under the name The Lalit Great Eastern Hotel in 2012, and is currently privately owned. *Great Eastern Hotel*

- The Grand Hôtel du Louvre, in Paris, France was built in 1855. Originally located in the building which is now known as the *Louvre des Antiquaires*, the Grand Hôtel du Louvre was the first luxury hotel in France and had 700 guestrooms. It was renowned for its French and international cuisine and was the first hotel to achieve recognition equal to its luxurious counterparts in New York and Switzerland. In 1887, the Hotel du Louvre was relocated to where it stands to this day. *Grand Hôtel du Louvre*

- The Fifth Avenue Hotel was a luxury hotel in New York City that was built in 1859. It developed a reputation as New York's most elegant hotel. It had five stories over a commercial ground floor and had the first passenger lift to be installed in a hotel in the United States. It also employed four hundred servants to serve the guests. It even had private bathrooms, which was considered extravagant in those days. It stayed in operation till it was demolished after closing at midnight on April 4th 1908. *Fifth Avenue Hotel*

- The Grand Hôtel, Paris, was originally built as part of the urban transformation of Paris at Napoleon's request in 1862. It was meant to help assure the world that Paris was ready to host the Universal Exposition of 1867. The hotel remains a French national historic landmark, having preserved every aspect of its original opulence. The hotel is made up of 470 luxurious rooms, all designed in 19th century French style. The hotel houses the famous *Café de la Paix*, which has one of the most illustrious terraces in all of Paris. It currently belongs to the Intercontinental Hotels Group. *Grand Hôtel*

- The Hôtel de Paris in Monte Carlo was quite an ambitious project for its time. As detailed in the specifications requested by François Blanc, who presided over the destiny of the Société des Bains de Mer, requirements were for 'a hotel which outstrips anything that has been built so far, even the Hôtel du Louvre or the Grand Hôtel in Paris. I want people to describe the Hôtel de Monaco as a real marvel, thus making it a powerful means of publicity'. The hotel was inaugurated in 1864, and has since undergone more than 6 expansions. It currently has 182 rooms, 74 suites and junior suites, 1 presidential suite, and 3 famous restaurants: the Louis XV, the Grill, and the Côté Jardin. It is part of the 'Leading Hotels of the World'. *Hôtel de Paris*

- The Hotel Victoria-Jungfrau in Interlaken, Switzerland. In 1856, 22-year old hotel pioneer Eduard Ruchti purchased the Pension Victoria, and in 1864 commissioned local architects Friedrich Studer and Horace Edouard Davinet to completely redesign the property. The new Hotel Victoria was opened for business in 1865, and in 1895 Ruchti acquired the adjacent Hotel Jungfrau (which had been built by Davinet in 1864). In 1899, the two buildings were linked and became the Victoria-Jungfrau. It offered standards of quality and comfort unparalleled at the time, including such innovative features as a telephone system, a hydraulic suspension lift *Hotel Victoria-Jungfrau* and electric lighting in all rooms. The hotel contains 212 luxury guest rooms, 105 of which are suites and junior suites, and is part of the 'Leading Hotels of the World'.

Mena House

- The Mena House in Cairo was initially a hunting lodge. It was built for the Egyptian King Isma'il Pasha in 1869, and was eventually sold to Frederick and Jessie Head as a private residence. It was expanded and sold to Ethel and Hugh Locke-King in 1885; they refurbished the building into the hotel that was opened as The Mena House in 1886. In 1890, the hotel opened Egypt's first swimming pool. In 1971, the hotel was purchased by Rai Bahadur Mohan Singh Oberoi. The Camp David Peace Agreement was a result of meetings at the Mena House in December 1977.

Palmer House

- The Palmer House in Chicago, USA has gone through four transformations. The original Palmer House, which had 225 rooms, was opened in September of 1870, while a second Palmer House was under construction nearby. Both buildings were destroyed by the Chicago Fire of 1871, however. The owner, Potter Palmer, quickly rebuilt, resulting in a 7-story, $13 million hotel, that was opened in 1875 and was presented as the nation's only fireproof hotel. It stood in that form until 1925, when it was replaced with the $20 million, 25-story multi-towered hotel that stands to date. The hotel has been part of the Hilton Hotel chain since 1945, and its lobby is considered one of the most magnificent in the world.

Hotel Minerva

- The Hotel Minerva in Baden Baden, Germany, began life in 1834 under the name *Stephanienbad*, and in 1872, a master tailor called Anton Brenner purchased the hotel and the adjoining land for his daughter and her husband. However, after the death of his son-in-law in 1875, Anton Brenner assumed the running of the hotel. In 1882, his son Camille took over, and helped enhance the hotel's status as a world-class grand hotel. Camille Brenner laid the groundwork for the modern Brenner's Park-Hotel & Spa, and his spirit is still felt throughout the hotel today. It is part of the Oetker Collection and is one of the 'Leading Hotels of the World'.

Hotel Imperial

- The Hotel Imperial is located in Vienna, Austria. It was designed by architect Arnold Zenetti, and built under the direction of Heinrich Adam in 1863. It was converted into a hotel in 1873. It is arguably Vienna's most exclusive five-star hotel. A speciality of the hotel is the Imperial Tart supposedly based on a secret recipe that is said to have been created when Emperor Franz Joseph opened the Hotel in 1873. The Imperial was acquired by the Compagnia Italiana Grandi Alberghi (CIGA) in 1985. In 1994, the Starwood Hotels and Resorts took over CIGA and transformed it into a branch of its high-end brand 'The Luxury Collection', to which the Hotel Imperial now belongs.

Hotel Grande Bretagne

- The Hotel Grande Bretagne in Athens, Greece traces its roots back to 1842, when Antonis Dimitrios acquired a plot of land opposite the Palace of King Otto, and built an impressive 90-room mansion that was the first incarnation of the current hotel. This mansion was bought by the hotelier Savvas Kentros together with Efstathios Lampsas in 1874, and was transformed into the Hotel Grande Bretagne, which was considered one of the most luxurious hotels in south-eastern Europe. The hotel is now part of 'The Luxury Collection' hotel chain, managed by Starwood Hotels & Resorts, containing 321 rooms and a 400 m² Royal Suite on the fifth floor. The Hotel Grande Bretagne is pictured in Figure 1.6.

FIGURE 1.6 The Hotel Grande Bretagne

- The Palace Hotel in San Francisco, California, USA was built by William Chapman Ralston and William Sharon in 1875, and was arguably the largest, most luxurious and costly hotel in the world. It was officially opened on 2 October, 1875, containing 755 guest rooms. It had hydraulic suspension lifts, and each guest room had an electronic call button that allowed guests to ring for anything they needed. The original hotel was destroyed by the fire that followed the 1906 San Francisco Earthquake. It was rebuilt and has undergone multiple renovations over the years. It now has 553 rooms and suites and is part of 'The Luxury Collection' hotel chain, managed by Starwood Hotels & Resorts. Palace Hotel
- The Grand Hotel Europe, Saint Petersburg, Russia, opened its doors to the public on 28 January, 1875, replacing an earlier inn. It was designed by Italian architect Carlo Rossi who used an impressive Neo-Baroque façade to join together neighbouring properties dating back to the 1820s to create one magnificent building for the Evropeyskaya Hotel Company. Its marble-and-gilt interiors, sweeping staircases and elegant furniture have attracted crowds of well-to-do visitors over the centuries. In the 1910s, the hotel was remodelled in the Art Nouveau style thanks to designs by Swedish-Russian architects Fyodor Lidval and Leon Benois. The latest major renovation was done between 1989 and 1991 and it currently has a total of 291 rooms and suites. The Grand Hotel Europe is affiliated with the 'Leading Hotels of the World'. Grand Hotel Europe
- The Sagamore, Lake George, New York, USA, is located on the shores of Lake George, and was built in 1883 as a country retreat for the wealthy. It provided luxurious and spacious accommodations that attracted a select, international clientele. It has twice been destroyed by fire and reconstructed (1893 and 1914), but eventually fell into disrepair before closing its doors in 1981. In 1983, Norman Wolgin purchased and restored the hotel to its former stateliness with 137 elegant guestrooms and 54 suites under the banner of the Preferred Hotels and Resorts Group. Sagamore
- The Grand Hotel, Mackinac Lake, Michigan, USA, began in 1886 when the Mackinac Island Hotel Company was formed with designs to create an appropriate accommodation to cater to the influx of people to the is- Grand Hotel

land following its popularity as a summer getaway. They acquired land and started the construction of the Grand Hotel which was officially opened in 1887. It featured the longest front porch in the world at more than 201 meters, and is a US National Historic Landmark. With multiple renovations over the years, it currently offers 385 guest rooms, no two of which are alike.

Hotel del Coronado

- The Hotel del Coronado, San Diego, California, USA, was built in 1888, and may be one of America's most beautiful beach resorts. It has been a US National Historic Landmark since 1977. The Coronado Beach Company hired architect J. W. Reid to design the hotel in which his masterpiece, the Crown Room, has a wooden ceiling which was installed with only pegs and glue. It had the world's first oil furnace and had electric lighting installed under the final inspection of Thomas Edison. It originally contained many amenities such as an Olympic-sized salt water pool, tennis courts, a yacht club, a Japanese tea garden, an ostrich farm, billiards, and bowling alleys. It currently has 679 guestrooms and suites in various categories and is owned by the Blackstone Group LP, Strategic Hotels & Resorts Inc., and KSL Resorts.

Savoy Hotel

- The Savoy Hotel, London, UK was built by famous impresario Richard D'Oyly Carte and opened on 6 August, 1889. It was designed by architect T. E. Collcutt. One of London's most iconic hotels, it is the epitome of class, sophistication, and glamor till this day. It was the first luxury hotel in Britain with electric lighting, electric lifts, *en-suite* bathrooms, and pressurised hot and cold running water. Its first famous manager was the Swiss, César Ritz, who was hired in 1890 and who came along with the French Auguste Escoffier as chef; the *maître d'hôtel* was Louis Echenard. They established an unprecedented standard of quality in hotel service, entertainment and elegant dining, which attracted royalty and other wealthy guests and diners. Following extensive renovation and reopening in 2010, the hotel currently has 62 suites and 206 guestrooms and is managed by the Fairmont Hotels and Resorts. The main entrance to the Savoy is shown in Figure 1.7.

César Ritz

Auguste Escoffier

Brown Palace Hotel & Spa

- The Brown Palace Hotel & Spa, Denver, USA was opened on 12 August, 1892. It was begun by and named after its owner by H. C. Brown, and was designed by architect Frank E. Edbrooke in the Italian Renaissance style. It had an atrium lobby, with balconies rising eight floors above ground, and was considered the second fire-proof building in America. It had 400 guest rooms (compared to only 241 today). Many changes have taken place over the years, but one thing remains the same – it is one of Denver's most elegant hotels, and has been open every day since its inauguration in 1892. It is privately owned and managed.

Waldorf Astoria

- The Waldorf Astoria New York, USA, started as two separate hotels belonging to two cousins: one of 13 stories, owned by William Waldorf Astor, known as the Waldorf Hotel, and opened in 1893; the other of 17 stories, owned by John Jacob Astor IV, known as the Astoria Hotel, and opened in 1897. The latter was designed so that it could be connected to the Waldorf. The architect was H. J. Hardenbergh and both hotels were placed under the management of George Boldt. The combined Waldorf-Astoria became the largest hotel in the world at the time and became significant for transforming the contemporary hotel from a facility for travellers into a social centre as well as a prestigious destination for visitors and a part of popular culture. The Waldorf Astoria was the first hotel to offer room service. The original buildings were demolished and

FIGURE 1.7 Main entrance to the Savoy Hotel

the current structure was rebuilt on another New York site in 1931. The present building at 301 Park Avenue in Manhattan is a 47-story, Art Deco landmark, designed by architects Schultze and Weaver, and was able to maintain the original name due to the fact that its former manager L. M. Boomer had been able to obtain exclusive rights to the name and transfer it to the new hotel. The hotel was bought by Conrad Hilton in 1949 and is a member of Hilton's Luxury and Lifestyle Brands along with Waldorf Astoria Hotels & Resorts and Conrad Hotels & Resorts. The Waldorf Astoria New York and The Waldorf Towers offer a total of 1,416 guest rooms, including 303 suites, all featuring original Art Deco motifs. Each room is decorated individually. The hotel has its own railway platform as part of the Grand Central Terminal in New York.

- The Hôtel Ritz in Paris, France, is a grand palace hotel in the heart of Paris. After César Ritz and Auguste Escoffier were dismissed from the Savoy London in 1897, Ritz purchased and transformed the former Hôtel de Lazun building, creating a 210-room hotel designed by architect Charles Mewès. The hotel was opened on 1 June, 1898 and it was reportedly the first hotel in Europe to have an *en-suite* bathroom, with telephones and electricity in each room. It quickly established a reputation for luxury. Today, the hotel is ranked highly among the most prestigious and luxurious hotels in the world, and is a member of the 'Leading Hotels of the World'. One of its restaurants, L'Espadon, is world-renowned and attracts

Hôtel Ritz

L'Espadon

aspiring chefs from all over the world who come to study at the Ritz Escoffier School of French Gastronomy. The best suite of the hotel is called the Imperial and it has been listed by the French government as a national monument in its own right.

The 20th Century

The birth of the 20th century ushered in a new phase in the development of the hospitality industry. This phase can be identified as that of the creation of the present day global hotel businesses, the introduction of franchising and management contracts, the growth in mass tourism, the introduction of social and welfare systems, the growth in salary levels, and the increase in average life span. All of these had an important impact on the hospitality industry. Unlike the previous section, in which the iconic hotels of the previous era have been highlighted, this section establishes some important facts, concepts and events within the context of their related decades.

The 1900s came with the expansion of steam heating, gas burners, electric bells, baths and water closets on all floors, and games rooms in most hotels. In-room telephones started appearing in some hotels. This decade was particularly significant because it brought with it what is considered to be the precursor to the modern business hotel. Ellsworth M. Statler (1863 – 1928), who had made a fortune in the restaurant business, opened his first hotel in Buffalo, New York, USA, in 1908; it was called Statler House and had 450 rooms. Its main target was the economic middle class. Unlike most hotels of the period, Statler's hotels, which numbered 6 at the time of his death in 1928, had many innovations for the time: fire doors, electric light switches by the door inside each room, private bathrooms, personal telephones, keyholes above the door knobs, hot and cold water in each room, full-length mirrors, free morning newspapers, and later, built-in radios in every room. Statler's genius in providing luxury-like amenities to middle and working class people helped his hotel chain become popular with everyday Americans. His formula was later adopted by the other hotel pioneers, such as Hilton. This decade also saw the creation of the magnificent *Taj Mahal Hotel* in Bombay, India; the *Hôtel du Palais*, Biarritz, France; the Ritz in London, UK; the Plaza in New York, USA; the *Beau Rivage Palace* in Lausanne Switzerland; and the new look *Hôtel de Crillon* in Paris, France.

The 1910s were disturbed by the First World War, but overall witnessed an expansion of modern amenities within all hotels instead of only in the luxury ones. It ushered in the increased use of electricity for cooking purposes within hotels as well. This decade witnessed the arrival of such hotels as the Ritz in Madrid, Spain; the *Négresco* in Nice, France; and the *Plaza Athenée* in Paris, France. The decade ended with the arrival of Conrad Hilton in the hospitality industry, when he purchased his first hotel, the Mobley, in 1919 in Cisco, Texas, USA.

The immediate post-war years of the 1920s brought some rapid expansion to the hospitality industry, which ended with a bang after the 1929 Crash that led to the Great Depression of the 1930s. This decade was also characterised by the introduction of the Prohibition in the United States, which was a national ban on the manufacture, transportation, and sale of alcohol between 1920 and 1933. Hospitality innovations included the expansion of in-room radios in hotels, and the creation of the first roadside motels, as

Statler House

Innovations

Ritz

Plaza

Ritz

Conrad Hilton

Mobley

Prohibition

well as airport hotels. Of note during this decade is that J. W. Marriott began business as a restaurateur in Washington D.C., USA, in 1927. The decade also introduced the construction of hotels in mountain ski-resorts thanks to the introduction of funiculars (inclined plane or cliff railways) that permitted tourists to be transported up and down steep slopes. Some hotels of note that started during this decade include La Mamounia in Marrakech, Morocco; the Hotel Ambos Mundos in Havana, Cuba; the Gleneagles Hotel near Auchterarder, Perth and Kinross, Scotland; the Gran Hotel Bolívar in Lima, Peru; the Westin Book Cadillac Detroit, Michigan USA; the Grand Hotel Niagara, in Niagara Falls, Niagara County, New York, USA; the Hotel President in Kansas City, Missouri, USA; Grosvenor House Hotel, London UK; and the Hotel Alfonso XIII in Seville, Spain.

The 1930s was highly affected by the Great Depression, which had a very negative impact on the hospitality industry. There was very little liquidity around, one result being that more than 80% of US-based hotels went into receivership, in which they were held by receivers who had custodial responsibility for the hotels' tangible and intangible assets. The Great Depression had devastating effects around the globe: incomes, revenues, profits and prices all dropped. International trade fell by more than 40%, and unemployment in some areas was at more than 35%. There was little construction activity in most countries and this situation lasted for the most part till the Second World War. Overall guest occupancy levels in hotels hit their historical low at around a mere 50%. This decade also had some good news for the hospitality industry. In 1935, American businessman Howard Dearing Johnson, in association with Reginald Sprague, created the first modern restaurant franchise by letting an operator use the name, food, supplies, and logo of his business, in exchange for a fee. It was also the decade of the invention of air-conditioning, as well as the construction of such hotels as the Imperial in New Delhi, India; the *Belvédère du Rayon Vert* in Cerbère, France; the Treetops Hotel in Aberdare National Park, Kenya; the Sheraton Hotel in Springfield, USA; as well as the reconstruction of the new Waldorf-Astoria already mentioned in the previous section. The Statler Hotel in Detroit, Michigan, USA, was the first to install air-conditioning in all its public spaces in 1934, and in 1937 Marriott started with the first in-flight food service to airlines.

The 1940s were not years of great constructional development within the hospitality industry, since they were highly affected by the ravages caused by the Second World War; yet they saw some innovations that have lasted to date. The decade was marked by the expansion of the installation of air-conditioning in hotels, the building of hotel swimming pools, the arrival of television sets in rooms, and the use of guest credit cards. The decade also saw the beginning of the use of an automated booking system that was first installed by American Airlines in 1946, and eventually adopted by other businesses, with the Sheraton Hotels becoming the first in the industry to adopt it. In the previous year, Sheraton had also become the first ever US hotel company to be listed on the New York Stock Exchange. The birth of the modern day hotel chains started when the InterContinental was founded as a hotel brand by Pan American World Airways (Pan Am) in 1946, for the purpose of improving tourism and increasing accommodation capacities in Latin America. It purchased its first hotel in Belém, Brazil. Conrad Hilton followed by receiving a contract in 1948 in which his company became responsible for the management of the first large hotel in Puerto Rico. Some ho-

J. W. Marriott
Ski-resorts
Gleneagles Hotel
Gran Hotel Bolívar
Westin Book Cadillac Detroit
Grand Hotel Niagara
Hotel President
Grosvenor House Hotel
Hotel Alfonso XIII
Great Depression

Restaurant franchise

Treetops Hotel
Sheraton Hotel
Waldorf-Astoria

Statler Hotel

Second World War

Credit cards

Flamingo Hotel
& Casino

Ledra Palace
Hotel Nicosia

Tidewater Inn

Club village

tels to have seen the light during these times include the Flamingo Hotel & Casino in the Las Vegas Strip, Nevada, USA; the Ledra Palace Hotel Nicosia, Cyprus; and the Tidewater Inn in Easton, Maryland, USA.

The 1950s came along with a new boom in construction for the hospitality industry, with new types of resorts such as the 'club village', as well as an increase in the use of cars as a means of transport. Arguably the first all-inclusive resort, the *Club Méditerranée* was created by Gérard Blitz in 1950; its first club village was opened on the Spanish island of Mallorca. The Club Med invented a new way to bring people together in a unique vacation style: the all-inclusive holiday in resorts in the world's most beautiful venues, where every guest or *'Grand Membres'* (GM) could unwind through contact with nature, sports and others, surrounded by friendly staff or *'Gentils Organisateurs'* (GO). Figure 1.8 is a photo of the entrance to the Club Med La Medina in Marrakech, Morocco.

FIGURE 1.8 Entrance to the Club Med La Medina in Marrakech, Morocco

Motels

Charles
Kemmons Wilson

The expansion of automobile travel led to the explosion of the 'motor hotel' (motel) concept, especially across the USA. Motels often provided free parking facilities, were inexpensive, and targeted people travelling between two destinations on a low budget. A pioneer in this domain was Charles Kemmons Wilson, the founder of the Holiday Inn chain of hotels, who came up with the idea after a family road trip to Washington, D.C., during which he was disappointed by the lack of quality and consistency provided by roadside motels of that era. He advocated for properties that were standardised, safe, clean, easily accessible, and family-friendly. The first Holiday Inn motel was opened in Memphis, Tennessee, USA, in 1952. It was franchised in 1957 as Holiday Inn of America, and within twenty years it had become the largest hotel chain in the USA. Other firsts of note that happened during the decade included the installation of television sets in all guestrooms by the

Hilton hotel chain in 1951; the creation of the first lodging franchise by Howard Dearing Johnson in 1954; the purchase of the Statler Hotel Company by Conrad Hilton in 1957; the opening of the Twin Bridges Marriott Motor Hotel in Arlington, Virginia, USA, by J. W. Marriott in 1957; the purchasing of the Hyatt House Hotel, Los Angeles, California, USA, by Jay Pritzker in 1957; and the introduction of the 'Reservatron', an automated electronic reservation system, by Sheraton in 1958. This made Sheraton the first hotel chain to centralise and automate its reservations function.

The 1960s can easily be characterised as the beginning of the expansion of the hotel chains, as well as the expansion of referral associations. This decade was marked by developments in modes of transportation, especially air travel, which had a tremendous positive effect on the expansion of tourism as a whole and the inclusion of new destinations. New resorts flourished around the Mediterranean region from Spain to Turkey; several hotels were opened specifically for the northern European summer guests in need of relaxation and sunshine. This expansion supported the internationalisation of transactions in the hotel industry and boosted the expansion of franchise agreements as well as various types of hotel management contracts. As hotel chains began dominating the worldwide hotel industry scene based on their stronger brand awareness and marketing power, small independent hotel operators began finding it more and more difficult to fill their rooms. These smaller operators thus began banding together in referral groups in which the individual properties became associated with certain chains such as the Leading Hotels of the World or Best Western. They normally refer guests to each other's properties, and may share the same logo, use the same central reservation system, or share similar advertising slogans, for which they pay service fees. The major expansion in the industry was driven primarily by US-based companies such as Marriott, InterContinental, Hilton, and Holiday Inns.

Referral associations

Hotel chains

The decade also witnessed the introduction of market segmentation and product differentiation within the hotel industry. Market segmentation led to the creation of homogenous customer categories, whereas product differentiation was principally carried out within three dimensions: concept, location and target group. Some hotels that started life during this decade include the Amsterdam Hilton Hotel, Amsterdam, the Netherlands; the *Estudiotel* Alicante in Alicante, Spain; the Hilton Portland & Executive Tower in Portland, Oregon, USA; the Parsian Esteghlal Hotel in Tehran, Iran; the Hilton on Park Lane, London, UK; and lastly the Sheraton New York Hotel and Towers in New York City, New York, USA. The decade also saw the introduction of the first refrigerated mini-bars in hotel rooms, an innovation by German company Siegas; not all previous mini-bars were refrigerated. It was also the period that saw the creation of rooms accessible to wheelchair-users by Travelodge in the USA, the beginning of desegregation in US hotels, the introduction of ice and vending machines, business lounges, and 24-hour room service begun by Westin.

Market segmentation

Refrigerated mini-bars

Desegregation

The 1970s continued the trends that had begun in the 1960s, introduced the notion of the construction of hotels especially meant for the business class, and was both positively and negatively affected by the energy crises. The decade ushered in a new era for the construction of hotels specifically destined for business class visitors; these hotels featured spectacular designs and architecture. A good example of such a hotel is the Hyatt Regency Hotel in Atlanta, Georgia, USA, whose hotel, convention, and tradeshow fa-

Business class

1

cilities offer luxurious accommodations and cordial hospitality. This movement towards business hotels was supported by the willingness of airline corporations extending their efforts in the domain of hotel expansions, as well as the sudden prosperity of Middle Eastern countries which attracted business class visitors from the entire world warranting major hotel developments in the region.

China

POS

Middle Eastern countries

Green movement

The decade was also influenced by China opening up to foreign tourists; this paved the way for spectacular developments in this domain to occur in the years following this opening up. During this period, hotels started offering a broader variety of services that had hitherto not existed, such as point of sales (POS) systems, keyless locks, free in-room movies, name-brand guest amenities, and in-room colour television becoming the standard. Hotel rooms became bigger and there was an upgrade in the quality of food offered to the guests. The sudden prosperity of Middle Eastern countries was enhanced by two events that happened during the period – the 1973 oil crisis, and the 1979 energy crisis. Due to these events, worldwide energy prices soared and the hospitality industry reacted by introducing measures that were precursors to the current green movement in the industry, such as asking guests to reduce electricity consumption or cutting off heating to unoccupied guestrooms.

Some of the hotels that began life during this decade include the Capital Hotel in London, UK; the Coast Edmonton House, in Edmonton, Canada; the Disney's Polynesian and Contemporary Resorts in Lake Buena Vista, Florida, USA; the Carlton Tower Hotel, Dubai; the Sheraton Dubai Creek Hotel & Towers, Dubai; the Empire Landmark Hotel in Vancouver, British Columbia, Canada; the Hilton San Francisco Union Square in San Francisco, California, USA; the Koreana Hotel in Taepyeongno, Jung-gu, Seoul, South Korea; the Peppermill Resort-Spa-Casino in Reno, Nevada, USA; the Shangri-La Hotel in Orchard Road, Singapore; the Atlantis Casino Resort Spa in Reno, Nevada, USA; the Izmailovo Hotel in Moscow, Russia; the Hilton London Metropole in London, UK; the Eldorado Hotel Casino in Reno, Nevada, USA; the Grand at Yuanshan, Zhongshan District, Taipei, Republic of China (Taiwan); Harrah's Las Vegas, Nevada, USA; the Hilton Springfield in Springfield, Illinois, USA; and the Mariston Hotel in Johannesburg, South Africa. Figure 1.9 is a picture of the Tower wing lobby of the Shangri-La hotel in Singapore.

Shangri-La hotel

Niche marketing

Competitiveness

Deregulation

The 1980s came along with another rapid hotel industry expansion phase fuelled by increased niche marketing, advances in technology, deregulation, and full product segmentation. During this period, hotels expanded their surveys of potential guest markets and were able to build networks and systems around the needs of recognised segments. This was made possible with the great advances in technology that occurred during this decade. Examples of such advances included the possibility to make reservations and checkout using credit cards; the invention of the optical electronic key card; and the development of the first chain-wide property reservations systems. The 1980s brought in structural reform programmes in many countries in Europe, as well as in the Americas and Oceania. These programmes all had the aim to raise the level of competitiveness in these economies in the hopes of resulting in higher productivity, increased efficiency and lower prices. This deregulation, which resulted in fewer and simpler regulations, mainly affected economic sectors such as energy, finance, agriculture, com-

FIGURE 1.9 The Tower wing lobby of the Shangri-La hotel in Singapore

munications, and transportation. The overall influence on the hospitality industry was that it helped boost their operating efficiency. For example, hotel telephone departments became transformed from exclusively being cost centres into being profit centres.

Operating efficiency

This decade ushered in a complete segmentation within the hospitality industry, with brands that ranged from budget hotels to boutique hotels to mega-hotels. Figure 1.10 is a picture of the Belle Époque Bar at the Pudi Boutique Hotel (that belongs to the Accor chain) in Shanghai, China.

Pudi Boutique Hotel

Choice Hotels was at the forefront of this concept of market segmentation, which involved dividing customers/guests into various subsets based on their common needs or desires. Each of these subsets was expected to respond differently to the marketing mix of the organisation. This decade also witnessed the Far East opening up to the West, with countries such as Japan, China, South Korea, and Thailand welcoming private tourists and business groups in particular. Some hotels that were constructed, renewed or opened during this decade include the Harrah's Reno in Reno, Nevada, USA; the Sokos Hotel Ilves in Tampere, Finland; the Jules' Undersea Lodge in Key Largo, Florida, USA; the Koryo Hotel in Pyongyang, North Korea; the Peabody in Orlando, Florida, USA; and the Çırağan Palace Kempinski Istanbul, Turkey.

Far East

For the hospitality industry, the 1990s can be considered the decade of the environment programmes revolution in terms of sustainability, greater advances in related technology, and an explosive increase in real estate investment trusts (REITs). Other defining features would be total quality management, prestige projects, and a recession. The environmental programmes at the forefront of hotel sustainability aimed at reducing a hotel's ecological footprint. These programmes were not only aimed at improving their environmental performances but their image as well. Consequently, hotels of all siz-

Sustainability

FIGURE 1.10 The Belle Époque Bar at the Pudi Boutique Hotel in Shanghai, China

es, classes, and locations joined the 'green revolution' in the hopes of ensuring their long term sustainability, as well as gaining the loyalty of the increasingly environmentally-conscious customers.

Examples of advances in related technology can be seen in the adoption of the internet by hotel chains, with Hyatt creating one of the first internet sites, TravelWeb.com's creation of the first online hotel catalogue, the introduction of guests' real-time access to central reservations systems, and interactive visitor guides and weather reports. Additionally, the first hotel room management systems were launched on a European level, and these were linked to the popular property management systems. The reservation systems became more efficient and opened up a new avenue for hotels to enhance their customer loyalty: the database, which contained all data related to a guest permitted hotels to make much more informed and individualised decisions in order to be better able to serve their guests. A real estate investment trust (REIT) is a real estate company that qualifies for some predefined tax benefits if it follows certain rules. Firstly, its main business should be the ownership and management of income-producing properties; secondly, it should distribute almost all of its taxable income as dividends. This new property ownership structure was made possible thanks to new tax laws; initially limited to the USA, these later expanded to other regions such as in Europe and Australia. In the USA, this led to the creation of many hotel REITs, for example; this resulted in multiple mergers and acquisitions. It helped in increasing the sector's combined market capitalisation to more than $9 billion at the end of the decade.

The decade also witnessed the adoption of total quality management (TQM) principles and techniques within the hospitality industry. Adopted and adapted from the manufacturing world, TQM was embraced by service industries, in particular by the hospitality industry. Some benefits of the adoption of TQM techniques within the hospitality industry include enhanced operational and financial performances, improved employee morale, increased customer

Real-time access

REIT

TQM

satisfaction, and greater competitive advantage. The decade, despite the fact that it saw some spectacular hotel projects such as the construction of the Jumeirah Beach Hotel and the Burj Al Arab in Dubai shown in Figure 1.11, was negatively affected by the recession caused by reductions in travel budgets by big multinational companies and the negative effects of the Gulf War on travelling in general. Some hotels that were constructed, renewed or opened during this last decade included the Aquarius Casino Resort in Laughlin, Nevada, USA; the Excalibur Hotel and Casino in Paradise, Nevada, USA; the Hyatt Regency Albuquerque in Albuquerque, New Mexico, USA; the Hyatt Regency Birmingham in Birmingham, UK; the Panda Hotel in Tsuen Wan, New Territories, Hong Kong; the Lanesborough Hotel in London, UK; the Rio All Suite Hotel and Casino in Paradise, Nevada, USA; the Trump Taj Mahal in Atlantic City, New Jersey, USA; the Atlantis Casino Resort Spa in Reno, Nevada, USA; the Hotel Adlon in Berlin, Germany; the Bellagio in Paradise, Nevada, USA; the Mandalay Bay Resort and Casino in Paradise, Nevada, USA; and lastly the Hilton Hanoi Opera Hotel in Hanoi, Vietnam.

Spectacular hotel projects

Recession

FIGURE 1.11 The Burj Al Arab in Dubai

The 21st Century

As the 19th century was characterised by the industrial revolution and the 20th century by the transport revolution, so the 21st century will be known as that of the technological revolution. This technological revolution, especially in the domain of IT, is having and will continue to have a great impact on what the hospitality industry will be, and how it will evolve in decades to come. The trend of spectacular projects initiated in the previous decade has continued since the turn of the century, with new types of developments rising to the

Technological revolution

1

foreground, such as the Hilton Corporation's 'dualtel' concept. In this concept, two of their brands, with separate general managers, are placed under one roof, and thereby help to provide mutually beneficial support to each other, for example in accounting, housekeeping and maintenance. Today's guests have an insatiable appetite for new and excitingly designed hotels in which there is a blurring of the borders between lodging, lifestyle and living. At the same time these guests request the discretion, style and grandeur that epitomised the hospitality industry of the 19th century.

Blurring of the borders

New concepts of luxury are now central to the 21st century lifestyle. There is now a greater interest in eco–resorts, spas, wellness hotels and retreats, and hotels have now become trendsetters as well as providing solutions to some of the negative aspects of modern day living. The IT revolution increased the exposure of the industry in which potential customers and guests began making more use of the web for sharing information. Potential customers make more of their decisions based on other peoples' reviews and blogs, transforming social networks such as Twitter and Facebook as well as review sites like TripAdvisor into powerful tools not to be ignored by the industry. Figure 1.12 clearly illustrates the influence of the use of social networks and review sites.

21st century lifestyle

Social networks

For example, guests now demand wireless internet access as standard even in budget hotels. Yet the IT revolution also opened massive avenues for the industry in the area of online sales and distribution. While the online travel agencies attract the highest numbers of visitors to their sites, hotels also carry out promotional campaigns on their own sites, offering lower-price guarantees and various loyalty programmes. Just two years into the new century, the industry was shaken to its core by the attacks on the USA on 11 September 2001. This event had a profound impact on sales, as business travel to the USA fell by more than 21% during the decade, for example. Leisure travel was also negatively affected due to the stricter rules imposed by the authorities. Other terrorist attacks around the world equally exerted negative influence on business/tourist travel. Examples include the 2002 attacks in Mombasa, Kenya, the bombings of two Bali nightclubs in 2002, and the 2008 attacks on two hotels in Mumbai, India. This period also witnessed the sustained growth of some emerging global economies, commonly referred to as the BRIC (Brazil, Russia, India, and China), where annual growth rates consistently hovered around 10%. This had a positive effect on the industry as more and more individuals moved into upper income levels and as such had potentially higher discretionary incomes. China hosted in 2008 the Beijing Olympics, the run-up to which had resulted in the construction of at least 50 brand new 5-star hotels in the Beijing area alone.

11 September 2001

BRIC

This period is also that of a serious financial crisis that originated in the US housing market in 2008. Initially, it spread throughout the financial systems of the US and Western Europe before expanding to other regions of the world. It negatively affected the hospitality industry due to the reduction of investment funding as well as reduced spending on both corporate and individual levels. The effect of the global crisis can be visualised using the average daily room rate, which was around 14% lower in 2009 than in 2008 globally, for example (based on the 'Hotel Price Index' at Hotels.com). Policies aimed at tackling the crisis on principally three fronts were enacted in various countries. These three fronts were: regulating financial markets;

Financial crisis

FIGURE 1.12 Using social networks and review sites

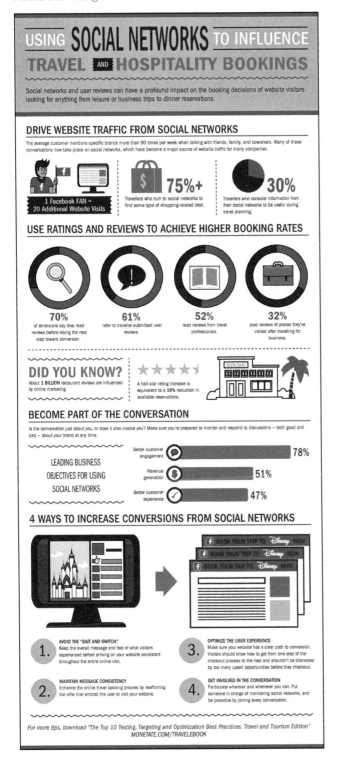

fighting tax evasion; and creating a global standard for ethical behaviour. These policies have had a positive effect on the global economies and, by extension, on the hospitality industry. Current forecasts are optimistic, with many international chains launching expansion programmes into key emerging markets, especially with the establishment of upper-midscale to luxury hotels. Text 1.1, an article by Patrick Ford from Hotel and Motel Management, dated 1 February 2012, illustrates this optimistic outlook.

TEXT 1.1

Global pipeline snapshot: U.S., Asia-Pacific lead

Global pipeline snapshot: U.S., Asia-Pacific lead

1 Feb, 2012 by Patrick Ford, Hotel and Motel Management

Globally, there are a total of 7,078 hotel projects/1,277,339 rooms in the construction pipeline as of the end of Q3 2011. Seventy-seven percent of the world's total pipeline projects and 76 percent of rooms are in the Top 10 countries. With 1,385 projects and 396,804 rooms at the end of Q3, China's total pipeline has surpassed that of the United States by 48,874 rooms. China's economy weathered global recessionary trends with minimal impact. As such, the pipeline rebounded quickly from modest declines and now exceeds the previous Q2 2008 peak, with totals up 12 percent by projects and 22 percent by rooms.

Top 10 countries: Total construction pipeline Q3 2011

Country	Projects	Rooms
China	1,386	396,804
United States	2,851	347,930
India	375	70,668
Brazil	208	32,406
United Kingdom	207	27,144
Saudi Arabia	78	24,933
Dubai	67	20,805
Russia	84	17,725
Canada	141	17,461
Abu Dhabi	58	17,205
All other countries	1,624	304,258
Total global pipeline	7,078	1,277,339

Source: Lodging Econometrics Q3 2011

UNITED STATES

The United States' construction pipeline has a total of 2,851 projects and 347,930 rooms. The lack of available financing and continued economic uncertainty remain major obstacles to construction pipeline growth. At 1,609 projects and 201,576 rooms, 56 percent of U.S. pipeline projects and 58 percent of rooms are in the early planning stage. This is largely due to the fact that new project announcements are entering the pipeline at this stage and not being fast-tracked, as developers wait for the overall economy to recover more substantially and financing to become more available.

INDIA

India's total pipeline is at 375 projects and 70,668 rooms. New hotel openings in India have accelerated and should reach a new high in 2012, which will likely draw down pipeline totals.

BRAZIL

Brazil, with a total of 208 projects and 32,406 rooms, now has the world's fourth-largest pipeline. Franchise companies and developers are eager to get a foothold in the country, especially since it will be hosting the 2014 World Cup and the 2016 Olympic Games. A high 51 percent of pipeline rooms are currently under construction, which will lead to rising new hotel openings through 2013 and beyond.

UNITED KINGDOM
At 207 projects and 27,144 rooms, the United Kingdom's total pipeline is the fifth largest for a country. Twenty-eight percent of the UK's total projects and 32 percent of rooms are in London, which is in the midst of preparing for the 2014 Olympic Games.

ASIA PACIFIC
Lodging Econometrics projects a total of 513 new hotels and 147,974 rooms to open in this region. We also adjusted forecasts for 2011 and 2012 upward due to the continued escalation in the number of pipeline projects currently under construction.

854 hotels and 135,644 rooms are now expected come online in 2011, then 646 hotels comprising 148,216 rooms in 2012.

A lion's share of the region's new openings belong to China, which will have the largest number of hotels entering current supply of any country in the world over the next three years. LE's forecast expects a total of 707 new hotels and 111,118 rooms in 2011, 467 hotels and 114,466 rooms in 2012, then 345 hotels and 113,705 rooms in 2013. While the number of rooms coming online is holding essentially flat, the number of hotels is trending down significantly. This is due to the number of larger-scale projects slated to exit the pipeline, with the average new hotel size doubling from 157 rooms in 2011 to 330 rooms in 2013.

(Source: ftp.hotelmanagement.net/pipeline/ global-pipeline-snapshot-us-asia-pacific-lead)

Considering the large number of hotels involved, only a selection of hotels (or mixed developments that contained hotels) constructed, renewed or opened during these early decades of the 21st century are listed here:

- The 41 Hotel in London, UK
- The AC Hotel Barcelona Forum in Barcelona, Spain
- The Altira Macau in Macau, China
- The Angsana Hotel & Suites in Dubai, UAE
- The Atlantis, the Palm in Dubai, UAE
- The Burj Khalifa in Dubai, UAE
- The Centara Grand Hotel in Bangkok, Thailand
- The Charles Hotel in Munich, Germany
- The Copperhill Mountain Lodge in Åre, Sweden
- The Dubai Marriott Harbour Hotel & Suites in Dubai, UAE
- The Dusit Dubai in Dubai, UAE
- The Encore Las Vegas in Paradise, Nevada, USA
- The Executive Towers in Dubai, UAE
- The Four Points by Sheraton in Dubai, UAE
- The Four Seasons Hotel and Tower in Miami, Florida, USA
- The Four Seasons Hotel Hong Kong in Hong Kong, China
- The Four Seasons Resort in Bora Bora, French Polynesia
- The Gran Hotel Bali in Benidorm, Spain
- The Guangzhou International Finance Centre, China
- The Hanging Village of Huaxi in Jiangyin, China
- The Hilton Diagonal Mar Barcelona Hotel in Barcelona, Spain
- The Hilton San Diego Bayfront in San Diego, California, USA
- The Hotel Barcelona Princess in Barcelona, Spain
- The Hotel Catalonia Plaza Europa in Barcelona, Spain
- The Hotel Porta Fira in Barcelona, Spain

Overview over Dubai

1

The W Barcelona in Barcelona, Spain

- The Howard Johnson Hotel in Bucharest, Romania
- The InterContinental in San Francisco, California USA
- The InterContinental Warsaw, in Warsaw, Poland
- The International Ocean Shipping Building in Shanghai, China
- The Jin Jiang Oriental Hotel in Shanghai, China
- The Jumeirah Emirates Hotel Tower in Dubai, UAE
- The JW Marriott Absheron Baku Hotel in Baku, Azerbaijan
- The Khalid Al Attar Tower 2 in Dubai, UAE
- The Kingkey 100 in Shenzhen, China
- The Lanko-Grand Hyatt Hotel in Chongqing, China
- The Le Royal Hôtel d'Amman in Amman, Jordan
- The Mardan Palace Hotel in Antalya, Turkey
- The ME Barcelona in Barcelona, Spain
- The MGM Macau in Macau, China
- The Nanning Marriott in Nanning, Guangxi, China
- The Palazzo in Paradise, Nevada, USA
- The Planet Hollywood Las Vegas in Paradise, Nevada, USA
- The Pullman Shanghai Skyway Hotel in Shanghai, China
- The Revel in Atlantic City, New Jersey, USA
- The Rose Tower in Dubai, UAE
- The Shangri-La Hotel in Dubai, UAE
- The Sheraton Phoenix Downtown in Phoenix, Arizona, USA
- The St. Regis Bali Resort in Bali, Indonesia
- The Tamani Hotel Marina in Dubai, UAE
- The THEHotel at Mandalay Bay in Paradise, Nevada, USA
- The Tokyo Disneyland Hotel in Tokyo, Japan
- The Trump Hotel Las Vegas in Paradise, Nevada, USA
- The Venetian Macao in Macau, China
- The W Austin Hotel & Residences in Austin, Texas, USA
- The W Barcelona in Barcelona, Spain
- The W Boston Hotel and Residences in Boston, Massachusetts, USA

The Four Seasons Hotel Hong Kong in Hong Kong, China

- The W Hong Kong in Hong Kong, China
- The Water Club in Atlantic City, New Jersey, USA
- The Wynn Las Vegas in Paradise, Nevada, USA
- The Yas Viceroy Abu Dhabi Hotel in Abu Dhabi, UAE
- The Zifeng Tower in Nanjing, China

1.2.3 Outlook for the Hospitality Industry

The previous sections described the evolution of the hospitality industry from ancient times to the current decades. Historically, the industry has been growing continuously in line with the overall growth in world economies, but more specifically with the rapid expansion of global tourism. According to projections by the World Tourism Organisation shown in Text 1.2, as noted in their Tourism 2020 Vision, travel and tourism will become the world's largest industry in the twenty-first century.

Rapid expansion

TEXT 1.2

World Tourism Organisation's Tourism 2020 Vision

Tourism 2020 Vision
Tourism 2020 Vision is the World Tourism Organisation's long-term forecast and assessment of the development of tourism up to the first 20 years of the new millennium. An essential outcome of the Tourism 2020 Vision are quantitative forecasts covering a 25 years period, with 1995 as the base year and forecasts for 2010 and 2020.

Although the evolution of tourism in the last few years has been irregular, UNWTO maintains its long-term forecast for the moment. The underlying structural trends of the forecast are believed not to have significantly changed. Experience shows that in the short term, periods of faster growth (1995, 1996, 2000) alternate with periods of slow growth (2001 to 2003). While the pace of growth till 2000 actually exceeded the Tourism 2020 Vision forecast, it is generally expected that the current slowdown will be compensated in the medium to long term.

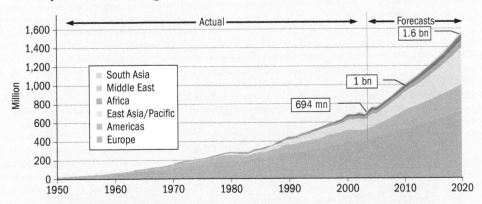

UNWTO's Tourism 2020 Vision forecasts that international arrivals are expected to reach nearly 1.6 billion by the year 2020. Of these worldwide arrivals in 2020, 1.2 billion will be intraregional and 378 million will be long-haul travellers.

The total tourist arrivals by region shows that by 2020 the top three receiving regions will be Europe (717 million tourists), East Asia and the Pacific (397 million) and the Americas (282 million), followed by Africa, the Middle East and South Asia.

East Asia and the Pacific, Asia, the Middle East and Africa are forecasted to record growth at rates of over 5% year, compared to the world average of 4.1%. The more mature regions Europe and Americas are anticipated to show lower than average growth rates. Europe will maintain the highest share of world arrivals, although there will be a decline from 60 per cent in 1995 to 46 per cent in 2020.

	Base Year	Forecasts		Market share (%)		Average annual growth rate (%)
	1995	2010	2020	1995	2020	1995-2020
		(Million)				
World	565	1006	1561	100	100	4.1
Africa	20	47	77	3.6	5.0	5.5
Americas	110	190	282	19.3	18.1	3.8
East Asia and the Pacific	81	195	397	14.4	25.4	6.5
Europe	336	527	717	59.8	45.9	3.1
Middle East	14	36	69	2.2	4.4	6.7
South Asia	4	11	19	0.7	1.2	6.2

Long-haul travel worldwide will grow faster, at 5.4 per cent per year over the period 1995-2020, than intraregional travel, at 3.8 per cent. Consequently the ratio between intraregional and long-haul travel will shift from around 82:18 in 1995 to close to 76:24 in 2020.

(Source: www.unwto.org)

This expansion in travel is expected to continue in the future and as such one can extrapolate its implications for the hospitality industry. Predicting the future is nearly impossible; but one can look around at the current trends and hypothesise what the future might be expected to look like, at least. This future may be guided by certain trends, and professionals in the industry should have some mastery of the skills, tendencies, and actions needed to operate within it. Some projections for the future that will impact the hospitality industry include:

Implications

- A shift towards ecotourism, sustainability and green hospitality;
- Advanced encryption technology will enhance the security of on-line transactions;
- Advertising will move away from printed media to the Internet;
- Apart from in the emerging markets, there will be fewer and fewer new hotels, but there will be increased existing hotel property transformation and refurbishment;
- Crime and terrorism will render some traditional tourist destinations unsalable;
- Customer share and customer profitability analysis will overtake market share and product profitability analysis as measures of marketing effectiveness;
- Data warehousing and data mining will open up unimaginable vistas for marketing departments;
- Energy and water consumption will be monitored and charged at room levels;
- Erosion of the distinction between business and leisure hotel;
- Increased sharing of technological services to enhance cost efficiency;
- Increasing reliance on social networking as a marketing technique;
- Redesigning hotels to cater to the needs of the elderly;
- The concentration of hotel real estate assets, particularly within the hands of private equity funds;
- The eventual disappearance of business centres within hotels due to the integration of advanced telecommunication devices within larger hotel rooms;
- The eventual elimination of human contact in budget operations due to credit card check-in and check-out, self-cleaning bathrooms, and food and beverage vending machines;
- The expansion of capsule-cocoon hotels within airport terminals;
- The expansion of e-hospitality with total solutions related to the distribution, service and support of the hospitality product;
- The expansion of franchising across the globe as hotel companies try to strategically reposition themselves from 'hotel businesses' into 'the business of hotels';
- The Internet will become the dominant distribution channel and hand-held devices will play a great role in leading to the elimination of the intermediaries;
- The introduction of Antarctica as an ecotourism tourism destination;
- The introduction of space as a destination for the very wealthy;
- The primacy of management companies in the control of the global inventory of branded hotel rooms;

- There will be more advanced revenue management systems with applications in new environments such as in restaurants and in sports stadia;
- Transformation of cruise ships into large mobile resorts;
- Usage of more sophisticated audience targeting advertising technology as well as direct text-messaging.

Summary

▶ The hospitality industry belongs to the larger business group called the travel and tourism industry and generally includes the service organisations that cater to people's needs in terms of food, drinks, and accommodation, as well as recreation, travel and entertainment.

▶ The hospitality industry has existed since ancient times, and is founded on such inventions as writing, money, and the wheel, which allowed people to move from place to place for pleasure and enabled them to pay for services received. This is in contrast to nomadic peoples who travelled as a way of life, who could only experience convenience if they found it.

▶ The hospitality industry has greatly evolved over time and every epoch has affected the industry in a peculiar way from pre-industrial revolution days to modern times.

▶ During the pre-industrial revolution era, while the Greeks developed thermal baths in villages designed for rest and recuperation, the Romans developed extensive networks of roads, and thermal baths throughout their empire. Caravanserais, monasteries and abbeys, relay houses and many inns appeared. Laws requiring hotels to keep a register of the visitors were established. The first travellers' guide books were written. Stagecoaches services based on regular schedules began operating. Clubs and lodges became widespread.

▶ The period from the Industrial Revolution to 1899 was characterised by a proliferation in the construction of hotels everywhere in Europe and America. These hotels were needed to cater to the needs of the rising establishment of managerial and middle classes taking care of new companies, as well as a growing demand for both leisure and business travel. This led to the appearance of a new style of hotel that provided luxurious amenities. While this period saw the birth of the Grand Tour, it also signalled the slow decline of the highway inns.

▶ The 20th century, characterised as that of the transport revolution, can be identified as the starting point for present day global hotel businesses, the introduction of franchising and management contracts, the growth of mass tourism, the introduction of social and welfare systems, a growth in salary levels, and an increase in average life spans – all of which have greatly affected the hospitality industry.

▶ The 21st century is characterised as that of the technological revolution, which is having and will continue to have a great impact on what the hospitality industry is, and how it will evolve in decades to come.

▶ Over time, the hospitality industry has continuously grown in line with the overall growth in world economies, but more specifically with the rapid expansion of global tourism. This expansion in travel is expected to continue in the future, and may be influenced by certain tendencies.

Questions and assignments for reflection

1   As lodging facilities appeared around the world, they were invariably known by different names. Using the text in this chapter, identify the various names that have been used over time to designate lodging facilities all over the world.

2   What were the main causes that triggered the creation of the hospitality industry?

3   In what major ways did the industrial revolution affect the expansion of the hospitality industry?

4   How did the transport revolution affect developments within the hospitality industry?

5   Without resorting to fortune telling, what directions do you think the hospitality industry is heading into?

2

Rating Systems and the Structure of the Hospitality Industry

M. N. Chibili

2.1 Introduction

There is no standardised set of rules for classifying hotels on a universal level, and this chapter discusses the ratings, classifications and structures of hotels as the predominant type of hospitality accommodation. Rating systems are as varied as the organisations employing them, but over the years several of these systems have proven to be of greater value to guests in helping them make their accommodation decisions. There are multiple classification criteria, including price, function, location, particular market segment, and distinctiveness of style or offerings. The diversity and changing patterns of the use of hotels often impede precise classifications, and new forms of accommodation are being introduced to cater to specific needs. Structurally speaking, no matter the size or type of the hotel, it will have a formal structure that permits it to distribute responsibility and authority amongst the different levels of management and staff.

2.2 Rating systems

Hotel ratings are often used to classify hotels according to certain objective standards such as the available facilities or the level of services provided. This normally does not include other criteria, such as ambiance or charm. There are many rating schemes and organisations worldwide, many of whom use the star symbol to categorise hotels. The greater the number of stars (or other symbols, such as diamonds as used in the USA by the American Automobile Association – AAA), the higher the expected levels of luxury.

Objective standards

2.2.1 The emergence of rating systems

One of the first known rating systems is the Michelin Red Guide, which started in 1900 and is the oldest and best-known European hotel and restaurant guide. It was created to encourage travelling by road in France, and

United Arab Emirates, Dubai: The Rose Rayhaan Tower

Michelin Stars

began reviewing restaurants anonymously by means of a three-star system in 1926. It awards the much-coveted Michelin Stars, which are granted on the basis of five criteria: the quality of the ingredients, the flair and skill used in preparing them in a combination of flavours, the chef's personality as revealed through his cuisine, value for money, and the consistency of culinary standards. The stars reflect 'what's on the plate and only what's on the plate'. In other words, their award does not take into consideration the restaurant's décor, or the quality of the service, amenities and equipment or availability of valet parking provided. The Michelin Red Guide is designed on

Premise

the premise that only reviews by anonymous, professionally-trained experts can be trusted to be accurate. A brief history of the Michelin Guide (an excerpt from the Michelin Guide Dictionary Page 7) is presented in Text 2.1.

2

TEXT 2.1

Brief history of the Michelin Guide

HISTORY

1900: André and Edouard Michelin publish the first MICHELIN guide. The brothers foresaw that, for the automobile to become successful, motorists had to be able to find places to refuel, charge their batteries or change their tires wherever they travelled. The MICHELIN guide was therefore created to offer drivers useful information, free of charge.

1904: First MICHELIN guide Belgique

1910: First MICHELIN guides España and Deutschland

1911: First MICHELIN guide Great Britain & Ireland

1920: The Michelin guide is no longer offered free of charge.

1926: The first MICHELIN stars are awarded.

1937: First MICHELIN guide Paris

1956: First MICHELIN guide Italia

1997: The Bib Gourmand distinction is introduced in France.

2000: Descriptions of selected establishments are added.

2001: The selection is published online on the ViaMichelin website.

2005: The first US guide is published, in the form of the MICHELIN guide New York City.

2007: The first Asian guide is launched, in the form of the MICHELIN guide Tokyo, and the Bonne Petites Tables France guide is introduced.

2009: The 100th edition of the MICHELIN guide France; first iPhone application launched; first MICHELIN Bib Gourmand guide in the Benelux countries and Buenas Mesas in Spain; first MICHELIN guide Hong-Kong Macau.

2011: The US selection is extended by the addition of Chicago, and the Japanese selection is extended by the addition of Kobe to the Kyoto Osaka guide and Yokohama and Kamakura to the Tokyo guide; the first MICHELIN Bonnes Petites Tables Tokyo guide is published.

2012: New Japanese cities are added, with Nara in the Kyoto Osaka Kobe guide, Shonan in the Tokyo Yokohama Kamakura guide, and the new Hokkaido guide.

(Source: travel.michelin.co.uk)

The Michelin Guide chooses the best hotels and restaurants in each comfort and price category. Establishments are ranked from one to five pavilions for hotels and from one to five fork-and-spoon pictograms for restaurants; or from 'quite comfortable' to 'luxury in the traditional style'. Symbols shown in red indicate particularly pleasant establishments in terms of atmosphere, décor, customer reception, and/or level of service. As for gastronomy, the stars, which are universally recognised as symbols of quality cuisine today, are defined as follows:

- One star: A very good restaurant in its category;
- Two stars: Excellent cooking, worth a detour;
- Three stars: Exceptional cuisine, worth a special journey.

The AAA copied the Michelin Tire Company example, and in 1937 started its own independent rating system for hotels and restaurants based on a system of standards and guidelines using professionally trained inspectors. The AAA rates hotels in the United States, Canada, Mexico and the Caribbean. Hotels do not pay to be included in the ratings, but can submit an application. To become AAA Approved, the hotel must first meet 27 basic requirements covering comfort, cleanliness and safety. If the hotel is approved, AAA sends out anonymous inspectors to evaluate the hotel and assigns a diamond rating from one to five. In 1963, AAA began assigning lodging ratings from 'good' to 'outstanding'. In 1977 the Diamond Rating system was introduced for lodgings, with restaurants included 12 years later.

Diamond Rating

In the lodging domain for example, the following criteria are used by the AAA to define the diamonds:

- One Diamond
  These establishments typically appeal to budget-minded travellers. They provide essential, no-frill accommodations. They meet basic requirements pertaining to comfort, cleanliness, and hospitality.
- Two Diamonds
  These establishments appeal to the traveller seeking more than the basic accommodations. There are modest improvements to the overall physical attributes, design elements, and amenities of the facility when compared to the one diamond establishments - typically at a moderate price.
- Three Diamonds
  These establishments appeal to the traveller with comprehensive needs. Properties are multifaceted and have a distinguished style, including marked improvements to the quality of physical attributes, amenities, and levels of comfort provided.
- Four Diamonds
  These establishments are upscale in all areas. Accommodations are progressively more refined and stylish. The physical attributes reflect an obvious enhanced level of quality throughout. The fundamental hallmarks at this level include an extensive array of amenities combined with a high degree of hospitality, service, and attention to detail.
- Five Diamonds
  These establishments reflect the characteristics of the ultimate in luxury and sophistication. Accommodations are first class. The physical attributes are extraordinary in every respect. The fundamental hallmarks at this level are to meticulously serve and exceed all guests' expectations while maintaining an impeccable standard of excellence. Many personalised services and amenities enhance an unmatched level of comfort.

(Source: Approval Requirements & Diamond Rating
Guidelines – Lodging, AAA Publishing, 2008)

There are more than 100 rating systems in use across the globe today, some of which have a governmental or supranational affiliation, while some are from self-rating and privately-run organisations. Others are run by tour operators or internet booking websites. Examples include:

- The Forbes Travel Guide (formerly Mobil Travel Guide);
- The Nordic/Baltic Rating Board;
- The North Star Travel Media;
- The Automobile Association (UK);
- The Royal Automobile Club (UK);
- The National Tourist Board (UK);
- The Japanese Travel Bureau;
- Various national tourism organisations.

Hotelstars Union

Many European countries are now a part of the Hotels, Restaurants and Cafés (HOTREC) in Europe organisation established in 2004 to help unify European hotel rating systems. Under the banner of the Hotelstars Union, the hotel associations have been committed to applying almost identical criteria for their hotel classification since 2010. Countries belonging to the Hotelstars Union were originally limited to Austria, Czech Republic, Germany, Hungary, Netherlands, Sweden and Switzerland, but have more recently been joined by Estonia (2011), Latvia (2011), Lithuania (2011), Luxembourg (2011), Malta (2012), and Belgium, Denmark and Greece (2013).

Text 2.2 lists the 21 HOTREC principles for the process of setting-up and/or reviewing national/regional hotel classification systems in Europe adopted by the HOTREC General Assembly in Barcelona, 6 November, 2009.

TEXT 2.2

21 HOTREC principles

1 Classification systems must ensure that accurate information is provided to the guests.
2 Classification systems should display their criteria (summary and full list) online to the guests via www.hotelstars.org at least in English and their national language.
3 Information about the star category of each individual hotel as well as the classification system on which this rating is based should be made transparent for the consumer.
4 Compliance with legal requirements is a prerequisite to classification.
5 Classification systems must ensure cleanliness and proper maintenance of the establishments in all the star categories.
6 Classification systems should encourage the use of quality management tools.

7 Tour operators and travel agents, as well as hotel booking and review sites are invited to use the official classification. If they use their own rating scheme alongside, they should specify so.
8 Classification systems should ensure that accurate and up-to-date data on the rating of establishments are provided to tour operators, travel agents, hotel booking and review sites.
9 The number of stars obtainable shall be one to five.
10 Stars must be granted/confirmed only after a control.
11 This control must take place regularly.
12 This control must take place on site.
13 Complaints by customers relating to classification should be dealt with in a systematic manner.
14 Explanation for classification decisions have to be made available to the hotel concerned.

15 Every classification system must allow for an appeal by the hotel concerned against the result of the classification.
16 Classification systems should have some range of flexibility in the application of their criteria.
17 Classification criteria should be regularly adjusted to market requirements. A systematic inventory process of the criteria should take place regularly.
18 Whenever research on consumer expectations in relation to classifications is carried out in one country, it is desirable that the results are made available to all HOTREC member associations.
19 When classification systems are set up/reviewed, equipment and service criteria should be emphasised in order to facilitate European and international harmonisation efforts.
20 When classification systems and criteria are set up/reviewed, co-operation with other countries is encouraged in order to facilitate European and international harmonisation efforts.
21 Classification systems should always involve the hospitality industry. In the countries, where the classification system is regulated and/or operated by public authorities, it is essential that the public authorities work in close partnership with the private sector.

(Source: www.hotelstars.eu)

There have been attempts made to set up a rating system operating on a more global level. An example is the creation of the World Hotel Rating (WHR) project that aims to set international classification standards and rating criteria along the lines of a world star-rating system. In a November 2011 declaration, the WHR created its 6 pillars as listed in Text 2.3. It should be noted that such attempts at the creation of a global rating system have historically been met with much resistance from organisations like the International Hotel & Restaurant Association (IH&RA).

World Hotel Rating

TEXT 2.3

The 6 pillars of World Hotel Rating

Declaration of intention (November 2011)

1 Universal language of hospitality
   – To develop a universal language of hospitality, together with common standards, criteria and indicators for classification, rating and labelling of hotels
   To help level the playing field between all hotels across the world as regards quality and compliance with regulatory requirements, in order to eliminate potential distortions of competition
   – To consolidate the overall image of the hotel industry

2 Diversity, multiculturalism and innovation
   – To encourage diversity of hotel services by stimulating innovation
   – To safeguard multiculturalism by maintaining the integrity and heterogeneity of local traditions
   – To participate actively in the protection of multilingualism

3 International transparency
   – To increase international transparency and comparability of information on hotels
   – To increase individually the international visibility of accommodation establishments
   – To enable travellers from all parts of the world to select quality hotels to stay in, in all destinations

4 Satisfaction of guests of all ages and enhanced quality
   - To boost quality of hospitality services and reinforce guests' confidence and satisfaction
   - To increase individually the international visibility of accommodation establishments
   - To enable travellers to select hotels which suit the purpose of their stay, which best match their preferences and meet their specific needs, as seniors, the disabled and families travelling with kids

5 Sustainable Tourism
   - To play a key role in the harmonious development of sustainable tourism
   - To contribute to the preservation of the world cultural and natural heritage

6 Equitable Tourism Declaration
   - To contribute to value tourism as a means of bringing communities closer together
   - To promote the Global Code of Ethics for Tourism in the hotel industry

(Source: www.worldhotelrating.com)

The WHR seeks to organise the overall transparency of hotel services, to create a universal language for the hospitality industry, and to be a direct interface between travellers, hotels and tourism professionals.

The WHR has created descriptive categories to use in classifying hotels. These categories (subject to possible change over time) that range from stopover hotels to grand resort hotels are listed in Text 2.4.

TEXT 2.4

The descriptive hotel categories of the WHR

Grand Resort Hotel: Large-scale hotel which provides extended or luxury services containing a combination of meeting facilities and recreational & leisure activities.

Grand Hotel: Large-scale hotel which is distinguished by a formal style and provides full, traditional hotel services including meeting and conference facilities.

Leisure Resort Hotel: Hotel located in a quiet and pleasant environment, providing relaxing retreats with leisure infrastructure generally including a swimming pool.

Eco-Resort Hotel: Hotel located in an idyllic, natural environment, providing full service and catering for ecotourism or active holidays.

Holiday Resort Hotel: Hotel located in a pleasant environment and offering sporting or active holidays, with a choice of recreational activities, individual and group.

Boutique Hotel: Medium-sized hotel, usually located in an urban or semi-urban environment, and distinguished by personal service and a stylish or sophisticated décor.

Hotel With Charm: Small-scale hotel, usually located in a rural or semi-rural area, and offering an intimate and authentic atmosphere.

Eco-Lodge Hotel: Hotel located in a natural and wild environment, providing select or limited service and catering for adventure or for activities related to the discovery of nature.

Apart-Hotel: Residential hotel where accommodation is provided in studios and apartments and particularly suited for travellers who are making an extended stay, who require housing that includes kitchen facilities and who may be satisfied with limited service.

Stopover Hotel: Easily accessible hotel mainly designed for stopovers and short stays within a functional infrastructure and suited for travellers who may be satisfied with limited service.

2.2.2   The Importance of rating systems

Current literature indicates eight benefits of a well-planned and administered rating system:

Benefits

- It assists government planning by supplying authoritative and reliable statistical data for different types of accommodations;
- It helps identify the need for developing certain categories of establishments;
- It improves marketing strategies by enabling tourist board promotion of hotels in particular geographical locations (e.g. resort, city, riverside, mountain);
- It allows the travel trade and visitors to more easily and accurately identify the types of hotels they are looking for;
- It encourages hoteliers to improve standards and the range of facilities by pinpointing weaknesses in operational services;
- It eliminates poor hotels which harm the good reputation of better hotels;
- It lets the hospitality industry cope with the age of information technology since contemporary guests base their purchasing decisions on information published on websites;
- It increases opportunities for local, independent hotels.

2.2.3   The effectiveness of rating systems in assessing quality

Nowadays, consumers make more use of the Internet to arrange their travel plans while websites use the existing rating systems to aid consumers in making their lodging or dining decisions. Consumers automatically react to changes in the ratings of properties with a lower rating, possibly indicating that the quality was less than desirable, and vice versa. In trying to evaluate whether ratings are really effective in assessing quality, it has been indicated that systems focus on criteria which are too detailed to allow hoteliers to innovate or position their properties in their own unique market segments (Ryan, 1998); that the use of size, room price, quality of management, and other features to describe a hotel do not relate directly to the quality offered, leading to controversy (Callan & Fearon, 1997; Hensens, 2001; Mintel, 2004); and that there are discrepancies between the rating system and the facilities the guests actually use, want, or appreciate. It has become clear that conventional rating systems have not been very successful in assessing the quality of hotels in providing realistic expectations for prospective travellers (Hensens, Struwig & Dayan, 2011). This ineffectiveness may partially be due to the limited input of the actual guests in the development and execution of the rating.

Controversy

The reliability of a hotel's rating depends on how frequently such a hotel is reviewed. Some countries, such as Germany, review hotels every three years to ensure that the quality levels are maintained; others have less strict requirements and only conduct on-site reviews by request or after receiving numerous complaints.

Reliability

© Noordhoff Uitgevers bv

2.3 Classification

Definition

The Oxford Advanced Learners' Dictionary (online) defines a hotel as 'a building where people stay, usually for a short time, paying for their rooms and meals'. On the other hand, according to the Hotel Proprietors Ordinance of Hong Kong (1997, p. 1), a hotel is an 'establishment held out by the proprietor as offering sleeping accommodation to any person who appears able and willing to pay a reasonable sum for the services and facilities provided and who is in a fit state to be received'. This definition now introduces the aspects of the physical ability, the financial ability and mental state of mind of the customer into the definition of what comprises a hotel. As most types of accommodation in the hospitality industry are classified as hotels, this section is primarily based on how hotels are universally defined and classified.

There are two main reasons for classifying hotels:
Firstly: to analyse the market sector and as such help in making comparisons, carrying out performance analyses, determining customer needs, identifying market gaps and establishing future strategies; and secondly: to describe the type of hotel for advertising purposes.

Criteria

Difficult

Lodging properties can be categorised according to various criteria. Classification criteria can include price, function, location, particular market segment, and distinctiveness of style or offerings. The diversity and changing patterns of hotel use often make precise classification difficult, and new forms of accommodation are being introduced to cater to specific needs, examples being condominiums and timeshares. The line between business and private has become increasingly blurred, with many business executives bringing along other members of their family on business trips. Hotels have become aware of this and try to provide all the facilities and services that both business and leisure travellers would enjoy. It should be emphasised that many types of hotels can fall into more than one category. The traditional classification of hotels was as shown in Figure 2.1.

FIGURE 2.1 The traditional classification of hotels

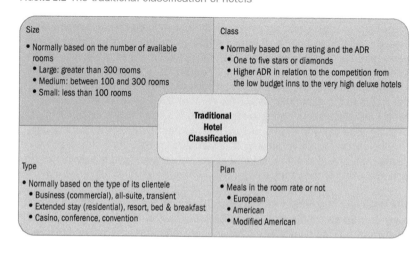

Size
- Normally based on the number of available rooms
  - Large: greater than 300 rooms
  - Medium: between 100 and 300 rooms
  - Small: less than 100 rooms

Class
- Normally based on the rating and the ADR
  - One to five stars or diamonds
  - Higher ADR in relation to the competition from the low budget inns to the very high deluxe hotels

Traditional Hotel Classification

Type
- Normally based on the type of its clientele
  - Business (commercial), all-suite, transient
  - Extended stay (residential), resort, bed & breakfast
  - Casino, conference, convention

Plan
- Meals in the room rate or not
  - European
  - American
  - Modified American

The classification of hotels in this text is done according to the perspectives illustrated in Figure 2.2: location; ownership and management; facilities and functions; target groups and types of client; price and standard; rating; and distinctiveness of the property, theme, and alternative accommodation.

FIGURE 2.2 Modern perspectives for hotel classification .

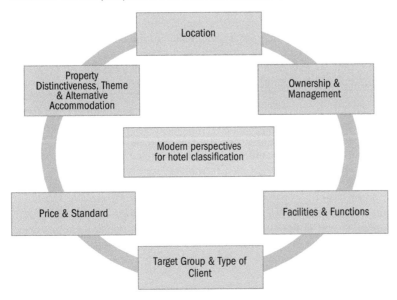

Size has not been included in these perspectives, due to the fact that it is difficult to generalise. Some countries or cities would consider properties of more than 200 rooms to be large, whereas in other areas properties are considered large only at 500 rooms or more. Some hotels, such as The Izmailovo Hotel in Moscow, are so large that using size as a benchmark makes for very difficult comparisons. Several such mega hotels, with over 5000 rooms, are shown in Figure 2.3.

Mega hotels

Tourist Hotel Complex IZMAILOVO ('Gamma', 'Delta'), Moscow

© Noordhoff Uitgevers bv

FIGURE 2.3 Some mega hotels around the world

Name	City / Country	Rooms & Suites
The Venetian & The Palazzo	Las Vegas, Nevada, USA	8,108
The Izmailovo Hotel	Moscow, Russia	7,500
The MGM Grand	Paradise, Nevada, USA	6,582
The First World Hotel	Genting Highlands, Malaysia	6,118
The Disney's All Star Resort	Orlando, Florida, USA	5,524

2.3.1   Location

Geographic position

This generally refers to the geographic position of the hotel. Mostly determined in relation to towns and cities, hotels in this category generally include downtown (city centre) hotels, suburban hotels, highway hotels, resorts, airport hotels, floating hotels, and rural hotels.

Downtown hotels

Downtown hotels (also called inner city hotels or city centre hotels) are mostly located within city centres and have the notable advantage of proximity to office complexes, retail stores and night entertainment centres. One main disadvantage in old cities for downtown hotels is the lack of parking spaces; they try to overcome this disadvantage with well-run valet and shuttle services. Downtown hotels charge comparatively higher room rates.

Suburban hotels

Suburban hotels are located further towards the outskirts of the cities and are generally not far from the main transport arteries. Suburban hotels often compensate for their distance from city centres by offering slightly better rates and generally spacious, secure parking facilities.

Highway hotels

Highway hotels (or motorway hotels – motels) are located along major highways, generally providing inexpensive, easily accessible overnight accommodation while offering only minimal banqueting and meeting spaces, with or without food and beverage facilities.

Resort hotels

Resort hotels are usually located in remote scenic settings and provide a broad selection of recreational facilities, as well as a wide variety of food and beverage outlets from informal to fine-dining. Resorts can be either 'destination resorts' which require long distance travelling to reach, or 'regional resorts' which require shorter trips. Resorts can be 'year-round', open all through the year; or 'seasonal', operating according to certain seasonal characteristics (for example ski resorts that are only open during winter).

Airport hotels

Airport hotels are specifically designed to accommodate air travellers and airline crews, and can vary depending on the size and location of the airport they are servicing. Airport hotels typically offer their guests shuttle services and courtesy vans to and from the airports.

Floating hotels

Floating hotels, as their name implies, are those hotels that are located permanently on rivers, seas or big lakes.

Rural hotels

Rural hotels are those usually found in remotely located, non-resort areas that cannot be categorised under any one of the previous categories. They are generally small and offer limited service.

2.3.2   Ownership and management

Forms of ownership and management are regarded from two different perspectives. Firstly, type of ownership, which has four aspects: sole proprietorships, partnerships, limited liability companies, and corporations. Secondly, management perspective, which also has four aspects: owned and managed privately; managed under a franchise agreement; managed under a lease agreement; and managed under a management contract.

A *sole proprietorship* is when one individual owns the property and runs the hotel. Its main advantage is that it grants the owner the freedom to operate as desired, but it has the major disadvantage that the owner has unlimited liability. This means that the owner is fully responsible for all debts incurred by the hotel and there is no distinction between what belongs to the hotel and what belongs to the owner.

Sole proprietorship

A *partnership* is when two or more individuals own and run the hotel. There are various forms of partnerships but the most common are general partnerships (where the degree of responsibility is similar to that in sole proprietorships), and limited partnerships (where limited partners enjoy some degree of limited liability and are thus not held personally liable for debts incurred by the hotel).

Partnership

A *limited liability company* is when many individuals own and run the hotel, and it principally differs from the various partnership forms in that the liability of the owners in a limited liability company is limited to the extent of their investment in the hotel.

Limited liability company

A *corporation* is when a hotel has its own separate legal rights and liabilities as defined by the laws of a specific area. These rights and liabilities are separate from those of the shareholders who own the hotel and control the hotel through an appointed board of directors. Shareholders can transfer their shares to others.

Corporation

In a *privately owned* and managed hotel, the owner operates independently and bears all the risks related to running the business. A privately owned and managed hotel may have other investors, but the ownership structure is in one person's or company's name. All decisions related to running the business are carried out by the owner. These decisions might concern human resources, the technology to be used, how the operation should be run, how to deal with customers and marketing issues or financing issues.

Privately owned

If a hotel is managed under a franchise agreement, it is privately owned but uses the successful business model of another company. The use of the business model is based on the payment of certain fees to cover for royalties and other related aspects, such as training and consultancy, a specific time period, or a specific location. The term franchisor designates the company whose business model is being used. The term franchisee designates the company or individual that uses the business model according to the terms of the agreement. A franchise has both advantages and disadvantages. The main advantages relate to the recognition of the brand name by consumers, the successful business model, and greater marketing potential. The main disadvantage relates to the owner's (franchisee's) reliance on the brand name for their business success. The franchisee also receives

Franchise

Franchisor
Franchisee

no guarantee for success and has no control over the overall quality and image of the brand. Franchise fees vary greatly across the industry, and as shown in Figure 2.4, the HVS-2011 US Franchise fee guide for first class brands can range from as little as 1% of the total rooms revenues to more than 15%.

FIGURE 2.4 Ranking of first-class brands franchise fees as a percentage of total rooms revenue (Source: HVS Global Hospitality Services)

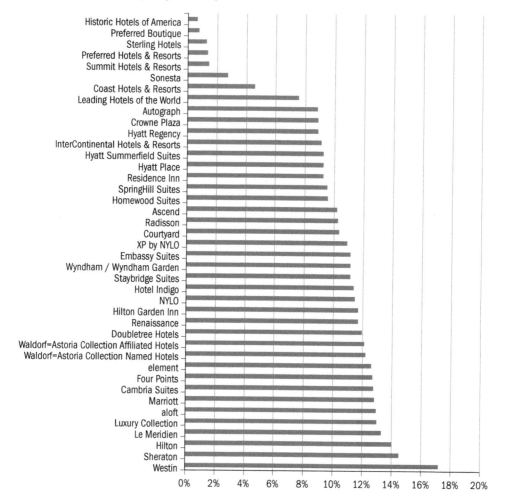

Lease agreement

If the hotel is managed under a lease agreement, the management company (the lessee) leases a hotel building from its owner (the lessor) for the rights to run the hotel and keep the profits, while also carrying the risks associated with running the hotel. Generally speaking, the lease agreement will have two components: a variable rent clause under which the lessee is obligated to pay a variable rent based on a percentage of the total revenue generated by the hotel, and a minimum rent payment requirement that is not dependent on the revenues generated by the hotel. Leases are generally long term in duration and are very popular during good economic periods.

In contrast to lease agreements, a hotel can also be managed under a management contract. This generally occurs with already existing hotels entering into agreements with other hotel operators to provide professional management services, thereby agreeing to pay fees for these services. A management service contract is usually a long-term agreement, and the operator assumes full responsibility for the management of the business, while the ultimate legal and financial responsibilities and rights of ownership of the assets, the profits or losses, remain those of the owner of the property. Managing hotels are frequently well established brands and they generally charge fees based on total revenues, ensuring fees are paid whether profit is made or not. The basic advantages and disadvantages of hotel management agreements (HMA) to both the owners and operators can be seen in Figure 2.5, designed by Ielacqua & Smith (2012, p. 3).

Management contract

Well established brands

FIGURE 2.5 Advantages and disadvantages of hotel management agreements

Owner		Operator	
Advantages	**Disadvantages**	**Advantages**	**Disadvantages**
Quality management and recognition	The owner had limited operational control (although this can be addressed in HMAs)	Opportunity for an inexpensive and rapid expansion which would guarantee a critical mass for optimising performance	The operator does not enjoy the residual benefit of ownership and does not capitalise on the value created
The owner retains ownership benefits (such as cash flows, depreciation deductions, tax benefits and so forth)	The owner is liable for all expenses (operational, fixed and fees to the operator)	Low downside risk	Minimal control over owner's decisions
	Premature termination of HMAs might result in very high expenses	The operator maintains all operational control	Dependence on owner's financing
	More difficult disposition of the property if it's encumbered with a HMA (although this can be addressed in the HMA)		The agreement can be terminated at any time by the owner (albeit at very high costs)
	The owner suffers higher downside risks (which are shifted to the operator in the case of a lease) – this can be limited by guaranteed return/subject to debt service		

2.3.3   Facilities and functions

Within this classification category, hotels can be defined as all-suite hotels, apartment hotels, bed and breakfast hotels, boutique hotels, casino hotels, commercial hotels, conference hotels, convention hotels, extended stay hotels, full service hotels, leisure hotels, limited service hotels, residential hotels, resort hotels, select-service hotels, and spa and health hotels. The classification is based on the resources available in the hotels as well as the types of activities that can be organised within these hotels.

Resources

Activities

All-suite hotels	In *all-suite hotels*, all rooms (or a very large proportion) are suites. They generally have their own separate living areas, which may also include a compact kitchenette or even a full kitchen. The décor in the suites is typically of very high standard, and the suites are aimed at rich customers who can afford the high rates.
Apartment	*Apartment hotels* are fully furnished and serviced apartment complexes that use a hotel-style booking system. It is like renting an apartment in which the 'tenants' can check out whenever they like. These apartment hotels normally contain everything an average home would have. Apartment hotels allow tenants to live as if they were at home, doing such things as cleaning, cooking and laundry; guests are not provided with services such as restaurants and bars.
B&B	*Bed and Breakfast* (B&B) *inns or hotels* are generally small in size, operated within family homes, and they do serve breakfast, which is automatically included in the room rates. A typical B&B has up to 7 rooms. A B&B inn will have between 8 and 15 rooms, while a B&B hotel will have between 16 and 30 rooms, but will only serve breakfast. Most B&Bs are independently operated, with the owners and their families living on the premises of the B&B. B&Bs are all unique in size, atmosphere, and attractiveness. They mainly serve the leisure group of clients and as such have higher weekend and holiday occupancy figures. Some bigger B&Bs now offer other services, such as restaurants and other catering activities.
Boutique hotels	*Boutique hotels* (also called design or lifestyle hotels) are hotels which often combine luxury facilities in unique or intimate settings with full service accommodations. They are typically furnished in a stylish and themed manner, and are most frequently operated independently. They are focussed on offering their services in cosy, friendly, and warm settings.
Casino hotels	*Casino hotels* are hotels that predominantly offer gambling facilities in addition to their rooms, bars and restaurants. Most also provide extravagant entertainment and sports events and even arrange all the transportation needs of their guests. They typically operate around the clock, all days of the year.
Commercial hotels	*Commercial hotels* (also called business or transient hotels) are hotels that offer their services to short-term visitors, especially business class visitors. They generally provide a high quality standard of rooms with internet connectivity, business centres, and banqueting or conference facilities. They are mostly situated in busy urban commercial areas, in order to benefit from high business flows. They can therefore be found in city centres, around ring-roads, in research parks, around airports and even in large shopping centres.
Conference hotels	*Conference hotels* are hotels that cater to the needs of conference delegations. Such hotels must comply with the guidelines of the International Association of Conference Centres as denoted in their Quality Assurance Checklist. These guidelines cover such areas as priority of business, design, services, food and beverage, technology, and guest rooms. These hotels are typically large, provide a high quality standard of services, and generally offer packages that include accommodation and meeting facilities.

Convention hotels are those hotels which do not form part of the conference hotels group, yet provide facilities and services geared to meet the needs of large meetings and trade exhibitions delegations. These hotels are typically bigger than conference hotels and have large unobstructed exhibit areas, often including conference rooms, hotel accommodations, restaurants, and other facilities such as public address systems. Convention hotels are often located close to convention centres and other convention hotels.

Convention
hotels

Extended stay hotels are a type of lodging with features unavailable at standard hotels, designed to provide a more domestic feeling and matching amenities, such as fully-fledged kitchens, dishes, refrigerator and laundry facilities. Extended stay hotels cover the range of hotels from economy to luxury. In such hotels, room rates are determined based on duration of stay, and they have no on-site food and beverage outlets.

Extended stay
hotels

Full-service hotels are those hotels that offer a wide range of on-site facilities and amenities. These facilities might include food and beverage outlets and services, a cocktail lounge, entertainment, conference facilities, shops, spa, health, sports, recreational, and parking facilities. The number of facilities also differs based on whether the hotel is economy or luxury.

Full-service
hotels

Leisure hotels are generally large hotels situated near important tourist destinations far from cities, offering a 'great escape' from the bustle of modern life. Hotel areas are usually spacious and have facilities such as golf courses, tennis courts, gardens, spas, saunas, and swimming pools. They offer luxurious environs and the finest in modern amenities, with highly personalised service delivered with the utmost care.

Leisure hotels

Limited-service hotels typically offer rooms-only operations, optionally with very limited food and beverage services. Limited-service hotels typically do not have public spaces or meeting spaces. The services and amenities offered in limited-service hotels vary depending on how low the hotel is on the budget scale.

Limited-service
hotels

Residential hotels are generally apartment buildings that offer accommodation for long durations and are patronised by 'tenants' who stay for a long period of time. They typically offer services such as maids, dining rooms, and room service. Residential hotels range from the moderately priced to the luxurious. In this type of hotel, there is some degree of permanent occupancy and there is a landlord-tenant relationship that is different from the normal hotelier-guest relationship found in other hotels.

Residential
hotels

Resort hotels have already been explained under the location classification section. Half-way between limited-service hotels and full-service hotels are what have been termed *select-service hotels*. These hotels present clients with the basics offered by limited-service hotels in combination with an assortment of services and amenities offered by full-service hotels. These generally include some restaurant and banquet facilities but on a smaller scale than would be the case for full-service hotels, including for example limited menus or limited opening days and times for meals.

Resort hotels

Select-service
hotels

Lastly, there are *spa and health hotels*. Spa and health hotels are hotels which are very often found in resort areas. They provide professionally ad-

Spa and health
hotels

ministered spa services, fitness and wellness components and spa cuisine menu choices. The staff in such hotels may often include dieticians, exercise physiologists, masseurs, physicians, physiotherapists, and various other therapists. With an ever-ageing global population, spa and health hotels are becoming more and more popular. The amount of facilities offered differs based on the whether the hotel is economy or luxury. Typical spa and health treatments offered in such properties are shown in Figure 2.6.

FIGURE 2.6 Some typical spa treatments

Some typical spa treatments

Acupuncture
Aromatherapy
Ayurveda (Indian folk medicine)
Body wraps
Facial cleansing
Hot springs
Hot tub
Hydrotherapy
Manicures and pedicures
Massage
Mud bath
Nutrition and weight guidance
Onsen (Japanese hot springs)
Peat pulp bath
Sauna
Shiatsu (Japanese mud bath)
Skin exfoliation
Steam bath
Thermae (Roman hot springs)
Waxing
Yoga and meditation

2.3.4   Target groups or type of clients

In this category, the emphasis is on the type of clients targeted by the various hotels unlike the functions and facilities as denoted in the previous section. Note that this does not take into account the special group of clients that are considered non-guests, such as the various intermediaries who purchase hotel rooms in bulk to then sell or distribute them to the final clients. As before, there are no clear-cut distinctions, and hotels are required by law to accept any person who, as defined at the beginning of this section, 'appears able and willing to pay a reasonable sum for the services and facilities provided and who is in a fit state to be received'. There are three primary sub-divisions in this category – business, groups and leisure.

Non-guests

Hotels that cater to business clients are typically full service hotels. Business clients average multiple trips per year and they account for a good percentage of hotel revenue overall. Business oriented hotels provide special amenities, facilities and business support services, such as complimentary newspapers, internet access and fax machines, free local telephone calls, business centres, meeting space, rentable office space, and in-room safes.

Business

Hotels also cater to group clients, which can either be business or leisure groups. These hotels are typically very large, such as with the convention hotels and resorts described in the previous section. The business groups include all those who travel for commercial, governmental or educational purposes, such as to attend management meetings, new product launches, training seminars, or shareholder meetings. The leisure groups include those who travel for recreational, educational, sightseeing, and relaxing purposes as well as for the sake of experience. Here, individuals purchase the group package.

Group

Hotels also cater to the leisure clients, who very often depend on the attractions, products and services offered by hotels; these clients are very price sensitive. They are attracted by low rates and discouraged by high ones. Leisure clients may visit an area for a specific pre-defined reason or because they are travelling to other destinations. Leisure clients may be individuals, couples, families, or groups as discussed in the previous paragraph. Leisure demand is often seasonal and in some market areas, this demand may be limited to weekends or holiday periods.

Leisure

2.3.5   Price or standard

Based on price or standard, hotels can be classified into budget and economy hotels, mid-price hotels (with or without food), upmarket hotels, and luxury hotels. There is a general belief that in a given market, the higher the prices charged for the goods and services provided, the better the quality or standards of these goods and services. Smith Travel Research (STR) uses a flexible format that relates the levels of the actual or estimated average daily rate to the number of hotels within the given market to define the class of hotels found there. Based on this format, they have defined different classes of hotels within the US hospitality industry depending on whether the hotels are metro-based or non-metro-based as shown in Figure 2.7.

Flexible format

Using this way of classifying hotels, it becomes clear that hotels might be classified differently if it were possible for them to be transferred from one place to another, or if the dynamics of the ADR within the specific market were to change. The various classes of hotels are explained in the following paragraphs.

Budget hotels are generally low-priced, and are normally part of a large branded hotel group. They are very often purpose-built. They are characterised by good quality, and adopt the 'no-frills principle', offering the ambience and comfort of star hotels but at much lower rates. They are most often located along major tourism routes or outside urban settings, often providing limited services, and enjoying relatively high occupancy levels. They are considered good value for money for travellers and groups on a limited budget. One step up are the economy hotels, which are not very different from budget hotels. The key difference between the two is that, on average, economy hotel prices are slightly higher than those found in the budget category within any specific environment. The article in Text 2.5, taken from the *Financial Times*, starkly illustrates how hard it is to separate the two.

Budget hotels

No-frills principle

Economy hotels

FIGURE 2.7 STR's ADR-based hotel classification

ADR level in the metro market	Class of hotel
Top 15%	Luxury
Next 15%	Upscale
Middle 30%	Mid-price
Next 20%	Economy
Lowest 20%	Budget

ADR level in the non-metro (rural) market	Class of hotel
Top 30%	Upscale
Next 30%	Mid-price
Next 20%	Economy
Lowest 20%	Budget

TEXT 2.5

Accor to rebrand economy hotels

September 13, 2011 7:24 am

Accor to rebrand economy hotels
By Jennifer Thompson in Paris

Accor is to rebrand its economy hotels, Denis Hennequin, chairman and chief executive, told the Financial Times, as Europe's largest hotels group by number of rooms attempts to assert a new identity after a period of restructuring.

The group's three current economy brands – Ibis, Etap Hotel and All Seasons – are to be grouped around a single Ibis 'megabrand,' a move aimed at trimming operating costs and making the division more recognisable to tourists and businesses looking for ways to make travel budgets stretch further.

The move will affect more than 1,500 hotels, or over a third of the group, and will require an investment of €150m ($205m, £129m). It will be completed by early 2013. Mr Hennequin wants to capitalise on the recognisability of Ibis's distinctive pillow-shaped red and dark green logo, which will be applied to signs, bedding and advertising across the segment.

The transformation will see Etap Hotel rechristened Ibis Budget, while All Seasons will be renamed Ibis Styles.

'Now Ibis is to become the iconic name of the economy segment – the Big Mac of Accor', Mr Hennequin said.

With a previous career in retail, Mr Hennequin's conversation is peppered with references to brands with identities he admires such as Uniqlo and Coca-Cola, but most notably McDonald's, where he spent 26 years latterly as head of the European division of the US fast-food chain.

'The restaurant business is of course different from the hotel business but there are strong similarities – the importance of brands, the direct contact with the customer', Mr Hennequin, 53, says.

He joined Accor's board in 2009, during a period of upheaval for the group. His predecessor, and nephew of the group's founder, Gilles Pélisson, announced his resignation in late 2010, the same year the group was split in two following the spin-off of its vouchers business into a separately listed company, Edenred.

Mr Hennequin took the reins of Accor earlier this year and is pursuing a strategy of asset sales to cut group debt and focus on a model favouring management contracts and franchises.

Net debt, which stood at €559m at the end of June, should be 'close to zero' by the end of the year.

Accor, which is aiming to open 100,000 new rooms by 2015, did not give guidance on the capital it could raise through disposals for acquisitions. However while cash would be earmarked for renovating existing hotels, the group would also consider making 'targeted acquisitions' with a focus on Latin America and China, Mr Hennequin said. Neither did he rule out an increase in Accor's dividend. The group would also examine opportunities 'with a focus on franchises in Europe', in order to maintain its leadership position in the region.

The group has not seen late summer and early autumn bookings dented by fears of a recession, but Mr Hennequin admitted that a sale of Motel 6, the group's US economy chain, was a possibility. 'If there is appetite for M6, I won't close the door,' he said.

(Source: www.ft.com)

Mid-price hotels

Mid-price hotels (with or without food) are those hotels that offer some modest services, such as room service, shuttle service, meeting rooms, and bar and dining facilities – services the budget/economy hotels do not provide. These hotels form a very large proportion of hotels in the industry, and can either be full service or limited service hotels. They are generally patronised by business travellers, individuals, and groups of all sorts for small conferences and conventions.

Upscale and luxury hotels

Upscale and luxury hotels are generally luxurious properties that provide the ultimate in hotel experience, while placing major emphasis on the quality of the products and services offered to guests. These hotels target society's rich and affluent, offering them world class products and personalised service of the highest standards. These hotels provide such services and amenities as multiple restaurants and lounges, concierge service, 24-hour room service, large and opulent rooms, and well-appointed sports and leisure facilities, just to name a few. General tendency in such hotels is for a high employee to guest ratio, which in some cases can be up to two employees per guest. They are able to compensate for these high quality services by charging high rates.

2.3.6 Rating

Rating systems have been extensively explained at the beginning of this chapter. At this point, it would suffice to indicate that rating establishments using stars is one of the most widely accepted systems worldwide. An excerpt of criteria applicable within the countries of HOTREC (2015) in attributing the various hotel star levels is shown in Text 2.6 (transitional arrangements might be in place).

Criteria

TEXT 2.6

HOTREC's star rating criteria

One star
- 100% of the rooms with shower/WC or bath tub/WC
- Daily room cleaning
- 100% of the rooms with colour-TV together with remote control
- Table and chair
- Soap or body wash at the wash basin
- Reception service
- Publicly available telephone for guests
- Extended breakfast
- Beverage offer in the hotel
- Deposit possibility

Two stars
- Breakfast buffet
- Reading light next to the bed Internet access in the room or in the public area
- Payment via card
- Body wash or shower gel at the shower/ bath tub
- Linen shelves
- Offer of sanitary products (e.g. toothbrush, toothpaste, shaving kit)

Three stars
- Reception open 14 hours, accessible by phone 24 hours from inside and outside, bilingual staff
- Lounge suite at the reception, luggage service
- Beverages on offer in the room
- Telephone in the room
- Hair-dryer, cleansing tissue
- Dressing mirror, adequate place or rack to put the luggage/suitcase
- Sewing kit, shoe polishing utensils, laundry and ironing service
- Additional pillow and additional blanket on demand
- Systematic complaint management system

Four stars
- Reception open 16 hours, accessible by phone 24 hours from inside and outside
- Lobby with seats and beverage service
- Breakfast buffet or breakfast menu card via room service
- Minibar or 16 hours beverages via room service
- Upholstered chair/couch with side table
- Bath robe and slippers on demand
- Cosmetic products (e.g. shower cap, nail file, cotton swabs), vanity mirror, tray of a large scale in bathroom), heating facility in the bathroom
- Internet access and internet terminal
- 'À la carte' restaurant

Five stars
- Reception open 24 hours, multilingual staff
- Valet parking service
- Concierge, page boy
- Spacious reception hall with several seats and beverage service
- Personalised greeting for every guest with fresh flowers or a gratuity in room
- Minibar and food and beverages on offer via room service 24 hours
- Personal care products in flacons
- Internet-PC in the room on demand
- Safe in the room
- Ironing service (return within 1h), shoe polish service
- Turndown service in evening
- Mystery guesting

(Source: www.hotelstars.eu)

It should be noted that some hotels claim to have more than 5 stars (seemingly for advertising purposes), but there is currently no globally recognised formal organisation that awards more than 5 stars (or diamonds) to hotels.

2.3.7   Property distinctiveness, theme, alternative accommodations

As noted in the earlier sections of this chapter, the diversity in services and facilities offered in the hotel industry makes it very difficult to classify hotels; as such, this section only lists some of those types that would be found in some areas of the world, and which do not easily fit any of the previous categories and have not previously been mentioned in this chapter. The following would be examples of hotels belonging to this classification: bunker hotels, eco lodges, exclusive use hotels, famous landmark and heritage hotels, ice hotels, retreats, tree house hotels, secret hotels, trophy hotels, underwater hotels, vacation ownership, water park hotels, and youth hostels.

Difficult

Bunker hotels are usually former military or nuclear defence bunkers converted into hotels. They may also fit other categories, such as lifestyle or eco lodges. The story in Text 2.7 paints a good picture of the story of one such bunker in Switzerland. Having briefly operated as a hotel, it was transformed into a museum called the Null Stern Hotel (German for 'zero star hotel').

Bunker hotels

TEXT 2.7

The Null Stern spirit

The Null Stern spirit - coming soon to a location near you

The world's first Null Stern Hotel in Teufen, Switzerland, closed its doors on June 4, 2010 – exactly one year after opening – to focus on opening in urban locations. The Null Stern Hotel in Teufen has been converted into a museum.

'We started with a Beetle but the Null Stern engine has grown and we need a truck' states, Daniel Charbonnier (Minds in Motion, SA). The overwhelmingly positive response from guests requesting additional Null Stern Hotel locations has led the three Swiss founders of the brand 'Null Stern – the only star is you', Frank and Patrik Riklin (Atelier für Sonderaufgaben) and Daniel Charbonnier to dedicate their efforts on the expansion strategy. 'The operating performance as well as market research collected in the past year has confirmed the demand to open a full size Null Stern Hotel', explains Daniel Charbonnier.

The current evolution of the socio-economic environment creates opportunities to develop the business model to its fullest potential. Due to on-going negotiations, the next Null Stern Hotel location cannot be disclosed. 'For sure it is a location where you don't expect a Biedermeier bed', says Patrik Riklin.

Museum
The Null Stern Hotel Biedermeier beds have welcomed guests from 29 countries in one year. The hotel is now open as a museum and is ready for visitors to experience and discover the birthplace of the world's first Null Stern Hotel. The founders will personally escort you on a tour to explain the unique features of the Null Stern Hotel such as the wheel of fate, the virtual window or the second check in. Additionally, you will have the opportunity to watch documentaries and exclusive footage of the making of the Null Stern Hotel brand.

(Source: www.null-stern-hotel.ch)

Eco lodges

Eco lodges are ecologically-themed hotels which provide accommodation, but differ from normal hotels in that they are designed to reduce humanity's environmental impact and provide support to their local community. They generally use non-toxic cleaners, greywater, renewable energy sources, locally produced organic food and eco-friendly forms of transportation.

Exclusive use hotels

Exclusive use hotels provide accommodation exclusively for one customer or group of persons with a minimum let of one day. They are required to have a certain minimum number of rooms to qualify for certification, and must be able to provide the full range of services that guests require, including food and beverage services.

Landmark and heritage hotels

Famous landmark and heritage hotels are hotels found in buildings or sites of historical significance, such as palaces, lodges, mansions, castles, forts, prisons, lighthouses, etc. They are generally situated in buildings that have been marked for preservation on a local, national or international level. The façade, architectural features and general (re)construction of these hotels should maintain their time-honoured distinctive qualities, ambience and décor.

Ice hotels

Ice hotels are found mainly in countries bordering the northern polar zone. Most of these hotels are designed and sculpted almost entirely out of ice and snow during the beginning of the northern winter, and are allowed to thaw away with the onset of the next spring. The unusual story of the first ice hotel is told in Text 2.8.

TEXT 2.8

The story of the first ice hotel

How it all started

If you can build a hotel of snow and ice in a village 200 kilometers above the Arctic Circle, which strikes the world with amazement – nothing is impossible. Listen to Yngve Bergqvist, the founder of ICEHOTEL, tell his story.

I started working for the company in the 1970's. It all began under the direction of the local folklore society. Love and the close vicinity to nature and the clean water is what made me stay in Jukkasjärvi.

In the 1980's the local folklore society started a joint-stock company. This company however was later owned by 'Kaamos' – a group of employees that were intent on tourism in Jukkasjärvi. We're still here.

The summer was a fortunate tourist season throughout the 1980's and in the beginning of the 1990's. Our most popular product was white water rafting, at the same time we developed other products such as survival training, fishing and canoeing. Everybody visited Jukkasjärvi – conference groups, leisure travellers and guests flying up for one night just to see the midnight sun. But we had no guest wintertime.

The ones that we tried to lure up here defended themselves by saying - What's there for us to do in all that cold and darkness? We might come for the summer when it's warm and we get to see the midnight sun. Only our own tracks could be spotted in the snow.

In 1989 I set out on a journey to frostbitten destinations, to see how they succeeded to attract guests. I went to Japan, among other places, and visited the town of Sapporo during their annual snow and ice festival. And I

established the fact that we had the entire Torne River full of ice, but not using it.
In November 1989 we arranged the first ice seminar together with the society for snow and ice sculptors in Kiruna. It was a two weeks course in Jukkasjärvi. I invited two Japanese chefs and ice artists to teach us the craft of working in ice. We built the first snow building the year after, in February – a 60 square meter arched building where we hosted an art exhibition.

The first guests stayed overnight in 1992 and the story goes: One of my clients wanted to visit us with his company. But our lodging had run out of availability that particular week. I solved the problem by suggesting that they would overnight in the snow house. We arranged sleeping bags and held survival training with detailed instructions before the guests headed for their lodging. Some staff members worried about how the guests would handle toilet visits and feel about the comfort of the room – everyone was in the same room.

The following morning we anxiously awaited the guests' reactions. After a morning sauna and breakfast we handed out diplomas as proof that the guests had survived a night in -5 C. They were fascinated by the experience and their faces lit up with joy. That's how ICEHOTEL came about.

There are still many things left to do - most is undone and many exciting challenges are waiting. We will dig where we stand.

(Source: www.icehotel.com)

Retreat hotels are hotels that afford peace, quiet, privacy, or security, thereby permitting the guests some degree of seclusion, retirement, or solitude. Some of these hotels might be used as rehabilitation centres for rich and famous substance or alcohol abusers.

Retreat hotels

The secret hotel concept relates more to the booking process than to the hotel itself. During this booking process, customer books a hotel online and is only informed of which hotel has been booked once the reservation is confirmed. The information made available to the customers include the location of the hotel and its rating, but its name remains a mystery until the customer has booked and paid for it. Text 2.9 provides a contemporary example of this concept.

Secret hotel concept

TEXT 2.9

Secret Cinema launches the Secret Hotel

People attend the Secret Cinema Lawrence of Arabia film event

Pioneers of popular immersive cinema experiences, Secret Cinema, today added a Secret Hotel element to the event, letting moviegoers stay on at themed mystery lodgings complete with staff in character.

Immersive theatre and cinema experiences are all the rage ... thanks to pioneering companies Punchdrunk and Secret Cinema.

More recently the likes of the Experimental Food Society and Poietic have created immersive restaurants that turn dining out into a theatrical experience (levitating canapés, anyone?). So, it was only a matter of time before some clever clogs came up with the concept of immersive, or theatrical, accommodation. Welcome to the Secret Hotel. Tickets went on sale today at 1pm for an overnight experience created by the founders of the hugely popular Secret Cinema – the Secret Hotel gives audience members the chance to become guests at a curated themed 'hotel' inspired by the film they've just watched.

As you would expect, the Secret Hotel is shrouded in mystery. All we know is that it's

somewhere in central London and that of the 450 or so people per night attending the film experience this autumn, 80 will stay at the hotel. The only other hint as to what the hotel might be like is in the price: tickets cost £30 per person.

In other words – you won't be sleeping in a king-size four-poster. Beds will be in dorm rooms for up to six people, and breakfast, we assume, will be basic. 'The most important thing is that it will be an experience ... the building and the staff will be in full character', says Fabien Riggall, creative director and founder Future Cinema, creators of Secret Cinema.

On the face of it paying in advance for a hotel in an unknown location doesn't sound that appealing. But Riggall says the hotel concept is a natural extension of the film events, another way of injecting some excitement and spontaneity into a familiar experience. 'Life's become a bit mundane ... we wanted to create something adventurous and fun.'

(Source: www.guardian.co.uk)

As their name implies, tree house hotels are constructed in trees or forests. They aim at providing people with a chance to experience nature amongst the tree-tops, combining ecological values and uniquely designed houses. Modern tree house hotel suites and rooms have all the trappings of normal hotels, such as air-conditioning, private bathrooms, balconies, but provide in addition tree top bars and restaurants and extensive elevated walkways among the trees.

Tree house hotels

Hotels can also be classified as trophy hotels when they meet certain criteria which might relate to their location, name, reputation, or ownership. Hotels that enjoy a prime location in a destination considered difficult to emulate or improve upon might be considered 'trophies'; as such, they are very desirable to investors. Hotels that enjoy some architectural prominence may be considered trophy hotels; the same holds for hotels that are monuments, or hotels considered to be a symbol of their location. Hotels that, in time, have developed a reputation for providing very high levels of faultless service in beautiful surroundings can also be considered trophy hotels. Some trophy hotels, however, in fact only satisfy the interest of ego-driven investors much more interested in owning the property than running the hotel in a profitable manner. Trophy hotels all share a quality of timeless elegance, ultimately defined by the guests who choose the hotel and over time build up its reputation by virtue of their loyalty to the 'experience' the hotel provides. Relating to trophy hotels, Rushmore (1993, p. 16) indicates that 'the reputation and name recognition are acquired through a long and successful operating history that creates the trophy image and a significant repeat clientele. As a result, it is rare that new hotels are accorded trophy status'.

Trophy hotels

Timeless elegance

For thrill seekers, underwater hotels could be the way forward. These are hotels that have accommodation facilities underwater. Current underwater hotels are very small, with some even requiring scuba diving gear to access them. However, there are some very ambitious projects in parts of the world aimed at building entire resorts and hotels below sea level, with some even designed to allow guests to stay bone dry throughout their stay.

Underwater hotels

More on the level of an occupation plan than of a type of hotel, vacation ownership (also called timeshare) refers to the period of time (days or weeks per year) that a customer can buy a specific property, thereby having the right to use the property during that specific period only. It is like owning the property instead of renting the property for part(s) of the year. There are multiple formats of this sort of ownership and it is becoming more and more popular in resort areas around the world, with the big hotel companies leading the way in developing the idea. In many cases, when a timeshare is purchased, the buyer receives a title deed allowing usage for the number of years indicated in the deed, and the purchase can be handed down to the buyer's heirs.

Vacation ownership

From amusement parks to theme parks entertainment facilities have evolved over the years. A currently popular iteration is the water park. Water park hotels or resorts belong to a category of hotels (or resorts) that have been designed specifically for integration with (either indoor or outdoor) water parks. Water parks are favoured for holiday days out, especially by families and groups. Figure 2.8 has been taken from page 17 of the TEA/AE-

Water park hotels

COM 2014 Theme Index: The Global Attractions Attendance Report published by the Themed Entertainment Association (TEA), and shows the top 20 water parks worldwide and the evolution in their attendance between 2013 and 2014.

FIGURE 2.8 The Global Attractions Attendance Report's Top 20 water parks and attendance (Source: www.aecom.com)

Rank	Park and Location	% change	2014	2013
1.	CHIMELONG WATERPARK, Guangzhou, China	4.0%	2,259,000	2,172,000
2.	TYPHOON LAGOON AT DISNEY WORLD, Orlando, FL	2.0%	2,185,000	2,142,000
3.	BLIZZARD BEACH AT DISNEY WORLD, Orlando, FL	2.0%	2,007,000	1,968,000
4.	THERMAS DOS LARANJAIS, Olimpia, Brazil	17.5%	1,939,000	1,650,000
5.	OCEAN WORLD, Gangwon-Do, South Korea	−5.7%	1,604,000	1,700,200
6.	AQUATICA, Orlando, FL	1.0%	1,569,000	1,553,000
7.	CARIBBEAN BAY, Gyeonggi-Do, South Korea	−8.0%	1,493,000	1,623,000
8.	AQUAVENTURE WATERPARK, Dubai, U.A.E.	16.0%	1,400,000	1,200,000
9.	HOT PARK RIO QUENTE, Caldas Novas, Brazil	0.3%	1,288,000	1,284,000
10.	WET 'N WILD, Orlando, FL	2.0%	1,284,000	1,259,000
11.	RESOM SPA CASTLE, Deoksan, South Korea	2.4%	1,218,000	1,189,000
12.	WET'N'WILD GOLD COAST, Gold Coast, Australia	−4.0%	1,200,000	1,250,000
13.	SHENYANG ROYAL OCEAN PARK — WATER WORLD, Fushun, China	6.5%	1,172,000	1,100,000
14.	SUNWAY LAGOON, Kuala Lumpur, Malaysia	0.0%	1,100,000	1,100,000
15.	SCHLITTERBAHN, New Braunfels, TX	1.0%	1,037,000	1,027,000
16.	PISCILAGO, Girardo (Bogotà), Colombia	−1.6%	1,018,000	1,035,000
17.	THERME ERDING, Erding, Germany	0.0%	1,000,000	1,000,000
18.	ATLANTIS WATER ADVENTURE, Jakarta, Indonesia	−2.0%	960,000	980,000
19.	BEACH PARK, Aquiraz, Brazil	−1.6%	949,000	964,000
20.	WOONGJIN PLAYDOCI WATERDOCI, Gyeonggi-Do, South Korea	−5.2%	945,000	997,000
TOTAL		**2.8%**	**27,627,000**	**26,887,000**

Hostels

Hostels (or 'youth hostels' when they limit guest age to the maximum of 18 years old) provide budget-type, sociable accommodations where guests can rent a bed in a dormitory-like setting. Guests share common spaces such as the bathroom, lounge, play room or kitchen. The rooms can be either mixed or single-sex, but in some cases private rooms are available. Occasionally, hostels also provide meals; this is then indicated in the price. Some hostels have long-term residents who may deliver some services in exchange for their accommodation. Hostels as described in this section should not be confused with those types of hostel which, in some areas of the world, is synonymous to a dormitory or student hall of residence that provides much longer term accommodation.

2.4 Hotel organisation

An organisation has been defined in multiple ways, such as 'an organised group of people with a particular purpose, such as a business or government department', 'the action of organising something', 'the quality of being systematic and efficient' or 'the way in which the elements of a whole are arranged' (Oxford Dictionary – online). When combining these definitions while relating it to the hotel industry, a hotel should be regarded as an organised group of people with the purpose of providing goods and services to guests in a manner that would entail the use of its resources while realising its own pre-established objectives. No matter the size or type of hotel, it will have a formal structure that allows it to distribute responsibility and authority amongst its different levels of management and employees. For hotels to be able to cater to their guests, they should have a well-organised structure, which will provide them with advantages such as:

Formal structure

Advantages

- Providing guidance to employees in explicating official reporting relationships within the hotel;
- Enhancing easier, faster and more effective communication between hotel departments;
- Making it easier to add new (or remove old) functions and positions when the need arises in response to business growth (or decline) requirements of the hotel;
- Improving operational efficiency allowing the various hotel departments to focus their time and energy on really productive tasks;
- Providing a road map to employee advancement within the hotel, thereby providing clarity, and enhancing employee motivation and desire to excel;
- Making it easier for hotel management to implement its goals and objectives, thereby enhancing the overall quality of their service delivery.

To be able to understand any organisation, it is necessary to have an understanding of its mission, vision, values, goals, objectives and strategy.

2.4.1   Mission, vision, values, goals, objectives and strategy

Mission and mission statement

The mission of an organisation states the purpose or reason for the organisation to exist. The mission explains what the organisation provides to the world. Understanding an organisation's mission will help management to better conceptualise and design its products and services. Organisations should avoid establishing missions that are too broad, because it might lead them into areas in which they have no expertise. Nor should organisations establish missions that are too narrow, because this might limit their growth potentials. The mission statement is simply the declaration of the organisation's mission. Wheelen and Hunger (2008, p. 12) indicate that a 'well-conceived mission statement defines the fundamental, unique purpose that sets a company apart from other firms of its type and identifies the scope of the company's operations in terms of products (including services) offered and markets served'. In the absence of specifically laid down criteria to be used in defining mission statements, well established mission statements should attempt to answer some (if not all) of the following questions:

Mission

Unique purpose

Mission statement

- What is our reason for being in business?
- What is unique about our organisation?
- Who are (or who will be) our principal customers or key market segments?
- What are (or what will be) our principal products and services?
- What is the philosophy of our organisation?
- What makes our organisation distinctive?
- How socially responsible is our organisation?

- What is our organisation's commitment to growth and financial stability?
- How does our organisation view its employees?

An example of the mission statement of a global hospitality company is that of the Wyndham Hotel Group, which states: 'We will be the global leader in travel accommodations welcoming our guests to iconic brands and vacation destinations through our signature *Count On Me!* service.'

The excerpt in Text 2.10, taken from the Christian Foundation Grants, illustrates some of the advantages of establishing a good mission statement early in the life of an organisation.

TEXT 2.10

Benefits of a good mission statement

Developing a clear and concise mission statement early in an organization's development is critical to its success. The first three benefits stated are tied to the process of creating the mission statement itself.

First, the process of creating a mission statement is tremendously valuable to the founders. This process helps define the company's goals to a concise and clear statement that is easy to share with the internal organization as well as to its customers.

Second, the process of defining the mission statement will help founders determine the scope of their effort; helps clarify competition and focus on their real market opportunities.

Third, create a better version of something that's already being done, help clearly differentiate your company from its competition.

Other benefits include direction, focus, policy, meaning, challenge, and passion. Direction states what the organization does and what it wants to be successful in. Focus concentrates on the company's strengths and competitive advantages and tells people how to obtain them. Policy is a guideline of what a company finds acceptable and unacceptable and states organizational values. Meaning shows what a company strives to achieve and why they wish to do so. Challenge is the setting up of goals and measurements of achievement for employees. Passion makes everyone involved with the organization show feelings of enthusiasm, pride, and commitment.

(Source: www.christianfoundationgrants.com)

A good mission statement should be very clear in terms of its intentions as well as its achievability. The mission statement should help management develop well-focussed goals and objectives that allow the organisation to achieve its mission.

Vision and vision statement

Vision

An organisation's vision describes what the organisation aspires to become. In other words, the vision provides a future direction for the organisation. It describes where the organisation desires to be in the future. The vision establishes an ideal that stretches the organisation's resources but is both inspiring and attainable. Establishing a vision is just like setting a desired destination on a GPS device. Explained in a vision statement, it describes a dynamic and persuasive view of the organisation at some point in the fu-

Future

Vision statement

ture. It will be an emotional driver for some important challenges that motivate those within the organisation aim for and achieve that future direction. A vision statement is not intended to be used by those outside the organisation. A vision statement describes the future direction of the organisation without determining the means needed to reach that desired direction.

An example of a vision statement of a global hospitality company is that of Marco Polo Hotels: 'Exceptional and personalised service, exceeding expectations, and inspiring a connection to our brand in the experiences we provide.'

In general, not all organisations develop both a mission statement and vision statement. Some simply choose to develop one or the other. Some organisations, meanwhile, have started developing what they call their value statements.

Values statements

The values statement tries to answer the basic questions of what an organisation stands for and what its core rules are. The values statement indicates the boundaries imposed on management and employees when carrying out their activities in their desire to conform to the overall mission and vision of the organisation.

Core rules

Text 2.11 indicates some basic requirements needed in the development of values statements.

TEXT 2.11

Basic requirements in developing a values statement

Developing a Values Statement

1 Values represent the core priorities in the organization's culture, including what drives members' priorities and how they truly act in the organization, etc. Values are increasingly important in strategic planning. They often drive the intent and direction for 'organic' planners.

2 Developing a values statement can be quick culture-specific, i.e., participants may use methods ranging from highly analytical and rational to highly creative and divergent, e.g., focused discussions, divergent experiences around daydreams, sharing stories, etc. Therefore, visit with the participants how they might like to arrive at description of their organizational values.

3 Establish four to six core values from which the organization would like to operate. Consider values of customers, shareholders, employees and the community.

4 Notice any differences between the organization's preferred values and its true values (the values actually reflected by members' behaviours in the organization). Record each preferred value on a flash card, then have each member 'rank' the values with 1, 2, or 3 in terms of the priority needed by the organization with 3 indicating the value is very important to the organization and 1 is least important. Then go through the cards again to rank how people think the values are actually being enacted in the organization with 3 indicating the values are fully enacted and 1 indicating the value is hardly reflected at all. Then address discrepancies where a value is highly preferred (ranked with a 3), but hardly enacted (ranked with a 1).

(Source: www.managementhelp.org)

Hilton Worldwide has a combined example of all three types of statements discussed above on its website, here shown in Text 2.12.

TEXT 2.12

Vision, mission and values of Hilton Worldwide

Our Vision
To fill the earth with the light and warmth of hospitality.

Our Mission
To be the preeminent global hospitality company - the first choice of guests, team members, and owners alike.

Our Values

Hospitality	We're passionate about delivering exceptional guest experiences.
Integrity	We do the right thing, all the time.
Leadership	We're leaders in our industry and in our communities.
Teamwork	We're team players in everything we do.
Ownership	We're the owners of our actions and decisions.
Now	We operate with a sense of urgency and discipline.

(Source: www.hiltonworldwide.com)

Goals, objectives and strategy

Once a hotel organisation has succeeded in establishing its mission and vision, its next target should be to define and set its goals, objectives and strategy. Goals are the activities and standards that a hotel must achieve in order to successfully carry out its mission and vision. In many instances, the goals and objectives are considered to be synonymous to each other as both have measurable end results. However, if results are to be viewed in the short term they are considered goals; if results are to be viewed in the long(er) term they are considered objectives. Goals and objectives are much more specific than the mission of the organisation, and they should very obviously be observable, measurable, reasonable, clear and consistent. These goals and objectives are essential for the success of the organisation and they help with, for example:

- Providing direction for the organisation;
- Evaluating the results achieved by the organisation;
- Providing a platform for effective planning and control within the organisation;
- Pointing out what should be considered priorities for the organisation;
- Revealing the synergy generated by the organisation.

Many hotels evaluate their goals and objectives frequently, and establish yearly, quarterly or monthly targets that have to be attained. The method put in place by a hotel in order to achieve its goals and objectives is called its strategy. A sample strategy, such as that indicated in the summary of the strategic vision of Accor for 2015, is shown in Text 2.13.

Must achieve

Specific

Strategy

TEXT 2.13

Accor's strategic vision

AccorHotels, the world's benchmark hotelier

Present in 92 countries. More than 3,700 hotels and 480,000 rooms. An extensive brand portfolio, with a comprehensive range of options from luxury to economy: Sofitel, Pullman, MGallery, Grand Mercure, The Sebel, Novotel, Suite Novotel, Mercure, Mama Shelter, Adagio, ibis, ibis Styles, ibis budget, hotelF1.

Today, AccorHotels is much more than a global leader, it's a group of 180,000 hoteliers who share the same passion.
Our ambition is to be the world's benchmark hospitality player so we can offer our guests, employees and partners a unique experience. In order to fulfill this ambition, on 3rd June 2015, the Group announced that it was entering a new playing field, and would be more open, more connected and more assertive, so it can continue to shake up hospitality industry conventions.

Spurred by Sébastien Bazin, its Chairman and CEO, the Group's strategy is based on several fundamentals:

- a new name, AccorHotels, and a new promise, Feel Welcome, expressed through an updated visual identity.
- two fields of expertise: operating and franchising hotels (HotelServices) and owning and investing in hotels (HotelInvest);
- a large portfolio of internationally renowned brands covering the full spectrum, with luxury (Sofitel, Pullman, MGallery, Grand Mercure, The Sebel), economy (ibis, ibis Styles, ibis budget, adagio access and hotelF1), and midscale (Novotel, Suite Novotel, Mercure, Mama Shelter, Adagio) establishments;
- A powerful marketplace and a well-known loyalty programme Le Club AccorHotels
- Almost half a century's commitment to corporate citizenship and solidarity with the PLANET 21 programme.

(Source: www.accor.com)

2.4.2   Hotel organisational structures and charts

A hotel needs a formal structure, called the organisational structure, for it to be able to carry out its mission and objectives as stated in the previous section. The organisational structure tends to differ depending on the type, size, and functions of the company. Organisational structures are illustrated in organisational charts, which are diagrams that show the hierarchical relationships between the various positions in the organisation, as well as the lines of responsibility and the division of roles. Large hotel organisations will tend to have tall organisational structures containing many management levels, while small organisations will have flatter organisational structures. The fewer the management levels, the more effective the organisation will be in completing its tasks and projects. As all hotel organisations are unique, the organisational structures depicted in their charts are, too. Organisational charts are also subject to change over time as changes occur within the organisations for whatever reason. Figures 2.9 and 2.10 illustrate two types of organisational structures: a full service hotel, and an independent small roadside motel with rooms-only facilities.

Taking into account the fact that Figure 2.9 has been limited to the levels contained within the hotel's management team, the chart does show four levels of responsibility – for example moving from the reservations supervisor through the conferences and events manager, then via the director of

Formal

Hierarchical relationships

Change

Levels of responsibility

FIGURE 2.9 Organisational Chart of the Mövenpick Hotel, Amsterdam City Centre.

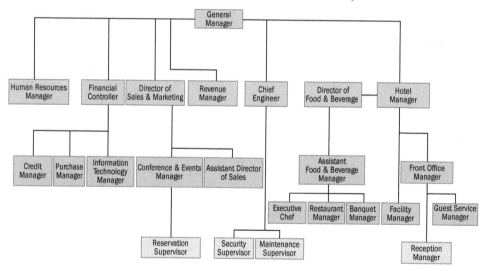

Levels of authority sales and marketing manager before reaching the general manager. It is also apparent that there are three different levels of authority as differentiated by different shades of colour used in the organisational chart. The lines indicate the reporting relationships within the hotel.

In the case of an independent and small roadside motel with rooms-only facilities, the organisational chart will demonstrate a much flatter structure. Degrees of responsibility are also limited to supervisor levels.

FIGURE 2.10 Sample organisational chart of an independent and small roadside motel

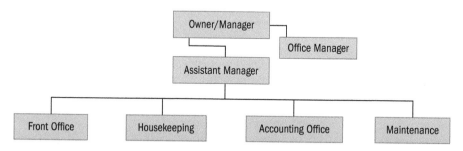

In full service hotels that have leased parts of their operations to other companies (such as their housekeeping activities or their food and beverage outlets), these leased divisions will consequently not feature in the hotels' own organisational charts since these operations are being carried out by other independently-owned and operated companies. In such instances, there should be a very accessible and transparent communication between the various companies concerned in order to ensure that the hotel's operations are not negatively affected.

Within the hospitality industry, levels of management are commonly split into three: top, middle and supervisory. Top managers have the highest responsibilities and determine the direction of the organisation. They are also responsible for establishing strategic plans. Middle managers have a little less responsibility than top managers and are also present in greater numbers. Middle managers are expected to have good relational skills and they are responsible for the coordination and implementation of the organisation's plans. Supervisory managers or line supervisors are at the bottom of the management ladder. Line supervisors have the primary role of planning and managing work; they are generally in close contact with frontline staff, whose activities are supported, coordinated and facilitated by frontline supervisors.

Top managers

Middle managers

Supervisory managers

2.4.3 Functional areas

Hotel functional areas or departments are as varied as the different types of hotels described in the previous sections. Today's hotel organisations are very complex and comprise many different departments. This complexity notwithstanding, certain methods have been designed to be used in classifying hotel departments. On the one hand, functional areas could be classified as either profit centres or cost centres. A profit centre is one that has costs but also generates revenues that are directly related to the department, such as the Front Office and the Food and Beverage outlets. In contrast, a cost centre is one that generates no direct revenues, such as maintenance and human resources, but exists in order to give support to profit centres. Profit and cost centres are also known as revenue centres and support centres respectively.

Profit centre

Cost centre

Alternatively, functional areas can be classified as front-of-house or back-of-house. Front-of-house covers those areas of the hotel in which the guests have the possibility to interact with employees, such as the front desk, lobby, or bar. Back-of-house covers those areas in which there are generally little or no contact points between guests and employees, such as in housekeeping where, although employees may come into contact with guests, their primary role is not to service guests directly.

Front-of-house

Back-of-house

In this section, the typical and major departments of a hotel will only be discussed briefly, since they form major parts of the next chapters of this book. Each department in a hotel has a role to play in delivering its services and products to guests, and departments each have a set of specific responsibilities when it comes to satisfying their guests.

The Rooms Department

Also referred to as Accommodation Services or Front Office and Housekeeping, this is one of the main operational areas in a hotel; a properly functioning rooms department is vital to the success of the hotel. Every hotel, motel or resort has a rooms department which generates most of its revenue (with a notable exception being casino hotels, which generate most of their revenue from gaming, gambling and entertainment activities). Most activities of the Rooms Department involve working closely with guests, for example greeting them on arrival, helping them check in, or assisting them with other needs. There are, however, some areas of little face-to-face guest contact activities within the Rooms Department, including in reservations, housekeeping and maintenance.

Vital

The Food and Beverage (F&B) Department

This normally forms an integral part of a full-service hotel and is designed to provide food and beverages to both guest and non-guest visitors to the hotel. The department is made up of multiple outlets which can include bars, cafés, restaurants, employee dining facilities, lounges, mini-bars, outside catering, banquets and room service. The F&B Department generally has the greatest number of employees in a hotel and is normally split between the production areas (such as the kitchen) and the service areas (such as the café or restaurant). The F&B Department relies on the other departments of the hotel for its smooth functioning; as such, there should be a properly coordinated line of communication between the various departments.

The Human Resources Department

This is the department concerned with the way a hotel treats its employees in order for them to be able to achieve the goals and objectives of the hotel. Some of the duties of the Human Resources Department include:
- internal and external recruitment;
- orientation;
- calculating and processing salaries, wages, benefits, and taxes;
- monitoring attendance and sickness;
- ensuring labour-related legislation, employment relations and collective bargaining agreements are respected;
- providing training.

It should be noted that some of these duties are performed by managers within their various departments, meaning that HR functions need not be exclusively limited to the Human Resources Department.

The Sales and Marketing Department

This is principally involved with creating new business for a hotel and ensuring that it is able to create levels of awareness, interest, desire and action among potential customers and guests, and as such influence their choices. The function of the Sales and Marketing Department is to create and retain profitable hotel customers and guests. Some of the responsibilities of the Sales and Marketing Department include:
- finding new target groups and market segments;
- designing and implementing effective sales and marketing plans;
- carrying out market research and providing relevant results to hotel management;
- building and reinforcing the image quality of a hotel towards its customers and guests.

The Finance and Accounting Department

This department is responsible for monitoring all financial activities of a hotel. In some areas, the department is known as the Finance and Control Department. The responsibilities of the department include:
- overseeing the accounts receivable system, the accounts payable system, the night audit, the payroll system, and the cost control system of the hotel;
- maintaining the records of the assets, the liabilities and all other financial transactions of the hotel;
- preparing required financial statements and reports;

Multiple outlets

Duties

Function

Responsibilities

- coordinating with other departments and carrying out required payments and bank transactions on their behalf;
- handling queries by suppliers, customers and guests related to bills and invoices;
- ratifying inventory items of the departments.

The Facilities Maintenance and Security Department

This is responsible for two major aspects of hotel operations – maintenance and security. On the one hand, this department is responsible for maintaining the physical state of the hotel and taking care of repairs and engineering work required to ensure that the equipment, machines, furniture, fixtures and fittings are in good mechanical and technical condition. The department is responsible for the electrical, plumbing, air conditioning, heating and lift systems in the hotel, and is at the forefront of ensuring that efforts are geared towards energy and water conservation. On the other hand, the department is responsible for implementing procedures aimed at protecting the safety and security of hotel employees and guests as well as hotel assets. Their responsibilities may include patrolling the property and monitoring surveillance equipment. In larger hotels this department can be split into two separate departments.

Major aspects

2.5 Guests and segments

Hotels exists in order to provide products and services to guests; and for hotels to be able to appropriately provide these products and services, they need to understand the nature, profile and financial ability of the various types of guests they serve. As indicated earlier in this chapter, hotels can be classified in various ways; over time, hotels have also developed various ways of classifying guests. This classification results in the segmentation of the market into various guest groups, with each group having its own behavioural patterns. This segregation helps the hotels offer guests those products and services that match their nature, profile and financial ability.

Segmentation

2.5.1   Types of hotel guests

This introductory section classifies hotel guests according to their numbers, the purpose of their trips and their origins. Figure 2.11 illustrates the classification types, and it should be noted that a hotel guest can be categorised under the three main headings of purpose, numbers and origin at any given time.

Classification types

FIGURE 2.11 Classifying hotel guests

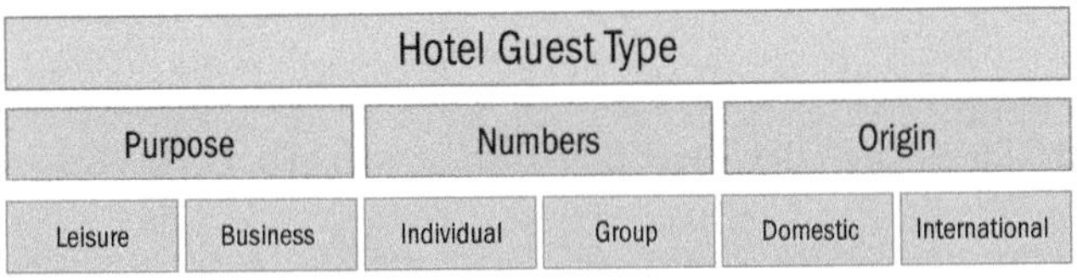

Trip purpose – leisure or business

This category consists of hotel guests who may have travelled either for leisure or for business purposes. A leisure traveller is an individual, whose

Leisure traveller

2

travels have come about from motivations such as taking a vacation, engaging in leisure activities, participating in some form of outdoor recreation, visiting family or friends, or attending organised events, such as sports matches or music concerts. As discussed earlier in this chapter, hotels guests in this category very often depend on the attractions, products and services offered by hotels; they are very sensitive to price. They are attracted by low rates and discouraged by high rates. Leisure clients may visit an area for a specific pre-defined reason or because they are travelling to other destinations.

Business traveller

A business traveller, however, is an individual whose travels have come about for reasons of work requiring them to visit another location to that of their regular place of business. Business travellers normally make multiple trips per year and they do account for a good portion of hotel revenue. Business travellers require some special amenities, facilities and business support services, such as complimentary newspapers, internet access and fax machines, free local telephone calls, business centres, meeting spaces, rentable office spaces, and in-room safes.

Numbers – individual or group

Individual traveller

This category includes hotel guests travelling either individually or as part of a group. An individual traveller is someone who could be travelling for either leisure or business and who is staying in a hotel for reasons that are not related to any function that may be taking place in the hotel at the time.

Group travellers

Group travellers can also be travelling for either business or leisure. Group travellers are people who travel together and are usually participants in the same type of activities. Business groups are those who travel for commercial, governmental or educational purposes, such as to attend management meetings, new product launches, training seminars, or shareholders meetings. Leisure groups are those who travel for recreational, educational, sightseeing, and relaxing purposes as well as for the sake of experience, and in which the individuals purchase a group package.

Origin – domestic or international

Domestic traveller

This category includes hotel guests who could be travelling either from domestic or from international sources. Domestic travel can be local, regional, or national. As per the definition formulated by the World Tourism Organisation (WTO):

> 'A domestic traveller is any person residing in a country who travels to a place within the country, outside his or her usual environment for a period not exceeding 12 months and whose main purpose of visit is other than the exercise of an activity remunerated from within the place visited'.

For 2008, the WTO estimated that more than 83% of travellers worldwide were domestic travellers; domestic travel provided the following statistics (taken from: Frédéric Pierret, UNWTO Executive Director – Some points on Domestic Tourism, 2011):
- 73% of total overnight stays;
- 74% of all arrivals and 69% of overnight stays at hotels;
- 89% of all arrivals and 75% of overnight stays in other (non-hotel) accommodations.

If a hotel guest has travelled from a country other than their normal country of residence, they are considered to be an international traveller, specified by the WTO as:

International traveller

'Any person who travels to a country other than that in which s/he has his/her usual residence but outside his/her usual environment for a period not exceeding 12 months and whose main purpose of visit is other than the exercise of an activity remunerated from within the country visited, and who stays at least one night in a collective or private accommodation in the country visited'.

2.5.2   Rooms differentiation

The previous sections noted that there are various ways of classifying hotels. Similarly, within the industry, the types of rooms have no universal classification system. Hotel guest rooms have been categorised differently and inconsistently in order to suit the profiles or financial ability of the different types of guests that visit the hotels. Some common bases that have been used to classify the different types of guest rooms include: room size; type of bed in room; number of beds in room; layout of room; view as seen through room window; position of room within hotel; interior decoration and theme; possible number of occupants; possible services available. Text 2.14 provides an insight into types of guest rooms commonly in use in the United States, the Caribbean, Canada and Mexico.

Common bases

TEXT 2.14

Common guest room types

Based on size and amenities

Standard: the most basic room type, with basic, standard amenities and furnishings

Moderate: usually better than standard, but still not deluxe. It may refer to the room view as well as the size and type of furnishings offered

Superior: subject to interpretation, it is supposed to mean superior to a standard room in both size and furnishings, but it often refers to just the view

Deluxe: supposed to be deluxe in every way: view, location, furnishings and size

Run of House: this can mean anything the hotel wants it to mean, but typically the interpretation should be 'standard room or better at time of check in; any location within the hotel'

Junior suite: typically a larger room with a separate seating area

Suite: usually two or more rooms clearly defined; a bedroom and a living or sitting room, with a door that closes between them.

Studio: usually configured like a junior suite, but has the added advantage of a 'kitchenette,' or cooking facilities.

Based on bedding categories

King: king-sized bed that measures 72 by 72 inches (US)

California King: king-sized bed that's longer than it is wide – 72 inches wide by 78 inches long (US)

Queen: a bed that is 60 inches wide and 72 inches long (US)

Double: a bed that is 54 inches wide and 72 inches long (US)

Twin: a bed that is supposed to be 36 inches wide and 72 inches long (US), but it can also describe a bed that is only 32 inches wide. It is also sometimes called a 'single'

Based on room views

Partial ocean view: you can actually see a bit of the ocean from inside your room or by craning your neck out of the window.

Ocean view: either you have a full view down the beach and can see the ocean but you don't face the ocean, or you are in a hotel several blocks away and on a high enough floor that you can see the ocean from your room.

Ocean front: you have a full ocean view from your windows

Beach front: you should be able to walk out of your room and onto the sand

City view: it could mean on a higher floor with a broad view over the city, or it could mean a city view instead of a more desirable ocean view or mountain view etc.

Mountain view: looking out at the mountains

Water view: the room looks at or has a view of a featured body of water in the destination. It is sometimes replaced with such specifics like lake view, or lagoon view or river view

Island view: used in Hawaii and the Caribbean for no ocean view at all

Pool view: view over the pool

Garden view: usually means lower floors, facing landscaping

Other categories

Handicap Accessible, Smoking, Non-Smoking, Concierge (or Tower) Level, Club Level, Balcony etc. which are pretty self-explanatory.

(Source: www.sleeping-around.com)

Categories

In addition to the categories mentioned in Text 2.14, the following categories are also globally used:

- *Cabana*: generally a shelter used as a bathhouse on a beach or at a swimming pool, but adapted by some hotels for occupation by guests, sold at slightly lower rates than standard rooms;
- *Double room*: containing a double bed designed for two persons;
- *Double-double room* (or twin double): containing two double beds or two queen beds, occupied by two or more persons;
- *Duplex*: rooms are not on the same level but connected by an internal staircase, with the sitting area generally on the lower level while the sleeping area is located upstairs;
- *Efficiency room*: commonly found in motels and residential hotels with some kitchen facilities;
- *Executive room*: more spacious, and has a sitting area furnished with chairs and usually a sofa;
- *Family room*: accommodates a small family, with at least one double bed and one or more single beds;

- *Hollywood twin*: a twin room variation where the two beds can be merged if required;
- *Interconnected rooms*: two rooms adjacent to each other with an inter-connecting door;
- *Quadruple room*: accommodates four persons in either two twin beds or two double beds;
- *Single room*: a single bed for a single occupant;
- *The Sico room*: very useful when space is limited, it has special beds which can be adjusted according to the needs of the guest. Can be used both as a meeting space and a sleeping space at night;
- *Triple room*: accommodates three persons either in one double bed and one roll away bed or two single beds and one roll away bed;
- *Twin room*: features two single beds for two people with one bedside table separating the beds;
- *Economy room*: given out at an economy rate, lacking in such facilities as air conditioning or television;
- *Executive suite*: designed for top executives;
- *Honeymoon suite*: designed for newlyweds;
- *Hospitality suite*: used for entertaining visitors;
- *Penthouse suite*: located on the top floor of a hotel.

2.5.3   Market segmentation

As indicated in the previous sections, the hospitality industry is a very diverse industry; and although the clients that the industry serves are considered its guests, the industry has also been able to categorise guests according to market segments. A market segment is an identifiable group of buyers who share similar needs, characteristics or behaviour, and who will respond in a similar and predictable way to a given set of marketing or promotional stimuli. Market segmentation is the process of defining and separating groups of buyers into identifiable subgroups having the same needs, characteristics or behaviour. *Identifiable group*

Segmenting the market is more important in today's hospitality industry because of the constant modifications in guest needs and the large variety in different products offered. Since the segments of a hotel depend on the type of hotel and the type of market it wants to operate in, no two hotels have exactly the same type of segmentation overview. Consequently, every hotel has to decide what segmentation best fits its corresponding market and property. There are two broad market segment categories – groups and transients – which can both be sub-divided into multiple sub-groups based on other criteria, as clearly demonstrated in the segmentation overview of the Mövenpick Hotel Amsterdam City Centre – October 2011 in Figure 2.12. *Categories*

The overview in Figure 2.12 identifies 28 possible market segments. Segmenting the market provides some advantages such as a better match between hotel resources and the needs of the identified group; a better usage of available resources; an improved ability to recognise available market opportunities; and an improved ability to provide guests with what they require, thereby increasing guest satisfaction levels. Hotels hope that by understanding guest segments, they will be better able to stand out from the competition, leading to competitive advantages. *Advantages*

FIGURE 2.12 Segmentation overview of the Mövenpick Hotel Amsterdam City Centre – October 2011

Segmentation Overview - Mövenpick Hotel Amsterdam City Centre – October 2011				
1st criteria	2nd criteria	3rd criteria	4th criteria	Segment description
Main segment	Nature of stay	Contract agreement with hotel?	Specific market segment	Short description each segment
TRANSIENT	BUSINESS	CONTRACTED	ICR	All accounts for which a chain contract has been agreed
			LCR	All accounts where a local contract with our hotel has been agreed by the hotel
			GOV	Government rate
		NON CONTRACTED	BBR	BAR on business
			BBP	Advance purchase rates with business purpose
	LEISURE	CONTRACTED	FIT	All FIT contracts with wholesalers/tour operators
		NON CONTRACTED	PKG	All package rates
			LBR	BAR on leisure
			LPP	Advance purchase rates with leisure purpose
			OPA	Rates booked via 'opaque' channels
	OTHER		LON	Long stay guests
			SOD	Staff of Mövenpick on business purposes
			SOV	Staff of Mövenpick staying in our hotel on leisure purposes
			DAY	Day use rooms
			FFT	All other rates
GROUPS	BUSINESS		GFA	Groups sold during citywide event periods
			GIN	Groups coming to our hotel for an incentive programme
			GME	Corporate group rooms that are booked in combination with meeting space
			GCD	Room only corporate groups - no meeting attached
	LEISURE		GTS	Tour/Cruise Series
			GIT	Groups coming to our hotel for leisure purposes
			GLE	Ad Hoc leisure groups
AIRLINE			CRE	Contracted airline crews
			LAY	Stranded Flights
			ATR	N/A
OTHER			HUS	House use rooms
			COM	Complimantary rooms
			PAY	Paymaster

Market segments are generally established based on the following factors and examples:
- Behavioural factors such as benefits, features, loyalty, occasion and usage;
- Demographic factors such as age, gender, income, lifestyle and occupation;
- Geographic factors such as climate, population, region and size;
- Psychographic factors such as activities, social interests and values.

Summary

▶ There is no universally accepted rule for classifying hotels. Existing rating systems are as varied as the organisations that create them. There is a multitude of classification criteria, including price, function, location, market segment, and distinctiveness of style or offerings.

▶ There are many rating schemes and organisations worldwide, many of whom use star or diamond symbols to categorise hotels.

▶ The Michelin Red Guide awards Michelin Stars, granted on the basis of five criteria.

▶ The AAA rates hotels in the United States, Canada, Mexico and the Caribbean, and hotels must meet 27 basic requirements covering comfort, cleanliness and safety.

▶ The World Hotel Rating project aims to set international classification standards and rating criteria along the lines of a world star-rating system, and their November 2011 declaration consists of 6 pillars.

▶ Though a well-planned and administered rating system is recognised as having various benefits, conventional rating systems have thus far not been very successful in assessing the quality of hotels. The reliability of a hotel's rating depends on how frequently a hotel is reviewed.

▶ The two main reasons for classifying hotels include the need to analyse the market sector and the need to describe the type of hotel for advertising purposes.

▶ While traditionally hotels were classified based on size, class, type and meal plan, modern perspectives are now more varied and include: location; ownership and management; facilities and functions; target groups and types of client; price and standard; rating; and the distinctiveness, theme, and alternative accommodation provided by the property.

▶ Location refers to the geographic positioning of the hotel in relation to towns and cities, and differentiates between downtown (city centre) hotels, suburban hotels, highway hotels, resorts, airport hotels, floating hotels, and rural hotels.

▶ Regarding ownership, hotels can be classified as belonging to one of four groups, including sole proprietorships, partnerships, limited liability companies, and corporations. Classification from a management perspective also assigns hotels to one of four groups, including owned and managed privately, managed under franchise agreement, managed under lease agreement, and managed under management contract.

▶ Based on the resources available in hotels as well as types of possible on-site activities , hotels can be separated into all-suite hotels, apartment hotels, bed and breakfast hotels, boutique hotels, casino hotels, commercial hotels, conference hotels, convention hotels, extended stay hotels, full service hotels, leisure hotels, limited service hotels, residential hotels, resort hotels, select-service hotels, and spa and health hotels.

▶ Hotel classification via the target group or type of clients is primarily done within the three subgroups of business, groups and leisure.

▶ On the basis of price or standard, hotels can be classified into budget and economy hotels, mid-price hotels, upmarket hotels, and luxury hotels. STR uses a flexible format, however; this relates the levels of actual or estimated average daily rates to the number of hotels within the given market to define the class of hotels found there.

▶ Not all hotel types fit the general classification criteria and some of them are very exceptional. Examples include bunker hotels, eco lodges, exclusive use hotels, famous landmark and heritage hotels, ice hotels, retreats, tree house hotels, secret hotels, trophy hotels, underwater hotels, vacation ownership, water park hotels, and youth hostels.

▶ All hotels have a formal structure that allows them to distribute responsibility and authority among different levels of management and staff. All hotels have missions, visions, values, goals, objectives and strategies (though in some cases these may not have been explicitly expressed).

Questions and assignments for reflection

1   Having read this chapter, why do you think it is relevant to have rating systems for hotels?

2   How would you adjust the definition of a hotel as an establishment 'held out by the proprietor as offering sleeping accommodation to any person who appears able and willing to pay a reasonable sum for the services and facilities provided and who is in a fit state to be received'? Why?

3   How does the traditional classification of hotels compare to and contrast with modern perspectives used in classifying hotel as shown in this chapter?

4   Why should a hotel have a mission, vision, goals, objectives and strategies?

5   Compare and contrast the various behavioural patterns of types of hotel guests as discussed in this chapter.

3
Hotel Management – Viewed from Above

M. N. Chibili

3.1 Introduction

In the hotel industry, the general manager is the head executive responsible for the overall operation of an individual hotel establishment, including its financial profitability. The general manager holds ultimate managerial authority over the hotel operation and usually reports directly to the owners or some other higher authority in the case of chain hotels. As head executive, the general manager's job comes with a lot of responsibilities and requires certain competences. Additionally, in order to be able to successfully carry out the activities required, the general manager is supported by the executive team who, while possibly as one-of-kind as the hotel itself, will generally consist of the most common positions as defined in this chapter.

3.2 General Management

In the previous chapters we have shown how varied the hospitality industry is; yet despite this propensity for variation, every hotel or similar facility has an individual within its managerial structure who is the leader at the property level (unit level). This individual, who makes the final decisions related to the property's day-to-day operations, is usually called the General Manager (GM); in some areas of the world, they are also known as Managing Director or General Director. Whatever the size of the unit, the GM reports to the owners either directly or through regional offices, and is ultimately responsible for the unit's success, image and reputation.

Leader

3.2.1 The General Manager's job

The GM's job differs for the type and size of the property as well as for the services offered by the property. For example, the GM of a large hotel may have little guest interaction but will frequently meet with other department managers in order to better monitor, coordinate and lead the execution of

Differs

© Noordhoff Uitgevers bv

China, Macau: The Venetian Macao

hotel strategies. On the other hand, the GM of a small property may be more of a host that guests regularly interact with, such as at reception or even serving meals, and whose personality and presence leave a serious mark on the identity of the property.

Nebel and Ghei (2011, p. 93) have argued that the hotel GM is the central management figure in the hotel business and have developed a conceptual framework of the hotel GM's job based on job demands and relationship issues in the short-, intermediate- and long run, the generic managerial work roles, and the specific job functions – this framework is shown in Figure 3.1.

FIGURE 3.1 Conceptual framework of the hotel General Manager's job

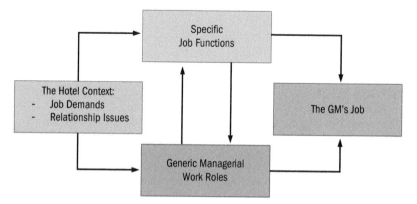

In their study, Nebel and Ghei arrived at these three important conclusions (p. 100):

1 By their nature, major modern-day hotels provide GMs with a variety of challenges that require careful attention is paid to short-run, intermediate-run, and long-run time frame issues. Thus, GMs must be able to successfully carry out three separate and different job functions. They must be effective as operational controllers, organisational developers, and business maintainers if they are to enjoy long-term success as effective GMs.
2 To be effective at all three job functions, a GM is required to perform a large variety of managerial work roles. While the GMs perform all ten of Mintzberg's managerial work roles, they must be particularly effective at seven of them to be considered successful operational controllers, organisational developers, and business maintainers. They must develop a wide variety of skills necessary to perform the roles of leader, liaison, monitor, disseminator, disturbance handler, entrepreneur, and resource allocator.
3 The importance of communication in the hotel GM's job becomes apparent from the analysis. Every job function and every managerial work role carries with it a communications requirement. GMs must be adept at gathering, analysing and disseminating external and internal information, and they must be able to effectively communicate laterally, downward, and upward. Without good communication skills, GMs cannot possibly be effective in any of their three job functions.

Taken from an internet blog, the abbreviated excerpt in Text 3.1 illustrates how difficult it is to understand what the job of a hotel GM really entails at times:

Difficult

TEXT 3.1

Hotel General Manager – Typical job responsibilities

Several years ago I invited a guest speaker to my class. This person was the general manager of a local inn in our community. He was very well prepared for the lecture and described the organization chart and staff he had developed. After he explained the work that goes on in the various departments and the responsibilities of the respective supervisors, a student asked, 'What do you do as the general manager if all the work is being done by your staff?' This type of honest question has always made me terribly aware that the role of the general manager is not easy to understand. Indeed, detailing this managerial role could fill volumes, encompassing decades of experience. However, the legitimacy of the question still compels me to be specific in describing this very important job in the organization chart.

The leadership provided by the general manager is undoubtedly the most important quality a person brings to this position. He or she orchestrates the various department directors in meeting the financial goals of the organization through their employees. The general manager is required to use the full range of managerial skills—such as planning, decision making, organizing, staffing, controlling, directing, and communicating—to develop a competent staff. Performance is judged according to how effectively supervisors have been directed to meet the goals of the organization. Efficiency depends not on how well tasks are performed, but on how well employees are motivated and instructed to meet the goals and objectives of the plans the general manager and staff have formulated.

What does a general manager do? He or she provides leadership to meet organizational goals of profitability and service. It is acquired by studying theories of management and the behaviour of other managers as well as actually practicing leadership and receiving constructive criticism from superiors on efforts expended. The role of general manager is a professional position. It is a career goal based on operations experience and education. The role of the general manager, whether in a full-service or limited-service property, must encompass the concepts previously discussed. The general manager in a limited-service property may perform additional hands-on responsibilities, but he or she is required to provide leadership to the other members of the management team. The use of total quality management (TQM) concepts, which involve application of managerial concepts to understand operational processes and develop methods to improve those processes, allows managers in full-service and limited-service properties to extend their role of leadership to frontline supervisors and employees. In full-service and limited-service properties, where profit margins are based on lean departmental budgets, total quality management is encouraged.

(www.hotelmule.com)

In summarised form, the main responsibilities of the hotel GM include taking full responsibility for the performance of the hotel; coordinating the activities of all hotel departments; leading the staff of the hotel towards attaining their communal, environmental and financial responsibilities; participating in determining the hotel's policies and strategies; and providing leadership of and guidance to the hotel's executive team.

Responsibilities

Text 3.2 is an advert for the position of a hotel GM, and it details some key responsibilities and attributes required by a world renowned brand.

TEXT 3.2

Job Role - Hotel General Manager

HOTEL GENERAL MANAGER - NATIONAL HOSPITALITY RETAILER
Detail 2 Group Job Reference: E2E-431972a
Employer/Agency Name: Detail 2 Group
Location: Birmingham
Job Sector: General Management; Travel, Leisure, Entertainment
Salary/Package: £40k-£50k
Date Posted: 22/11/2012

Apply Now: HOTEL GENERAL MANAGER - NATIONAL HOSPITALITY RETAILER
Hotel General Manager required to take over a flagship site for this market leading value hotel chain. The site is a high profile venue closely associated with quality & value. The company offers opportunities for career progression and personal development. A world renowned brand, this is an amazing opportunity for anyone currently working within the hotel business.

The Company:
Our client is a national hospitality retailer who is operating an instantly recognisable hotel brand which has a global presence. They are a dynamic company, whose aim is to provide first class service and exceptional value to each and every guest.

Job Role - Hotel General Manager – National Hospitality Retailer:
To be responsible for the overall management of your site in order to maximise sales and profit through effectively leading your team, maintaining brand standards and driving great customer service. Your key responsibilities will be to:
- Maximise sales and profit within your business and deliver your agreed targets and sales plan.
- Manage and control the costs of your business.
- Ensure compliance with cash handling, accounts, licensing, company property, security and stock procedures in your site.
- Hold regular meetings with your team in order to encourage open communication at all levels and ensure they know everything they need to know.
- Develop and manage your team through regular feedback and reviews, agree action plans and timescales for follow up.
- Take full responsibility for the brand at your site. Ensure your team consistently maintains company brand standards and expectations through utilisation of company policies and procedures.
- Keeping customers happy will be the most important thing to you - ensure your team deliver and recognise the importance of great customer service in line with company best practice.
- Recruit and induct the right people for your team in line with company policy and provide ongoing development to help them reach their full potential.
- Analyse and benchmark the performance of your site, sharing best practice, and drive ongoing improvements in all areas.
- Ensure that all legislation is adhered to within your site, including employment law, health and safety, food hygiene, COSHH.
- Be friendly and helpful at all times, leading by example.
- Treat your colleagues in a fair and friendly way.
- Be prepared to muck in and help out where needed.

Key Attributes - Hotel General Manager – National Hospitality Retailer:
- Previous hotel general management experience preferably within a branded property

© Noordhoff Uitgevers bv

- Strong leadership quality
- Totally guest focused
- Outgoing, exceptional interpersonal skills
- People Manager - inspires and develops the team
- Financial awareness - proven record of full P & L responsibility and control
- Ambition to continually drive and develop the business
- Understanding of the value hotel market
- Proven planning and organising skills.
- Able to work in a fast-paced environment.

(Source: www.exec2exec.com)

3.2.2   Competences required of a hotel General Manager

The previous section discussed the responsibilities and attributes of a hotel GM. For hotel GMs to be able to carry out these responsibilities, they need to be able to show that they have the required knowledge, skills, abilities and behaviour needed to successfully carry out these duties. Over the years, determining relevant competencies and skill sets has helped human resource managers improve hiring and selection practices, develop strategies to retain managers, and set up career planning initiatives (Chung-Herrera, Enz, & Lankau, 2003). In this way, the hospitality industry has tried to identify valid job competencies and skill sets required for future leaders in an effort to reduce turnover, overcome the challenges encountered in the recruitment and retention of quality hospitality managers, and remain competitive. As the hotel GM is the leader of the property, the competencies model devised by Chung-Herrera et al. (2003, p. 23), which is one of many such studies, is used here to illustrate the types of competencies required in this respect. Their study identified the required key competencies for hospitality leaders. Based on a 5-point Likert-type scale, the mean scores of the factors and dimensions are shown in Figure 3.2 in order of importance.

Competencies

Due to the ever changing external environment, the current hotel GMs should be people who are continually seeking to improve their skills and knowledge base, and they should also be able to transfer newly gained knowledge to their subordinates through practical means in order to improve service to their guests and enhance their profitability.

FIGURE 3.2 Leadership competency model for the hospitality industry

Leadership Competency Model for the Lodging Industry			
Factor	**Mean**	**Dimension**	**Mean**
Self-management	4.32	Ethics and integrity	4.58
		Time management	4.28
		Flexibility and adaptability	4.22
		Self development	4.12
Strategic positioning	4.17	Awareness of customer needs	4.39
		Commitment to quality	4.25
		Managing stakeholders	4.21
		Concern for community	3.67
Implementation	4.16	Planning	4.23
		Directing others	4.15
		Re-engineering	4.02
Critical thinking	4.15	Strategic orientation	4.24
		Decision making	4.18
		Analysis	4.17
		Risk taking and innovation	4.03
Communcation	4.12	Speaking with impact	4.27
		Facilitating open communication	4.14
		Active listening	4.06
		Written communication	4.06
Interpersonal	4.09	Building networks	4.20
		Managing conflict	4.07
		Embracing diversity	4.01
Leadership	4.09	Teamwork orientation	4.25
		Fostering motivation	4.19
		Fortitude	4.14
		Developing others	4.02
		Embracing change	3.98
		Leadership versatility	3.97
Industry knowledge	4.09	Business and industry expertise	4.09

3.2.3   The behavioural patterns of General Managers

The behavioural patterns of general managers have been researched in the last decades. One of the best known such studies was that carried out by Kotter (1982), the highlights of which are indicated in this section. From a detailed study of 15 successful American general managers, he concluded that despite the differences in their jobs and in the way they carried them out, they all had two significant activities in common: agenda-setting and network-building:

Activities

- Agenda-setting, in which the managers figure out what to do despite uncertainty, great diversity, and an enormous amount of potentially relevant information.
- Network-building, in which the managers try to get things done through a large and diverse set of people despite having little direct control over them.

Kotter (1982) found the following features of a typical pattern of daily behaviour for a GM (pp. 158-159):

1 They spend most of their time with others. The average GM manager spends only 25% of his working time alone, and that time is spent largely at home, on airplanes, or while commuting. Few spend less than 70% of their time with others, and some spend up to 90% of their work time this way.
2 They spend time with many people in addition to their direct subordinates and their bosses. They regularly see people who may appear to be unimportant outsiders.
3 The breadth of topics in their discussions is extremely wide. GMs do not limit their focus to planning, business strategy, staffing, and other top-management concerns. They discuss virtually anything and everything even remotely associated with their businesses.
4 GMs ask a lot of questions. In a half-hour conversation, some will ask literally hundreds of them.
5 During conversations, GMs rarely seem to make 'major' decisions.
6 Their discussions usually feature a fair amount of jocular content and often concern topics that are not related to work. The humour often relates to others in the organisation or industry. Non-work discussions are usually about people's families and hobbies.
7 In more than a few of these encounters, the issues discussed are relatively unimportant to the business or organisation. GMs regularly engage in activities that even they regard as a waste of time.
8 In these encounters, executives rarely give orders in a traditional sense.
9 Nevertheless, GMs often attempt to influence others. Instead of telling people what to do, however, they ask, request, cajole, persuade, and even intimidate.
10 GMs often react to others' initiatives; much of the typical GM's day is unplanned. Even GMs who have a heavy schedule of planned meetings end up spending a lot of time on topics that are not on the official agenda.
11 GMs spend most of their time with others in short, disjointed conversations. Discussions of a single question or issue rarely last more than ten minutes. It is not at all unusual for a general manager to cover ten unrelated topics in a five-minute conversation.
12 They work long hours. The average GM studied works just under 60 hours per week. Although GMs can do some of their work at home, while commuting to work, or while travelling, they spend most of their time at their places of work.

Later on, building on the work of Kotter and others, Luthans and Associates (1988) investigated the true nature of managerial work through the observation of 44 'real' managers from all levels and many types of organisations. They sorted out four managerial activities performed by real managers split into 12 descriptive behavioural categories as shown in Figure 3.3.

FIGURE 3.3 Descriptive behavioural categories of managers

Managerial activity	Descriptive Behavioural Category
Communication	Exchanging information; Paperwork
Traditional Management	Planning; Decision-making; Controlling
Networking	Interacting with outsiders; Socializing/Politicking
Human Resource Management	Motivating/Reinforcing; Disciplining/Punishing; Managing conflict; Staffing; Training/Developing

Following the definition of the nature of managerial activity, Luthans studied a different set of 248 real managers in order to determine the relative frequencies of the four main activities. Time and effort spent on the four activities varied among different managers, but the 'average' manager spent 32% of their time and effort on traditional management activities; 29% on communication activities; 20% on human resource management activities; and, lastly, 19% on networking activities. Concluding this section in Text 3.3 are the views of Mr Xhali, General Manager of Stenden Hotel, describing his role as a GM.

TEXT 3.3

Concise views of a hotel GM on the position

From a practical perspective, a General Manager (GM) is the executive head of a property with the responsibility of implementing and managing agreed strategies. The management of said strategies typically includes, but is not limited to, financial objectives, sales and marketing, human resources and public relations.

I view the GM as a conduit that channels the talents of the department heads and operational team by ensuring that the correct people are in their intended positions with adequate resources available. By understanding that the hotel is not just bricks and mortar, but rather a living entity that is a part of, and affected by, the immediate and global community, a GM fosters engagement guaranteeing the property's relevance through understanding markets, trends and industry developments.

Thulani Xhali
General Manager – Stenden University Hotel

3.3 Other members of the Executive Team

Executive
Committee

The organisational chart of the Mövenpick Hotel Amsterdam City Centre, Amsterdam, given in Figure 2.9, was limited to the levels of the hotel's management team headed by the Executive Committee. This committee is made up of all senior managers of the functional areas reporting directly to the GM; the committee is responsible for directing, coordinating, and implementing the vision and objectives of the hotel. The composition of the executive committee differs per hotel as the organisational structures of no two hotels are the same. Chapter 2 covered the main functional areas; here, the people who lead these functional areas will briefly be discussed. Due to the importance of information technology and revenue management nowadays, the additional positions of Information Technology Manager and Revenue Manager are also briefly covered.

3.3.1   Rooms Department Manager

Depending on the hotel, this position is called the Rooms Division Manager, the Hotel Director, the Director of Rooms, or the Resident Manager. The Rooms Department Manager answers to the GM for the effective leadership and smooth operations of all activities performed by the departments that make up the Rooms Department. In most cases when there is no Deputy GM, the Rooms Department Manager acts as the GM in case of the GM's absence. A Rooms Department Manager is expected to be clear and concise in their written and verbal communication, and should also possess strong organisational skills, excellent time management skills and technical skills. The Rooms Department Manager ensures that the Rooms Department meets hotel guests' needs, and ensures acceptable levels of employee satisfaction, revenue growth and financial performance.

Rooms Division Manager

3.3.2   Food and Beverage Director

The Food and Beverage Director (or Manager) answers to the GM and is responsible for the overall supervision, planning, control and coordination of the activities and the personnel of the Food and Beverage Department. Concerned with managing various teams of people, the Food and Beverage Director is expected to have excellent management and organisation skills. The Food and Beverage Director is normally also required to have strong interpersonal and communication skills combined with a passion for customer service with a focus on details and high quality service. The Food and Beverage Director should be able to provide strong leadership skills, and is responsible for running the food and beverage outlets within the hotel, forecasting future demand and ensuring that policies and procedures are respected.

Food and Beverage Director

3.3.3   Human Resources Manager

The Human Resources Manager answers to the GM and works very closely with the GM as well as all the other department heads with the main aim of developing and maintaining very good team spirit and an excellent working environment. The Human Resources Manager manages the human resources department and ensures compliance with the hotel's human resources policies, procedures and practices, as well as labour-related laws and employment relations. The Human Resources Manager is expected to have strong procedural and administrative skills, and must be able to effectively generate action plans and long term human resource strategies.

Human Resources Manager

3.3.4   Sales and Marketing Manager

Depending on the size of the hotel, this position can be a single position or can be split between the two positions of Sales Manager and Marketing Manager. The Sales and Marketing Manager answers to the GM and over-

Sales and Marketing Manager

sees sales and marketing activities of the hotel in order to ensure that the hotel creates new business, and also generates and increases levels of awareness, interest, desire and action among potential customers and guests of the hotel. The Sales and Marketing Manager is expected to employ participative management, using it to monitor and motivate the sales and marketing force in order to help increase revenues and maximise the hotel's market and/or media profile.

3.3.5   Financial Controller

The Financial Controller answers directly to the GM (or in some cases to a higher regional manager) and is responsible for monitoring the financial activities of the hotel. In other words, the Financial Controller is responsible for preparing, reviewing and establishing hotel budgets, forecasts, operating results, financial reports and statements, and tax returns in compliance with government regulations. The Financial Controller also coordinates and administers financial systems, internal control systems, and the hotel's capital expenditure plans. A Financial Controller is expected to have excellent planning and organisational skills, strong leadership and training skills, with the ability to multi-task and work under pressure. The Financial Controller should also have a thorough knowledge of the hotel's operations and administration as well as applicable government laws and regulations.

3.3.6   Chief Engineer

The Chief Engineer (or Director of Engineering and Security) is intimately concerned with the state of the physical property of the hotel as well as with related security issues of both guests and staff. The Chief Engineer answers to the GM and ensures that the hotel is a safe and comfortable environment for both guests and staff. Some large hotels may have a separate department with its own Director of Security in charge of security. The Chief Engineer is mainly responsible for maintaining the physical state of the hotel and takes care of the repairs and engineering works required to ensure that equipment, machines, furniture, fixtures and fittings are in good mechanical and technical condition, and are fully operational. The Chief Engineer may also be responsible for implementing procedures aimed at protecting the safety and security of hotel employees and guests as well as hotel assets. The Chief Engineer is expected to have a thorough understanding of the laws and regulations of the area, especially those related to environmental protection, construction, and safety.

3.3.7   Information Technology Manager

As hotels are becoming increasingly reliant on technology, the position of the Information Technology (IT) Manager is becoming more and more important for business success. Also answering to the GM, and working closely with other department managers, the IT Manager advises the hotel on information technology solutions that will help the hotel to grow and carry out its activities much more efficiently. The IT Manager is most often involved in the planning and execution of information technology-related projects within the hotel. An IT Manager is therefore expected to have excellent project management and organisational skills, and to have excellent analytical and problem solving skills. They should also be flexible and able to manage tight deadlines, as well as operate within certain financial constraints. Lastly, the IT Manager should be able to explain complex information technology terms and systems in layman's terms.

3.3.8 Revenue Manager

The Revenue Manager answers directly to the GM and works closely with the department heads of the profit centres. The Revenue Manager is responsible for planning, establishing, and implementing the strategies of the hotel that will help maximise revenues. As such, they have a great impact on the hotel's profitability. The Revenue Manager collects data and creates a database related to prices, bookings and events. They also analyse the hotel's prices and performance vis-à-vis the competition and the overall market. The Revenue Manager is also responsible for providing forecasted data to be used in drafting budgets and strategy establishment processes. A Revenue Manager is expected to have a strong understanding of customer and market dynamics, and to have advanced logical and analytical thinking abilities.

Revenue Manager

The standard job description of a revenue manager position at Kempinski (obtained from a third-party site) is given in Text 3.4.

TEXT 3.4

Standard revenue manager job description at Kempinski Hotel

Prime Objectives
She/he is also responsible for maximising overall revenue through development and implementation of effective inventory and pricing strategies based on demand and competitor analysis in order to gain market shares

Responsible for
- Drive Market Share and Revenue Performance
- Develop overall pricing strategy to include all market segments and distribution channels
- Effectively manage and be in control of all inventory
- Responsible for effective implementation and compliance with Kempinski Revenue Management Standards and initiatives
- Ensure all distribution channels are optimized
- Share best RM practices and key learning's with peers and management.
- Play a leader role on the property's weekly RM & operation meetings
- Produce accurate forecast on weekly and monthly basis (+/-5%)
- Recruit, train and mentor the Reservations Manager (when applicable) and/or a strong second with a view to contingency
- Assist in developing a career path for direct reports

Experience
- Opera central systems knowledge is an advantage.
- Knowledge of either Fidelio V6 or Opera PMS is imperative.
- A minimum of 2 years' experience in revenue management, including electronic distribution.
- A proven track record of increasing revenue streams or strengthening the performance of a property or several properties.
- Experience with revenue management reports and market performance reports.

Competencies, Skills & Personality Traits Required
To fill this position the candidate must have strong leadership and analytical skills. Specific requirements include:
- Be proactive in achieving Rooms Revenue goals

- Relevant experience in Revenue Management. Hotel Operations experience a plus
- Detail orientated and hands on
- Team player with strong interpersonal skills
- Effective ability to supervise, motivate, train and develop associates
- Ability to develop and deliver effective presentations
- Ability to train people and convey complex systems functionalities to a broad audience.
- Demonstrate self-confidence, energy, enthusiasm and be a motivator.
- Ability to investigate systems malfunctions or user-input errors.
- Ability to analyze data, make meaningful conclusions and base sound decisions and strategies on these.

- Knowledge of industry-specify terminology such as ADR, RevPAR, on-the-books, etc.
- Ability to adapt to a frequently changing market environment. Be proactive and able to 'think outside of the box'.
- Ability to work under pressure

Other Skills:
- Fluent English language skills, both verbal and in writing. A second language is required.
- Good Keyboard skills and proven working knowledge of Microsoft Office to include MSWord, MSExcel and MSPowerPoint.
- PMS, Opera, IDEAS and EZYield

(Source: lifeofarevenuemanager.wordpress.com)

3.4 The Property Management System

Management information

This chapter on hotel management has so far covered the position of GM as well as provided a brief overview of other members of the Executive Committee. For this management team to be able to carry out its activities effectively, it should be possible for them to be brought up-to-date of all management information generated from within the hotel property, and at times even from outside. Nowadays, management should be able to obtain all data or reports needed for their decision-making activities at the click of a button. The hotel's property management system (PMS) nowadays makes it possible for management and other employees to be able to use computers within an integrated system (depending on level of access required). This system allows its users manage and control almost all operations within a hotel and even links them to other worldwide information networks.

Property management system

Software

A hotel PMS is software used to automate its operations. It is the heart of property operations – processing activities like guest bookings, online reservations, check-ins and check-outs. A hotel PMS can keep track of how many rooms are left to be sold and at what rates. It can handle front office accounting and marketing, as well as interface with other systems such as central reservation, revenue or yield management, front office, back office, point of sale, door-locking, pay-per-view movies, energy management, payment card authorisation, and channel management systems. Possible benefits of implementing a PMS in a hotel can include a reduction of repetitive tasks; the ability to provide more accurate information; making up-to-date data easily available to management; and improving the ease of controlling operations. Having a PMS is important, regardless of the size of the property. There are systems that have been designed to cater to properties of all sizes, and the number of PMSs available is almost as numerous as the types of hotels in the world.

Benefits

3.4.1   Pre-PMS days

Before the invention of personal computers, hotels were managed in what is nowadays known as the 'manual environment'. All information had to be recorded on slips or sheets of papers to be stored in various ways and means destined for later consultation and use. Simple activities, like checking the current room status of the property, had to be done by way of housekeeping staff regularly contacting the front desk clerk for updates either by phone or in person. Similarly, all accounting processes and reports had to be generated by manual systems that required the use of many clerical employees working on typewriters or other record-keeping devices. All sales transactions were posted manually through handwritten or typewritten postings, for example.

Manual environment

The hospitality industry experienced a marked change for the better with the advent of the computer age though, according to Diehl (1973), the integration of computers in the industry was comparatively slower than that of other business segments. He also recognised that computer miniaturisation provided the industry with the realistically-priced tools needed to finally accomplish the goal of developing a powerful real-time hotel management information system.

Text 3.5 contains the synopses of two interviews of employees who experienced working in hotels in the days immediately leading up to the introduction of PMSs. Their observations also confirm what Diehl (1973) earlier noticed about the difficulties of adopting computers experienced by the hospitality industry.

TEXT 3.5

The old way: Manual reservations

Ms. Joke Tasma

Before computers were introduced within the hospitality industry, every single activity, from making a reservation to billing, had to be done by hand. For example, in order to process a reservation, a lot of hand writing was involved with employees starting very early in the morning with processing all the reservations in order to complete everything on time, and then placing the related cards on the planning board.

One could argue that the old fashioned way of processing reservations was not the most effective; however it had its advantages such as the fact that the employees were more focussed on the guests, they were more involved and customer focussed. These days on the contrary, employees are sometimes more focussed on the screens of their computers than on the people who really matter – the guests.

Once the digital age came and the reservation planning boards were replaced by computers, at first there was a lot of hesitation, concerns and feelings of insecurity – especially from the management. The management preferred to do things the old fashioned way and by hand because nobody could assure them that the digital system could really be trusted and that serious business-damaging mistakes would not be made. *'And in what way would the digital system be better than the way things had always been?'* they asked themselves. So as you might imagine, it took a long while before the management dared to rely on the digital system.

Once, in 1993 our hotel had no PMS for almost five days, and as such we had no access to any information related to the arriving and departing guests. Thanks to my previous manual environment knowledge, I was able to process everything by hand, and despite the heavy toll and time it took, we were able to continue with our operations with no negative impact on the guests and their satisfaction levels. Sometimes it is better to first learn things by hand and later on with the computer; than the other way around.

Joke Tasma (left) and Roelien Bos

Ms. Roelien Bos

In my case, I worked in a hotel in which a planning board was used which covered the reservations of one entire month. It was an enormous board on which the room numbers and dates were listed. You might think this would be a bit exaggerated and not useful, but the opposite was true. Just by taking a quick look at the board, every staff member had a good overview of what was happening in the hotel and what was still on the agenda for the coming month. In the board, small cards were inserted and each card had its own definition. For example with a group the same colour was used, and by using several cards the entire reservation was explained on the board. And when you had to overbook, you just put in an extra card behind the original reservation. And in the case when a guest stayed several days, you just blocked the room with one big card. The whole reservation processing was just a matter of writing the right reservation on the right card and inserting them at the right day and room slots.

Occasionally it was quite scary and thrilling if something went amiss. Sometimes a card fell off the board or the reservation was incorrectly written. And the challenge would then be to determine for example where the card had fallen from. Also some regular guests had only a little card (no confirmation on paper), and in case such a card got lost and not put in the system again, the whole reservation would not exist anymore. This could even happen while the guest was standing in front of you and confirming they had made a reservation.

For new employees, it was pretty difficult to get the hang of the planning board, but once understood its many advantages came to the forefront. If you understood the planning board, it was a much quicker way of working and you were immediately up-to-date. This cannot always be said about the digital reservation system. With the digital system you have to process everything as well which will cost some time.

When my hotel switched from the old planning board to the digital system, I noticed that this transfer was easier for the reservations department than for the other departments. Reservations already knew how the system worked manually, now they simply had to do almost the same thing but with some reduced proceedings because the computer had taken over from them. However for the other employees, the transfer was not that easy. First of all, they had always had access to the highly visible planning board, which was an important guideline for them. These employees could immediately be well informed and see if they were on the right track. However, with the digital system, these employees did not have any direct access to the formerly highly visible information, which made them at times confused and sometimes even irritated.

When comparing the old fashioned way to the digital age, one notices massive changes. And although it took some effort and as well a lot of motivation, they managed it. Everything has become more effective and efficient. You have to take the risk and dare to change.

(Source: Interviews and synopses by Ms. Lilian van der Ham)

These days, software is crucial to the entire hospitality experience, from enhancing the experiences of the guests to increased service offerings (such as real-time reservations) and connectivity to other departments and areas. As information technology (IT) is assumed to create value for hospitality companies, certain important considerations must be taken into account before adopting it. Text 3.6 is a list of important and essential questions to be considered when adopting IT, established by Connolly and Haley (2008, p. 348).

Create value

TEXT 3.6

Important considerations for evaluating IT usage in a hospitality firm

- Is the proposed IT project aligned with the hospitality firm's business strategy, and is there technology/task congruency?
- Will an IT-driven business strategy create business barriers to entry or create lag time effects, making it difficult and more time-consuming for competitors to copy?
- What are the IT project's anticipated benefits, and how will they be measured?
- What are the IT project's critical success factors?
- What risks are associated with the IT project, and how can these be mitigated?
- How can IT be used to change the competitive dynamics and industry structure?
- What position has the competition taken with respect to IT, and what effects should this have on one's own strategy?
- If the IT project is undertaken, how might competitors react (i.e. what might be their likely responses or defence tactics)?
- Can the hospitality firm gain economies of scale using IT and better leverage and use its resources more efficiently?
- Will IT reduce costs and change the hospitality firm's cost structure to provide advantages in the market place?
- Can IT create new revenue opportunities, generate new revenue streams, and help the hospitality firm focus on more profitable lines of business?

- Can IT provide access to new markets and new market segments?
- Can IT extend the hospitality firm's reach and, in doing so, lower costs and increase conversion rates?
- Will IT enable the hospitality firm to differentiate itself among its competitors in a demonstrable way that can be easily and effectively communicated to guests?
- Can IT provide business intelligence that will lead to better and more timely decisions and provide knowledge asymmetry that will lead to unparalleled market advantages?
- Will IT enhance or improve guest service, lead to more loyal guests, and allow the hospitality firm to charge rate premiums?
- Will IT increase the revenues generated per guest per visit and allow the hospitality firm to focus on more profitable guests and market segments?
- Will IT positively shift the balance of power away from guests and suppliers in favour of the hospitality firm?
- Will IT create a more flexible, agile hospitality firm, one that is capable of sensing and responding to changes in the marketplace to capitalize on opportunities and thwart threats quickly?
- Will IT enhance and extend the hospitality firm's core competencies, resources, and capabilities?
- Will IT provide an enabling platform for growth, new functionality, and new business capabilities?
- What are the costs associated with the IT project, including hardware, software, training, implementation, etc.?
- Do the IT project's benefits outweigh the costs?

Needs analysis   When the answers to such questions have been provided, analysed, reviewed, and the decision is made to proceed with the adoption of IT within the property, the first port of call will be related to the PMS. However, selecting the right PMS can be a difficult thing. The question then arises of how to select the right PMS. This begins with performing what is termed a needs analysis, which is carried out by front-line staff members; it should focus on the flow of guests through the hotel and on the communication between departments concerned.

3.4.2   Needs analysis

The first step in the decision making process of adopting computers in the workplace in order to help in organising data and performing business transactions, is to carry out a needs analysis. A needs analysis is the process of identifying and evaluating needs in a community or other defined population of people. The identification of needs is a process of describing problems of a target population and the possible solutions to these problems. Witkin and Altschuld (1995) describe a need as a gap between what is and what should be. Reviere, Berkowitz, Carter, and Gergusan (1996), however, describe a need as a gap between the real and the ideal both acknowledged by community values and potentially amenable to change. Also called needs assessment, it should focus on the future – what should be done rather than what was done.

Gap

In summarised form, Bardi (2011, p. 105) identifies the following steps in performing a needs analysis for adopting a PMS in a lodging property:

Steps

1 Select a team to analyse needs. This team should include employees at both management and staff levels.
2 Analyse the flow of guests through the lodging property. This should cover all issues related to reservations, registration, guest accounting, checkout, night audit, and guest history.
3 Analyse the flow of information from other departments to the front office. This should cover such diverse issues as reporting on occupancy status, reporting on guest charges, or monitoring energy use.
4 Analyse the administrative paperwork produced by other departments. This should cover such issues as maintaining employee files and records, and processing work orders.
5 Review the information gathered in Steps 2, 3, and 4, with management reviewing compiled information to in order to determine if needs are being met.
6 Evaluate the identified needs—such as control reports, communication, and administrative paperwork produced by other departments—in terms of importance.
7 Combine needs to determine desired applications. In this last stage, the operational and administrative needs are combined in order to determine which computer applications will be appropriate for the property.

In this analysis, all processes the hotel requires from its PMS have to be documented, and factors such as location, target groups and markets, and the size of the property will affect the needs analysis. A large hotel with many departments and outlets inevitably needs a much more robust and comprehensive PMS than a small roadside motel. Establishing a PMS for independent hotels is much easier than for hotels that are managed through franchise agreements or under other forms of management contracts because of contractual restrictions related to the use of PMS. Thus, while an independent hotel may freely choose a PMS that best suit its needs, a chain hotel might be bound to adopt the PMS of its chain because the chain's management hopes to generate savings by implementing the same PMS in its affiliate hotels.

Processes

3.4.3   Considerations in selecting a PMS

When the needs analysis has been completed, and the operational and administrative needs have been combined to determine which computer applications are appropriate for the property, the next action is to acquire appropriate software combined with required hardware. Looking for a hospitality PMS is easier said than done, with a plethora of vendors promising to provide flawless service and technology. Before selecting a PMS, management must ensure that the technology selected and bought is their best pick. There are so many fresh and innovative technologies in the hospitality management niche that are both tempting and imaginative, but hospitality decision makers should recognise that new technologies can provide both unique new features and hidden shortcomings at the same time.

Hardware

Best pick

For the hotel management to know which PMS and related software and hardware are appropriate for their property, certain crucial considerations need to be looked into. Listed here are several questions that hotel management must ask of PMS developers and vendors before making any decisions related to the acquisition of their products:

Crucial considerations

1 Are there any security concerns and loopholes related to this PMS?
2 Does this PMS have any constraints or operational limitations?
3 Does this PMS provide answers to the specific requirements and needs of the hospitality property?
4 How compatible is this PMS to existing Customer Relationship Management services and networks currently in use by the hospitality property?
5 How cost-effective is this PMS and what would its requirements be in terms of upgrades and maintenance?
6 What are the contractual terms for the acquisition, maintenance, payment, and renewal of this PMS?
7 What is the detailed return on investment (ROI) for the hospitality property for this PMS?

The information received from the PMS developers and vendors in answer to these questions should act as an indicator to the hotel management on how to proceed. Proceeding entails the acquisition of appropriate software and hardware packages related to the selected PMS. However, before selecting the software and hardware, it is essential to confirm the operating platform in use. An operating platform can simply be defined as a place to launch software. Some common operating platforms are Linux/Unix; Mac OS; and Microsoft Windows. Software is the collection of programmes and related data stored in the computer; this data provides instructions telling a computer what to do and how to do it. Software is the set of programmes, procedures, algorithms and its documentation concerned with the operation of a data processing system. Whereas software cannot be touched, computer hardware is tangible; it consists of the physical interconnections and devices required to store and run the software. In general, software dictates hardware needs based on processing speed requirements or memory capabilities. The usefulness of a PMS hinges on selecting software that permits management to attain their guest satisfaction goals and also to access all data needed for control purposes.

Operating platform

A well-chosen PMS can provide a hotel with standardisation of its processes and procedures on a single platform, advanced reporting possibilities, seamless integration between all the departments and outlets, revenue management, and e-commerce enhancements, as well as connections to

Standardisation

third-party revenue management systems and global distribution systems (GDS), at no extra costs.

3.4.4   PMS applications

A PMS is organised into modules which are at the core of the hotel's ability to deliver excellent service to its guests. The selected modules summaries found in this section are imported from the product information of the cloud solution *protel Air*, produced by Protel GmbH (this reproduction has been officially authorised by Protel GmbH). Apart from these basic descriptions and functions, several of the main software features included in some of the PMSs available are shown in Figure 3.4, with several other providers and vendors of PMS listed in Figure 3.5.

Modules

FIGURE 3.4 Some main software features found in PMS

Some main software features found in PMS

Account/invoice transfer	Guest management	Post à-la-carte charges
Automatic backup	Incident management	Reporting
Call accounting	Individual/group check inn	Reservations management
Catering	Inventory management	Room availability accounting
Conference centre support	Maintenance management	Room feature classification
Content Management System	Marketing management	Room key manager
Custom user interface	Mobile access	Social Media Commerce
Customizable functionality	Multi-currency	Software development kit
Data import/export	Multi-language	Staff management
E-mail confirmation	Multi-property functionality	Travel Agent commissions
Extended stay options	Online booking	Vacation rental management
GDS/IDS	Payroll management	Wait list management
Group management	POS integration	Walk-in registration

FIGURE 3.5 Some providers and vendors of PMS

Some providers and vendors of PMS

Amadeas PMS	http://www.amadeus.com/hotels/hotels
Globekey Systems	http://www.globekey.com
GuestCentrix	http://www.cmshop.com.au/Products/Guests/CentrixPMS
Hotelogix	http://www.hotelogix.com
Infor Hospitality Group	http://www.infor.co.uk/solutions/hospitality
Innkeeper	http://www.ehospitalitysystems.com
Micros Systems	http://www.micros.com/Solutions
Optima PMS	http://www.silverbyte.com/optimapms
Protel Hotel Software	http://www.protel.net
SumiT	http://www.choicehospitalitysolutions.com
SynXis CRS	http://www.sabrehospitality.com
Visual One	http://www.agilysys.com/home/Hospitality/Solutions
WebRezPro PMS	http://www.webrezpro.com

Overall, the cloud solution *protel Air* is a highly integrated and cost-effective hotel management system for hotels that do not want to take on the burden of maintaining their own technical infrastructure. The concept behind *protel Air* is to use software via an Internet browser, instead of having to buy software and install it on the hotel computers. *protel Air* is a web-based hotel management solution that supports all areas of front office work and saves staff valuable time to focus on their most essential assets: the rooms and the guests. Some of the main benefits of using such a cloud-based solution as PMS and provided by Protel GmbH are that it is:

- Easy: Only requires an Internet browser
- Free: Stationary and mobile usage
- User-friendly: User interface is similar to standard desktop solutions
- Sustainable: Latest technologies
- Independent: Windows, Mac OS, iOS, Android
- Open: Smooth interaction with other applications
- Safe: Data is stored in secure data centre
- Flexibly priced: Available as needed
- Convenient: Full Protel support 24/7

Some protel Air functionality is as shown in the screenshots in Figures 3.6 through 3.13:

FIGURE 3.6 protel Air Active Desktop

FIGURE 3.7 protel Air Room type plan

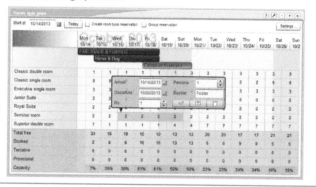

FIGURE 3.8 protel Air Room plan

protel Air Room plan

In the multi-functional room plan you can book rooms for single guests or a group, change reservations and directly access all guest data. Even a guest moving from one room to another no longer means additional work for you: protel Air will automatically change all relevant details such as room status, invoicing and availability.

▼ Multi-functional room plan

▼ Create and change reservations anytime

▼ Direct access to all guest data

▼ Automatic update of all details such as room status and availability

▼ Display of all reservation data

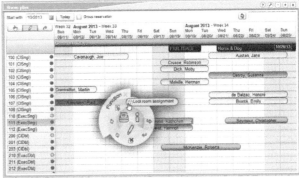

FIGURE 3.9 protel Air guest profiles

protel Air Profiles

The clearly structured tabs of the protel Air guest profiles allow easy and fast access to address and contact data and provides the reservation and invoice history of each guest, including graphs displaying generated revenue. Individual notes and keywords facilitate personal and individual guest service.

▼ All guest information and specific guest wishes at your fingertips

▼ Clear overview through tabs for easy access to address and contact data

▼ Personal service by entering notes and adding guest codes

▼ Allocation of VIP codes in the guest profile (longstay, regular guest, VIP)

▼ Private, businesses- and other profiles

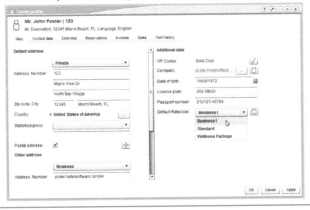

FIGURE 3.10 protel Air Reporting

protel Air Reporting

The hotel's daily routines generate a vast amount of data. The protel Air reporting gathers and manages this data to support your operative business. This enables you to make quick and safe decisions for every facet of your business.

▼ Various daily and manager reports

▼ Various filter options per report for a precise search

▼ Retrieval of reports either as PDF or Excel spreadsheet

▼ Cost-effective through Open Office connection, MS Word is not required

▼ Comfortable distribution of reports using the online cloud storage tool "Dropbox"

FIGURE 3.11 protel Air payment instructions

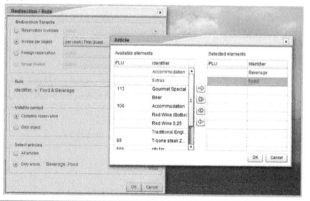

protel Air
Payment Instructions

The Payment Instructions module enables you to create an invoice to fit your guest's needs. The automatic redirection of charges to different invoices or a collective invoice facilitates the billing process especially when dealing with group or company reservations. By using such rules, the invoices are perfectly prepared for check-out.

▼ Automatic booking to the correct invoice

▼ Redirecting certain items or item groups

▼ Finished invoice at check-out, even when the guest has special wishes

FIGURE 3.12 protel Air rate availability

protel Air
Rate availability

Finding the "right" prices is an art in itself. Achieve better prices by adjusting the rate availability flexibly for each day and situation. protel Air's ingenious price management system enables you to implement your desired strategies to all of your booking channels at the snap of a finger.

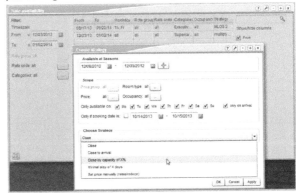

- ▼ Manage your prices from one place
- ▼ Differentiated strategies for all occasions
- ▼ Central rate management for all booking channels
- ▼ Price strategies automatically valid for online-sales
- ▼ Make full use of revenue potentials

FIGURE 3.13 Online sales with protel Air

Online-sales with protel Air

"Book Online" – This button should always be visible to the guest. And when he clicks it, things ought to happen quickly: Check availability, book room and other offers! protel Air's online booking function makes sure that guests who want to make a booking on your hotel website can do that quickly.

A number of additional interfaces which open the door to the entire world of online sales and marketing are at your fingertips. Imagine how many more potential guests will notice your room deals if you not only offer your rooms on your website, but also on the websites of tourism organisations and via booking portals such as booking.com, hotels.com, etc.

Whether you directly or indirectly connect with certain sales channels or use a channel manager such as Cultuzz, all reservations will automatically be transferred to your protel Air hotel management, without you having to even lift a finger. The availabilities will then automatically be adjusted accordingly and taken into account for further enquiries.

You can centrally manage your online rates and availabilities for your rooms via protel Air; changes will be taken into account in all channels. You won't need to worry about constantly updating availabilities and rates per sales channel, as protel Air will take care of that for you.

Summary

3

▶ Either called General Manager (GM), Managing Director or General Director, the GM reports to the owners either directly or through regional offices, and is ultimately held responsible for the unit's success, image and reputation.

▶ The job of the GM differs by property type and size, as well as by its services offered. The GM's job can be conceptualised based on job demands and relationship issues in the short-, intermediate- and long run, generic managerial work roles, and specific job functions.

▶ The main responsibilities of the hotel GM include taking full responsibility for the performance of the hotel; coordinating the activities of all hotel departments; leading the staff of the hotel towards conform to their community, environmental and financial responsibilities; participating in determining the hotel's policies and strategies; providing leadership of and guidance to the hotel's executive team.

▶ The leadership competency model for the lodging industry establishes various dimensions for competencies required by hospitality leaders in eight factors.

▶ The Executive Committee consists of the senior managers of the functional areas who report directly to the GM; this committee is responsible for directing, coordinating, and implementing the vision and objectives of the hotel. The executive committee composition differs by hotel as the organisational structures of no two hotels are the same. Apart from a GM, it generally features a Rooms Division Manager, a Food and Beverage Director or Manager, a Human Resources Manager, a Sales and Marketing Manager, a Financial Controller, a Chief Engineer, an Information Technology Manager, and a Revenue Manager.

▶ A hotel's property management system (PMS) is software used to automate operations; a PMS makes it possible for management and other employees to use computers within an integrated system permitting them to manage and control almost all operations within the hotel, even linking them to other worldwide information networks.

▶ Since selecting the right PMS for a hotel is not always easy, it is essential to start with a needs analysis carried out by front-line staff members; this analysis should focus on the flow of guests through the hotel and on the communication between departments. This should be followed by a crucial evaluation of PMSs and their developers before making a final decision.

© Noordhoff Uitgevers bv

Questions and assignments for reflection

1   Briefly describe the (most) important job-related roles of a hotel GM.

2   Why should hotel GMs be people who are continually seeking to improve their skills and knowledge base?

3   Discuss the relevance of the leadership competency model for the hospitality industry as described in this chapter for contemporary hospitality managers.

4   Why is it important for a hotel to own and use a PMS?

5   What are the questions faced by hotel managers when trying to determine which PMS to obtain for their properties?

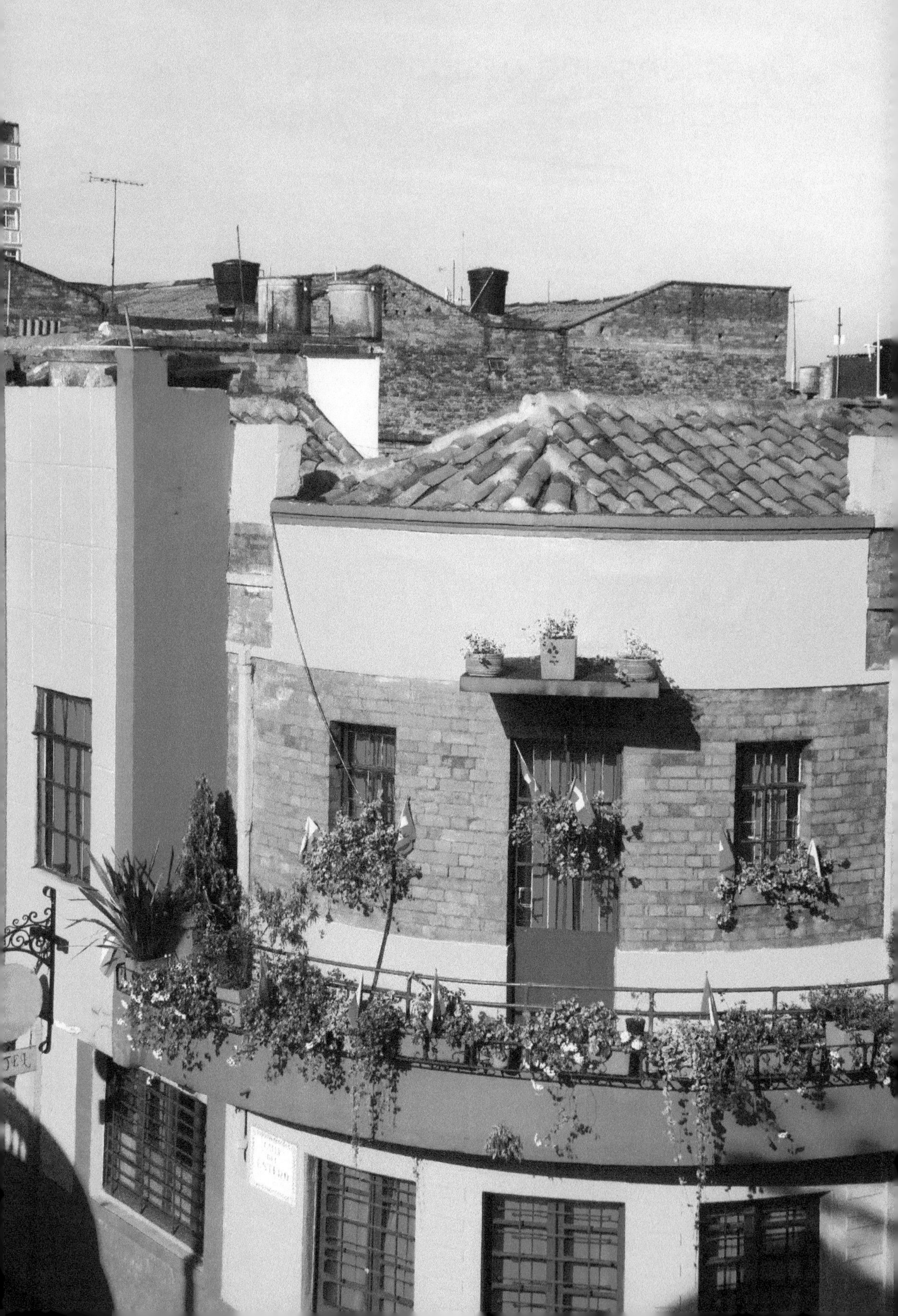

4
The Rooms Department

S. Penninga and M. N. Chibili

4.1 Introduction

As previously indicated in Chapter 2, the hotel industry has a colourful palette of different hotel types, from small-sized independently-owned hotels to
mega-sized hotels belonging to a chain. For all their numerous variations
and differences related to size, products and services, target groups, location and quality, all hotels have a common denominator: they have hotel
rooms, which need to be cleaned and sold. For a hotel to fill up its rooms,
guests need to be able to find it (distribution channels), be welcomed in it
(Front Desk), and have a wonderful stay in a decent room (Housekeeping
and Front Desk), before departing. This process is what all hotels worldwide
have in common, and it is part and parcel of the tasks and responsibilities
of the Rooms Department.

4.2 A guest's journey

Figure 4.1 depicts a guest's journey from the moment of booking to the
moments after leaving the hotel.

Guest's journey

FIGURE 4.1 A guest's journey

Guest service touch point	Hotel departments involved
Booking	Distribution channels, (Central) Reservation Department
Arrival and check in	Uniformed Services and Front Office
Entering hotel room	Uniformed Services (and Housekeeping)
Facilities	For example Food and Beverage outlets, Spa and Fitness facilities, Business facilities, and Hotel Shops
Check out and departure	Uniformed Services and Front Office
After sales and guest loyalty programme	Front Office, Reservations, Guest Relations

Colombia, Bogota: Hotel in La Candelaria

Vital role

As shown in Figure 4.1, the Rooms Department plays a vital role at several moments during the guest's journey. The organisation of the Rooms Department is explained in the following sections; this explanation includes several of the most important standard operating procedures applicable to some of the Rooms Department activities.

Organising

Now more than ever, hotels organise their Rooms Departments differently depending on hotel size and levels of outsourcing of hotel activities. Hotels therefore need to determine what would be the most cost effective and efficient way of organising their processes for ultimate guest satisfaction. Different organisational charts show that not one single organisational chart can fit all hotel types. What all hotels have in common is that the Front Office and Housekeeping are the two main components of the Rooms Department. In several hotels, reservations is an activity branch that belongs to the Rooms Department, and since the guest's journey most likely begins at the booking stage, the Reservation Department is discussed first.

⬤4.3 Reservations

Reservation requests

Centralising

The Reservation Department responds to reservation requests, and creates reservation records. Every hotel can have its own Reservation Department. However, hotels in a chain may organise the Reservation Department more efficiently by centralising activities. For example, the NH Hotel Group in Amsterdam, the Netherlands has a central reservations office called the Amsterdam Booking Office, which is responsible for all group reservations made for the other NH Hotel Group properties in the Amsterdam area. This centralisation also applies to their revenue management policies and decisions. In addition, all individual reservations for NH Hotel Group properties are processed via their Central Reservation Office in Madrid, Spain. Figure 4.2 shows how the central reservation office is connected to the NH Grand Hotel Krasnapolsky, Amsterdam, the Netherlands, where the Amsterdam Booking Office (one of their central services) is linked to the hotel by a single dotted line.

FIGURE 4.2 Linking the Amsterdam Booking Office to the NH Grand Hotel Krasnapolsky (2015)

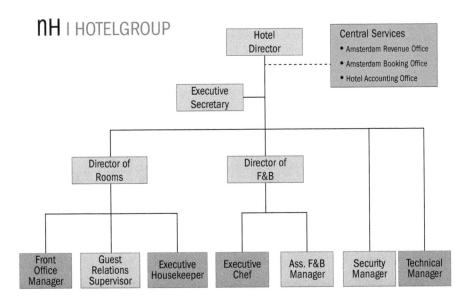

The NH Grand Hotel Krasnapolsky example uses a so-called cluster reservation office. Hotel chains with several hotel properties in a geographic area may choose for a cluster reservation office to serve one specific destination instead of the entire hotel company. Apart from this Amsterdam cluster reservation office, the NH Hotel Group also has an affiliate central reservation system (CRS) or central reservation office (CRO). The CRO for the NH Hotel Group chain permits guests to book at any NH hotel property worldwide. An affiliate reservation network is therefore a hotel chain reservation system in which all participating properties are involved. Other examples of hotel chains that use CROs are Hilton, Marriott, Sheraton, Holiday Inn, and many other franchises to accept reservations for hotels within the chain.

Cluster reservation

Central reservation system

Affiliate

A non-affiliate reservation system is a subscription network designed to connect independent and non-chain hotel properties. A non-affiliate reservation system offers its participants the same kind of benefits as an affiliate reservation system, like advertising their services. Examples of non-affiliate reservation systems are The Leading Hotels of the World, Preferred Hotels & Resorts Worldwide, and Distinguished Hotels (Kasavana & Brooks, 2009).

Non-affiliate

Although any hotel would like to be filled with guests obtained through own network, it is actually not realistic for a hotel to expect to be filled with guests obtained only through their own CRO the year round. Co-operating with third parties and connecting to electronic distribution systems to enlarge the scope of the available market is inevitable for the majority of hotel properties.

In addition to CROs, two other modes of electronic distribution are the Global Distribution Systems (GDS), and the Internet Distribution Systems (IDS). A GDS is defined by Tranter, Stuart-Hill and Parker (2009, p. 104) as 'a computerized reservation system facilitating the sale of hospitality products and

GDS

services primarily to organisational buyers, such as travel agents'. Some current major global distribution systems are Sabre, Apollo, Worldspan, and Galileo (Forgacs, 2010). These GDSs were initially developed by the airline industry, and although the airlines no longer own them exclusively, GDSs remain a powerful distribution channel. Hospitality providers, such as hotel chains, cruise lines, and car rental agencies connect directly to each GDS through an interface or link. A travel agent booking via the GDS may then access the provider's inventory directly (for example to book a hotel room directly from the available rooms of the hotel property concerned). An IDS is an electronic system that facilitates purchases of hospitality products and services by consumers. Examples of IDSs are a hotel's own website, or websites like Hotels.com, Booking.com or Expedia.com. IDSs consist of different components. Figure 4.3, based on Hayes and Miller (2011), shows these different components and by whom they are controlled.

IDS

FIGURE 4.3 The control of the different components of IDS

IDS Type	Content Controlled By
Property websites	Hotel / Hotel Franchisor
Third-party websites	Intermediaries
Web 2.0	Guests / Room Buyers

The first component is the property website, which is a web address whose content is fully controlled by the hotel's own executive team. A great advantage of this type of IDS is that the hotel does not need to pay any fees or commissions to third parties.

There are different types of third party websites arrangements (Tranter et al., 2009; Forgacs, 2010):

Agency model
- The Agency model or retail operations: an arrangement in which a hotel pays a commission (historically 10% of selling price) to an intermediary

for selling its rooms. The advantage of this model is the lack of commitment in terms of capacity allotment or rate for any of the parties. This model also affords hotels a high level of control over availability and price. However, the volume of guests hotels can expect from this model is less significant than that from other models;

- The Merchant model: a system in which an intermediary obtains the rooms inventory at wholesale rate (also known as net rate), and then acts as merchant by selling the rooms to buyers at retail rates. Some examples are Travelocity.com, Hotels.com and Expedia.com. Travelocity, for example, obtains 40 rooms from Hotel X at €100. Travelocity then offers these 40 rooms for sale on its website at €120. The difference is their mark up on the inventory. For this model, a capacity allotment contractual agreement is established between the parties – the agreement is particularly related to the management of the volume of the inventory, and any unsold capacity;   *Merchant model*
- The Auction model: the selling price of a hotel room is determined by the winning bid on a website. Examples are Vakantieveilingen.nl, Priceline, and Luxury Link;   *Auction model*
- The Opaque model (also known as reverse auction): a system in which the room buyer does not know the name of the hotel they have chosen until after they have committed to the purchase price of the room. Examples are Hotwire, Travelocity Packages, and Priceline. In addition, some websites offer mystery hotels in which the principle is the same: the name of the hotel is revealed only after the booking has been confirmed;   *Opaque model*
- The Referral site: a web site that searches for and reports information found on other web sites. Also known as scrapping sites or Meta search engines. These sites scour other sites for the best prices or deals. Figure 4.4 is an overview of some Meta search engines.   *Referral site*

FIGURE 4.4 Some Meta search engines (Source: www.metasearchmanager.com)

Web 2.0

Web 2.0 is the term used to describe social networking sites, video sharing, tweets, blogs and review sites. In the hospitality industry, Web 2.0 describes sites that emphasise user-generated content, usability, and interoperability; it is of major importance, since consumers share their experiences via Web 2.0 possibilities more and more.

4.3.1   The reservation process

Guest's perspective

Hotel's perspective

From a guest's perspective, the most important outcome of a reservation process is a hotel having a room available and ready when the guest arrives. The reservation process from a hotel's perspective starts with identifying what the guest requires, checking the availability, recording and acting on the reservation details, promoting hotel facilities and services, closing the sale, and confirming the reservation.

Reservation process

Based on Kasavana and Brooks (2008), the steps in a reservation process from a hotel's perspective in those instances when the guest makes a phone call can be summarised as follows:

1 Greet the guest. A friendly start of the conversation, for example: 'Thank you for calling the Stenden hotel, this is Anna of the Reservation Department speaking, how may I help you?'
2 Identify the guest's need. Appropriate questions to ask in this stage are: does the guest know this hotel property, has the guest been here before, what are the expected dates of arrival and departure, does the guest have room and/or bed preferences or dinner and travel needs, will they be accompanied by other guests (business or family), what is the purpose of the stay. To acquire valuable information, such open-ended questions like: what; when; why; who; and how questions are crucial.
3 Offer the guest the features the hotel has, based on the needs (obtained through the previous step) and emphasise the benefits. Based on the identification of guest needs, the reservation agent can suggest a hotel room which bests suits the guest's wishes or requirements. At the same time, the agent should stress the advantageous benefits the hotel may have. An example would be free parking places at a city centre hotel.
4 Overcome any objections. In this stage it is important for the reservation agent to check if the offer is actually what the guest wants. If not, perhaps another room can be offered or an available package may be explained to help convince the guest. Guests may start having second thoughts when being informed of price, especially when it is more than initially thought or expected, but price objections may also in fact be questions that need to be clarified.
5 Close the sale. 'I am happy to book the hotel suite, arrival 1st of October, departure 2nd of October, 1 night stay for 2 persons, including breakfast'. By summarising the agreements, the reservation agent can check if everything is fully understood, and the guest has the time to check if all requirements have been taken care of.
6 Gather reservation information. Record and establish reservation information by repeating the name of the hotel guest, arrival and departure dates, room type, rate agreed, special requests, payment instructions, guarantee of reservation, and a confirmation number.

7 Thank the guest and make arrangements to confirm the reservation as agreed. Thank the caller for the reservation in a friendly way, leaving the caller confident that the right hotel has been selected. The agent should also act on any promise to send a confirmation mail or letter, if such was agreed upon.

Figure 4.5 shows a sample reservation display screen as used in *protel Air*.

FIGURE 4.5 Sample reservation form – protel Air

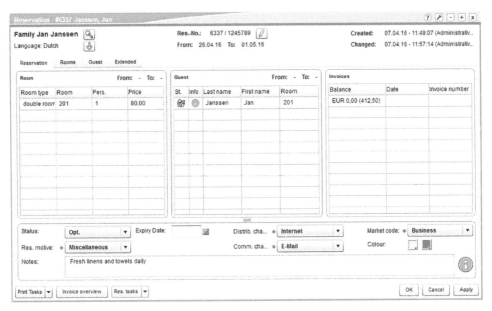

4.3.2 Revenue management

When working at the Reservation or Front Office Department of a hotel, staff are inevitably confronted with the application of revenue management. In daily operations, this means that hotels are trying to sell the right room (implying that hotels offer different room types, for example standard, deluxe and suite) to the right guest (implying that there are different types of guests and target groups) at the right time (hotels face high and low occupancy and different booking patterns of the different target groups) for the right price (the same hotel room is offered at different rates to different target groups and different prices in different seasons) for the right duration of stay (prices may be different based on duration of stay) from the right distribution source (nowadays there are many distribution channels to choose, so a hotelier must decide which channels sell most the rooms at the lowest commission). The main purpose of practicing revenue management is to maximise revenue and profit.

Revenue management

Right room

Right guest

Right time

Right price

Right duration of stay

Right distribution source

4.3.3 The history of revenue management

Hayes and Miller (2011, p. 17) indicate that:

'The foundation of contemporary revenue management is to be found in the nineteen eighties in the airline industry as yield management: a technique used to maximize the revenue or yield, obtained from a service operation, given limited capacity and uneven demand.'

Yield management

Yield management was innovative and successful in a time where consumers' price-related knowledge was limited. Text 4.1 illustrates the use of yield management in the airline industry.

TEXT 4.1

Application of yield management in the airline industry

An airplane with 100 seats with the price set at €200 per seat

Assumption:
60 seats sold at €200 leads to €12,000 revenue per flight. If the price remains at €200 and no customer is willing to buy another ticket at €200, the revenue remains at €12,000 and the airplane will take off with 60 occupied seats as well as 40 empty seats.

Results of applying yield management
60 seats × €200 =	€12,000
20 seats × €150 (sold 1 week before take-off) =	€ 3,000
10 seats × €100 (sold 1 day before take-off) =	€ 1,000
Total revenue per flight =	€16,000

Conclusion with the support of yield management €4,000 extra revenue is generated
Revenue with Y.M. =	€16,000
Revenue without Y.M =	€12,000
Extra Revenue =	€ 4,000

4.3.4 Conditions of implementing yield management successfully

The yield management principles of the airline industry were quickly adopted by the hotel industry. Selling seats for an airplane is comparable with selling hotel rooms for a hotel. To be able to implement yield management successfully, several conditions should apply. These conditions are the same for the airline industry as for the hotel industry, and they are:

Conditions

Fixed

Inventory

- There is a relatively fixed amount of inventory. It is hardly possible to expand the amount of hotel rooms for one night when demand is high or decrease the amount of hotel rooms when demand is low;

Perishable

- The inventory is perishable. If hotel room 213 is not in use on day 1, the revenue missed as a result cannot be reclaimed on day 2. The possibility for hotel room 213 to have generated revenue on day 1 is gone forever. Hotels cannot compensate for this loss, since their capacity for guests remains the same as mentioned in the previous point. In other words, hotel rooms cannot be stored for times when demand is high;

Market segments

- There are differences in market segments or types of guests. For example, the leisure market is generally more price-sensitive than the business market segment. The business guest is more interested in a location nearby a conference and is willing to pay for this convenient location; the leisure guest is more price-sensitive, and therefore more willing to travel longer to the city centre while paying less for the accommodation;

- There is a possibility of pre-selling the products. Hotel rooms can be sold in advance, for example placing Christmas bookings in summer;   *Pre-selling*
- The demand is changeable. Demand in the hotel industry is almost never consistent throughout the entire year. The majority of hotels face periods of high demand and periods of low demand (high-season and low-season).   *Changeable*

Over the years, yield management has evolved into revenue management, where the consumers' price-related knowledge is no longer limited. Tranter et al., (2009, p. 9) define revenue management as 'the act of skilfully, carefully, and tactfully managing, controlling, and directing capacity and sources of income, given the constraints of supply and demand'. Following this definition, supply refers to the available hotel rooms the hotels would like to sell. Demand refers to the guests who would like to make a reservation for the hotel concerned. Capacity is related to the total amount of rooms that the hotel has available. According to Hayes and Miller (2011, p. 122): 'Revenue management is the application of disciplined tactics that predict buyer response to prices, optimize product availability, and yield the greatest business income'.   *Definition*

4.3.5   Room rates
To be able to attract different market segments, hotels need to offer different rates to satisfy the needs of the different guests and to stay occupied throughout the year, while at the same time maximising revenues. The following are some of the most frequently used types of rates established by hotels: *Different rates*

- Rack rate – historically speaking, hotels established a rack rate, which means full rate. The established rack rate is the highest rate a hotel charges for unconstrained demand. Since revenue management is more common for both hotels and hotel guests, this rack rate has developed into the BAR;   *Rack rate*
- BAR – the best available rate, or price that is the lowest while still offering an attractive enough value proposition, to generate sufficient volume of business for the hotel. The BAR depends on the high/low demand of the hotel and can even vary per day. If Monday, for example, is regularly a high demand day, the BAR for Monday can be higher than that for Tuesday. BAR is actually the best rate until market conditions force the hotel to change it;   *BAR*
- Corporate rate – a reduced price for hotel rooms that are offered to companies or organisations. It is in reality a price agreement between the hotel and a company. The discount is based on the volume of room nights the organisation books at a particular hotel;   *Corporate rate*
- Group rate – a special rate offered to groups. Every hotel will establish the parameters of what constitutes a group booking. A common parameter for groups is 10 hotel rooms or more. Groups bring volume to a hotel, and in return groups want a discount;   *Group rate*
- Government and military rate – in the United States of America, hotels establish a special rate for guests working for the US Government or US Army, often also extending to former members of the armed forces – the veterans;   *Government and military rate*
- Tour operator rates – a specially reduced rate for tour operators and travel agencies. Tends to include a travel package. Next to offering a reduced price, hotels need to pay commission to the tour operators and travel agencies for the service of booking a group into the hotel;   *Tour operator rates*
- A day rate – established in hotels where guests may use a hotel room for only a few hours per day or only during the day time instead of during the night. Airport hotels in particular need to establish day rates;   *Day rate*

Complimentary rate

- Complimentary rate – guests staying in a hotel room pay nothing; their stay is free of charge. This rate can be offered to compensate for a complaint, to offer a free room to very important guests, or for publicity reasons.

4.3.6   Key performance indicators

To measure whether hotels are successful in managing their capacity to maximise their revenue, some familiarity with several different key performance indicators (KPIs) is required when applying revenue management.

Occupancy

The first key performance indicator is occupancy.

Occupancy:

Definition: the percentage of available rooms sold during a specific time period.

Calculation: demand (number of rooms sold) divided by supply (number of rooms available).

Occupancy = Demand / Supply
or
Occupancy = Rooms Sold / Rooms Available

Occupancy is indicated as a percentage and as such the result is multiplied by 100. See for example the calculations in Figure 4.6, which are based on the Smith Travel Research (STR) Hotel Math Fundamentals (STR Global, 2015).

FIGURE 4.6 Occupancy percentage calculation

	A	B	C	D	E	F
1	Month and Year	Supply in number of Rooms	Demand in number of Rooms	Revenue	Formula	Occupancy percentage
2	Jan-16	3100	2345	€ 198,765.00	C2 / B2 *100	75.60%
3	Feb-16	2800	2002	€ 175,432.00	C3 / B3 *100	71.50%

ADR

The second key performance indicator is the average daily rate (ADR). ADR is a common abbreviation in the hotel industry, and will be used from here on.

ADR:

Definition: a measure of the average rate paid for rooms sold during a specific time period.

Calculation: revenue from rooms divided by demand (rooms sold), the result is an amount in the applicable currency.

$$ADR = Revenue / Demand$$

Figure 4.7 shows an example of ADR calculations.

FIGURE 4.7 ADR calculations

	A	B	C	D	E	F
1	Month and Year	Supply in number of Rooms	Demand in number of Rooms	Revenue	Formula	ADR in €
2	Jan-16	3100	2345	€ 198,765.00	D2 / C2	84.76
3	Feb-16	2800	2002	€ 175,432.00	D3 / C3	87.63

The third key performance indicator is yield percentage.   Yield percentage

Yield percentage:
Definition: a percentage indicating the realised percentage of revenue achieved in relation to the potential maximum revenue. The maximum potential revenue is determined by multiplying the supply of rooms by the rack rate.

Calculation: revenue from rooms divided by potential revenue from rooms multiplied by 100.

$$Rooms\ revenue / Potential\ rooms\ revenue \times 100.$$

Figure 4.8 shows examples of yield percentage calculations assuming a rack rate of €150.00.

FIGURE 4.8 Yield percentage calculations

	A	B	C	D	E	F
1	Month and Year	Supply in number of Rooms	Demand in number of Rooms	Revenue	Formula	Yield percentage
2	Jan-16	3100	2345	€ 198,765.00	D2 / (B2 *150) *100	42.75%
3	Feb-16	2800	2002	€ 175,432.00	D3 / (B3 *150) *100	41.77%

The fourth key performance indicator is revenue per available room (RevPAR).   RevPAR

RevPAR:
Definition: a measure of revenue generated by a property in terms of rooms available. This differs from the ADR in that RevPAR is affected by the amount of unoccupied rooms, while ADR only shows the average rate of rooms actually sold.

Calculation: rooms revenue divided by the total number of rooms available (the supply), the result is an amount in the applicable currency.

$$\text{RevPAR} = \text{Revenue} / \text{Supply}$$

Figure 4.9 shows examples of RevPAR calculations.

FIGURE 4.9 RevPAR calculations

	A	B	C	D	E	F
1	Month and Year	Supply in number of Rooms	Demand in number of Rooms	Revenue	Formula	RevPAR in €
2	Jan-16	3100	2345	€ 198,765.00	D2 / B2	64.12
3	Feb-16	2800	2002	€ 175,432.00	D3 / B3	62.65

GOPPAR

The fifth and last key performance indicator discussed in this chapter is the gross operating profit per available room (GOPPAR).

GOPPAR: Definition: GOPPAR compares gross operating profit for a certain period to rooms available during that period. The calculation can be done on a monthly, quarterly, semi-annual or annual basis.

Calculation: gross operating profit for a certain period divided by the total number of rooms available during that period.

$$\text{GOPPAR} = \text{Gross operating profit for a certain period} / \text{available rooms during that period}$$

A 350 bedroom hotel with an annual gross operating profit of €4,650,000 will, for example, have a GOPPAR of € 4,650,000 ÷ (350 rooms × 365 nights) of € 36.40. GOPPAR assesses cost efficiency because it takes into account management control and containment costs, and it is useful in comparing gross operating profits across properties within the same competitive set (see Chapter 7 of Chibili, 2016 – *Basic Management Accounting for the Hospitality Industry*, 2nd edition). While RevPAR measures revenue performance, there is a growing interest in evaluating overall profitability, with GOPPAR seen as a clearer indicator of overall performance.

4.4 The Front Office

The Front Office is the core of hotel operations. O'Fallon and Rutherford (2011, p. 120) indicate that 'the student of hospitality management will find the hotel's front office referred to as the *hub*, the *nerve centre* or the *brain* or some other name suggesting centrality'. This department has intense traffic and it is the most important access point for guest complaints, information and requests. It is the area where guests have their first and last encounter with hotel staff, and this encounter is of major influence on guests' impressions, guests' satisfaction, and their willingness to share this satisfaction and experiences with other guests or friends on social media via a review, for example.

Core

Access point

4.4.1   Departments and positions related to the Front Office

Figure 4.10 is an example of an organisational chart of the Rooms Department adapted from Hayes and Ninemeier (2007, p. 24). Hotels can organise their Rooms Departments in various ways. Several factors, such as size, type and location, may have an influence on how hotels actually organise their operations. As already indicated in previous sections, there are at least two major departments that belong to the Rooms Department: the Front Office, and Housekeeping.

Factors

FIGURE 4.10 Organisational chart Rooms Department

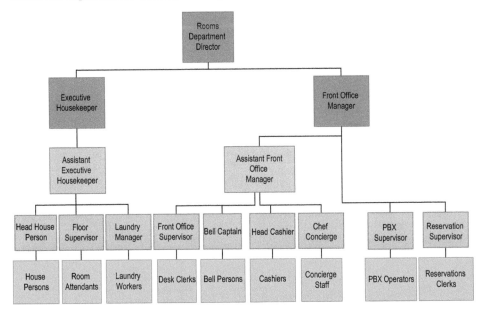

Rooms Department Manager

Responsibilities

The Rooms Department Manager or Director is responsible for the daily operations of the Rooms Department of the hotel and reports directly to the hotel property's General Manager. Their main responsibilities are achieving (or exceeding) budgeted revenue for the department, maintaining or reducing costs, achieving positive guest satisfaction as well as a positive employee satisfaction of the staff working within the department: happy staff serves happy guests. The job of a Rooms Department Manager can be very challenging and varied. For an impression of a day in the life of a Rooms Department Manager, refer to Text 4.2: a summarised story of the Rooms Department Manager of the Crowne Plaza Amsterdam City Centre, Mr Maurice Janssen.

Front Office Manager

The Front Office Manager is responsible for the daily operations of the Front Office. The Front Office Manager needs to think about the schedule, who is working when and how many front desk staff members need to be scheduled based on the expected amount of guests and the occupancy percentage of the hotel. Furthermore, the Front Office Manager ensures a proper, efficient and profitable functioning of the front office, maintaining its policies, procedures and technological equipment. The Front Office Manager also provides the support and the training that the Front Office staff require to fulfil the hotel's mission towards its guests.

TEXT 4.2

A day in the life of Maurice Janssen, Rooms Department Manager

Maurice Janssen is the Rooms Department Manager at the Crowne Plaza Amsterdam City Centre, Amsterdam, the Netherlands since 2011. He graduated from Hotel school The Hague, The Netherlands and has since held positions at the Waldorf Astoria Rome Cavalieri, Italy; The InterContinental New York Barclay, USA; InterContinental Boston, USA; Fitzpatrick Manhattan Hotel, New York, USA; and the InterContinental Mark Hopkins, San Francisco, USA. He loves to experience cultures through food and cooking.

To describe a typical day out of a Rooms Department Manager's life is almost impossible. Every day is a complete different scenario and whatever you planned is never how it really maps out. I am not a manager to sit in my office working on my computer all day. I still love the interaction with my guests hence I am walking through the hotel a lot to seek interaction with our guests: how they are enjoying their stay; what they are planning to do; or seeking to know if there is

anything that my team or I can do to enhance their stay. Covering for breaks might seem to be an unusual thing to do however once in a while I like to cover my team's breaks. That takes me back to hotel procedures and I can see where we can improve our services even more. It also enables me to sit with the Reception Manager and Training Manager to discuss where the team can improve its services.

My day starts at home. When I wake up, I quickly check my mails to see if there is anything pressing. Once at work, I firstly greet the team members on the floor followed with analysing the results from the previous day checking out especially the occupancy figures, the ADR, the RevPAR and of course the comparisons with the competitive set. I also look at the occupancy for the coming month to see where we can improve our numbers in conjunction with the Revenue Manager. The issues we ponder over concern such topics like the levels of the rates (too high or too low), the upcoming city activities and how they will affect bookings, and the pace at which reservations are coming in. Then there are our current in-house guests. A look at the guest report tells me which guests might have had challenges during the previous day. This will trigger such questions like:

- Is follow up needed?
- Is there a trend in the complaints?
- How can we prevent them from happening in the future?

The Managers-on-Duty would have previously placed notifications related to any situation in which the guests might have had hitches during their stay caused either through the fault of the hotel, or by a third-party such as taxi-drivers, bookers, or bus companies. Anything that might affect a guest's stay is important for my team and me to follow up and talk them over with our guests. This even goes as far as following up on a guest who tripped over the wobbly Amsterdam cobble stone pavement.

On a daily basis I liaise with the Guest Relations team to review the VIP situation. We review the VIP arrivals and possibilities of maintaining their room assignments, the amenities to be placed in the rooms, the cards that might need to be written, and the VIPs that I would personally want to welcome. Various meetings take place during the day designed to ensure that the strategic targets are set and met. A sales meeting is held to discuss all potential returning business or to capture corporate accounts by the Front-of-house departments. Social Media, guest reviews and guest correspondences are analysed and responded to on a daily basis ensuring that the guests feel heard and any challenges during their stay are overcome. We hope with this to be able to improve guest service with the feedback that is provided.

In between these meetings, I hold conversations, take part in laughter, and share cups of coffee with my colleagues at the Reception, Guest Relations, Concierge and Housekeeping to ensure that they feel valued, trained, informed and heard as well.

Depending on its size, a hotel might employ an Assistant Front Office Manager to assist the Front Office Manager, or to replace them in case of absence.

Front Desk

The Front Desk manages room inventory, assigns rooms to newly arrived guests according to their personal preferences, and manages the check-in (and check-out) processes. Another responsibility of the Front Desk is answering all questions the guests may have which may cover topics from finding a restaurant or fitness centre to questions regarding breakfast times or local tourist information. Another task is to maintain room availability information. Cashiers handle money, post charges, manage guest accounts settlements, and conduct check-out procedures. In small-sized hotels, these different positions and responsibilities may be combined and executed by one and the same Front Desk employee.

Concierge

A Concierge is specialised in providing personalised service to guests. In order to do so, the Concierge must be very well aware of the area where the hotel is located, and have knowledge of local specialties, touristic attractions, unique selling points, restaurants and events. The concierge, in other words, is a destination specialist. Modern hotels, in collaborations with technology experts, have developed apps that function as digital hotel concierge systems that are made available for hotel guests. Text 4.3 explains the responsibilities and added value of a concierge for hotel guests according to the Golden Key Association (Les Clefs d'Or).

TEXT 4.3
A concierge according to Les Clefs d'Or

In Service through Friendship

You can recognize any Concierge Clefs d'Or by the keys they display on the collar of their uniforms. These crossed gold keys are more than just the symbol of the organization — they are the symbol of guaranteed, quality service.

Concierge Clefs d'Or will accommodate every guest request so long as it is morally, legally, and humanly possible. Their services run the gamut from the mundane to the

extraordinary, yet each request is fulfilled with vigour to the guest's full satisfaction. Concierge Clefs d'Or handle all duties with zeal: mail and messages, recommendations and reservations, travel and meeting planning, personal shopping and professional communications. They are also supreme social advisors, business expediters, and personal confidantes.

On those rare occasions when guests' requests cannot be fulfilled single-handedly, Les Clefs d'Or Concierges have the necessary back-up: a never-ending network of

acquaintances, friends, and colleagues from around the world to see to it that guests' demands are met.

Les Clefs d'Or members have dedicated many years of hard work and training to the concierge profession. They are pleasant and welcoming in appearance, they remain calm in a hectic environment, and they always display integrity. Indeed, discretion is the hallmark of a Concierge Clefs d'Or.
Les Clefs d'Or Concierges have their fingers on the pulses of their cities, able to advise guests on restaurants, night life, sporting and theatre events, sightseeing tours, shopping, etc. They can direct guests to any location, to any product, at any time of day or night.

Les Clefs d'Or Concierges are motivated by a genuine desire to serve. They are prudent, patient, kind toward guests and staff alike, self-confident, tenacious, persistent, adaptable, ingenious, disciplined, and flexible.
The global environment of today's business world demands that concierges be able to converse with all travellers, from Albania to Zaire. Many Clefs d'Or members are multilingual and most are well-versed in many cultures.
Les Clefs d'Or Concierges have worked hard to obtain their keys. Whether requesting something simple or complex, you can be sure they are trusted resources to business travellers and vacationers alike, always keeping guests' safety, enjoyment, and satisfaction in mind.

(Source: www.lesclefsdor.org)

The concierge is part of the Uniformed Services, a high visibility department in full-service luxury hotel properties, and can employ various members. The Valet Parking Attendant greets guests while driving their cars to the front of the hotel or to the parking lot, opens car doors, and escorts and assists guests to the front door. The Door Attendant assists with transferring luggage from the car until a Bell Person retrieves it for delivery, and of course opens the door for the hotel guest. The Bell Attendant retrieves the luggage

Uniformed Services

from the lobby area and delivers it to the hotel rooms. The Concierges, as indicated in Text 4.3, are dedicated to welcoming the guests at the hotel personally, thereby ensuring that guests have a lasting positive service impression upon departure. In an era of rising labour costs, the distinction between these positions may become more blurred, with various tasks being integrated and combined into the single position of concierge.

Private Branch Exchange

PBX is short for Private Branch Exchange. The PBX takes care of telecommunications within the hospitality property. PBX employees answer all phone calls and distribute these calls to the appropriate extensions.

For very large hotels, additional supervisory positions may be added to the organisational chart in order to manage the sphere of influence of certain departments, with examples including Front Office Supervisor(s), Bell Captain, Head Cashier, Chef Concierge, PBX Supervisor and Reservation Supervisor(s).

Guest Relations Desk

Hotels may employ a Guest Relations Desk in the Lobby area. These days, Guest Relations or Guest Services are of great importance to any hotel, because although there is little joy in receiving complaints, it is better for hotels to deal with complaints immediately, giving them a chance to resolve complaints rather than to have to read about them on various social media platforms or review sites. At the Guest Relations Desk, a guest can be moved away from the Front Desk, giving the Guest Relations Officer ample time to carefully listen and try to provide a solution to the complaint without being overhead or disturbed by other guests.

Night Auditor

The Night Auditor (not featured in Figure 4.10) is a position that belongs to the Rooms Department in some hotels, but to Finance in others (see Section 8.5). The main reason that hotels organise this position differently is due to its character. In many hotels, working shifts at the Front Office are organised as follows:

Working shifts

• 07.00 – 15.00 hrs = Early shift
• 15.00 – 23.00 hrs = Late shift
• 23.00 – 07.00 hrs = Night shift

From the perspective of covering all shifts at the Front Desk, the Night Auditor belongs to the Rooms Department. However, looking at the main activities of this position, the Night Auditor, who audits and ensures the accuracy of transactions that have taken place during a period at the Front Office, is therefore a Finance associate. Hotels need to determine what would be a **End of day** convenient and efficient time at end of day to make up the financial accounts, check the financial transactions of the previous day, and compile account balances. This moment is mainly during the night shift, when guests are no longer checking-in or checking-out. Apart from financial transactions, the Night Auditor also checks the room status of the rooms. If, for example, a room is listed as vacant, but the system indicates room charges for that particular room, the Night Auditor must find out who is staying in that room. Alternatively, the system may list a room as occupied, while it actually appears to be empty; this has to be verified as well. This situation, identified by Kasavana and Brooks (2009) as a sleep-out, leads to lost room revenues for the hotel. Any difference between room status according to the PMS and **Discrepancy** the actual situation is termed a discrepancy. Towards the end of the night shift, the Night Auditor compares the information about the ADR and the occupancy percentage with the performance of other hotels in its competitive range. A hotel is only able to measure and judge its success if it can compare its data to that of hotels of similar character and facilities in the area (Jansen, 2008). The activities of the Night Auditor are made much easier in hospitality properties that have adopted modern PMSs.

4.4.2 Main procedures at the Front Office

The main procedures at the Front Office are the check-in procedure, the check-out procedure, dealing with guest complaints and providing service when anticipating the demands and wishes of the guests.

Check-in procedure

Early check-in requests come from guests who would like to check-in before the regular check-in time of the hotel property. Most hotels have regular check-in times, somewhere between 13.00 and 16.00 daily. If guests wish to check-in earlier, a Front Desk employee needs to check whether the room can be assigned to the guest and whether the status of the room indicates it is clean.

Check-in times

4

One of the first steps in the check-in procedure is in asking the guest to fill in all required information on the registration card. The purpose of the registration card upon arrival is to record a guest's arrival and to confirm their personal details, as well as to satisfy legal requirements (Baker, Huyton & Bradley, 2000). As indicated by Vallen and Vallen (2013), in some countries this document is known as the police document. This document allows concerned parties to keep track of the whereabouts of visitors, and may help hotels to trace guests who did not pay their bills, forgot something at the hotel, or caused damage to hotel property. The registration card currently functions as a form of contract between the guest and the hotel since it contains important statements by the hotel. It could state, for example, that the hotel cannot be held responsible for any loss of guest property unless such property was stored in a safe. It could also state guests are liable for all costs incurred during the stay, and are required to accept responsibility for these costs (for example if a guest smoked in a non-smoking room). Guests need to sign the registration card to indicate that the contractual statements have been read, understood and accepted (Jansen, 2008).

Registration card

Police document

Contract

Sign

Based on Vallen and Vallen (2013), many things might simultaneously be happening at the Front Desk during check-in, as listed below:
- Guests are being welcomed;
- Reservations are located;
- Accommodation needs are determined or checked;
- Registration cards are offered to guests to be filled in;
- Some small talk may take place, while at the same time the Front Desk agent may be trying to up-sell (proposing a more expensive and luxurious room) or cross-sell (making table reservations for dinner at the restaurant) services or facilities to the guest;
- Guests identities, including correct spelling of names and addresses, are verified;
- Other hotel services and facilities are promoted (restaurant, room service, fitness area), and guests are informed of breakfast and dinner times and possibilities;

- Anticipated departure dates are verified;
- Credit cards are validated, payment instructions are checked;
- Any mails or messages are handed over;
- The Bell person is called and guests are escorted to their rooms. In less luxurious hotel properties, directions to the hotel rooms are shared with guests, after which guests must find their own way to their hotel rooms.

Credit card authorisation

In some hotels, credit card authorisation is requested during the check-in procedure in order to guarantee payment. Hotels may also ask for a cash deposit or cash payment upon arrival. The development of technology in combination with the need of guests for speed of service, self-check-in, and self-check-out kiosks or terminals are becoming more common in the hotel industry.

Check-out procedure

Check-out procedure

The check-out procedure also sees a lot of activity in a relatively short period of time. Kasavana and Brooks (2009, pp. 340-341) indicate the following procedures designed to simplify check-out and account settlement:

- Inquiring about additional recent charges (for example mini bar use or breakfast consumption);
- Posting outstanding charges (for example newspaper);
- Verifying account information;
- Presenting the guest folio;
- Verifying the method of payment;
- Processing the account payment;
- Checking for mail or messages;
- Securing the room key;
- Updating the room's status;
- Inquiring about guests' stay and experience;
- Requesting guests complete a guest satisfaction survey or a review;
- Updating the guest history file.

Folios

Digitally

For sustainability reasons, hotels do not print guests' folios as a rule. Hotels may ask guests if a printed folio would be appreciated and then print one by request only. Invoices can also be sent to debtors digitally.

Important functions

To summarise, the Front Desk is responsible for at least four important functions during the check-out procedure:

- Resolving outstanding guest account balances;
- Updating room status information;
- Recording guest history;
- Maintaining guest relationships by stimulating guest loyalty and asking guest for positive reviews.

Dealing with guest complaints

Guest complaints

One procedure used to deal with guest complaints is known by its acronym, LEARNT. Easy to remember and apply, its steps are listed in Figure 4.11.

FIGURE 4.11 LEARNT in dealing with guest complains

L	Listen to the guest, what the complaint entails.
E	Empathise and emphasise, show the guest that the complaint is understood and that the hotel representative is feeling sorry for the inconvenience suffered by the guest.
A	Apologise on behalf of the hotel.
R	React upon the complaint.
N	Notify involved departments what happened and take measures to prevent these complaints from occurring again.
T	Thank the guest for taking the effort to share the complaint with the hotel organisation and to give them a chance to resolve the issue.

Figure 4.12 lists regular do's and don'ts when dealing with guest complaints.

FIGURE 4.12 Guidelines for handling guest complaints

Do's	Don'ts
Listen with concern and empathy.	Do not deny, become defensive or hostile - 'That is not true...'
Isolate the guest, so other guests will not overhear.	
Stay calm.	Do not argue with or insult the guest.
Show interest in the guest and use the name of the guest frequently. Take the complaint seriously.	'It is not your fault...' 'It is not a big deal, is it?' 'We heard this all the time'.
Give the guest undivided attention.	'You have to...'
Take notes, the guest will probably slow down as well and it might give the guest a feeling of reassurance.	Do not blame the guest. My colleague wrongly did it of forgot about it.
Inform the guest what can be done. Offer choices if possible.	Do not promise the impossible.
Set an appropriate time for completion of corrective actions and monitor the progress.	Do not exceed your authority.
Follow up. Contact the guest to ensure that the problem was solved satisfactorily.	
Record the entire event, including the actions taken.	

4.4.3   Review sites

Nowadays, almost equally important to official hotel classification and rating systems as indicated in Chapter 2 are the review sites for hotels. Instead of an official institute classifying the hotel's facilities and services, hotels are rated by guests who have previously visited the hotel properties. Their opinions are highly appreciated by potential guests and are used in their decision making processes. As a result of these developments, many hotels have created new job positions, such as those of Social Media Managers or Reputation Managers. The aim here is not to list all review sites in this chapter, but two examples (in addition to Figure 1.12 of Chapter 1) are provided to illustrate the powerful influence of social media on the performance of hospitality operations. Text 4.4 shows its positive effects, whereas Text 4.5 shows that it can also have negative influences.

Review sites

Opinions

Social Media Managers

Positive effects

Negative influences

TEXT 4.4

Reviews increasingly drive booking decisions, October 8 2014

By Jason Q. Freed, HNN contributor

Positive reviews increase conversion rates and allow hoteliers to charge higher rates. But with different customer segments come different booking behaviours.

Highlights

- Travellers are 3.9 times more likely to choose a hotel with higher review scores.
- Negative reviews are not deal breakers for business travellers.

Leisure travellers care more about online reviews because their travel is more experiential, one revenue manager said.

Online reviews increasingly are affecting booking decisions, although not all traveller segments behave the same way, according to research and various industry sources. Multiple studies recently have highlighted the importance of guest reviews and ratings in the booking funnel.

A study conducted by TrustYou and Donna Quadri-Felitti, clinical associate professor at New York University's Preston Robert Tisch Center for Hospitality and Tourism, concluded that guest reviews have a significant impact on hotel conversion rates as well as the rates that travellers are willing to pay. Given equal prices, travellers are 3.9 times more likely to choose a hotel with higher review scores, the study showed. And when hotel prices are increased for hotels with better review scores, travellers are more likely to book the hotel with the higher score despite the higher rate.

A different report conducted by PhoCusWright on behalf of TripAdvisor showed that more than half of global respondents do not want to book a room until they've read reviews to find out what other travellers think about the property. In addition, 87% of TripAdvisor users agree that an appropriate management response to a bad review improves their impression of the hotel, and 62%

agree that seeing hotel management responses to reviews generally makes them more likely to book the hotel.

Other research shows that not all guests respond to online reviews the same way. One such study conducted by Breffni Noone, associate professor at Penn State University, and Kelly McGuire, executive director of hospitality and travel for SAS, showed that while more business travellers reported reading reviews most of the time before they booked, leisure travellers were more likely to shy away from hotels that didn't get the highest scores.

Business and leisure travellers 'both cared about (user-generated content), but used it in different ways. ... Leisure travellers would not consider a hotel with negative reviews, but with business travellers, although reviews were strong drivers of value, they weren't deal breakers,' McGuire said.

Key takeaways from a study on the effects of user-generated content on purchasing decisions.

Real-world context

Numbers often can tell one story while real world experience might tell another.

Mark Molinari is VP of revenue management and distribution at Las Vegas Sands, where the flagship hotel-casino in Las Vegas does 35% to 40% group business. He said transient guests 'for sure' care more about user-generated content because their travel is more experiential.

'They're going to demand the best experience,' he said.

© Noordhoff Uitgevers bv

Conversely, Molinari said business travellers would stay where their conference or meeting is being held and are less likely to rely on user-generated content when making decisions.

McGuire and Noone's research tells a slightly different story, with business and leisure travellers indicating the order of importance of various factors when booking:

- **Business traveller:** review sentiment (positive or negative); brand; aggregate ratings; price; and finally review language (descriptive or emotional).
- **Leisure traveller:** review sentiment (positive or negative); price; aggregate ratings; brand.

'As you can see, there are some interesting differences in how these two segments assess value and make decisions, yet review sentiment is most influential for both segments,' McGuire said.

Michelle Davis, director of revenue management for Hospitality Ventures Management Group, which operates 38 mostly corporate-driven hotels, echoed McGuire's findings. She said HVMG's leisure customers look at reviews first, then at price and finally loyalty program affiliation. HVMG's business travellers, on the other hand, first consider hotels in their loyalty programs, then look at reviews and finally weigh price.
Both McGuire's study and revenue managers said there is a big difference between one negative review and a string of negative reviews.

'According to our study, a pattern of negative reviews, especially when others in the market have better reviews, would negatively impact demand,' McGuire said.

'One negative review doesn't hurt on either the business or the leisure side,' Davis said, 'as long as you've got a mixture of positive reviews in there.'

The next step
The next step for the industry is taking those positive and negative reviews into account when setting rates. Molinari said Las Vegas Sands isn't quite there yet but noticed software developers are innovating in the space.
Davis said she has developed her own metrics and is taking ratings and reviews into account when determining her price positioning, although she admits her process is a bit subjective and does not rely on a specific algorithm, such as a software program might.
McGuire offers a bit of caution: 'Given a pattern of negative reviews, my study indicates that lowering the price does not make up for the negative impact of negative reviews for both business and leisure travellers. When a hotel has negative user-generated content, they should not be focused on pricing. They need to fix the problem.'

(Source: www.hotelnewsnow.com)

TEXT 4.5

The most-hated hotel chains on social media, 23 Jun, 2015 by Esther Hertzfeld

While hotels have tried to embrace social media as much as possible, it can backfire on them. When it comes to getting beat up on social media, the Hilton chain is on top, according to a new survey by Crimson Hexagon.

The research analyzed Twitter posts over an almost six-month period to see how 10 of the world's largest hotel chains (based on number of rooms, employees, properties, and social media buzz) fared. Hilton had a 17 percent negative rating; customers com-

plained about charging for Wi-Fi, connection speeds, poor customer service, getting spammy phone calls and billing problems, according to the survey.

Hilton was the most hated, with 17 percent of tweets being negative. Tying for second place, with 14 percent of tweets being disparaging, are Marriott, Sheraton, Westin, DoubleTree and Crowne Plaza, reports Business Insider.

For hotels, success is measured in large part, by positive ratings on social media. Radisson (62 percent) and Best Western (57 percent) led the pack, followed by Marriott (45 percent). Radisson also has the lowest negative sentiment, at just 4 percent. The reason? Loyalty, said John Donnelly, the senior vice president of global sales and marketing at Crimson Hexagon.

'In the hotel industry, customer loyalty is paramount,' he told Fortune. 'Social media gives hotel brands the opportunity to deepen engagement with their customers, build an emotional connection and amplify loyalty initiatives to new platforms.'

The full breakdown:

Brand	Tweet Volume	Positive Sentiment	Neutral Sentiment	Negative Sentiment
Hilton	25,020	40	43	17
Marriott Hotels	89,092	45	41	14
Sheraton	26.056	33	54	14
Westin	25,899	40	36	14
Double Tree	10,736	41	45	14
Crowne Plaza	7,981	33	53	14
Best Western	16,568	57	31	12
W Hotels	8,968	44	43	13
Holiday Inn*	49,231	33	60	8
Radisson	40,531	62	34	4

*Includes Holiday Inn Express

(Source: www.hotelmanagement.net)

4.4.4   Developments

As indicated in many previous instances in this book, particularly in Chapter 3, one of the major developments currently impacting the hotel industry is that of technological innovations. Hotels use technology to impress, and anticipate on the needs of their guests. Self-check-in, for example, or the use of apps on mobile phones for various access possibilities such as entering hotel rooms (visible keys no longer required) are some examples. A major benefit of technology is the support it can provide to Rooms Department Managers in making their strategic and operational decisions. In this section, some systems used by Rooms Department Managers are highlighted.

Technological innovations

Support

Systems

IDeaS (www.ideas.com) is a revenue management system that offers support to hotels in terms of optimising rates, improving operational results, understanding the value of revenue management, and accurate forecasting. This system supports hotel properties in making price decisions to optimise their room revenue. Figure 4.13 shows an example of an IDeaS information sheet.

IDeaS

FIGURE 4.13 IDeaS – Hampshire Eden Oranje Hotel Leeuwarden, the Netherlands

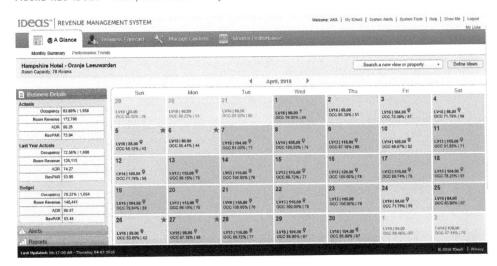

The calendar in IDeaS RMS provides a way to understand and review rate decisions, occupancy forecasts, special events, and overrides for the displayed time period. For past dates, the calendar displays rate decisions and actual occupancy for that date.

Olery (www.olery.com) offers its services to big and small companies in the leisure and hospitality industry in order to understand how guests experience their services (reputation management). The different Olery products are:

Olery

- Hotel Review Data API that provides access to data from millions of guest reviews;
- Hotel Review Summaries that provide auto-generated summaries of reviews for consumer sites/apps;
- Custom Reports that analyses review data for unique applications;

- Reputation for Hotels which is an online tool for monitoring and managing online guest reviews;
- Feedback for Hotels which is a simple survey tool for gathering real insights from guests.

Revinate

Revinate (www.revinate.com) is another such company, whose product is called the Guest Feedback Suite. This product has two major components: online reputation management and post-stay surveys. The Guest Feedback Suite supports hotels in improving guest experience before, during and after a stay using mobile and desktop solutions, thereby making guests more accessible and approachable. Through the Guest Feedback Suite, hotels can communicate and engage with hotel guests directly. The system shows a ranking of the hotel compared to its competitors. Another feature of this system is the Sentiment Analysis, which shows the trending topics guests are talking about on social media. Figure 4.14 shows an overview of some of the information the Revinate product can compile for hotels using the software.

FIGURE 4.14 Guest satisfaction overview Revinate

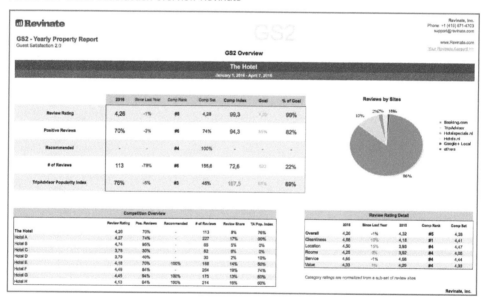

Sprinklr

Sprinklr (www.sprinklr.com) is another technology company that has multiple products aimed at helping hotels and other big companies in various domains. In regards to social media management, Sprinklr features a product called Engagement, which can manage massive volumes of complex social conversations, distribute workload across teams, automate complex workflows, and enforce compliance rules. It makes social media a core function for all business lines including Sales, Marketing, Customer Services, Public Relations, Events and Crisis Management. Sprinklr supports hotel management in determining the most ideal moment for engaging with guests. Messages can be prepared in advance and sent virally just at the right moment.

Text 4.6 is a case study of how Starwood Hotels & Resorts uses Sprinklr to deliver great customer service.

TEXT 4.6

Case study of Starwood Hotels & Resorts using Sprinklr

SPRINKLR – STARWOOD HOTELS AND RESORTS CASE STUDY
Co-authored by Sandra Henriques and Marcella Nicotera, Starwood Hotels & Resorts

Business Challenge
Recognized as the world's most global, high-end hotel company, Starwood Hotels & Resorts Worldwide is comprised of nine internationally renowned brands and an award-winning loyalty program. The company's social media presence spans several global regions across various local teams. To effectively manage the approximated 300,000 incoming messages per month, across 10 brands, Starwood needed to coordinate its social media efforts across brand, regional, and team structures while minimising redundancy. Message responsiveness and timing was critical to accomplish the overriding objective of excellent customer care. Starwood needed a solution that was scalable across divisions, robust enough for content performance analysis, but simple enough for everyday monitoring of social channels, which includes global brand channels and 1200+ hotel channels.

Being a social business means collaborating internally and externally. By improving processes internally, the brand has more time to focus on its customers externally. If less time is spent searching for conversation history, paired with the ability to collect details about guests as the brand interacts with them, those learnings can be shared internally enabling Starwood to enhance its communication across channels with those who matter the most – their guests.

Starwood recognizes that customer service is imperative to continued brand growth and leadership. Moderating social conversations throughout brands, regions, and teams has the power to meaningfully enhance guests' booking and travel experiences.

What They Did
Starwood's team monitors their social channels globally, across 15 languages, 24 hours a day, 7 days a week through Sprinklr. To solve business challenges in an always-on situation, Starwood identified measurement, monitoring, and workflow processes as key elements of a solution. In order to grasp the full impact of social customer service, the team first needed to measure it in a way that enabled comparison with more traditional customer care channels, such as phone, e-mail, and chat. Then, integrating comprehensive monitoring of social channels with Starwood's workflow processes would provide the ability to automatically categorize content and assign messages. Additionally, analytics provided by the platform, such as inbound volume, response volume, volume by category, language, and profile tags could help Starwood identify employee superstars.

Processes
Processes were critical to have in place before implementation 'to set the foundation, but we recognized that we had to be flexible in order to be more efficient and deliver a better customer experience.' For example, approvals – such as external agencies, internal partnerships, and legal – had been col-

lected via e-mail on excel sheets. But with Sprinklr, these processes were adjusted and approvals now route to the right people before publishing. Starwood processes (like approvals) were converted into workflows in Sprinklr to ensure consistency.

Monitoring

An agent's daily routine includes monitoring channels, listening, and engaging across legal, PR, brands, and hotel properties to deliver the right messages. Color-coding incoming messages allows teams to quickly recognize and assign items on moderation dashboards and also visually categorize them. Starwood responds to guest complaints, but also engages in pivotal opportunities to make great moments even better with Surprise and Delights. A negative customer experience, for example, could be coded in red and automatically routed to the hotel team. Specific crisis keywords are routed to appropriate queues and handled accordingly. A Surprise and Delight moment, on the other hand, could be coded in orange and automatically routed to the global care team.

Coordination across Starwood properties is also easier. For example, when responding to a guest directly @mentioning or tweeting a specific property, the social care team looks up their reservation, adds appropriate tags to the guest's Sprinklr user-record, reaches out (or assigns the message) to the specific hotel, and then responds to the customer with an answer based on information received.

Measurement

Starwood heavily utilizes analytics for operational and strategic direction. Instead of gathering social metrics natively from each channel, Starwood now utilizes Sprinklr reporting for one single source of truth on social measurement on their channels. Key metrics such as Average Response Time, First Response Time, Volume by Reason, Sentiment, and Surprise and Delight Executions provide fact-based indications of how to improve and adjust. Starwood has these metrics (and others) custom reporting dashboards so teams and executives align on the most relevant data to their business.

The Results

'Success is a happy guest, and a happy team that can execute brilliantly on every piece of social media verbatim received combined with the time saved in moderation,' shares Sandra and Marcella. Starwood feels successful in both aspects.

Reporting, for example, used to take an entire day every month at Starwood, but now it only takes 20 minutes.

Time saved provides the Starwood team more resources to focus on advanced analysis and internal feedback, and ultimately, a world-class guest experience.

STR   STR and STR Global (www.strglobal.com) track supply and demand data for the hotel industry and provide market share analyses for international or regional hotel chains as well as independent hotels. With more than 50,000 hotels participating in their hotel performance surveys worldwide, they are the world's foremost source of historical hotel performance trends on a daily and monthly basis. STR and STR Global offer standard reports and customised data sets that help their clients understand historic and forecasted market performances and supply and demand dynamics of the hotel industry.

With such a plethora of service providers, today's managers face a serious challenge in selecting the best system to support them in making the right decisions for their hotel properties.

4.5 Housekeeping

In Section 2.4.3, the various departments within a hotel organisation were shown as being classifiable in various ways. While within the Rooms Department the Front Office is classified as a revenue (or profit) centre, the Rooms Department also has a very important support centre: Housekeeping. A hotel room cannot be sold until it is cleaned according to the quality standards of the hotel. Housekeeping plays a vital role in this cleaning process, and it is classified as a support centre due to its supporting role in the generation of the hotel's revenue. According to Nitschke and Frye (2008, p. 3), the 'Housekeeping Department not only prepares clean guestrooms on a timely basis for arriving guests, it also cleans and maintains everything in the hotel so that the property is as fresh and attractive as the day it opened for business'.

Support centre

Housekeeping

4.5.1   Departments and positions related to Housekeeping

The Executive Housekeeper is responsible for ensuring efficient operations of the Housekeeping Department, as well as for supervising the entire Housekeeping Department staff. For the housekeeping staff to be able to effectively carry out their cleaning activities that, apart from laundry, include such areas as hotel rooms, front-of-house areas, back-of-house areas, public areas, the Executive Housekeeper has the responsibility of structuring staff, and dividing the work in such a way that everyone gets a fair task and that everything that needs to be done is finished on time.

Executive Housekeeper

The Assistant Executive Housekeeper is employed in some large hotels that experience high occupancy levels, thereby necessitating some support for the Executive Housekeeper. The Assistant Executive Housekeeper also replaces the Executive Housekeeper in case of the latter's absence.

Assistant Executive Housekeeper

The House Person performs a combination of tasks (cleans, washes, sweeps, mops, waxes, dusts and polishes) in order to maintain guest rooms, working areas, and the hotel premises, in general, are presented to guests in a clean and orderly state. A Houseman is employed in mega-sized hotels. To ensure that Room Attendants can efficiently continue to clean hotel rooms, the Housemen take care of the heavy work, such as carrying clean linen to the floors and taking dirty linen to the laundry areas. Housemen also take care of heavy garbage bags and the removal of furniture from rooms in need of refurbishment. In some large hotels, the House Persons or Housemen report to the Head House Person.

House Person

Houseman

The Floor Supervisor is responsible for controlling and maintaining quality standards on guest floors. The Floor Supervisor allocates rooms to be cleaned to scheduled Room Attendants. Room Attendants perform routine duties in cleaning and servicing the hotel rooms under the supervision of the Floor Supervisor.

Floor Supervisor

Room Attendants

Although many hotels have outsourced their Laundry Departments in order to save costs, other hotels may still have an on-premise laundry. In these cases, a Laundry Manager may be employed; this individual manages the Laundry Department that is responsible for cleaning bed linen, bath towels, restaurant linen, guest laundry, uniforms and dry cleaning.

Laundry Manager

© Noordhoff Uitgevers bv

4.5.2   Room status

Occupancy report

Within the Rooms Department, communication between the Front Office and the Housekeeping Department is often about the status of the rooms. Every night the Front Desk Agent or Night Auditor compiles an occupancy report. This report lists rooms that are occupied during the night, and indicates the names of guests who are expected to check out the following day. The occupancy list is picked up by the Executive Housekeeper who schedules the occupied rooms for cleaning. Figure 4.15 shows an example of a housekeeping status report taken from *protel Air*. Note that it is always possible to customise the housekeeping status report based on the desired information.

Housekeeping status report

FIGURE 4.15 Housekeeping status report of Stenden Hotel Leeuwarden

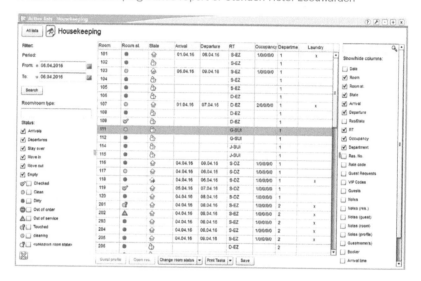

Once guests have checked-out, the Front Office notifies the Housekeeping Department that the room status has changed. The Housekeeping Department prioritises cleaning the checked-out rooms, making sure they are readily available for newly arrived guests. Nowadays, this notification process is done by the PMS automatically. At the end of any housekeeping shift, the Housekeeping Department prepares a housekeeping status report based on an actual physical check of each room. This housekeeping status report indicates the current housekeeping status of each room. If the housekeeping status report is compared to the Front Office occupancy report, any differences should be brought to the attention of the Front Office Manager. A room status discrepancy is a situation in which the Housekeeping Department's description of the room status differs from the room status information from the Front Office. In other words: a discrepancy is a deviation from the actual room situation when compared to the situation in the PMS. Some examples of discrepancies can be summarised as follows:

Physical check

Room status discrepancy

Sleep-out
- A Sleep-out – a guest is registered to a hotel room, yet the bed has not been used;

Skipper
- A Skipper – the guest has left the hotel without making arrangements to settle the account (also called a walk-out);

- A Sleeper – the guest has settled the account and left the hotel, but the Front Office staff has failed to correctly update the room's status.

Sleeper

Since more and more PMSs are web-based (which means that all information is accessible from every computer with an internet connection), as well as for sustainability reasons ('please be green and read from the screen'), historical occupancy, housekeeping and discrepancy reports are no longer (always) printed; required information is simply retrieved from the PMS by the different departments.

4.5.3 Planning and organising the Housekeeping Department

Nitschke and Frye (2008, pp. 67-68) indicate that for most hotel properties the areas cleaned by the housekeeping departments are:

Areas cleaned

- Guestrooms;
- Corridors;
- Public areas, such as the lobby and public restrooms;
- Pool and patio area;
- Management offices;
- Storage areas;
- Linen and sewing rooms;
- Laundry rooms;
- Back-of-house areas, such as employee locker rooms.

Housekeeping Departments of hotels offering full service are generally responsible for additional areas, such as:

Additional areas

- Meeting rooms;
- Dining rooms;
- Banquet rooms;
- Convention exhibit halls;
- Hotel-operated shops;
- Game rooms;
- Exercise rooms.

The responsibility of the Housekeeping Department related to the cleaning of Food and Beverage areas varies from property to property. In most hotels, the Housekeeping Department has limited cleaning responsibilities with regards to the food preparation, production, and storage areas. In these areas, special cleaning and sanitation tasks are usually carried out by kitchen staff themselves.

Limited cleaning responsibilities

As such, it is the responsibility of the General Manager (possibly delegating to the Executive Housekeeper) to identify which areas belong to the responsibility of the Housekeeping Department. In planning department work, the Executive Housekeeper starts by creating an area inventory list, which indicates the items in each area that need to be cleaned or maintained. It is recommended to set up the area inventory list according to the sequence of

Area inventory list

Sequence of rooms

Frequency schedules

rooms that the attendant follows. Once the area inventory list has been drafted, the Executive Housekeeper defines frequency schedules, which indicate how often/frequent the items in the area will have to be cleaned or maintained. Those items that must be cleaned on a daily or weekly basis become part of routine cleaning and should therefore be incorporated into standard work procedures. Other tasks related to cleaning or housekeeping, such as cleaning chandeliers and windows or rotating mattresses, can become part of a deep cleaning programme, or periodical cleaning programme.

Performance standards

Productivity standards

Once the frequency schedules have been established, performance standards need to be set. Performance standards indicate *what* must be cleaned in a particular area and *how* the job must be done. In other words, performance standards establish the expected (minimum) quality of the work to be done. Once these standards have been formulated, the productivity standards need to be determined. Productivity standards indicate the acceptable (minimum) quantity of work to be done, and determine how long it should take to perform an assigned task according to the defined performance standards. Figure 4.16, based on Nitschke and Frye (2008, p. 77), illustrates productivity standards calculations.

Sufficient quantities

The final step in the planning phase in the Housekeeping Department is to ensure that housekeeping staff have equipment and supplies in sufficient quantities (inventory levels) required for them to meet the performance and productivity standards of the department.

FIGURE 4.16 Sample productivity standards calculation

Step 1

Determine how long it should take to clean one hotel room according to the department's performance standards.

Assumption: 27 minutes*

Step 2

Determine the total shift time in minutes.

8 hours shift × 60 minutes = 480 minutes

Step 3

Determine the time available for hotel room cleaning.

Total shift time	480 minutes
Less:	
Beginning-of-Shift Duties	20 minutes
Break	30 minutes
End-of-Shift Duties	20 minutes
Time available for hotel room cleaning	410 minutes

FIGURE 4.16 Sample productivity standards calculation (*continued*)

Step 4
Determine the productivity standard by dividing the result of Step 3 by that of Step 1.

The result indicates that one room attendant can clean 15.2 hotel rooms in an 8-hour shift

*Performance standards vary per hotel property for many reasons: labour costs; the qualification of the room attendants; the size of the rooms, suites, or apartments; the number of amenities in the room; the fixtures and furniture; the luxury level of a hotel; and quality standards. This sample productivity standard of 27 minutes is illustrative only and should not be considered as a suggested time for hotel room cleaning.

Assume that a 456-bedroom hotel has an occupancy of 80%. How many room attendants need to be scheduled to be able to clean the hotel rooms?

0.80 × 456 hotel rooms = 365 hotel rooms need to be cleaned

365 hotel rooms divided by 15.2 results in the need to schedule 24 room attendants to be able to clean the hotel rooms with the given productivity.

4.5.4   Cleaning rooms and public areas
Nitschke and Frye (2008, p. 369) confirm that the:

> 'Condition of the guestroom conveys a critical message to guests. It shows the care that the hotel property puts into creating and maintaining a clean, safe, and pleasant environment for its guests. This places a big responsibility on the Housekeeping Department. After all, the guestroom is the main product that a property sells.'

Critical message to guests

For the Housekeeping Department staff to be able to conveniently carry out their duties, they usually start work very early in the morning. In most properties, a Room Attendant's workday begins in the linen room with a briefing. Following this briefing, the Room Attendants collect their fully equipped service carts. The rooms that have already been vacated are serviced first, thereby making sure these rooms are available for newly arrived guests. These rooms are followed by those occupied by guests who have expressed a request for early service, rooms with expected check-outs (due outs), stay-over rooms, and lastly those with requests for late(r) servicing (Casado, 2012).

Briefing

Service carts

Hotel room cleaning starts by the attendant approaching the hotel room door; if no 'DO NOT DISTURB' sign can be identified, the room attendant knocks on the door, announcing 'housekeeping' at least twice prior to entering the room. The service cart is placed in front of the door. This is for the safety of the room attendant while at the same time alerting the hotel guests to the presence of someone in the room should they come back to their room from elsewhere.

Safety

Nowadays, all hotel properties have standard operating procedures (SOPs) designed to provide instructions on how all housekeeping activities should be carried out within the hotel. Overall, housekeeping activities are scheduled and performed in sequence, though the order, details and frequency of

Standard operating procedures

the cleaning activities can deviate for different hotel properties. Guest room cleaning activities can be performed following this example of an established sequence: opening windows so the room can air out while being cleaned; checking amenities; checking the condition of the room and equipment; emptying the trash; stripping the bed; making the bed; dusting and wiping the bedroom; cleaning the bathroom; replacing guest supplies; vacuum cleaning; and finishing with a final check. See Appendix A for a sample SOP for dusting hotel rooms.

Sequence

Once the rooms have been cleaned by the Room Attendants, the hotel rooms are then checked by a Floor Supervisor or other qualified (members of) staff before they are indicated as clean in the PMS. All hotels have a checklist or hotel room inspection form for checking and registering any deviations from required quality standards. Appendix B shows a sample hotel room inspection checklist in which the various components receive marks based on a correctly serviced room earning 100 points; thus a final comparative percentage score can be attributed to the rooms.

Checklist

Casado (2012, p. 147) indicates that 'if the hotel property provides turndown service, the evening team will perform tasks like unfolding bedsheets, drawing drapes, restocking used towels, tidying the hotel room, emptying waste baskets, and fluffing the pillow'. Some properties leave fresh flowers, chocolates, or messages on the pillow. The evening team of Housekeepers will also carry out any further guest requests such as delivering extra pillows and towels, providing baby cots and roll away beds.

Public areas

Establishing and maintaining cleaning procedures for public areas is just as important as it is for hotel rooms. Cleaning procedures for these areas may vary among different hotel properties because of differences in architectural configurations, lobby space allocations or guest traffic. Public areas include public restrooms, entrances, lobbies, the front desk, corridors, elevators, swimming pools, exercise rooms and spas. Apart from these front-of-house public areas, the back-of-house areas or employee areas (employee locker rooms, rest rooms, hallways and employee cafeteria) are also important, and should be cleaned and maintained because, as indicated in this chapter earlier, the condition of these areas also reflects the company's concern for its employees.

4.5.5   Linen par stock levels

To be able to run a Housekeeping Department efficiently, sufficient inventory levels of linen need to be available. The sufficient level of linen inventory is called the linen par and it is defined as the amount of linen needed to outfit the hotel property at 100% occupancy. It is the standard number of linen items that must be on hand to support daily housekeeping operations. Clearly, only one linen par is not sufficient to run efficient laundry operations, thus the Executive Housekeeper must determine how many par levels are required to efficiently run the department. When establishing linen par levels, Nitschke and Frye (2008, p. 169) indicate the following major elements need to be taken into consideration:

Sufficient inventory

Linen par

Major elements

- The laundry cycle;
- The replacement of worn, damaged, lost or stolen linen;
- Emergency situations.

Another important issue to consider when determining linen par levels is the number of times sheets are changed in a hotel room. In luxury and upper-class hotel properties, this may be daily. However, due to sustainability practices, some hotels may follow environmentally-friendly measures to limit the use of water and energy (for more information on the use of water and energy in hotels, see Chapter 9). Such hotels place cards in the rooms asking stay-over guests to notify the Housekeeping Department if they want their sheets to be changed daily, for example. Figure 4.17, based on Nitschke and Frye's example (2008, p. 170), demonstrates how to calculate linen par stock levels.

Sustainability practices

FIGURE 4.17 Calculating linen par stock levels

Establishing a par stock level for king-size beds for a hotel that uses an external laundry operation, and supplies three sheets for each of the property's 300 king-size beds.

300 king-size beds × 3 sheets per bed = 900 sheets per par number

One par in the guest room	1 × 900	=	900
One par in floor linen closets	1 × 900	=	900
One par soiled in the laundry	1 × 900	=	900
One par replacement stock	1 × 900	=	900
One par for emergencies	1 × 900	=	900
One par for linen in transit	1 × 900	=	900
	Total number of sheets		5400

Thus 5400 sheets ÷ 900 sheets per par = 6 par

Note that if such a hotel uses an on-premises laundry operation, 5 par will be sufficient.

In the domain of linen management for the hospitality industry, Blycolin, a leading service provider for the industry, has as its core activity the rental of professional linen and textiles for beds, baths, tables and kitchens. Text 4.7 is an indication of par stock calculation by Blycolin, and Text 4.8 is a short review of how the linen services provided by Blycolin fit the operations of the Carlton Hotel Collection.

TEXT 4.7

Par stock levels and factors used by Blycolin

The following calculations are applied by Blycolin

For hotel occupancies of 70% or more, par stock level: 5
For hotel occupancies below 70%, par stock level: 4
For extremely high hotel occupancy levels (e.g. 95%) or when there is a high percentage of short stays, par stock: 6

Blycolin uses their own laundry facilities as well as external laundry partners. These par stock calculations therefore include external laundry services for hotel properties.

Factors influencing par stock calculations are:
- Occupancy of the hotel
- Frequency of delivery of clean linen and pick up of dirty linen by the laundry service
- Average length of stay
- Application of turn down service

TEXT 4.8

Review – Blycolin fits the operations of the Carlton Hotel Collection

'Blycolin's logistical process fits us like a tailor-made suit' according to Hans van der Heijden, Manager of Operations of the Carlton Hotel Collection.

The Carlton Hotel Collection is a special group of ten hotels. Seven are located in the Netherlands, two in Great Britain and one in Belgium. Although they operate under one flag, all of these four star hotels have their own identity for both the professional and recreational guest. 'We always present our hotels in relation to its surroundings, the location and the décor,' Hans van der Heijden explains. His job means that he is, among other things, responsible for the hotel group's linen management in the Netherlands and Belgium. For a large part, he has outsourced that into the trusted hands of Blycolin. 'And I can recommend doing so to anyone.'

'Like a tailor'
Especially because the Carlton Hotel Collection hotels each have and guard their own specific characteristics, there are great demands on linen management. For instance, a very efficient logistic process. 'That's right,' the Manager of Operations confirms. 'From our linen partner, we expect that they completely attune the logistical process to the individual requirements of our hotels. That process should fit like a tailor-made suit for every location. Blycolin does this like a true tailor. The frequency of collecting and delivering linen, the right amounts, the means of transport, the arrangement of the

linen transport in containers and the time schedule which fits the 'clock' of any individual hotel. Moreover, Blycolin is also very flexible in these things.'

'Solid and reliable'
The Carlton Hotel Collection chose Blycolin in order not to worry about linen management. 'To entertain our guests with quality, we need to have complete faith that linen is available carefree. To put it in other words, the linen has to be there in the quality we want, it has to be clean, without defects, folded and sorted correctly in the right amounts. Also when you need more linen for an unexpected higher occupation. When you don't have to look after these things and you work with a partner that does these things for you, that's one less thing to worry about. What we also consider as carefree is the fact that we do not have to invest a small fortune in our linen. Blycolin takes care of the investments, so we can use our resources for other things. Sustainability is also an issue. Blycolin is very active in Corporate Social Responsibility and translates that into a number of products and services. To us, it is an advantage that we 'hitch along for the ride' and can let that be a part of our own sustainability policy.'

'For all these reasons, Blycolin is truly an added value to us. The company offers carefree continuity at a very attractive price. We hold this co-operation in high esteem. Solid and reliable.'

4.5.6   Outsourcing

Outsourcing has become common practice in the hotel industry. Hotels can now choose to outsource several tasks, positions, or even entire departments. Outsourcing is basically the process of establishing and managing a contractual relationship with an external supplier or service provider for the provision of capacity that had previously been provided in-house. Some definitions of outsourcing emphasise strategy, such as that of Lam and Han (2005, pp. 42-43) who define outsourcing as 'a management strategy in

Common practice

Outsourcing

which a hotel utilizes and forms strategic alliances with specialized out-sourcing supplier to operate certain hotel functions, in an attempt to reduce costs and risks and to improve efficiency'. When outsourcing is applied to the Housekeeping Department, this may be strictly for tasks (such as like window washing); for broader services (such as planning and payment of room attendants); or even for all activities of the department (including laun-dry, supervision and management). Hotels can selectively choose what to outsource – room attendants only, for example – while keeping the manage-ment functions of the department on their own payroll in order to have more control over the cleaning quality.

Major reasons

Whatever the various reasons for outsourcing, Agyemang-Duah, Aikins, Asi-bey and Broni (2014) found that there are two major reasons for outsourc-ing the Housekeeping Department: to maintain a competitive advantage, and to focus on core activities. They also identified some of the benefits, challenges and difficulties related to outsourcing hotel non-core functions as illustrated in Figure 4.18 (Agyemang-Duah et al., 2014, pp. 41-42), but it should be noted that since not all hotels are the same, individual hotel management – should they be interested in outsourcing some of their non-core functions – must be able to determine what is most efficient for their property after a serious cost-benefit analysis.

Cost-benefit analysis

FIGURE 4.18 Benefits, challenges and difficulties of outsourcing non-core functions

Outsourcing of non-core functions in hotels	
Major benefits	**Major challanges and difficulties**
Efficient service delivery	Risk of losing sensitive data and the loss of confidentiality
Highly specialised workforce	Losing management control of business functions
Services delivery at a reduced cost	Possible delays and inaccuracies in the work output
	Hidden costs and legal problems may arise
Promptness of delivery	Post-contract processes and decision rights not understood
Operational flexibility	Poor mutual understanding of the contract
	Client retained team lacks required skills
	Loss of key talent
	Culture clash between the client and the service provider

Outsourcing can have both advantages and disadvantages. Hotels need to consider what is most beneficial in their specific situation. In some situa-tions, outsourcing is more expensive than operating in-house. However, ho-tels may still choose outsourcing for quality reasons, or with regard to avail-able time for other businesses. Other hotels, though outsourcing may be a cheaper option, may still choose to retain their own in-house Housekeeping Department due to possible relations their staff may have with regular guests and as such the influence they may have on guest satisfaction. Text 4.9 is an article that reflects the advantages and disadvantages related to outsourcing in the hospitality industry.

TEXT 4.9

Pros and cons of hospitality outsourcing

Pros and cons of hospitality outsourcing, by Elaine Yetzer Simon, HNN contributor, April 26 2010

When done the right way, outsourcing can provide a hotel or company with a host of benefits.

REPORT FROM THE U.S.—The decision whether to outsource is a question nearly all hotels will have to address at some point.

The practice of outsourcing has been increasing every year in the hospitality industry, according to Mark Hoare, a partner with The Prism Partnership, a Boston-based travel and leisure consulting company.

'The argument for outsourcing is, in the majority of cases, driven by a desire to reduce cost while at the same time maintaining or even elevating quality of service,' he said.

'This is especially true where the function being outsourced is very labor intensive.

'Payroll is the largest cost centre for almost all functions within the hospitality industry, so any opportunity to outsource functions that can be performed off-property to lower-salary areas of the country, or world, is attractive.'

Thomas Morone, a principal in Los Angeles with Warnick + Company, a strategic advisory firm, said outsourcing is a fairly widespread practice.

'Anything that saves labor is outsourcing,' he said. 'At the end of the day, we do outsource a lot of stuff in the hotel business.'

A number of hotel executives declined to be interviewed for this story.

When should hotels not outsource? When a function involves direct guest contact at the property, such as bell staff, housekeeping and front desk employees, according to Morone.

'The rule is if you can touch it, it has to be real, such as never put a fake plant within reach of the guest,' he said. 'You need to have consistency in the guest experience.'

Advantages of outsourcing

Hoare said the drivers for outsourcing are many, and he believes in today's market every hotel would benefit from some form of outsourcing.

Probably the biggest push behind outsourcing is cost, according to Morone.

'You outsource because you can get the best talent in a highly specialized area and not have to carry them on your payroll,' he said. 'If you're installing a new computer system, you might have one IT person and outsource beyond that. The big benefit is it's a contracted price and a predictable cost.'

Outsourcing can help hotels see the forest for the trees, said Leora Lanz, director of New York-based HVS Sales & Marketing Services.

'(Hotels) like someone from the outside driving the momentum, to help them think outside the box and think of other methods,' she said. 'It can be very refreshing for the hotel to have someone push them to act proactively instead of reactively all the time.'

Hoare said another benefit is maintaining competitive advantage when competing with larger competitors who have the budget, in-house skills and technology to go it alone.

Morone also cited these benefits:
- The contract typically is terminable at will or after 30 days' notice. 'You have the chance to test drive things,' he said. 'If you don't like it, you get rid of it and bring in someone else;'
- you don't have to own and maintain highly specialized equipment that's not used every day; and
- there's no training or retraining involved.

'It's a plug-and-play model,' he said. 'It's almost like going to the Yellow Pages. You hire somebody, you wind them up and let them go.'

Disadvantages of outsourcing

The hotel's loss of control when outsourcing is one disadvantage, Morone said.

'GMs really like to control what's going on in their shop,' he said. 'When you outsource, you lose some control. You have absolutely no control over those employees. They are not your employees.'

Another disadvantage, particularly for luxury customers, is the perception that people who aren't on the payroll are a guest security issue, according to Morone.

Then there's the question of service. A number of hospitality companies that outsourced their guest contact centres, central reservation offices and other functions have brought the jobs back in-house because of declining service levels, Hoare said.

'For those that outsourced to an offshore provider to realize even further cost reductions, they have in many cases found that the degradation in quality of service – language, accent, cultural, etc. – has been a proven cause of loss of business, and therefore the original outsourcing return on investment has been completely overturned,' he said.

Another issue to be aware of is the ramp-up period when knowledge transfer takes place, Hoare said.

'During this interim period, the fully expected ROI may not be realized,' he said.

'This isn't a reason not to outsource, but is something that must be factored to your short-term outsourcing expectations.'

Functions *most likely* to be outsourced
Laundry
Pool maintenance
Grounds keeping / landscape management
Equipment maintenance
Restaurant / foodservice
Painting
Some maintenance contracts, especially air conditioning and boilers
Public relations and marketing
Elevator maintenance
Floral arrangements
Revenue management
Information technology
Reservations
Project management
Capital projects
Furniture, fixture and equipment purchasing
Operating supplies purchasing
Help-desk support
Loyalty program management
Distribution management
Accounts
Finance Service

Functions *least likely* to be outsourced
Bell staff
Housekeeping
Front desk
Switchboard operations
Concierge
Front office

4

Summary

▶ A guest's journey begins at the moment of booking and ends once the guest has left a hotel; the rooms department plays a vital role at several moments during this journey.

▶ Rooms departments within different hotels are organised differently depending on size and levels of the outsourcing of their activities. Each rooms department will, however, have at least the front office and housekeeping components.

▶ The reservation department responds to reservations requests and creates reservations records; chain operations usually centralise their reservations activities and even create clusters or reservation networks.

▶ The use of GDSs and IDSs by hotels has become more and more popular.

▶ The reservation process can be viewed from two perspective – that of the guest and that of the hotel.

▶ The main purpose of revenue management is to help hotels maximise revenue and profit; it evolved from yield management.

▶ Effective yield management has several prerequisites: a relatively fixed amount of perishable inventory, differences in market segments or types of guests, the possibility of pre-selling the products, and a changeable demand.

▶ The most frequently applied room rates include the rack rate, the BAR, the corporate rate, the group rate, government and military rate, tour operator rates, the day rate, and the complimentary rate.

▶ Hotels use different key performance indicators to measure how successful they are in managing ability to maximise revenue; these include occupancy, average daily rate, yield percentage, revenue per available room, and gross operating profit per available room.

▶ The front office is the core of hotel operations; with its intense traffic, it is the most important access point for guest complaints, information and requests.

▶ Hotels all organise their rooms departments differently, with such factors as size, type and location having an influence on the organisation. This organisation is clearly shown in the department's organisational chart.

- The main procedures at the front office are performing check-in and check-out procedures, dealing with guest complaints, and providing service when anticipating the demand and wishes of the guests.

- Hotel review sites are of great importance nowadays; using these sites, guests who previously visited hotel properties rate the hotels concerned. Their opinions are highly appreciated by potential guests and are used in guest decision making processes with both positive effects and negative outcomes.

- The executive housekeeper is responsible for the very important support centre of housekeeping. Housekeeping plays a vital role in ensuring that hotel rooms are clean and that quality standards of the hotel are maintained.

- Room status is constantly monitored via occupancy and housekeeping status reports to establish if discrepancies exist. Examples of discrepancies are sleep-outs, skippers and sleepers.

- While most housekeeping departments are responsible for cleaning many areas of the hotel, their responsibilities related to cleaning food and beverage areas vary from property to property. In most cases, housekeeping departments have limited cleaning responsibilities in relation to food preparation, production, and storage areas, where special cleaning and sanitation tasks are usually carried out by kitchen staff themselves.

- Planning housekeeping activities begins with drafting an area inventory list. This is followed by defining the frequency schedules, developing performance and productivity standards. It ends with ensuring enough equipment and supplies are available (inventory levels) for housekeeping staff to carry out their activities.

- Housekeeping activities generally follow well-established standard operating procedures, and for housekeepers to be able to conveniently carry out their duties, they usually start very early in the morning with briefings and collecting their fully equipped service carts. The room cleaning sequence beings with rooms that have already been checked out, followed by rooms whose guests have expressed some request for early service, expected check-outs (due outs), stay-over rooms, and lastly those whose guests requested late(r) servicing.

- Once the rooms have been cleaned, they are checked using a checklist or hotel room inspection form by a qualified staff member before they are indicated as clean in the PMS.

- A sufficient level of linen inventory is called the linen par; it is the standard number of linen items that must be on hand to support daily housekeeping operations. Major elements that need to be taken into consideration in determining linen par are the laundry cycle, the replacement of worn, damaged, lost or stolen linen, emergency situations, and the number of times sheets are changed.

4

▶ Factors that influence the linen par stock calculations are the occupancy of the hotel, the frequency of delivery of clean linen and pick up of dirty linen by the laundry service, the average length of stay, and the application of turn down service.

▶ Outsourcing is the process of establishing and managing a contractual relationship with an external supplier or service provider for the provision of capacity previously managed in-house. When applied to the housekeeping department, this may either be strictly for tasks, for some broader services, or even for all activities of the department.

▶ Whatever the reasons for outsourcing, there are two major reasons for outsourcing the housekeeping department; and though it has its benefits, it also comes with challenges and difficulties.

4

Questions and assignments for reflection

1   What is the difference between an affiliate central reservation system and a non-affiliate reservation system?

2   Describe a hotel guest's journey from the moment of booking till the moment of departure.

3   What are the steps in a hotel's reservation process when selling products and services?

4   Hotel Enjoy has 802 rooms. Each room attendant works approximately 7 hours and 30 minutes a day. During the day, a coffee break of 15 minutes and a half-hour lunch break are obligatory and unpaid. The beginning-of-shift duties take about 20 minutes while the end-of-shift duties take about 10 minutes. According to the productivity standards of Hotel Enjoy, it takes 24 minutes to clean one hotel room.
Calculate the productivity standard for a room attendant and indicate how many room attendants should be scheduled when the hotel is at 75% occupancy.

5   What are the considerations a hotel manager needs to take into account when making possible outsourcing decisions?

© Noordhoff Uitgevers bv

5

The Food and Beverage Department

S. de Bruyn and M. N. Chibili

5.1 Introduction

Aside from the lodging possibilities offered by hospitality organisations, the provision of food and beverage products is also of paramount importance. The Food and Beverage Department is in charge of this service, meaning it has a key role to play within the hospitality industry. More and more people enjoy a meal or drink outside of their homes nowadays. Where traditionally the 'lady of the house' would take care of the cooking, and 'going out' used to be reserved for special occasions only, it is now considered entirely normal and part of everyday life to enjoy food and beverage products at one of many available establishments. This chapter provides a short discussion of the hospitality concept, fundamentally important to all food and beverage service operations, followed by an insight into different food service companies and various food and beverage provision and support departments, as well as an outline of their scope and processes.

5.1.1 A guest's perspective (demand)

The main reason guests visit a food service company is to eat or drink, both components of their primary needs. Also called innate, basic, or physiological needs, these needs are important for survival. Everybody needs to eat or drink, for example. But there are other needs that make a guest want to go out and have a meal, snack or drink. These can be the need for contacting other people (including service staff), or the need to have a good time with family or friends. Such needs are called secondary needs, and they are also referred to as either social, acquired or psychological needs. Furthermore, needs and wishes differ depending on the person as well as other factors, such as age, profession, education, relation to the company, income, or nationality (culture). Subsequently, the purposes, in conjunction with the occasion and the time of day, play a very important role in the needs and wishes of guests. If a guest visits a restaurant for a business lunch in order to discuss and finalise a very important deal, for example, the guest's wishes and demands will surely differ from those in situations where the same guest

Eat or drink
Primary needs

Secondary needs

Inner Mongolia, Helan Mountains, Yurt Lodge

visits the same restaurant with family or alone. In the case of the business lunch, a guest's main objective is to please the business partner with a meal, and very hopefully get a deal finalised. In such a scenario, the service staff should be present, but also silent and discrete. In the case of a guest's visit with family, it would be wiser for service staff to also focus their hospitality offering on the children. In those cases where the guest is alone, the guest may now be expecting a more social and sociable interaction with the service staff.

5.1.2   A company's perspective (supply)

As indicated in the previous paragraph, the offerings of hospitality organisations go beyond lodging possibilities, and include food and beverage elements, both tangible products. Additionally, these very tangible products are offered within a certain surrounding: the building itself; the restaurant; the bar; the meeting rooms. It should also be remembered that it is not only the décor, inventory, lighting, and music that make the surrounding, but other guests are also part of – and do influence – these surroundings (ambiance). There is also the matter of hospitality – an intangible, behavioural aspect provided by the persons that serve the tangible products on offer. These 3 elements (products, surrounding, and hospitality) form the foundation of the hospitality formula of a food service company. A mixture of these elements should be adapted by any food service company and should be recognisable to guests or potential guests.

Tangible products

Surrounding

Hospitality

5.1.3   The hospitality model

Hospitality model

To get a better insight into matching demand and supply perspectives, the Hospitality Institute developed the hospitality model as shown in Figure 5.1.

FIGURE 5.1 The hospitality model (Source: www.hospitalityinstitute.nl)

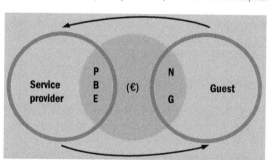

The model shows the interaction between the needs and goals of the guests (N and G) and the product, behaviour and environment of the service provider (P, B, and E), leading to a certain guest experience as well as returns for the service provider. When the needs of the guest have been met (or even exceeded), a guest is likely to return. If the expectations have not been met, this guest will probably not pay another visit and may in fact share this negative experience with other people, with possible negative effects for the service provider.

In order for a company to be successful in the hospitality industry, it is crucial for it to be able to assess the different needs and wishes of its guests and adapt its service offering to these needs. For a more detailed discussion on services and hospitality, see Chapter 11 – Managing Hospitality Services. As this chapter concerns the Food and Beverage Department, however, it is worthwhile to note that, according to Dictionary.com, service is defined as 'the performance of duties or the duties performed as or by a waiter or servant'. In addition, the Oxford Advanced Learners Dictionary (online - www.oxfordlearnersdictionaries.com) defines hospitality in two ways. Firstly as 'friendly and generous behaviour towards guests', and secondly as 'food, drink or services that are provided by an organisation for guests, customers, etc.'. | Service

There are similarities between service and hospitality, yet there is one major difference. Providing service is by nature a type of transaction (economic activity); the provider obtains something in return for services rendered, which is money. Guests receive products and service, and in return pay the bill. Hospitality is the superlative of service, more in the manner of 'a way of life', which is not only shown at work but also in relation to other people in one's private life. For more on this distinction, see Section 14.6 on hospitableness.

Hospitality is about seriously considering one's guests, having a genuine interest in them, and doing the utmost to fulfil and, if possible, exceed their wishes. Hospitality is about making a choice to be helpful, friendly and having a positive impact on the people one encounters. It is about taking responsibility, making a choice to serve others instead of oneself, getting satisfaction out of solving problems. Receiving payment can certainly be a desired result when providing hospitality, but hospitality goes beyond merely making money: hospitality is about going the extra mile, and it is something that is or has to become part of the DNA of any hospitality industry employee. Gunnarsson and Blohm (2003) suggest a modified level of hospitality called hostmanship, which is based on the following fundamentals: interaction; the big picture; dialogue; responsibility; consideration; and knowledge. Text 5.1 is an extract from Gunnarsson and Blohm (2003, p. 25), in which hostmanship is summarily explained. | Hostmanship

TEXT 5.1

Hostmanship is an attitude

I usually think of hostmanship as an attitude. A way to live.

Never forgetting that people who have contacted you are an extension of yourself.

Hostmanship is about giving. It's about sharing a part of yourself and your knowledge.

Hostmanship is an art. The host is an artist.

This artist, for which there is a growing demand these days, is an important aspect of sustainable business relationships that allow hospitality organisations and individuals to make the deciding difference beneficial to both guests and organisations.

Considered as a lifestyle attitude, De Zwaan has conceived 6 pillars to explain hostmanship as indicated in Text 5.2.

TEXT 5.2

Six pillars of hostmanship

A basic serving attitude (I really like to serve people)

A care reflex (when a glass falls over, you already get a towel)

Make contact – start with eye-contact, and make sure you are really listening

Consideration (have empathy for the other, place yourself in the other person's shoes – without judging)

Knowledge of what you pour or serve (this gives power, certainty, and credibility)

Not only putting the above into practice during working hours, but also when you see a mature citizen with a rollator walker hesitating to cross over at a crosswalk.

Brenda de Zwaan regularly writes on hospitality related issues, and can be found at bdezwaan.blogspot.nl

Symbol of hospitality

This subsection ends with a short story related to one symbol of hospitality as shown in Text 5.3, the pineapple, and its commonplace nature in many food and beverage outlets.

TEXT 5.3

Pineapples: a symbol of hospitality

Pineapples are traditionally a welcome gift in the tropics. Centuries ago however, modes of transportation were relatively slow and fresh pineapples (being perishable) were a rare luxury and coveted delicacy.

The fresh pineapple was highly sought after, becoming a true symbol of prestige and social class. In fact, the pineapple, because of its rarity and expense, was such a status item that all a party hostess had to do was to display the fruit as part of a decorative centerpiece, and she would be awarded much social awe and recognition. Colonial confectioners sometimes rented pineapples to households by the day. Later, the same fruit was sold to other, more affluent clients who actually ate it.

King Charles receiving a pineapple.

During the 20th century, the pineapple primarily symbolized hospitality. American Sea Captains placed the fruit outside their homes to signal to friends that they had returned after a voyage. It was this act that began the trend of stone pineapples being placed at the entrance of fine properties.

Pineapples appeared frequently in the decorative arts on gates, bedposts, crockery, napkins, tablecloths and door knockers. This pineapple fountain can be found in Charleston, South Carolina, USA.

Did you know: The pineapple was used by political cartoonists during the Napoleonic Wars to symbolize extravagance.

(Source: www.kingoffruit.com.au)   Pineapple fountain in Charleston

▬5.2▬ Types of Food and Beverage Service Operations

Classification

There is a large variety of service companies providing an extended selection of food and beverage products designed to satisfy all needs and wishes. These can range from a small ethnic restaurant in a city centre to a fish-and-chips stall around the corner, or from a school canteen to a fine-dining Michelin-starred restaurant. Since the structure of the hospitality industry was classified and rated principally with a bias towards hotels in Chapter 2, the current subsection provides a brief discussion related to the specific classification of food and beverage service operations, which can be either small or large. A small enterprise can be a person selling spring rolls at a street market, for example, while a large business can be a buffet restaurant at a holiday park selling more than 1,000 meals every day.

FIGURE 5.2 Categories and examples of food service operations

Categories			Some examples (based on the Dutch market)
Commercial	Quick Service	Fast food restaurants (drive-throughs)	McDonald's, KFC, Burger King
		Lunchrooms/coffee shops	Subway, Bagels & Beans, Delifrance, Bakker Bart, Starbucks
		Take-away places (often offering delivery services)	Chinese, Indian, Indonesian restaurants, Domino's Pizza, fish & chips kiosks, sushi bars etc.
		Cafeterias and motorway restaurants	La Place, Haje
		Buffet restaurants	Chinese, Indian, Indonesian restaurants, holiday parks etc.
		Street vendors	Food trucks etc.
		Ice cream parlours	Min 12, Toscana, Australian Homemade
	Full Service	Casual	Many Dutch restaurants
		Bistro	Humphreys, De Beren
		Brasserie	Flo
		Single item	Pancakes, chicken, steak or sushi etc.
		Ethnic	Greek, Italian, Chinese etc.
		Family	Van der Valk
		Theme	Hard Rock Café, Rainforest Café, Theatre restaurants
		Beverage-offering food service	Pubs, coffee bars, wine bars, cocktail bars
		Fine-dining	De Zwethheul & De Librije
	Catering	Fixed location	Hotels, banquet companies, clubs
		Outdoor catering	Customer-desired locations
Non-commercial	Institutional food service	In-house	Schools, universities, companies, factories, military installations, and prisons, etc.
		Contracts	Sodexo, Aramark, Compass Group
Hotels and other lodging companies			Hotels, B&B, holiday parks, etc.
Food service within consumer-based companies		Leisure attractions	Sports clubs, cinemas, theaters, museums, zoos, fun parks, music festivals, etc.
		Retail stores	Shopping malls, retail stores, gas stations, traiteurs.
Travel food service		During travel	Food and beverage services on board planes or cruise ships
		At the stations	Restaurants and bars at airports, bus, and train stations

There are two basic types of food service: commercial food service and non-commercial food service. Commercial food service is offered by companies aiming to make a profit, and non-commercial food service is provided by organisations that exist for some other reason, but do offer food and beverage to their employees or other people as a service. To provide a better insight into this complex world of food and beverage service companies, they can be categorised using the basic criteria in Figure 5.2. One should keep in mind that there are many food service businesses that will not fit any single category exactly, instead requiring more than one at a time.

Commercial food service

Non-commercial food service

It is important to understand that there are both independent restaurants and chain restaurants. A chain restaurant, also called multiple-unit business, has more than one location operating under the same name and ownership. There is also a type of chain restaurants operated as franchises, which is a concept that allows an entrepreneur to start or continue a restaurant without taking too many risks. This allows the franchising company to expand rapidly without having to finance the operation itself. The franchise chain owner (or franchisor) lends certain rights to the entrepreneur (or franchisee) running the location. These rights can refer to the use of the concept, trademark, logo, operating systems, distribution channels, reservation systems, marketing expertise, purchasing discounts, etc. In return for these rights, the franchisee pays a fee and signs a franchise contract stipulating they will operate in accordance with the guidelines set by the franchisor.

Chain restaurant

Franchises

5.2.1   Quick service restaurants

As their name implies, these restaurants provide guests with speed, convenience, and low to medium service at relatively low prices. This service is most often 'self-service' – implying that guests have to collect their food or drinks themselves before proceeding to their tables. There are usually only few employees in relation to the number of guests. Quick service restaurants include fast food restaurants, lunchrooms, take-aways (including delivery service), cafeterias, buffet restaurants, 'street food' stalls, and ice-cream parlours.

Quick service restaurants

Fast food restaurants

A fast food restaurant usually has a counter at which orders can be placed. The menu consists of a limited number of products, which can be prepared very quickly. The production process is mainly capital intensive, necessary for a speedy production. Kitchen routes and *mise en place* are designed to

Fast food restaurant

Capital intensive

make processes run smoothly and efficiently. Production times of incoming orders take no longer than 5 minutes. Once prepared, orders can be picked up and paid for at the same counter, and either enjoyed at one of the tables in the dining room or taken for consumption elsewhere. These restaurants, especially those that belong to a chain, also offer drive-through windows catering for guests in a hurry or not wishing to consume their food and beverage items in the restaurant. Within this domain, the best known example is McDonald's, being one of the largest restaurant chains at over 34,000 restaurants in 119 countries. It is remarkable that a Big Mac in Amsterdam tastes exactly the same as does one in Hong Kong. It should however be noted that such companies also adapt their products or services that are available all over the world to make them suitable for local needs in what is termed *glocalisation*. Such consistency raises questions. How do they do it? How do they get such a consistent product and quality with so many outlets? The answers are related to the systems and standards implemented to ensure the quality of service, and to employees, who are offered intense training programmes for different positions. Lastly, the ability to adapt to market conditions also enables them to adequately react to the demands of the guests.

Consistency

Lunchrooms

Lunchrooms

Lunchrooms are mainly located in shopping areas, and operate following the opening times of surrounding shops. Lunchrooms can also be found in other places where there is heavy pedestrian traffic, such as at airports or train stations. These facilities offer different kinds of breads, like sandwiches, buns, French bread, bagels, and croissants, with a variety of fillings. Both hot and cold bread products are offered. Soups, salads, hot dishes, pastries, cold and warm drinks are also served. Average spending is low to medium, and the service varies from take-away to table service. Catering and takeaway within this domain are expanding, making it possible for businesses to generate revenue during off-peak hours with the help of the Internet, which enables consumers to order their products online.

Nowadays, there is a wide range of lunchroom type businesses available: small outlets in bakeries with a few tables; traditional privately-owned lunchrooms; franchise chains like Subway; and non-franchise chains like Pret a Manger. Because consumers are becoming increasingly health conscious, lunchrooms have become a major competitor to the relatively more unhealthy fast-food sector. At the time of writing, the Subway franchise chain has overtaken McDonald's in terms of number of branches worldwide, having more than 43,500 branches in 109 countries, compared to McDonald's 34,000 restaurants in 119 countries as indicated above.

Health conscious

Coffee shops
Quick service businesses that offer coffee as a core business, in addition to other products like cold and warm drinks, pastries, and other food items like sandwiches. An well-known example of a coffee shop is Starbucks. All Starbucks branches have one or more 'baristas' (coffee professional) in service to ensure a high standard of specialty coffee. There are more than 21,500 Starbucks locations in 64 countries worldwide at the time of writing, and their very interesting mission statement intimates that their aim is 'to inspire and nurture the human spirit – one person, one cup and one neighborhood at a time'.

Coffee shop

Take-away restaurants
These food service operations offer food for guests to take home or elsewhere. Some take-away places also offer delivery service. While, not so long ago, the majority of food available in-store or by delivery was limited to pizza, Chinese food, and kebabs, there is now a huge variety of dishes and snacks from which guests can make their choice; these range from different types of pizzas to exotic dishes, and from sushi to vegetarian dishes. Quality and pricing can differ enormously, and these companies tend to flourish, particularly in cities,

Take-away

Huge variety

where a large concentration of people works long hours, earns good salaries, and cannot find the time to cook. The nature of take-aways can vary from traiteurs to (ethnic) grocery shops, and from restaurants offering take-away and/or delivery services to full take-away or delivery services.

Cafeterias

Cafeterias are food service providers where food and drinks are displayed on counters, placed in a line, or in an arbitrary fashion (islands). Guests take a tray and walk along the service line, picking up the food and drinks, paying at the check-out, and finally picking out a table at which to consume their meals. Guests are often required to clear the table of their tray, plates, cups, glasses etc., and place them on a trolley in a designated clearing area. Cafeterias are designed in such a way that many guests can be provided with food and drink in a short period of time. Compared to a regular restaurant the amount of covers is high, there is little or no service (the food and beverage items do not have to be served at guests' tables), and speed of any available service is high. Prices are usually lower because labour costs can be kept low. To avoid waiting lines, the service line or routing is designed in such a way that little or no time is lost.

Cold food items and warm snacks are usually ready to be picked up. Warm dishes take a maximum of a few minutes to be assembled on a plate, or are prepared quickly to be served very fresh. Drinks are offered either in bottles or as empty containers to be filled with soft drinks, juice or coffee once the guests has paid at the check-out. There are many different types of cafeterias, but the most common characteristic is that they are located in areas where there is enough pedestrian traffic to cater to. They are most common in the institutional food service (see 5.2.5), but there are also many commercially operated cafeterias and other motorway restaurants.

Buffet restaurants

Similar to the cafeterias, buffet restaurants also require guests to collect food themselves instead of being served. Drinks, however, are often served at the table, and plates are cleared by the waiting staff. Buffet restaurants, or buffet-style service in other food service companies, allows many guests to be served in a short time. In most cases, food is pre-prepared, saving preparation time. There are also buffet restaurants which offer most food items as ready-to-take, with a few items to be prepared on the spot, however. In some Asian themed restaurants, dishes are prepared in a wok; in

Margin notes:
Cafeterias

Time

Pedestrian traffic

Buffet restaurants

© Noordhoff Uitgevers bv

others, food preparation is finalised on a barbeque. This activity is performed either by kitchen staff or left to guests themselves in some restaurants. The extensiveness of buffets ranges runs from hotel breakfast buffets to lavish buffets with ice-carved figures on display on 5-star cruise ships. The key to offering a quality buffet is to have quality and tasty products and dishes, present them in a fine, creative manner, while at the same time refilling and maintaining the buffet selection. There is little more disappointing than a messy, half-empty buffet; guests coming last should get the same quality as those arriving first.

Extensiveness

Key

Street food
Street food is food (or drink) sold on the street, and is ready-to-eat or prepared very quickly. Vendors or hawkers offer their food and drinks from stalls, carts, or food trucks. They are located at places like markets, festivals, squares and other public places where there are enough people passing by. These small enterprises have two advantages in terms of location. Firstly, they are not tied to a single location – when sales are disappointing they can easily move elsewhere. Secondly, they are not attached to high fixed rents. Another of their advantage is their relatively low labour costs, since they often operate as independent entrepreneurs or have only one or a few staff members. Lastly, the prices of the snacks and dishes offered are relatively low.

Street food

Advantages

5

In the world of street food there is a wide variety of different food types and styles worldwide, ranging from well-known hot dogs and hamburgers to region-specific specialties such as Spanish bocadillo, Japanese chicken katsu curry, or Thai chicken meatballs. There are also food trucks specialised in serving coffees, wines, cocktails; the possibilities are endless. The current trend is for locally-sourced, sustainable and healthy street food.

Wide variety

Ice cream parlours

Ice cream parlours are food service businesses that often produce and sell ice-creams, sorbets or frozen yoghurt to consumers. It is common for several flavours and various toppings to be on offer. Parlours sometimes also offer soft serve (a type of ice cream softer than regular ice cream as a result of air being introduced during freezing), which is dispensed by a machine, offering a limited amount of flavours. There are different types of ice cream parlours, with some having only a window and a few seats with others having complete indoor facilities. Most ice cream parlours operate seasonally, for example from March to October in the Northern Hemisphere, while others are available the year round in hotter climes. Ice cream parlours vary in size and in ownership. While most of them are privately owned, there are also major enterprises such as Ben & Jerry's and Haagen-Dazs.

5.2.2   Full service restaurants

This restaurant category seats guests at a table, after which the order is taken and food and drinks are served at the table as well. There is a huge diversity of full service restaurants, ranging from popular local bistros to high class Michelin-starred restaurants, and from trendy brasseries to classical Italian restaurant. There are also restaurants that cater to particular types of guests, like family restaurants. The basic sub-division within this category of restaurants is between casual and fine dining. As shown in Figure 5.2, however, there are many other sub-categories as outlined in the following sub-sections. It should be noted that, in spite of the comprehensive nature of this list, there are always those restaurants that do not completely fit any one category, but are a mix of more than one category. Combinations in service styles are also possible, with some restaurants offering buffet service during specific days (for example Mother's Day brunch), and regular service on others. There may even be combinations of self-service and table-service. Restaurants may even offer a take-away window or delivery services. Service styles can also depend on the time of day, with breakfast served buffet style and dinner served as fine-dining within the same restaurant, for example.

Ice cream parlours

Seasonally

Full service restaurants

Combinations

© Noordhoff Uitgevers bv

Bistro

A bistro is a small, cosy location where food and drink is provided, originally decorated in French style. The menu offers a limited number of dishes which are traditional, simple, and relatively low-priced. The bistro falls in between the food service categories of pub and restaurant. The ambiance of a classical bistro is one of mood lighting and intimacy, with no posh interior, table linen, or luxurious tableware, but with wooden tables, place mats, candles in wine bottles, and wine served from carafes. A few examples of classical dishes served in a bistro include onion soup, escargots, pâté de campagne, rilette, bœuf bourguignon, entrecote with chips, tarte tatin, and cheese platters.

Bistro

Ambiance

Brasserie

Brasseries are bright, spacious, restaurants with large windows, mirrors, and are often extended with a terrace where people can eat and drink. Tables are laid up with white linen, the furniture is trendy, and the atmosphere is lively with waiters running to-and-fro. They generally have open kitchens,

Brasseries

5

menu cards, and closely grouped tables. In summation, they can be defined as bustling restaurants. Unlike bistros, which are more intimate, brasseries are more outgoing places. The speed of service is high and the prices range from average to high. The menu is inspired by typical French cuisine and traditional craftsmanship. There is often an extended seafood buffet available, featuring a wide choice of shellfish and crustaceans from which guests can make their selection. Nowadays, the original meaning behind the brasserie concept has faded slightly, and the term 'brasserie' is often used for small bars and restaurants and displayed on their facades. Some examples of classical dishes served in brasseries include choucroute, quiche lorraine, pieds de porc, salade niçoise, steak tartare, foie gras, crème brûlée, and mousse au chocolat.

Single item restaurant

As the name indicates, these restaurants focus on and specialise in one specific item of food. Examples include; pancakes, pizza, steak, seafood, chicken, and sushi.

Ethnic restaurant

There are many ethnic restaurants, specialising in foods from different nations, offering a diverse range of cuisines including Italian, Ethiopian, Chinese, Lebanese etc. Traditionally, ethnic restaurants emerge where immigrants begin to cater to the culinary needs of their own ethnic groups, setting up restaurants in the countries they move to. The best-known examples of such restaurants are those with Chinese, Indian and Italian cuisine, which have all become very popular. Ethnic restaurants provide something different, exotic and adventurous to the original local community, and offer a taste of home to people from similar ethnic backgrounds. There are both independent operators as well as large restaurant chains for guests to choose from. These restaurants are available in different styles, price categories and levels of service. Some restaurants also offer take-away and

Outgoing
Menu

Faded

5

One specific
item

Ethnic
restaurants

Exotic

delivery service. In order to meet guests' ever-changing preferences, some of these restaurants have had to be flexible enough to integrate new or fusion cuisines. Fusion is the blending of flavours, techniques or elements from two or more different culinary traditions.

Flexible

Fusion

Family restaurant

Some of the more casual family restaurants, like pancake restaurants, Chinese restaurants, and buffet-style restaurants, have already been discussed. The main features of a family-orientated restaurant have yet to be explained, however. There are various restaurant concepts targeting families while using multiple service styles and products, at price and service levels ranging from low to medium. Among the most common features of these restaurants is the fact that they primarily focus on the wellbeing of children, offering an informal setting with a children's menu consisting of dishes that children like in small portions. A second common feature is that dishes have to be prepared quickly. Thirdly, available amenities include colouring pencils and books or paper, or even smaller or larger play-pens for little children. Small presents may be offered as give-aways. It is very important for serving staff working in a family-orientated restaurant to take speed of service into account; this has to be quicker than in a normal restaurant, because most of the times it is difficult for kids to sit still at a table for extended periods of time. All these services and facilities offered by family restaurants ensure that both children and their parents can have a good time.

Family restaurants

Multiple service styles

Informal setting

Prepared quickly

5

Theme restaurant

These restaurants combine food and drink with a certain theme. They offer a totally immersive experience for the guest, where entertainment, ambiance, decoration, menu, serving staff, and music all provide a unique dining experience. The total concept in these restaurants is that guests are served a theme, and this theme often takes precedence over the food and bever-

Theme

Total concept

age products. These restaurants attract guests largely on the basis of the theme itself. A well-known example is the Hard Rock Café, where the theme is rock & roll and pop music. Each café plays this music and is decorated with photos of rock stars, guitars and other instruments played by the legends of these musical genres. The Hard Rock Café chain has about 198 cafés in 63 countries, and has also started operating casinos and hotels, but there are also privately-owned theme restaurants. Another example of a theme restaurant is a theatre restaurant, serving dinner for guests visiting a theatre show after dinner. Dessert is sometimes served following the show. Both restaurant and dishes served are completely kept in the style of the theatre show.

Beverage-offering food service

Beverage-offering

In beverage-offering food service companies, beverages are the main products served. Some of these establishments also serve food, ranging from bowls of peanuts to 3-course meals. Service is usually provided at the level of the bar, but some such companies also offer table service. Prices vary from low to medium. Beverage-offering food service companies can be privately owned or part of a chain. These companies include pubs, coffee bars, wine bars, and cocktail bars.

Pub/Café

One of the most well-known types of beverage-offering food service provider is the pub. Usually open afternoons and evenings, and in some places and countries all through the night, pubs offer a range of beers, wines, spirits and non-alcoholic drinks, and frequently also snacks. Some may offer different draft beers and/or ales poured directly from the draft system. Many pubs are owned by breweries, allowing pub owners to reduce risk due to the fact that the breweries take up the majority of investments in exchange for exclusive pouring privileges. In many villages and towns, a pub is a social place where people come not only to have a few drinks, but also to socialise with each other or with the owner. All pubs have a bar; depending on size this may be supplemented with a few tables or a whole seating area. There is often a pool or billiards table or darts lane available. Music often plays an important role and some pubs organise live music evenings. The bar as a hotel department is discussed in Section 5.7.

Pub

Social place

5

Coffee shop

Note that for the purposes of this text, the term coffee shops only applies to those establishments as indicated in 5.2.1, and which primarily focus on serving coffee, tea and other hot beverages, particularly during the daytime. Where a cup of coffee was a cup of coffee not so long ago, most modern coffee shops offer a wide selection of specialty, quality coffees to choose from. These coffees are made from fresh top quality coffee beans (produced in different countries) using high standard equipment and machines.

Coffee shops

Specialty

Coffee beans may be freshly roasted for a specific coffee shop exclusively, or coffee shops may roast coffee beans themselves, allowing guests to choose their favourite blends. Coffee beans, teas, and even machines and equipment needed to make the same tasty coffees and teas at home are also regularly on sale in the coffee shops. Delicious pastries, fresh sandwiches, and other finger foods are often featured on the menu. Coupled with a comfortable and cosy atmosphere and seating, coffee shops entice guests to return more frequently. Some coffee shops mainly focus on offering fast service and offer coffee-on-the-go, such as Starbucks (see 5.2.1).

Blends

Wine bar

Wine bar

A wine bar (also called bodega) is a bar where wine lovers can select from a wide assortment, with wines served by the glass as well as in bottles (which can be taken home in those cases where the country's licensing laws allow, thus effectively functioning as both a wine bar and as a wine shop). Wine bars fill the gap for knowledgeable guests who really appreciate a good glass of wine before or after a meal and novices to the world of wines looking for a good introductory setting. The carefully selected and stocked wines come from many countries and are available in a wide range of different tastes.

Fill the gap

The staff in a wine bar mostly have both a good knowledge of wines on offer as well as a passion for wine in general, and in most cases might have completed a course in wines. Aside from enjoying a glass or a bottle of wine, special 'tastings' can be ordered, featuring a selection, or 'flight', of several different wines. These wines are combined according to a certain theme, for example 'grape variety' where 3 or 4 different wines of similar or different grape varieties can be tasted. Other themes can be region, aging, style (fresh or ripe), complexity, etc. Apart from wines, there is usually a small menu with snacks and appetisers like tapas, charcuterie, and cheese boards on offer. Combined wine and food tastings may be available. While many wine bars are private, stand-alone businesses, wine bars are occasionally associated with specific wine retailers or other wine outlets to provide additional marketing for that retailer's wine portfolio. Text 5.4 is the first in a series of four excerpts highlighting some food and beverage experts, this one featuring Ernest Lefebvre and his wine bar.

TEXT 5.4

Expert in Food and Beverages Ernest Lefebvre (Owner 'Wine Bar Lefebvre' Utrecht, IHM 1994 cohort alumnus)

Ernest Lefebvre started his successful wine bar together with his business partner Wim Wiersma in the historic city centre of Utrecht in 2011. Wine Café Lefebvre has become a major hit, a booming place packed with enthusiastic guests enjoying a nice glass of wine with some tasty finger food. There is a fine, lively atmosphere, with plentiful choice of available 'house wines' in three different price ranges: €3.50, €4.50 and €5.50 per glass. There are over 100 wines on offer, of which more than 60 are served by the glass. Furthermore, there are various Belgian beers and a variety of tapas-style foods available. Trade journals and other media have been full of praise, and the financial results exceed all expectations. The crowning glory of the work by Wine Café Lefebvre was the Dutch 'Wine Bar of the Year' award in 2014.

As a student, Ernest already knew that someday he would start his own business. He knew his type of business would be in the food and beverage industry. After finishing his education at the Hotel Management School in Leeuwarden, the Netherlands, he worked in various management positions in different types of food service companies, mostly in hotels and catering in the Netherlands and the United States. Before he started his wine business, he worked for a large catering company in The Hague and met his current business partner and former employer, Wim Wiersma. Wiersma owned a number of restaurants in a separate company, as well as a trading company dealing in wine, olives and water, called WOW for short.

Ernest had always had an affinity with wines, and while he was working as operations and sales manager at Brasserie and Banqueting 'De Kloosterhoeve' in Harmelen, the Netherlands during the day, he helped in the wine business during the evening hours. He wrote a plan to set up a wine café, and his part-

ner Wiersma was immediately attracted to the idea. Thus, Lefebvre's dream slowly started coming true.

Instead of employing a sommelier or wine connoisseur, Ernest likes to work with students who enjoy working part-time, are hos-

5

pitable, and are eager to learn about wine. Employees are given in-house training on the background of the wines before they are allowed to serve at the tables. Staff wine tastings are essential according to Ernest, as this is the way to gain knowledge, develop a palate, and create a mental database.

Because of the huge success of the Wine Café Lefebvre, entrepreneurs started coming to Ernest for advice on their plans for similar businesses. That is why he also setup a small consultancy business where he offers supervision in exchange for a small fee, and on the condition that they buy their wines from WOW.

Regarding his success, he has one important piece of advice:
'No Guts, No Glory'

Cocktail bar

Cocktail bar

Shaken or stirred, straight up or neat, nightcap or pick-me-up are all terms encountered in the cocktail bar. A cocktail is a mix of at least two ingredients, one of which officially has to be a spirit – the exception being non-alcoholic cocktails. Cocktails are made using finest liquors and spirits. They are finished off with colourful garnishes and served in beautiful glasses, mugs or other containers. Some cocktails are even served in very spectacular ways, such as those presented in a smoke screen or even set on fire. Staff working these bars know what flavours pair well with each other, and which ones do not. They have a well-developed database of different spirits, drinks, sodas, sours, and other ingredients, allowing them to also develop new cocktails. A shaker is one of the items often used to mix ingredients to make cocktails.

Flavours

5

Fine-dining restaurant

A fine-dining restaurant is a restaurant where the quality of the dishes, wines and service is on a high level, with prices to match. It is a restaurant with a stylish décor and atmosphere, ranging from classy and formal to hip and trendy. It is the top class of the full service restaurants category. Dishes are created with the greatest care and attention, using fresh ingredients and multiple cooking techniques. The different food items are plated, or even composed, by the head chef with the utmost care, in the manner of an artist applying the finishing touches to a masterpiece.

Fine-dining restaurant

Top class

Most of the chefs working in these restaurants have years of culinary experience in the field, combined with an extensive education in cooking. Most fine dining restaurants are based on some variety of international cuisine, including French, Italian, Chinese, Japanese, Latin-American, and Spanish. Some chefs even cook according to some variant of fusion cuisines. In such establishments, the drive for perfection in both cooking and hospitality is evident. The service staff has to be of a high standard, since they are in direct contact with guests and are responsible for giving the best in hospitable service. The majority of these restaurants employ a sommelier responsible for suggesting good wine and food pairings, and serving quality wines during the service. Text 5.5 illustrates this type of food and beverage expert in the form of Erik van Loo, an Executive Chef.

Sommelier

TEXT 5.5

Expert in Food and Beverages Erik van Loo, Owner and Executive Chef (SVH Master Chef) of 2 Michelin Starred Restaurant Parkheuvel

My kitchen is all about quality. Real food. Taste is knowledge, taste is emotion and feeling, taste is memory.

As chef, you have to dive into a dish. Every single taste you experience you process in a dish in such a way that it gets the most out all these aspects. Cooking is establishing flavour. By cooking, you show something of yourself.

Fortunately, the trend has returned to seasonal food. I meet many guests who would like to know the story behind the ingredients I use. In the kitchen of Parkheuvel, only the best is good enough. To be able to guarantee quality, I have built good relations with my suppliers over many years. They know exactly what I want and what my demands are, and they also know what to leave out. We approach life the same way, we share the same ideas about flavour and quality. These relationships grow; time gives them flavour, and their quality intensifies.

Erik often compares his profession to the UEFA Champions League. 'Cooking is top sport. You always have to try to be in peak condition. Every single day you have to score, and that is only possible if you use the best ingredients; otherwise it doesn't work. Along with that, the people I work with are indispensable. Your team has to be as one, one unit. You have to put all the wood behind one arrow, otherwise you will not accomplish anything.'

5.2.3   Catering

Catering is the provision of food and beverage products for special events. This is usually done for a large number of people at the same time. Depending on the quantities involved, guests might either all have a set menu, or a limited selection to choose from. Special events can be divided into two types: business events and social events. Business events are conventions, business meetings, receptions, special company celebrations, and award dinners, for example. Social events include birthday parties, anniversaries, weddings, graduations, proms, and charity related events. Catering can also be provided at special events such as festivals and fairs. There are numerous caterers either offering one or several specialties or complete ranges of food items and beverages. Caterers can specialise in anything from high teas or high quality hors-d'oeuvre to all-round service including complete meals up to supplying service equipment and staff for the event. Catering companies can be large and have many employees working for them, while others can be small and work on their own. Most of the smaller entrepreneurs principally work from their homes, whereas larger enterprises often have separate business locations from where they operate.

There are two types of catering: on-premises and off-premises. On-premises catering takes place where the caterer is located. The caterer has the facilities and equipment necessary to operate, like a banquet room and a kitchen. On-premises catering can also take place at restaurants and hotels. In hotels, the catering department is often called the banquet department or conference and banquet department – see Section 5.6 for additional information related to this department. Other organisations, like clubs and churches, may also provide on-premises catering. There are many different clubs, mostly associated with hobbies or sports, that offer on-premises catering. Examples include golf clubs, tennis clubs, yachting clubs, hunting clubs, military clubs, and country clubs. Off-premises catering takes place at locations away from the caterer's business location. Off-premises catering requires good planning and logistics, because the tables, chairs, materials, equipment, and food and beverages have to be taken to the location. Sometimes, entire kitchen areas have to be set up.

The world of catering can be exciting but also stressful, and last minute changes can occur on a regular basis. These last minute changes may be caused by guests arriving late, programmes running early or late, or the weather suddenly changing, for example. Catering companies must work very closely with the different parties involved, including the decorator, the entertainers, and the event coordinators; all parties must be involved in order to ensure an event is run smoothly.

5.2.4   Institutional food service

Institutional food service is a food service that supplies meals and other food and beverage products within institutions like schools, universities, hospitals, military installations, prisons, and companies. This type of food service mostly serves people staying at these institutions, because they do not have the possibility or time to have a meal at a commercial restaurant or food service business.

Institutional food services can be managed either in-house or based on a contract. If a food service is run by the organisation itself, it is called in-house food service. This means that the institution is totally responsible for

Catering

Business events

Social events

On-premises

Off-premises

Stressful

Institutional food service

In-house

5

Contract

the food service, including purchasing, production, service, staff, as well as carrying financial obligations that come with it. Contract food service involves an outside food service company hired by the institution. These companies have a lot of experience in this type of business and can arrange the whole food service department from A to Z. Most of the on-site food services are non-commercial – available because they are convenient and beneficial for employers. This tendency is changing, however; the food service operations increasingly have profit-making goals.

5.2.5   Food and beverage within a consumer-based company

The provision of food and beverage products in these companies can be found in the following domains.

Leisure attractions

Attraction

Large numbers of people

Such provision is very often not fully visible, because the food service operation is part of the attraction or event. This event could be a football match, a festival or a pop concert, an international golf tournament, or it could be akin to the food services placed in an attraction like a zoo. Wherever there are large numbers of people, this offers opportunities to provide food services. The following are examples of some of the different leisure facilities in which the provision of food services is very much present.

Stadiums and arenas

Stadiums and arenas

Fixed outlets

Hawkers

There are mostly sporting events organised in stadiums and arenas. These locations also feature other large entertainment events like concerts and shows. There are usually some fixed outlets where food and beverage products are offered, with mobile food and beverage service points are set up depending on the event, in order to serve masses of people. Visitors can sometimes buy snacks from hawkers without having to leave their seats. Stress levels usually go up during breaks and intermissions, during which many guests may have to be served at once in a short period of time, inevitably leading to long queues. There are also special food and beverage facilities for business-related guests, called VIP areas or VIP boxes; these are principally reserved for the main sponsors and other important dignitaries.

Fairs and festivals

Festivals

There are countless festivals attracting lots of people, including music festivals, dance festivals, and the currently very popular food festivals. In such situations, most of the food and beverage provision is done using mobile units that have been strategically placed so as to serve visitors as quickly as possible. Products offered consist of food that can be produced quickly.

Theatres

Theatres

This includes such locations as movie theatres, where the food offered can vary from popcorn and soda to hamburgers, sandwiches and other finger foods, which may be served at the seat of the guest. At other theatres, food and beverage products are most commonly served from fixed service points before and after shows and during breaks. There are also theatres where guests can enjoy a complete meal during the show (also called a dinner show).

Other recreational operations

Horse racing tracks, car racing tracks, parks (national and state), zoos, museums, and aquariums are examples of other recreational operations where food and beverage operations can be successfully run.

© Noordhoff Uitgevers bv

The large operations and the frequently organised events are most frequently operated by contract management companies. Smaller and less frequently organised events are most commonly managed by the facility's management.

Retail

Businesses like shopping malls, gas stations, traiteurs, and other retail stores also generate revenue from their sales of food and beverage products intended for immediate consumption. Many chain restaurants have franchises in major department stores. Nowadays, the formerly fixed borders between the retail and restaurant business are fading. A lot is changing in the world of retail, where consumers are thinking more in terms of needs than of channels. People no longer buy all of their vegetables at a greengrocer's or their bread at a bakery, but prefer to go somewhere where their needs are capable of being fulfilled simultaneously. Consumers are willing to pay more when the experience is enhanced. This blurring of borders has led to new retail concepts like the food courts found in several large cities worldwide, where shopping, dining, parking, and working are all organised under one roof. Browsing, tasting, eating, cooking, buying and selling: they all happen there.

Retail

Blurring of borders

5.2.6   Travel food service

Food service offered within the travel industry is not bound to fixed locations. Examples of travel businesses were food services are offered during transportation include airplanes, trains, and cruise ships. As shown in Chapter 2, there are principally two types of guests making use of the different means of transport – business guests and leisure guests.

Travel Industry

Airplanes

Both types of guests travel by plane, and food and beverage products are on offer on most flights. Depending on the airline, there are generally two or three different categories of passengers: business class; first class; and economy class. The food and beverage service might range from a sandwich

Flights

in economy class to a culinary dinner in business class. Sometimes, mostly on low-cost flights, passengers have to pay for the food services offered themselves. Food served on airplanes is not prepared aboard the airplanes, but mainly in large kitchens at airports (or near the airports), before bringing them on-board. Such operations require detailed procedural and logistical planning and organising.

Trains

Trains

Another example of travel food services can be found on trains. Most long distance or international trains have a special dining area serving food, snacks and drinks. On shorter trips, there may be a vendor selling coffee, tea, snacks and sandwiches, while on longer trips the selection of food and beverage products on offer may be more extensive. Long distance trains, such as the Trans-Siberian Express, are in themselves considered a holiday destination, and offer breakfast, lunch and dinner.

Cruise ships

Cruise ships

Wide range

Cruise ships are well-known for their fantastic food offerings, with wide varieties of food and beverage products to be enjoyed at the different on-board restaurants. There is a wide range of outlets available: different types of bars, à la carte restaurants, casual or fine-dining restaurants, and restaurants offering lavish buffets. The cost of the food and the basic beverage products served is usually included in the price of the travel package. Depending on the cruise line and the category of the trip, supplementary charges can apply for dining in the à la carte restaurant and/or partaking of certain alcoholic beverages. In the early years of the cruise industry, cruise lines were merely offering holidays for upscale and luxury markets, but nowadays cruising has become popular among all layers of society.

Other outlets

Airports

Food and beverage product are also offered in various food service outlets at airports, train stations, and bus stations. One example of a food service company operating in airports worldwide is the HMSHost, exploiting more than 70 restaurants and food service outlets at the Amsterdam Schiphol Airport alone, for example. Their brands include those shown in Figure 5.3, and the services offered vary from self-service to counter-service to table-service, with some of them operating round the clock every day of the year.

FIGURE 5.3 HMS Host brands

5.3 The restaurant business

The restaurant business can be one of the most interesting and exiting businesses imaginable. It is one of the largest businesses worldwide, employing millions of people. As discussed earlier, there are numerous restaurants, offering many different concepts, services and flavours. It is a people business, where contact and communication between guests and service staff take place constantly. Because of the nature of restaurants, where 'production' (product and service offering) and 'consumption' take place at the same time, it offers its share of challenges, making the restaurant business a vibrant and lively workplace. To get a better insight into the restaurant business, the following section begins by outlining the restaurant's formula, followed by highlighting the restaurant's layout, and lastly by describing developments within the food and beverage domains.

People business

5.3.1   The restaurant's formula

As indicated in Section 5.1, the guest is the party that forms the 'demand', and the restaurant is the party that represents the 'supply'. In order to make 'demand' and 'supply' match up, an entrepreneur has to make sure that a clear restaurant profile is communicated to the (potential) guest before the guest sets foot in the restaurant. This is because guests will have developed expectations prior to a restaurant visit. These expectations are based on what a restaurant may have communicated such as impressions about the dishes, service levels, ambiance, comfort, and price levels. If expectations are not met, guests will most likely be disappointed and not return. The company's profile, also called its formula, gives an impression or image of the restaurant which enables guests to form a picture of the company; this picture is the basis of a guest's decision-making process. A restaurant's formula is the sum of the following six elements: location; ambiance; menu; staff; price; and promotion.

Profile

Expectations

5

Location
This is a key part of the restaurant's formula, because the location of the restaurant determines the possibilities and limitations of the business. The location determines approximately how many guests can be expected and when they are most likely to come. If, for example, the restaurant is situated in a part of the city with many young, dual income couples, it would not be wise to open a coffee shop with opening times from 10am to 6pm. In such an environment, it would be advisable to open a restaurant where a good meal is offered at a reasonable price, with take-away possibilities readily available. Important locational factors include demographics, average income levels, convenience, parking, visibility, and accessibility.

Location

Ambiance
The atmosphere has an immediate effect on the guest. It has to do with how tables are arranged (very close together or leaving room for some privacy). Furnishings, lighting, music, noise, and the way the restaurant is decorated all form the ambiance and are very important in a guest's decision making process.

Atmosphere

The menu
The menu of the restaurant is one of the most important factors of its formula. Guests want to eat tasty food of consistent quality, but it has to be clear what the menu offerings are. This depends on restaurant type as well

Menu offerings

the needs and wishes of local target groups the restaurant is focussing on. Furthermore, the capabilities of the staff, the layout and equipment capacity, and the availability of menu ingredients play a role in the decision making process concerning the dishes and the menu.

Staff

Staff

Similar to the menu, the type of staff found in a hamburger stall is different to that found in a brasserie, for example. Training plays a major role in the quality of staff. To be able to deliver consistently good quality products and services, a lot is required from both cooks and servers. Figure 5.4, adapted from Ninemeier and Perdue (2005, p. 178), illustrates the traits of professional food and beverage servers; these qualities are applicable to all professional food and beverage servers whatever the type of restaurant concerned.

Traits

FIGURE 5.4 Traits of professional food and beverage servers

Price

Price

The price of a restaurant visit is the compensation paid by a guest for the menu, wines, and other food and beverage items consumed, together with the hospitality offered. The price should be representative of the whole restaurant visit. Awarding value to every individual element of the restaurant's formula leads to the end price.

Promotion

By means of advertising or promoting the restaurant, potential guests have to be informed about its existence. Promotion actually tells the story of the 5 previously mentioned elements (location, ambiance, menu, staff, and price).

Advertising

A restaurant's success is not based on luck, but mostly on hard work, putting in long hours, and making sure that the 6 elements described are well attuned to each other. Note that since restaurant formulas are not everlasting but instead are subject to changing needs and trends, it is advisable to keep track of what is happening in the market and adjusting formulas as the needs arise.

Hard work

5.3.2 Restaurant layouts

While hospitality layouts are more extensively discussed in Chapter 13, suffice to note that layout is of utmost importance when planning a restaurant. The layout depends on restaurant concept and its major goals (see also Chapter 12). The ingredients of the concept, like the menu, guests, and price levels, play an important role in the process of deciding how the restaurant and kitchen are to be set up. A good layout avoids having both kitchen staff and service staff make unnecessary and unproductive movements, and enables them to work as efficiently as possible. The layout should be as convenient and attractive as possible for the guests, and there should be a seamless incorporation of the restaurant's design into the entire layout of the business operation. It should be noted that a perfect layout of a restaurant might not always be possible, however; restrictions imposed by the presence of a previously existing restaurant may influence possible layout options. Budgetary constraints also have an influence on the extent to which alterations can be made. Important issues to consider regarding a restaurant's layout are indicated in the sections that follow.

Layouts

Concept

Convenient

Costs

It is always wise to avoid focussing on the short term and the temptation of cheap alternative solutions leading to unnecessary renovations when it comes to costs; instead, costs should be approached as a long term investment issue.

Costs

Entrance

Because it is the first and last area guests encounter during their visit, the entrance has to be well designed. It should be inviting and able to capture the essence of the restaurant.

Entrance

Kitchen (including the dish-washing areas)

All equipment like ovens, stoves, fryers, cooling spaces, hot benches, working spaces, and the like, has to be placed in a way that allows chefs to operate quickly and efficiently. Preparation areas also have to be taken into account. The dish-washing areas have to be designed in such a way as to leave enough room to place items, while still working at optimum efficiency. There should be enough space for both kitchen staff and stewarding staff to move around at a fast pace when business is hectic. A crucial element is hygiene and safety issues; these issues should be taken into account and integrated when designing the layout.

Equipment

Enough space

Food storage areas

There has to be enough room to store products. A large walk-in fridge, freezer, and appropriately spacious dry storage facilities should be integrated in the layout.

Dining room

The layout of the dining rooms very much depends on the type and concept of the restaurant; here, issues such as target groups, services style, or even the need for private dining may be taken into account. As such, restaurants have to be set-up with high or low tables, chairs, or stools, without forgetting the work stations.

Employee-related issues

Employee productivity

As mentioned earlier, restaurant layout has to be efficiently designed to help in enhancing employee productivity. This also contributes to improved employee satisfaction, thereby having a positive influence on the restaurant's revenue: 'happy staff leads to happy guests', meaning more guest spending.

Restrooms

Restrooms

Influence

Restrooms are very important but remain an underrated aspect of restaurant design. Almost all guests visit the restroom at least once during their visit. A dirty restroom has a negative influence on the guest's view of the restaurant, and may lead to doubts about levels of cleanliness in those areas not accessible to guests, including the kitchens and storage spaces. Restrooms have to be large enough to accommodate many guests at the same time, but should not take up too much restaurant space.

Bar

The bar area should be laid out in such a way as to allow bartenders easy access to all beverages, ingredients and equipment needed to quickly and efficiently carry out their activities.

Other areas

The layout of other areas is also of paramount importance in restaurants. Such areas include the staff canteen, the staff dressing room (including lockers), as well as the offices of managers and other staff.

5.3.3   Some trends affecting the restaurant business

Direction

A trend is a general direction in which something is developing. It indicates the direction in which a customer's preferences are going. It is hard to predict a certain trend, and while trends are usually initiated by the industry itself, they can also come from individuals who have had a moment of insight. Based on trends, hospitality professionals can adjust their operations with the goal to attract more guests and consequently generate more revenue. An example of a trend would be that more and more consumers are becoming very savvy and critical about what they eat and drink, or are concerned about the sourcing of ingredients used. The following are some trends as noticed in 2015.

Technology

Technology

Because of developments in technology, restaurants are profoundly changing in the ways they operate. From using a tablet for a menu card to setting up special buzzers on every table, enabling guests to have direct contact with waiters to either make orders or request their bills. Waiters are equipped with special devices such as watches so they can be alerted to the signals and wishes of their guests. Using a mobile phone, guests can reserve a table, pre-order dinner, and even use special apps tracking how long it takes to get to a restaurant. Adding to that is some restaurants now using touchscreens letting guests customise their orders by dragging icons of various toppings onto their virtual pizza, for example. Technological developments used in restaurants allow for an acceleration of the dining process and a reduction in the number of errors. They even transform ordering into a game the entire family can take part in.

Acceleration

Celebrity Chefs running a restaurant in a hotel for a period of time only

When hotel restaurants want to boost their sales, they can hire a top chef to either work alongside the existing crew (designing the menu, among others), or to run the restaurant for a period of time. This creates massive exposure for the restaurant and boosts turnover.

Internet

Potential guests increasingly turn to the reviews of restaurants on websites or via other sources before actually deciding to visit the venue. Restaurants also use social media like Facebook and Twitter more frequently when it comes to informing guests of special promotions, and to communicate with (potential) guests. When complaints about restaurant visits are shared online, it is crucial that a company acts quickly and decisively.

Reviews

Sustainable, organic, and local products

An ongoing trend which remains in vogue. Text 5.6 introduces the third in the series of food and beverage experts, and discusses the principles of the very trendy New Dutch Cuisine.

New Dutch Cuisine

TEXT 5.6

Principles of New Dutch Cuisine – Albert Kooy

Expert in Food and Beverages Albert Kooy (SVH Master Chef, and Executive Chef at Stenden Hotel)

Albert Kooy developed and is responsible for Restaurants Wannee and Stones as well as food service outlets Canteen and Café IF. Albert has a passion for cooking, food and beverages. He is a chef who worries about

food, which is why he developed the idea of 'New Dutch Cuisine' which led to the establishment of 'Dutch Cuisine' as an association of various chefs who actively back the principles of the New Dutch Cuisine. Albert's vision on food and beverage is based on the ingredients required for better, fresher, healthier, and more honest food embodied in the 5 principles of the New Dutch Cuisine:

- Culture – the Dutch culinary culture; vegetables from the cold soil, regional, seasonal, recognisable, kitchen traditions. From what is on the plate, one should be able to visualise the country and be able to recognise the season.
- Health – healthy food for the body and the mind (and the planet). A healthy eating habit promotes well-being. A distribution between vegetables and meat/fish in an 80:20 ratio.

- Nature – eating what the land and seas provide, seasonally, without artificial additives, as a whole. An entire chicken from which different dishes are cooked, not merely using a filet.
- Quality – with respect to the ingredients one eats and the people producing them. Recognise the quality of ingredients used to produce a meal: organic, fair-trade, animal-friendly, fresh, seasonal and local.
- Profit – profit for oneself, the farmer, the producer, and the planet. Quality comes with a price tag, but if one eats more vegetables and less meat and fish, net spending will be lower. A small portion of good quality meat is still cheaper than a large portion of poor quality meat.

Master Chef Kooy fuses these elements not only in the kitchen, but also in the restaurant. From his use of materials to the lighting, from the service delivery to the styling, these 5 principles are very clearly noticeable in all his food concepts.

Bringing back craftsmanship to cooking and serving, with passion and care – that is Albert Kooy.

For sale

Products (including furniture) are up for sale in restaurants
Similar to mixing retail with hospitality, this is hospitality mixing with retail.

Less formal service staff
The time of the classical, formal approach to servants is over for most restaurants, even when looking at the appearance and grooming standards of front-line employees. If properly presented or kempt, tattoos, beards, and piercings are more frequently allowed based on the idea that employees will feel more comfortable, and thus perform better.

Appearance

The reappearance of the service professional
The job of a waiter is becoming more of the profession it used to be. The front stage position of chefs is slowly disappearing, with chefs being directed back to the kitchen. The true role, skills and craftsmanship of the host are making a come-back, and hosts are running the show more and more,

Host

putting the finishing touches to dishes at a station or table in the restaurant. Examples of these table presentations include steak flambé, crêpe suzette, filleting sole, carving beef, or grey mullet prepared on a hot salt stone à la minute.

Service tsunami/rhythm

One of the most frequently heard complaints in restaurants is the time guests have to wait before the first dish is served. Bread may be served after the first course, water is only poured after a guest may have asked for it twice, or first courses take an unreasonable amount of time to be served. The trend now is to overwhelm guests with a speedy service of aperitifs, appetisers, and water and bread within the first 10 minutes of their arrival. Speed of service can be slowed down after that, and the natural rhythm of the restaurant service can continue. Natural rhythm refers to the speed of service adapted to the guest.

Overwhelm guests

This subsection on trends concludes with Text 5.7, which introduces the fourth food and beverage expert, Maartje Nelissen, a partner in the Food Line-up, here giving her views on food and beverage trends.

5

TEXT 5.7

Maartje Nelissen's views on food and beverage trends

**Expert in Food and Beverages Maartje Nelissen
(Partner – The Food Line-up, and IHM 2005 cohort alumnus)**

Maartje Nelissen

The Food Line-up organises food line-ups at (professional) events, festivals, and public places, with more than 200 temporary and craft food entrepreneurs. Each entrepreneur shares the same vision of food, and has specialised in one signature dish or one type of cuisine. As connector and overall organiser, the Food Line-up arranges an ever-changing and complete food concept for 100 to 25,000 guests every day. Between 2012 and 2015, the Food Line-up introduced more than a million people to better, fresher, authentic, and more sustainable food.

According to Maartje, the following topics in food and beverages are currently trending:
1 Specialism – as transparency, knowledge and understanding are becoming more important in a time of global trends and issues, consumers look for more specialist advise. Apart from taste, experts specialising in one particular type of cuisine or dish have the possibility to offer a great sustainable product. So, if one makes the best potato wedges, for

example, then that should be it. It makes purchasing accessible and easy to trace, and due to the required volumes of the ingredients, substantial agreements can be struck with the farmer or the supplier directly. If focussed on one particular dish, a chef will have more affinity with it and excel at that dish. This in turn leads to the best possible flavour due to the constant need to aim for improvement and the drive to serve the best product available.

2 Great, no-nonsense food – great, no-nonsense food with advances in haute friture is the next level. Gone are the days of frothed mousses and pretentious foods like caviar made from eggplant, for example. This trend has been around for some time now, as has the trend for Scandinavian cuisine, which is good and has a great respect for nature, making use of ingredients that lend themselves to quality products. If this standard is upheld, and chefs have the best ingredients, they do not need to bother too much in order to stand out.

3 Drinks get front-stage – guests do not go to a restaurant for an extensive menu focussing solely on brunch or dinner. One does not get by in this business by only having a food menu; hence the need for a gin and tonic menu, a tea menu, or a selection of cocktails based on Japanese whiskeys. It is good to check out the versatility of magnificent drinks on offer. At the BAR-BAR – our own mobile bar concept – we celebrate local taste heroes; our motto is 'Think Global, Drink Local.'

4 More blurring – retail, café, restaurant, hotel, online: they are all coming together. We live life on the go, online, fast paced. The existing hospitality industry, food and retail will have to intermingle more and more, and adapt to that fast lifestyle.

5 Food with a face – this does not refer literally to serving a whole fish from the grill or roasting an entire pig on a spit; instead, it refers to the notion that our food tastes better if we know who has prepared it and why. Knowing that the saté babi from one of our entrepreneurs has been based on an authentic, 80-year-old Indonesian family recipe by Granddad Kisman adds to the flavour and experience. In addition, the fact that food is locally sourced is one of the most important aspects of preservation; it lends value to the area.

6 Become big by staying small, valuing the little things – fixed scale formulas indicate that times are changing, and consumers need all of the aspects mentioned above: authenticity, local initiative, and specialisation. Precisely those issues

© Noordhoff Uitgevers bv

where great formulas have been set through (speed of) innovation and flexibility. The goodwill factor is now more important than ever, and entrepreneurs must not be afraid to spend big. Today's competition could be tomorrow's ally; working together or in tandem may be mutually beneficial. Major Dutch caterers like Sodexo, Maison van den Boer but also NS Retail and Albert Heijn add experience to their concepts by staying small scale, using local suppliers (hiring third parties); and as a result they improve their market position.

5.4 Restaurant operations

As noted in Section 5.2, there are many different types of restaurants defined under various categories and subcategories. This section discusses the structure of a fine dining restaurant, outlining the different tasks and responsibilities of the staff working in the restaurant, and clarifying the processes taking place. While other types of restaurants may have similar structures, existing positions are usually less specialised. Restaurant operations are most commonly divided into front-of-house activities and back-of-house activities. Front-of-house is defined as the staff serving and being in contact with the guest; back-of-house are the kitchen, responsible for the production of food, and stewarding, responsible for cleaning materials and equipment.

Structure

To be able to manage restaurant operations, it is important to have a good understanding of the organisation of a restaurant. To keep the quality of both products and services at a high level, the processes and procedures have to be safeguarded by using SOPs. Furthermore, tasks and responsibilities of the restaurant staff have to be clear so that employees know what is expected of them and what they have to do. In the end, a good organisation contributes to a restaurant's success and positive financial performance. Since profit margins in the restaurant business are relatively low, close attention must be paid to financial issues, like costs and revenues. In the following sections, front-of-house and back-of-house activities and positions will be explained further, including description of the tasks and responsibilities of the Restaurant Manager and the Kitchen Manager (Executive Chef).

SOPs

Profit margins

5.4.1   Front-of-house

Restaurant General Manager

The person responsible for the overall restaurant's operations is the Restaurant General Manager – RGM (who in many cases is also the owner of the restaurant). The RGM is responsible for all service and kitchen departments. The RGM supervises the Restaurant Manager and Head Chef directly. If a restaurant is part of a chain, the RGM is responsible for informing headquarters on the running of the restaurant. The Restaurant Manager

Maître d'hôtel

(*Maître d'hôtel*) is responsible for the front-of-house operations of the restaurant. A more detailed summary of the profile of a Restaurant Manager/ *Maître d'hôtel* is provided in Section 5.4.2. In larger restaurant companies, Headwaiters are responsible for a part of the dining room. In smaller companies, this position does not exist, and is instead incorporated into the

Chef de rang

tasks of the *Chef de rang*. The *Chef de rang* is also called Supervisor and runs an area of the restaurant. *Chefs de rang* are responsible for their areas, and have to lead and guide the *Demi Chefs de rang* and the *Commis* (also called Waiters). A Restaurant Manager can delegate certain activities to a *Chef de rang,* such as providing a menu, explaining specialty menus and dishes, and taking and processing orders to the kitchen through a cash-

Demi Chefs de rang

iering system. *Demi Chefs de rang* assist a *Chef de rang* in serving dishes and drinks. A *Commis*, also called Runner, is responsible for transporting dishes to the restaurant, and clearing the used and empty plates. In some traditional restaurants, serving is done with the help of trays which are brought to the restaurant and put on work stations or trolleys from which

Commis

the dishes are served. Traditionally, *Commis* are not allowed to serve the dishes themselves. To maintain quality standards, this is done by a *Chef de rang* or *Demi Chef de rang* because of the notion that *Commis* do not have full knowledge of the ingredients and cooking techniques used to produce the dishes. This is done differently in many restaurants, however, there are

Runners

Runners that serve at tables. It is crucial, however, that the *Commis* knows the dishes, ingredients and cooking techniques used. During peak hours, the owner or RGM can be seen at the 'pass', communicating with the Head Chef, directing the *Commis* (Waiters/Runners), and making sure that the right dishes go to the right tables at the right time. *Commis* may also be responsible for serving the aperitif, water and bread. It should be noted that there are many variations of the division of labour in a restaurant. Last but

Sommelier

not least, there is often a *Sommelier* (Wine Steward), who is responsible for serving wines and providing guests with advice to help them make their selections. A *Sommelier* is in charge of selecting, purchasing and storing wines for a restaurant, as well as arranging wine and food pairings. Figure 5.5 is a basic organisational chart of the main positions in a fine-dining restaurant.

The activities of the front-of-house can be divided into 5 phases: the pre-service phase; the welcoming phase; the staying phase; the farewell phase; and the post-service phase.

Pre-service phase

Tasks

Pre-service phase

This is the period before the service, during which all necessary preparations are carried out to ensure a smooth service. The tasks that have to be executed include: setting up the tables; refilling the stock of wines and beverages; polishing and refilling glassware, cutlery and chinaware; and stocking other materials needed to run the operation. In some luxury restaurants, the silverware also needs to be polished. To work efficiently, service stations

FIGURE 5.5 Main positions in a fine-dining restaurant.

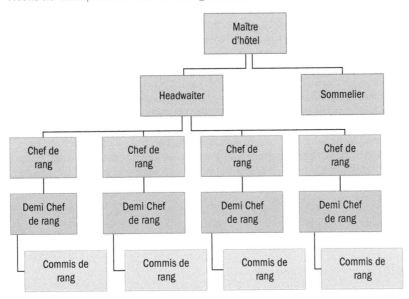

have to be prepared with all required items (wines, glassware, trays, serving plates, bread and butter, and equipment used for table preparations). The bar or pantry also needs to be made ready for service. If there are trolleys (such as for cheeses or digestives), these also need to be prepared, restocked and maintained. The coffee area has to be refilled with the products and materials needed. In short, everything has to be cleaned, organised and prepared before the first guests enter.

To make it easier, a start-up checklist can be used, which sums up pre-service tasks for them to be ticked off when completed. If there is time left before the first guests arrive, training sessions can take place, including practicing the service sequence (the different steps in restaurant service), handling complaints, managing wine or food tastings, or a combination of both. Right before the opening time, staff are briefed on several topics regarding the shift: the division of staff; (VIP) guests; special wishes; dietary requests; (specialty) dishes and wines etc. – this ensures service proceeds fluidly.

Start-up checklist

Welcoming phase
This is a very important phase of the guest's visit to a restaurant – it has a great influence on the overall impression a guest has of a restaurant. Guests have to be welcomed in the most hospitable manner, at the entrance, holding the door when possible, using eye contact accompanied by a smile with an open attitude. Next, guests' coats have to be taken, and reservations have to checked (if applicable). Guests are subsequently guided to the restaurant or other areas, like a bar, where an aperitif (a drink prior to the meal) can be offered, often served with a few nuts, olives or other light snacks. Guests are then placed at a table in the dining room (with hosts assisting by holding the chairs, for example). In some restaurants, the menu card (and/or wine card) are presented with the aperitif. The real first contact

Welcoming phase

Great influence

Real first contact

with the guest is usually when they make a reservation, which can be done by phone or online. The way in which the reservation is handled is actually the guest's real first impression. In both cases (when making the reservation and when entering the restaurant) a guest has to feel welcome and comfortable. As the saying goes, 'one never gets a second chance at a first impression'.

Staying phase

Staying phase

This is the period during which the actual meal takes place. Once the aperitif (with snacks) is served, bread, butter and water need to follow quickly.

Wait too long

This way, guests do not have to wait too long before getting something to eat and drink. Once presented with the above-mentioned items, guests are presented a menu card and/or wine menu, and informed of specialty menus and dishes. Staff should also enquire after special dietary requests at this point. Staff presenting the menus is expected to have good knowledge of the ingredients used in the dishes, as well as the tastes and the various methods of preparation. The presentation of the menus is followed by tak-

Food and wine orders

ing the food and wine orders, and processing them through the PMS. To make sure that the order is correctly taken, staff is advised to repeat the order for the guest's approval.

Taking the order is a very important aspect of the service. A staff member

Clear to everyone

taking the order has to make sure that it is clear to everyone which guest ordered which dish(es). This is to pre-empt such questions as 'Who ordered the scallops?' when the food is delivered. Such situations are considered very unprofessional, and a good system should be used to avoid it from happening altogether. Suggestions are the use of chair numbers attached to the dishes ordered, making a small table plan, or using the cashiering sys-

Bridge the time

tem to indicate who ordered what. To bridge the time until the first course is served, guests are presented with appetisers (one or more, depending on quality levels and prices).

During this phase, the selected wine (glass or bottle) is served by the *Sommelier* while providing any additional information related to the wine. This is followed by serving the first dish. Once dishes are served, they are described to the guests at the table. Other ordered dishes, accompanied by their appropriate wines and other beverages, follow suit. Once guests

Appropriate techniques

finish their dish(es), the empty plates have to be taken away using the appropriate techniques, and transported to the Stewarding Department. Before the dishes and wines are brought to the table, the required cutlery and glassware have to be ready and on the table. Following the last dish, usually a dessert or cheese platter, guests are offered coffee; if accepted, this is usually served accompanied by a selection of homemade chocolates and cookies. After dinner, guests are offered drinks (digestives), sometimes using a trolley containing a variety of liqueurs, cognacs, and other spirits.

To make sure that all members of staff follow the same guidelines, a ser-

Service sequence

vice procedure or service sequence is often used. Text 5.8 is an adjusted example of the dinner service procedure used by Restaurant Wannee.

TEXT 5.8

Service Procedure Restaurant Wannee

Before the guests arrive make sure you have checked the table according to the standards.

- Welcome the guest upon arrival.
- Ask the guest if you can take his/her coat.
- Guide (the guest to the restaurant) and place the guest at the table.
- Try selling an aperitif (special suggestion).
- Book the ordered aperitif in the PMS.
- Serve the aperitif.
- Serve the crisps with bell pepper mayonnaise.
- Serve bread and butter.
- Present the à la carte menu and the 6-dish menu and wine pad, explain the menus/wine pad, explain the concept and promote the wine suggestions *(before elaborating on the concept, ask if the guest is familiar with our concept, or if he/she has visited us before)*.
- Take the food order, write the food docket (with an overview of who ordered what), and ask for wines and water.
- Request for the 1st appetiser at the Front Kitchen.
- Give the food docket to the Supervisor and communicate any specialties.
- Book the food order and beverages in the PMS.
- Clear the crisps when finished.

- Serve the water (and wine/beverage, depending if the aperitif is finished). Serve the 1st appetiser.
- Request for the 2nd appetiser at the Front Kitchen.
- Clear the 1st appetiser.
- Serve the 2nd appetiser.
- Request for the 1st course.
- Clear the 2nd appetiser.
- Serve the wine/other beverages, (*take away the wine glasses when you are sure they will not be used*).
- Adjust the cutlery.
- Serve the 1st course.
- Carry out a Satisfaction check.

Depending on what is ordered, the following steps should be repeated with each new course:

- Remove the dirty plates and cutlery from the previous course.
- Request the next course from the Supervisor (check preparation times to ensure a smooth service).
- Adjust and replace the cutlery when necessary so that the guests have what they need.
- Prepare the *mise en place* for serving the course.

- Book the food and beverage items in the PMS.
- Serve any ordered wine before the course is served.
- Serve water and/or other beverages.
- Take away the used glasses.
- Serve the next course.

In addition to the other steps, after serving the last warm dish:
- Carry out a Satisfaction check.
- Clear the main course.
- Put the dessert (cheese) cutlery on the table.
- Try selling a glass of dessert wine/port.
- Book the beverages in the PMS.
- Serve the dessert wine/port.
- Serve cheese or dessert.
- Clear the empty plates.
- Ask if the guest would like extra coffee/tea.

- Try to sell an additional digestive and serve the drink.
- Book the coffee or tea, friandises and digestives in the PMS.
- Serve the coffee or tea with the friandises (from the cookie box).

Finally these last steps should be followed:
- Serve the second cup of coffee or tea if desired.
- WHEN THE GUEST ASKS FOR IT, present the bill (check the bill before printing).
- Escort the guest to the door, help him/her with his/her coat.
- Thank the guest for visiting our restaurant, and wish him/her a good day/evening.

After the guests have left:
- Clean and relay the table for the next guests.

Farewell phase

Farewell phase
The bill

Once a guest requests to settle the account, the bill needs to be presented very rapidly. One major source of aggravation among guests is having to wait too long before being allowed to settle their bills. Before bringing the bill,

Correct

staff must ensure that it is correct. Once the bill is confirmed, it should be presented to the guest in a folder (or in any other acceptable way). It is con-

Appropriate distance

sidered to be professional for staff to keep an appropriate distance while the guest checks the bill. The guest then pays using either a debit card, credit card or cash. There are situations when guests do not need to pay im-

On account

mediately afterwards; there, the bill is put 'on account', and it can be settled later (most often based on company arrangements). Once guests indicate that they want to leave, the host has to escort them and help them into their coats. The host then shows them the door, and extends their goodbyes appropriately, by wishing them a pleasant evening or a safe jour-

Last impression

ney home. This is the last impression the guests get of the restaurant, and it is therefore as important as the first impression.

Post-service phase

Post-service phase

Once the guests have gone, the restaurant has to be cleared and cleaned.

Cleared and cleaned

Depending on when the last guests leave, the restaurant is set up for the next shift. Some luxury restaurants set up tables of guests that have left during service, while some wait until the last guests leave. There may be situations in which part or all of the tables are set up only the following day.

Not allowed

In upscale restaurants, it is not allowed to start moving tables around while guests are still dining. It is considered unprofessional, giving the impression that guests should leave as soon as possible. Additionally, beverages and wines have to be restocked either immediately or the following day.

Shift closed

Lastly, the end-of-shift financials have to be taken care of, and the shift closed while respecting the normal operating procedures related to such activities.

5.4.2 The Restaurant Manager

In addition to the position of the Food and Beverage Director already indicated in Chapter 3, as well as the introduction of the position in Section 5.4.1, the individual responsible for the management of front-of-house operations is the *Maître d'hôtel*, also called the Restaurant Manager in more casual restaurants. A Restaurant Manager is responsible for keeping the restaurant running efficiently and profitably. A Restaurant Manager has to make sure that guests visiting the restaurant will leave with a positive impression about their lunch or dining experience, and are likely to come back or even tell others. This can only be ensured by the Restaurant Manager possessing the various characteristics and knowledge needed to be a good manager. Ten key characteristics for the position of Restaurant Manager are described here:

- Drive – if a Restaurant Manager is lacking in enthusiasm and passion, it is impossible for them to be successful in leading a restaurant. The Restaurant Manager has to be determined to be successful. Drive is the engine that will make things happen.
- Hospitality mindedness – a Restaurant Manager has to be excellent in customer service. A Restaurant Manager is the face of the restaurant, and has to be able to adapt the service to different types of guests and moments. A Restaurant Manager also has to set an example towards service staff, radiating hospitality and creating an atmosphere of excellence in service.
- Responsibility – for a manager, hospitality starts with taking responsibility for the entire operation and the processes and people involved. It starts with using self-discipline and making a choice to do the right thing in the interest of the restaurant. Once again, the *Maître d'hôtel* is a role model for the team.
- Planning and organising – because the Restaurant Manager has many responsibilities, good planning and time management are crucial. These aspects enable the Restaurant Manager to manage operations proactively instead of reactively. It is also wise to look ahead when planning, thereby avoiding stress and last minute activity – 'to govern is to see ahead'.
- Leadership skills – a must for all Restaurant Managers. Restaurant Managers need to have a clear vision of the direction the restaurant has to go in, and should be able to guide employees into whichever direction leads to service excellence and profitability. A Restaurant Manager therefore has to put the right people in the right places, know the strengths and the weaknesses of their colleagues, and to inspire and motivate them to be the best they can be. A Restaurant Manager should offer training sessions on various topics that are important in a restaurant for the support of their colleagues, instructing them on such issues as hospitality, service sequence, complaint handling, product knowledge, wine-food pairings, etc. A Restaurant Manager is responsible for the development of the employees. Furthermore, a Restaurant Manager has to create a positive atmosphere of co-operation, teamwork, and sympathy, empowering servers to work on shared goals leading to a successful operation. As control is an extremely important aspect of management, delegating and leaving responsibility to employees is a good thing, though the final check should always be performed by the Restaurant Manager.
- Communication – good communication at different levels is essential. First and foremost, a Restaurant Manager has to communicate effectively with the waiting staff on the work floor. This is best done by having a briefing before service starts. But Restaurant Manager should not only

Maître d'hôtel

Key characteristics

Drive

Hospitality mindedness

Responsibility

Planning and organising

Leadership skills

Inspire and motivate

Communication

5

© Noordhoff Uitgevers bv

perform everyday briefings; they should also organise staff meetings on a regular basis, 4-6 times a year, to discuss any other issues that need attention. The Restaurant Manager subsequently has to maintain good communication lines with the kitchen and the Head Chef. Daily one-to-one sessions with the Head Chef and good teamwork with the kitchen are crucial in running good service. It is also advisable to have meetings with both kitchen staff and service staff to discuss any necessary subjects, and to solve any issues that might have arisen. Lastly, the Restaurant Manager has to communicate with guests and suppliers, enhancing good and lasting relationships to assure repeat business.

Knowledge and expertise

- Knowledge and expertise – it is often said that 'knowledge is power.' For a Restaurant Manager, knowledge is indeed very important. They must have a good knowledge of the products being served, spending time in the kitchen to talk to Chefs in order to know the ingredients and preparation techniques used for the different dishes. Knowledge of wines and other beverages can be gained by collaborating closely with the *Sommelier* and staying up to date by attending wine and other beverage tastings. Furthermore, expertise related to basic skills, etiquette, and processes taking place in a restaurant is a requirement for all Restaurant Managers. The different food serving methods should also be part of their expertise.

Profitability awareness

Up-selling techniques

Waste and spillage

- Profitability awareness – this is a very important characteristic of a Restaurant Manager, since it directly concerns the restaurant's profit. A Restaurant Manager has to increase revenue by attracting new guests, and maximising the average amount spent by guests by using up-selling techniques. A Restaurant Manager can help reduce costs by looking closely at waste and spillage, and by training staff in pouring the right measurement of drinks. To illustrate the possible effects of using incorrect measurements, assume that a 70 cl bottle of Remy Martin VSOP costs €40.00, and that the standard amount poured for each drink is 35 ml. Also assume that this standard pouring of 35 ml is not respected, and instead 45 ml is poured and sold at the same price of €5.00 per drink in the PMS. The annual effect of this mistake is shown in Figure 5.6, assuming a year of 365 days and 5 drinks sold daily.

FIGURE 5.6 Cost effects of incorrect drink measurements

	Remy Martin VSOP 70 cl. pouring 35 ml	Remy Martin VSOP 70 cl. pouring 45 ml
Servings (700 ml/X)	20	15.56
Price per drink (€)	5.00	5.00
Revenues per bottle (€)	100.00	77.78
Drinks sold annually (5 sold daily)	1,825.00	1,825.00
Annual servings in ml (drinks * serving size)	63,875.00	82,125.00
Bottles served	91.25	117.32
Annual cost of the Remy Martin VSOP 70 cl (€)	3,650.00	4,692.86
Extra costs (€)	1,042.86	
Excess bottles sold	26.07	

The simulation in Figure 5.6 represents lost revenues of 22.22% per bottle; quite a considerable shortfall for any restaurant. It is also extremely important for a Restaurant Manager to control staff costs; one of the largest items of expenditure in a restaurant, which therefore has to be monitored closely.

A Restaurant Manager generally should have a good overview and understanding of all financial figures, and has to maintain them on a regularly basis to ensure timely and adequately management. Drafting the yearly budget, forecasting the revenues and expenses, is also part of a Restaurant Manager's job; they should be the first to be aware of the bottom line – profit. Financial figures

- Flexibility – is also very important for Restaurant Managers. For a manager, it is crucial to stay calm and organised and not to get stressed when multiple tasks have to be performed at the same time, for example during peak hours. While setting priorities is key, a positive but realistic approach to unforeseen circumstances is also essential. A Restaurant Manager has to be flexible both in terms of working days and working hours. They often work between 10 and 14 hours a day, without being able to take time off during special days or holidays like Christmas. Flexibility
Unforeseen circumstances
- Creativity – coming up with new ideas is crucial for a Restaurant Manager. In order for a restaurant to stay popular and keep guests interested, a Restaurant Manager needs to be inventive. A good knowledge of the market and a good feeling of what guests would like are key elements in staying on top. A Restaurant Manager should know what the trends are, and incorporate new successful concepts on a regular basis, thereby attracting new business and enhancing the loyalty and repeat patronage of existing relations. Creativity
Inventive

Besides these basic characteristics, there are many other tasks and responsibilities that a Restaurant Manager has to fulfil. These may include hiring the right staff, staff who preferably have the right attitude, skills and knowledge. Furthermore, a Restaurant Manager has to carry out performance appraisals and assessment interviews with staff members. A Restaurant Manager is also responsible for scheduling staff members in anticipation of (expected) business levels. In addition, the Restaurant Manager is responsible for the cleanliness of the restaurant according to HACCP rules and ISO norms (more on these in Chapter 16). Tasks and responsibilities

Before service starts, a Restaurant Manager has to make sure that all preparations needed to run a smooth service are carried out, and that everybody knows their tasks and duties. During service, the Restaurant Manager has to maintain an overview and check on the quality of service while being the host of the restaurant. In small to medium sized luxury restaurants, the Restaurant Manager is usually responsible for presenting the menu card and informing guests of special menus or dishes available. After service is complete, the Restaurant Manager has to take care of the cashier's closure and rounding off other financial activities. Quality of service

5.4.3 Back-of-house

The person responsible for the kitchen operations is the Executive Chef, who has to make sure that the food coming out of the kitchen is of a high standard, tastes delicious, and is presented in an original way. The Executive Executive Chef

Good reputation

Chef, who might have earned a good reputation over the years, is often the major reason guests come to a restaurant. There are many guests who, when making a decision to eat somewhere, base it on the 'Cuisine' of the Executive Chef. The tasks and responsibilities of the Executive Chef are indicated in Section 5.4.4. Reporting to the Executive Chef is the Sous Chef,

Sous Chef

who helps prepare the different food items needed for several dishes, and who organises and supervises the kitchen's operations before, during and

Aboyeur

after service. The Sous Chef also often takes on the role of *aboyeur*, calling orders to the *Chefs de partie*, continually instructing them on what needs to be made and when it has to be ready. This is to ensure that all individual orders of a party of guests are available simultaneously, and that dishes are finished and sent to the right tables by communicating with the runners or *commis*.

Chefs de partie

Chefs de partie are cooks who, like Chefs de rang in the service areas, are responsible for a section of the kitchen. In large upscale restaurants and

Traditional titles

hotel kitchens, the division is often made based on the traditional titles and responsibilities developed by the great and memorable French Chef Auguste Escoffier – 1846-1935 (see Section 1.2.2), and may include the following stations still found in some form or other in kitchens today:
- *Boucher* – the butcher, responsible for meats, poultry (and sometimes fish);
- *Boulanger* – the baker (breads and breakfast pastries);
- *Confiseur* – the candy chef;
- *Décorateur* – the chef responsible for making large show pieces;
- *Entremetier* – the chef in charge of entrées – might also take care of activities for the *légumier* and the *potager*;
- *Friturier* – the fry chef, responsible for chips as well as other deep fried items;
- *Garde-manger* – pantry chef in charge of all cold starters;
- *Glacier* – the ice cream chef;
- *Grillardin* – the grill chef, responsible for all grilled meats;
- *Légumier* – the vegetable chef;
- *Pâtissier* – the pastry chef, responsible for dessert items;

© Noordhoff Uitgevers bv

- *Poissonnier* – the fish chef, responsible for all fish and seafood preparations;
- *Potager* – the soup chef, in charge of soups;
- *Rôtisseur* – the chef in charge of roasts;
- *Saucier* – the sauté chef, responsible for the sauces;
- *Tournant* – swing cook or roundsman, fills in at the various stations as needed.

Nowadays, most kitchens in fine-dining restaurants use a more simplified version of the traditional *partie* system. In small to medium kitchens of fine-dining restaurants, some of the stations and the duties are usually combined. Some stations, like those of the *boucher, boulanger*, and *confiseur*, are mostly outsourced.

Simplified version

In most kitchens, there are also trainees, who go to school and work in the kitchen part-time in order to learn the skills and knowledge required to work as *Chef de partie*. This is the starting point in climbing the ladder in the kitchen brigade.

Trainees

Lastly, there are the dishwashers, responsible for cleaning used and dirty crockery, cutlery and kitchen materials, as well as making sure that cleaned materials are made available at the right locations. This job is often highly underestimated, but it is one of the most important jobs in the restaurant; if the plates are not clean, the kitchen cannot prepare the dishes and the guests cannot be served.

Dishwashers

To better understand the back-of-house activities, the kitchen timeline is divided into 3 phases: the preparation phase; the service phase; and the rounding off phase.

Kitchen timeline

Preparation phase

This is the period before guests arrive, during which all preparations of the different sections are carried out. This is also called the *mise en place*. During this phase, the quality and freshness of products in the fridges has to be checked. If the required food items are not prepared and ready for use, this will have to be done during the service phase, thus jeopardising the service. This may cause mistakes or long waiting times, and eventually results in unsatisfied guests. Good time management by the *Chef de partie* and good control by the *Sous chef* are crucial in ensuring that the *mise en place* is completed before service begins. It is important that the products prepared have to be covered, labelled with product name and date, and stored in the section's fridge or the much bigger *mise en place* fridge.

Preparation phase

Mise en place

Service phase

This is the phase during which dishes are prepared for guests already seated in the restaurant. During the service phase, the co-operation between the kitchen brigade and the service team in the restaurant determines the success of the service. Dishes have to be prepared, plated, and served to the guests at enormous speed and on a high quality level. Good team work, precise time planning, and good leadership help in enhancing the simultaneous assembly of all the food items on the plates and their delivery to the service teams. The communication between the *Sous Chef* (or Executive Chef), and the *Maître d'hôtel* (or *Chef de rang*) has to be extremely good to

Service phase

Co-operation

Communication

Mistakes

avoid errors. In the restaurant, mistakes can be turned around much more easily than in the kitchen – if the wrong glass of wine is poured, it does not take long to correct the mistake and pour a new glass, for example – but if a dish is ruined, does not taste well, or is cold, it takes much more time to prepare it anew. This means that the entire kitchen brigade has to be sharp and focussed, and they have to work together as a well-oiled machine in tandem with the equally well-focussed restaurant service team.

Rounding-off phase

Rounding-off phase

Cleaning and organising

Next shift

After service, the necessary cleaning and organising activities have to be carried out. The work stations as well as the fridges need to be cleaned and organised. Any exposed products need to be covered and stored, and those products about to reach their best-before-dates should be disposed of. If there is time, *mise en place* activities can already be carried out for the next shift, and necessary products taken from the store room or ordered from the suppliers.

5.4.4   The Executive Chef

Executive Chef

The person responsible for the management of the operations in the back-of-house is the Executive Chef. An Executive Chef is responsible for the food production and everything else that has to do with the back-of-house, including the Stewarding Department. The following list consists of 10 characteristics that an Executive Chef preferably should have:

Passion

- Passion – an Executive Chef has to have great passion for food and cooking, combined with a need to constantly attain high quality standards in the kitchen, using the best ingredients to create high quality dishes. An Executive Chef should be eager to get the best of their employees, willing them to improve every day. An Executive Chef should enjoy the whole process of developing dishes, creating menus, selecting food, and preparing dishes. What is also typical of an Executive Chef is the drive to reach 'perfection' in everything they do.

Creativity

Critical success factors

- Creativity – this is a very important characteristic that an Executive Chef should possess. Creativity is needed to develop new dishes, consisting of different components that make these dishes tasty, unique, and balance, finally resulting in a full menu. A variety of ingredients should be used, with different tastes textures, using different cooking techniques. To support creativity, Klosse (2004), in a study with 18 Master Chefs, analysed 63 different dishes and concluded that there are 6 critical success factors that increase the chance that a dish is 'good'. Although subjective, it can still increase the success chances of any dish.
  - A name and presentation meeting the expectations
  - An attractive smell that fits the dish
  - A decent balance of flavour components
  - The presence of Umami
  - A mixture of hard and soft textures in the mouth
  - High flavour content

Planning and organising

- Planning and organising – because of the two great challenges found in the kitchen (working with perishable products and working with people), it is highly important that there is a clear schedule of what tasks need to be executed for what period of time. An Executive Chef therefore needs a good overview is of all the complex processes and work that need to be done by the various parties.

- Leadership skills – an Executive Chef is the person responsible for leading the entire kitchen brigade. An Executive Chef should be an example to all subordinates and be able to translate the underlying vision to the team, resulting in serving top quality dishes. The Executive Chef is responsible for motivating, training and coaching staff in order to get make them all they can be. The Executive Chef understands that everyone should work in harmonious to ensure that dishes are served on time, especially because staff often works under (time) pressure, in hectic and busy circumstances. This also means that the Executive Chef sometimes has to intervene directly and decisively. If certain situations or problems occur, the Executive Chef has to be able to handle them quickly and make the appropriate decisions. By acting immediately, guests will be kept satisfied and operations will continue to flow fluidly. Leadership skills
Example
- Communication – apart from management skills, an Executive Chef should also have good communication skills. Firstly, it is essential for an Executive Chef to communicate clearly to the Sous chef, who is the main assistant, and to lead the *chefs de partie* directly. Besides that, the Executive Chef needs communication well with other back-of-house staff. Secondly, there has to be sound communication with the service brigade, especially the *Maître d'hôtel*. This is essential in order to avoid mistakes, and to ensure a smooth service. Thirdly, the Executive Chef has to have good contacts with suppliers, which often benefit from lifelong relationships. Lastly, the communication with guests is extremely important. As mentioned before, the guest often comes for the 'Cuisine' of the Executive Chef, which means that the role of host is not only reserved for the *Maître d'hôtel* but also for the Executive Chef (regarded as 'the face' of the restaurant). Communication

Good contacts
- Knowledge and expertise – an Executive Chef has to have a wide knowledge of the products and their characteristics, the materials used to produce dishes, and the different cooking techniques. But knowledge and expertise in the field of health and safety are also must-haves, as the Executive Chef is responsible for the hygiene and cleanliness of the kitchen. To keep up with new trends and developments, Executive Chefs should stay up-to-date with food industry developments, and if possible attend master classes and other courses to keep their knowledge and expertise current. Knowledge and expertise

Up-to-date
- Business mindedness – it is the Executive Chef's task to not only run a kitchen producing quality food and dishes, but also to do this in an efficient and cost effective manner. The Executive Chef has to reduce waste to the barest minimum, and if possible re-use products that can no longer be used for their original purposes. Leftover vegetables may be used in making sauces or soups, for example. The Executive Chef is responsible for the cost calculations of all dishes. This means that the cost of every single ingredient used in the dish is calculated, so that when the total is added up, the costs (cost price) compared to the selling price (excl. VAT) should indicate cost percentages varying between 25% and 40%. Very often, food cost percentage targets are set by the General Manager or Owner. The productivity of the workforce also has to be closely monitored to avoid high labour costs. Business mindedness
Reduce waste

Cost calculations
- Multi-tasking – an Executive Chef regularly thinks about and handles many things at the same time. While a single *Chef de partie* is responsible for a few items of a dish, the Executive Chef has to maintain the Multi-tasking

5

overview, and ensures that everything needed is brought to the various sections and completed simultaneously.

Stress-resistant

- Stress-resistant – a busy kitchen is often a very stressful environment. An Executive Chef has to be able to deal with moments of stress, and stay alert and focussed in the fast pace of the kitchen, constantly producing top quality dishes under pressure.

Flexibility

- Flexibility – the working times and hours of an Executive Chef are not ideal. If lunch service is offered, hours can go up to 16 hours a day. The busiest periods are usually the weekends and festive moments, when most other people are off work. Although this is part of the job, it still requires flexibility. On the work floor, the Executive Chef has to be flexible as well. The guests in the front-of-house have a major influence on how an evening is going to run. If guests have certain wishes or requirements – for example dietary requests or allergies – the kitchen needs to adapt to these quickly and should try to satisfy guests with alternative dishes. This requires the Executive Chef to have a flexible mentality as well.

5.5 Room service

Room service

Room service is a service offered by a hotel, offering guests the option of having food and beverages delivered to their rooms. This service is available in most full service hotels, making it possible for guests to enjoy their meals and drinks in their own private setting. While some hotels provide this amenity 24 hours per day, others may only offer breakfast for room service. The **Reasons** reasons for guests preferring to order room service instead of having a meal in the restaurant can vary; from a business guest who needs to get some work done, preferring to work in a private surrounding not to be disturbed to a couple wanting to have a cosy dinner for two. Sometimes, complete meetings are organised in hotel rooms (suites) where room service is required. **In-room dining** Room service can also be presented as 'in-room dining', which sounds much more appealing and emphasises the dining experience of the guests. In large hotels, there is a separate room service department serving high volumes of room service. The person in charge of this department is the Room **Room Service Manager** Service Manager, who is responsible for the quality of every aspect that concerns room service. The Room Service Manager has to set and maintain the SOPs, plan the room service menu, and make sure the room service ordertakers, attendants, and cooks are doing their jobs well. Furthermore, the training and development of all room service staff is part of the responsibili- **Room service process** ties of the Room Service Manager. The room service process can be divided into four parts: order taking; preparation and setting up the cart; delivery; and clearing. To be able to offer a constant quality of service, it is important that there are guidelines on how to operate for all four parts of the room service process; these should be provided in the SOPs. Figure 5.7 is an example of a room service SOP, indicating what a server should do when delivering a room service order to a hotel room at Stenden Hotel.

In smaller hotels, room service activities are incorporated into the Food and Beverage Department. The staff member in charge of room service activities is then the Food and Beverage Manager, and food items are produced by the restaurant's chefs, with the delivery being carried out by the restaurant's waiters.

FIGURE 5.7 SOP serving room service

Stenden hotel
★ ★ ★ ★

Standard operating procedure – Serving room service in the hotel room

Department: Room Service   **What: Serving room service in the hotel room**

Position: Server   **Nr.: 2015/241**

Steps	How should we do it?	Why do we do it?
Knocking on the door.	Knock on the hotel room door twice and announce yourself as 'room service'.	To announce yourself professionally.
	If there is a 'Do Not Disturb' sign on the door, call the room from the nearest telephone, and inform the guest of the situation (the guest might have forgotten to remove the sign).	To respect the DND sign and the privacy of the guests.
	Greet the guest, introduce yourself using your name, and use the guest's name if possible.	To make the guests to feel comfortable in the room environments.
Entering the room.	Always request the guest's permission if you may enter the room.	To make the guests to feel comfortable to allow a third party to enter their hotel rooms and private spaces.
	If you are entering with a cart, place the door stopper under the door to leave the door open when you enter the room.	
Serving the order.	Ask the guest where in the hotel room the order is to be placed.	
	Explain all the served dishes.	Informing and educating the guests about the ordered food and beverage products, and ensuring that the order is complete.
	Remove the plate covers from the plates when you are explaining the dishes.	
	Ensure that the order is complete.	
Explaining dirty dishes clearing, signing of the bill, and leaving the room.	Explain the removal procedure of the dirty dishes.	Ensuring dirty dishes will be removed from the room properly and efficiently.
	Present the bill to the guest, and request to have it signed by the guest. Retrieve it after it has been signed.	In order to avoid any possible dispute of the charges.
	Ask the guest if there is anything else you can assist with.	
	Wish the guest a pleasant meal, and a good (time of) day and leave the room. Use the guest's name. Make sure you close the door properly.	

5.5.1   Profitability concerns

The provision of room service creates some profitability concerns for hospitality operations. Because of the time involved in the whole process from taking orders to clearing the dirty dishes, room service labour costs are comparatively high. In particular, the transportation of the ordered food and bev-

Profitability concerns

erage items can take a long time, certainly if the room is located in a remote area. In addition, the investment costs for the equipment like room service carts and hot boxes can be significant. Another profitability concern is that guests sometimes take souvenirs home from the carts, including glassware, cutlery, or other materials; these then have to be replaced. Because of the high costs involved, room service operates at a loss in many hotels, even when the prices of the menu items are of a higher level and a room service fee is charged. On the other hand, some guests also select hotels on the basis of availability of room service, so it can generate revenue as well.

5.5.2   Menu planning

Room service menu

Sales and marketing tool

The room service menu firstly contains the list of food and beverage items available for sale; guests can make their selection from this list. Secondly, the room service menu can serve as a sales and marketing tool, which can increase a guest's average spending. The design of the room service menu has to be in line with what the department (or even hotel) wants to communicate. In some hotels, there are special breakfast menu cards placed in the room to be filled in by guests and hung on the door handles. These menu cards are picked up at a later stage and given to the room service cook and attendant to prepare.

Quality

Because of the distance covered from the (room service) kitchen to the room, and the challenges this brings regarding quality, the room service menu has to be carefully planned. The quality of the dishes on the room service menu should be maintained as best as possible. That is why the room service menu should only offer dishes or menu items that cannot be affected during the transportation of the items from the (room service) kitchen to the guest room. Cold dishes and drinks should be served cold, and hot dishes and drinks should be served hot. Often 'hotboxes' and plate covers are used; these are placed underneath the cart and ensure that the hot dishes remain hot during transport. There are, however, some popular products that are always found on room service menus although they very easily get cold; examples include chips and omelettes.

Adapted

It is essential when planning the menu that the room service menu is adapted to the capacity of the (room service) kitchen. If beautiful, complicated dishes are available from the menu but the (room service) kitchen is not able to produce them, rooms service overall will be considered a failure. It is also important, especially if room service activities are integrated in the Restaurant Department, that ingredients used are also usable in the restaurant. This prevents products having to be thrown away if the dishes on the room service menu are not ordered. It is often better to have a room service menu with a limited selection of dishes which can be easily prepared while safeguarding their quality, than offering an extended menu where both timely service and quality cannot be guaranteed.

5.5.3   Operating issues

Operating

Unpredictable

Unfortunately, there are some operating issues involved in the room service offering. The first one is scheduling room service attendants. The unpredictable nature of room service, combined with slow periods, makes it difficult for the Room Service Manager to schedule the shifts efficiently. A restaurant is able to spread out the flow of guests by managing reservations and, for example, by using the bar as an aperitif area – room service employees do not have these opportunities. They have to take the orders as they come

Room #

_____

*S*TART YOUR DAY OFF RIGHT WITH OUR BREAKFAST
PRE-ORDER. MAKE YOUR BREAKFAST SELECTIONS
TONIGHT, THEN HANG IT OUTSIDE ON THE DOOR KNOB
BEFORE 3:00 A.M.

Select a delivery time:

☐ 5:00 - 5:30 a.m.   ☐ 6:30 - 7:00 a.m.   ☐ 8:00 - 8:30 a.m.
☐ 5:30 - 6:00 a.m.   ☐ 7:00 - 7:30 a.m.   ☐ 8:30 - 9:00 a.m.
☐ 6:00 - 6:30 a.m.   ☐ 7:30 - 8:00 a.m.   ☐ 9:00 - 9:30 a.m.

CONTINENTAL BREAKFAST
Please indicate quantity in the box next to each item.

JUICES
☐ Orange
☐ Apple
☐ Grapefruit

BREADS AND PASTRIES
☐ Fresh Fruit Bowl
☐ Danish Pastries
☐ Assortment of Muffins
☐ Croissants
☐ Doughnuts
☐ White Toast
☐ Whole Wheat Toast
☐ English Muffins
☐ Bagel

CONDIMENTS
☐ Selection of
   Jams and Honey
☐ Margarine
☐ Butter
☐ Cream Cheese

COLD CEREALS
Served with Milk:
☐ Whole
☐ Skim
☐ Low Fat

☐ Corn Flakes
☐ Raisin Bran
☐ Rice Krispies
☐ Froot Loops
☐ Special K
☐ Frosted Flakes
☐ Low-Fat Granola

BEVERAGES
☐ Low Fat Milk
☐ Whole Milk
☐ Skim Milk
☐ Chocolate Milk
☐ 100% Columbian Coffee
☐ 100% Columbian
   Decaffeinated Coffee
☐ Selection of Teas
☐ Hot Chocolate

5

and spring into action. A partial solution would be to train staff to be able to work in other departments, in order to mitigate labour costs.

Language barriers

Another operating issue is caused by language barriers, because hotels often house international guests. Some guests may be unable to read a menu written in the local language, and thus will have difficulties ordering from the menu. This can be solved using new technology, for example by providing a fixed computing device in the rooms with software that can translate menu items into multiple languages. The use of pictures can be also very helpful to guests.

Communication

As in other departments, communication can also be an operating issue. For room service, the risk of not receiving the order as meant by the guest is higher because, at times, communication takes place over the phone. That is why – just like in a restaurant – the order has to be repeated to make sure it is correctly understood. A room service order taker also has to have a room service menu card with relevant questions for all dishes. Should, for example, a steak be rare, medium, or well-done; should an omelette be served with cheese, etc.

Opportunity

A room service order taker can also use the opportunity to up-sell the food and beverage items, for example by suggesting a drink, some bread, a starter, or even a dessert. This opportunity for up-selling may not always be used, and is thus an operating issue in the Room Service Department.

Contact

In offering room service, the contact with guests takes place in the guest rooms. Its duration is only a limited period in the whole room service process, especially when compared to the restaurant where employees are constantly in contact with guests. It is crucial that a room service attendant provides good quality service, knows how to set up the room service cart or tray, has the skills necessary to serve drinks (such as opening a bottle of wine), explains the procedures of clearing the room service items, presents the bill and secures payment or gets a signature and, most importantly, is professional and offers genuine hospitality to guests. Clear SOPs and proper training ensure the constant delivery of good quality room service.

5.6 Conference and Banqueting

Function rooms
Food and beverage services

The Conference and Banqueting Department offers function rooms and other areas in the hotel, together with food and beverage services for groups of people visiting an event in the hotel. Examples are conferences, meetings, product presentations, dinners, receptions, parties, weddings, etc. There are two types of groups that use conference and banqueting facilities within a ho-

Business-related

tel. The first group is business-related, such as companies or professional associations, often having conventions and business meetings within the hotel

Social-oriented

during which food and beverage items are provided. The second group is social-oriented, such as weddings, anniversaries, special birthdays, christenings, award ceremonies, graduations, proms, charity events, etc. The person responsible for making sure all aspects of this department run smoothly is the

Conference and Banqueting Manager

Conference and Banqueting Manager, who reports directly to the Food and Beverage Manager. It is of utmost importance that the appointments made between clients and the hotel's sales department are followed up by the ban-

Fact sheet

queting operations. Whatever the event, it requires an established fact sheet (or function sheet) containing all the information of the event like the event programme, the food and beverage items to be served, special requests, room set-ups, audio-visual equipment needs, and other important information. The Conference and Banqueting Manager has to lead and supervise the Banqueting Supervisors (Captains), who are responsible for the direct operations and contacts with the contact persons of the meetings and events.

It is essential that the event or meeting principals are welcomed in a hospitable fashion, and that the service during the meeting or event is of a high standard. To assure this quality of service (as with all other areas of hospitality operations), SOPs are used. Text 5.9 is an SOP emphasising one aspect – hospitality guidelines for all Conference and Banqueting Department waiters.

Event or meeting principals

TEXT 5.9

Showing Hospitality Guidelines for Banquet Waiters (taken and adapted from Mövenpick Hotel Amsterdam City Centre's Banquet Waiter Manual)

Showing Hospitality

- Mövenpick addresses the interaction between the guest and the employee with the 'Yes with Pleasure!' philosophy. Within Mövenpick each and every employee looks for, responds to, and exceeds the needs of the guests.
- Always greet the guests that you encounter, and leave everything else when recognising a guest.
- When communicating with a guest, show initiative, ensure eye contact, listen carefully, show interest, and mention the guest's name if possible.
- Help them if they have any questions. If you do not know the answer to the question, inform the guest that you do not know and ask somebody that does know the answer.
- Walk with the guests if they ask for a direction. Never point.
- You are responsible that the food and beverage products are placed on time.
- Communicate with other departments (kitchen) about amounts, and times etc. when necessary.
- A smoothly-run operation depends on the co-operation of all departments, and close teamwork between all staff members. Remember the word 'TEAM' stands for Together Everyone Accomplishes More.
- Inform management if the guests want any additional food and beverage products.

Banqueting
Supervisors

The Banqueting Supervisors have to lead, guide and work alongside the servers responsible for serving coffee, tea, lunches, dinners, and other food and beverage products during meetings and conferences, as well as dishes, snacks and beverages during banquets. Having a good, detailed planning is necessary for the Conference and Banqueting Manager to make sure that all tasks are performed on time. Furthermore, the banquet servers have to set up the rooms with tables and chairs prior to the conference or banquet event, sometimes even during the event if the layout needs to be changed.

Last minute
changes

Last minute changes occur regularly, requiring a flexible attitude from the servers. Meetings and banquets often use audio-visual equipment such as projectors, screens, sound equipment, and music equipment. It is essential that all equipment works properly. At the end of any event, rooms have to be set-up for the next event, and food, beverages, room rent, equipment and other costs have to be charged appropriately.

5.6.1   Sales

Banquets Sales
Manager

Conferences, meetings and banquets are booked through the Sales Department. The Banquets Sales Manager is responsible for filling up the different rooms in the conference and banquets department. They have to attract new business, maintain regular clientele, and make sure that the process of organising a conference or event is correctly handled, making sure that the information required by the conference and banquets operations and guests is accurate, clear and complete.

Banquet Event
Order

In order to organise a successful meeting or event, the Salesperson and Banqueting Manager need to know the details of their guests' wishes. These details include numbers of guests, event programmes, service style, room set-ups, selected food and beverages, decorations, entertainment, speakers, audio-visual requirements, and any dietary requests, etc. Once these details are known, the Sales Department puts everything on paper and sends a Banquet Event Order (BEO) to the event principal. This BEO is based on the correspondence with the event principal, and the notes made during their visits. The BEO is sent in two copies: one for the client to sign and return to the hotel, the other for their own administration. Since this concerns a contractual arrangement, it is important that the BEO covers such topics as:

- a final date until which the room is held available without a signed contract;
- a date by which the number of guest has to be established;
- cancellation policies;
- payment agreements;
- special arrangements related to prices and discounts;
- health and safety regulations (for example relating to alcohol consumption by minors);
- other information relevant to the event, such as signage, etc.

Text 5.10 is taken and adapted from the BEO of NH Hotels, and relates to conference and event cancellation conditions.

TEXT 5.10

General conferences and events cancellation conditions NH Hotels

General cancellation conditions

Cancellation should take place in writing and is to be dated. The customer cannot derive any rights from a verbal cancellation. The date on which the written confirmation of the cancellation is received will be considered the definite date of cancellation. The cancellation fee will be based upon the total value of the reservation, as within the most recent confirmation letter of the group, event or conference.

This cancellation clause applies to the following types of cancellations:
a When the entire event is cancelled
b When cancelling a part of the facilities for the event (e.g. meal, break-out room)
c Reduction of the duration of the event as result of which the reservation value is reduced
d Reduction in the contracted number of guests
e When the entire event is rescheduled to a different date

Cancellation conditions of hotel bedrooms
a Up to 90 days before the arrival date, no charges.
b Between 89 and 30 days before the arrival date, 10% of the contracted rooms may be cancelled without any costs.

All cancellations above this percentage will be charged at 30% of the cancelled reservation value.
c Between 29 and 14 days before the arrival date, 10% of the remaining rooms may be cancelled without any costs. All cancellations above this percentage will be charged at 50% of the cancelled reservation value.
d Between 13 and 8 days before the arrival date, 5% of the remaining rooms may be cancelled without any costs. All cancellations above this percentage will be charged at 80% of the cancelled reservation value.
e All rooms cancelled 7 days or less before the arrival date will be charged at 100% of the cancelled reservation value.
f No shows will be charged at 100% of the cancelled reservation value.

Considering our cancellation policy, we advise you to inform us as soon as possible about any changes in your reservation.

5.6.2 Profitability opportunities

Because the Conference and Banqueting Department mostly hosts groups of guests at events of which the date, programme, number of guests (formally guaranteed), and food and beverage products (menus) served are known in advance, it is easier to schedule the right amount of staff, both in service and in the kitchen. This leads to an efficient input of hours, thus contributing to lower labour costs. Labour costs are also lower because part-time banquet servers can be called in as needed, such as during peak times. As such, the basic banqueting team can be kept relatively small.   *Known in advance*

The costs of sales of the food products can also be kept low since, because of the high volumes concerned, a better price can be agreed with the suppliers. The menu ordered by the guests is usually also more expensive because of the festive nature of most such banqueting events, generally leading to a better contribution margin. Beverage costs can also be reduced by   *Costs of sales*

buying in bulk. Drinks served during receptions, parties and dinners contribute to the department's revenue and profitability to a large extent. The amounts of drinks consumed at social events like weddings or other parties is generally higher than normal. It also depends if drinks have been paid for by the hosts or company, or if drinks are to be paid for by individual guests. Whatever the case, these events offer a great opportunity to not only offer great quality service, but also to increase revenue by actively serving drinks, contributing to the financial success of the department.

Higher than normal

Commissions

More income through commissions can also be generated through the use of third-party companies, such as bakers, florists, photographers, or entertainers, offering their products and services during events. These third-parties sometimes pay commissions as preferred partners/suppliers, or the hotel charges the event taking into account third-party supplier costs.

5.6.3   Menu planning

Banquet menus

Menu planning is slightly different in the Banqueting Department than in the Restaurant. The banquet menus are often limited in their offering and are communicated to the person hosting the event to make a choice in advance. Menu suggestions can differ depending on the nature of the event: a menu suggestion for a wedding is different from a menu suggestion for a business dinner. The Chef in charge of developing the menus has to make sure that these are of good quality, that the dishes are reasonably easy to make, are presented in a fine manner, and contain enough nutritious ingredients. Because many guests have to be served simultaneously in a short period of time (especially where hot dishes are concerned), the speed of preparing and plating up the dishes has to be of a much higher level than in a Restaurant. The points of contact involved in plating the dishes should be limited to 5 or 6. At peak moments when courses are served, there is usually a line-up of cooks putting one menu item on the plate, and then moving the plate onward (like a conveyor belt). It is crucial that the chefs have the right materials to put the food items on the plates, and that the products are supplied in time so that the train of movement does not come to a standstill. The speed of the servers has to be in tune with the speed of plating up in the kitchen. A good coordination of the service staff is necessary to ensure fluid service.

Speed

Peak moments

5.6.4   Service methods

Styles

For banquets, as in restaurant service, there are various methods (or styles) used in serving food and beverage products. When it comes to food, the major table styles are commonly denominated in the French language and consist of:

French language

- *le service plat sur table;*
- *le service à l'assiette;*
- *le service à l'anglaise;*
- *le service à la française;*
- *le service à la russe.*

Apart from these, non-table-based service styles exist as well. For coffee, tea, water, and other beverages, multiple styles are also in use, and these styles are summarily explained in the following sub-sections.

Le service plat sur table (the plate service method)

Service plat sur table

This method is used quite frequently for sit-down dinners. Dishes are prepared on the plate, and the guest is served at the table from their right-hand side. A popular version of this method is the walking dinner, where a menu of 6-12 small dishes, prepared on plates and transported on trays, is quickly served one dish after the other. This method is labour intensive but, compared to a buffet style service, food costs are kept relatively low.

Le service à l'assiette (le service à l'américaine or the tray method)

This is a variation of the plate service method and includes a serving tray. Plates are put on a tray in the kitchen, carried into the restaurant and put on a service station by the *Commis du rang* or Runner. Plates are then served to the guests from the tray. There are various methods used in carrying plates, and Figure 5.8 adapted from the Mövenpick Banquet Waiter Manual illustrates some common methods.

Service à l'assiette

FIGURE 5.8 Methods for carrying plates

Methods for Carrying Plates

Upper hand carrying method

The first plate is held with the thumb, index finger and middle finger (of left hand).
The thumb should be as much as possible at the edge of the plate, and pointing to the right.
The index finger is positioned underneath, but within the edge of the plate.

The ring finger, and the little finger that stick out of the plate, build up with the mouse (ball) of the hand, and the forearm into one horizontal surface.
On this surface it is possible to place the second plate.

Underhand carrying method

The first plate should be held in the same way as in the upper hand carrying method.

The second plate is placed underneath the first plate.
The edge of the second plate is placed against the index finger, underneath the edge of the first plate.
The middle finger, ring finger, and the little finger hold the second plate from below.

The hand (with the 2 plates) is turned inside through the wrist. Because of this, the edge of the second plate, the mouse (ball) of the hand, and the forearm form a horizontal surface upon which the third plate is placed.

Le service à l'anglaise (serving out method)

This method involves the server bringing and posing a plate in front of each guest, which is later served from their left-hand side. Food is artistically plated in the kitchen, brought to the guests, and skilfully served using serving cutlery. This style requires skill and training, is labour intensive, but gives an extra dimension to the service.

Service à l'anglaise

Le service à l'anglaise avec guéridon (guéridon or trolley service method)

À l'anglaise avec guéridon

This service style is a variation on the serving out method. A guéridon is a movable service or trolley on which food can be carved, filtered, flambéed or prepared and served. It is, in other words, a movable side board which has sufficient equipment for the immediate operation at hand; however, it should also carry essential equipment, e.g. crockery or cutlery service gear. It includes equipment for carving, salad preparation, preparation of fresh fruit, etc. This method is not often used at banquets but mostly at relatively small private settings. This method is very labour intensive, demands great skill and craftsmanship of the servants, but offers a fantastic experience for the guests. Figure 5.9 is a picture of a guéridon.

Small private settings

FIGURE 5.9 A guéridon

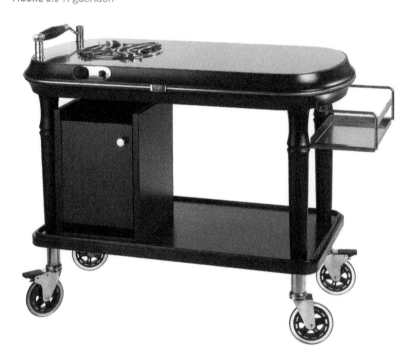

Le service à la française (presentation method)

Service à la française

For this method, food items and dishes are presented to the guests on the condition that guests take their own food instead of being served. Originally, the meal was divided into three services: soups and fish; roasts; and desserts. Each service included a variety of dishes, all served at the table at the same time as the desserts and appetisers. Guests gathered round the table and helped themselves to foods that suited them while standing. Tables were set and food was served before the arrival of guests, with waiters bringing in new serving dishes as needed to replace emptied dishes ensuring food was always available. If a buffet service is used, food items are attractively displayed on a buffet, where warm dishes are kept warm in chafing dishes or on hot plates (*rechauds*), and guests can help themselves while walking along the buffet. It is important that the food items are refilled in a timely manner. This method requires less service staff than the plate service method, for example, but food costs will generally be higher.

© Noordhoff Uitgevers bv

Le service à la russe (combined or platter method)

This is a method that involves courses being brought to the table in sequence. This is an elaborate silver service, much along the lines of *le service à la française*, except that food is portioned and carved by the waiter at the guéridon in full view of the guests in the restaurant. Display and presentation are a major part of this service. The principle is to present guests with whole joints, poultry, game and fish which has been elaborately dressed and garnished, which is then carved and portioned by the waiter. As there are multiple variations; for the most correct *service à la russe*, (source: www.wikipedia.org) the following rules must be observed:

- The place setting for each guest includes a service plate, all the necessary cutlery except those required for dessert, and stemmed glasses for water, wines and champagne. This setting is called a cover. On top of the service plate is a rolled-up napkin, and on top of that is the place card. At the top of the plate are a saltcellar, nut dish, and a menu;
- From the outside in, the cutlery to the right of the service plate consists of the oyster fork resting in the bowl of the soup spoon, the fish knife, the meat knife and the salad knife (or fruit knife). On the left, from the outside in, are the fish fork, the meat fork and a salad fork (or fruit fork);
- Guests are seated according to their place cards and immediately remove their napkins and place them in their laps once seated. Another accepted variation holds that the napkin is only removed once the host/hostess has removed theirs. Similarly, the host/hostess is the first to start eating, and guests follow. The oyster plate is then placed on top of the service plate. Once cleared, it is replaced by the soup plate. Once the soup course is finished, both the soup plate and service plate are removed from the table, and a preheated plate is put in their place;
- The fish and meat courses are always served from platters; a filled plate is never placed before a guest in correct service, as this would indirectly dictate how much food the guest is to eat;
- Right before dessert, everything but the wine and water glasses is removed from the place settings. Crumbs are dusted. The dessert plate is then brought out with a doily on top of it, a finger bowl on top of that, and a fork and spoon, the former balanced on the left side of the plate and the latter on the right. Guests remove the doily and finger bowls, move them to the left of the plate and place the fork to the left side of the plate and the spoon to its right. Guests do not actually need to use the finger bowl, since they may not have used their fingers to eat with, unless they also had bread with the meal.

Other common service methods in the hospitality industry

Snack-bar service

Tall stools are placed along a counter so that guests may eat the food at the counter itself. In up-market establishments, the covers are laid out on the counter. Food is either displayed behind the counter for guests to choose from or displayed on either screens or menu cards.

Buffet service

In this method, guests enter the dining area and retrieve the food from a buffet counter either individually or partly assisted by servers. Food is displayed on tables and guests take their plates from a stack at the end of each table, or request service from the servers behind the buffet tables. For sit-down buffet service, tables are laid with crockery and cutlery as in a restaurant. Guests may serve themselves at the buffet table and return to eat at the laid out guest tables. Servers may serve a few courses, like appetisers or soups, at the table. See Section 5.6.5 for further details related to set-up styles at banquets.

Self-service

Self-service

In this method, guests enter the dining area, select their own trays with cutlery, and collect food from the food counter before proceeding to their seating places.

Cafeteria service

Cafeteria service

This method is normally applied in industrial canteens, colleges, hospitals or hotel cafeterias. To facilitate quick service, a fixed menu is displayed on large boards. Guests may have to buy coupons in advance, and present them to the counter attendant who then serves the requested item. Food is sometimes displayed behind the counter and guests may indicate their choice to the counter attendant. Food is served pre-plated, and cutlery is handed to the guest directly. Guests may then sit at tables and chairs provided by the establishment or, if high tables are provided, stand up to eat.

Coffee, tea and water service

Coffee, tea and water service

Different methods

Similar to serving food, there are also different methods of serving beverages. For conferences and meetings, coffee and tea service depends on the kind of meeting, the set-up of the meeting room, the location of the breaks, the time available, and the preferences of the guests. When coffee and tea are served inside the meeting room or in a separate area, they are usually served in flasks; depending on the set-up, they are available either at a coffee/tea station or on top of the tables of the set-up. Depending on guests' wishes, coffee and tea may only be served while guests are being welcomed or during breaks. Establishments often offer package deals where coffee, tea and water are included in the price. Coffee and tea corners are frequently utilised, where freshly ground and brewed coffee or hot water and various teas can be collected by guests themselves. Another method of coffee and tea service is that serving staff pour the coffee and tea for the guests from the flasks. Cups are placed on a service station and servers pour coffee or tea before handing them over to guests. A variation of this service is that the coffee is already in cups, freshly produced from a coffee machine, and then served using a tray. Water is commonly served in bottles, placed in the meeting rooms, and guests can serve themselves.

Other beverages

At dinner, one common service method for beverages is to serve wines from the bottle, from a guest's right-hand side. At receptions, it is more common to serve the beverages from a tray. To offer guests a variety of drinks, beverages placed on the tray are mostly white and red wine, orange juice, soft drinks, and water as part of the standard assortment. Beer is usually served upon request because beer cannot hold its foam for extended periods of time. Another method is to serve drinks from a beverage buffet where guests can take the drinks from appropriate glasses that have previously been filled by service staff. There may be a person handing out beverages and making sure new drinks are poured.

There is also the bar service where bar staff provide a wide range of drinks. There are different ways beverages can be charged, with wine poured at dinner often charged per bottle. Beverages served by the glass are mostly charged by the glass, either to the account of the principal event organiser, or individually using cash or tokens. Some establishments offer package deals on the basis of an estimated average number of drinks per person, or an hourly rate per capita.

5.6.5   Conference and Banquet set-ups

Depending on the type of meeting or conference and the amount of attendees, the Conference and Banqueting Department may offer one of many basic types of set-ups as described in this subsection. It should be noted that room capacity and aisle size are regulated by local fire departments, and Figure 5.10 indicates the various conference rooms and their different capacities depending on set-up as used by the Mövenpick Hotel Amsterdam City Centre's conference facilities.

(Margin notes: Other beverages; Standard assortment; Bar service; Set-ups; Regulated)

FIGURE 5.10 Dimensions and capacity of Mövenpick Hotel Amsterdam City Centre's conference facilities

MÖVENPICK
Hotels & Resorts

Convention rooms - Amsterdam City Centre

(data of the Foyers 1 & 2, and Atrium excluded)

Dimensions

Room	Length	Width	Height	Area	Theatre	Classroom	U-shape	Carré	Boardroom	Banquet	Cabaret
					Conference seating capacity						
Matterhorn 1	15.45 m	8.33 m	3.10 m	128.70 m²	110	50	32	38	-	96	40
Matterhorn 2	15.45 m	8.97 m	3.10 m	138.60 m²	130	56	32	38	-	96	60
Matterhorn 3	13.88 m	8.26 m	3.10 m	114.65 m²	120	42	28	36	-	88	40
Matterhorn 1-2	15.45 m	17.29 m	3.10 m	267.13 m²	250	120	44	64	-	192	100
Matterhorn 1-2-3	15.45 m	25.55 m	3.10 m	394.75 m²	450	160	66	-	-	280	175
Matterhorn 2-3	15.45 m	17.23 m	3.10 m	266.20 m²	250	98	40	60	-	184	95
Zurich 1	14.30 m	10.68 m	3.10 m	152.72 m²	130	72	38	44	-	96	60
Zurich 2	14.30 m	12.82 m	3.10 m	183.33 m²	150	60	38	44	-	128	80
Zurich 1-2	14.30 m	23.50 m	3.10 m	336.05 m²	300	130	66	-	-	256	160
Basel	7.50 m	5.11 m	3.10 m	42.52 m²	-	-	-	-	16	-	-
Geneva	7.50 m	5.11 m	3.10 m	42.52 m²	-	-	-	-	16	-	-
Luzern	7.50 m	4.68 m	3.10 m	38.94 m²	30	12	15	-	16	16	12
St. Gallen	7.50 m	4.70 m	3.10 m	36.39 m²	30	12	15	-	16	16	12
Lausanne	7.50 m	4.50 m	3.10 m	38.08 m²	30	12	15	-	16	16	12
Monte Rosa	7.40 m	6.20 m	2.20 m	45.88 m²	50	22	16	20	16	40	20
Winterthur	7.50 m	4.50 m	3.10 m	37.77 m²	30	12	15	-	16	16	12

Theatre or auditorium style

This style requires only chairs, which are set up in rows facing the stage or speakers; it is mainly used for small or large groups that require little or limited note-taking by participants.

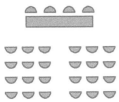

Classroom or schoolroom style

This style requires tables, set up in conjunction with rows of chairs all facing the stage or speakers; it is used for sessions in which note-taking by participants is required, such as during training sessions. Figure 5.11 is an illustration of the schoolroom set-up at the Stenden Hotel.

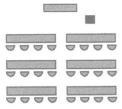

FIGURE 5.11 Schoolroom set-up at one of the Stenden Hotel meeting rooms

U-shape or horseshoe style

This style requires tables are set up in a u-shape with chairs behind the tables, in situations where small groups require face-to-face interaction. Figure 5.12 shows the horsehoe style of the Mövenpick Hotel Amsterdam.

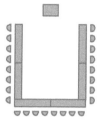

FIGURE 5.12 Horseshoe set-up – Mövenpick Hotel Amsterdam City Centre

Carré or hollow square style

This style is similar to the u-shape, except that the open end is now closed; it applies for situations where neither a head table nor a projector are required, or alternatively when multiple screens are set up within the hollow for comfortable viewing by the participants from all seats.

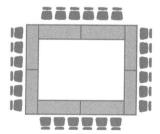

Boardroom or conference style

This style consists of one large meeting table or several smaller tables set up as block of tables with chairs around them. Some hotels have permanently outfitted boardrooms. In some companies, there are specially placed boardrooms for the management of the companies to meet on a regular basis. Boardrooms are generally well decorated, have beautifully designed tables and comfortable chairs, and are set up with all the trappings of top level quality used in the domain.

Boardroom

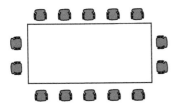

Cabaret

In this style, chairs are set up around the tables, with many variations depending on table sizes and shapes (rectangular or circular), which will have an influence on the maximum number of seats to be placed around each. Figure 5.13 shows the cabaret set-up of the Mövenpick Hotel Amsterdam City Centre, placing 8 persons per table.

Cabaret

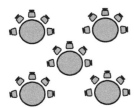

For clients, it is very important that the hotel or banqueting service provides them with an overview of the different rooms and available set-ups, enabling guests then to make the right choices to match the requirements for their specific events or functions. Furthermore, the hotel or banqueting service must ensure that all required audio visual equipment is in good working order, and that lighting and temperature are set up appropriately.

Match

FIGURE 5.13 Cabaret set-up – Mövenpick Hotel Amsterdam City Centre

Banquet

Banquet

Concerning the banquet set-up styles, there are many possibilities depending on the nature of the party or event. There is also a number of issues to closely look at before deciding on the set-up. Most importantly, guests all need to have enough space to sit down or stand up comfortably. There also needs to be enough space for servers to be able to walk around. In addition, it may be necessary to reserve space for buffets, portable bars, entertainment, bands, dance floors, and any other required activities. If there are buffets and beverage serving points involved, enough walking space has to be arranged to make sure the flow of guests proceeds fluidly. These serving points should also be placed strategically, so that guests not only have easy and relatively quick access to the food and beverages offered, but that refilling the buffets and bars can be done efficiently. To safeguard smooth proceedings, it is advised to make a table plan and go through the event programme with the organisers in advance, asking how things should be done at every step. The most common set-up styles used at banquets, weddings, receptions and parties include the following:

Seated banquet

- Seated banquet in which guests are seated at tables, usually round ones with seating capacity ranging from 8 to 12 persons. Cutlery, glassware, napkins, flowers, pepper and salt, menu cards, butter and bread are placed on the tables before the guests arrive;

Seated buffet

- Seated buffet in which guests are also placed at tables. The same items are placed on the tables, but there may be little or no cutlery and glassware on the table; alternatively, nothing besides the main attributes is set up. Cutlery can be taken from the buffet, and wine is served from trays;

Standing buffet

- Standing buffet is a set-up that is used so that guests can socialise. High tables are placed in the room, where guests can place their drinks and plates. Food can vary from hot to cold and sometimes even include a dessert buffet, or can be limited to a finger food type buffet. Buffets can be placed as with a seated buffet or can be scattered around the room. A combination of a seated buffet and standing buffet can also be used; a good alternative especially if there are elderly guests;

Walking dinner

- Walking dinner is a set-up similar to the standing buffet set-up. Small dishes and drinks are served to guests standing at high tables;

Weddings

- Weddings depend on the wishes of the organisers in terms of room lay out. The traditional seating arrangement at the head table of a wedding set-up is displayed in Figure 5.14.

FIGURE 5.14 Traditional seating arrangement at a wedding head table

Other tables are set up like at a seated banquet, and these are decorated according to the wishes of the organisers. Dishes and wines are served at the tables like at a seated banquet;

- For receptions and parties, standing tables are generally used, especially round the dance floor. In quieter areas, there may be some seating tables available. Servers serve the drinks and snacks at the tables. A variation of this set-up is the walking dinner mentioned above.

Receptions and parties

5.7 Hotel bars

Hotel bars provide multiple types of service for guests, such as offering them a cup of coffee with a nice piece of apple pie, serving them a refreshing drink and some finger food after an intensive meeting, or letting them unwind while sipping a cocktail in a relaxing ambiance. The hotel bar is usually the central place of the hotel where both individual guests and groups of guests, leisure or business related, meet up and socialise while enjoying food and beverages. At a bar, there are usually bar stools at bar counters behind which the bartender is making and serving drinks; some bars offer seating possibilities in the bar area. The bar is often the starting place and ending point of a meeting, event or restaurant visit. This is why it is crucial for the waiting staff to offer good quality and speedy service. Because bars are more beverage-oriented, and because drinks contribution margins are generally higher than food contribution margins, bars greatly contribute to hotel profits. The person responsible for the bar (or bars) is the Bar Manager, generally responsible for:

Hotel bars

Central place

Crucial

Contribution margins

Bar Manager

- the quality of overall running of the bar;
- leading and guiding bar staff (or Bar Supervisors/Captains in large hotels);
- supervising service processes (maintaining and updating SOPs when needed);
- keeping track of bar revenue and profit (cost-control);
- providing proper training to bar staff;
- offering hospitality as a host when required;
- assisting operations during peak hours;
- possessing a good basic knowledge of different types of drinks and food;
- maintaining hygiene and ISO standards;
- developing bar cards, specialties and bargain deals;
- organising entertainment in the bar areas.

The Bar Manager reports to the Food and Beverage Director (or to the Beverage Manager in large hotels). Bartenders and bar staff are responsible for serving beverages and food items appropriately. One of the key qualities of bar staff is hostmanship. Guests often do not come just for a drink, but also for a chat with the bartender. Business guests who travel alone and stay in a hotel are often particularly interested in social contact. A good bartender can identify the different types of guests, and can adapt to the type of contact and interaction desired. Another imperative bartender quality is a good memory, allowing them remember guests' names and favourite drinks. Text 5.11 is a description of bartenders by H. L. Mencken (1880 - 1956), published in the Baltimore Evening Sun on 11 May 1911, which captures the essence of a skilful bartender:

Key qualities

5

TEXT 5.11

H. L. Mencken on bartenders

The average bartender, despite the slanders of professional moralists, is a man of self-respect and self-possession; a man who excels at a difficult art and is well aware of it; a man who shrinks from ruffianism as he does from uncleanliness; in short, a gentleman ... the bartender is one of the most dignified, law abiding, and ascetic of men.

He is guided by a rigid code of professional ethics; his work demands a clear head and a steady hand; he must have sound and fluent conversation; he cannot be drunken or dirty; the slightest dubiousness is quick to exile him to the police force, journalism, the oyster boats or some other Siberia of the broken.

The core qualities of a bartender still remain the same to date. Some responsibilities of bartenders include:

- Providing good and speedy service of beverages and food;
- Preparing consistent, good quality, attractive looking drinks;
- Maintaining cleanliness of bar and bar area according to hygiene (HACCP) rules;
- Checking guests' alcohol consumption, and preventing alcohol intoxication;
- Maintaining a profitable outlet, guarding against waste, and minimising other costs.

5.7.1   History of bars

Different names

There have been many different names for public drinking places throughout history, where such names as saloon, tavern, pub or club were all used for what is now called the bar. During US colonial times till the mid-19th century, saloons, for example, provided food and lodging, and were open to all members of the community including women and children. Saloons were very important meeting places, where social issues, politics, and other news were

FIGURE 5.15 Classic bar

shared and discussed. They functioned as community centres. These saloons cannot be compared to the London coffee houses or Paris saloons, which were bourgeois meeting places reserved only for a select few. In saloons, different people of different working classes would mingle together, with workers drinking alongside employers. Prices were also pretty much fixed to prevent them from catering just to the wealthy. Later, dedicated saloons started mixing cordials and spirits at a long bar (as opposed to drink initially being served from cages). The sale and/or consumption of alcoholic beverages was prohibited in several countries including the United States during the first half of the 20th century. During this so-called 'Prohibition' period (1920-1933), people began illegal bars which they called speakeasies or blind pigs. Today's bars form an integral part of almost every community, and a wide variety of different styles of bars offers an atmosphere, service and assortment suited to every guest and occasion. Figure 5.15 illustrates a classic bar, while Figure 5.16 is a picture of a modern bar.

FIGURE 5.16 Modern bar

5.7.2   Types of bars

Within hotels, different types of bars offer beverages and food according to their location in the hotel and the type of hotel. The choice of bar type also depends highly on the location of the hotel itself.

Types of bars

Lobby bars

These bars are usually placed around the front entrance, next to hotel reception. This type was popularised by Conrad Hilton when he wanted to generate revenue using hotel lobbies; these are not exclusively available for hotel guests, but offer a great range of drinks and snacks to non-lodging guests as well.

Lobby bars

Restaurant bars

Restaurant bars

These bars are often incorporated into (or situated next to) the restaurants, and are used for serving drinks before and after the meals of the guests. As discussed earlier, they also allow restaurants to spread the flow of guests during peak hours, allowing staff the necessary time to have tables available and ready.

Service bars

Service bars

These bars are found in large hotels, where drinks are prepared for the restaurants and for room service.

Catering and banquet bars

Catering and banquet bars

These bars are specifically used for serving drinks to conference and banquet guests. The bars can be permanently situated in function rooms or in corridors close to the function and conference rooms. Depending on the nature of the event and guest wishes, flexible bars (pop-up bars) can be set up and used at a variety of locations. Multiple bars may be needed to serve enormous quantities of drinks especially during large events.

Pool bars

Pool bars

Pool bars are popular at resort hotels where guests can enjoy a variety of exotic cocktails while relaxing pool side. Special events and theme parties are often organised around pool bars. Figure 5.17 is a picture of a pool bar.

FIGURE 5.17 Pool bar

Night clubs

Night clubs

Some hotels offer the service of dancing and entertainment in the evenings. Usually, these bars offer full beverage service. Some are only accessible to hotel guests, especially for safety and security reasons, but many hotel nightclubs do welcome outside guests. An entrance fee is generally charged, and entertainment is often arranged in the form of a DJ or live bands or other forms of live entertainment.

Sports bars

These popular bars have also become widespread in hotels, and they feature large television screens where guests and visitors can watch the latest sports and news action. There is often an informal, bustling yet relaxed atmosphere where beers, wines and other drinks can be ordered. Bars also often offer a menu of snacks and platters that can be ordered throughout the day.

Sports bars

Casino bars

These bars provide drinks at relatively low prices. Casino bars are not expected to generate revenue, but should ensure that guests keep gambling. The real source of income is the casino itself. Some hotel casinos offer free drinks, snacks and lavish entertainment to entice patrons to keep on gambling.

Casino bars

5.7.3 Legal Restrictions

As mentioned under the core qualities of bartenders, one of the major responsibilities of bar staff is to keep a close eye on guests' alcohol consumption, and to prevent alcohol abuse and even intoxication. Places that serve alcoholic beverages usually have an alcohol service policy and procedures to prevent alcohol-related problems from occurring. The Food and Beverage Director (or Manager) is responsible for setting up these policies, and has to see to it that these guidelines are followed by service staff. All bar and other staff serving alcoholic beverages have to be trained to prevent problems; they need to know how to recognise and deal with potentially problematic situations in such a way they do not get out of hand while avoiding embarrassment to guests involved at the same time. Policies can include subjects like drinks measurements or minimum legal age. Depending on the country, serving alcohol to persons below the age of 18-21 is illegal. Appendix C lists the various legal alcohol drinking and purchasing ages for various European countries (valid for 2015, and sourced from www.wikipedia.org).

Alcohol service policy

Legislation related to serving drinks should be well understood by service personnel. In the Netherlands, for example, if a guest becomes intoxicated and is still served alcohol by a bartender, or if a minor is served alcohol and causes an accident that involves a third party, then the bartender and the management are liable for anything that happened to that third party. Furthermore, individual cities and towns normally have legal restrictions on where bars may be located and on the types of alcoholic drinks allowed to be served.

Liable

Summary

▶ From a guest's perspective, the main reason for visiting a food service company is to eat or drink, both components of their primary needs. They also have secondary needs, however; whatever the case, these needs and wishes differ depending on the person, with such factors as age, profession, education, relation with the company, income, or nationality (culture) all influencing the overall decisions.

▶ The offerings of hospitality organisations include food and beverage elements, which are offered within a certain surrounding by people exuding hospitality, with other guests also being an influential part of the surrounding. The products, surrounding, and hospitality are at the foundation of the hospitality formula of a food service company.

▶ The hospitality model shows the interaction between the needs and goals of guests with the product, behaviour and environment of the service provider, leading to a certain guest experience as well as returns for the service provider. Hostmanship is based on interaction, the big picture, dialogue, responsibility, consideration, and knowledge.

▶ There are two basic types of food service – commercial food service and non-commercial food service. The commercial can be split into the quick service, full service and catering categories. Non-commercial is basically institutionalised food service which can be in-house or contract-based.

▶ Quick service includes fast food restaurants, lunchrooms/coffee shops, take-away places, cafeterias and motorway restaurants, buffet restaurants, street vendors, and ice cream parlours. The full service category includes casual, bistro, brasserie, single item, ethnic, family, theme, beverage-offering food service, and fine-dining restaurants. Catering can take place at a fixed location or outdoors.

▶ In addition, food and beverage may be available in other surroundings such as hotels and other lodging companies, or within consumer-based companies, leisure attractions, retail stores, with a travel food service available during travel or at stations.

▶ In order to ensure demand and supply match, a restaurant entrepreneur has to make sure that a clear restaurant profile is communicated to (potential) guests. This company profile is also called its formula, and it is the sum of location, ambiance, menu, staff, price, and promotions.

▶ When planning a restaurant, the layout is of utmost importance. Important issues to consider regarding layout are costs, entrance, kitchen (including the dish-washing areas), food storage areas, the dining room, employee-related issues, restrooms, the bar and other areas.

▶ Some trends affecting the restaurant business are the developments in technology, celebrity chefs temporarily running restaurants, a greater use of the internet for guest reviews, the use of sustainable, organic, and locally sourced products, product-exposure within restaurants, less formal service staff, the reintroduction of the service professional, and service tsunami/rhythm.

▶ Restaurant operations are most commonly divided into front-of-house activities and back-of-house activities. Front-of-house is the staff serving and having contact with guests; back-of-house are the kitchen, responsible for the production of food, and stewarding, responsible for cleaning the materials and equipment. The activities within front-of-house can be divided into the pre-service phase, the welcoming phase, the staying phase, the farewell phase, and the post-service phase.

▶ The person responsible for the management of operations within front-of-house is the *maître d'hôtel*, also called restaurant manager in more casual restaurants. Ten key characteristics of a restaurant manager are drive, hospitality mindedness, responsibility, planning and organising, leadership skills, communication, knowledge and expertise, profitability awareness, flexibility and creativity.

▶ The person responsible for kitchen operations is the Executive Chef, who has to make sure that food coming out of the kitchen is of a high standard, tastes delicious, and is originally presented. An Executive Chef should possess characteristics such as passion, creativity, planning and organising, leadership skills, communication, knowledge and expertise, business mindedness, multi-tasking, stress-resistant, and flexibility. The kitchen timeline is divided into the preparation phase, the service phase, and the rounding off phase.

▶ Room service, also referred to as in-room dining, is offered by hotels for so guests can have food and beverages delivered to their rooms; while some hotels provide rooms service 24/7, others only offer breakfast. There are various reasons guests prefer to order room service, and the room service process can be divided into order taking, preparing and setting up the cart, delivery, and clearing.

▶ The provision of room service comes with its profitability, menu planning, and operating concerns.

▶ Under the supervision of the conference and banqueting manager, the conference and banqueting department offers function rooms and other areas in the hotel together with food and beverage service for groups of people attending an event in the hotel. There are two types of attendant groups – business-related and social-oriented. Since the department mostly hosts events of which the date, programme, number of guests, and food and beverage products served are known in advance, it is generally considered a profitable department thanks to its lower labour and sales costs and improved contribution margins.

5

▶ There are various service methods including *le service plat sur table, le service à l'assiette, le service à l'anglaise, le service à la française, le service à la russe,* snack-bar, buffet, self, and cafeteria; equally, there are various ways of serving coffee, tea, water, or other beverages.

▶ For conference rooms, the basic types of set-up are the theatre or auditorium style, the classroom or schoolroom style, the u-shape or horseshoe style, the *carré* or hollow square style, the boardroom or conference style, the cabaret, the seated banquet, the seated buffet, the standing buffet, the walking dinner, and weddings or other receptions and parties.

▶ Under the responsibility of the bar manager, hotel bars provide multiple services for guests; bars are usually the central place of the hotel where both individual guests and groups of guests, both leisure or business related, meet up and socialise. There are diffident types of hotel bars such as lobby bars, restaurant bars, service bars, catering and banquet bars, pool bars, night clubs, sports bars, and casino bars. All bars have to respect an alcohol service policy, and should employ procedures to prevent alcohol-related incidents from occurring.

Questions and assignments for reflection

1   Explain the hospitality model and how it works.

2   In your own words, indicate the traits a good waiter should possess. Compare your answers to the traits of a professional server as listed in Figure 5.4. What are the differences and similarities?

3   What is a restaurant's formula? Why is it important to constantly review this formula?

4   In your own estimation, what are the five major characteristics that a restaurant manager should possess?

5   Why would hotels keep offering room service even when the room service department operates at a loss?

6

Hospitality Human Resource Management

Dr. B. Rowson

6.1 Introduction

Most hospitality managers and management academics will agree that Human Resource Management (HRM) is an important function of an organisation. Human Resource Management involves five main functions, which are planning, organising, staffing, leading and controlling. All these elements are important functions for a business to be competitive and successful. Collectively, these five functions represent the managing process of human resource departments and companies in general.

This chapter focusses on many areas of Human Resource Management (HRM) in a hospitality business setting. At its simplest, HRM is the process of acquiring, training, appraising and compensating employees, as well as employee relations, health and safety, and fairness at work. The aim of this chapter is to provide the concepts and techniques required to be a good people manager in the hospitality industry. These concepts and techniques comprise understanding of employee training, workforce planning, motivation, performance evaluation, compensation, labour turnover, employee retention, recruitment and selection of employees, as well as legal aspects surrounding employment.

6.2 Human Resource Management functions

Dessler (2013) defines the specific activities involved in the HRM functions as follows:
- Planning, which involves establishing goals and standards, developing rules and procedures, developing plans, and forecasting employee needs and numbers for the business.
- Organising, which is done by arranging subordinates' tasks, establishing business departments, delegating chains of command or authority,

HRM functions

Planning

Organising

China, Shenzhen: The Kingkey 100

establishing channels of communication, and co-ordinating subordinates' work.

Staffing
- Staffing, which involves determining what kind of people should be hired
for the different job roles, recruiting prospective employees, selecting
employees, training and developing employees, setting performance
standards for the organisation, setting performance standards for employees, evaluating performances (by appraisals and other methods),
counselling employees about pensions and other benefits, and compensating employees in the form of rewards and pay.

Leading
- Leading, which is motivating and leading employees at all levels to get
the job done, maintaining morale in the business, and motivating employees to achieve their potential.

Controlling
- Controlling, which is done by creating strategies for setting standards
such as sales quota, quality standards, or production levels, checking to
see how actual performances compare to the standards, and taking corrective actions as needed.

6.3 The importance of Human Resource Management to hospitality managers

Recruitment mistakes
Human resources (HR) concepts and techniques are important to all manag-
ers for an array of reasons but probably the most important reason is to
avoid recruitment mistakes. By having a command of HR knowledge, a hotel
or restaurant manager can make sure they recruit the right people for the
right job at the right time. For example, no manager wants to:
- Hire the wrong person for the job;
- Experience high labour turnover;
- Have employees not do their best;
- Waste time on interviewing;
- End up in court because of discriminatory actions;
- Endure employee disputes about salaries; or
- Allow lack of training to undermine employee potential.

Careful study of this chapter can help managers to avoid such mistakes,
and can help improve profits and performance in the business. Similarly,
effective human resource management can help ensure that getting the
right results, through people.

6.4 New approaches to organising human resources

The world is a fast changing place and as change impacts upon hospitality
businesses, it impacts upon their HRM departments. Employers are also
offering human resource services in new and innovative ways. For example,
some organise their HR around various groups such as transactional, corporate, or embedded groups, or as centres of expertise (Dessler, 2013), and
as shown hereafter:

Transactional HR
- In the transactional HR group, the organisation basically forms a centre
to deal with all HRM issues, often in the form of a call centre that supports the day-to-day HR services and activities (such as changing benefit
plans, employee assistance and counselling). Many of the larger hotel
groups use this method.

- The corporate HR group focusses on assisting top management in 'top level' big picture issues such as developing and explaining the personnel aspects of the company's long-term strategic plan.   *Corporate HR*
- The embedded HR unit assigns HR generalists (sometimes known as 're-lationship managers' or 'HR business partners') directly to departments like rooms or food and beverage. They provide the localised human re-source management assistance that the departments need.   *Embedded HR*
- Centres of expertise are like specialised consulting firms within the com-pany or corporate framework. For instance, they provide specialised as-sistance in areas such as organisational change (recruitment, training existing employees and change management techniques).   *Centres of expertise*

6.5 Trends shaping human resource management in the hospitality industry

The role of human resource managers in the hospitality sector is changing. There are many reasons for the changes, some of which are obvious and others much more complicated. One of the main changes is caused by tech-nology where, for example, many leading hospitality companies (hotel chains) allow employees to deal with benefits plans, working time, holiday bookings via the companies' intranets. Other trends shaping human re-source management are globalisation, deregulation by governments, chang-es to the demographics of populations (Chartered Institute of Personnel and Development (CIPD), 2015), and the nature of work (Dessler, 2013).   *Changes* *Technology*

Globalisation refers to the tendency of hospitality firms to extend their sales, ownership and business to new markets abroad. Examples are Mar-riot Hotels, Starwood's Group, Hilton, and Ritz-Carlton. Companies expand abroad for several reasons but sales expansion is the main one in the hos-pitality industry. For hospitality businesses, globalisation often means more competition; more competition means more pressure to perform at one's peak. This often calls for business streamlining, getting the best perfor-mance from employees while striving to maintain and improve quality and service levels. The bottom line is that the growing integration of the world economy into a single, huge marketplace is increasing the intensity of com-petition in a wide range of manufacturing and service industries (Dessler, 2013). Clearly, both workers and companies have to work harder and smart-er than they did before globalisation took hold. Also, it must be noted that a significant number of hospitality organisations are small independent busi-nesses, often with no formal business structure, unlike the larger hospitality businesses. In these small hospitality businesses, HRM is often barely rec-ognisable when compared to their larger counterparts. The business owner or manager often makes all HR decisions from recruitment to investment. Research undertaken by Lashley and Rowson (2004) points to the fact that, typically in small hospitality businesses, recruitment is often done very in-formally and includes limited introduction or training opportunities, hence frequent high labour turnover in the organisation.   *Globalisation* *Competition*

Globalisation therefore brings both benefits and threats for hospitality or-ganisations. For consumers of hospitality, it means lower prices and higher quality products and services. But for workers in the hospitality sector, it

6

Off-shore jobs

means the prospect of working harder and perhaps less securely as employers off-shore jobs by recruiting employees from cheaper labour countries instead. Text 6.1 clearly illustrates the situation.

FIGURE 6.1 Trends shaping Human Resource Management in Hospitality (Source: Dessler, 2013)

Trends	So companies must be	Employers will expect that HR managers
• Globalisation • Increased competition • Increased indebtedness • Technological innovation • More high tech jobs • More service jobs • More knowledge work • An ageing workforce	• More competitive • Faster and responsive • More cost effective • Human capital-oriented • Quality conscious • Downsized • Empowered teams	• Focus more on the big picture issues such as helping the company achieve its strategic goals. • Find new ways to provide transactional services such as benefits administration • Create high performance work systems

TEXT 6.1

HR distribution in Dubai hotels

Modern Dubai has a large number of luxury hotels and accommodates wealthy guests in abstract luxury. Yet careful observation shows that the nationalities of employees vary greatly by job role and position in the hotel. Most senior managers are European or American. Most duty managers are European. Front-of-house staff, for example receptionists, greeters to the luxury restaurants, are Eastern European or Chinese. Most of those serving in the restaurants are from the Philippines. For employees working in the maintenance section, once again the managers and engineers are usually European or American while the porters, cleaners, and gardeners are often of Indian or Sri Lankan descent.

© Noordhoff Uitgevers bv

6.6 Trends in the nature of work

For much of the 20th century, personnel managers in the hospitality sector typically focussed on day to day transactional types of activities. In larger hotel organisations, for example, personnel managers took over the role of hiring and firing from supervisors and managers, began to run the payroll department, and arranged pension plans. However, typically in hospitality firms (often small, independently-owned businesses), one manager wears all the hats, and is HR, Accounts, and GM rolled into one. Only in bigger hospitality businesses like the large hotel chains do HRM departments come into their own right. This is often because, as the hotel businesses have grown, it has become impossible for owners to control all the processes that take place; and thus different departments are formed to deal with these functions. Today we see the impact of trends like globalisation, indebtedness, and technology advances on all hospitality businesses, but it is perhaps the larger hospitality organisations that feel the most impact. Over the last two decades, hospitality business owners and employers have faced many new challenges, such as squeezing more profits from existing hospitality operations. Corporate hospitality employers now expect their human resource managers to have what it takes to address these new trends and challenges.

Personnel managers

6.7 Recruitment and Selection

The hospitality business is a people business and therefore recruiting and selecting people to fill new or existing positions in the sector are crucial elements of human resource activity in all hospitality organisations, irrespective of size, structure or activity. Although it has been noted how the importance of service quality and delivery has increased the pressure on hospitality businesses to select the right kind of individuals, it is widely and frequently suggested that, too often, recruitment decisions are made in an informal, ad hoc and reactive manner (Lashley & Rowson, 2004).

People business

Recruitment decisions

This deduction is especially true in smaller hospitality organisations that may not have well developed HRM functions or recruitment and selection systems, and many small hospitality firms may recruit irregularly with heavy reliance on informal systems and methods. Indeed, within the context of the hospitality sector, Price (1994) found that, out of 241 hotels sampled in her research, a third never used job descriptions or person specifications. In their work, Lashley and Rowson (2002) said that hospitality firms often use poor recruitment strategies with no formal process and that in fact this is typical of many small firms in the hospitality sector. Additionally, when Lockyer and Scholarios (2005) surveyed over 80 hotels, they similarly found a general lack of systematic procedures for recruitment and selection. This lack of systemisation may seem strange when many writers point to the cost of poor recruitment and selection being manifested in such things as:

Lack of systemisation

- Expensive use of management time;
- Recruiting replacements for individuals who leave very quickly;
- High labour turnover;
- Absenteeism;
- Low staff morale;
- Ineffective management and supervision

Clearly then, it is important for organisations to consider how they approach recruitment and selection to increase the likelihood of a successful appointment decision and to do so in a cost effective manner. Reflecting on this latter idea of cost effectiveness, it is important to recognise the contingent nature of recruitment and selection. Thus, although there may be good practice approaches to recruitment and selection, these are not going to be appropriate for all positions available in an organisation. Take, for example, a management traineeship in a major hotel; the company may use a variety of sophisticated and costly mechanisms culminating in an assessment centre. On the other hand, for part-time seasonal positions in an organisation, managers in the hospitality industry face real challenges in recruiting, developing and maintaining a committed, competent, well managed, and motivated

Cost effective manner

Appropriate

TEXT 6.2

Skills shortage: the case for hospitality and tourism in the UK

Despite the sector spending £2.7bn on training, 21% of employers report skills gaps and the sector's spend per employee has reduced by 24%. This leads to question what impact training investment is having on a business. Recent data suggest that 83% of employers had provided training in health and safety in the previous year, compared to 32% who have provided training in new technology or 9% in personal development (UKCES, 2014). Once employers have been able to fill their vacancies, the next problem is retaining the workforce. The sector has a 20% labour turnover rate which costs the industry £274m a year but is particularly a problem in the pubs, bars and nightclub sector (26%) and the restaurant sector (23%). (People 1st, 2014). This is largely due to employers continuing to recruit transient workers such as students (15%) and migrants (25%) who are typically not looking for a career in the industry.

---

workforce to serve their guests. As the customer base becomes ever more discerning, the challenges increase, and more customer-facing soft skills are required. Text 6.2, taken from the UK's Labour Force Survey 2014, illustrates the situation of skills shortage within hospitality and tourism in the UK.

6.7.1   The need for effective recruiting

Effective recruiting

There is a need for effective recruiting. When the CEO asks for a human resource manager to be recruited, that position should be filled by the right person for the role. Effective recruiting is important and it is hard to overemphasise its importance to the company. If there are two jobs to fill and only two applicants apply, there may be little choice but to hire both of them. But if 10 or 20 applicants appear, techniques like interviews and tests can be employed to filter out all but the best. Even in times of high unemployment it is not necessarily easy to find good candidates. A 2013 survey by the UK's Institute for Personnel and Development (IPD), for example, found that about half the responses from industry managers indicated they had difficulty finding qualified applicants, and about 40% said it was hard to find good candidates. Figure 6.2 shows the links between the skills required of managers during the recruitment and selection process, and the various processes.

Skills

FIGURE 6.2 Skills involved in the recruitment and selection process

Recruitment and Selection Process	Skills required
Job description	Evaluation of the vacancy
Person specification	Drafting the criteria
Advertisement	Summarizing
Shortlist	Fair discrimination
Interview	Questioning skills
Selection tests	Listening skills
References	Assessment skills
Decision	Evaluation

6.7.2 What makes recruiting a challenge?

It is easy to assume that recruiting is easy, and what is needed is to place a few ads on the internet and in local newspapers and trade magazines. The following two things make it more complex, however:

- Firstly, some recruiting methods are superior to others, depending on the type of job one is recruiting for;
- Secondly, recruitment success depends on non-recruitment issues and policies. For example, paying 10% more than what most firms in a location offer can usually result in a bigger candidate pool to select from. Many of the lower end jobs in hospitality are often not very well paid, and a small difference of just £0.50 per hour can attract suitably trained candidates from competitors in the local area.

6.7.3 Organising recruitment

There are currently two management schools of thought on recruitment policy in the hospitality sector. Firstly, centralising the company's recruitment policy, or letting each unit do its own recruiting. For many large hospitality firms, it is better to use a combination of both methods. For specialised roles, such as supervisors, managers, chefs, accountants, it is better to recruit centrally, because one can advertise on the internet or in specialist trade magazines sure to attract the attention of the right type of candidates with the skills required. On the other hand, for unskilled service employees it is often much better to recruit from the local labour market, because in the local economy sensitivity to payment will make it easier to attract the right kind of candidates for the roles that need to be filled.

Schools of thought

Using internal sources: pros and cons

Filling open positions with inside candidates has several advantages. First, there is foreknowledge of the candidates and an assumed understanding of their strengths and weaknesses. Current employees may have more commitment to the company. Morale amongst employees will rise if current employees see possible promotions for loyalty and competence. However, hiring from within can also have its downside. Employees who apply for the jobs and are not hired can become discontented, in their eyes having been passed over. When hiring managers in this way, there is a risk that existing managers may want to maintain the status quo; whereas new managers hired from outside the organisation may want to develop new ideas and move company thinking forward or in a different direction.

Inside candidates

Hiring in the open job market

Open job market Firms cannot always get the employees that they need from their current staff. This may be due to business expansion, or because current employees do not have the skills required and re-training is expected to take too long; here, it may be easier to hire the necessary employees from the open job market.

Recruiting via the internet

E-recruitment For many hospitality firms, job recruitment can be done via internet-recruitment, especially for supervisor or management level jobs. Online recruitment, or e-recruitment, refers to the use of technology to attract candidates. An organisation's website is one of the most frequently used recruitment methods. According to a 2009 Industrial Relations Services (IRS) survey, employers feel there is a certain logic to using their own websites in recruitment. They believe that these websites provide better informed candidates at a lower cost than other recruitment methods. Almost nine out of ten of respondents (88%) said that using their own websites increases the likelihood that candidates know about the company and their work, thus enhancing good employer branding (Gilmore & Williams, 2013).

6.7.4   Future challenges for recruitment in the hospitality industry

Soft skills shortage

Soft skills Research suggests that four of the top five skills applicants are lacking are soft skills (UKCES, 2014). Such a shortage is increasing the challenge of recruitment for employers, with hard-to-fill vacancies having risen by 12% between 2011 and 2013 (People 1st, 2014). On top of that, soft skills gaps in the existing workforce are affecting businesses' ability to compete, with 61% of hospitality and tourism businesses experiencing gaps in customer handling skills, resulting in 26% of those businesses reporting a loss of business to competitors (UKCES, 2014).

Personal attributes Soft skills are personal attributes that enable someone to interact effectively and harmoniously with other people, be they customers or fellow team members; these skills are closely associated with emotional intelligence (see Chapter 15). Soft skills are critical to the sector. The sector cannot have an effective workforce without these skills and there are differing opinions about whether companies should recruit those already possessing the soft skills, or if soft skills can be developed. The figures are concerning, as a recent report by Development Economics, commissioned by McDonalds UK, warns that in five years' time more than 122,000 workers in retail and food services in the UK will be held back by a lack of soft skills. This compares to almost 53,000 workers in the health and social care sector, and almost 41,000 in professional services (Development Economics, 2015).

Other research has also identified the importance of soft skills. Recently, the CIPD (2015) Learning to Work Skills Survey found that the top three key skills that employers were concerned about developing in young candidates during their first year in the job were: communication (64%), teamwork (60%), and confidence (45%). Also cited frequently were time management (45%), business awareness (26%), and problem-solving (20%) (CIPD, 2015).

Soft skills – a challenge for the hospitality and tourism sector

To illustrate this challenge, the case of the UK situation is highlighted. The *Challenge* problem of applicants lacking soft skills has become more acute as the economy has picked up. During the recession, the hospitality and tourism sector was one of the few sectors to recruit in significant numbers; as a result, it was able not only to attract more, but also higher skilled applicants. In the past two years, however, there have been fewer applicants for sector vacancies. As a consequence, the number of vacancies sector businesses considered to be hard-to-fill rose by 12% between 2011 and 2013. Similarly, *Hard-to-fill* the number of vacancies that were considered skill shortages rose by 10% between 2011 and 2013.

The challenge for the sector is in being able to compete in a competitive job market when it is associated with much higher numbers of zero-hour contracts, less visible career progression opportunities, and comparatively low pay levels.

The other challenge is that a lack of soft skills is often associated with younger people and as previously indicated, the hospitality and tourism sector employs three times the proportion of 16 to 24 year olds compared to the economy as a whole, with 34% of the workforce being under 25. Businesses are increasingly recognising a lack of soft skills in younger applicants. A recent survey showed that over half the employers questioned (57%) said that young people lack basic soft skills, such as communication and team work (ONS, 2014). Figure 6.3 shows the percentages various hospitality and tourism companies with hard-to-fill vacancies who find applicants to be lacking in various soft skills.

FIGURE 6.3 Soft skills lacked by applicants as noted by hospitality and tourism businesses with hard-to-fill vacancies

6.8 Training

Training

It is necessary that the organisation aligns its training programmes to its strategy. The employer's strategic plan should ultimately govern its training goals. In essence, the task is to identify employee behaviours that the firm requires in executing its strategy.

6.8.1   Induction training and developing employees

New employees

For new employees to work effectively in the company, it is essential that they go through an induction/orientation training course as soon as possible once they start with a company (CIPD, 2015). Carefully selecting employees does not guarantee they will perform effectively. Even high-potential employees cannot do their job if they do not know what is expected of them. Making sure that employees know what to do is part of orientation training, often referred to as induction training. The hospitality industry has high labour turnover, and companies often refrain from providing quality induction training, often leading to even higher labour turnover (Lashley & Rowson, 2002).

Orientation training

Purpose

The purpose of orientation/induction training includes:
- Making sure that new employees feel welcome and part of the team;
- Making sure that new employees have the basic information needed to function effectively, including e-mail access and an understanding of personnel policies and benefits offered by the company;
- Helping employees understand the organisation in its broadest sense (its past and present culture, its vision and strategies for the future;
- Socialising the employees into the firm's culture, values, and strategies.

Company handbook

The usual format is an induction day covering all of the above. In some cases, half a day is sufficient to cover the training material. The company usually presents the new employee with a company handbook at this time.

6.8.2 Training and Performance

Creating a training programme involves more than contracting with an on-line training provider and requiring employees to take the course. An employer should use a rational training process. The gold standard here is still the basic analysis-design-development-implement-evaluate (ADDIE) training process model that training experts have used for years. The ADDIE acronym stands for:

Rational training process

- Analysing the training need;
- Designing the overall training programme;
- Developing the course (actually assembling/creating the training materials);
- Implementing training (actually training the target group of employees, using methods such as on-the-job training and off-the job training);
- Evaluating the training course's effectiveness.

A training needs analysis should address an employer's strategic/longer term training needs/or current training needs. If the programme is to use technology, the manager also needs to review the technology they plan to use for presenting the training programme.

6.8.3 On-the-job training

An on-the-job approach to training is consistently popular with hospitality businesses, especially when organisations face difficult economic times (CIPD, 2011). Cannel (1997) has described it as training that is planned and structured, and occurs at the employees' workplace. It varies in format and complexity, with the most commonly used methods being observing a skilled employee. At its most basic level in the hospitality industry, this can be as limited as shadowing another member of staff, e.g. working with a housekeeping team for a few days to gain the knowledge of how rooms are prepared at the hotel. On the other hand, in-house training can be very formal, such as monitoring an employee while they carry out a series of tasks and then evaluating the work done. It is common practice in the hospitality industry to use self-learning training manuals (paper-based or, more recently, computer-based and online).

On-the-job

Varies

6

TEXT 6.3

Improving training at Pontins

Pontins is a British company that has a number of holiday centres which are catering primarily for families. The vast majority of Pontins' employees are seasonal workers, many of whom will only work for the company for a short period of time. Despite the relatively high turnover of staff that this situation creates the company's commitment to the Investors in People (IiP) Standard means that all employees have the opportunity to improve, no matter how short their stay is with the company. Drawing on the IiP Guidelines the company now has a structure which means that every employee will have a personal development file with job description and aims, access to NVQs, access to funding for vocational training, assistance with professional qualifications and assessment of aims and goals and help achieving them. So even those employees who only stay a short period of time can gain a new qualification. As well as increasing the amount of training and delivering higher standards of service, the company has also seen improved employee retention, resulting in greater productivity and reduced costs.

(Source: www.investorsinpeople.co.uk)

6.8.4   External training

Off-the-job

This is sometimes referred to as off-the-job training. It usually consists of courses organised by internal or external training providers, with training held away from the workplace. While off-the-job training can provide a training experience away from the workplace and introduce employees to new ideas, it is commonly perceived to be less effective if it is not directly related to the organisation and workplace environment. Text 6.3 is an illustration of some of the positive effects of training.

6.8.5   Evaluation of training

Evaluation

Quantitative measures

The final stage of any training cycle is its evaluation. While it is a key activity, literature suggests that there is no consensus as to the best way to perform evaluations (Anderson, 2007). One approach, often used by hospitality businesses, is to adopt quantitative measures to measure costs and benefits of any intervention, ascertaining whether or not a 'return on investment' can be calculated. CEOs and senior managers often know the cost of training to the exact figure from the profit and loss accounts, but are often unable to assess the more intangible areas where value is added to the business (Lashley & Rowson, 2004). Text 6.4 is an excerpt illustrating the costs attributable to attaining an Investing in People award.

TEXT 6.4

Investing in people: at what cost?

Amanda Scott, the General Manager of the Copthorne Hotel in Glasgow, suggests that in many respects IiP embodied what any good manager should be doing – investing in their people. However, she also outlined a number of criticisms. Many companies that have attained the IiP Standard often already have good HR systems and procedures in place so gaining the award may simply be nothing more than a 'badging' process. Moreover it is a badging process that generates a lot of paperwork and bureaucracy, with the awarding body often using obscure and confusing jargon. She also suggests that the cost of IiP accreditation may well be prohibitive, 'As a management model it can deliver, but in my opinion £4000 for the privilege of a branding exercise ... cannot be justified. It if was my personal money? I don't think so'. This latter point concerning the costly nature of IiP accreditation could be particularly important for smaller companies who predominate in tourism and hospitality. The CIPD has recently estimated that the total cost of seeking IiP is between £5000 and £15000 depending on the size of the organization and how much consultancy support the organization uses.

Different methods

Other evaluation approaches seek to measure at different individual departmental or organisational levels within the company. Different degrees of evaluation use different methods, becoming more complex and involving a wider range of stakeholders (Guerci & Vinante (2011). However, with the advent of more individualistic approaches to training and development and increasing focus on continuous development, however, organisations are using different forms of evaluation which are more learner-centric than provider-focussed (Edelenbos & Van Buuren, 2005). Many hospitality organisations now measure more intangible elements which are difficult to measure financially with the balanced scorecard method (Rowson & Lashley, 2007), such as customer satisfaction, repeat business (return visits by cus-

Balanced scorecard

tomers), employee satisfaction, reduced labour turnover, value of sales per customer. The balanced scorecard method, developed by Kaplan and Norton (1996), is a very prominent performance management model, and for this reason it is worth looking at in detail by all hospitality organisations. It has gained in popularity to such an extent that it now dominates the field of performance management (Kennerly & Bourne, 2003).

6.9 Motivation

6.9.1   The nature of motivation

Motivation

All hospitality organisations are concerned with achieving sustained high levels of quality standards and performance through people. This means paying close attention to how individuals can best be motivated through such means as incentives, rewards, leadership and, importantly, the value of the work they do within the context of the organisation; in short, the way individuals carry out their work in line with company policy. The aim is to develop motivation processes and a work environment that helps to ensure individuals deliver results in accordance with the expectations of management.

6.9.2   Understanding motivation

Motivation theory examines the process of motivation. It explains why people behave in a certain way while at work, what they do in terms of efforts and directions taken. It describes what organisations can do to encourage people to apply their efforts and abilities in ways that further the organisation's goals as well as satisfy their own needs. Motivation theory is also concerned with job satisfaction, the factors that create it, and its impact on performance.

Theory

In understanding and applying motivation theory, the aim is to obtain added value through people in the sense that the value of their output exceeds the cost of generating it. This can be achieved through discretionary effort. In most if not all roles, there is room for individuals to decide how much effort they want to exert. They can do just enough to get away with it, or they can throw themselves into their work and deliver added value to the business. Discretionary effort can be a key component in organisational performance.

Added value

Discretionary effort

6.9.3   Methods for motivating employees

Motivation at work can take place in two ways. Firstly, people can motivate themselves by seeking, finding and carrying out work (or being given work) that satisfies their needs or at least leads them to expect that their goals can be achieved. Secondly, people can be motivated by management through such methods as pay, promotion, personal praise and one-off rewards.

There are two types of motivation as originally identified by Herzberg, Mausner, Peterson and Capwell (1957):
- Intrinsic motivation – self-generated factors that influence people to behave in a particular way or to move in a particular direction. These factors include responsibility (feeling that their work is important and having control over their own resources), autonomy (freedom to act), scope to use and develop skills and abilities, interesting and challenging work, and opportunities for advancement;

Intrinsic

Extrinsic

- Extrinsic motivation – what is done to or for people in order to motivate them. This includes rewards, such as increased pay, praise, or promotion, and punishments, such as disciplinary action, withholding pay, or criticism of individual performance.

Extrinsic motivators can have an immediate and powerful effect, but it will not necessarily last long. The intrinsic motivators, which are concerned with the quality of working life (a phrase and movement that emerged from this concept and is sometimes referred to as work-life balance), are likely to have a deeper and longer-term effect because they are inherent in individuals and not imposed from outside.

Work-life balance

6.9.4   Motivation theories

Motivation theory

Approaches to motivation are underpinned by motivation theory. The most influential theories, many of them quite old but still the underpinning theories for many newer business models in this domain, are classified as follows:

Instrumentality

- Instrumentality theory, which states that rewards or punishments (carrots or sticks) serve as the means of ensuring that people behave or act in a desired way at work;

Content

- Content theory, which focusses on the content of motivation. It states that motivation is essentially about taking action to satisfy needs, and identifies the main needs that influence behaviour. Needs theory was originally developed by Maslow (1954), and in their two-factor model Herzberg et al. (1957) listed needs they termed 'satisfiers';

Process

- Process theory, which focusses on the psychological processes which affect motivation with reference to expectations, goals, and perceptions of equity.

6.10 Performance Management

6.10.1   What is performance management?

Managing performance

The terms managing performance and performance management are widely used in the literature, raising the important question: do they mean the same thing? 'Managing performance' is typically applied in a wider organisational context, and is used to refer to the ways that organisations plan, coordinate and use their resources, including their human resources, to achieve business aims and goals. The term performance management tends to be used when referring to specific methods and processes linking people management to organisational goals. This method proposes that employee performance is best developed through practical challenges on the job with guidance from managers in the organisations. This is typically the method used by most hospitality employers.

Performance management

Performance management as a process

Flexible process

Performance management should be regarded as a flexible process, not as a system. The use of the term system implies a rigid, standardised and bureaucratic approach that is inconsistent with the concept of performance management as a flexible and evolutionary, albeit coherent, process that is applied by managers working with their teams in accordance with the circumstances in which they operate. As such, it involves managers and those whom they manage acting as partners, but within a framework that sets out how they can best work together.

Performance management as a cycle

Performance management can be described as a continuous self-renewing cycle, as illustrated in Figure 6.4 and summarily explained thereafter.

Self-renewing cycle

The five stages in the cycle are: plan, manage, review, reward and renew, and depending on the type of organisation, the performance management cycle may take place over different period lengths, ranging from monthly to yearly. They are explained as follows:

Five stages

1 Planning involves getting together with an employee and evaluating expectations for a set period of time. The first stage in the planning process is to evaluate an employee's current role and performance, establishing an initial idea of areas of improvement and realistic targets;

Planning

2 Managing by providing support to an employee at all times and ensuring that the appropriate systems and tools are available to maximise performance expectations;

Managing

3 Reviewing by making sure that the performance structure set out in the first stage is being adhered to; this may be particularly useful if there are any performance barriers that could have a direct effect on other areas of the organisation;

Reviewing

4 Rewarding if all of the objectives have been met; the reasons for and types of rewards should be discussed during the first stage when the objectives are outlined;

Rewarding

5 Renewing involves analysing the previous objectives and looking at ways to improve on them, planning for the next cycle.

Renewing

6

FIGURE 6.4 The Performance Management Cycle (Source: www.love2reward.co.uk)

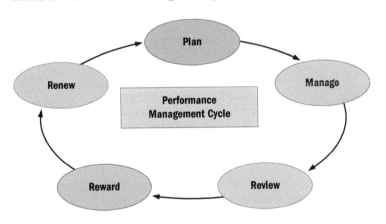

6.10.2 Performance agreements

Performance agreements form the basis for development, assessment and feedback in the performance management process, often referred to as performance appraisal. They define expectations in the form of a role profile that sets out role requirements in terms of key result areas and competencies required for effective performance. The role profile provides the basis for agreeing objectives and methods of measuring performance and assessing the level of competency reached. The performance agreement incorporates any performance improvement plans that may be necessary, as well

Performance agreements

Role profile

as a personal development plan. It describes what individuals are expected to do but also indicates what support they can receive from their line managers. Performance agreements emerge from the analysis of role requirements and the performance review, often referred to as appraisal. At its most basic, this is an assessment of an employee's past performance leading to an analysis of future requirements. The two processes can take place at the same meeting (Armstrong, 2012).

Appraisal

The 12 golden rules

12 Golden rules

The 12 golden rules for HR managers when conducting performance appraisal meetings are:

Prepared

1 Be prepared. Managers should prepare by referring to a list of agreed objectives and their notes on performance throughout the year. They should form views about the reasons for success or failure and decide where to give praise, which performance problems should be mentioned and what steps may be undertaken to overcome them. Any changes that may have taken place or are contemplated in the individual's role should also be given some thought, as should work and personal objectives for the next period. Individuals should also prep to identify achievements and problems, and be ready to assess their own performance at the meeting. They should prepare any points they wish to raise about their work and prospects.

Clear structure

2 Work to a clear structure. The meeting should be planned to cover all the points identified during preparation. Sufficient time should be allowed for a full discussion – hurried meetings are ineffective. An hour or two is usually necessary to get maximum value from the review.

Right atmosphere

3 Create the right atmosphere. A successful meeting depends on creating an informal environment in which a full, frank, but friendly exchange of views can take place. It is best to start with a fairly general discussion before getting into any detail.

Good feedback

4 Provide good feedback. Individuals need to know how they are getting on. Feedback should be based on factual evidence. It refers to results, events, critical incidents and significant behaviours that have affected performance in specific ways. The feedback should be presented in a manner that enables individuals to recognise and accept its factual nature – it should be a description of what has happened, not a judgement. Positive feedback should be given on things the individual did well, in addition to areas for improvement. People are more likely to work at improving their performance and developing their skills if they feel empowered by the process.

Time

5 Use time productively. The reviewer should test understanding, obtain information, and seek proposals and support. Time should be allowed for the individual to express his or her views fully and to respond to any comments made by the manager. The meeting should take the form of a dialogue between two interested and involved parties, both of whom are seeking a positive conclusion.

Praise

6 Use praise. If possible, managers should begin with praise for some specific achievement, making sure it is sincere and deserved. Praise helps people to relax – everyone needs encouragement and appreciation.

Talking

7 Let individuals do most of the talking. This enables them to get things off their chest and helps them feel that they are getting a fair hearing. Use open-ended questions (i.e. questions that invite the individual to think about what to reply rather than indicating the expected answer). This is to encourage people to expand.

8 Invite self-assessment. This is to see how things look from the individu- Self-assessment
al's point of view and to provide a basis for discussion – many people un-
derestimate themselves. Ask questions such as:
- How well do you feel you have done?
- What do you feel are your strengths?
- What do you like most/least about your job?
- Why do you think that particular project went well?
- Why do you think you didn't meet that target?

9 Discuss performance, not personality. Discussions on performance Not personality
should be based on factual evidence, not opinion. Always refer to actual
events or behaviour and to results compared with agreed performance
measures. Individuals should be given plenty of scope to explain why
something did or did not happen.

10 Encourage analysis of performance. Don't just hand out praise or blame. Analysis
Analyse jointly and objectively why things went well or badly and what can
be done to maintain a high standard or avoid problems in the future.

11 Don't deliver unexpected criticisms. There should be no surprises. The Criticisms
discussion should only be concerned with events or behaviours that have
been noted at the time they took place. Feedback on performance should
be immediate. It should not wait until the end of the year. The purpose of
the formal review is to reflect briefly on experiences during the review period and on this basis to look ahead.

12 Agree on measurable objectives and a plan of action. The aim should be Measurable
to end the review meeting on a positive note. These golden rules may
sound straightforward and obvious enough, but they can only function
properly in a culture that supports this type of approach, hence the importance of getting and keeping top management support and the need
to take special care in developing and introducing the system and in
training managers and their staff.

Managers conducting appraisals should be objective and open in addressing poor performance. The use of SMART goals and performance data enable managers to apply rational criteria and conduct appraisals objectively,
which helps to make the process more acceptable to employees. This approach also allows the employee being appraised to acknowledge that poor
performance is an issue and to be receptive to addressing the problem
(Gilmore & Williams, 2013).

The cause and extent of the performance problem should be understood by
both parties, as this is a fundamental and crucial step in dealing with the Both parties
problem. There are many causes for poor performance which may or may
not be workplace-related; sometimes, they are a combination of both. A
good hospitality manager must be able to identify the genuine cause of poor Genuine cause
performance. This can be a serious challenge to many managers in the hospitality sector, as their own personal training often does not cover this phenomenon. Recent studies of organisational practice confirm that there are
three new key areas being developed in many organisations. Firstly, organi- New key areas
sations appear to be concerned with giving employees more involvement
with the process of performance management, for example by exercising
more influence on how performance objectives are set. Secondly, there is a
focus on developing more sophisticated performance objectives, particularly
those relating to the way employees realise their objectives and targets.
Thirdly, many organisations have now moved to give front line managers

6

more influence over the ownership and performance management process for their department (Incomes Data Service, 2011).

6.11 Managing wages and salaries

6.11.1 Reward management

Rewards

Reward management is an essential activity, because pay and benefits, together with non-financial intrinsic rewards, can have a powerful influence on the recruitment and retention of employees. Reward management is concerned with the formulation and implementation of strategies and policies, the purposes of which are to reward people fairly, equitably and consistently in accordance with their value to an organisation, thus helping it achieve its strategic goals. It deals with the design, implementation and maintenance of reward systems (reward processes, practices and procedures) that aim to meet the needs of both organisation and stakeholders. Instrumentality is the belief that actions work along the lines of cause and effect. In its very crudest form, instrumentality theory states that people only work for money, and that the job role that they perform is instrumental to receiving pay.

Instrumentality theory

6.11.2 The relationship between motivating strategies, job satisfaction and money

Job satisfaction

The basic requirements for job satisfaction can include comparatively higher pay, an equitable payment system, real opportunities for promotion, considerate and participative management, a reasonable degree of social interaction at work, interesting and varied tasks, and a high degree of autonomy: control over work pace and work methods. The degree of satisfaction obtained by individuals, however, depends largely upon their own needs and expectations, and the working environment (Armstrong, 2006).

6.11.3 The aims of reward management

Aims

The aims of reward management are to:
- Reward people according to what the organisation values and wants to pay for;
- Reward people for the value they provide;
- Reward the right things to convey the right message about what is important in terms of behaviours and outcomes;
- Develop a performance culture;
- Motivate people and obtain their commitment and engagement;
- Help attract and retain the high quality people the organisation needs;
- Create total reward processes that recognise the importance of both financial and non-financial rewards;
- Develop a positive employment relationship and psychological contract;
- Align reward practices with both business goals and employee values.

Alignment

The 2013 People 1st State of the Nation Report emphasises the importance of the alignment of reward practices with employee values and needs, which is every bit as important as the alignment with business goals; is the former is critical for the realisation of the latter. A reward system needs to be seen to operate fairly, and people need to feel they are treated justly in accordance with what they are due because of their value to the organisation (Armstrong, 2012).

The reward system also needs to apply equitably, so that people are reward-   Equitably
ed appropriately in relation to others within the organisation; relativities between jobs should be measured as objectively as possible and equal pay
should be provided for work of equal value. The system needs to function
consistently, so that decisions on pay do not vary arbitrarily or occur without
due cause to different people or at different times. The reward system
needs to operate transparently, so that people understand how reward processes operate and how they are affected by these processes.

6.11.4   Rewarding people

The philosophy of reward management recognises that it must be strategic   Strategic
in the sense that it addresses longer-term issues relating to how people
should be valued for what they do and what they achieve within the organisation. Reward strategies and the processes that are required to implement
them have to flow from the business strategy. Reward management adopts
a total reward approach, which emphasises the importance of considering   Total reward
all aspects of reward as a coherent whole integrated with other HR initia-   approach
tives designed to achieve the motivation, commitment, engagement and development of employees. This requires the integration of reward strategies
with other HRM strategies, especially those involving human resource development. Reward management is an integral part of an HRM approach to
managing people (Armstrong, 2012).

The philosophy of reward management is affected by the business and HR
strategies of the organisation. The significance attached to reward matters
by top management and the internal and external environment of the organisation can make the organisation the employer of choice. The external envi-   Employer of
ronment includes the levels of pay in the labour market (market rates), and   choice
it is helpful for all hospitality managers to be aware of the economic theories that explain how these levels are determined. A classic reward system   Classic reward
consists of: system
- Policies that provide guidelines on approaches to managing rewards;
- Practices that provide financial and non-financial rewards;
- Processes concerned with evaluating the relative size of jobs (job evaluation), and assessing individual performance (performance management);
- Procedures applied in order to maintain the system and ensure that it operates efficiently and flexibly and provides value for money.

A market-related pay strategy signifies an approach where pay and benefits   Market-related
practice is sharply responsive to the rates of pay in the external labour mar-   pay
ket. This means that pay rates reflect the market price for labour and incorporate the philosophy of a particular job being worth what the labour market
commands at any given time or location (Gilmore & Williams, 2013). In the
UK, for example, the labour and pay market for waiting staff in a small city
in the Midlands dictates an hourly pay rate of just over the National Minimum Wage (NMW), which in October 2015 was £6.70 per hour for workers
aged 21 years old and over, and £5.30 per hour for workers aged 18 to 20
years old. Waiters in London, however, because of the demand and high living costs, are paid the London living wage rate of £9.40 per hour, which applies to all employees 18 years old and over.

TEXT 6.5

Hospitality has a poor reputation on pay

The hospitality sector in the UK suffers from a poor reputation, with the general perception that it is both low skilled and low paid. This perception does not take into account the huge range of career opportunities in the sector, particularly at higher skilled and management levels, but at the same time across a range of measures, the sector performs poorly. Pay rates are low, with the average salary in the sector being £13,930 p.a., compared to an economy average of £27,174.11 (Reed UK Data, 2015). Similarly, the number of workers not on the living wage is comparatively high, as are the number of people on zero-hour contracts. As a result, hospitality is less attractive as a career destination than other sectors. Another factor undermining the skills of the sector is the poor impact of training. People 1st's research has found that a significant proportion of training is not providing a return on investment as it is not linked to a business output and the learning from training is not sufficiently embedded back in the business.

(Source: People 1st, 2014)

Market-related pay is based on classical economic theory where pay decisions are influenced by market supply and demand for labour (as in the previous example). The hospitality sector is well known for its low pay – particularly at the lower end of the job scale, e.g. waiters, bar staff, porters - with many low level jobs in the hospitality sector set at minimum wage levels.

Paradox
There is a paradox here in that the hospitality industry suffers from a bad image in that it is often considered to be a low paid, low skilled job filled by transient workers waiting for better jobs or students helping to pay the cost of university, whereas there is opportunity for those willing and able to learn or graduate to quickly move into reasonably well paid mid-level management roles much earlier than in many other service industries, such as retail, in-

surance or banking. However, this poor image needs to be recognised by hospitality managers, as it makes it far more difficult to recruit and retain employees at the low jobs end of the labour market. Text 6.5 illustrates the hospitality industry's reputation, while Figure 6.5 is a summary of average hospitality and catering salary levels for 2015 compared to their values in 2014, taken from Reed.co.uk data (2015).

FIGURE 6.5 UK 2015 hospitality and catering average salaries

Role	2015 Level	Change since 2014
Hotel Management	£35.234	£3.169
Contract Catering Management	£35.215	−£6.957
Head/Executive Chef	£32.504	£2.632
Restaurant Manager	£31.111	−£1.616
Events Management	£26.852	£1.788
Bar Management	£26.785	−£1.885
Other Hospitality & Catering	£26.596	−£ 277
Sous-Chef	£26.101	£1.356
Duty Manager	£25.356	£2.968
Restaurant Deputy Manager	£25.207	−£ 542
Pastry Chef	£24.608	£ 234
Chef Manager	£23.989	£ 253
Concierge	£23.512	£2.788
Assistant Manager	£23.163	−£ 125
Conference & Banqueting	£22.806	−£ 201
Chef de Partie	£20.533	−£ 34
Chef de Rang	£20.099	£2.633
Housekeeper	£19.562	−£3.263
Receptionist	£18.512	£1.344
Waiting & Bar Staff	£17.964	£ 595
Commis-Chef	£16.960	£ 109
Kitchen Staff	£15.642	−£1.986

6.12 Other matters

6.12.1 Labour turnover and retention
Historically, the hospitality sector has always had a high labour turnover rate, with many transient employees including university students and travellers (backpackers) working in the sector whilst travelling the world. This often happens because there are usually basic jobs available in a hotel, and there is normally a large labour pool willing to fill these job roles. Text 6.6 shows the poor staff retention rates of the UK hospitality sector.

Labour turnover

6.12.2 The changing nature of hospitality skills needs
The growth of the hospitality sector has brought with it increased diversity. Sometimes referred to as the hospitality and tourism sector, this is because in many parts of Europe, the term tourism includes hospitality and refers to hotels, restaurants and bars, rather than tourism management. In hospitality, the growth has largely been found in the mainstream restaurant industry, which is recruiting in significant numbers. In most cases, the demand is for entry level staff with good customer service and teamwork skills rather than high levels of craft skills. Similarly, food production chefs need to be able to maintain consistency and deal with high volumes rather than having to demonstrate high level culinary skills. This means that many of these roles can

Diversity

TEXT 6.6

Poor staff retention levels in the UK

Many hospitality employers are investing heavily in recruitment and training and development, and there are some fantastic examples across the hospitality sector of businesses that have highly successful recruitment and training interventions. These not only contribute to the growth of their businesses but, given the low barriers to entry for some roles and the development opportunities available, they also play an important role in supporting social mobility. However, despite the huge investment made, training and development is undermined by labour turnover.

Recent data from People 1st shows that the hospitality sector has one of the highest levels of labour turnover across the UK economy at 20%. This is a fall of 10% when compared to turnover rates in 2008, when they were at 30%. However, some researchers consider this to be a gross under estimate of the real labour turnover rate in the hospitality sector (Lashley & Rowson, 2003).

However, based on the current figures this means that approximately 365,675 people are leaving the sector each year. Clearly, the high rate of staff turnover is impacting on skills in the following ways:

- It is increasing the amount of recruitment the sector requires, exacerbating the existing recruitment challenges.
- Investment in training and development is not being maximised as staff are not staying long enough with the company.
- Training budgets are being directed at initial training rather than towards areas where skills gaps have been identified to address the ongoing recruitment demand.

(Source: People 1st, 2014)

---

be filled without any prior experience or qualifications. Yet the demand for craft skills has increased across the hospitality industry. This has been driven by growing consumer demand for more authentic products and higher levels of service, along with a growing emphasis on pub food. As a result, there is an increased requirement for skilled front- and back-of-house staff (UK's Office for National Statistics – ONS, 2013).

6.12.3 Recruiting skilled migrants

Skilled entrants

As the hospitality and tourism sector is not attracting sufficient numbers of skilled entrants into the sector, it is currently addressing its recruitment issues by hiring international workers. In the case of the UK, just over a quarter of the workforce was born outside of the UK with 12% coming from other EU member states and the remainder coming from outside the EU. Recent figures show that nearly 11% of all EU migrants end up working in the sector, with the most common roles including kitchen assistants, retail assistants, chefs and waiting staff. EU migrants not only fill lower skilled craft roles, but also higher craft and management roles. Figures needed to really understand their impact on skills shortages rather than broader vacancies are unavailable, but as an indication nearly 13,000 EU migrants are working as restaurant and catering managers (ONS, 2013).

Larger urban areas are more likely to attract a higher percentage of migrants than rural or coastal areas and, as a result, reported hard-to-fill vacancies and skills shortages are higher outside major cities. The largest percentage of non-EU migrants is from the Indian sub-continent, and often found in Asian restaurants. However, current UK immigration policy means that few employers can afford to bring in skilled staff from outside the EU; this is beginning to have an impact on skills shortages in this area, in particular for companies that are seeking to grow. The reliance on non-UK nationals to fill skilled roles is likely to continue, unless there is a significant increase in the number of apprenticeships and full-time students on relevant sector specific programmes (People 1st, 2014).

6

Summary

► Human resource management involves five main functions, which are planning, organising, staffing, leading and controlling; its concepts and techniques are important to all managers, especially in avoiding recruitment mistakes.

► Common approaches to organising human resources include the transactional HR group, in which organisations form centres to deal with all HRM issues; the corporate HR group, which focusses on assisting top management; the embedded HR unit, which assigns HR generalists directly to departments; and centres of expertise, which are like specialised consulting firms within the organisation.

► Some trends affecting HRM are globalisation, increased competition, increased indebtedness, technological innovation, more high tech jobs, more service jobs, more knowledge work, and an ageing workforce.

► Recruiting and selecting people to fill new or existing positions in the hospitality sector are crucial elements of human resource activity, though recruitment decisions are too often made in an informal, ad hoc and reactive manner, especially in smaller hospitality organisations.

► Poor recruitment and selection practices lead to expensive use of management time, recruiting replacements for individuals who leave very quickly, high labour turnover, absenteeism, low staff morale, and ineffective management and supervision.

► In recruiting, filling open positions with inside candidates has several advantages as well as downsides. As firms cannot always get the employees they need from their current staff, they need to recruit externally using both traditional as well as online means.

► The problem of applicants lacking soft skills poses a serious challenge for recruiters within a hospitality and tourism sector already fraught with such problems as higher numbers of zero-hour contracts, less visible career progression opportunities, and comparatively low levels of pay.

► Organisations should align their training programmes with their strategies. For new employees to work effectively in any company, it is essential that they go through an induction/orientation training course as soon as possible once they start with the company. The purposes of such an induction course are:
• Making sure that new employees feel welcome and part of the team;
• Making sure that new employees have the basic information needed to function effectively;

6

- Helping employees understand the organisation in its broadest sense;
- Getting the person socialised into the firm's culture, values, and strategies.

▶ Training programmes should be set up to be rational, such as by using the analysis-design-development-implement-evaluate training process model.

▶ On-the-job training is planned and structured, and occurs at the employees' workplace; it can vary in format and complexity. It is common practice in the hospitality industry to use self-learning training manuals.

▶ Off-the-job training usually consists of courses organised by internal or external training providers and the training is held away from the workplace.

▶ There is no consensus as to the best way of evaluating training. One approach is to adopt quantitative measures while other evaluation approaches seek to measure more intangible elements difficult to measure financially using the balanced scorecard method.

▶ Motivation theory, based on instrumentality, content or process, examines the process of motivation, and seeks to explain people's behaviour and directions taken at work. Motivation can be intrinsic or extrinsic, and while extrinsic motivators can have an immediate and powerful effect, they will not necessarily last long. Intrinsic motivators are likely to have a deeper and longer-term effect because they are inherent in individuals and not imposed from outside.

▶ Performance management tends to be used when referring to specific methods and processes linking people management to organisational goals; it should be seen as a flexible process which can be described as a continuous, self-renewing cycle of five stages – planning, managing, reviewing, rewarding, and renewing.

▶ Managers conducting appraisals should be objective and open in addressing poor performance. The 12 golden rules for HR managers conducting performance appraisal meetings are: be prepared; work to a clear structure; create the right atmosphere; provide good feedback; use time productively; use praise; let individuals do most of the talking; invite self-assessment; discuss performance, not personality; encourage performance analysis; don't deliver unexpected criticisms; establish measurable objectives and a plan of action.

▶ Reward management is the formulation and implementation of strategies and policies in order to reward people fairly, equitably and consistently in accordance with their value to the organisation, thus helping the organisation in achieving its strategic goals.

▶ A classic reward system consists of: policies that provide guidelines on approaches to managing rewards; practices that provide financial and non-financial rewards; processes concerned with evaluating the relative size of jobs, and assessing individual performance; and procedures

6

applied in order to maintain the system and ensure that it operates efficiently and flexibly and provides value for money.

▶ Market-related pay is based on classical economic theory where decisions regarding pay are influenced by market supply and demand for labour; a market-related pay strategy signifies an approach where pay and benefits practice is sharply responsive to the rates of pay in the external labour market.

Questions and assignments for reflection

1. What are the specific activities contained in the five main functions of the human resource management? Why should all managers be acquainted with human resource management?

2. Compare and contrast the various ways in which human resources services are organised within organisations. If you were the owner of a national motel chain, which way of organising the human resources services will you prefer? Why?

3. Why is recruitment and selection a thorny issue within the hospitality and tourism sector?

4. Compare and contrast on-the-job and off-the-job training. Which would you prefer if you were a departmental manager? Provide arguments to justify your choice.

5. Explain how the growth of the hospitality sector and its increased diversity have affected the nature of hospitality skills needed by employees.

7
Marketing for the Hospitality Industry

Dr. B. Rowson

7.1 Introduction

This chapter is about marketing in the hospitality industry. First of all, what is marketing? Simply put, marketing is managing profitable customer relationships. The aim of marketing is to create value for customers and capture value from customers in return. Essentially, there are five steps in the marketing process: understanding customer needs, designing customer driven strategies, integrating marketing programmes, and building customer relationships whilst capturing value for the firm.

7.2 What is marketing?

Marketing, more than any other business function, deals with customers. Although in this chapter more detailed definitions of marketing and how it is used in the hospitality sector will be explored, perhaps the simplest definition is this: Marketing is managing profitable customer relationships. The twofold goal of marketing is to attract new customers by promising superior value, and to keep and grow numbers of current customers by delivering satisfaction (Lovelock & Wirtz, 2011).

Definition

Walmart, for example, has become the world's largest retailer and company by delivering on its promise, 'Save money, Live better.' Nintendo surged ahead in the video-games market behind the pledge that 'Wii would like to play,' backed by its wildly popular Wii console and a growing list of popular games and accessories for all ages. And McDonald's meets its 'I'm lovin' it' motto by being 'our customers' favourite place and way to eat' the world over, giving it a market share greater than that of its nearest three competitors combined (Kotler & Armstrong, 2013).

Russia, Caucasus, Dombai: Wooden Hotel

7.2.1 The service revolution

Service sector

Across Europe and indeed around the world, the service sector of the economy is going through a period of almost revolutionary change in which established ways of doing business continue to be shunted aside. At the second decade of the 21st century, all ways of life and work are being transformed by new developments in services. Innovators continually launch new ways to satisfy existing needs, and meet these heretofore unknown needs as well. The same is true of services directed at corporate users.

Progress

Although many new service ventures fail, a few succeed. Many long-established firms are also failing or being merged out of existence; but others are making spectacular progress by continually rethinking the way they do business, looking for innovative ways to serve customers better and taking advantage of new developments in technology. This is as true for the hospitality sector as for any other business sector.

7.2.2 Services marketing

People use an array of services every day, although some of these, like talking on the phone or using a credit card, even taking a bus ride, or withdrawing money from an ATM, are often so routine they almost escape notice unless something goes wrong. Other service purchases may involve more forethought and may be more memorable experiences, for instance booking a cruise vacation, getting financial advice, or having a medical examination. The use of these services is an example of service consumption at the indi-

B2C

vidual, or business-to-consumer (B2C), level (Lovelock & Wirtz, 2011).

B2B

Hospitality organisations also use a wide array of business-to-business (B2B) services, varying according to the company size to some degree, but usually involving purchases on a much larger scale than those made by individuals or families. An independent restaurant business, for example, will often purchase their food from various suppliers, most of which deliver to the business. In the restaurant business, food provenance is everything nowadays; customers often want to know the origin of the seafood, meat or vegetables used. This can be part of a marketing plan for the business. Having the source of one's produce on the menu, for example, can be a particular selling point to restaurant customers (Ball, Rimmington, & Rowson, 2007).

Core business

Time-based performances

Current trends suggest firms are outsourcing more and more tasks to external service providers in order to focus on their core business. So what are services? The formal definition of services is: economic activity offered by one party to another, most commonly employing time-based performances to bring about desired results in recipients themselves or in objects or other assets for which purchasers have responsibility (Lovelock & Wirtz, 2011). Time-based means something a firm does within a certain time period, for

Desired results

example providing dinner for customers in the restaurant that evening. Desired results are outcomes desired by a customer, e.g. the wish to have dinner with friends that evening. Other examples are going to a theatre to be entertained, to a university to get an education, to visit a hotel to have somewhere safe to stay and sleep when away from home. These are desired results of service activities. Put simply: in exchange for their money, time and effort, service customers can expect to obtain value from access to goods, labour, professional skills, facilities, networks and systems. However, they do not normally take ownership of any of the physical elements involved (Lovelock & Wirtz, 2011).

7

What is so special about services marketing? Service marketing focusses on the distinctive characteristics of services and how these affect both customer behaviour and marketing strategy. Many hospitality services, for example, are produced and delivered with the customer present at the service firm's facility (staying in a hotel or eating at a restaurant). The presence of the customer in a service facility means that capacity management becomes an important driver of a firm's profitability. If too few customers are present, for example, the high fixed costs of operating and staffing the facility cannot be covered. If too many customers show up, their service experience often deteriorates as service providers get busier; customers who have to be turned away may not want to come back having been disappointed by not being able to stay in the hotel or eat in the restaurant a first time.

To address this constant struggle of having the right number of customers show up, pricing of services tends to be highly dynamic and complicated. Consider the pricing of airline tickets and the terms and conditions attached to a discounted ticket. Prices change all the time, and typically depend on time and date of travel, how long in advance a flight is booked, the duration of the stay, whether tickets are flexible and allow for changes in travel dates and itinerary, and whether they are refundable. Such pricing is also called 'revenue management' or 'yield management', previously discussed in Chapter 4.

In hospitality services marketing, the traditional 4 Ps of the marketing mix (product, pricing, promotion/market communications, and place/distribution) are adapted to the distinctive features of hospitality services; because of the personalised nature of hospitality services, these differ from other services marketing concepts (e.g. car hire or banking services) in that, in the hospitality sector, customers are very much part of the service delivered. Then, there are the additional 3 Ps of services marketing: people, physical evidence and process.

The process of service delivery is often as important as the function of the service. A service is a process from an organisation's point of view, but from a customer's perspective it is an experience. The quality of the experience is a function of the careful design of customer service processes, adoption of standardised procedures, rigorous management of service quality, high standards of training and automation. Services marketing helps ensure that these processes are designed to be viewed from the customer's perspective (Kotler & Armstrong, 2013).

Physical environment includes the appearance of buildings, landscaping, interior furnishing, equipment, uniforms, signs, printed materials and other visible cues that provide evidence of service quality and guide customers through a service process. The design of a physical environment can have a profound impact on customer satisfaction and service productivity. People relate to the frontline employees of the firm. From a hospitality customer's point of view, when service employees are involved, the people are the service. This means that frontline employees need to possess the required technical and interpersonal skills and a positive attitude. People can be a key competitive advantage for many service firms. Services marketing includes building customer loyalty, managing relationships, complaint handling, improving service quality and productivity of service operations, and how to become a service leader in the hospitality industry.

Special

Customer

Pricing of services

Traditional 4 Ps

7

Additional 3 Ps

Process

Experience

Frontline employees

Key role

Furthermore, frontline employees play a key role in anticipating customers' needs, customising the service delivery, and building personalised relationships with customers. Effective performance of these activities should ultimately lead to customer loyalty. How attentive employees can be in anticipating customers' needs is shown in Text 7.1, borrowed from Berry (1999, pp. 156-159) as an example. This, and many other success stories of employees showing discretionary effort makes a difference, have reinforced the truism that highly motivated people are at the core of service excellence. They are increasingly a key variable for creating and maintaining competitive positioning and advantage.

Service excellence

TEXT 7.1

Cora Griffiths, the outstanding waitress

Cora Griffith, a waitress for the Orchard Café at the Paper Valley Hotel in Appleton, Wisconsin, is superb in her role, appreciated by first-time customers, famous with her regular customers, and revered by her co-workers. Cora loves her work – and it shows. Comfortable in a role she believes is right for her, Cora follows nine rules of success:

1 **Treat Customers Like Family.** First-time customers are not allowed to feel like strangers. Cheerful and proactive, Cora smiles, chats, and includes everyone at the table in the conversation. She is as respectful to children as she is to adults and makes it a point to learn and use everyone's name. 'I want people to feel like they're sitting down to dinner right at my house,' she says. 'I want them to feel they're welcome, that they can get comfortable, that they can relax. I don't just serve people, I pamper them.'

2 **Listen First.** Cora has developed her listening skills to the point that she rarely writes down customers' orders. She listens carefully and provides a customized service: 'Are they in a hurry?' 'Do they have a special diet?' 'Do they like their selection cooked in a certain way?'

3 **Anticipate Customers' Wants.** Cora replenishes beverages and brings extra bread and butter in a timely manner. One regular customer, who likes honey with her coffee, gets it without having to ask. 'I don't want my customers to have to ask

for anything,' says Cora, 'so I always try to anticipate what they might need.'

4 **Simple Things Make the Difference.** Cora manages the details of her service, monitoring the cleanliness of the utensils and their correct placement. The fold for napkins must be just right. She inspects each plate in the kitchen before taking it to the table, and she provides crayons for small children to draw pictures while waiting for the meal. 'It's the little things that please the customer,' she says.

5 **Work Smart.** Cora scans all her tables at once, looking for opportunities to combine tasks. 'Never do just one thing at a time,' she advises. 'And never go from the kitchen to the dining room empty-handed. Take coffee or iced tea or water with you.' When she refills one water glass, she refills others. When clearing one plate, she clears others. 'You have to be organized, and you have to keep in touch with the big picture.'

6 **Keep Learning.** Cora makes an ongoing effort to improve existing skills and learn new ones.

7 **Success Is Where You Find It.** Cora is content with her work. She finds satisfaction in pleasing her customers, and she enjoys helping other people enjoy. Her optimistic attitude is a positive force in the restaurant. She is hard to ignore. 'If customers come to the restaurant in a bad mood, I'll try to cheer them up before they leave,' she says. Her definition of success: 'To be happy in life.'

8 **All for One, One for All.** Cora has been working with many of the same co-workers for more than eight years. The team supports one another on the crazy days when 300 conventioneers come to the restaurant for breakfast at the same time. Everyone pitches in and helps. The waiting staff cover for one another, the managers trade down to wait the tables, the chefs garnish the plates. 'We are like a little family,' Cora says. 'We know each other very well and we help each other out. If we have a crazy day, I'll go in the kitchen toward the end of the shift and say, 'Man, I'm just proud of us. We really worked hard today."

9 **Take Pride in Your Work.** Cora believes in the importance of her work and in the need to do it well: 'I don't think of myself as 'just a waitress' ... I've chosen to be a waitress. I'm doing this to my full potential, and I give it my best. I tell anyone who's starting out: 'take pride in what you do.' You're never just an anything, no matter what you do. You give it your all ... and you do it with pride.'

7.2.3   Marketing theories, the marketing mix: from 4 Ps to 7 Ps

Marketing is a continually evolving discipline and as such can be one where companies find themselves left very much behind the competition if they stand still for too long. One example of this evolution has been the fundamental changes to the basic marketing mix. Where once there were 4 Ps used to explain the mix, nowadays it is more commonly accepted that the more developed 7 Ps add a much needed additional layer of depth to the marketing mix, with some theorists going even further. Before getting carried away, the first order of business should be to address the marketing mix and the original 4 Ps principle.

Evolving discipline

Marketing mix

The marketing mix

Simply put, the marketing mix is a tool used by businesses and marketers to help them determine a product or brand's offering. The 4 Ps have been associated with the marketing mix since their creation by E. Jerome McCarthy in 1960, and they are listed in Figure 7.1.

FIGURE 7.1 The 4 Ps

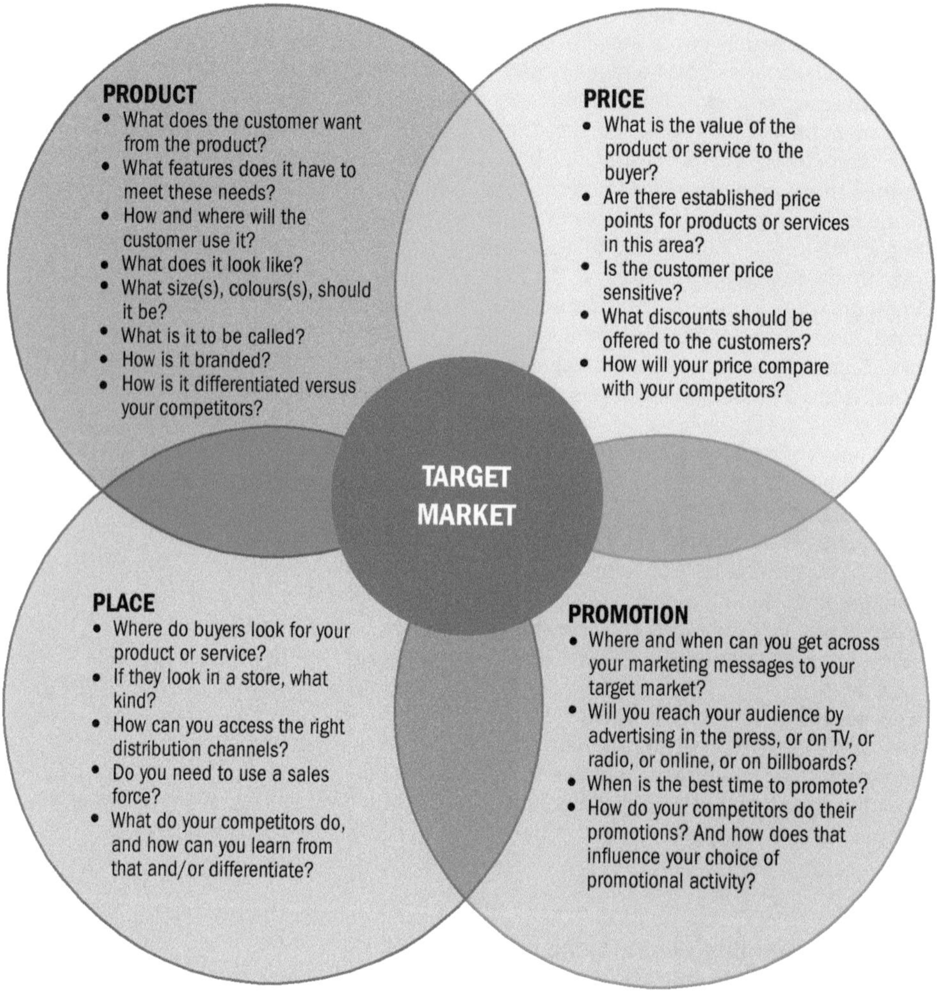

PRODUCT
- What does the customer want from the product?
- What features does it have to meet these needs?
- How and where will the customer use it?
- What does it look like?
- What size(s), colours(s), should it be?
- What is it to be called?
- How is it branded?
- How is it differentiated versus your competitors?

PRICE
- What is the value of the product or service to the buyer?
- Are there established price points for products or services in this area?
- Is the customer price sensitive?
- What discounts should be offered to the customers?
- How will your price compare with your competitors?

TARGET MARKET

PLACE
- Where do buyers look for your product or service?
- If they look in a store, what kind?
- How can you access the right distribution channels?
- Do you need to use a sales force?
- What do your competitors do, and how can you learn from that and/or differentiate?

PROMOTION
- Where and when can you get across your marketing messages to your target market?
- Will you reach your audience by advertising in the press, or on TV, or radio, or online, or on billboards?
- When is the best time to promote?
- How do your competitors do their promotions? And how does that influence your choice of promotional activity?

The 4 Ps

Product
- Product – A product should fit the task consumers want; it should work and it should be what consumers are expecting to get.

Place
- Place – A product should be available from where target consumers find it easiest to shop. This may be a high street, mail order or the more current option of e-commerce or online shopping.

Price
- Price – A product should always be seen as representing good value for money. This does not necessarily mean it should be the cheapest available; one of the main tenets of the marketing concept is that customers are usually happy to pay a little more for something that works really well for them.

Promotion
- Promotion – Advertising, PR, sales promotion, personal selling and, in more recent times, social media are all key communication tools for an organisation. These tools should be used to put across the organisation's message to the correct audiences in the manner they would most like to hear, whether it be informative or appealing to their emotions.

In the late 70s, it was widely acknowledged by marketers that the marketing mix needed to be updated. This led to the creation of the extended marketing mix, which added 3 new elements to the 4 Ps Principle as shown in Figure 7.2. This allowed the extended marketing mix to also include products that are services instead of being limited to physical things (Kotler & Armstrong, 2013).

© Noordhoff Uitgevers bv

FIGURE 7.2 The extended marketing mix

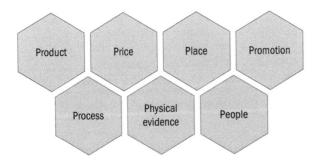

The extended 7 Ps
- People – All companies are reliant on the people who run them, from front-line sales staff to Managing Director. Having the right people is essential, because they are as much a part of business offering as the products/services on offer. *People*
- Process – The delivery of service is usually done with the customer present, so, how the service is delivered is once again part of what the consumer is paying for. *Process*
- Physical evidence – Almost all services include some physical elements, even if the bulk of what the consumer is paying for is intangible. A hair salon, for example, provides their customers with a finished haircut, and an insurance company provides their customers with some form of printed material. *Physical evidence*

Though used since the 1980s, the 7 Ps are still widely taught due to their fundamentally sound logic in the marketing environment as well as marketers abilities to adapt the marketing mix to include changes in communications. Examples of the latter include the use of social media, upgrades of the places where a product/service can be sold, or customers' expectations in a constantly changing commercial environment.

Is there an 8th P?
Some schools of thought hold that there are 8 Ps in the marketing mix. The final P is Productivity and Quality, which came from the old services marketing mix and is folded in to the extended marketing mix (Lovelock & Wirtz, 2011). *8th P*
The 8th P of the Marketing Mix
- Productivity and Quality – 'is the customer being offered a good deal?' This is less about a business improving its own productivity for cost management, and more about how it passes this on to its customers. *Productivity and Quality*

After over half a century, the marketing mix is still very much applicable to a marketer's day to day work. Good marketers will learn to adapt the theory to fit not only with modern times but with their individual business models as well (Kotler & Armstrong, 2013). Text 7.2 illustrates the type of questions to be generated in using the 7 Ps when seeking to open a new restaurant.

TEXT 7.2

Opening a new restaurant

Imagine you want to open a new restaurant. Services marketing would then guide you through the 7 Ps, being the:
- (Core) product: What is your value proposition? What sort of dining experience do you wish to deliver: one that is ideal for romantic fine-dining or geared towards business lunches?
- Pricing: What price levels and menu designs, such as lower priced off-peak menus, do you want to offer?
- Promotion/market communications: How do you reach your target audience and shape their visitation behaviour?
- Place: Where do you locate your restaurant?

- People: How do you select, train, motivate and retain your front-line employees?
- Physical evidence: What will the interior of the restaurant look like?
- Process: How do you design service processes to satisfy customers? This can range from seating to preparing the bill?

Services marketing would also help guide your thinking about how to develop long-term profitable relationships with your customers, design complaint handling and service recovery processes and policies, and help you to systematically improve the quality of your service and the productivity of the entire operation.

7.3 Hospitality marketing and sales

7.3.1   Designing a customer-driven marketing strategy

Marketing strategy

Once hotel management fully understands consumers and the marketplace, hospitality marketing management can design a customer-driven marketing strategy for that particular hotel business. Marketing management is defined as the art and science of choosing target markets and building profitable relationships with them. The hospitality marketing manager's aim is to find, attract, keep, and grow target customers for the hotel or restaurant sector by creating, delivering, and communicating superior customer value. To design a winning marketing strategy, a marketing manager must answer two important questions:
- What customers should be served (what is the target market)?
- How can these customers be served best (what is the value proposition)?

7.3.2   Selecting customers to serve

Segments

A hospitality company must first decide whom it will serve. It does this by dividing the market into segments of customers (market segmentation) and selecting which segments it will pursue (target marketing). Some think of marketing management as finding as many customers as possible and increasing demand (Kotler & Armstrong, 2013). But marketing managers know that they cannot serve all customers in every way. By trying to serve all customers, they may end up not serving some customers properly (Ball et al., 2007). A company should therefore strive to select only customers it can serve properly and profitably. The Ritz-Carlton Hotel group, for example, profitably targets the group of affluent professionals and business people, whereas Jury's Inns profitably target the group of families with more modest means. Ultimately, hospitality marketing managers must decide which customers they want to target and on what level, timing, and nature of their demand.

Simply put, hospitality marketing management is a trade-off between customer management and demand management (Lovelock & Wirtz, 2011). The first three steps in the marketing process are: understanding the marketplace and customer needs; designing a customer-driven marketing strategy; and constructing a marketing programme. These lead up to the fourth and most important step: building profitable customer relationships.

Trade-off

7.3.3   Customer satisfaction

Customer satisfaction depends on a product's perceived performance relative to a buyer's expectations. If a product's performance falls short of expectations, the customer is dissatisfied. If performance matches expectations, the customer is satisfied. If performance exceeds expectations, the customer is highly satisfied or delighted. Outstanding marketing companies go out of their way to keep important customers satisfied. Most studies show that higher levels of customer satisfaction lead to greater customer loyalty, which in turn results in better company performance. Smart companies aim to delight customers by limiting promises to what they can deliver, and then delivering more than they promise. Delighted customers not only make repeat purchases but also become willing marketing partners and 'customer evangelists' who spread word of their good experiences to others (Kotler & Armstrong, 2013).

Perceived performance

Expectations

7.3.4   Creating customer loyalty and retention

Customer delight   Good customer relationship management ensures customer delight. In turn, delighted customers remain loyal and talk favourably to others about the company and its products. Studies show big differences between the loyalty of customers who are less satisfied, somewhat satisfied, or completely satisfied. Even a slight drop from complete satisfaction can create an enormous drop in loyalty. The aim of customer relationship management, there-

Loyalty   fore, is to create not only customer satisfaction but also customer delight. The recent economic recession has put strong pressure on customer loyalty. It created a new consumer frugality that will last well into the future. Business travellers, for example, are now more aware of what they spend, and in many cases have traded down from 4 star hotels to budget hotels, often flying economy instead of business class. One recent study found that, even in an improved economy, 55% of consumers say they would rather get the best price than the best brand. Nearly two-thirds say they will now shop at a different, lower priced store even if it is less convenient. Lee Resources International Inc. indicated that marketing managers know that it is five times

Cheaper   cheaper to keep an old customer than to acquire a new one. Companies today should therefore shape their value propositions even more carefully and treat their profitable customers well.

Losing a customer means losing more than a single sale. It means losing the entire stream of purchases that customer would make over a lifetime of

Lifetime value   patronage. Text 7.3 is a dramatized illustration of customer lifetime value.

TEXT 7.3

Customer lifetime value

Tom Price, who is GM at a 5 star hotel in London, says he potentially sees £10,000 flying out of his hotel when he sees an upset customer leave the hotel. Why? As he says: 'Assume this customer's average spend is about £500 per visit, and he stays with the hotel twice a month while conducting business in the local area. That is £1000 per month, or £12,000 per year if this customer is lost to another hotel competitor.' Furthermore, if this customer works in business in this region for ten years, that is a potential loss of £120,000 in revenue over that period of time. So if a customer has an unhappy experience at the hotel and switches to another hotel, Tom Price has lost a potential £120,000 in future revenue.

The loss can be much greater if the disappointed customers share their bad experiences with other customers and cause them to switch loyalties. The hospitality business, therefore, needs to find ways to ensure customers come back.

Hospitality companies interested in delighting customers with high service standards, exceptional value, and quality service should be aware that it can take many years for this level of service to become part of overall company culture and brand identity. Year after year, Ritz-Carlton, for example, ranks at or near the top of the hospitality industry in terms of customer satisfaction. Its passion for satisfying customers is summed up in the company's marketing credo, which promises that its luxury hotels deliver a truly memorable experience, one that 'enlivens the senses, instils well-being, and

fulfils even the unexpressed wishes and needs of our guests'. Text 7.4 is adapted from Kotler and Armstrong (2013), and illustrates customer satisfaction at the Ritz-Carlton.

There is a down side to exceeding customer satisfaction, however, and this is cost. Although a customer-centred hospitality firm can seek to deliver high customer satisfaction relative to its competitors, it does not attempt to maximise customer satisfaction because of the high costs associated with

Down side

TEXT 7.4

Customer satisfaction the Ritz-Carlton case

Check into any Ritz-Carlton hotel around the world, and you'll be amazed by the company's fervent dedication to anticipating and meeting even your slightest need. Without ever asking, they seem to know that you're allergic to peanuts and want a king-size bed, a non-allergenic pillow, the blinds open when you arrive, and breakfast with decaffeinated coffee in your room. Every day, hotel staffers - from those at the front desk to those in maintenance and housekeeping - discreetly observe and record even the smallest guest preferences. Then, every morning, each hotel reviews the files of all new arrivals who have previously stayed at a Ritz-Carlton and prepares a list of suggested extra touches that might delight each guest. Once they identify a special customer need, Ritz-Carlton employees go to legendary extremes to meet it. For example, to serve the needs of a guest with food allergies, a Ritz-Carlton chef in Bali located special eggs and milk in a small grocery store in another country and had them delivered to the hotel. In another case, when the hotel's laundry service failed to remove a stain on a guest's suit before the guest departed, the hotel manager travelled to the guest's house and personally delivered a reimbursement check for the cost of the suit. According to one Ritz-Carlton manager, if the chain gets hold of a picture of a guest's pet, it will make a copy, have it framed, and display it in the guest's room in whatever Ritz-Carlton the guest visits. As a result of such customer service heroics, an amazing 95 percent of departing guests report that their stay has been a truly memorable experience. More than 90 percent of Ritz-Carlton's delighted customers return.

it. A company can always increase customer satisfaction by lowering its prices or increasing its services. But this may result in lower profits. The purpose of marketing, after all, is to generate customer value profitably. This requires a very delicate balance: the marketer must continue to generate more customer value and satisfaction but not 'give away the house' in doing so (Kotler & Armstrong, 2013).

7.4 Current trends in hospitality marketing

Sustainable marketing

7.4.1   Sustainable marketing

Hospitality businesses face governmental and consumer pressures for socially and environmentally responsible actions that meet present needs of consumers and businesses while also preserving or enhancing the ability of future generations to meet their needs. The marketing concept recognises that organisations thrive from day to day by determining the current needs and wants of target groups of customers and fulfilling those needs and wants more effectively and efficiently than competitors do. It focusses on meeting the company's short-term sales, growth, and profit needs by giving customers what they want today. Satisfying consumers' immediate needs and desires does not, however, always serve the future best interests of either customers or businesses. Text 7.5 clearly illustrates this issue.

TEXT 7.5

Criticism of McDonald's early decisions

McDonald's early decisions to market tasty but fat and salt-laden fast foods created immediate satisfaction for customers and sales and profits for the company. Critics, however, assert that McDonald's and other fast-food chains contributed to a longer term national obesity epidemic, damaging consumer health and burdening the national health system. In turn, many consumers began looking for healthier eating options, causing a slump in the sales and profits of the fast-food industry. Beyond issues of ethical behaviour and social welfare, McDonald's was also criticised for the sizable environmental footprint of its vast global operations, from wasteful packaging and solid waste creation to inefficient energy use in its stores. Thus, McDonald's strategy was not sustainable in terms of either consumer or company benefit.

In recent years, however, McDonald's has responded with a more sustainable 'Plan to Win' strategy of diversifying into salads, fruits, grilled chicken, low-fat milk, and other healthy fare. Also, after a seven-year search for healthier cooking oil, McDonald's phased out traditional artery-clogging trans fats without compromising the taste of its French fries. The company also launched a major multifaceted educational campaign called 'it's what I eat and what I do ... I'm lovin' it' to help consumers better understand the keys to living balanced, active lifestyles (Kotler & Armstrong, 2013).

7.4.2   Green retailing

Greening up

Today's hospitality businesses are increasingly adopting environmentally sustainable practices. They are greening up their hotels and restaurants, promoting more environmentally responsible products, launching programmes to help customers be more responsible, and working with channel partners to reduce their environmental impact. McDonald's Golden Arches are now going green. Its new eco-friendly restaurants, designed from the bottom up with a whole new eco-attitude, is illustrated in Text 7.6.

TEXT 7.6

The new green McDonald's

A new 'green' McDonald's in Cary, North Carolina, has been built and furnished mostly with reclaimed building materials. The parking lot has been constructed with permeable pavers, which absorb and clean storm water and filter it back into the water table. Exterior and interior lighting use energy-efficient LEDs, which consume up to 78 percent less energy and last 10 to 20 times longer than traditional lighting. The restaurant is landscaped with hearty, drought-resistant native plants, which require less water. What little water they do need comes from rainwater channelled from the roof and condensation from the super high-efficiency HVAC system. Inside the restaurant, solar-tube skylights bring in natural light and reduce energy use. A sophisticated lighting system adjusts indoor illumination based on light entering through the skylights. The dining room is filled with materials made from recycled content (recycled floor tiles, for example, and counters made from recycled glass and concrete), with paints and cleaning chemicals chosen for low environmental impact. Other green features include high-efficiency kitchen equipment and water-saving, low-flow faucets and toilets. The restaurant even offers electric vehicle charging stations for customers.

7.4.3   Sustainable marketing: the call for more social responsibility

Hospitality marketing managers are re-examining their relationships with social values and responsibilities and with the very planet that sustains us. As worldwide consumerism and environmentalism movements mature, today's marketers are being called to develop sustainable marketing practices. Corporate ethics and social responsibility have become hot topics for almost every business, including the hospitality sector. Few companies can ignore the renewed and very demanding environmental movement and the impact on social and business policies. Clearly, every company's action can affect the customer relationship and brand. But today's customers expect companies to deliver value and quality in a socially and environmentally responsible way.

Social values

7.4.4   Social media as a marketing tool

Over the last decade, social media usage has accelerated at high speed. 2015 was another year of rapid evolution in online hotel marketing. Thanks to quickly growing online travel agency presence, and expanding mobile space, social media and corporate channels, travellers have more options for researching and booking travel than ever before. They consult high-quality images and videos while doing their travel shopping on different devices, through different platforms, and from multiple locations.

Social media

7.4.5   Notable social media trends

As users engage across multiple platforms and devices, cross-channel consistency and optimisation are key. Businesses that engage in cross-channel marketing, leveraging traditional, social, mobile, and other websites are more profitable than those that do not (Kasper, Helsdingen, & Gabbot,

Cross-channel

2006). Users expect relevant, targeted content. All web users, not just travellers, are inundated with a near-constant stream of content. Relevant content, meaningful to a specific user, stands out.

🔵 7.5 Planning and creating service products

7.5.1   The need for marketing plans for hospitality businesses

Hospitality can be defined as a combination of activities and services that delivers a pleasant service experience for customers. Effectively marketing these experiences to potential customers can be challenging, especially if one is unaware of the strengths and weaknesses of one's business, or what the competition is doing in the market place.

Choices
    All hospitality organisations face choices of how to present their product offer and deliver it to their customers. To better understand the nature of hospitality services, it is useful to distinguish between core products and supplementary elements (see Chapter 12 for more on this topic). It is also essential to recognise that, in the hospitality sector, it is very difficult to offer something for everyone. Basically, a marketing plan should be about focussing on who should be the targeted customers, because it is impossible to appeal to all target groups simultaneously. It is better to understand a business' target groups and aim at these groups with a well-constructed marketing plan. This makes the best use of available resources and should, if done properly, produce the best results for the company. Text 7.7 is a slightly adjusted actual marketing plan case study based on the Enchanted Vineyard (a B&B outlet).

Marketing plan

TEXT 7.7

The Enchanted Vineyard (a Bed and Breakfast outlet)

The Enchanted Vineyard is a charming Bed & Breakfast located in the Lorane Valley, outside of Eugene, Oregon. The valley is well known for its beauty and concentration of vineyards and wineries. The B&B will be run by Missy Stewart in the Stewart's newly renovated home. The Inn itself is a work of art. Each of the five guest rooms has walls that are 65% glass providing a breath-taking view of the valley. In addition to the views, the Inn offers a huge patio and vineyard for the guests to explore. The Enchanted Vineyard Bed & Breakfast has two competitive advantages that will ensure profitability. The first is Missy's relentless attention to personal service. Missy recognizes that her most important job is to pamper the guests, allowing them to have an excellent stay. The other sustainable competitive advantage is the facilities, handcrafted and simply beautiful. The

house and adjoining land are magnificent. Missy will turn leads into customers through attention to callers on the phone and through the use of a comprehensive website with all details of the bed & breakfast experience listed therein. The Enchanted Vineyard Bed & Breakfast will begin to make a profit by month nine and will grow steadily from month to month.

Situation Analysis
The Enchanted Vineyard Bed & Breakfast is a start-up business. The basic market need is a delightful B&B serving the Eugene area. The physical structure that houses the B&B has been specially engineered to please the most discriminating travellers.

Market Summary
The Enchanted Vineyard Bed & Breakfast possesses good information about the mar-

ket and knows a great deal about the common attributes of the most prized and loyal customers. The Enchanted Vineyard Bed & Breakfast will leverage this information to better understand who is served, their specific needs, and how The Enchanted Vineyard can better communicate with them.

Target Markets

- ■ Weekend getaway customers
- □ Travellers
- ■ University of Oregon travellers

Market Demographics

Geographic
One target group is the geographic target of the city of Eugene with a population of 130,000 people. Another target population is travellers from the US (90%), with 10% from other countries.

Demographics
Male and Female
Ages 35-55
College or graduate education
Income over $50,000

Behaviour Factors
Enjoy travelling for the sake of seeing new things and meeting people. Tend to use B&Bs when travelling instead of hotels. Enjoy meals at restaurants once a week.

Market Needs
The Enchanted Vineyard Bed & Breakfast seeks to fulfil the following benefits that are important to their customers:
- *Selection:* The Enchanted Vineyard has several different rooms, each with its own unique, breath taking view of the countryside.
- *Accessibility:* The B&B is located within 10 minutes of the city of Eugene, providing accessibility for people from Eugene,

travellers in the Willamette River Valley, and guests of the University of Oregon.
- *Customer Service:* The customers will be impressed with the level of attention that they receive.
- *Competitive Pricing:* All rooms will be competitively priced relative to similar B&Bs.

Market Trends
Within the last two years, people have begun to discover B&Bs and appreciate the additional services that they offer relative to traditional accommodations. The industry has seen an increase in occupancy, from out-of-state or out-of-region travellers, as well as and more importantly, local people that are looking for a place to escape from their homes.

Market Growth
In 1999, the national B&B market reached $543 million dollars. Sales are expected to grow by 9% for the next few years. This growth can be attributed to a couple of factors. The first factor is an appreciation for the services that a B&B provides. Another factor driving market growth is the increase in airfare that makes non-local vacations less practical and cost effective. People are turning to B&Bs in unique locations as vacation spots instead of flying. Lastly, as the number of work hours Americans perform has increased in the last few years, people are relying on weekend getaways as a way to distance themselves, albeit briefly, from their workweek.

SWOT Analysis
The SWOT analysis related to The Enchanted Vineyard.
- *Strengths:*
  Great location
  Fantastic facilities
  Owners who are passionate about their work
- *Weaknesses:*
  Brand visibility
  Limited number of rooms
  The struggle with taking care of everything with low labour overhead
- *Opportunities:*
  Growing market

Increase in sales from university-related events

The ability to become more efficient over time

- *Threats:*
Competition from new B&B entrants
The introduction of a B&B-style hotel
A slump in the economy

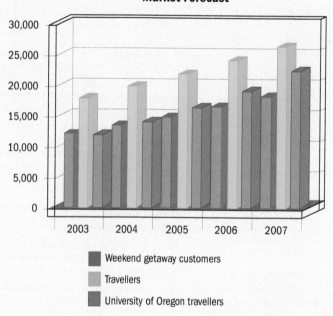

Market Forecast

Legend:
- Weekend getaway customers
- Travellers
- University of Oregon travellers

Competition
Competition comes in several forms:

Other B&Bs
Typically B&Bs have a set of unique features, something that makes them stand out. Some B&Bs will create uniqueness down to the level of different rooms within the B&B. On average, most B&Bs have only four to six rooms and are often booked up in advance. Particularly during special events, demand outstrips supply. B&Bs differentiate themselves by personal service offerings and the general ambiance. Finally, B&Bs usually have a nice sit down breakfast for their guests. This is not a simple continental breakfast of juice, coffee, and a bagel, but an elaborate spread of gourmet food such as quiche with portabella mushrooms, fresh roasted garlic and sun dried tomato omelettes, or some sort of fresh smoked fish.

Hotels/motels
These facilities are generally much more sterile in character relative to B&Bs. The rooms are typically the same throughout the facility (unlike B&Bs where each room is typically quite different). The guests of hotels generally use the hotel as a place to stay at night. The operator will usually see the guest when they check in and when they check out. This differs from a B&B where the guests are encouraged to spend time in communal rooms and socialize with the operators and other guests. Breakfast, if included at all in hotels, is sparse.

Services
The Enchanted Vineyard Bed & Breakfast is a small, attractive B&B that offers travellers a relaxed setting for weekend getaways, change of scenery, sports or cultural events, family occasions, University of Oregon events, etc. The Enchanted Vineyard Bed & Breakfast has a large central gathering room that allows travellers to socialize. The customers will receive the personal attention of the Stewarts who will meet any need a traveller has (within reason of course!).
The Enchanted Vineyard Bed & Breakfast

provides a wonderful breakfast feast and can meet any dietary restriction. The B&B is centrally located about 15 minutes from downtown Eugene in the heart of Lorane Valley wine country. In fact, The Enchanted Vineyard Bed & Breakfast has their own vineyard which grows grapes for local wineries and the clients are encouraged to explore The Enchanted Vineyard Bed & Breakfasts ten acres of land.

Keys to Success
The key to success will be based on customer attention. The facilities for the Enchanted Vineyard are already complete and are far nicer than anything around. The key is then to treat the customer properly so they are amazed at the level of attention that they receive. The Enchanted Vineyard will generate repeat business and increase the length of stay per customer.

Critical Issues
The Enchanted Vineyard is still in the speculative stage as a B&B. Its critical issues are:
Continue to build brand awareness, which will drive new customers to The Enchanted Vineyard
Gain operating efficiencies
Develop a strong relationship with the University of Oregon

Marketing Strategy
The Enchanted Vineyard Bed & Breakfast has a three-pronged strategy:

Association membership and advertising
A large number of visitors will look to regional B&B associations for information about the different B&B's in the area. Most associations publish a guide to the local B&B's and The Enchanted Vineyard Bed & Breakfast wants to be in this guide. One of the other perks of membership is visibility on the association's website with a link to ours. Additionally, we will be a member of the chamber of commerce because people typically inquire with the local Chamber when planning a vacation.

Website
The Enchanted Vineyard Bed & Breakfast will have a full-service website that allows the visitor to view the B&B, read details about what it has to offer, provide information on regional activities, even allow the visitor to book a reservation. With the growing use of the Internet, the Web has become an indispensable tool people have for planning vacation to areas that are not close enough to check out in person.

Strategic relationship with the University of Oregon
The Enchanted Vineyard Bed & Breakfast will develop a partnership with the university so when the school is in need of finding rooms for guests they will use The Enchanted Vineyard Bed & Breakfast. We will also be advertising with the university so when students are searching for places for their parents to stay, they will come across The Enchanted Vineyard Bed & Breakfast in school-related publications and feel more comfortable with booking a reservation sight unseen because of the trust bond they have formed with the university.

Mission
The mission of The Enchanted Vineyard Bed & Breakfast is to provide the finest B&B experience. We exist to attract and maintain customers. When we adhere to this maxim, everything else will fall into place. Our services will exceed the expectations of our customers.

Marketing Objectives
Maintain positive, steady growth each quarter
Experience a growth in new customers who are turned into long-term customers.
Realize an increase in occupancy each subsequent year

Financial Objectives
A double-digit growth rate for each future year
Reduce the variable costs per guest
Continue to decrease the fixed costs

Target Marketing
Our customers can be broadly divided into three groups (please note that it is possible to divide the customers into much smaller

groups, but we have chosen not to):

- **Weekend getaway customers:** These people are from the region and are looking to get away so they come to The Enchanted Vineyard Bed & Breakfast to be pampered and escape.
- **Travellers:** These people are passing through Eugene and prefer to stay in a B&B instead of a hotel or motel.
- **University of Oregon travellers:** The University brings a large number of people through Eugene, and The Enchanted Vineyard Bed & Breakfast believes that a good portion of their business will be from the university. Occasions include parents' weekend, orientation, parents visiting, and graduation. Lastly, the university will often set up rooms for administrative visitors.

Positioning

The Enchanted Vineyard Bed & Breakfast will position itself as an upscale B&B with a gorgeous facility and unmatched customer attention.

The Enchanted Vineyard Bed & Breakfast will leverage their competitive edge:

Attention to Personalized Service
While anyone at a B&B should reasonably expect good service, there are ways of setting yourself apart from this already high level of service. This will be done through the unrelenting pursuit of personal attention. In the Eugene area there are several larger (more than six room) B&B's that offer outstanding service, but it is not personal. What is meant by that is that the service is provided by employees, not the owner. At The Enchanted Vineyard Bed & Breakfast all interactions with the customer will be with Missy or John who see it as their duty to do whatever it takes to make the customer feel at home. The feeling of personal attention, or more accurately defined as a sense of personal concern, not just mere personal attention, really adds a very positive dimension to the B&B experience. Not only will the Stewarts be offering personal concern, but they will also be providing the concern, not some employee.

Uniqueness and Beauty of the Facility
The Enchanted Vineyard Bed & Breakfast will be housed in the Stewart's home. The Stewart's will be renovating their farmhouse to accommodate their new guests. They will be building two more bedrooms with private baths, building a patio, and enlarging the common area. One unique aspect of The Enchanted Vineyard Bed & Breakfast is the setting within the Lorane Valley region, known for its outstanding wine production, housing both vineyards and wineries. To complement this setting, The Enchanted Vineyard Bed & Breakfast will have a large outside patio allowing guests to spend time relaxing outside with a nice view of the valley. The guests also have the option to wander through The Enchanted Vineyard Bed & Breakfast's own vineyard. Each room in the B&B is 65% glass, overlooking the hillside and vineyard. Basically there is not a room in the house that doesn't have a breath taking view.

Strategy Pyramids

The single objective is to position The Enchanted Vineyard Bed & Breakfast as the upscale B&B located in Eugene, reaching generally full occupancy within the first three years. The marketing strategy will seek to first create customer awareness regarding the services offered, develop that customer base, and work building customer loyalty and strategic relationships with the university.

The message that The Enchanted Vineyard Bed & Breakfast will seek to communicate is that The Enchanted Vineyard is the premier B&B in the Eugene area with the finest facilities. The message will be communicated through a variety of methods. The first will be advertising in the B&B association newsletter. The next method will be a robust website with a comprehensive amount of information. The last method will be developing strategic relationships with the university. While this will require a budget for assorted activities, these activities are basically networking activities, taking people out to lunch and schmoozing.

Marketing Mix

The Enchanted Vineyard Bed & Breakfast's marketing mix is comprised of the following approach to pricing, distribution, advertising and promotion, and customer service.

- *Pricing:* The pricing scheme is based on a room rate. The rate is arrived at in terms of by its market value.
- *Distribution:* All services will be provided at the B&B.
- *Advertising and Promotion:* The most successful traditional advertising will be with the B&B association. Developing strategic alliances with the university is a non-traditional method of marketing, but it will be quite efficient. The website will also be used in marketing activities.
- *Customer Service:* Obsessive customer attention is the mantra. The Enchanted Vineyard's philosophy is whatever needs to be done to make the customer happy must occur, even at the expense of short-term profits. In the long run, this investment will pay off with fierce customer loyalty.

Marketing Research

During the initial phases of the marketing plan development, several focus groups were held to gain insight into a variety of B&B patrons. These focus groups provided useful information into the decision-making processes of consumers.

An additional source of dynamic market research is a feedback mechanism based on a suggestion card system. The suggestion card has several statements that patrons are asked to rate in terms of a given scale. There are also several open-ended questions that allow the customer to freely offer constructive criticism or praise. The Enchanted Vineyard will work hard to implement reasonable suggestions in order to improve their services as well as show their commitment to the customer in that their suggestions are valued.

(Source: www.mplans.com)

7.6 Importance of service employees in sales and marketing

7.6.1 Service employees are crucially important

Among the most demanding jobs in service businesses are the so-called front-line jobs. Employees working these customer-facing jobs span the boundary between inside and outside the organisation. They are expected to be fast and efficient in executing operational tasks while remaining courteous and helpful when dealing with customers. In fact, front-line employees are a key input for delivering service excellence and competitive advantage. Therefore, most of today's successful service organisations uphold a firm commitment to effective management of human resources (HR), including recruitment, selection, training, motivation, and retention of employees (as indicated in Chapter 6). Organisations that display this commitment understand the economic payoff from investing in their people. These firms are also characterised by a distinctive culture of service leadership and role modelling by top management. It is probably harder for competitors to duplicate high performance human assets than any other corporate resource (Lovelock & Wirtz, 2011).

Front-line jobs

Key input

7.6.2 Service personnel as a source of customer loyalty and competitive advantage

There exist many horror stories of consumers having dreadful experiences with a service business. If pressed, many of these same consumers will also be able to recount really good service experiences. Service personnel

Horror stories

Service personnel

usually feature prominently in these tales. They feature in roles either as un-caring, incompetent villains or as heroes who went out of their way to help customers by anticipating their needs and resolving problems in a helpful and empathetic manner. From a customer's perspective, the encounter with service staff is probably the most important aspect of a service. From a firm's perspective, the service levels and the way service is delivered by the front-line personnel can be an important source of differentiation as well as competitive advantage. The main reasons service employees are so impor-tant to customers and a firm's competitive positioning are because front-line employees in hospitality services:

Reasons

- are a core part of the product. Often, service employees are the most visible element of the service, deliver the service, and significantly deter-mine service quality.
- are the service firm. Front-line employees represent the service firm, and from a customer's perspective, they are the firm.
- are the brand. Front-line employees and the service they provide are of-ten a core part of the brand. Employees determine whether the brand promise is delivered.
- affects sales. Service personnel is often crucially important for generat-ing sales, cross-sales, and up-sales.
- determine productivity. Front-line employees have heavy influence on the productivity of front-line operations.

Furthermore, front-line employees in the hospitality sector play a key role in anticipating customers' needs. By customising service delivery and building personalised relationships with customers, they help to increase repeat business, e.g. return visits by the customers who are pleased with the ser-vice received. Clearly, effective performance of these activities ultimately leads to customer loyalty. The level of attentiveness employees can show in anticipating customer needs was indicated in Text 7.1, citing the example of Cora Griffith. Her story, along with many others of employees showing dis-cretionary effort making a difference, reinforces the truism that highly moti-vated people are at the core of hospitality service excellence. Customer-fac-ing employees in the hospitality sector are increasingly a key variable for creating and maintaining competitive positioning and advantage for the busi-ness.

Discretionary effort

Quality

The quality of a service firm's employees, especially those working in cus-tomer-facing positions, plays a crucial role in determining market success and financial performance of organisations in the hospitality sector. This is why the People element of the 8 Ps is so important. Successful service or-ganisations are committed to effective management of human resources and work closely with marketing and operations managers to balance what might otherwise prove to be conflicting goals. They recognise the value of investing in HR and understand the costs resulting from high levels of turno-ver. In the long run, offering better wages and benefits may be a more finan-cially viable strategy than paying less to employees who have no loyalty and soon defect. The market and financial results of managing people effective-ly for service advantage can be phenomenal. Good HR strategies allied with strong management leadership at all levels often lead to a sustainable com-petitive advantage.

7.6.3 The role of the sales force

Personal selling in the hospitality sector is the interpersonal arm of the promotion mix. Advertising consists largely of non-personal communication with large groups of consumers. By contrast, personal selling involves interpersonal interactions between sales people and individual customers, often up-selling. Whether face-to-face, by telephone, via e-mail, through video or web conferences, personal selling can be more effective than advertising in more complex selling situations. Sales people can probe customers to learn more about their problems and then adjust the marketing offer and presentation to fit the special needs of each customer.

Personal selling

7.6.4 Coordinating marketing and sales

Ideally, the sales force and other marketing functions (marketing planners, brand managers, and researchers) should work together closely to jointly create value for customers. Unfortunately, however, some hospitality companies still treat sales and marketing as separate functions. When this happens, the separate sales and marketing groups may not get along well. When things go wrong, marketers blame the sales force for a poor execution of what they see as an otherwise splendid strategy. In turn, the sales team blames the marketers for being out of touch with what is really going on with customers. Neither group fully values the other's contributions. If not repaired, such disjoint between marketing and sales can damage customer relationships and company performance (Kotler & Armstrong, 2013).

Work together

Put simply, the sales and marketing department devises strategies for increasing the use of the hotel by businesses, conventions, academic conferences, and individuals. They will create and deliver presentations to corporations about why the hotel would be perfect for a business event; inform universities of why the hotel is perfect for holding a conference; or will send out information to people (including travel agents) in distant cities about travellers should choose this hotel when visiting the area. They also do research on customer satisfaction with the hotel, points of attention or room for improvement for the hotel, and public perception of the hotel. The sales and marketing department in a hotel is responsible for finding ways to bring in customers, and may offer package deals with free tickets to nearby attractions, or two-for-one stays during weekdays. They also try to use advertising to entice customers.

Strategies

7.6.5 Organisational chart: hotel Sales and Marketing Department

Hotel sales and marketing departments vary with the size, budget, and type of hotel organisation. But all hotels, large or small, should have a sales and marketing department to take care of the hotel's sales and marketing strategies. Figure 7.3 shows a typical organisational chart of a hotel's Sales and Marketing Department. At smaller hotels, a sales executive handles businesses from all market segments. They may deal with travel agents, tour operators, event planners, corporate guests, online travel agents and travel consortia. Large hotels have specialised sales managers and executives to handle different market segments, for example with one sales manager and sales executive team assigned to handle corporate clients, another to handle travel and trade.

Organisational chart

FIGURE 7.3 A typical organisational chart of a hotel's Sales and Marketing Department

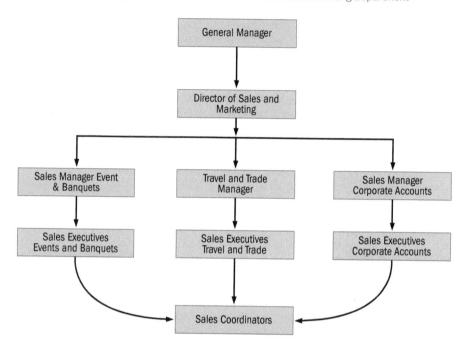

7.7 Digital marketing in the hospitality industry

Digital marketing

Digital marketing for hotels is becoming increasingly complex. Hotel managers must not only serve guests, manage rooms, availabilities and pricing, but are also expected to compete for guests using new channels and digital communities that emerge every day. Many hotel managers are therefore asking themselves how they can expand their brands online while still having the time to run their businesses.

The obvious choice is to hire additional staff, but this tactic is just a temporary solution: demand for digital marketing is unstoppable and the problem will continue to grow. The breakthrough solution for this complex problem is having a digital marketing architecture and tools that provide a consistent multi-channel experience to hotel guests and prepare hotels for future digital marketing demands.

7.7.1 Prioritise hotel website and booking engine

Hotel's website

A hotel's website is their best opportunity to engage with and sell to their guests. On average, guests spend 6 minutes on hotel websites, which is an ample opportunity to use to engage future guests with bold pictures, easy-to-read room descriptions and attractive offers that make the decision to book simple and predictable. It is also important to show what guests will experience when they visit the destination. Hotels are advised to use video as part of their web strategy; video will let them mesmerise their guests. Considering the rapid pace at which possibilities for online content continue to develop, hotels should regularly and frequently (re)evaluate their websites in order to ensure they do not become outdated.

© Noordhoff Uitgevers bv

7.7.2   Aim at social travellers (60% of consumers)

Research has shown that 60% of guests use one or more social networking platforms during their search, shop and buy processes. It is therefore critical to manage TripAdvisor ratings, have a professional-looking presence on Facebook, and allow guests to engage over Twitter. Hotels should use the social network to amplify their messages, ensuring that good guest experiences are shared on different digital communities. The medium used partly dictates the platform. For photos, best results are obtained using Flickr; for videos, a dedicated YouTube channel is most effective (www.guestcentric.com). E-mail, lastly, is still the most widely used mechanism for sharing itineraries and ideas for trips.

Social network

7.7.3   Provide optimised content for mobile consumers

Mobile traffic is the fastest growing category in digital marketing and, unsurprisingly, also in travel. Research states that as many as 19% of all hotel searches are currently executed on a mobile device. Entrepreneurs who deployed a mobile solution in 2015 will by now realise that mobile consumers demonstrate much more utilitarian behaviour – they are looking for the hotel's address, phone number, or want to book a room for tonight or tomorrow night. Hence, the experience to conclude those tasks should be optimised by 2016. While success can be found using mobile as a stand-alone media, it provides the largest rewards when it is used as an integrated, multi-channel engagement platform. If entrepreneurs can provide consistent messages across web, social and mobile, while ensuring that the most relevant offers are prioritised, they will truly have provided multi-channel digital marketing.

Mobile consumers

7

7.7.4 Diversify online distribution channels

Online bookings

Recent studies indicate that booking.com is driving a whopping 50% of all hotel online bookings in Europe. This dominance is threatening to hotels as they become more dependent on (and therefore vulnerable to) a single channel already demanding higher commissions based on results. It is therefore critical to diversify one's channels. A manager of a boutique property should consider signing up with tablethotels.com, mrandmrssmith.com or jetsetter.com, for example. One good source of information for the latest trends in accommodation websites is tnooz.com's roundup of top travel websites per market.

7.7.5 Innovate with marketing campaigns

Campaigns

Digital marketing is not a one-time project. It is a new discipline to be embraced by hotel managers. Digital marketing does not, however, necessarily require learning to use many new tools or hiring many new staff members. Using the appropriate tools, hotel managers can use their existing e-commerce and reservations staff to create campaigns, and follow-up and reap the rewards of increased marketing exposure: more and better bookings. Tools should be chosen to minimise setup costs and provide maximum flexibility when creating campaigns.

7.7.6 Deliver content marketing as an engaging customer journey

Content marketing

Content marketing starts with understanding the audience and the customer journey. Content should engage, inspire and enhance the user experience. The audience should be empowered with engaging content, including local attractions and activities, visuals and trending topics. Content should be optimised for local and conversational search and saturate diversified channels – from own website to blogs to Facebook. Key performance indicators time spent on page, bounce and click-through rates, and engagement patterns should be investigated. Once the top converting pages are determined, the content should be enhanced so as to encourage the path to purchase and ensure mobile responsiveness.

7.7.7 Optimise user experience

User experience

User experience is the human path to digital marketing. Audiences want to be engaged, be able to navigate the site, and tap into social influences. Conversion optimisation starts with usability factors such as speed and performance, information architecture, legibility, colours and images. With robust architecture, clear design and navigation, and engaging content, a site will increase conversion. A smart way to see how user experience relates to

A/B testing

the conversion funnel is to implement A/B testing – (sometimes called 'split testing') comparing two versions of a web page to see which one performs better. Two web pages are compared by showing one variant ('A') to one set of visitors, and the other variant ('B') to a different set of similar visitors over a certain period. The variant that gives the better conversion rate wins. Points of interest concerning pages that perform better are based on simple design and content evolution, such as floating buttons, drop-downs, marketing messages, and banners.

7.7.8   Improve hotel social media marketing

In the contemporary connected online community, the synergy of social engagement empowers a hotel's digital marketing. Most of the world uses social media sites, including Google+, Facebook, Instagram, Pinterest and LinkedIn. Social media is a driver of brand awareness and customer relationships and retention. To be in the social conversation and derive traffic from social platforms, therefore, web content must be interesting, build connections, and inspire conversion. Ensure a site is optimised for mobile and sharing across devices, and add open graph (OG) tags and Twitter cards. The business needs to stand out with robust hotel social media outreach, engaging content and visual media.

Social engagement

7.7.9   Expand the hotel's paid search presence

The key to a highly successful hotel paid search campaign is in maximising business outreach and diversifying channels – via Facebook, Google, Yelp, and HotelFinder. Hotels should make sure to build on brand or hotel name, leverage social channels, and allocate budgets to tap into mobile conversion, which is higher than ever. Sending out customised marketing messages and focussing on the customer journey helps entrepreneurs address their specific target audiences.

Key

7.7.10   Attribute the hotel's ROI across all touch points

The customer journey is evolving, so businesses need to alter their approach to measuring digital marketing return on investment (ROI). With the dramatic spike in mobile search and social signals, the conversion funnel is not linear; the purchase journey can begin at any point along the decision path. It is important for hotels and businesses to tap into this dynamic, target the audience journey, and personalise the content with innovations in digital tracking software that can attribute ROI to every channel. By understanding the conversion path, attributing ROI, and integrating a dashboard to break down the data, managers can see the value of each touch point.

Return on investment

7.7.11   Understand the hotel customer journey

From travel inspiration to research to booking to post-stay social; understanding the customer journey is paramount to a viable digital marketing strategy. In hospitality and tourism (and just about any industry or business) customers use search engines, websites, social channels, and reviews to plan a trip or book a room. That is why a hotel's website has to be optimised for organic and paid search, connected to social channels, and designed for conversion. Being present on every layer of the customer journey gives a business the edge. Text 7.8 illustrates this issue and shows its effects.

Customer journey

TEXT 7.8

The digital marketing case for the Townhouse Hotel, in Maastricht, the Netherlands

Our 2014 hotel internet marketing actions:

1 **SEO** (search engine optimization): penetrating both short-tail and long-tail destination keyword combinations to optimise the organic positioning on search engines. Adjusting and fine-tuning meta-tags, page titles, content and internal links, plus seeding content on themed blogs to build up a strong overall infrastructure both internally and externally.

2 **Brand Protection**: submitting the hotel's trademark to Google to block ads with the hotel name / brand.

3 **SEM** (search engine marketing):
   – Keyword bidding / advertising on the hotel's name, to divert more traffic to the hotel website from 3rd party websites.
   – Remarketing with banner adds to visitors of the hotel website.

4 **Reputation Management**: here we have a 4 fold approach:
   – Monitoring reviews with review management tools to structurally identify areas of improvement
   – Post-stay e-mails to all guests requesting their feedback on public review websites (TripAdvisor, Google+, Zoover, etc.).
   – Responding to reviews by the hotel manager (without exception)
   – Marketing on the hotel website the external review scores to emphasise on what our guests think about the hotel.

5 **Meta-search**: Displaying direct hotel rates in price comparison websites including TripAdvisor, Google HPA (hotel price ads) / HotelFinder, Trivago, Kayak, Hotels Combined.

How did we do? Let's have a look at the results...
- website sales up 20%
- more than €50.000 in incremental website sales
- direct sales 30% of total sales

(Source: www.guestcentric.com)

In conclusion, a successful digital marketing strategy must provide a consistent multi-channel experience to hotel guests. This can be achieved by using a multitude of tools or an all-in-one hotel digital marketing platform. But no matter which tools are selected, at the core of the strategy should be a digital marketing architecture that prepares a hotel for future digital marketing demands.

Summary

▶ Marketing is basically managing profitable customer relationships with the main goals of attracting new customers by promising superior value and keeping and growing numbers of current customers by delivering satisfaction.

▶ People use an array of services every day, although some are often so routine that they are hardly noticed unless something goes wrong. This use of services is an example of service consumption.

▶ In the restaurant business, food provenance is important; customers often want to know the origin of seafood, meat or vegetables used.

▶ Formally, services are an economic activity offered by one party to another, most commonly employing time-based performances to bring about desired results in recipients, or in objects or other assets for which purchasers have responsibility.

▶ To address the constant struggle of having the right number of customers show up, pricing services tends to be a highly dynamic and complicated process, and using revenue management or yield management can be very helpful.

▶ In hospitality services marketing, the traditional 4 Ps of the marketing mix (product, pricing, promotion, and place) are adapted to the distinctive features of hospitality services since the hospitality sector customer is very much part of the service delivered. The marketing mix is a tool used by businesses and marketers to help them determine a product or brand's offering. The original 4 Ps marketing mix has been extended to include people, process, physical evidence, and productivity and quality.

▶ From a hospitality customer's point of view, where service employees are involved, the people are the service. Front-line employees therefore need to possess required technical and interpersonal skills and a positive attitude.

▶ The hospitality marketing manager's aim is to find, attract, keep, and grow numbers of target customers by creating, delivering, and communicating superior customer value.

▶ Customer satisfaction and loyalty is very important, and since losing a customer means losing the entire stream of purchases they would make over a lifetime of patronage, it is imperative that companies shape their value propositions even more carefully and treat their profitable customers well.

7

▶ Hospitality businesses are increasingly adopting environmentally sustainable practices by greening up their hotels and restaurants, promoting more environmentally responsible products, launching programmes to help customers be more responsible, and working with channel partners to reduce their environmental impact.

▶ A marketing plan is about focussing on who should be the target customers, because it is impossible to properly reach out to all target groups at once.

▶ Front-line employees are a key input for delivering service excellence and competitive advantage

▶ Service employees are important to customers and firms' competitive positioning: front-line employees in hospitality services are a core part of the product; are the service firm; are the brand; affects sales; and determine productivity

▶ Compared to advertising, personal selling, which involves interpersonal interactions between sales people and individual customers, can be more effective in more complex selling situations.

▶ In an ideal situation, the sales force and other marketing functions should work together closely to jointly create value for customers; this is usually not the case, leading to friction within firms.

▶ Hotel sales and marketing departments vary with the size, budget and type of hotel organisation. All hotels, however, should have a sales and marketing department to take care of the sales and marketing strategies of the hotel.

▶ Hotel managers should not serve guests, manage rooms, availabilities and pricing, but are also expected to compete for guests in new channels and digital communities that emerge every day. A digital marketing architecture and tools that provide a consistent multi-channel experience to the hotel guests can prepare hotels for future digital marketing demands.

Questions and assignments for reflection

1   How has the service revolution changed the landscape of the hospitality industry?

2   How can hospitality firms develop effective marketing strategies?

3   Are sustainable marketing and green retailing simply tactics used by hospitality companies to position themselves in the market without any real belief in these ideals? Explain your views.

4   What is the importance of a marketing plan to hospitality companies?

5   Why are front-line sales and marketing personnel very important to customers in the hospitality industry?

7

8

Financial Control and the Accounting Department

M. N. Chibili

8.1 Introduction

A hotel's financial management starts in the front office in close collaboration with the accounting office. Financial management is primarily based on the accurate and timely processing of guest accounts. For this processing to be appropriately carried out, the accounting system, principles, financial statements and reports should be well understood, applied, developed, and distributed to the stakeholders concerned. These activities have nowadays been made much easier with advances in technology and programming of sophisticated software.

8.2 The accounting function and systems

Accounting is generally recognised as the language of business. It is concerned with reporting, summarising and recording the transactions of the business in monetary terms. At the level of hospitality operations, accounting is used to control activities, plan acquisition of finance, plan future activities, and report on activities and successes to other users of the accounting information. Users of accounting information are broadly split into two categories: internal users and external users.

Language of business

Internal users are principally the hospitality operation's management. They use the information for planning, controlling, stewardship and decision making; this type of accounting is by nature managerial. External users are generally the other stakeholders in the hospitality operation. These other stakeholders include employees, owners, lenders, suppliers, customers, local community, investment analysts, media, and government entities. The accounting information they receive is generally found in the hospitality operation's annual reports; this type of accounting is by nature financial. An additional component is tax accounting, which helps to ensure proper tax

Internal users

External users

Chili: Los Rios: Montana Magica Lodge

planning as well as properly establishing a hospitality operation's taxable income and tax liabilities.

Business values   There are four major business values contained in the various branches of accounting: planning, communicating, controlling, and determining profit (or profit determination). Accounting information based on the uniform language of numbers helps communicate the hospitality operation's current status and its future plans. As a control system, accounting provides information needed to perform tasks in accordance with the hospitality operation's long-term goals. The profits of the hospitality operation depend on the accuracy of the accounting information, however.

8.2.1   Generally accepted accounting principles – GAAP

To ensure that users of a hospitality operation's financial data may have faith in the information, the principles and practices used must be known.

Accounting principles   The basic accounting principles form the foundation for understanding accounting methods. These are called the 'generally accepted accounting principles' (GAAP); they provide the basis for the preparation of financial statements. Figure 8.1 contains a summary description of some of the most important principles.

FIGURE 8.1 The GAAP and their basic meanings

Principle	Meaning
Cost principle	This principle indicates that a transaction should be recorded at its acquisition price or cash cost and this should represent its accounting value.
Business entity principle	This principle indicates that accounting and financial statements are based on the concept that each business maintains its own set of accounts and that these accounts are separate from those of the owners.
Time period principle	This principle indicates that a company has to complete its analysis to report the financial condition and profitability of its business operation over a specific operating time period.
Going concern principle	This principle indicates that at the time the business is preparing its statements, it is expected to live forever and that liquidation should not be a prospect.
Monetary unit principle	This principle indicates that the financial statements should be based on transactions expressed in the primary monetary unit of the area.
Objectivity principle	This principle indicates that all accounting transactions should be justified as much as possible on objective evidence.
Full disclosure principle	This principle indicates that the financial statement should provide all information necessary for the understanding of the financial statement.
Consistency principle	This principle indicates that once an accounting method has been chosen by management, this should be used from period to period unless a change is necessary and this change must be disclosed.
Matching principle	This principle indicates that expenses should be related to their revenues.
Conservatism principle	This principle indicates that expenses should be recognised as soon as possible whereas revenues should be recognised only when they are verified.
Materiality principle	This principle indicates that events or information must be accounted for if they make a difference to the user of the financial information.
Realisation principle	This principle indicates that revenues are only recognised only when they are earned.

The GAAP must be adhered to when a hospitality operation distributes its financial statements to external users. If a hospitality operation's shares are publicly traded, the financial statements must also adhere to other rules as established in the jurisdiction where the shares are traded. One such important rule is that financial statements should be audited by an independent accounting firm.

8.2.2　USALI

Most organisations in the hospitality industry (hotels, motels, resorts, restaurants, and clubs) use the Uniform System of Accounts for the Lodging Industry (USALI). This system was originally initiated by the Hotel Association of New York in the shape of the Uniform System of Accounts for Hotels (USAH) in 1925. The system was designed for classifying, organising, and presenting financial information so that uniformity prevailed and comparing financial data among hotels was possible. A major advantage of accounting uniformity is that information can be collected and compared between similar organisations within the hospitality industry. Changes to the USALI are being made constantly in order to keep pace with the evolving hospitality business environment. The current version of the USALI is its 11th revised edition (2014).

USALI

8.2.3　International financial reporting standards – IFRS

An accounting standard is a set of rules and regulations containing detailed guidance on the preparation of financial accounts. Since the 1970s, the International Accounting Standards Committee (IASC), replaced by the International Accounting Standards Board (IASB) in 2001 has been responsible for the establishment and maintaining of international standards, known as International Financial Reporting Standards (IFRS). IFRS began as an attempt to harmonise accounting across the European Union but the value of harmonisation quickly made the concept attractive around the world (www.ifrs.org).

IFRS

Accounting provides companies, investors, regulators and others with a standardised way of describing the financial performance of a given entity. Accounting standards present preparers of financial statements with a set of rules by which to abide when preparing an entity's accounts, thus ensuring standardisation across the market. Companies listed on public stock exchanges are legally required to publish financial statements in accordance with relevant accounting standards.

International Financial Reporting Standards (IFRS) is a single set of accounting standards, developed and maintained by the IASB with the intention of those standards being capable of globally consistent application – by developed, emerging and developing economies – thus providing investors and other users of financial statements with the ability to compare financial performance of publicly listed companies on a like-for-like basis with international peers.

Accounting standards

IFRS are designed as a common global language for business affairs enabling company accounts to be understandable and comparable international boundaries. They are a consequence of growing international shareholding and trade, and are particularly important for companies that have dealings in several countries, as is the case with many hospitality operations that have chains and brands operating internationally at the same time. IFRS are progressively replacing the many different national accounting standards, and are now mandated for use by more than 100 countries, including the European Union and over two-thirds of G20 countries. The

Global language

G20 and other international organisations have consistently supported the work of the IASB and its mission of global accounting standards. Since 2005, the European Union has decided that all listed companies should prepare their financial statements in compliance with these international standards (www.ifrs.org).

8.2.4   Centralised and decentralised accounting systems

In Chapter 3, the position of the Financial Controller was introduced as a member of the Executive Team within a hospitality operation. It was also noted that a Financial Controller may answer directly to the GM or to a higher regional manager. This generally depends on the type of accounting system applicable within the hospitality operation.

Centralised accounting

In a centralised accounting system, accounting functions are completed from head office, or from one single unit in which there is a dedicated team of employees using one system and set of procedures to record and analyse data. In most cases, the team has direct access to the management team. Alternatively, a decentralised accounting system has employees at different individual units handling the paperwork at their unit levels; here, employees have independent reporting accountability. Each of these systems has its specific benefits.

Decentralised accounting

For a centralised accounting system, benefits include:
- a dedicated central resource for finance activities,
- consistency of systems and procedures,
- improved control and visibility,
- easy access to documentation,
- less risk of document loss and staff inefficiency.

A decentralised system has the benefits of:
- increased engagement by local managers,
- increased skill levels of staff at site level,
- all information demanded by local managers is available,
- all documents are locally seen and matched,
- reduced potential loss through re-routing of financial documents.

Outsourcing

Centralised accounting systems are mostly used in hospitality operations that have multiple units (multi-property hotels or restaurant companies) and, generally, Financial Controllers heading such units are certified public accountants. Decentralised accounting systems are prevalent within small operations, and the GM and Financial Controller play a large role in the preparation of financial documents. Recently, some of these small hospitality operations have begun outsourcing their accounting activities to external accounting specialists in order to ensure their financial statements are drafted according to accepted standards and expected reliability. As the excerpt in Text 8.1 illustrates, outsourcing of finance and accounting activities has benefits for all types of companies (see also Section 4.5.6, Chapter 4).

© Noordhoff Uitgevers bv

TEXT 8.1

The Benefits of Outsourcing Finance and Accounting activities

Jul 12, 2013 @ 09:13 AM
By Joe Mullich (Xerox Contributor, Xerox)

Finance and accounting (F&A) was one of the first processes that companies outsourced, and the practice continues to boom: Ed Thomas, an analyst for Ovum research, found the number of F&A outsourcing projects valued at $1 million or more increased in 2012 compared to the year before.

As the market matures, companies contracting for outcomes are exploring fresh ideas and seeking new answers to streamline F&A processes. They are expanding outsourcing to new areas of finance and accounting, new industries, and new sizes of companies than in the past.

Driving efficiency is a high priority for CFOs who want to outsource F&A processes, according to an Ovum study of 150 large companies in the United States, United Kingdom and Canada. Most survey respondents saw the main strategic aim of the accounting department as delivering efficiencies, whether that is within the department itself or across the company as a whole.

'This is a wider trend in outsourcing as a whole,' Thomas explains. 'Cost reductions are the table stakes, and companies want to know what else their outsourcers can do to make their processes and technology run more efficiently.'

The most commonly outsourced services within accounting are payroll accounting, accounts payable, and accounts receivable. The Ovum study found companies are 'moving up the value chain' in the types of F&A functions they outsource.

'They are looking to move from relatively basic transactional processes, such as accounts payable to more strategic functions, like budgets, forecasts and internal audits,' Thomas says. 'More than a third of respondents had outsourced internal auditing, which is a high-level function.'

Simplifying and standardizing F&A processes is a key characteristic of well-run companies, and by instilling good F&A processes these companies can achieve a variety of good outcomes—such as more information, more service and more cash. By simplifying their F&A processes, companies have found they can reduce the cycle it takes to close books, and they can develop better benchmark and baseline financial processes to help them meet regulatory requirements. Expanding the scope of outsourcing can multiply such benefits, some experts say.

'One simple example is accounts payable and receivables,' says Jag Dalal, managing director of thought leadership at the International Association of Outsourcing Professionals (IAOP). 'If you outsource only one function, you limit your benefits. If you outsource both, you get a value beyond improving the transactional component because the outsourcer can see when cash comes in and goes out. That can help the company take best advantage of the cash on-hand and optimize internal processes.'

As companies look to leverage the power of their data, they are turning to outsourcers with greater expertise and technology resources than they have in-house. 'An outsourcer is going to have access to state-of-the-art technology, and experts who use those software packages every day,' says Greg LaFollette, a spokesperson for CPA-2Biz.

More and more, companies are looking for end-to-end F&A capabilities from outsourcers. Consider how outsourcing can help a company get a better handle on its pay-to-procure process. Powerful analytics can help a company better understand their spending through the entire supply chain in order to control budgets and standardize procedures company-wide.

This approach allows companies to identify cost savings through supplier consolidation and duplicate payment analysis. Automating the process can improve policy compliance and reduce order errors by ensuring employees around the world can order what they need when they need it, while enforcing business rules and limits that prevent employees from making costly mistakes.

While CFOs of large companies are focused on outsourcing to improve far-flung global operations, smaller companies, who have typically eschewed outsourcing of F&A, are beginning to embrace it as well. Outsourcers have expanded their offerings to the small- and mid-size company segments and developed solutions targeted toward specific vertical industries.

A recent report from the Association of Chartered Certified Accountants (ACCA) found that companies using F&A outsourcing believe they will reduce costs but lose control. However, as they realize those cost advantages, they see that quality is rising because benchmarks are being applied to their performance. In the end, the report concludes, companies could see control was improving, too.

'Many companies don't realize going in that they manage an outsourced provider more stringently than their in-house resources were managed,' Dalal says. Outsourcing outcomes are more likely to use clear metrics, such as savings and service-level achievement. That allows a company to have continuous improvement in their accounting and finance operation, while the company itself can focus on its core competencies.'

(Source: www.forbes.com)

8.3 Principal financial statements

Principal statements

Financial statements are the records that summarise the financial activities of a business, an individual or another entity. For hospitality operations in particular, these statements have to be prepared by the Accounting Department on a regular basis. Financial statements let the hospitality operation's management review past activities, as well as use them as a basis for making decisions about future operations. The Accounting Department ensures that the information contained in these statements is presented as clearly and concisely as possible. The following sections will look at the principal statements meant for both external and internal use and generated by the Accounting Department. These principal financial statements are the balance sheet, the income statement, the statement of comprehensive income, the cash flow statement, and the statement of retained earnings.

8.3.1 Balance sheet

Balance sheet

Very specific date

Equation

The balance sheet, also called the 'statement of financial position' is a list of all of a hospitality operation's owned assets, its incurred debts, and the sum of investments by the owners. Despite the fact that the balance sheet is the result of a hospitality operation's activities over time, it is a representation of the worth and obligations of the hospitality operation at a very specific date. The balance sheet shows the balance between the assets and the liabilities and owners' equity of the operation. This balance is symbolised in the fundamental accounting equation in which the assets are equal to the sum of liabilities and owners' equity at all times. For this fundamental equation to be respected, an increase in one asset must be accompanied by a corresponding decrease in another asset or an increase in either a liability or an owners' equity item. The balance sheet is the only one of the major accounting statements established at a given point in time that shows a balance between its two halves. The major sections of the balance sheet are defined in the fundamental accounting equation.

An asset is anything of value owned by the hospitality operation. On a balance sheet, all things owned are recorded in their monetary values. There are two major classes of assets: tangible and intangible assets. Tangible assets are those that have physical substance, whereas intangible assets lack physical substance but have value to the hospitality operation. For hospitality operations, assets are further sub-divided into the following categories: current assets; non-current receivables; investments; plant, property and equipment; and other assets. While most assets on the balance sheets are recorded at their acquisition values, the value of the accumulated depreciation affecting plant, property and equipment indicates how much of their value has been used up since their acquisition.

Asset

A liability is an amount a hospitality operation is under obligation to pay to other persons or organisations. Liabilities generally have the following characteristics:

Liability

- They result from all types of borrowing;
- They represent a duty or responsibility to others that entails settlement by future transfers;
- The duty or responsibility obligates the entity, leaving it little or no discretion to avoid it;
- The transaction or event obligating the event has already taken place.

Liabilities are generally divided into the two sub-categories of current liabilities and long term liabilities. Current liabilities are those obligations which, on the balance sheet date, are reasonably expected to be paid back within the next 12 months. They generally consist of one of five types:

- payables resulting from the acquisition of goods, services, and labour with applicable payroll taxes;
- payments received in advance for the delivery of goods or services;
- obligations to be paid relating to fixed assets purchases;
- dividends payable;
- income tax payable.

Long term liabilities obligations on the date of the balance sheet are expected to be paid back at some point after the next 12 months. Common hospitality industry-related long term liabilities are:

- mortgage notes, other notes, and similar liabilities;
- obligations under capital leases;
- other long-term liabilities;
- deferred income taxes (non-current);
- commitments and contingencies.

Owners' equity represent the funding brought into the hospitality operation in order to finance the acquisition of assets. Based on the fundamental accounting equation, all acquired assets have been funded either through debt (liabilities) or by the owners themselves (owners' equity). Once all liabilities are accounted for, the positive difference is considered to be the owners' interest in the business. The details of the owners' equity section as shown on the balance sheet are a function of the type of organisation in which the business operates – sole proprietorship, partnership, limited liability company or corporation.

Owners' equity

A simplified balance sheet of a small hospitality operation (in this case a restaurant) is shown in Figure 8.2.

FIGURE 8.2 Simplified balance sheet for the Sense of Taste Restaurant on 31/12/20XX

Sense of Taste Restaurant
Balance Sheet
December 31 20XX

Assets			Liabilities & Owners' Equity		
Current Assets:			**Current Liabilities:**		
Cash	€	31,500.00	Accounts Payable	€	11,500.00
Restricted cash	€	1,050.00	Accrued Expenses	€	30,850.00
Receivables	€	2,500.00	Income Taxes Payable		€ 200.00
Operating Equipment	€	6,500.00	Current Maturities of Notes Payable	€	23,676.00
Prepaid Expenses	€	23,190.00	Current Maturities of Mortgage Payable	€	15,054.00
Inventory	€	17,500.00			
Total Current Assets €		*82,240.00*	*Total Current Liabilities* €		*81,280.00*
Fixed Assets:			**Long-Term Liabilities:**		
Land	€	25,000.00	Notes Payable	€	151,324.00
Buildings	€	275,000.00	Mortgage Payable	€	184,946.00
Furnishings and Equipment	€	200,250.00			
less Accumulated Depreciation	€	140,000.00	*Total Long-Term Liabilities* €		*336,270.00*
Net Property & Equipment €		*360,250.00*			
			Total Liabilities €		*417,550.00*
Other Assets:					
Intangible Assets	€	7,560.00			
Cash Surrender Value of Life Insurance	€	75,000.00	**Owners' Equity**	€	107,500.00
Total Other Assets €		*82,560.00*	*Total Owner's Equity* €		*107,500.00*
Total Assets		**€ 525,050.00**	**Total Liabilities and Owners' Equity**		**€ 525,050.00**

8.3.2   Income statement and statement of comprehensive income

Income statement

The income statement, also known as the 'profit and loss statement', the 'statement of earnings', and the 'statement of operations' (in the case the statement reflects a net loss) describes a company's financial performance

Period

for a period of time, and in many cases is considered the most important financial statement. The income statement is prepared by the Accounting Department with the main goal of providing users of the financial state-

Profitability

ments with information relating to the profitability of the hospitality operation over a particular period of time; this could be on a weekly or monthly basis for internal management use, or on a quarterly, semi-annual or annual basis for external users. An extension of the income statement is the statement of comprehensive income, which indicates the change in equity [net assets] of a business enterprise as a result of transactions and other events and circumstances from non-owner sources during a given period. It includes all changes in equity during that period except those resulting from investments by owners or distributions to owners.

As of 1 January 2009, a business entity adopting IFRS must include:
- a statement of comprehensive income, or
- two separate statements comprising:
  - an income statement, and
  - a statement of comprehensive income

The major elements of an income statement are:

Under operating activities
- Revenues, which represent the amount of assets created by the hospitality operation during normal business activities of delivery or production of goods and services over a specific time period. Revenues are usually presented as sales minus all sales discounts, returns and allowances.

  Revenues
- Expenses, which represent the amount of assets consumed in the performance of normal business activities of the hospitality operation while delivering or producing goods and services over a certain period. Generally, the most prominent expense item is the cost of items sold to customers. Other expenses may include salaries, utilities, supplies, transportation, marketing, insurance, research and development, commissions, rent, interest, repairs and maintenance, depreciation and taxes, to list a few.

  Expenses
- Net income or net loss, which represent the difference between revenues and expenses. If revenues are more than the expenses, there is a positive net income or profit. If the expenses are more than the revenues, on the other hand, there is a negative net income or loss.

  Net income or net loss

Under non-operating activities
- Gains or other revenues represent what the hospitality operation makes from activities other than its primary business activity. This could include items such as rent or patents.

  Gains
- Losses or other expenses represent expenses or losses not related to the primary business activity, for example a loss caused by an act of nature.

  Losses

Within the hospitality industry, revenues, gains, expenses, and losses are all reported distinctly from each other. Management is generally held primarily responsible for their success in operations determined by revenues and expenses. On the other hand, management is only held secondarily responsible for gains and losses.

Responsible

For management purposes, the summary operating statement prepared for owners by the Accounting Department in conformity with the USALI 11th Revised Edition contains the revenues and expenses analysed during operating periods and including forecasts as shown in Figure 8.3.

The design of the income statement destined for internal management's use lets management use a single sheet to compare their current performance to their past performance, as well as showing the relation of their current performance to originally budgeted plans as denoted in the forecast column. This comparison allows management to identify significant variations that may warrant urgent corrective action.

Design

FIGURE 8.3 Summary operating statement in conformity with the USALI 11th Revised Edition

Summary Operating Statement [For Owners]						
	PERIOD OF					
	CURRENT PERIOD			YEAR-TO-DATE		
	ACTUAL	FORECAST/BUDGET	PRIOR YEAR	ACTUAL	FORECAST/BUDGET	PRIOR YEAR
ROOMS AVAILABLE: ROOMS SOLD: OCCUPANCY: ADR: ROOMS REVPAR TOTAL REVPAR						

	PERIOD OF												
	CURRENT PERIOD						YEAR-TO-DATE					
	ACTUAL		FORECAST/BUDGET		PRIOR YEAR		ACTUAL		FORECAST/BUDGET		PRIOR YEAR	
	€	%	€	%	€	%	€	%	€	%	€	%
OPERATING REVENUE												
Rooms												
Food and Beverage												
Other Operated Departments												
Miscellaneous Income												
TOTAL OPERATING REVENUE												
DEPARTMENTAL EXPENSES												
Rooms												
Food and Beverage												
Other Operated Departments												
TOTAL DEPARTMENTAL EXPENSES												
TOTAL DEPARTMENTAL PROFIT												
UNDISTRIBUTED OPERATING EXPENSES												
Administrative and General												
Information and Telecommunications												
Systems												
Sales and Marketing												
Property Operations and Maintenance												
Utilities												
TOTAL UNDISTRIBUTED EXPENSES												
GROSS OPERATING PROFIT												
MANAGEMENT FEES												
INCOME BEFORE												
NON-OPERATING INCOME AND												
EXPENSES												
NON-OPERATING INCOME AND EXPENSES												
Income												
Rent												
Property and Other Taxes												
Insurance												
Other												
TOTAL NON-OPERATING INCOME AND												
EXPENSES												
EARNINGS BEFORE INTEREST, TAXES,												
DEPRECIATION, AND AMORTISATION												
INTEREST, DEPRECIATION, AND												
AMORTISATION												
Interest												
Depreciation												
Amortisation												
TOTAL INTEREST, DEPRECIATION, AND												
AMORTISATION												
INCOME BEFORE INCOME TAXES												
Income Taxes												
NET INCOME												

All revenues and expenses should be shown as a percentage of total operating revenue, except departmental expenses, which should be shown as a percentage of their respective departmental revenue.

The USALI emphasises the reporting of the income statement accounting information based on the operating centres within the hospitality operation. These operating centres are generally those areas that are in direct contact with guests and customers. Figure 8.4 shows the basic income statement format of a standard hotel in conformity with the USALI 11th Revised Edition and destined for external users.

Operating Centres

FIGURE 8.4 Basic statement of income in conformity with the USALI 11th Revised Edition – external users

STATEMENT OF INCOME

	Period	
	Current Year	Prior Year
REVENUE		
Rooms	€	€
Food and Beverage		
Other Operated Departments		
Miscellaneous Income*		
Total Revenue		
EXPENSES		
Rooms		
Food and Beverage		
Other Operated Departments		
Administrative and General		
Information and Tellecommunications Systems		
Sales and Marketing		
Property Operations and Maintenance		
Utilities		
Management Fees		
Non-Operating Expenses		
Interest Expense		
Depreciation and Amortisation		
Loss or (Gain) on the Disposition of Assets		
Total Expenses		
INCOME BEFORE INCOME TAXES		
INCOME TAXES		
Current		
Deferred		
Total Income Taxes		
NET INCOME	€	€

* For the Statement of Income, Miscellaneous Income includes non-operating inconme. This differs from Miscellaneous Income on the Summary Operating Statements.

8.3.3   Cash flow statement

Like the income statement, the cash flow statement (CFS) is established by the Accounting Department over a certain period of time. The CFS reflects the flow of money into and out of the hospitality operation over time. It is established based on the actual cash flows experienced during the given period. The primary function of the CFS is to provide required information to management as well as to other concerned stakeholders – especially investors, suppliers, and creditors. This information indicates where the cash in the hospitality operation comes from and how it is used. The CFS excludes transactions that do not directly affect cash movements.

Cash flow statement

Period

Cash

The main features of the CFS can be summarised as follows:
- Showing the hospitality operation's ability to generate positive future cash flows. Despite the fact that the CFS is historical in nature, it does provide information on how the hospitality operation generated its cash in the past; this may be used to evaluate the hospitality operation's ability to generate cash in the future.
- Showing the hospitality operation's ability to honour its obligations to its debtors. By providing information on the hospitality operation's liquidity and solvency, concerned stakeholders are better able to make decisions on future transactions with the hospitality operation.
- Showing the difference between the hospitality operation's profit and its cash movements. The CFS clearly indicates sources of cash within a company, as it displays such information under the 3 headings of direct operating activities, investing activities and financing activities. Concerned stakeholders are much more interested in hospitality operations that generate most of their cash from their primary operating activities.
- Showing the effect of both cash and non-cash financing and investing activities during the accounting period.
- Highlighting the comparability of different hospitality operations' operating performance in eliminating the effects of different accounting methods. This is a result of the fact that the CFS is established according to the 3 major categories of activities – operating, investing, and financing.

For the Accounting Department to be able to adequately establish a SCF, the following documents and information are required:
- The income statement for the period concerned;
- The statement of retained earnings for the period concerned;
- The balance sheet established at the beginning date of the period concerned;
- The balance sheet established at the ending date of the period concerned;
- Any details relating to all transactions that affected fixed asset elements of the organisation in the period between the two balance sheet dates.

When all of the above documents, statements and information are available, the Accounting Department establishes the SCF by determining the net cash flows from the three main sections as indicated in Figure 8.5 in conformity with the USALI 11th Revised Edition.

FIGURE 8.5 Determining the statement of cash flow

Net Cash Provided by (Used In) Operating Activities
+
Net Cash Provided by (Used In) Investing Activities
+
Net Cash Provided by (Used In) Financing Activities
=
Increase (Decrease) in Cash and Temporary Cash Investments
+
Cash and Temporary Cash Investments, Beginning of Period
=
Cash and Temporary Cash Investments, Ending of Period

8.3.4   Statement of retained earnings

A statement of retained earnings, is also called an 'equity statement', a 'statement of owner's equity' for sole proprietorships, 'statement of partners' equity' for partnerships, 'statement of financial position', and 'statement of retained earnings and stockholders' equity' for corporations. This statement explains the changes in a company's retained earnings from the end of one accounting period to the end of the next. The statement reconciles the opening and closing balances in the equity accounts as found in the two ends of period balance sheets.

Retained earnings are part of the balance sheet (within the owners' equity section) and they are mostly affected by the net income earned by a company during a certain period minus any dividends paid to the company's owners within that same period. In its IAS 1, the IFRS requires all business entities to present a separate statement of changes in equity as one of the components of their financial statements. According to the USALI, the statement of owners' equity is designed according to the type of hospitality operation (sole proprietorships, partnerships, limited liability companies, and corporations). Figure 8.6 is an example of a statement of owner's equity of a sole proprietorship and based on the USALI 11th Revised Edition.

Statement of retained earnings

Reconciles

Designed

FIGURE 8.6 Statement of owner's equity of a sole proprietorship based on the USALI 11th Revised Edition

STATEMENT OF OWNER'S EQUITY

	Owner	Accumulated Other Comprehensive Income (Loss), Net of Income Taxes	Total
BALANCE AT BEGINNING OF PRIOR YEAR	€	€	€
Add (Deduct)			
Net Income			
Contributions			
Change in Unrealized Gain (Losses)			
Withdrawals			
Other			
BALANCE AT END OF PRIOR YEAR	€	€	€
Add (Deduct)			
Net Income			
Contributions			
Change in Unrealized Gain (Losses)			
Withdrawals			
Other			
BALANCE AT END OF CURRENT YEAR	€	€	€

Cumulative foreign currency translation adjustments should also be reflected in this statement

The configuration of the statement shown in Figure 8.6 is the same for partnerships and limited liability companies (with changes only in titles: statement of members' equity; or statement of partners' equity – in which there is a distinction between general and limited partners). For public corporations, the configuration is different, and includes volume and values of different types of shares outstanding (preferred or common), additional paid-in capital, retained earnings and treasury stock. The Accounting Department of the hospitality operation knows which type of equity statement to create depending on their ownership structure. If desired, small hospitality operations can omit the statement of changes in equity if the hospitality operation has no owner investments or withdrawals other than dividends; they may decide to present a combined statement of comprehensive income and retained earnings instead.

8.4 Management reports

Management reports show the worth of a business over a specific period of time. The quality of management information is critical in delivering the best possible basis for decision-making to business managers. Price Waterhouse Coopers (www.pwc.com) indicate that leading companies are already starting to confront some fundamental issues, such as:

- Is the right information to run the business available at the right time?
- Is too much time spent producing numbers rather than gaining real insight?
- Are the performance measures transparent? How can accountabilities for performance management across the business be clarified?
- How can rewards be aligned with performance, thereby driving the right actions?
- How is a performance language that fosters non-threatening analysis and discussion of business issues and opportunities best developed?

In order for managers to find answers to such questions, they must ensure they have the relevant information required to make adequate decisions.

8.4.1   Some frequently used reports

Advances in information technology and widespread use of advanced PMSs have changed the basic reporting possibilities for hospitality organisations. Most required or necessary reports or statistics are now simply generated at the click of a button; the system then proceeds to retrieve the required information and produce the relevant report. A report produced by the *protel Air* PMS reporting module has been given as an example in Figure 8.7.

Since a hospitality operation's daily routines generate a vast amount of data, versatile reporting capabilities in a PMS enable managers to make quick and safe decisions for every facet of their operation. Some frequently used reports are:

- The accounting report, which provides an overview of all revenues and payments for individual accounts over a selected month. All postings within a specified period of time are displayed, regardless of whether an invoice was created. The report can be printed along with end-of-day reports for a given day, or accessed digitally for a defined period of time;
- The discount groups report, which shows the number of guests grouped by discount group for a defined period of time. This shows management how many children or seniors are guests of the hotel, for example;
- The distribution channels report, which allows management to evaluate the success of individual distribution channels. It creates a report used for

---

Margin notes:

Management reports

Issues

8

Reporting possibilities

Decisions

Accounting

Discount groups

Distribution channels

FIGURE 8.7 Partial screenshot of protel Air's reporting possibilities.

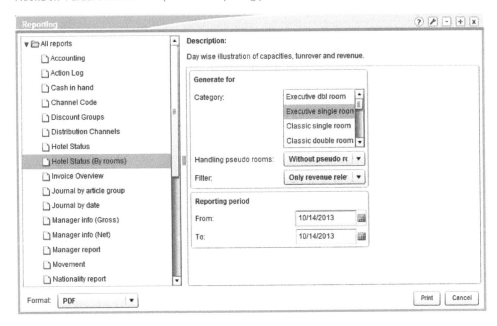

analysing the distribution channels management has assigned to its reservations. It includes information such as the number of reservations per distribution channel and the revenues achieved per distribution channel;

- The invoice overview report, which shows all invoices created over a selected period of time;

Invoice overview

- The journal by article group report, which provides a list of booked items by article group over a selected period of time;

Journal by article group

- The hotel status report, which provides day-to-day illustrations of capacities and revenue, which can be generated for specific rooms, categories or states;

Hotel status

- The Manager's report, which provides all important data (e.g. number of guests, rooms, capacity and revenue) at a glance, and can be generated for specific rooms, categories or states;

Manager's report

- The movement report, which shows the movements for one day in a single report. The report shows all arrivals, departures, staying guests, and moves for the selected day;

Movement

- The nationality report, which provides details about guests' nationalities. Many hotels are subject to national or regional legislation that requires them to provide this list to responsible registration authorities on a monthly basis;

Nationality

- The payments report, which shows all payments posted for a selected period of time. It can be used to perform a simple comparison of credit card payments posted in the PMS to statements from the credit card terminals. It also allows management to check on accounts receivable by further processing all payments 'on account', for example. The report can also be displayed for each individual method of payment, and can be restricted to one or more users. If a particular user is selected, only payments entered by that user are included;

Payments

Rate overview
- The rate overview report, which evaluates the turnover the operation have reached in a selected time-span for a certain rate code. This displays the turnover made by the room rate. Turnover made from extra services is displayed separately;

Revenue
- The revenue report, which lists all revenues posted for a specific period of time. The information is broken down by various tax rates, product groups, and individual posted articles. Management can use the revenue and sales figures to create targeted statistics, or use them as a basis for implementing required marketing or sales measures;

Revenue to previous year
- The revenue to previous year report (gross/net), which shows daily, monthly and yearly revenues grouped by product ranges. The booking date is vital for the revenues displayed. Current revenues are compared to revenues of the previous year. Differences are shown in percentages;

Top bookers
- The top bookers report, which lists the top guests/bookers generating the most turnover.

8.5 Some accounting issues

The profitability of a hospitality operation does not only rely on efficient sales, professional attitude, or quality standard of services provided to guests, but also mainly on following procedure and correctly using an accurate guest ac-

Responsibility
counting. It is the responsibility of the Front Office to prepare and present a guest's bill, and ensure that it is paid. This involves a lot of record keeping, because a guest may generate a lot of separate charges during a stay.

8.5.1   Billing and the guest accounting process

Account
An account is a record of a business transaction; as a document, it records, accumulates and summarises financial data. Increases and decreases to an account are calculated and the result is called the 'account balance'. In the hospitality industry, guest accounting relates to all transactions involving

Guest accounts
money received from guests, costs paid by guests. Guest accounts are created when guests make their reservations or when they check in at the Front Desk. Guest account management is done by the Front Office, who try and ensure that the account is either fully or partially settled before guests

check out of the property. There also exist non-guest accounts, which refer to all in-house charged privileges extended to local businesses or others, such as the use of banqueting and conferencing facilities. These are usually called 'house accounts' or 'city accounts', and if set up for groups, they are termed 'master accounts'. Such accounts are also set up when former guests fail to settle their account at check-out; from this point onward, the duty of ensuring the settlement of the account is handed over from the Front Office to the Accounting Department.

Non-guest accounts

Depending on a hospitality operation's size and type, various systems (such as manual, mechanical or fully automated) may be used in the accounting procedure. Notwithstanding the system employed, the basic objectives of a good accounting system are:

Basic objectives

- Maintaining accurate and up-to-date guest accounts;
- Ensuring payments are received in full and as promptly as possible;
- Providing management with accurate and up-to-date financial reports.

The guest bill and methods of communication

In operations with manual or mechanical systems, the guest bill is updated immediately once received from the various departments or sales outlets. In operations with fully automated systems, guest bills are updated automatically as part of a guest folio. As hotel guests are traditionally entitled to credit facilities for purchases regarding accommodation, food and beverages, telephone or other facilities during their stay, it is important to maintain a minutely detailed record of guests' accounts. Figure 8.8 (retrieved from protel Air) shows some articles contained in a guest bill. It clearly notes sources such as accommodation, food and beverages, spa package, recreational rides, and newspapers.

Guest bill

FIGURE 8.8 Guest bill sources

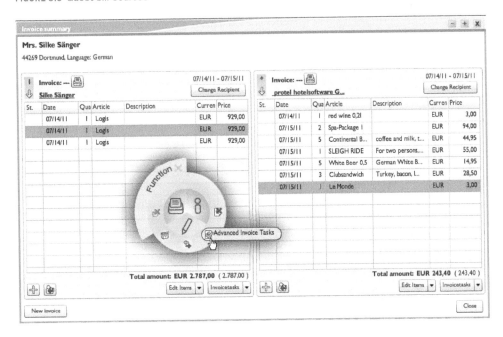

Speed and accuracy in managing guest accounts is very important. It helps to prevent belated charges. To improve guest account management speed and accuracy, an effective communication system between the billing section and the various sales outlets must be established. Depending upon the type of hotel, the communication methods can be:

Communication methods

1 Manual systems: in small operations, employees at the sales outlet can physically move to the billing section to enter the data into a guest's folio;

Manual
Mechanical

2 Mechanical systems: some hospitality operations use pneumatic tubes (pressure suction tubes) that transport signed guest vouchers from sales outlets to billing sections;

Fully automatic

3 Fully automatic systems: in most modern hospitality operations using a good quality PMS, very efficient and convenient point-of-sale (POS) terminals are connected directly to a central computer server, and all guests' transactions are automatically updated and stored in their respective folios.

The guest accounting process

Concepts

The guest accounting process is centred on the following concepts:

1 A financial transaction leading to the creation and maintenance of accurate accounting details. This transaction can be in the form of a cash payment by the guest (with no further influence on a guest's outstanding balance), an acknowledgement of debt by a guest (as 'account receivable'), or an advance payment by a guest;

2 The recording of transactions on relevant documents. These documents generally include cash receipts, folios, and vouchers. A 'cash receipt' is a document issued to the guest by the cashier when the cashier receives a cash payment from the guest. A 'folio' is an account statement created at the time of a guest's arrival; starting with an initial balance of zero, it is an ongoing record of a guest's transactions. These transactions either increase or decrease the balance of the account. The process of recording transactions on a folio is called 'posting'. 'Vouchers' are documents – signed by guests – that detail guests' transactions at points of sales, and are used to transmit guests' charges which still need posting to the Front Office. The use of vouchers is currently experiencing a significant decline due to the use of point of sale systems that directly transmit the transactions of guests to their folios;

3 The verification of the accuracy of transactions. This is also called 'auditing', and it is usually done by a night auditor at night or at a time when business is relatively slow, which is why the process is usually called

Night auditing

'night auditing'. The activities of the night auditors are important in ensuring that there are no discrepancies between the various account balances. Hotels with fully automated systems do not require large night audit teams, since most of the audit functions (system updates) are automatically carried out by the PMS; but to prevent problems resulting from system errors, at least one person is required to physically verify the accounts and vouchers;

4 The settlement of the account either by cash or credit card charge. This is an important phase in the guest accounting process, and it leads to 'zeroing-out' the folio balance; neutralising the outstanding debit balance with a settlement credit balance.

© Noordhoff Uitgevers bv

8.5.2   Important internal control proposals

An important activity of the Accounting Department is the creation and maintenance of appropriate internal control systems used to prevent fraud or embezzlement. For the department to carry out this essential activity, they require the development of policies and procedures designed to ensure the safety of the operation's assets. This section indicates a global over-view of basic internal accounting control proposals based on the AHMA-FMC (1997) Hotel Internal Control Guide. It should be noted that individual hospi-tality operations should review the various areas and determine which con-trol proposals are best suited to their needs.

Internal control systems

Front of house internal control proposals

a   Room revenue

  I   Establishing prices
   1 Authorise room rates to be charged
   2 Communicate approved room rates to appropriate parties
   3 Authorise deviations from approved rates

  II Accepting reservations
   1 Obtain complete and accurate reservation information
   2 Accept reservations in accordance with established policies

  III Checking-in guests
   1. Receive reservation information in a timely manner
   2 Establish approved methods of payment
   3 Obtain necessary guest information
   4 Train front desk personnel
   5 Obtain evidence of guest check-in
   6 Maintain current room status information

  IV Recording room revenue
   1 Bill all occupied rooms
   2 Post charges in a timely and accurate manner
   3 Provide guests with a statement of charges
   4 Authorise rebates and allowances

  V   Checking-out guests
   1 Close out guest records in guest ledgers
   2 Update the current room status

b   Food and beverage revenue

  I   Planning and pricing the menu
   1 Plan, price, and periodically update menu items and product lists
   2 Authorise prices to be charged
   3 Authorise officers' cheques, complimentary meals and discounts
   4 Document guest reservation procedures
   5 Establish staffing guidelines based on forecasted business
   6 Establish seating rotation procedures
   7 Establish and maintain adequate par stocks
   8 Establish and implement suggestive/up-selling techniques
   9 Establish and implement hospitality training programmes
   10 Set up a shopping service – establish an independent review of guest service and control procedures

  II Recording revenue
   1 Establish order/entry procedures and train staff in proper use of the POS system
   2 Authorise and account for void cheques and transactions/adjust-ments
   3 Verify cash transactions and settlements

    4 Prove the mathematical accuracy of F&B cheques and verify posting of revenues and settlements

    5 Calculate beverage sales potentials

    6 Independently control guest/cover counts

    7 Establish additional cheque controls for the restaurant buffet

    8 Audit banquet cheques

    9 Establish procedures for banquet cash bars

    10 Balance, post, and verify all F&B transactions through night or income auditor

    11 Record daily minibar consumption

    12 Authorise steward sales

  III Minimising general risks

    1 Establish a food safety programme

    2 Establish an alcohol awareness programme

c Telephone revenue

  I Establishing prices

    1 Select a telephone switch

    2 Select a long-distance carrier and rate structure

    3 Select a call-accounting vendor

    4 Establish a mark-up margin

  II Recording revenue

    1 Post charges in a timely and accurate manner

    2 Reconcile total charges from call-accounting vendor reports to total posted telephone charges

    3 Establish procedures for operator-assisted calls

    4 Provide a statement of charges to guests

    5 Authorise rebates and allowances

    6 Establish procedures for manual systems

    7 Restrict outside operators without restricting emergency calls

  III Reviewing the long-distance invoice to guest charges

    1 Review mark-up margins

    2 Review potential operator-assisted calls (e.g., overseas, third-party charges) to guest postings

    3 Review for unusual charges (e.g., premium rate numbers)

    4 Review call-accounting configurations

    5 Review the call-accounting database

d Other revenue

  I Establishing services provided by external vendors

    1 Selecting services and vendors

      a Determine whether to provide services using parties internal or external

      b Authorise vendors

      c Obtain written contracts from vendors

      d Establish a commission rate

      e Review vendor insurance limits

    2 Recording revenue

      a Establish procedures for accepting vendor charges

      b Post charges in a timely and accurate manner

      c Provide guests with a statement of charges

      d Authorise rebates and allowances

    3 Reviewing vendor invoices charged to guests

      a Reconcile vendor invoices with guest postings and allowances b Review the commission rate for accuracy

    c Audit concessionaires and outside vendors

    d Ensure that vendors have the necessary licenses and permits

II Services provided internally

  1 Establishing prices

    a Select a recording method for sales and receipts (e.g., separate outlet or through front desk)

    b Develop a system to accumulate applicable expenses

    c Authorise rates to be charged for services

  2 Recording revenue

    a Bill all applicable services

    b Post charges in a timely and accurate manner

    c Provide guests with a statement of charges

    d Authorise rebates and allowances

  3 Managing expenses

    a Train appropriate personnel

    b Compare revenue to related expenses

e Cashiering

  I Maintaining cash receipts – house funds

    1 Provide a secure storage area

    2 Limit access to cash monies

    3 Define terms and conditions for maintenance of the house fund

    4 Establish accountability for the house fund

    5 Perform periodic, independent check-ups

II   Maintaining cash receipts – cash banks
1   Provide a secure storage area
2   Limit access to cash monies
3   Define the terms and conditions for maintenance of cash banks
4   Establish accountability for operating banks
5   Perform periodic, independent check-ups

III   Maintaining cash receipts – cash transactions
1   Post all guest payments immediately upon receipt
2   Establish a cheque log for cheques received in the mail
3   Establish accountability
4   Provide guests with receipts for payments on accounts

IV   Maintaining cash receipts – cheque cashing
1   Establish standards for cheque-cashing approval
2   Establish cheque-cashing procedures
3   Train cashiers to be alert to characteristics that may indicate bad cheques

V   Maintaining cash receipts – petty cash
1   Define criteria for the use of petty cash
2   Establish standards for authorising the use of petty cash
3   Record the payment of petty cash
4   Record expenses represented by petty cash payments on a timely basis

VI   Maintaining cash receipts – pay-outs
1   Establish standards authorising pay-outs
2   Establish accountability
3   Post all pay-outs in a timely and accurate manner

VII   Maintaining cash receipts – deposits
1   Establish a system of deposits
2   Establish accountability
3   Ensure the accuracy and timeliness of cash deposits
4   Account for and secure cash deposits

VIII   Maintaining cash receipts – cheque payments
1   Accept cheques for payment of accounts, advance deposits, and miscellaneous income in accordance with established policies
2   Post cheque payments in a timely and accurate manner
3   Provide guests with a credited folio as receipt of payment

IX   Maintaining cash receipts – credit card transactions
1   Apply all credit card payments to guest accounts
2   Approve credit cards
3   Post payments in a timely and accurate manner
4   Provide guests with a credited folio as receipt of payment

X   Managing food and beverage revenue
1   Bill all food and beverage charges
2   Post charges in a timely and accurate manner
3   Provide guests with a statement of charges

XI   Managing banquet and meeting room revenue
1   Bill all banquet and meeting room charges
2   Post charges in a timely and accurate manner
3   Provide guests with a statement of charges

XII   Managing miscellaneous revenue
1   Bill all miscellaneous charges
2   Post charges in a timely and accurate manner
3   Provide guests with a statement of charges

XIII Managing adjustments
    1 Authorise all adjustments
    2 Post all adjustments in a timely and accurate manner

Back of house internal control proposals
a Purchasing
  I Ordering
    1 Establish and authorise purchase specifications
    2 Communicate requirements to vendors
    3 Select optimal vendors and establish bid procedures
    4 Implement the use of authorised purchase orders or contracts and requests
    5 Establish and maintain purchase procedures
  II Receiving
    1 Advise receivers as to goods expected
    2 Check the quality and quantity of goods or services received
    3 Record the receipt of goods or services and establish procedures for errors, returns, and goods received without invoice
    4 Communicate the receipt to stores and accounts payable
    5 Match receivers' reports and related purchase documentation
  III Paying vendors
    1 Ensure purchases are properly recorded, valued, classified, and accounted for
    2 Authorise disbursement vouchers
    3 Restrict access to critical forms, records, and processing areas
    4 Ensure that cash disbursements are valid, accounted for, properly recorded, in the correct amount, and classified

b Inventories
  I Managing the storeroom
    1 Establish storeroom checks for inventory items – based on hotel size and availability of sufficient storage space (food and beverage; general supplies; guest supplies; engineering supplies; non-circulating operating equipment – china, glass, silver, and linen)
    2 Use forms and procedures to record receipt and issue of inventory stores
    3 Maintain physical protection; safeguard assets
  II Managing inventory count and valuation
    1 Perform inventory counts and adjust physical records accordingly; ascertain reasons for discrepancies
    2 Reconcile perpetual records with general ledger control accounts monthly, where applicable
  III Managing operating equipment
    1 Establish procedures for the control of and accounting for reserve and in-use operating equipment

c Food and beverage costs
  I Purchasing and receiving
    1 Establish purchase specifications to maintain consistency in food and beverage purchases
    2 Establish guidelines for determining quantities of food and beverage purchases
    3 Establish procedures for the creation and maintenance of purchasing records
    4 Establish procedures for receiving food and beverage items

    5 Establish procedures for goods received without invoice, for delivery errors, and for returns

  II Storing and issuing

    1 Establish physical controls and standards for the storage and retention of perishable and non-perishable food and beverage items

    2 Secure storage areas; restrict access to authorised personnel

    3 Establish requisition procedures

    4 Establish procedures for transfers from one storeroom to another, and between storerooms and food and beverage outlets

  III Managing daily and monthly F&B cost reconciliations/potentials and yields

    1 Establish procedures for monitoring and verifying daily and monthly food and beverage costs

    2 Establish procedures for calculating and monitoring food and beverage pars, standards, yields, and potentials

    3 Establish procedures for recording sales values and cost equivalents for A&G or S&M food and beverage cheques for officers and other employees. Include guidelines and authorisations for application

  IV Managing banquets

    1 Establish procedures to monitor banquet food and beverage costs

d Personnel administration

  I Complying with government requirements

    1 Require new employees to complete necessary immigration forms

    2 Require minors to have work permits

    3 Comply with minimum wage requirements

    4 Comply with workers' compensation laws

    5 Comply with equal employment opportunity requirements

    6 Maintain necessary work related insurances

  II Following company guidelines

    1 Require applicants to complete job application forms

    2 Conduct reference and background checks on candidates

    3 Establish fair wage guidelines

    4 Monitor employees' eligibility for insurance benefits

    5 Monitor employees' eligibility for paid vacation time

    6 Conduct an annual review of each employee

    7 Complete a termination checklist

    8 Conduct exit interviews

    9 Keep detailed employment and termination records

e Payroll

  I Authorising wages, salaries, withholdings, and deductions

    1 Hire and retain employees only at rates, benefits, and perquisites determined in accordance with management's general or specific authorisations

    2 Determine payroll withholdings and deductions based on evidence of appropriate authorisations

  II Preparing and recording

    1 Compensate company employees only at authorised rates and only for services rendered (hours worked) in accordance with management's authorisations

    2 Correctly compute gross pay, withholdings, deductions, and net pay based on authorised rates, services rendered, and properly authorised withholding exemptions and deductions

  3 Correctly accumulate, classify, and summarise payroll costs and related liabilities in the appropriate accounts and periods

  4 Make comparisons of personnel, payroll, and work records at reasonable intervals for the timely detection and correction of errors

III Managing disbursements

  1 Remit net pay and related withholdings and deductions to the appropriate employees and entities respectively, when due

  2 Make disbursements only for expenditures incurred in accordance with management's authorisations

  3 Make adjustments to cash accounts only in accordance with management's authorisations

  4 Record disbursements at correct amounts in the appropriate period and properly classify disbursements in the accounts

  5 Restrict access to cash and cash disbursement records to minimise opportunities for irregular or erroneous disbursements

IV Separating functions and physical safeguards

  1 Assign function so that no single individual is in a position to both perpetuate and conceal fraud in the normal course of duties

  2 Limit access to personnel and payroll records to minimise opportunities for errors and irregularities

V Reconciling banks

  1 Make comparisons of detail records, control, accounts, and bank statements at reasonable intervals for the detection and appropriate correction of errors or irregularities

Administration internal control proposals

a General accounting and financial reporting

 I Ensuring the accuracy and completeness of the financial data provided to various parties

  1 Authorise accounting principles

  2 Authorise entries and adjustments

  3 Authorise the issuance of specific financial statements

  4 Prepare general journal entries

  5 Summarise general ledger balances

  6 Combine departmental information accurately

  7 Prepare appropriate disclosures

  8 Protect records from hazards and misuse

b Loss prevention and risk management

 I Keeping guests and employees safe

  1 Promote safety awareness

  2 Fill out and submit incident reports accurately and timely

 II Restricting access to the property

  1 Protect the perimeter

  2 Designate an employee entrance and exit

  3 Restrict access to interior areas

 III Protecting the guestroom

  1 Establish physical security in guestrooms

  2 Inform guests of guestroom safety features

 IV Managing keys

  1 Issue keys only to employees requiring access

  2 Document key issuance

  3 Rekey locks as needed

8

V   Protecting against fires and planning for emergencies
  1 Educate all employees in fire prevention and safety
  2 Maintain adequate fire protection equipment
  3 Institute an emergency response and evacuation plan
VI Evaluating the loss prevention programme
  1 Establish a protection committee
  2 Perform periodic safety audits
VII Reducing internal theft
  1 Verify applicant information
VIII Limiting property liability and loss
  1 Provide safe-deposit-box protection
  2 Obtain cost-effective insurance coverage
  3 Assign insurance coordination responsibilities to a qualified individual

c Computer systems

I   Control access to computer systems and applications
II   Protect sensitive company information from accidental or intentional misuse or disclosure
III Establish a security administration function for each major system
IV   Include security awareness training in employee training programme
V   Establish an appropriate environment for the equipment in the computer room
VI   Purchase sufficient insurance coverage for all computer assets
VII Cover all major hardware with preventative maintenance contracts, and arrange for the use of backup equipment in an emergency
VIII Ensure the reliable installation, maintenance, and physical security of all telecommunications
IX   Make sure all acquisitions of software and hardware are fully justified, approved, and compatible with the existing environment
X   Implement check-ups of all software and hardware changes
XI   Make sure computer systems are used effectively and for their intended purposes

d Administration

I   Managing annual forecasts
  1 Forecast revenue for each revenue centre by month, based on forecasted occupancy
  2 Forecast expenses based on the occupancy volumes used to generate revenues
  3 Review and compare monthly forecasts of revenues and expenses
II Managing capital expenditures
  1 Obtain, in writing, all approvals necessary to proceed with projects
  2 Prepare forms necessary for the initiation of projects: purchase orders, major expense forms, contracts, etc.
  3 Document any changes to the original project, purchase order, or contract
  4 Ensure proper payments for planned projects
  5 Compare budgets to actual expenditures and planned expenditures
  6 Prepare overviews of capital expenditures made in the previous seven years
  7 Prepare lists of all projects that may be desired or needed
  8 Prepare amounts in funding to be spent on projects
  9 Prioritise project listings by importance to ongoing operations and management objectives

8.6 Forecasting and budgeting

Another major function of the Accounting Department is the preparation of forecasts and budgets in collaboration with the departmental heads as well as the General Manager within an operation. Forecasts are the financial documents that are used to update an operation's operating budget. Forecasts are flexible and provide possibilities for management to carry out modifications to the operating budget during the operating cycle. This lets management take into consideration any changes caused by economic and market conditions; it also lets them adapt to current trends. Forecasts are used to update a budget so that it reflects current business levels and conditions. Forecasting involves using current information and combining it with established ratios and formulas to estimate or project future business levels and operations. Forecasting is the key management tool used to plan the details of daily operations in the very short term, such as tomorrow, next week or next month. Weekly activity forecasts, for example, are used to predict and develop weekly part-time employee schedules.

Forecasts and budgets

Key management tool

The income statement of the organisation is the main focus of forecasting for hospitality managers, as it presents the historical record of day-to-day activities. In the forecasting process, the actual financial performances of the past are projected onto the future through the development of an operations budget based on whatever forecasting method is used in the organisation. Though not found in the income statements, forecasts are included in the internal management reports generally reviewed daily and weekly. This includes reviewing actual revenues and labour costs and comparing them to the forecast, the budget, and last year's figures.

Main focus

Operations budget

The fact that forecasts are not generally included in the monthly or other periodic income statement does not mean they are not important. It means that they are used primarily as an internal management tool to plan, operate, and analyse the daily and weekly operations. In fact, operations managers spend more time with weekly financial information than with income statements. This is because they use the forecasts daily in their operations, critiquing variations daily and weekly, and making necessary changes to improve performance. Effectively using weekly forecasts and other internal management reports generally leads to better financial performance on monthly or other periodic income statements.

Internal

Forecasting includes projecting future revenues and scheduling future expenses to maintain productivity and profit margins. Forecasting is primarily based on volumes as expressed in rooms sold or guests served. The amount of activity in a hotel or restaurant requires an established level of wages and other operating expenses to deliver the expected products and services. As business volumes increase, additional wages and operating expenditures are necessary to properly deliver these expected levels of service. Likewise, when business levels decrease, these wages and operating expenses also need to be reduced to maintain productivity and avoid unproductive waste in wages or operating costs. It is important for the operations managers to possess adequate forecasting skills that enable them to adjust operating expenses with expected levels of business. For more on Forecasting methods, see Chapter 13 of Chibili, 2016 – *Basic Management Accounting for the Hospitality Industry,* 2nd edition.

Based on volumes

Business plan

The operating budget is a business plan converted into monetary terms. It may take the form of forecasted revenue and related expenses for the next months. A budget can also be stated in non-monetary terms, such as numbers of house-keeping staff needed next week. A business that operates without a budget (or a plan) makes decisions that do not contribute to the profitability of the business, because its managers lack a clear idea of the goals of the business. Forecasting and budgeting systems are expected to reflect realistic expectations. However, in practice, differences do arise between actual and projected performances. It is therefore necessary for the budgeting process to include systems that allow immediate feedback and control, ensuring corrective actions within the hospitality operations can be taken; the Accounting Department is obligated to ensure the implementation of an operating budget.

Realistic expectations

Corrective actions

8.6.1   The budget and the budget process

Budget

The budget is a listing of the amount of estimated revenues a company expects to receive, as well as a listing of related costs and expenses expected to be incurred in obtaining the estimated revenue over a particular period of time. The budget helps with:

- Providing organised estimates of future unit sales, sales revenues, expenses, net income, staffing requirements, or equipment needs, with estimates broken down by operating period and department;
- Providing management with both short-term and long-term goals, to be used to plan future activities;
- Providing information for control so that actual results can be evaluated against budget plans and, in case of differences, adjustments are made to correct the situation.

Planning

The budgeting process is essentially about planning for the future. Planning can be split into three categories:

Long-range

- Long-range planning (also referred to as strategic planning), which is about providing long-term vision and goals to the organisation. It is a planning process that attempts to coordinate the use of resources over time. Such plans may include decisions about future expansion or the creation of new markets and products;

Operational

- Operational planning, which is a sub-set of long-range planning. The operational plan describes short-term ways of achieving milestones and explains how, or what portion of, a strategic plan is to be put into operation during a given operational period. An operational plan is the basis for, and justification of, an annual operating budget request. A good operational plan should contain: clear objectives; promises to be delivered; quality criteria; desired results; resource requirements; and the time frame;

Project

- Project planning covers the detailed activities on how to accomplish a given project, such as opening a new catering outlet. Project planning is part of project management, which relates to the use of schedules such as Gantt charts to plan and subsequently report progress about the project. Good project planning involves the following steps: definition of scope; determination of methods to complete the project; creation of a work breakdown structure; identification of the critical paths using activity network diagrams; and the estimation and allocation of related revenues and expenses. Once established and agreed, the plan is then referred to as the baseline and is used to measure a project's progress.

8.6.2   Objectives of budgeting

A budget serves five main purposes – communication, coordination, planning, control, and evaluation.

Communication – during the budgeting process, managers in every department attempt to justify the resources requested to achieve their goals. They explain to their superiors the scope and volume of their activities, as well as how their tasks are to be performed. The communication between superiors and subordinates helps affirm their mutual commitment to company goals. In addition, different departments and units must communicate with each other during the budget process to coordinate their plans and efforts.

Coordination – different units in the company must also coordinate the many different tasks they perform. The number and types of packages to be marketed, for example, must be coordinated between the service and revenue centres to ensure that all tasks are performed appropriately.

Planning – a budget is an organisation's operational plan for a certain period of time. Many decisions are involved and many questions must be answered. Old plans and processes are questioned, and new plans and processes are evaluated. Managers decide the most effective ways to perform each task. They ask whether a particular activity should still be performed and, if so, how. Managers ask what resources are available and what additional resources are needed.

Control – once a budget is finalised, it becomes the operational plan for the organisation. Managers have authority to spend within the budget, and responsibility to achieve revenues specified by the budget. Budgets and actual revenues and expenditures are constantly monitored for variations, and to determine whether an organisation is on target. If performance does not meet the budget, action against existing activities can be taken immediately. Without constant monitoring, a company will not realise it is not on target until it is too late to make adjustments.

Evaluation – one way to evaluate a manager is to compare the budget to the actual performance: did the manager reach the targeted revenue within the constraints of the targeted expenditures? Other factors, such as market and general economic conditions, also affect a manager's performance, of course. Whether a manager achieves the targeted goals is an important part of managerial responsibility.

8.6.3   Types of budgets

Hospitality operations have different kinds of budgets (operations budgets, capital budgets, department budgets (profit and service centres), cash budgets and master budgets, to name but a few). Budgets can generally be either long-term or short-term. A long-term budget is a plan for a period from 1 to about 5 years. These long-term budgets are also called 'strategic budgets'. Short-term budgets may be for a day, a week, a month, a quarter, or a year. A summary of the various types is given here:

Operations budgets – an operations budget, also called the 'revenue and expense' budget, is management's plan for generating revenues and incurring expenses over a specific period. A monthly revenue forecast for a motel would be an example.

Capital budgets   Capital budgets – a capital budget is a plan for the acquisition of new – as well as the replacement of old – plant, property and equipment. A five year development plan to increase the number of rooms in a property would be an example.

Department budgets   Department budgets – a department budget contains the planned activities of a single department. For revenue and profit centres, a department budget includes all planned revenues as well as planned expenses for a given period. For service centres, however, a department budget only shows projected expenses for the given period. Department budgets are normally prepared for a year and then sub-divided into months.

Cash budgets   Cash budgets – a cash budget (also called 'cash flow budget') is the forecast of future cash receipts and expenditures for a particular time period, generally in the short term. It helps management to determine when revenues will be sufficient to cover expenses and when the company should seek outside financing.

Master budgets   Master budgets – once all organisational objectives, goals and strategies have been identified, the master budget is drafted to express the plans in monetary terms. It is the most comprehensive of all budgets and it serves as a tool for communication and coordination within the organisation. It is generally prepared for a year. An illustration of the interconnections between various budgets within the master budget of a mid-sized hotel is shown in Figure 8.9.

FIGURE 8.9 Parts of the master budget of a hospitality operation

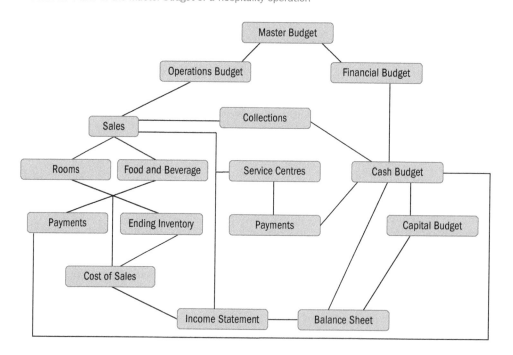

© Noordhoff Uitgevers bv

Figure 8.9 clearly demonstrates the two main parts of the master budget: the operations budget and the financial budget. The operations budget begins with the sales budget and ends with the budgeted income statement. The financial budget includes the capital budget along with the cash budget and the budgeted balance sheet. Collections and payments link the operations and financial budgets together, along with all budgeted changes in balance sheet accounts.

In very small owner-operated operations, budgets can be prepared by the owner with or without an external accounting assistant. At this level, the budget may be a written plan; it may simply be the owner's general idea, not formalised in writing. In larger operations, many individuals are involved in the budget preparation process (department managers and their employees). Very organised bottom-up operations may feature a budget committee consisting of departmental managers, financial controllers, and the general manager who gives the final approval. The committee coordinates the preparation of the budget to ensure a meaningful final budget package.

Budget
committee

Summary

▶ Accounting is the language of business and it is concerned with reporting, summarising and recording the transactions of the business by both internal users and external users in monetary terms.

▶ The four major business values contained in the various branches of accounting are planning, communicating, controlling, and determining profit.

▶ To ensure that users may have faith in the information provided, generally accepted accounting principles should be respected in the preparation of financial statements.

▶ A uniform system of accounts for the lodging industry, designed for classifying, organising, and presenting financial information, makes it possible for uniformity to prevail, and for hotels to compare their financial data.

▶ The international financial reporting standards is a single set of accounting standards, intended to be globally applicable on a consistent basis; they are designed as a common global language for business affairs so that company accounts are understandable and comparable across international boundaries.

▶ In centralised accounting systems, accounting functions are completed by head office, or by one single unit; these hold a dedicated team of employees using one system and set of procedures to record and analyse data. A decentralised accounting system, on the other hand, has employees at different individual units handling the paperwork at their unit levels; these employees have independent reporting accountability.

▶ Financial statements are the records that summarise the financial activities of a business, an individual or any other entity. These statements let a hospitality operation's management review past activities. They can also be used as a basis for making decisions about future operations. The principal financial statements are the balance sheet, the income statement, the statement of comprehensive income, the cash flow statement, and the statement of retained earnings.

▶ Management reports show the value of a business over a specific period of time. The quality of management information is critical in delivering the best possible basis for decision-making to business managers. Some frequently used reports are:
- accounting reports
- discount groups reports

- distribution channels reports
- invoice overview reports
- hotel status reports
- Manager's reports
- movement reports
- nationality reports
- payments reports
- rate overview reports
- revenue reports
- revenue to previous year reports
- top bookers reports

▶ Guest accounting relates to all transactions involving money received from guests, and costs paid by guests. Guest accounts are created when guests make their reservations or when they check in at the Front Desk.

▶ Non-guest accounts refer to all in-house charged privileges extended to local businesses or others, and are usually called 'house accounts', 'city accounts', or 'master accounts' in the case of groups.

▶ Depending on hotel size and type, the accounting communication system between the billing section and the various sales outlets can be manual, mechanical or fully automated.

▶ The guest accounting process is centred on the concepts of:
- establishing financial transactions leading to the creation and maintenance of accurate accounting details
- recording the transactions on relevant documents
- verifying the accuracy of transactions
- settling accounts either by cash or credit card charge

▶ An important activity of the Accounting Department is the creation and maintenance of appropriate internal control systems in order to prevent fraud and embezzlement. For the department to be able to carry out this essential activity, it requires policies and procedures designed to ensure the safety of the operation's assets; these should cover front of house, back of house, and other administrative tasks.

▶ Another major function of the Accounting Department is the preparation of forecasts and budgets. The income statement is the main focus of forecasting for hospitality managers, as it presents a historical record of day-to-day activities. Forecasting is primarily based on volumes as expressed in rooms sold or guests served. It is important for operations managers to possess adequate forecasting skills, enabling them to adjust operating expenses for expected levels of business.

▶ The operating budget is a business plan converted into monetary as well as non-monetary terms. Forecasting and budgeting systems are expected to reflect realistic expectations, but differences do arise between actual and projected performances.

▶ A budget serves five main purposes – communication, coordination, planning, control, and evaluation. As the budgeting process is essentially about planning for the future, planning can be split into long-range (strategic), operational, and project planning.

▶ The various types of budgets are operations, capital, department, cash, and master budgets.

8

Questions and assignments for reflection

1   Compare and contrast the USALI from the IFRS. Explain which of the two, in your opinion, is more likely to become the generally accepted norm in time?

2   If you were the general manager of an independent mid-sized hotel, why would you opt to outsource the accounting activities of the hotel?

3   What are the main differences between an income statement and a statement of comprehensive income?

4   Why are management reports very relevant for hospitality decision making?

5   Compare and contrast the various types of planning. Which would be more important for a small, local B&B? Explain your choice.

8

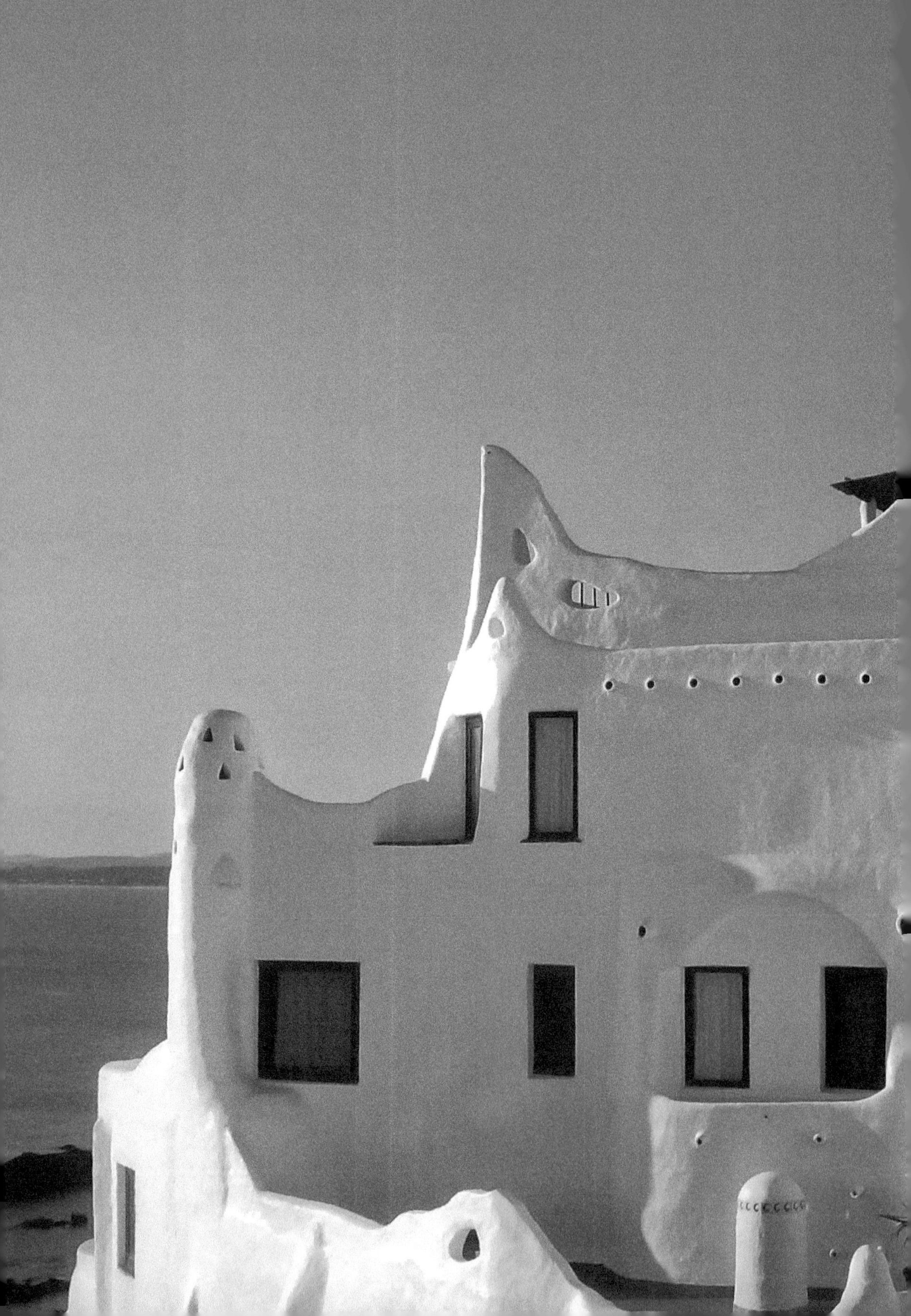

9
Facility Engineering and Maintenance

M. N. Chibili

9.1 Introduction

At the core of the activities of the Facility Engineering and Maintenance Department is ensuring that the operation's grounds, buildings and equipment are properly protected and maintained, to avoid dissatisfied guests consequently having negative effects on sales and profitability. Headed by a Chief Engineer, the roles and responsibilities of maintenance engineers have evolved over time. These roles and responsibilities are reviewed in this chapter, along with the main types of maintenance activities. Lastly, hotel energy and water usage and management is illustrated in an in-depth study.

9.2 Roles and responsibilities

The Facility Engineering and Maintenance Department is essentially responsible for the management of services and processes that support the core business of the organisation which, in the case of hotels, is the provision of goods and services guests require. The engineers ensure that a hotel has the most suitable working environment for its employees; they support the delivery of products and services to guests and other customers. While engineer duties may vary depending on the nature and size of the operation, engineers generally focus on using best business practices to improve efficiency by reducing operating costs while increasing productivity.

Core business

9.2.1 Roles

The roles of the Facility Engineering and Maintenance Department are concisely illustrated by this quote from an interview with a maintenance worker at the Mövenpick Hotel Amsterdam City Centre.

'I am Marcel, working with Maintenance. We keep all the sections of the building in good shape. From the bathrooms to the lighting sys-

9

© Noordhoff Uitgevers bv

Uruguay, Punta del Este: Casapueblo Hotel

> tems, through to all the technical areas. We carry out special inspec-
> tions, and we have to do our rounds. We commence every day at
> about 08:00 am, and start with checking the technical areas. After
> that we walk through the hallways carrying out all the required inspec-
> tions and repairs.'

The essence of the department's activities is to ensure that an operation's grounds, buildings and equipment are properly protected and maintained. These assets have a very strong influence on how guests or potential guests view and assess the quality or attractiveness of an operation. A poorly maintained operation will inevitably lead to dissatisfied guests who, by extension, have seriously negative effects on sales and profitability.

Chief goals

Hayes and Ninemeier (2005, p. 384) summarise the chief goals of the Facility Engineering and Maintenance Department as follows:
- Ensuring guest satisfaction
- Protecting and enhancing the financial value of buildings and grounds
- Supporting efforts of all other hotel departments through timely attention to their Engineering and Maintenance needs
- Managing maintenance and repair costs
- Managing energy usage
- Increasing the pride and morale of hotel's staff
- Ensuring the safety of those working and visiting the hotel

Chief Engineer

The Facility Engineering and Maintenance Department is headed by the Chief Engineer (or Director of Engineering and Security), whose place in the management team has already been indicated in Chapter 3. The Chief Engineer is mainly responsible for maintaining a hotel's physical state; they take care of the repairs and engineering works required to ensure that all equipment, machines, furniture, fixtures and fittings are in good mechanical and technical conditions, and are fully operational. In some cases, the Chief Engineer may also be responsible for implementing the procedures aimed at protecting the safety and security of hotel employees and guests as well as hotel assets. The Chief Engineer is expected to have a thorough understanding of the laws and regulations of the area, especially those related to environmental protection, construction and regulations on safety. This basic responsibility can be supplemented with detailed knowledge in the following areas, indicated by Brymer and Johanson (2011, p. 152):
- Systems and building design
- Systems and building operations
- Maintenance of guestroom fixtures and furnishings
- Equipment maintenance and repair
- Equipment selection and installation
- Contract management
- Utilities management
- Waste management
- Budget and cost control
- Security and safety
- Contractual and regulatory compliance
- Management and inventory of (spare) parts
- Renovations, additions and restorations
- Staff training
- Emergency planning and response

In the past, Chief Engineers were usually those who had worked their way up through the ranks from one of the crafts or from a position as engineering employee specialising in one of the building systems. They may have been in hotels for the length of their professional careers or may have come to a hotel company from engineering positions in any of various other organisations. Mounts and Meinzer (2011) indicated that, unlike their earlier counterparts, 25% of contemporary Chief Engineers had a university degree. Three-quarters of those degrees were in some area of engineering, suggesting that the sophistication of modern hotel building operations may be of a level of property management requiring a formal education more extensive than that of the past. The study by Mounts and Meinzer (2011) also ranked various components of the Chief Engineer's job, the top 10 of which are listed in Figure 9.1. As stated, the engineers ranked their knowledge of the maintenance of equipment as the most important aspect, closely followed by energy conservation and energy management.

FIGURE 9.1 Components of the Chief Engineer's job ranked by importance

Rank	Item
1	Knowledge of maintenance of equipment
2	Energy conservation
3	Energy management
4	Responsibility for communication with employees
5	Relations with top management
6	Responsibility for leadership
7	Responsibility for safety
8	Responsibilities of an effective organisational ability
9	Energy costs
10	Knowledge of the types of equipment

Mounts and Meinzer (2011, p. 199) concluded:

'Summing up, the engineering department, its management, and, to a certain extent, its staff and technical experts represent an organisational function of the modern hotel that is in the process of evolutionary change. This change is driven by a number of factors. The future of successful hotel organisations hinges, to a great extent, on the ability of hotel management to recognise the importance of the contributions of the engineering department to providing guest services and maintaining a high return on investment for property owners.'

Evolutionary change

9.2.2   Spending time with a Chief Engineer

The following is adapted from a transcript of an interview between M. Chibili (MC) and Chief Engineer R. Vis (RV) of the Mövenpick Hotel Amsterdam City Centre, recorded on October 21st 2011. It clearly illustrates the range of functions and responsibilities of a hotel's property operations and maintenance department.

- MC: As you are aware, I am continuing my rounds of all the departments of this hotel. Can you briefly tell me about your role in your department?
- RV: I am the chief engineer, responsible for engineering and security. My job is to plan and make appointments and contracts with outside contractors. Engineering contracts, security contracts, contracts with the fire brigade, contracts with the city of Amsterdam like building permits, etc. In order to conform to the rules, certifications like fire certifications are also needed, of course. The Green Globe certification is also my responsibility.
- MC: How is the Green Globe certification application proceeding?
- RV: It is going well. We hope to be certified soon. Last Wednesday saw the final audit and we hope to receive confirmation in 10 days. But it has been an almost one year process. We were lucky that we already had the Green Key certification, because that really helps. We are running a pilot for the entire Mövenpick chain, so we have had a lot of support from the chiefs of operations and other consultants from the start.
- MC: There is a BBC Programme called Rogue Traders, which is about technicians or building companies who dupe their clients. They pretend to work longer than is actually required, and then charge large sums of money for work that has not been done, or done very poorly. Have you had experience in similar situations with external companies you have dealt with and, if so, how do you manage these situations?
- RV: For one thing, I want to know when external parties are coming beforehand. I have a whole schedule for the year with all external companies and I know exactly who is coming in when. If they are planning a visit, I first want to know the exact date; once they come in, they register at the front desk, and before they start their work I discuss what they have to do. Once they are finished, I have them summarise and explain their activities, and I double-check.
- MC: Do you usually check their invoices?
- RV: Of course. This is part of my job because I am responsible for my own engineering budget, so I have to fight for my budget as well. There are the monthly costs, called the 'opex' – operational expenditures, as well as the 'capex' – capital expenditures. These are the shared responsibility of the financial controller, the general manager and, of course, myself. So we plan for refurbishments, investments, etc. together. This is a relatively new hotel at five years old, but what you notice is that, as the hotel gets older, you have to start investing in it for the coming years. So in the most recent few years, especially in a hotel's early stages, we have had to make some minor changes, because we may not have been thrilled with everything as it was for the pre-opening. I think we were not spending so much on 'capex' over the past two years, but in the coming years we will start having to spend more. Looking at the hotel as it gets older, you need to change the wallpaper, the carpets and other things like that.
- MC: Do you have a pre-organised schedule of what has to be done and when?
- RV: We have an overview for 15 years, but while it is set up for 15 years it is not so specific as to state that 'next year we are going to change the

carpets in the conference area. We have a general idea without going too much into specifics.

- MC: Do you have a depreciation schedule for every single item on the premises?
- RV: The answer to that is simple: 'Yes, we do.' In addition, we use a computer programme for our daily activities. When Housekeeping, F&B, or the Front Office fill in a request, such as for repair work, we immediately receive a notification. If there is a complaint from a guest that the TV does not work, and that same guest complains that no-one showed up to fix it later in the day, we can have a look at the timing. I can see exactly at what time the engineer or person on duty entered the room. That is an important tool.
- MC: How would you describe the relationship with the city council?
- RV: I would describe it as okay. Dealing with these councils is always difficult, but it is okay.
- MC: The building had already been built before you started your work here, so why do you need to be involved with the city council?
- RV: If there are changes to be made, I need building permits. Our fire-safety system, for example; some possible changes need the city's approval.
- MC: How many big changes did you have over the past five years?
- RV: In truth, only small ones; but we will now be verified for our certification every half year. If there are small changes, the company can approve those. But if they touch on something major, you certainly have to go to the city council and ask permission.
- MC: And what if it is something you really need, but the city council refuses to give you a permit?
- RV: That does not tend to happen, ever.
- MC: How about on an operational level?
- RV: We have a good relationship with the Amsterdam fire brigade, and that is really important. If the Fire Department is in agreement, then so is the city council.
- MC: Do you pay any special charges to the Fire Department?
- RV: No, we do not need to grease the wheels.
- MC: If there is an alarm triggered at your location and the fire department is summoned, you still do not have to push any money their way?
- RV: Possibly, if they had to be called out every week – but in this hotel, that is not the case. We have 24-hour security and we also have 24-hour reception available. An office building is totally different, because after 5 pm it is closed and vacated – meaning the fire brigade is required in case of alarms. They know that we have people on site; those people first check to see what kind of alarm it is, and immediately contact the fire brigade. It is only if they can confirm an emergency that we request the fire brigade's attention – and never at an additional fee.
- MC: So any payable fees are already included in city taxes?
- RV: That is correct.
- MC: What are your thoughts on your job? Is it an easy one?
- RV: I love my job, so that makes it easy. I enjoy my work; I stay in touch with employees, I stay in touch with outside contractors, and I stay in touch with guests. It is not only back-of-house, but front-of-house as well. I have 22 years' experience, so that helps. It was more difficult when I started, but there are still the occasional urgent and less easy to handle affairs.

9

- MC: Could you tell me a little bit more about your working experience?
- RV: I have been working for Mövenpick for three years now; before that, I worked for the InterContinental Amstel Hotel in Amsterdam for two years, and I worked for the Hilton organisation for 13 years, during which time I was part of a major refurbishment between 1998 and 2003; that was a really great job. It was tough but rewarding. Before that, I worked for Golden Tulip Hotels, and I opened a hotel near Utrecht almost 21 years ago. That is when I started in the hotel industry.
- MC: What were your original background studies?
- RV: Electrical engineering. I managed the electrical installations in the first hotel; I was working for an electricity company at the time. The hotel, it turned out, was looking for a chief engineer.
- MC: So, you worked for an electricity company to carry out the electrical installations at the hotel, and when the job in the hotel was finished they managed to pull you out of the electricity company?
- RV: Something like that.
- MC: What was your original employer's response?
- RV: They were fine with it, because the company was situated quite a long drive from where I lived. In fact, the hotel was located in the same city I lived in at the time.
- MC: Did you never feel you might come to regret your decision?
- RV: Not at all.
- MC: What do you expect of the engineers on your team?
- RV: Flexibility and friendliness, especially towards the guests; those are important characteristics of an engineer. In the past, engineers were always behind the screens, always back-of-house, working in technical rooms, etc. If I look back 15 or 20 years ago, a hotel like this had 25 engineers – because back then, all maintenance was in-house, nothing was outsourced. Over the years, that began to change: maintenance and other units are now outsourced, for example, and engineers are only on site for service maintenance. If the kitchen reports damages, or if a guest indicates the hotel room television is not working, or even if a light bulb needs to be changed, then that is what you'll see engineers actually working on. But in the past, you only saw them working in boiler rooms, for example. Times have definitely changed. We are more service-related to our guests. The engineers of the past did not seem to enjoy talking to guests at all, and that could not be further from the truth, now.
- MC: Can you explain what you mean by flexible?
- RV: If the engineers are at work, hanging up a painting, for example, and a guest reports that the TV does not work, the engineers should be able to immediately switch and carry out the necessary repairs to ensure that the guest remains satisfied. It can be really stressful for the engineers, especially in the evenings. They are all alone over the weekends, and have to be able to shift gears at a moment's notice. They also have to be flexible in terms of scheduling. We draft schedules for the coming four weeks, but if somebody calls in sick, then I need to be able to call on another engineer to replace that person. This hotel employs all-round engineers. They can do everything. We have one engineer who is an electrician by trade; painting, for example, is not his strong suit. But if push comes to shove, he still has to do it. It is our job to assist and train him.
- MC: So engineers are offered trainings?
- RV: Yes, they are; for us, the most important thing is that our engineers become even better-rounded.

- MC: Is there anything else about your job you would like to share?
- RV: One of the most important aspects of running a hotel is preventative maintenance, not only in front-of-house but also in back-of-house. Back-of-house is also important for our employees, because it lets them be proud of the area they work in. Preventative maintenance is incredibly important; without it, in about two or three years you will start to see the level of maintenance going down, costing you more and more money because the guests do not return.
- MC: What do you mean by preventative maintenance? Could you give some examples?
- RV: Maintenance is run using checklists. From a light bulb to a shower to a mini bar, we have to go in and check the rooms. Doing one floor every week, just to make sure everything is in working order: that is preventative maintenance, which is really concerned with inspections ensuring that everything is in order.
- MC: And are these checks part of your work here?
- RV: They are. But we are always running behind, because there are always guests checking in, even in rooms where a light happens to be broken, or where the shower is leaking.
- MC: You have your own team of four engineers, but do you use many outsourced specialists? Are there periods during which you rely more heavily on outsourced specialists, like for example during winters, when the hotel experiences lower occupancy rates. Do you make more use of outsourcing during such periods?
- RV: The majority of outsourcing tends to be done in the months of April and September/October. We outsource in spring and just before the summer and winter periods; it is scheduled that way. One or two weeks in advance I do have a peek at the expected occupancy levels, and if it should happen that we are at maximum capacity during the scheduled outsourcing period, then we move it forwards a little.
- MC: Just as an aside, this is a gorgeous property. And I cannot help but notice that many members of the staff here are graduates from my school.
- RV: Yes, that is true. Many of our department managers are from there. I even visited the school's hotel a few months ago for a business meeting.
- MC: And what did it seem like, to you?
- RV: I was really impressed. You can tell they are really young, still, but I was truly impressed. I was also impressed with how Executive Chef Albert Kooy runs the kitchen, and the food certainly was excellent. The service was great as well. The students knew that we were a hotel management team, so any nervous jitters were forgiven; but overall it was great to see. I loved it.
- MC: Back to your work here. Do you work in close collaboration with the finance department?
- RV: I certainly do. I am also responsible for power management.
- MC: This hotel is becoming more and more *green*; have you noticed the effects on your expenses?
- RV: Yes, we have. We have performed many adjustments over the past years, we installed a lot of LED lighting. I think we are already saving 8% to 10% off our previous annual bills. Looking at it in terms of direct savings, the results are still negligible – but we do see a difference in terms of usage volumes. Costs are more difficult to manage. They are controlled by the suppliers. We buy energy in advance. We bought it for

two years, with an option of a third year at a fair price, but we have no influence on taxes and energy transportation costs. Those are managed on a governmental level. We can, however, make the decision when it comes to who we buy energy from; and we certainly have an influence on its usage. Using energy saving systems is very important, of course. Instead of 9 litre flushes, toilets now use only 6 litres, for example. In terms of gas usage, there is a big difference between setting room temperature at 21 degrees or at 23 degrees.

- MC: What is the standard temperature level in this property?
- RV: A comfortable 21 degrees. We use a computer programme for this aspect of climate control. I enter in the times that the rooms are going to be occupied and the programme heats them automatically.
- MC: Who does the programming?
- RV: I do it, every morning. I look up which rooms will be occupied in the banquet and other occupancy sheets, and then I set the timers.
- MC: Do you have to do that yourself?
- RV: Yes, the other engineers are not authorised to tinker with all aspects of the engineering system. We need to be careful with that. You asked me earlier if it is a difficult job. It is not so difficult for me, with 22 years of experience – but even I sometimes stop and check if everything is operating within established parameters, in terms of fire and safety as well. If we are fully booked and the conference rooms are fully occupied, that can mean a maximum of 2,400 permitted guests in-house. On days like that, I do sometimes realise the enormity of my responsibilities and hope that I am up to the task.
- MC: Do you still manage a decent night's sleep? Or do you stay up thinking about the property?
- RV: I can confess to some restless nights, especially if there are several projects going on simultaneously; but I generally sleep well. I have a good, responsible team of engineers behind me, so that really helps. And there is a good security team available 24 hours a day. They know what they are doing and that really helps as well. You need a good team of people you can trust.
- MC: Would you say trust is key, then?
- RV: Yes, trust is essential, as is giving people their responsibilities. They may make mistakes, but we are all human.
- MC: I did two nights of night auditing during my first week here. There were only five members of staff managing the whole property at night. Isn't that too much of a responsibility? Two security and maintenance staff members, one night auditor, one person doing room service, and one cleaner – not including myself.
- RV: Yes, but you have to remember that is not unique to this hotel. All hotels have the same problem, but we have a very good system in case of fire and other emergencies.
- MC: During the past five years, how often have you had to use the system?
- RV: I have never had to use it. I feel it is a very safe building, certainly. But it is more than the building, it is also the security equipment.
- MC: I have seen the security equipment. It is really overwhelming.
- RV: If you show this to people, they tend to realise why hotels charge the rates they do. This hotel's selling point, of course, is its views. Sometimes, when I am working on the 24th floor, I see people looking out the windows at the cruise ships below – they are often tourists, taking pic-

tures. Then I tell them to come with me and I take them to the 21st floor and show them the platform area located there, and they are utterly overwhelmed. I love doing that, people really appreciate it.

Mövenpick Hotel Amsterdam City Centre, outside terrace

9.2.3   Specific financial responsibilities

The previous section outlined the roles and responsibilities of the Facility Engineering and Maintenance Department, and showed how vital it is to the hotel's activities. Hotels are comparable to cruise ships or hospitals; the majority operates twenty-four hours a day and seven days a week. When the guests are asleep, the building's systems continue to operate; everything has to work so that employees can do their jobs and guests are safe and comfortable. The Chief Engineer is faced with the major challenge of ensuring that the physical state of the property is constantly upgraded, while at the same time managing the use of limited financial resources. The Chief Engineer should also be knowledgeable in the relationships between design, maintenance, repairs and costs. This implies that the Chief Engineer must work in close collaboration with the Financial Controller as well as the General Manager. For this to be practicable, they have to establish a 'Property and Operations Maintenance Budget', also simply called the Engineering Budget.

Safe and comfortable

Engineering Budget

The engineering budget is usually split into two categories: heating, lighting, and power; and repairs and maintenance. Due to location and size differences for a full service hotel, the heating, lighting, and power costs might range from about 4% to 7% of the annual revenues of the property on an annual basis. Repairs and maintenance costs, on the other hand, might range from about 5% to 8% of the property's annual revenues. The major influences on heating, lighting, and power costs are expected room occupancy, weather conditions, purchasing price of the utility components, and banquet and restaurant occupancy and usage levels. A thorough knowledge of these variables and their evolution over time lets the Chief Engineer use the available forecasting resources or computer programmes to determine budget items and levels. The Chief Engineer should be able to keep track of utility costs as well as find ways to ensure that these expenditures are kept at a minimum. Keeping records of the utilities (electricity, natural gas, steam, water and sewage etc.), heating degree days, cooling degree days, guests in-house, and covers, for example, provide background information to evaluate against billing unit consumption. Meter readings should be collected on a daily basis to quickly detect any irregularities such as may result from major leaks or equipment malfunction. The repairs and maintenance portion of the engineering budget should cover the balance of the engineering expenses, such as labour expenses, buildings and mechanical equipment repairs, kitchen repairs, and work uniforms, to name but a few.

As with all budgets, the engineering budget is only a plan, based on concrete knowledge of the evolution of historical data of the property combined with weather conditions. Its end result reflects how a property should be managed in order to achieve the desired levels of maintenance. The Chief Engineer may also be called upon to evaluate capital projects that tend to lead to major uses of funds. There may be a need to acquire new equipment or replace old or broken down equipment. This entails a proper analysis of initial acquisition and installation costs, operating and fixed costs related to equipment, and possible tax implications such as tax credits and relevant depreciation rules.

9.3 Types of maintenance

The plant, property and equipment of most hotels are very complex, with many hotels delivering different types of services. The quality of service delivery is therefore dependent on the proper functioning of the plant, property and equipment. The different types of maintenance generally carried out in the hotel industry are indicated in the subsections that follow.

9.3.1 Scheduled maintenance

Scheduled maintenance refers to activities initiated by the Facility Engineering and Maintenance Department based on a formal work order that identifies a known problem or need. Scheduled maintenance attempts to solve the identified problem in an orderly and timely manner consistent with overall needs and demands. To complete scheduled maintenance activities, the department normally requires extended durations, as well as significant planning for the required manpower, tools and materials, coupled with good co-ordination with other departments or any outside contractors. The replacement or maintenance on a major piece of equipment could lead to the shutdown of one or more departments or blocks of guest rooms, for example. Projects such as building walls or refurbishing certain areas can be classified as scheduled maintenance.

Extended durations

9.3.2 Routine maintenance

Routine maintenance is a procedure to ensure that the hotel's property and equipment are kept in good condition, and provide a long operating life. For the Chief Engineer to help in protecting and enhancing the financial value of the building and grounds, routine maintenance is required. Routine maintenance may also help in discovering potential problems and preventing eventual equipment failures. Quality control procedures, ensuring correct operation and calibration, are also a part of routine maintenance. Carrying out routine maintenance works on hotel equipment leads to a good knowledge

Quality control procedures

of the equipment; in case of a problem, this knowledge can help rapidly locate the cause. Where there is a more serious problem, accurate reporting and requesting specialist assistance allows a faster and more cost-effective response in solving the problem. Routine maintenance activities also relate to the general upkeep of the property, both interior and exterior. Interior maintenance may include taking care of carpets, indoor plants, or burned-out light bulbs. Exterior maintenance can refer to snow removal, grass-cutting, hedge trimming, window cleaning, and painting in order to enhance property image and curb appeal. Routine maintenance is performed on a regular basis (daily, weekly, or monthly), requires minimal skills, and does not tend to require formal work orders or specific inventory of the time or materials used in maintenance activity. Appendix D shows examples of 5-day routine inspection checklists of the HP Hotels. These checklists are tailored to specific properties depending on the available facilities.

Regular basis

9.3.3 Preventative maintenance

In the interview with the Chief Engineer, the concept of preventative maintenance was briefly introduced. This type of maintenance comes down to taking care of and servicing the facilities and equipment of the hotel for the purpose of maintaining satisfactory operating conditions. This is done through the systematic inspection, detection, and correction of developing failures either before they occur or before they become major failings. Preventative maintenance consists of tests, measurements, adjustments, and parts replacement, carried out specifically to prevent major faults from occurring. Preventative maintenance is designed to preserve and restore equipment reliability by replacing worn components before they actually fail. Preventative maintenance activities can include partial or complete overhauls at specified periods, oil changes, or lubrication. Preventative maintenance activities are generally based on the guidelines received from the manufacturers of the equipment or those provided by the Chief Engineer. Preventative maintenance also allows engineers to record equipment deterioration, so they know when to replace or repair worn-out parts to avoid general system failures. If, during the course of preventative maintenance inspections, it is determined that major works may be required, work orders are generated to schedule specific maintenance. Hotels develop preventative maintenance annual plans such as those is shown in Figure 9.2.

Systematic

Guidelines

FIGURE 9.2 Sample annual preventative maintenance planner

Sample Annual Preventative Maintenance Planner

Schedule the activity under the month it should occur

Activity	Jan	Feb	Mar	Apr	May	Jun	Jul	Aug	Sep	Oct	Nov	Dec
Boiler												
Breakfast Equipment												
Building Cleaning												
Carpet Cleaning												
Circulating Pumps												
Elevator Inspections												
Exteriour Signage												
Fire Alarm Tests												
Fire Extinguishers												
Fire Pumps												
Generator Inspections												
HVAC Units												
Ice Machines												
Landscape Plantings												
Laundry Equipment												
Office Equipment												
Paint Railings												
Parking Lot Stripes												
Power Wash Building												
PBX System												
Rooftop												
Sidewalk Cleaning												
Smoke Detector Tests												
TV and Cable System												
Water Softener Equipment												
Window Washing												

9.3.4 Emergency and breakdown maintenance

Emergency maintenance involves the repair or replacement of equipment and components after they have failed and are liable to cause situations requiring immediate attention in or around the hotel's facilities. Unforeseen occurrences, such as flooding or tornadoes, may cause significant damage to the buildings and equipment. These situations can create unmanageable or unsafe conditions that could expose guests and staff to a significant possibility of harm. Examples of situations requiring emergency maintenance actions can be fire, trees falling on sections of the building or roof, flooding, sewage back up, power failures, and unexplained gas smells. In most cases, if the emergency is potentially life-threatening, emergency services should be summoned immediately. Most hotels have well-laid out contingency plans, such as back-up generators in case of a power failure, in case of emergencies (covered in Chapter 10).

Unforeseen occurrences

The breakdown maintenance approach, however, is typically employed when failures are unlikely to result in workplace injuries or excessive downtime. A policy of breakdown maintenance is sometimes instituted if a facility or business has decided to (temporarily) close or cease operations, especially if there are no plans to continue using the equipment afterwards. This is often a calculated risk, since the decision assumes that damaged or broken equipment will continue running long enough for the facility to be closed down. If there are plans to scrap the equipment at the end of the period, costly preventative maintenance can be seen as unnecessary. Unlike the preventative approach, breakdown maintenance is a reactive policy. This ap-

Downtime

Reactive policy

proach avoids the costs associated with inspections and pre-emptive repairs by simply allowing components to fail and then addressing the issue
after the fact. The term 'run-to-failure' is also used to describe this approach to maintenance, since that is what equipment is allowed to do.
Equipment typically receive lubrication and other minor attention under this
kind of maintenance policy. There are costs associated with a breakdown
maintenance policy. Since any component can fail at any time under this approach, maintenance staff must be ready to do many different types of repairs. This may involve maintaining a stock of replacement parts for every
piece of equipment in the facility, or paying for rush shipping on new components as the old ones fail. There are typically also costs associated with
downtime, so this approach to maintenance is not well-suited to any business operation that would suffer large monetary losses from the sudden
failure of any given piece of equipment (www.wisegeek.com).

For hospitality operations, breakdown maintenance can have both positive
and negative effects. The positive aspect is possible savings made by not
carrying out relatively expensive preventative maintenance activities. The
negative aspect is potential impact on guest comfort and safety, as well as
possible disruptions to a smooth flow of operations in the affected departments. Breakdowns can be very expensive if they occur after hours or require outside contractors to solve the problem.

*Positive and
negative effects*

9.3.5 Contract maintenance
Contract maintenance is one-off or periodically arranged maintenance performed by a third party under a contract. Contract maintenance is occasionally necessary if the expertise required for the repair of specific equipment
is beyond the capabilities of the hotel's maintenance staff. In some instances, such as servicing elevators, contract maintenance may be obligatory.
The reasoning behind this is to ensure that the work is performed by qualified technicians, who may also be required to carry licenses and or possess
specialist knowledge. Local regulations and insurance companies usually
demand such contracts, which also serves the purpose of making sure work
gets done regardless of budget limitations. Maintenance contracts or contracting out are almost always necessary to complement an undersized engineering department (www.maintenanceresources.com).

Expertise

Contracts are agreements in legal form, and fairness and honesty should be
a prominent part of any contract. Any valid contract contains clauses related
to a variety of topics, including: terms of agreement; definition of services,
charges and payment; ownership title and risk; indemnity and liability; warranties; confidentiality; termination; force majeure; business continuity; law
and jurisdiction; waiver; and invalidation. A contractor should be honest,
with no likelihood of employing inferior workmanship or using replacements
with cheaper parts. Text 9.1 provides some tips to help ensure a property's
contract maintenance experience is an effective one. Depending on the size
and qualifications of the property's maintenance engineers, contract maintenance services can include such activities as:

Legal

- Maintaining the elevators.
- Maintaining HVAC equipment.
- Filling or refilling fire extinguishers.
- Testing and adjusting fire alarm systems.
- Maintaining laundry machines.
- Maintaining kitchen equipment.

- Maintaining spa, gym and sauna equipment.
- Disposing of grease and other refuse.

Some advantages of contract maintenance are:
- Flexibility in taking care of emergencies.
- No union negotiations required.
- No employee recruitment or training required.
- Possible reductions in costs of supplies and equipment.
- Possible reductions in total labour-related expenses.
- Reductions in administrative time required for maintenance activities.
- The use of the latest techniques and methods for maintenance activities.

Contract maintenance also has some drawbacks:
- An increase in total maintenance expenses if there is no proper management.
- A possibility of missing out on the best terms due to opaque bidding.
- Perceived but false labour cost savings, unless employment levels are actually reduced.
- Loss of contact with the needs of facility and staff.
- Loss of control over employees in contract maintenance areas, resulting in loss of attention to guests, security matters, and identity with the property.

TEXT 9.1

Engineering 101: Maintaining Hotel Maintenance Contracts

By Richard Manzolina, February 29th 2012

One of the most important and high impact responsibilities of a hotel's engineering team is the administration of maintenance contracts and service agreements. Successful management of this critical function can streamline engineering operations, reduce operating expenses, and minimize downtime. However, when executed poorly, maintenance contracts can act as the proverbial tail wagging the dog, shortening equipment life cycles, raising expenses and increasing the risk of loss and exposure to liability. As such, choosing the right service professionals, creating appropriate contract documents, and pragmatically executing their scope of work, are some of the most vital responsibilities of the engineering team.

The potential benefits of maintenance contracts are numerous, and should be carefully considered when deciding whether to enlist the assistance of outside service professionals. Outsiders often bring specific and applicable expertise and are able to reduce staffing needs, and there are many other advantages including risk mitigation, access to specialized labour and parts inventories, and preferred labour rates. Yet despite these benefits, many hoteliers are often hampered by service agreements that fail to meet the needs of their properties. Contracts with obsolete provisions and terms, and automatic price escalations, can hinder the hotel engineer's ability to meet the quality and financial goals of the property. Below are seven tips to help ensure that the property's contract maintenance experience is an effective one.

1 Avoid, or at least seriously scrutinize, vendor-supplied contract documents
Service agreements written and provided by contractors are often extremely vendor-centric, and tend to include provisions that put an inordinate amount of responsibility or risk on the customer. These boiler plate contracts are designed to benefit the contractor, often at the expense of an equitable agreement. Instead, opt for standardized agreements offered by the hotel company's

© Noordhoff Uitgevers bv

legal department, or consider other standardized agreements that create a level playing field for both parties. A quick internet search for 'standardized maintenance contracts' can provide a great starting point, and can offer plug-n-play style contract creation. While these are no substitute for the advice of competent legal counsel, use of such documents can help to prevent committing a property to unfair and often detrimental contract terms.

2 Consider agreements for the long term

Contract terms vary greatly, from months to several years, and there are many good reasons for this variance. Longer term agreements can generate financial security for both parties, in the form of predictable expenses for the customer and predicable revenue streams for the contractor. A longer contract term can have value to both parties and may positively influence contract terms or reduce costs. In addition, a longer term may make it more palatable for a vendor to invest in equipment or training that positively affects the hotel, by knowing that the cost of such an investment can be amortized by them over a longer period of time.

3 Beware of automatic renewal; and 'boilerplate' renewal terms

Avoid automatic renewal clauses that keep parties bound to an agreement simply by doing nothing, or agreements that are designed to automatically renew unless prior notification to cancel is provided many months before a contract expires. At a minimum, include a provision that requires written notification of intent to exercise a renewal option. By doing so, it affords both parties a chance to review an agreement for its appropriateness and will prevent a contract's inadvertent renewal.

4 Don't forget the 'meat and potatoes'

Legalese and elaborate clauses aside, the purpose of a service agreement is to bind a vendor to provide specific, timely and appropriate maintenance services. Yet oftentimes even contracts that have undergone diligent legal review falter when it comes to their non-legal content. Such contracts typi-

cally include Scopes of Work that poorly define the contractor's responsibilities. Moreover, the absence of well-defined scopes of work clauses creates an opportunity for unintended contract interpretation, and can result in an inordinate amount of 'billable services' that were expected to be included in the agreement. To prevent this, be sure to have the Chief Engineer or other qualified personnel review a contract's scope of work to ensure its completeness and applicability.

Also, where necessary and/or appropriate, use a third party consultant to provide this review, especially for high risk or highly technical disciplines such as vertical transportation, water treatment, or life safety systems. Lastly, utilize manufacturers' recommended maintenance standards when defining a scope of work. By doing so, not only will there be an appropriate scope definition to aid in maximizing the reliability and longevity of hotel equipment, but it will also provide a system for ensuring manufacturers' requirements are met to maintain their specific warranties.

5 An educated consumer is often the best customer

Frequently, service professionals are relied upon exclusively to maintain a given system, a piece of equipment, or building component. While this is often appropriate, or even mandated, there are many instances where the limited use of building personnel to supplant contract maintenance can be extremely beneficial, even cost effective, in the ongoing execution of a service agreement.

One example is the hotel building automation system, often referred to as an energy management system. Frequently, the in-house staff lacks the training and skills to troubleshoot even the most basic building automation problems. Instead, a log of deficiencies is commonly kept to be shown to and addressed by a service technician, necessitating that the property will endure the problem until their next routine maintenance visit. This means that the technician's contractual maintenance time is spent fixing ru-

dimentary problems which are better addressed by in-house personnel, while long term system improvements that require the technician's care are deferred.

To combat this problem, include contract provisions that require contractors to provide training to in house personnel, training that not only makes the service provider's visits more efficient and effective, but also provides an invaluable investment in the development of the hotel staff.

6 Make it easy to do business together... and reap the rewards

After the outside service provider's sales person and the hotel GM have signed a contract, the hotel engineer and service manager are charged with its execution. But no matter how much time and effort go into the creation of a contract, its success is contingent in large part upon the relationship with the service providers. With this is mind, focus on creating an environment conducive to strong relationships with outside contractors, upon whom you regularly rely, and make it easy for them to service the hotel account. The creation of such good rapport will pay back many times over when the hotel has a guest stuck in an elevator, or the HVAC chiller fails on a hot summer night. Seemingly small considerations, such as

granting a contractor access to an employee cafeteria, or allowing them to park at the hotel loading dock, can go a long way in building strong, hospitable relationships with key service providers who might not otherwise be so punctilious in their adherence to the strict requirements of your contract.

7 Certification and competence

In some instances, hotels believe that the contract terms are so technical or complex that they are not qualified to objectively judge the performance of the service provider, or the quality of their services. Beyond a simple reference check, hoteliers are often limited to the use of third party consultants to inspect performance and ensure their compliance with contract specifications or industry standards. However, such consultants can be costly, and only provide a snapshot in time relative to a contractor's performance over the life of an agreement. Moreover, such an inspection would be inappropriate when trying to gauge a contractor's service quality during a bid review. Thus, hoteliers should consider utilizing the benefits of third party certification entities, which specialize in maintaining quality standards within a given industry. Many industries have well respected associations or governing bodies that are diligent in self-governing their industry and the quality of their members' products or services. Check to see if a service provider's ability to safely and effectively execute industry standards is certified by an appropriate entity.

Examples of such entities include the National Fire Protection Association (NFPA) for fire and life safety standards, the American Society of Heating, Refrigeration and Air Conditioning Engineers (ASHRAE) for mechanical standards, and the National Swimming Pool Foundation (NSPF) for pool operating standards.

Diligent contract administration makes for positive outcomes. So while the meticulous review and execution of service agreements may not be as alluring as a full house or as marketable as the chef's winning gumbo recipe, engineering managers who implement these tried and true methods can expect as much financial benefit and job satisfaction as their more visible counterparts - and in the process of doing so, they will play an invaluable role in helping their hotels to flourish.

(Source: www.hospitalitynet.org)

As indicated in Text 9.1, as well as previously discussed in the interview in the current chapter, a Chief Engineer has certain responsibilities where maintenance contracts are concerned. A Chief Engineer should ensure and verify that contractors have suitable insurance coverage for their employees working at the property. A Chief Engineer should ensure that maintenance contracts are carefully structured, and that contracts should specifically define both the work that has to be carried out and the frequency and times it has to be performed. A Chief Engineer should also be capable of reviewing existing contracts in order to determine and prevent unnecessary work. Work performed by contractors should be inspected to ensure that it meets contract standards. Contractor employee movements within the property should be monitored and limited to areas where they are needed to perform their maintenance works. Lastly, it is important that contractors perform the work in a manner consistent with the safety standards of the property and other relevant rules and regulations.

Insurance coverage

Consistent with the safety standards

9.3.6 Replacement

Replacement problems involve items that deteriorate with their use or the passage of time, or items that fail after a certain amount of use or time. Items that deteriorate are likely to be large and costly (e.g., air-conditioning units, laundry machines, or window flower boxes, as shown in Figure 9.3). Non-deteriorating items tend to be small and relatively inexpensive (e.g., light bulbs or ink cartridges). The longer a deteriorating item is kept in operation, the more maintenance it requires to maintain its efficiency; until it is too cost ineffective to maintain. Furthermore, the longer such an item is kept in use, the lower its resale value and the more likely it becomes obsolete. If an item is replaced frequently, however, its investment costs increase. The problem is therefore to determine when to replace such items and how much maintenance (particularly preventative maintenance) is needed so that the sum of the operating, maintenance, and investment costs is minimised.

Deteriorating item

FIGURE 9.3 A hotel employee applying the finishing touches to new window flower boxes

Non-deteriorating items

In the case of non-deteriorating items, the problem involves determining whether to replace them as a group (group replacement) or to replace them individually as they fail (spot replacement). Though group replacement is considered wasteful, the labour cost of replacements is greater when done individually. As such, light bulbs in a large property may be replaced in groups to save labour costs. Replacement problems that involve minimising the costs of items, failures, and replacement labour can be solved by the application of numerical analysis, simulation, or probability theory. The replacement procedure becomes economically unrealistic if labour costs are higher in relation to the costs of items being replaced. Labour costs include the preparation, removal, installation and clean-up man-hours required to replace the items.

ICODE conditions

Equipment that gradually deteriorates is replaced following the ICODE conditions. This acronym stands for:

- Inadequacy; in which existing machines or equipment are incapable of meeting increased demand, and alternative equipment or machines are installed so that new demand requirements can be met.
- Combination of Causes; in which equipment starts requiring more preventative maintenance requirements, or starts to operate at reduced levels of efficiency.
- Obsolescence; in which new equipment is continuously being developed, and performs much more efficiently than older models.
- Decreased Efficiency; in which equipment sometimes operate at initial peak efficiency but declining over time or use, thus leading to lower efficiency and more energy needed.
- Excessive Maintenance; in which, as machines and other complex equipment rarely incur uniform wear, some parts likely deteriorate so much faster than others, that it is impossible to carry out partial maintenance.

Maintenance log

It is important for the Chief Engineer to keep a maintenance log in which all repair requirements, costs, and energy consumption data of all equipment is recorded. Such a maintenance log helps management determine the most appropriate time to carry out replacement activities, and as such establish a replacement cycle.

© Noordhoff Uitgevers bv

9.3.7   Total productive maintenance

Though of much more relevance to manufacturing settings, this type of maintenance is worthwhile to discuss. The following information, adapted from a MoreSteam text (www.moresteam.com), indicates that total productive maintenance was developed in Japan in the 1970s as a method of involving machine operators in the preventative maintenance of their machines. Autonomous maintenance activities tap the knowledge and skills of the people who work with the equipment on a daily basis, and give the operators a stake in the performance of the equipment. Involving the machine operators also makes regular maintenance engineers more productive by focussing them on more extensive preventative maintenance (PM) tasks. The overriding objective of total productive maintenance is the elimination of losses or waste. These include equipment downtime, defects, scrap, accidents, wasted energy, and labour inefficiency. Equipment reliability is a cornerstone of a lean production system and by bringing together people from all departments concerned with equipment into a comprehensive PM system, equipment effectiveness is raised to the highest possible level.

Involving machine operators

Most total productive maintenance programmes are built upon autonomous small group activities – the people closest to the action. This requires the support and co-operation of everyone from top management downwards. Some benefits of effective total productive maintenance include:
- Better financial performance and job security for the company
- Improved equipment reliability – uptime
- Improved quality
- Increased capacity
- Increased productivity
- Safer working environment

The goal of total productive maintenance is to drive all waste to zero: zero accidents, zero defects, zero breakdowns: The Concept of Zero. On the surface, this may seem unachievable, but if it is can be considered possible to run for an hour with no accidents, defects, or breakdowns, would it be possible to do the same for two hours, a shift, a day? The Concept of Zero aims to find the limit of waste minimisation. It is built upon error-proofing activities (Poka-Yoke) in the design of the process to make it impossible to cause or pass on defects in all aspects of manufacturing, customer service, procurement, etc.

The Concept of Zero

Poka-Yoke

It employs visual signals that make errors clearly stand out from the rest, or devices that stop an assembly line or process if a part or step is missed.

Overall Equipment Effectiveness

The primary metric to measure total productive maintenance performance is Overall Equipment Effectiveness or OEE. OEE is a combined measurement that shows the impact of equipment availability, equipment performance, and quality of output. The metric is calculated by multiplying Availability x Performance x Quality, as detailed below:

Availability:
100% minus:
- All known losses (stoppages) due to equipment failures, measured in time.
- Losses (in time) due to process set-up and adjustments.
- Losses (in time) due to start-ups after shifts, breaks, lunch, and weekends.

Performance:
100% minus:
- Losses (in time) due to minor stoppages.
- Losses (in time) due to speed (Actual vs. Engineered Speed).

Quality:
100% minus:
- Losses due to defects and rework

For example, if Availability is 94%, Performance is 96%, and Quality is 97%, then OEE is 0.94 x 0.96 x 0.97 = 87.5%

Core elements

There are five core elements to a total productive maintenance programme:
1. Operator self-maintenance – Set up a basic programme of cleaning, lubrication, general inspection, and minor preventative maintenance to be completed by the production operators.
2. Conduct planned maintenance – Develop and execute planned maintenance activities. Establish standards for each piece of equipment, prioritise equipment based on relative importance to safety, quality, productivity and cost. Establish a maintenance plan for each piece of equipment, based on time, condition, overhaul, or predictive maintenance.
3. Small group Kaizen activities (see also Chapter 16) – Identify team activities that focus on eliminating losses by focussing on all elements of OEE. The 5-Why analysis is often used to guide small group actions.
4. Education and training – Systematically train all employees to provide awareness and improve skill levels.
5. Maintenance prevention – Adopt early equipment management: a system whereby shop-floor personnel participates in new equipment concept and design phases to develop equipment that requires less maintenance, and is more easily maintained when maintenance is required. As with all processes, the most leverage to effect change exists in the design phase.

Primary maintenance activities

In addition, there are seven primary maintenance activities to support the five core elements of total productive maintenance:

1 Education and training – Set up a programme to systematically enhance maintenance technical skills. Many organisations have effectively adopted pay-for-skills programmes.
2 Support and guidance for operator self-maintenance – Provide instructions to operators on cleaning, lubrication, safety, and contamination countermeasures. Support Kaizen activities.
3 Downtime countermeasures – Track breakdowns, analyse root causes, apply countermeasures. The goal is to increase mean time between failures (MTBF) and reduce mean time to repair (MTTR).
4 Preventative maintenance programme – Identify and number all equipment, establish standards for cleaning, lubrication, and inspection. Develop a schedule of PM activities and track conformance to this schedule – this includes lubrication programme activities.
5 Spare parts management – Establish inventory standards and reorder points for parts needed on a planned basis. Apply the 5-S principles (Sort, Set in Order, Shine, Standardise and Sustain) to the spare parts' storage area.
6 Maintenance cost analysis – Understand where costs are incurred for parts, indirect supplies, oils & lubricants, manpower, and outside contractors. Organise systematic actions to reduce costs – the goal is to reduce long term total cost – not to be sacrificed for short term cost improvement.
7 Maintenance efficiency improvement – Track maintenance activities by category: planned (time-based, condition-based, predictive), and unplanned (breakdown). The goal is to increase percentages of maintenance hours on planned vs. unplanned, and lower overall totals for both.

9.4 Hotel energy and water management

This is the practice of managing procedures, operations and equipment that contribute to efficient energy and water use in hotel operations. This can include electricity, gas, water and other natural resources. Because hotels can have complicated operations and extensive facilities, they utilise many different types of energy resources.

9.4.1 Practices
Modern practices of managing energy usage include contributions by guests themselves, popularised by information cards requesting guests to save water by letting hotel housekeeping staff know if they would care to re-use towels and bed linens. This reduces the amount of water and/or cleaning substances used by the hotel laundry department, which also reduces expenses. Recently, consultants have developed entire organisations around advising hotels operating inefficiently or using more energy than necessary. Some consultants participate by providing the products needed to implement their advice for a share of the cost savings. Other practices include using infrared motion sensors and door contacts to control heating, ventilation and air conditioning (HVAC) systems in case guests leave them on and leave the room or leave balcony doors or windows open. Text 9.2 is an article illustrating energy management activities currently carried out in hotels.

Information cards

Energy management in hotels by Esther Hertzfeld, 26 Feb, 2015

In the U.S., hotels spend in excess of $7.5 billion on energy each year according to the U.S. Environmental Protection Agency. This translates to an average spend of nearly $2,200 per available room each year on energy by the more than 47,000 hotels and motels in America, which, in turn, accounts for around 6 percent of all domestic hotel operating costs.

Robert Attaway, director of engineering for the Westin Buckhead Atlanta, has been continuously working on making his hotel the most efficient it can be in the past 16 years he's been with the property. Over the last

energy, water and waste, and then use that data to develop a multi-faceted approach to reduce our impact.' Starwood Hotels enabled a third-party energy and water audit in 2011 and looks for a return on investment of less than a year on energy-efficient projects and for capital projects with the lowest initial costs for the biggest impact.

The Westin Buckhead has initiated several low-cost, high-payback measures to save energy, such as using LED lighting throughout the hotel, replacing the kitchen exhaust hoods with those that automatically sense smoke or steam to run efficiently, and only

five years, Attaway has been collaborating with the hotel's owners to keep energy consumption down. 'If you waste energy, you're wasting money,' he said. 'But with increasing energy efficiency, we can actually increase guest comfort and save money.'

Starwood Hotels and Resorts Worldwide recently implemented a '30/20 by 20' Programme to reduce energy use by 30 percent and cut water consumption by 20 percent by 2020 at all its properties. 'We really think of energy efficiency by data first,' said Andrea Pinabell, VP of sustainability at Starwood Hotels and Resorts Worldwide. 'We track

operating the ice machines at night. The hotel has done larger-ticket items as well, such as installing a water pressure system, a guestroom energy management system and an energy recovery unit, which can change the inside air temperatures by up to 50 degrees in the winter and 30 degrees in the summer months, Attaway said.

Mike Prevatte, owner of Wilmington Development, which has a Sleep Inn and MainStay Suites in Wilmington, N.C., is a strong proponent of energy management systems. Prevatte built his properties with Lodging Technologies' energy management system in place.

© Noordhoff Uitgevers bv

The extended-stay MainStay Suites has an interface with its cook tops in guestrooms that will automatically turn it off if the guest leaves the room. 'Energy management products have a great ROI, and with the use of cellular activity instead of wiring, you can save a lot on installation costs,' he said.

How design impacts savings

Hotel lighting is accountable for a significant percentage of energy usage, and is something that impacts guests' perceptions of a space. Lighting is a great place for hoteliers to look when contemplating changes that might benefit both guests and the bottom line.

Many hoteliers are making subtle energy-saving changes, switching to LED and compact fluorescent lamp technology in their hotels.

Ross Burch, project director at design company Wilson Associates Dallas, said that the biggest impact designers can make in increasing a hotel's energy efficiency is in the lighting choices. 'Light-emitting diode [LED] lighting has become a huge component and part of our specifications,' he said. 'They have a longer life and use less energy. They require less manpower to replace when the time comes. We now use LED lighting in everything from desk lights, bedside lamps to huge light installations across the hotel.'

While LEDs are more expensive than incandescent bulbs, these lamps can often pay for themselves through energy and maintenance savings. Robert Attaway, director of engineering for the Westin Buckhead Atlanta, said his hotel now exclusively uses LED lighting throughout the property.

Many hotel operators now have green initiatives with standards that they require within design. 'This is so fantastic to see, because in the past, we as designers were required to take the lead on incorporating energy-saving techniques wherever we could, and now operators are issuing those standards to us,' Burch said. 'Products like keycards that shut off lights and A/C when you leave the room, dimmers, electric shade and LED lights all make a huge impact.'

How to make a hotel's energy efficiency easier

Many hotels have been able to complete their energy efficiency upgrades through partnerships, rebates and incentives from local, state and federal governments along with power companies. Late last year, the Energy Department announced $9 million to encourage investments in energy-saving technologies that can be tested and deployed in hotels and other types of commercial buildings.

Starwood Hotels and Resorts' The Phoenician, in Scottsdale, Ariz., partnered with NRG Energy to install approximately 2,000 solar panels at the resort. More installations are planned.

Mike Hardin, VP of asset management for Apple REIT Companies, makes a point to choose energy efficiency upgrades to hotels that have rebates available. 'We investigate all the things we can do to lower the overall costs so we can do as many upgrades to as many hotels as possible in a year,' he said.

Hardin uses a third-party utility consultant, which brings the utilities upgrade opportunities directly to him. 'Things like solar opportunities, ozone laundry systems—and they constantly review all the utilities for us,' he said. 'They will correct bills and notice where we may have leaks or broken meters. It saves us money and stops any bleeding as quickly as possible. It's definitely worth the relatively low-cost expense that I highly recommend.'

The MainStay Suites and Sleep Inn in Wilmington, N.C., was recently able to upgrade its outdoor parking lot lighting with a rebate and incentive from the local power company, said Mike Prevatte, owner of Wilmington Development. This was a move that Prevatte expects to generate significant savings, especially when the hotel reaches its peak April-to-September season.

The Phoenician, a Starwood Hotels and Resorts Worldwide resort in Scottsdale, Ariz.,
partnered with NRG Energy, Inc. to integrate
clean sustainable energy at the resort with
approximately 2,000 photovoltaic solar panels. The installation will offset a portion of
the resort's energy demand, and this project

is the first of several between NRG and Starwood. The partnership will also incorporate
solar installations at The Westin St. John
Resort in the U.S. Virgin Islands and The
Westin Maui Resort & Spa, Ka'anapali.

(Source: www.hotelmanagement.net)

9.4.2   Energy consuming activities and factors influencing energy consumption in hotels

Environmentally conscious

Nowadays, hotel operators are more environmentally conscious than ever before, because energy costs have a massive impact on the bottom line. Hotels
use significant amounts of energy for their daily operating activities. In many
facilities, energy costs are the second-highest operating costs after payroll.
Investments in more efficient use of energy or improved housekeeping practices can lead to significant reductions in operating costs and energy bills.

Research on hotel energy use, carried out by the Hotel Energy Solutions
(2011) on hotel energy use, is at the heart of this section. The main energy
consuming areas and activities in a hotel are (p. 4):
- heating rooms,
- cooling rooms,
- lighting,
- hot water use and other energy consuming activities by guests,
- preparing meals (especially warm ones),
- swimming pool,
- others.

The relative importance of different energy end-uses is defined as follows (p. 4):

- Space conditioning (heating/cooling, ventilation and air-conditioning) – the largest single end-user of energy in hotels, accounting
  for approximately half of the total consumption – it is thus widely
  accepted that outdoor weather conditions and floor areas are
  among the main factors affecting energy use in hotels. The indoor
  temperature levels also greatly influence the quantity of energy
  consumed in a building.

- Domestic hot water – commonly the second largest user, accounting
  for up to 15% of the total energy demand. Lighting can account for
  anywhere between 12 – 18% and 40% of a hotel's total energy consumption, depending on the type of establishment. Services such
  as catering and laundry also account for a considerable share of energy consumption, particularly considering that they are commonly
  the least energy-efficient. Sports and health facilities are typically
  high energy consumers. Broadly similar results have been reported
  by studies of Greek hotels: 72 – 75% of total energy consumption is
  used for space conditioning (heating and air conditioning) and for
  hot water production, 8 – 9% is used for lighting, 15% is used for
  catering. No specific data have been found in the literature on the
  specific energy consumption breakdown of SME hotels.

Hotel energy consumption is influenced by physical and operational parameters. Physical parameters common to most buildings include size, structure and design of the building (prevailing architectural/construction practices), geographical and climatic location, the age of the facility, the type of energy and water systems installed, the way these systems are operated and maintained, types and amounts of energy and water resources available locally, and energy-usage regulations and cost (Hotel Energy Solutions, 2011).

Physical and operational parameters

Operational parameters that influence energy usage in hotels include operating schedules for the different functional facilities in the hotel building, the number of facilities present (restaurants, kitchens, in-house laundries, swimming pools and sports centres, business centres, etc.), types of services offered, fluctuations in occupancy levels, variations in customer preferences relevant to indoor comfort, on-site energy conservation practices, and culture and awareness of resource consumption among personnel and guests (Hotel Energy Solutions, 2011).

The energy saving potential of hotels is significant, especially since a large part of energy consumption is due to unnecessary loss and wastage. For instance, guests are frequently given full control over thermostat settings and individual air conditioning units, and adjust these with little or no concern for energy conservation. Windows and doors are often opened while cooling or heating systems are also in operation. Furthermore, many rented rooms remain unoccupied for long periods of time – approximately 60 – 65% during the day – while HVAC systems are left running or in stand-by mode. Energy consumption by a hotel room therefore frequently reaches 24-hours-a-day, year-round, regardless of whether or not that room is occupied (Hotel Energy Solutions, 2011).

Energy saving potential

Various studies have estimated that hotels have the potential to save at least 10 – 15% of energy they consume, depending on the age and size of the hotel, types of equipment installed, and existing maintenance and operating procedures. An assessment of potential energy conservation in southern European hotels revealed that there is a potential for 25 – 30% energy savings, especially in hotels with high annual energy consumption. European studies have estimated savings of 15 – 20% for heating, 5 – 30% for cooling, 40 – 70% for hot water, and 7 – 60% for lighting (Hotel Energy Solutions, 2011).

Despite the recognition of the benefits of efficient energy use in hotels, there are barriers and drivers affecting energy efficiency investment by hotels. Hotels regard the lack of information about energy efficiency systems and best practices regarding energy efficiency to be a major barrier when it comes to investing. According to a report on 'Developing a Cleaner Production Programme for the Irish Hotel Industry' prepared for Ireland's Environmental Protection Agency in 2006, other barriers include a lack of management commitment, unskilled staff not properly trained to run existing energy facilities efficiently, market place confusion making it difficult for hotels to assess information provided by suppliers on energy efficiency measures and costs, and poor design of existing buildings resulting in energy losses (e.g. through poor insulation, draughts, etc.). Driving forces that have led to greater use of energy efficiency measures include provision of independent

Barriers and drivers

information, advice and training on energy efficiency, better understanding of costs and benefits of investments in energy efficiency measures, and increasing customer concern and awareness regarding energy use issues (Hotel Energy Solutions, 2011).

9.4.3   Managing energy in hotels

Monitor and control capabilities

An energy management system or 'EMS' is a system that combines monitor and control capabilities to provide optimum efficiency for energy use within the environment managed by the system. An EMS performs tasks such as automatically turning off lights or lowering temperatures during times of non-demand. Energy management systems in buildings are used to improve energy efficiency by monitoring building temperatures (indoor and outdoor), and controlling boilers and coolers.

Environmental challenges

According to Kapiki (2011) the energy hotels consume is not only expensive, but also contributes to well-known environmental challenges. Hotels are among the top five types of buildings in the service sector when it comes to energy consumption, preceded by food production, sales, and health care facilities. Europe has the world's largest hotel stock with approximately 5.45 million hotel rooms – nearly half of the world's total. A typical hotel annually releases between 160 – 200 kg of CO_2 per m^2 of room floor area. By reducing CO_2 emissions, hotels can make a positive contribution to the environment and, at the same time, reduce their operational costs. The EU Action Plan for Energy identifies the tertiary sector, including hotels, as having the potential to achieve 30% savings on energy use by 2020 – higher than savings from households (27%), transport (26%) or the manufacturing industry (25%) (Kapiki, 2011, p. 79). Figure 9.4 shows the typical total energy consumption by end use in hotels in 2008 from Hotel Energy Solutions (2011).

FIGURE 9.4 Typical total energy consumption by end use in hotels – 2008

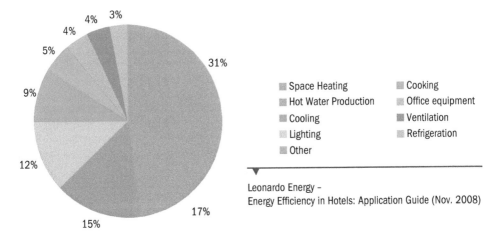

Leonardo Energy –
Energy Efficiency in Hotels: Application Guide (Nov. 2008)

There are great opportunities for the hotel sector to save on operational costs by taking advantage of potential energy efficiency and renewable energies. About 40% of energy used by hotels is electricity, and 60% comes from natural gas and oil fuels. Three-quarters of this energy is used for space heating, hot water production, air conditioning and ventilation, and lighting. These are all uses which lend themselves to dramatic increases in energy efficiency as well as easily harnessing renewable energies by using of simple, proven technologies.

Opportunities

EU hotels are in a strong position to access renewable energies, as over one third of the world's renewable power capacity is located in the European Union. Due to the number of clients they receive, hotels are in a good position to act as a beacon of energy responsibility for other industries, as well as for individuals (Kapiki 2011).

Technology is used in most hotels in order to extend in-room comfort while at the same time reducing the consumption of energy. At some hotels, guests can check-in with their web-enabled personal digital assistants (PDAs) and adjust the in-room temperature. Moreover, advances in technology have provided 'intelligent thermostats' which, when tied into a room motion sensor, can detect whether or not a room is occupied and maintain either an 'occupied' temperature, humidity and air quality (which the guest may have pre-selected), or an 'unoccupied' temperature (a temperature set by property management) (Kapiki, 2011).

Technology

The resulting reduction in energy consumption using such a system is not only immediate, but significant. Measurements indicate that passive infrared motion sensors and door switches can reduce energy consumption by 30% or more by automatically switching off lights and air-conditioning, thus saving energy when guests are out of the room (Kapiki, 2011). Intelligent energy management software tools used to monitor, control and optimise the performance of generation and transmission systems reduce energy consumption, improve the utilisation of the system, increase reliability, and predict electrical system performance as well as optimise energy usage to reduce cost.

Some innovative energy management systems could cut energy costs for hotel and commercial building owners by up to 65%. Moreover, they can be customised to meet individual needs and manage energy consumption effectively in one product. They come as either a simple package that turns off all energy supplies to a room once it is vacated, or as an on-line system which links to a computer and provides additional information about security, room occupancy rates, cleaning, staff monitoring and employee efficiency levels. Additional features include: minibar access reporting, guest control amenities, and smoke detector alarm reporting. Hospitality operators can save money by utilising this type of energy-saving software to reduce their energy costs. Such systems can have payback periods from 8 months to about 1 year 6 months, depending on the hotel facilities (Kapiki, 2011).

Efficient energy solutions

Kapiki (2011) equally indicates that there are several contemporary tools offering efficient energy solutions and significant cost reductions. Most solutions promise up to 30% of energy cost savings and return on investment of 20% to 50%. Given the increasing need for the hospitality industry to bring down overhead costs, more and more hotels are integrating energy management systems into their properties. It should be noted that installing traditional efficient energy systems typically causes interruptions in hotel operations due to required renovations. However, using wireless technology enables hotels to successfully integrate an energy management system without disrupting their day-to-day operations. An effective energy management system can provide 30% to 50% savings on guest room utility costs and return on investment (ROI) in about 2 years. When used in combination with back-office software for enhanced monitoring and control, hotels can manage their energy consumption more easily. This leads not only to cost savings, but to reduced environmental impact as well. Wireless energy management systems, consisting of flexible configurations of sensors, controls and devices, solve many of the issues that hold back facilities managers and owners from installing an energy management system:

Wireless

- Affordability – Wireless is more affordable to install than hard-wired solutions, often reducing costs to a quarter of what hard-wired installations would run.
- Speed and Convenience – Installations can go forward without having to move people out of their offices or rooms. They can also be completed in a very timely manner.
- Flexibility – With the growth of wireless technology over the past several years, applications now fit a wide range of buildings and business goals.
- Reliability – Wireless mesh has performed reliably in virtually every type of commercial building, including hotels, restaurants and other facilities.

9.4.4   Managing water in hotels

This section on water management as contained in Text 9.3, is with permission reproduced from the Know How Guide to Water Management and Responsibility in Hotels as published by Green Hotelier, a programme of ITP (the International Tourism Partnership).

TEXT 9.3

Water Management and Responsibility in Hotels

Posted By Holly Tuppen On March 22, 2013 (12:52 pm) In Know How Guides

In celebration of World Water Day here are our top tips for hoteliers looking to reduce their water consumption and address water issues responsibly.

An international day to celebrate freshwater was recommended at the 1992 United Nations Conference on Environment and Development (UNCED), and since then World Water Day has been held annually on 22nd March. The day aims to focus attention on the importance of freshwater and advocating for the sustainable management of freshwater resources.

Each year, World Water Day highlights a specific aspect of freshwater. In 2013, in reflection of the International Year of Water Co-operation, World Water Day is dedicated to the theme of co-operation around water, which is very in keeping with what the International Tourism Partnership (ITP) has been doing on the topic of water since establishing a Water Working Group in 2012.

ITP is currently working with its 16 global hotel company members to address how the industry should address water challenges. This collaboration is being conducted through a working group on water, with its first objective: *To produce a risk analysis of key water issues - present and forecast - of water availability and quality, along with an assessment of any cost and regulatory implications, in selected geographic regions, in order to increase awareness and understanding of how and where water issues present a significant risk to the industry's future.*

As part of this working group, ITP has engaged the help of SIWI, the Stockholm International Water Institute, to conduct a research piece on the above. More details of this research will be publicly available in early summer. However, for now, we've updated our practical Know How Guide to Water Management in the hotel industry.

Why the need to conserve water?

Water scarcity is a recognised global problem, with demand for water projected to exceed supply by 40% by 2030. By the same year, half the world's population will be living in areas of high water stress.

Most water (97%) is in the oceans, which cover 71% of the Earth's surface. 3% is freshwater, two-thirds of which is tied up as ice in glaciers and at the poles. This leaves approximately 1% as freshwater in rivers, lakes, the atmosphere and in groundwater.

However, with demand rising rapidly due to a growing global population with expectations of higher living standards and resource-intensive farming, that 1% is under threat. Climate change is adding to the problem because our weather patterns have become less predictable and more pronounced. While a number of areas are experiencing periods of prolonged drought, the rain that falls in some other areas is heavier. This leads to flooding without sufficiently replenishing groundwater stocks.

Hotel companies have both a strong commercial and moral imperative for addressing water use. Cost is a clear factor: water accounts for 10% of utility bills in many hotels. Most hotels pay for the water they consume twice – first by purchasing fresh water and then by disposing of it as waste water. According to the UK's Environment Agency, depending on their water efficiency, hotels can reduce the amount of water consumed per guest per night by up to 50% compared with establishments with poor performance in water consumption. The **moral reasons** are equally compelling: water is a scare resource in many resorts around the world so hotels have a responsibility not to use more than necessary; in rural or remote areas it ensures that local residents are not deprived of their essential supply; and by reducing the amount of waste-water that needs to be treated, this lessens the risk of water pollution.

According to the latest research conducted by

SIWI, almost 20 % of the world's population live in areas of physical water scarcity. A **water scarce region** is one where water resources development is 'approaching or has exceeded sustainable limits' and 'more than 75% of river flows are withdrawn for agriculture, industry, and domestic purposes'. By 2030, the world might face a 40% global demand/supply gap of accessible, reliable water supply for economic development. The private sector is a major water user and often completely dependent on water for production and service delivery. The Hospitality industry is one of these where water plays a determining part in everyday operations and potential growth.

Resorts have to be developed responsibly in water-stressed regions

Water efficiency: Establishing a water management plan

In order to set up and achieve relevant and realistic targets you will need to invest time and resources in careful planning, organisation, training and follow-up.

The first step to take when creating a water management plan is to start measuring water consumption and set some **tangible targets**. It's vital to know your start point and find out how much water you are currently using. Installing meters and taking regular readings will aid this and sub meters will help you see where the areas of greatest use are. These are obviously the areas where you will probably need to focus most of your efforts.

Another key part of understanding measurement and target setting is knowing your water costs. Work out what your potential cost savings may be and the payback period for any capital investment. Grounding a water management plan on costs, as well as environmental saving, will help gain the buy in of

key stakeholders and improve your property's overall efficiency.

Once measurement and targets have been set, you can establish a **water conservation plan**. Here are some suggestions of how best to go about this:

- Carry out a water audit to show where the major water costs are and where savings can be made
- Compare total and departmental consumption figures with hotel industry benchmarks to determine the potential for savings (see the diagrams below)
- Calculate the water used per guest per night by dividing the total water consumed in guest rooms by the number of guests for that month. If your utility bill is in cubic metres rather than litres, multiply the number of litres by 0.0001
- Check if funding / loans are available from government or other sources for investment in new technology or water reduction schemes
- On the back of the information gathered, establish realistic goals for each department and the entire hotel
- Communicate the management's commitment to water reduction and the subsequent objectives and goals to all employees
- Train staff so they understand how to make prudent use of water and how to maintain equipment for optimum energy-efficiency
- Encourage staff to put forward their own suggestions for water reduction
- Establish a monitoring and targeting system so that you can regularly report progress back to staff and other stakeholders. Motivate through feedback and reward success
- Join forces with other hotels and provide mentoring to help them reduce their water consumption

© Noordhoff Uitgevers bv

Area	Temperate m^3	Temperate %	Mediterranean m^3	Mediterranean %	Tropical m^3	Tropical %
Guest Rooms	18,088	34	17,075	33.3	120,312	34
F&B incl. Kitchens	11,704	22	8,614	16.8	48,168	13.5
Lockers/public toilets	10,640	20	8,255	16.1	17,840	6
Laundry	9,044	17	2,410	4.7	39,248	11
HVAC	532	1	1,231	2.4	57,088	1.6
Steam generation	2,128	4	205	0.4		
Pool	1,064	2			17,840	5
Gardens			2,054	4.2	3,568	1
Snack Bar			1,743	3.4		
Water supply treatment					24,976	7
Public areas					14,272	4
Boilers					3,568	1
Cold rooms					1,784	0.5
Others/not metered			9,589	18.7	7,136	2

DATA FROM: Fully sub-metered 300-room hotel in Germany with total annual water consumption of 53,200m^3 (620 litres per guest)

DATA FROM: Fully sub-metered 270-room hotel in Lisbon. Portugal with total annual water consumption of 51,276m^3 (819 litres per guest)

DATA FROM: Luxury fully-serviced hotel in Jakarta. Indonesia. with 800 rooms. 100 apartments. 25-acre gardens. sports centre and olympic-sized pool. Total annual water consumption of 356,800 m^3 (820 litres per guest)

Annual water consumption in hotels

Hotel profile	Climate zone	Water consumption (m^3 per overnight guest) EXCELLENT	SATISFACTORY	HIGH
Luxury serviced hotels	Temperate	< 0.3	< 0.45	< 0.7
	Mediterranean	< 0.4	< 0.6	< 0.8
	Tropical	< 0.8	< 1.0	< 1.4

Water benchmark for luxury fully serviced hotels, from EMH

© Noordhoff Uitgevers bv

Moving through areas of a hotel where water consumption is likely to be highest, here are some ways in which you can change your operational water use. Always test first to see that any measures taken will not compromise quality, health or safety.

Bathrooms

Bathrooms

- Shower flow should be no more than 10 litres / min. This can be very simply measured with a bucket and stopwatch.
- Low flow toilets use an average of just six litres per flush, compared to older models that use roughly two to four times more than that. Additionally, you can install dual flush toilets so guests can opt for a shorter flush. If it is not feasible to change all toilets, you can reduce the water used in flushing by placing a brick or full water bottle in the cistern (effectively displacing some of the water).
- Taps should have a maximum flow of six litres / min, or four in hand washing sinks in public bathrooms. Flow restrictors or better aerators can both help reduce tap flow.
- Maintenance is a key part of saving water consumption – a leaking toilet can lose 750 litres of water day.

Laundry

Laundry

- Where outsourced, ask your supplier what procedures they have in place to reduce water and energy use.
- Wash small quantities in a 5kg machine and always ensure machines are fully loaded.
- Minimise the rinse cycle as much as possible without reducing quality.
- Consider using 'intermediate extraction' between rinse operations.
- Consider the re-use of water from previous rinse cycles for the first wash of the next cycle by installing temporary holding tanks.
- Maintenance is also key: Check regularly for leaking dump valves, ensure that all water inlet valves are closing properly and check that level controls on water re-use tanks are working properly.
- 500-room-plus hotels could consider installing a continuous batch washer (CBW), which uses all the rinse water for pre-washing and main suds operation.
- Ensure that the water flow rates on tunnel washers and CBWs are adjusted to the manufacturer's recommended setting.
- When buying washing machines, look out for a good water consumption rating.
- Consider using ozone laundry systems. These inject ozone into the water, which works in conjunction with the laundry chemicals to provide a more efficient wash.

Swimming pools

Swimming pools

Having a swimming pool can increase fresh water consumption in a large hotel by up to 10% so think hard about whether it is really necessary before installing one. These steps will help ensure no water is wasted.

- Conduct regular maintenance to prevent leaks. Checking for leaks is best done by reading water meters last thing at night and first thing in the morning.
- Backwash the swimming pool every two to three days rather than daily. It is also best to opt for a backwash system where water can be recaptured and used for irrigation.

- Always cover swimming pools when not in use to prevent evaporation and reduce the need to empty and refill.
- Installing push-button showers by the pool will reduce water use.

Grounds

- Do not water grounds in the heat of the day. In hot climates, the best time to water is in the evening.
- It's best to avoid using automated watering systems, however if they do have to be used water can be saved by fitting timers on sprinklers to control water use. Moisture sensors in gardens and grounds can also be used to avoid over-watering.
- Put a procedure in place for manual watering and train gardening staff to reduce water use where possible.
- Use rainwater harvesting techniques to divert and capture rainwater from roofs and gutters. Water can be diverted into underground storage tanks or into water butts. Plants actually prefer rainwater to treated water from a tap.
- If possible, use grey water from baths and sinks for irrigation. Consider installing a treatment system that will enable you to use treated black water from toilets in the gardens. The treatment plant needs to be carefully positioned in relation to prevailing winds and screened from view. Management of these systems must be well controlled.
- A well-designed and controlled irrigation system will deliver water when and where it is needed.
- Using your own organic compost will add nutrients and help retain moisture in the soil.
- Placing wood chips on top of soil helps to reduce evaporation.
- Native species of plant often need less water so design and landscape your grounds in keeping with the existing environment.
  The Orchid in Mumbai has a Sewage Treatment Plant on its roof to treat all waste water.

9

Kitchens

Kitchens

- Taps in kitchens should have a maximum flow of 10 litres per minute.
- Only use dishwashers on full load.
- Pre-soaking utensils and dishes saves using running water. Similarly, wash vegetables and fruits in a sink of water rather than a running water rinse.
- Avoid thawing food under running water and avoid using running water to melt ice in sink strainers.
- Minimise the use of ice machines and adjust settings to dispense less ice.

Housekeeping

Housekeeping

- Put procedures in place and conduct training to inform housekeeping on how they can reduce water use. These procedures should include how many times to flush the toilet when cleaning, not to leave taps running or use excessive water, using a mop rather than hose when cleaning floors.
- Implement a linen re-use programme. As well as saving water, these pro-grammes mean less wear on fabrics, prolonging their life, and saves housekeeping staff time. Many hotels advertise a re-use programme but often do not adhere to them, leaving guests cynical, exasperated by the fact that guests often think this is just a cost saving exercise for the ho-tel. Rather than imposing a structured programme, the most successful policies are those that allow guests to opt out of having their linen changed on a daily basis.

Water efficiency systems

Water efficiency systems

- Greywater systems enable up to 50 per cent of wastewater to be re-turned to the hotel after treatment for toilet flushing.

Grey water systems

  Because of the separate pipe-work involved, grey water systems are ex-pensive to install and chemical treatment of the recycled water is some-times necessary for health and safety reasons (only in on-demand sys-tems). They are therefore best designed into the building at the outset, although increasingly hotels are choosing to retrofit them because of the savings to be made. Payback time is difficult to calculate, as it will de-pend on the type of systems installed and the relative cost of the potable water to that of the re-use water. The payback can be anything from two to fifteen years depending on the cost of water at your location.

Low-flow technology

- Low-flow technology installation can save huge volumes of water across bathrooms and kitchens, with minimal effect on the customer experi-ence.

  Adjustable flow restrictors on taps enable them to deliver a lower instan-taneous flow rate than screw-operated taps and can reduce water use by over 50%. Similarly, low-flow shower heads cost very little and use around 9.45 litres a minute compared with conventional heads (which typically use nearly twice that). If properly designed they should feel as effective as higher water volume models.

  An IHG property recently experienced huge savings by implementing this kind of technology. Holiday Inn in Flinders, Australia, recouped its AUD $22,000 (USD $19,500) investment in low flow technology after 18 months and cut water usage by 50%.

Spotlight on Starwood and incentivisation

Starwood Hotels have committed to reduce water consumption by 20% by 2020. All hotel brands owned by Starwood in the U.S. offer a $5 voucher to spend in the shop/restaurant/bar if guests don't have their room cleaned every day. Other hotels donate to charity when guests opt out of having rooms cleaned/linen changed. These rewards act as an incentive but also remove any cynicism from the customer – so they understand that not changing linen is the hotel's environmental policy, rather than simply a money saving scheme.

Spotlight on Soneva and sourcing water

Sourcing water from sustainable sources is a major priority for these luxury resorts in The Maldives and Thailand. Although water consumption in the resorts continues to rise, no water is taken from the public water supply with 60% coming from rainwater collection or wells and 40% from desalination. Since fresh water issues are a particular concern in Thailand, Soneva Kiri has built its own reservoir to collect rainwater.

Water and the stakeholder: Communicating and educating

Access to water is a human right and educating those around us about its fragility is therefore vital. Hotels have a responsibility in educating and communicating water issues to their stakeholders; employees, the local community and the customer.

Stakeholder

Key component

As we can see from the above, a key component of a water management action plan is communication with and the education of staff. Implementing simple procedures and setting targets can play a huge role in effecting the mind-set of employees when it comes to water consumption. Although this starts at the hotel, this shift in attitude is soon carried into home-life and in turn extends to others.

Where water is in short supply, being aware of competing demands for water and availability issues for a local community is vital. Hotels have to work with local communities when it comes to water use, rather than taking supplies from them.

- Get informed about local water issues through talking to local authorities, community and business groups and your staff.
- Conduct a water use and risk assessment of your property (see tools below).
- Be aware of and as a minimum, adhere to local regulations on water extraction and waste water disposal. Where standards are low or infrastructure poor, ensure yours are high and join with other businesses and community groups to lobby for better regulation and management.
- In areas where local people may have limited access to water, or where water quality is poor, consider supporting improvement schemes with local authorities and community groups or funding better access to water, such as water tanks or standpipes.

Educating customers

Hotels can also play a role in educating customers about water issues, and to some extent encourage reflection on their own water use at home and when travelling. Most simply, this can be done by communicating what the hotel does to minimise water consumption and why it is committed to doing so. This can be done by:

- Communicate to guests the importance of fresh water resources within the area and provide opportunities to allow guests to use water wisely.
- Encourage guests to shower instead of bath.
- Suggest they do not leave the tap running when brushing their teeth. It can save up to nine litres each time they do so!.
- Invite them to re-use their towels and linens by opting not to have them changed every day.
- Incentivise guests to change their behaviour through donations to charity or vouchers to spend at the hotel.
- Inform guests how the hotel reduces water consumption in other areas of the hotel.

Going one step further, hotels in particularly water-stressed areas can involve guests in their water policy. This is most successfully done in properties and places where guests are motivated to learn about the local area and community, and are environmentally aware. Initiatives include guest participation in local education or water infrastructure building and running educational tours of innovative water saving initiatives.

In some regions working with the local community on improving water infrastructure is essential.

Spotlight on Kempinski and staff education

Kempinski's Green Inspiration programme starts with raising awareness among guests and staff, inspiring them to adopt simple but impactful behaviours. The first of many initiatives is 'The Oak Tree':

> 'The oak tree is a symbol of strength, an ancient European tree, resistant to drought and disease. All Kempinski hotels participate in the Oak Initiative with a guest awareness programme: the small Oak Tree left on the bed by the guest invites their housekeeping attendant to make up the bed with the existing linens (reducing water used for laundry and the associated waste water), to use green cleaning products, and to turn off air-conditioning, lights and TV while the guest is not in the room. Staff contribute by purchasing goods responsibly and communicating this to suppliers - each decision to use FSC paper or buy local produce for the restaurants adds up. A hotel may also choose to support a local environmental conservation programme. Staff take part in Earth Hour each year, and a Green Day each month – where they will clean up the property and its grounds.'

Water and charity: Philanthropic approaches to water

Besides from the potential for an individual property to educate immediate stakeholders about water issues, many hotels/ hotel chains choose to interact and support broader water charity and conservation efforts. Larger hotel chains may set up their own water conservation groups, or become a primary sponsor of an existing one.

For smaller hotels, there are numerous charities and schemes that are always looking for partners. One example is Whole World Water, which encourages the tourism industry to filter, bottle and sell their own water supply and give 10% of the proceeds to the Whole World Water Fund, which seeks to provide clean and safe drinking water for everyone. Also find out about what Water Aid and Just a Drop are doing in your local area.

Spotlight on Marriott, Nobility of Nature

Marriott's 'Nobility of Nature' program works with Conservation International to protect the source of fresh water in Asia for more than 2 billion people. Located in Sichuan Province, an area hard hit by the 2008 earthquake and home of the giant panda, the program will help to improve water quality in the rural communities of Pingwu County.

> 'Worldwide, Marriott is investing in innovative, large-scale conservation projects that help address some of the most pressing environmental problems, such as water and rainforest preservation. In China, the need for fresh water is expected to exceed its supply by 25% over the next 15 years. Helping to develop viable ways to preserve the water supply and conserve water in our hotels is one way we can help.' J.W. Marriott Jr., Chairman and CEO of Marriott International.

Reporting and risk

Assessing water risk

Water security is a key issue for hotels. Water risk is not only about availability, but there are a host of other concerns such as infrastructure, governance,

Water risk

competing needs and water quality. A variety of tools are available online for companies and hotels that wish to take a deeper dive into assessing these risks. Most of these require water sources, annual consumption and discharge rates and the location of the property. From this they use a variety of data-sets to assess water risk. So whilst some effort would be required to gather data, the benefit is a clear picture to inform planning and investment going forward. The choice of tool will depend on the needs of the individual company so it is recommended to try these out.

World Business Council for Sustainable Development (WBCSD) Global Water Tool
Produces detailed assessment of water risk on a multi-site level and generates data for reporting mechanisms such as CDP Water Disclosure.

WWF Water Risk Filter
A comprehensive tool looking at water management issues as well as water risks and mitigation solutions in order to develop a holistic strategy for water use.

WRI Aqueduct
Produces maps based on property location which can be weighted against different risks such as flood risk and groundwater quality.

Global Environmental Management Initiative (GEMI). Collecting the Drops (2007)
An online tool to better understand what emerging water issues might mean for a business, given their operations, needs, and circumstances. Does not assess risk, though is a useful tool for overall strategy planning.

Reporting

Companies may wish to report on water management in order to demonstrate their commitment to sustainable water use. This may be in company reports, on their website or to a national or international reporting mechanism.

The Global Reporting Initiative
Provides globally applicable sustainability reporting guidelines and provides information on how and what to report.

CDP Water Program
Directed at large companies, however, companies of any size may choose to report under the largest water reporting system globally.

Carbon Trust Water Standard
Certification for UK companies who measure, report on and commit to reduce water use.

Accreditation and further reading
The Travel Foundation, *Greener Accommodations*
International Tourism Partnership, *Environmental Management for Hotels*
Tourism Concern, *Water Equity in Tourism: A Human Right, a Global Responsibility 2012*
United Nations, *UN Global Compact CEO Water Mandate*

Summary

- ▶ Led by a Chief Engineer, the roles, responsibilities and goals of the Facility Engineering and Maintenance Department can be summarised as follows:
  - Ensuring guest satisfaction
  - Protecting and enhancing the financial value of the building and grounds
  - Supporting efforts of other hotel departments through timely attention to their Engineering and Maintenance needs
  - Managing maintenance and repair costs
  - Managing energy usage
  - Increasing staff pride and morale
  - Ensuring the safety of those working for and visiting the hotel

- ▶ Within the financial domain, a Chief Engineer is faced with the major challenge of ensuring the physical state of the property is continually upgraded, while at the same time managing the use of limited financial resources. Chief Engineers must always work in close collaboration with Financial Controllers as well General Managers through the establishment of the Property and Operations Maintenance Budget.

- ▶ There are various types of maintenance:
  - Scheduled maintenance, which refers to activities based on formal work orders that identify a known problem or need.
  - Routine maintenance, which ensures that the property and equipment are kept in good condition, and provide a long operating life.
  - Preventative maintenance, which is the care and servicing the facilities and equipment in order to maintain satisfactory operating conditions.
  - Emergency maintenance, which involves the repair or replacement of equipment and components after they have failed and require immediate attention.
  - Breakdown maintenance, which is reactive and typically employed when failures are unlikely to result in workplace injuries or excessive downtime.
  - Contract maintenance, which is one-off or periodically arranged maintenance performed by a third party under a contract.
  - Replacement problems, which involve items that degenerate with use or with time, or those that fail after a certain amount of use or time.
  - Total productive maintenance programmes, which are built on autonomous small group activities with the goal of driving all wastes to zero.

9

▶ Hotel energy and water management is the practice of managing procedures, operations and equipment that contribute to efficient energy and water usage in a hotel operation.

▶ The main energy consuming areas and activities in a hotel are:
- heating rooms,
- cooling rooms,
- lighting,
- hot water use and other energy consuming activities by guests,
- preparing meals (especially warm ones),
- swimming pool,
- others

▶ Since the energy that hotels consume is not only expensive, but also contributes to environmental challenges, energy management systems are required. These systems use technological innovations by combining monitoring and controlling capabilities to provide optimum efficiency for energy usage within the environment managed by each system.

▶ Water management is similarly of huge importance to the hospitality industry and the following suggestions on how to establish a water conservation plan should be heeded by operators:
- Carrying out water audits
- Comparing consumption figures to hotel industry benchmarks
- Calculating water used per guest per night
- Checking if funding is available for investment in technology or other schemes
- Establishing realistic goals for each department and the entire hotel
- Communicating management's commitment to water reduction
- Training staff to make properly use water and maintain equipment
- Encouraging staff to make suggestions for water reduction
- Establishing a motivational monitoring and targeting system
- Co-operating with other hotels in reducing water consumption

Questions and assignments for reflection

1   This chapter looked at the roles and responsibilities of the Chief Engineer. Going through the responsibilities, indicate which you find to be the five most important ones. Which factors influenced your choices?

2   Compare and contrast scheduled maintenance with routine maintenance. Which would you prefer to have implemented in a property of which you were the manager? Why?

3   Compare and contrast in-house maintenance with contract maintenance. Which would you prefer to have implemented in a property in which you were the manager? Why?

4   Can you think of at least five reasons why total productive maintenance would be difficult to implement in the hospitality industry? Explain your choices.

5   What would you advise a hospitality operation to do in case they want to establish a water management plan? Why would this be your advice?

9

10
Managing Safety and Security Issues

M. N. Chibili

10.1 Introduction

Hotels are caught in the dilemma of having to keep their assets as secure as possible, while doing the same when it comes to keeping their properties open and welcoming. In a post 9/11 world (i.e. following the attacks on the Twin Towers in the US in 2011), safety and security issues have been made a genuine factor of concern for hotels worldwide; these issues are now a key responsibility of hotel management. In the recent past, hotels increasingly became targets for various terrorist acts leading to loss of life and substantial property damage. Examples are the attacks on the Taj Mahal Palace & Tower Hotel, and the Oberoi Trident in Mumbai, India (2008), the Islamabad Marriott Hotel in Islamabad, Pakistan (2008), the JW Marriott and the Ritz-Carlton in Jakarta, Indonesia (2009), the Breeze View Hotel in Mpeketoni, Kenya (2014), and the Radisson Blu Hotel in Bamako, Mali (2015). All members of hotel staff should be committed to ensuring a safe and secure environment in which guests as well as staff feel protected. This should, however, fall within the activities overseen by a safety and security manager (for large properties) or someone responsible for such issues in smaller properties. Managing the safety and security within a hotel is vital to delivering hospitality to guests. A safety and security manager is responsible for establishing plans related to bomb threats, emergency communication and evacuation, employee safety training, fire safety systems, guest and employee safety, and even room key security. Any negligence in the domain of safety and security could lead to financial losses as well as serious legal consequences for the hotel through civil suits, in which guests or others may seek compensation for alleged security deficiencies. In cases of civil suits, a hotel should attempt to have an out-of-court settlement in order to avoid wasting time and money as well as to avoid negative publicity.

10

Kenya, Nairobi: Giraffe Manor

10.2 Safety and security legislation and programmes

10.2.1 Rules and regulations

In all developed countries, rules and regulations have been established to ensure that practices and procedures carried out within hospitality operations are done in such a way that the environment in which guests are received and in which employees work in a safe one. Appendix E is an illustration of the principal hotel-specific laws in certain European countries related to health and safety issues only and adapted from the CMS Guide to Principal Hotel-Specific Laws in Europe, 2007. Hotel managers must be fully aware of their obligations towards their guests, employees, assets and local communities in these contexts at all times.

Obligations

Within the Netherlands, for example, safety and security issues are covered by the Establishment Design (Licensing and Catering Act) Decree. This decree stipulates basic design conditions to which hotel and catering activities should adhere, covering such topics as floor spaces, room sizes, room height, obligatory toilets and functionality. With the objective of ensuring safety and security, other topics covered in the decree include visibility issues (overall and through views), management and employee area monitoring, lighting conditions, storerooms, display cases, key management, cash register and money safe management, means of communication (mobile telephones and walkie-talkies), cameras, alarm systems, detection equipment, night porters, bouncers, company first aid, automatic external defibrillators, and fire prevention and management.

Design conditions

10.2.2 Safety programmes

In many countries, governments require hospitality establishments to have safety programmes. A health and safety programme is a process for managing health and safety in the workplace. It includes a written document that details health and safety policies and procedures for the property. The scope of a health and safety programme depends on the size of the business and hazards to which employees and guests may be exposed. The basic components of a health and safety programme for small hospitality operations are summarised as follows:

Components

- Management should control hazards and develop a safety plan. They should be able to identify hazards and hazardous elements within and around the workplace, and take steps to eliminate or minimise these elements. A safety plan should be developed in collaboration with the employees. Employees should be informed what is being done to ensure their safety as well as what is expected from them. Employees should also have access to first aid kits.
- Management should continuously inspect the workplace. All equipment and tools should be regularly checked to ensure they are well maintained and safe to use. Storage areas should be also checked, and safe working procedures should be reviewed.
- Management should thoroughly investigate incidents. They should look into the causes of accidents, including near misses where no one was injured. Management should try to find ways to change procedures or equipment to help prevent similar incidents from occurring in future.
- Management should maintain adequate records related to all first aid treatments, inspections, incident investigations, and training activities.

10

This information can help management to identify trends in unsafe conditions or work procedures.

- Management should make safety a fundamental part of the business. A strong commitment to health and safety makes good business sense because it is the only way to protect the greatest resource of the business — the employees.
- Management should regularly talk with employees. Regular meetings with staff to discuss health and safety issues should be held. Employees should be encouraged to share their ideas and thoughts on how to improve safety in the workplace.
- Management should train employees and provide them with written instructions and safe work procedures so they themselves can verify whether they are unsure of any tasks or have forgotten part of their training. Management should also ensure that the employees are well supervised to ensure that they are using their training skills effectively, and provide additional training if such seems necessary.

Larger hotel chains have much more elaborate safety and security procedures. Taken from The 2012 Rezidor Hotel Group's Responsible Business Report is such an example. TRIC=S is their formula for safety and security. TRIC=S stands for

- Threat assessment +
- Risk evaluation and mitigation +
- Incident response preparedness +
- Crisis management, communications and continuity =
- Safe, secure and sellable hotels.

Although TRIC=S is designed as a dynamic programme, guidelines are needed to ensure the safety and security of guests, employees and owners' investments while maintaining (or even enhancing) guest and employee comfort and satisfaction. Text 10.1 illustrates the development and implementation of TRIC=S at the Radisson Blu Gautrain Hotel, Sandton Johannesburg (South Africa).

Rezidor indicates that accurate threat assessment does not entail looking at a crystal ball and predicting the future. Their threat assessments are based on honest, open internal communication, news and media monitoring as well as intelligence supplied by third-party business risk analysis and alert services. Information is analysed and shared within the Group, along with experience and good practice. Rezidor also encourages hotels to actively contribute to keeping their local communities safe by engaging in safety and security related forums and crime prevention schemes.

Threat assessment

10

To evaluate and mitigate risk, Rezidor works very closely with partners such as risk engineers at Willis (Rezidor's insurance broker). The Willis Blue risk management benchmarking programme has been specifically tailored for Rezidor. It follows Rezidor's Four Cornerstone structure for Guest Safety and Security, Employee Safety and Security, Fire Safety, and Operational Security. Willis' fire risk engineers survey a percentage of the portfolio annually in order to measure performance against benchmarks. To ensure security risks are also addressed, risk engineers are accompanied by security professionals from Rezidor. All hotels carry out an annual operational safety and security self-assessment based on the same four cornerstones. In 2012, the self-assessment originally developed by Rezidor was upgraded and improved and is now accessible by all hotels around the world that are affiliated with the Carlson Rezidor Hotel Group.

TEXT 10.1

Development and implementation of TRIC=S at the Radisson Blu Gautrain Hotel, Sandton Johannesburg (South Africa)

Taking TRIC=S to the Public

TRIC=S is Rezidor's unique approach to safety and security: Threat Assessment + Risk Mitigation + Incident response capability + Crisis management, communication and continuity = Safe, secure and sellable hotels. TRIC=S In my Hotel is an equally unique and successful tool for hotels to communicate their safety and security preparedness both internally and externally.

In order to communicate their safety and security preparedness both internally and externally, the Radisson Blu Hotel Johannesburg (South Africa) developed TRIC=S In my Hotel.

A simple presentation, TRIC=S In my Hotel starts with a brief introduction to TRIC=S. Using simple diagrams, TRIC=S In my Hotel goes on to outline the safety and security features in guestrooms, back-of-house and public areas. The presentation also includes details of the local emergency services and specialised safety and security capabilities that are available.

During 2012, all Rezidor properties have been encouraged to create their own TRIC=S In my Hotel and keep it updated. TRIC=S In my Hotel can be shown internally to train

© Noordhoff Uitgevers bv

staff. As TRIC=S In my Hotel does not include details of sensitive areas in the hotel or how they are secured and accessed, it also can be shown to external parties such as corporate clients to demonstrate the safety and security features of each property.
There is an old saying that a picture paints a thousand words. Using images, TRIC=S In my Hotel presentations communicate a lot of information simply, efficiently and sefely.

TRIC=S In my Hotel was first used in Johannesburg as the introductory presentation to a delegation of very high-level security specialists representing an extremely important potential client. At the end of the 15-minute presentation the head of the delegation stood up and said: 'That was impressive! You just answered 99% of our questions.' The

potential client has since become a loyal guest. Their first visit alone generated more than EUR 200,000 in revenue.

Safety and Security team, Radisson Blue Gautrain Hotel, Sandton Johannesburg

(Source: The Rezidor Hotel Group's Responsible Business Report, 2012)

10.3 Security systems

Recent events have forcibly turned the hospitality industry's focus to safety and security issues. Prior to September 11th 2001, there had been fewer than 30 reported attacks on hotels in 15 countries around the world, ever. Within 15 years of 9/11, that number had gone up to 62 attacks on hotels in 20 different countries around the world. Security risks to hotels, employees and guests are expanding exponentially, and while the hospitality industry is stepping up their facilities in terms of employee and guest safety and data protection, the industry as a whole has been challenged with increasing safety and security levels without impacting day to day operations or guest experience. There are now many providers of advanced security systems designed specifically to improve hotels' ability to prevent, detect, respond to, and recover from serious security incidents.

Risks

These systems can have physical components that may include features such as landscaping and lighting systems; fire and security alarm systems; access control systems including card keys, locks, safes and biometric systems; closed-circuit television (CCTV) systems to monitor, record and store camera or video surveillance of a hotel premises; and various other devices or programmes to protect proprietary information of the property and its guests. Fast paced changes and significant improvements in physical security system technologies are evident in this domain. Analogue security systems are being converted to, or replaced by, digital systems with internet protocol. These systems now enable superior and advanced imagery, recognition and data storage. Advanced software enables observation cameras to detect incidents and incident patterns. Such systems can alert system monitors of actual or impending security breaches through the detection of 'patterns' that could signify a security incident.

Physical components

Physical security systems are being 'integrated' so that access control systems, alarms and cameras are coordinated. If, for example, an access

10

control device such as an exit door is breached, a camera is activated automatically to focus on the breached door. This results in a more efficient use of installed security systems through enhanced identification and response to potential and actual problems. Fire safety and security alarm systems are also becoming more sophisticated. Due to the complexity and variety of available physical security systems, hotel operators are recommended to select independent consultants to review the design, selection and installa-

Conduct due diligence

tion of their physical security systems. Hotel operators are advised to conduct due diligence in choosing a consultant, because physical security systems are highly varied, complex and are often available at substantial differences in price. Text 10.2 illustrates how the use of technology helps keep hotel guests safe.

TEXT 10.2

Security service – using technology to keep hotel guests safe, 24 March 2015

Modern technology plays a pivotal role in keeping hotels secure and safe. Arup's Gregoir Chikaher and Accenture's Kevin Richards outline how the latest developments provide protection, and why operators must be suitably proactive without seeming alarmist.

Ensuring a safe and secure environment for staff and guests is a priority for any hotel, and one in which modern technology plays an absolutely crucial role. The latest systems help to protect against physical threats, while the increasing frequency of data breaches makes cutting-edge technology an essential tool in tackling cybercrime. Security measures must be discreet, however, and it is essential to strike the right balance between safety and intrusiveness. For Gregoir Chikaher, global hotels and leisure business leader at engineering giant Arup, recent advances have allowed hotels to improve their systems without alarming customers.
'Security methods have become more technically advanced and, because of this, harder to breach,' he explains. 'Most hotels now allow guests to book online using credit cards, and, by doing so, can collect information to verify people as they check in. This system can also be used to run credit checks; if the guest has an unpaid bill at another branch, for example, this can help guard against incurring further financial loss.'
'Visiting a hotel should be a leisurely experience, where guests can slow down and

relax. They are not prisons, and therefore you can't restrain people too much.'
CCTV, long-established as a basic safety measure, is also becoming increasingly sophisticated.
'Systems have become much more proactive,' says Chikaher. 'Cameras not only provide a level of general surveillance, but can also now detect items such as bags abandoned in public areas, provide automatic number plate recognition for pre-registered guests and employee vehicles, and detect when a person is in a sensitive area.'
Collectively referred to as 'video content analysis', closed-circuit cameras now require less manned monitoring and only need responding to in exceptional circumstances. Likewise, other security measures, such as key card systems, have also reduced staffing requirements.

Wireless protocol
Data security is an increasingly important issue for hotels, with major brands falling victim to hackers. Late last year, security researchers uncovered a sophisticated industrial espionage campaign targeting business executives using Wi-Fi networks in luxury hotels across Asia that dated back as far as 2009.
'The hospitality industry has some unique challenges surrounding data protection, privacy and security,' says Kevin Richards, a managing director at Accenture and former

international president of the Information Systems Security Association.

'In many ways technology has increased the speed and volume, and therefore the impact, of attacks. Hotels manage a significant amount of personal data, including credit card numbers, addresses and affinity programme information.'

Guest internet access can certainly be a weak point in hotels' defences. 'Attackers can monitor and track guest activities and look for credit card information, user credentials and other sensitive data,' he adds. 'Because they are not attacking hotels' systems, many of these activities go undetected.'

There are, however, ways in which the industry can protect itself, such as separating the guest and hotel networks.

'Information security can be a challenge for any industry that wants to provide convenience to its customers,' continues Richards. 'The reality is that travellers want to be able to do business while staying at a hotel. They want to check their personal e-mail and social networking sites, and do everything they would in the office or at home.

'Hotels manage a significant amount of personal data, including credit card numbers, addresses and affinity programme information.'

Technology brought into the property by guests can also cause problems. 'The fact that hotels don't control end-point devices is a particular challenge, as computer malware can easily be introduced,' he adds.

'Furthermore, with data stores containing a potentially large repository of critical information, they are higher-profile targets for attackers to pursue.'

The introduction of security technology can be something of a delicate balance for hotels, however. On the one hand, it is necessary to create a safe environment, while on the other, security measures need to be unobtrusive.

'You can have the most sophisticated systems in place, but these can be circumvented if someone is determined and clever enough. You will always need people to be vigilant at reception, and other access points, to watch for suspicious behaviour.'

'Many issues, such as the risk of theft, are understood by the operator and the guest, who will expect a level of security that is representative of the threat posed,' says Chikaher. 'Not all methods of surveillance are seen as intrusive. For example, the presence of CCTV in public areas such as lobbies or corridors can often make people feel more secure. However, visiting a hotel should be a leisurely experience, where guests can slow down and relax. They are not prisons, and therefore you can't restrain people too much.'

People watching

Future security policies will continue to rely heavily on emerging technology.

'New measures such as people-recognition technologies, which may use PIN codes, or fingerprint, voice and iris readers, make it harder for people with ulterior motives to enter,' says Chikaher.

'When used to register a guest, this biometric information may then be used to authenticate room access, purchase goods and services, and allow access to additional or privileged facilities, such as gyms and spas.'

Operators shouldn't expect technology to reach a point at which it is able to manage every security concern, though; there are certain human skills and intuitions that machines will never be able to replicate. The very presence of staff on the front lines also goes a long way towards creating warm, welcoming environments that put guests at ease.

'You can have the most sophisticated systems in place, but these can be circumvented if someone is determined and clever enough,' Chikaher warns. 'People have caused atrocities by taking on fraudulent identities to avoid detection, for example.

'You will always need people to be vigilant at reception, and other access points, to watch for suspicious behaviour and guide people in the right direction to where they should and shouldn't be, especially in higher-risk establishments.

'In developing the use of technology in hotel security, the balance between protection and providing the right hospitality experience will always be an integral factor.'

(Source: www.hmi-online.com)

10.3.1   Security systems and equipment

Hotels are not designed with high-security in mind and, generally, do not need to be concerned with high-security at all. Hotels are built to accommodate a travelling public, and high-end resorts and hospitality facilities around the world have aesthetics and comfort, not security and safety, in mind. Hotels are now, however, considered soft targets, being much easier for terrorists to access. Since diplomatic missions have now been transformed into veritable fortresses, and in a world where airports scan every item passengers travel with, it behoves hotels to install adequate security systems to forestall or stop attacks. Taken and adapted from Clifton (2012), systems to be considered are summarised here:

Soft targets

Alarms

- Fire alarms, which have two main objectives: the notification and the suppression of fires. The notification component consists of automatic detectors, manual switches, a control panel, communications interface, and alert devices. The suppression component consists of detectors, water pumps, standpipes, chemical supplies, and sprinklers or chemical emitters.
- Panic alarms, which are manually activated alarms used to provide an extra layer of security in certain areas of the property, best combined with a closed-circuit television (CCTV). These should be installed in such a way as to be easily accessible but not activated accidentally, yet they should also be well-hidden and activated without an assailant's knowledge.
- Intrusion (or burglar) alarms, which are automatically activated through the actions of an intruder in an area that needs to be secured even if the property is open around the clock. Intrusion alarms use different types of sensors or switches. Upon activation, information is sent to a communications centre (external, such as the Police Department, or internal, such as an in-house monitoring system). Some intrusion alarms may be local, in the sense that they simply activate a bell, a light, or even a camera.

Monitoring devices

- Other monitoring devices, which are required for the monitoring of elevators, water boilers, generators, valves, HVAC, and pool equipment. In the past, most of these systems were monitored by humans, but nowadays technology has made it possible for most of these systems to be fitted with sensors, whose readings can be monitored remotely from a central control room. This results to a better and more efficient use of scarce resources.
- Access control, which is a core function of the security department in a hotel and includes locks on doors, remote switches that open locks, officers watching doors, and electronic access systems. Most hotels have access control systems on their guest rooms, and many bolster their security with access control to their restricted areas, elevators, and offices. Electronically controlled access requires a reader (tumblers or pins within a lock; magnetic strip; radio frequency chips; and biometrics), an authorisation (which differs depending on the type of reader), a mechanism (that opens the locks), and a procedure (detailing what should be done and when).

Key systems

- Key control, which is another crucial security responsibility. Key systems consist of a hierarchy of access levels that are generally classified as individual, group or sub-master, master, and grand master – or in some hotels as room, floor, section, zone, and master or emergency. Access is normally based on job requirements; an employee who cleans rooms on one floor does not need a key that fits every room in the property. It is very important that keys are issued and accounted for by one person or department and that only current employees have access to their specific areas.

- Closed-circuit television (CCTV), also known as video surveillance, which is the use of video cameras to transmit a signal to a specific place, on a limited set of monitors. In the recent past, CCTV systems underwent drastic technological development and improvement, especially due to the digital revolution. The main components of a video surveillance system are the camera (input), a switch (control), a recording medium (output), and a monitor (output). It should be noted that the use of CCTV raises issues related to the privacy of those people under surveillance, is covered by legislation in many areas.

  Video surveillance

- Documentation and reporting software, which consist of documenting all activities of the Security Department to show evidence that events occurred, how they occurred, and why they occurred. Daily logs of patrol activities and incident reports of unusual events are the most common and most important of the events that should be documented using paper logs, and a standard table or spreadsheet of date/time, location, officer, and activity is its general structure. Incident reports generally consist of a fact sheet with the statistics of the event and those involved, a narrative, supporting statements, and summary of evidence. Certain reporting software currently available has been specifically designed for the functions of security

- Tracking systems, which take the place of manually logging patrol routes and frequencies of security officers. Tracking systems date back to the middle of last century, when night watchmen would tour a building, wearing a large clock on a strap around their neck – every time they passed a designated check station, there would be a key hanging there. The watchmen would insert the key in their clock, which would log their presence at that time and place. Over the years, the concept has hardly changed; the three components of watchperson, clock, and key have only changed in size and technology. Keys have evolved from magnets to magnetic encoding to barcodes and radio frequencies. Most devices now use a radio frequency (RF) chip read by a handheld reader. RF chips or buttons are placed in strategic places around the property that require regular inspection, such as stairwells, linen rooms, boiler rooms, swimming pools, laundry rooms, and kitchens. Unless the reader has wireless capabilities, its data needs to be downloaded to a database on a regular basis. Once the data has been downloaded, the reporting software allows management to review the activities of patrol officers, taking into account acceptable exceptions such as exceptions if an officer has dealt with a noise complaint or a report in a guest room.

  Tracking systems

- Lost and Found management, in which there are many reporting software products offering modules that help log items left unattended by guests. Since hotels are responsible for these items left in their possession, they must protect the assets. Unlike reporting software, a Lost and Found database needs to have some security functions. A simple spreadsheet would be difficult to secure against having other users delete or edit entries. When creating a programme (or purchasing one), access rights, audit trails and user access should be taken into consideration.

- Employee lockers, which should also be placed under management of the Security Department, because they provide asset protection. Many hotels buy lockers, install them, and let employees use them as they

  Lockers

10

please. To prevent locker abuse, use for criminal activity, or become a nuisance for the company, however, management needs to regulate and manage them. Locks need to be of a type which management, should the need present itself, can open. For this reason, keyed padlocks with a master key are probably best. Combination locks may be too complicated for employees and are difficult to track and change. Lockers are best placed in open areas, such as hallways (due to frequent traffic), where theft can be kept to a minimum. Locker rooms should be avoided, because they may not be fitted with cameras; additionally, thefts are more likely when employees forget to properly secure their lockers in locker rooms.

- A key dispenser, which is generally a cabinet, such as that shown in Figure 10.1, which securely holds several key rings until they are individually unlocked from the cabinet electronically. Access methods can be numeric codes, print readers, magnetic swipes, or other types of access devices. Key dispensers can issue keys without having another human present, or can be set to require two or three people (with access codes) to be present to issue a high security key set. Key sets used in key dispensers are of a type that cannot be opened without damaging the ring, so none of the keys can be removed without authorisation. Key dispensers are expensive, but if a hotel spends a lot of time issuing keys, looking for them when lost, or figuring out who has what and for how long, they may be a wise investment.

FIGURE 10.1 A key dispenser

10.3.2 Managing accidents and emergencies in hotels

Accidents and emergencies can occur unexpectedly at any time in the 24 hours during which hospitality operations are normally in activity. As such, it is imperative that hospitality operations are able to employ adequate arrangements, knowledge and procedures to handle accidents and emergencies at a moment's notice. Hospitality operations therefore establish emergency operating procedure manuals that contain guidelines for guests and employees related to the building and emergency operations, assigning responsibilities and prescribing procedures to protect guests, employees, and other visitors to the property in case of unforeseen emergencies – including fire or other natural or external threats. The excerpt in Text 10.3 is a reminder of the threats to which hotels are exposed; fortunately, in this case no one was hurt and there was relatively little damage. Not all incidents end so well, as there have been instances of multiple deaths occurring over the years due to hotel fires in many parts of the world.

Procedure manuals

TEXT 10.3

Hotel on fire

The Metropolitan Park Lane Was On Fire Yesterday. Literally.

Where: 19 Old Park Lane, London, United Kingdom, W1K 1LB
March 4, 2015 at 9:25 AM | by juliab |

The Metropolitan on London's Park Lane used to be on fire. Everyone who was anyone hung out at the Met Bar, we couldn't get enough of the sleek white rooms, and not a day went by without us fantasizing about eating at Nobu one day.

These days, the scene is a little quieter. But yesterday the hotel actually caught fire, causing the evacuation of 180 guests, 120 staff and needing 40 firefighters to battle the flames. Luckily, nobody was hurt, and it looks like there wasn't a huge amount of damage.

The Evening Standard reports that the fire broke out on scaffolding on the outside of the building, at the first floor level (second floor in American) in the early evening. It started at 5.15pm and was under control by 6.30pm. 'A small amount of the external fascia' on the first floor has been damaged.

So what next? Nobu was closed last night, and though the hotel's Facebook page stated that 'all guests and staff are safe' and promised further updates, there's been nothing else. On Twitter they mention that it was a small fire. But if you try to book a room, there's no availability for either today or tomorrow night. It's an odd time of year to be booked up – maybe they're playing it safe? We'll keep an eye on it.

To prevent such negative consequences, the establishment of rules and procedures is a must for all types of properties ranging from the very small to the very large. Large properties establish fire safety or emergency operations plans, which cover actions to be performed in case of hazardous events like fires, medical situations, deaths, bomb threats, elevator malfunctions, civil unrest, severe storms and tornadoes, earthquakes, the presence of hazardous materials, and keeping guests and employees with disabilities in mind at all times. The following procedures have been adapted from the US state of Missouri City of Clayton's high-rise hotel emergency operating procedures, in which hotels are expected to have their emergency plans approved and constantly reviewed by the city's Fire Department. Each hotel should have a safety plan consisting of three components: a fire evacuation plan; a fire safety plan; and an emergency operations plan.

Large properties

Three components

Fire evacuation plans cover the following topics:

- **High rise buildings** generally sound the alarm on the reported fire floor and the floor above and below. These floors should follow the instructions provided by the alarm message and evacuate the building. If additional floors must be evacuated, the Fire Department will notify those floors using the building fire alarm voice communication system. In some high rise fires, the safest thing to do may be to shelter in place. Hotel management will have to assign emergency responsibilities to key personnel for a smooth and safe evacuation of the building. Management must describe how guests, visitors and employees are to evacuate the building, and should identify two evacuation routes for all occupants as well as provide written information describing the evacuation routes from each area to the designated meeting area outside the building. Signs should be displayed near each exit showing the two evacuation routes. The plan should include instructions like:

Emergency responsibilities

  - Staying calm and moving in an orderly fashion.
  - Notifying someone that you are trapped.
  - Knowing how many doors your office is away from the exits.
  - Staying close to the floor where there is cooler, cleaner air.
  - Covering your mouth with a wet towel or cloth to act as a filter.
  - Closing doors behind you to slow down the spread of smoke and fire.
  - Describing where occupants will be evacuated to. Provide a designated meeting place for occupants to report to after evacuating the building. This area should be outside the building, in an area that is protected and not liable to interfere with firefighting operations.
  - Keeping in mind that sheltering-in-place may be necessary.

- **Procedures for employees who must remain** to operate critical equipment before evacuating. Property managers and building engineers must meet with the Fire Department to provide critical building and tenant information. The Property Manager reports to the front of the building and ensures that:
  - The Fire Department has been notified.
  - Evacuation and emergency procedures are being followed.
  - The condition of the fire floor was reported to the Fire Department.
  - They remain at the front to assist the fire incident commander.

The Building Engineer also reports to the front of the building to:
  - Assume all of the duties described above, in the event of a property manager's absence.
  - Provide the Fire Department with building information.
  - Be prepared to assist the Fire Department in the activation or deactivation of utilities, pumps, generators, HVAC units, fans and other building mechanical equipment.
  - Be able to provide a working knowledge of any construction being done.

If there is no Property Manager or Engineer on site, then it is imperative that there is a valid emergency number and contact person available 24 hours a day.

Emergency number

- Management must develop **procedures for accounting for all occupants** after evacuation. If someone is not accounted for, management must indicate how the Fire Department is to be notified of the missing person or persons. It must be noted that Fire Department personnel will be assigned to search for any missing person or persons. It is critical that the accounting method is accurate, so that Fire Department personnel are not looking for someone who has exited the building but did not report to their assigned meeting area. This prevents wasting time and effort of firefighters which could be spent on firefighting efforts or other rescue operations.

Accounting method

- The management should provide **procedures for identification** and assignments for any **personnel responsible for rescue or emergency medical aid**. They may be assigned as searchers or monitors.

Searchers or monitors

Searchers should:
- Search all rooms (includes restrooms, conference rooms and remote areas).
- Advise all remaining personnel on the floor of the emergency and ensure their evacuation to the appropriate exits.
- Ensure that all non-employees are evacuated. Check the reception area and the elevator lobby.

Monitors for the disabled should:
- Know where disabled workers are and evacuate them.
- Know how to get them to safety (i.e. special ramps, manually leading them).
- Have an assigned place to evacuate the disabled to.
- Be able to recruit persons to assist with the safe evacuation of disabled persons and stay with them once outside if necessary.

Stairway monitors should:
- Take a position at an assigned stairway to assist in the evacuation of personnel.
- Make sure that stairway doors are closed when not in use so that pressurised stairways may render the exit route clear of smoke.
- Inspect stairways before and after evacuation of personnel.
- Instruct personnel to form a single file line, proceed down the stairs on the right side of the stairway to the exit, and meet at the designated outside area.
- Stay at the stairway until the searchers have rendered the floor clear and have started down the stairs.

- Management should describe the **means for notifying occupants and employees** of a fire or emergency. The building fire alarm will be used for fire emergencies only. Management will have to determine a method of notifying occupants of other types of emergencies in the building.

- Management should describe the **means for reporting** fire or other emergencies to the Fire Department. The fire alarm system must report fire

10

alarms to a listed central station alarm monitoring company. This company will then notify the Fire Department of the alarm. The alarm company should regularly test the alarm system and Fire Department notification. Management must also have a system in place to notify the Fire Department or Police Department in the event of emergencies other than fire.

- Management must **identify and assign personnel for emergency contacts** and personnel who can be contacted for further information or explanation of duties under the plan. They must provide a list of persons with appropriate phone numbers to be contacted in case of an emergency. They must also provide a list of personnel who can answer questions regarding the plan and assignment of personnel for emergency contacts.

Familiar

- The management must provide a **description of the emergency voice/alarm communication system** alert tone and pre-programmed voice messages, so that occupants will be familiar with the message and know what to do when they hear the message.

Fire safety plans include:

Fire is
discovered

- The procedure for reporting a fire or other emergency. When a fire is discovered:
  - Close the door to the fire area.
  - Pull the closest Fire Alarm. Pull stations are normally located near an exit from the floor or the building and will automatically notify the Fire Department.
  - Call the emergency number (note that you should not call from the fire floor)
  - Provide the following information, and do not hang up until told to do so:
    - Your name
    - Your company's name
    - The guestroom, suite and floor number
    - What is on fire – the exact location of the fire
    - Your telephone number
  - The operator should relay the information to the Fire Department and to management.
- Site plans indicating the following:
  - Occupancy assembly points
  - Locations of fire hydrants
  - Normal routes of Fire Department vehicle access.
- Floor plans identifying the locations of the following:
  - Exits
  - Primary evacuation routes
  - Secondary evacuation routes
  - Accessible egress routes
  - Areas of refuge
  - Manual fire alarm boxes
  - Portable fire extinguishers
  - Fire alarm annunciators and controls.
- A list of major fire hazards associated with the normal use and occupancy of the premises, including maintenance and housekeeping procedures.
- Identification and assignment of personnel responsible for maintenance of systems and equipment installed to prevent or control fires.

10

- Identification and assignment of personnel responsible for maintenance, housekeeping and controlling fuel hazard sources.

All employees must receive training on fire safety and evacuation plans during new employee orientation, and at least annually thereafter. Employees must be trained in fire prevention, evacuation, and safety.

The emergency operations plan
This plan addresses emergencies other than fire emergencies, such as medical situations, deaths, bomb threats, elevators, civil unrest, severe weather, earthquakes, hazardous materials, while keeping guests and employees with disabilities in mind at all times.

Medical emergencies
Medical emergencies may involve guests, employees, or visitors and can happen at any time. Management and staff should be prepared to act promptly if confronted with such an emergency. Time can be very crucial and hysteria can quickly hinder any good intentions. Management is suggested to keep an unlocked, fully stocked first aid kit and first aid guide centrally located on the premises. It is highly recommended that some employees take a First Aid or Cardiopulmonary resuscitation (CPR) course. It is also recommended that Automatic External Defibrillators (AEDs) are installed in the building. Apart from the regular horizontal response time to the building, high rise buildings have a vertical response time for emergency medical personnel as well. The vertical response time reflects the time it takes for the Emergency Medical Service (EMS) crew to get their equipment into an elevator and to the patient on the floor above or below the entry floor. Personnel trained in the use of AEDs can utilise these units to provide lifesaving defibrillation for persons in cardiac arrest prior to the arrival of the EMS crew. During a medical emergency, the following actions should be taken by employees:
- Remain calm. Remaining calm will help to keep the patient calm.

Training
Time

10

- Stay with the patient, if possible, no matter how minor it may seem. You might witness crucial changes in their condition.
- Send another person to call Security or the emergency number and supply the following information, and do not hang up until told to do so:
  - Building address
  - Room number, floor level, or other location
  - Nature of the problem
  - Condition of the patient
- Secure an elevator and meet the EMS crew in the lobby of the building.
- Try to gather the patient's medications, if any – the paramedics will need these.
- Gather or copy common information – name, address, phone number, birth date.
- Clear a path for the EMS crew and keep crowds from gathering.

Deaths

Mortal accident, homicide, or suicide

- Deaths can occur anywhere. They may be the result of any number of situations or circumstances, such as choking, having a heart attack, or any number of medical problems. Death can also be the result of an obvious mortal accident, homicide, or suicide. The safety plan should include the personnel plan with the following actions to be taken by employees:
- Stay calm. Do not add more confusion to the situation.
- Call the emergency department and explain the situation to the dispatcher. They will contact the appropriate city departments.
- If there are staff members or guests who have some medical training and feel they can help, and the scene is not an obvious crime scene involving a non-viable person, they can intervene.
- The dispatcher should be made aware of what is being done and their instructions, if any, should be followed.
- Try not to disturb the area around the deceased and keep crowds from gathering.
- Someone should gather information about the deceased, as incoming dispatched personnel will need this information promptly:
  - Name
  - Address
  - Date of birth
  - Phone number
  - Social security number or similar national identification number
  - Current medications
  - Medical history

Bomb threats

Anxiety and panic

Bomb threats are becoming universal, affecting occupancies large and small. The general rule is that a bomb threat caller desires to create an atmosphere of anxiety and panic, which will result in the disruption of normal work activities. The safety plan should include the following actions to be taken by employees:
- Remain calm
- Have the police notified immediately.
- Discreetly attract the attention of a co-worker.
- Keep the caller on the line as long as possible.

- Ask the caller to repeat parts of the message.
- Try to buy time – this is very important.
- Write down the following:
  - The complete message word for word.
  - Follow the checklist as shown in Figure 10.2.
  - Add any information you feel is relevant and not covered by the checklist.

FIGURE 10.2 Telephone operator checklist – bomb threat

TELEPHONE OPERATOR CHECK LIST - BOMB THREAT

If you receive a bomb threat, **keep calm**. Have a pre-arranged signal to alert a manager or supervisory personnel to listen to and, if possible, record the call. Advise the caller, if you can, that the detonation of the bomb may kill or injure innocent people. Obtain as much of the following information as possible:

Where is the bomb?

What time is it set to go off?

What kind of bomb is it?   If dynamite, how many sticks?

Method of activation? Mechanical, movement of clock, chemical action, etc.

What kind of package or box?

Method of deactivation?

What is your name, address, telephone number?

Is the call a hoax or legitimate? Hoax _____ Legitimate _____

Have there been, or will there be other calls? How old are you?

Why did you set the bomb?

Judge the Voice: Man _____ Woman _____ Child _____ Age _____ Drinking? Yes _____ No _____

Other: _____

Listen for Background Noise:

	CHECK IF HEARD	DESCRIPTION
MUSIC		
PEOPLE TALKING		
CARS OR TRUCKS		
AIRPLANE		
CHILDREN OR BABIES		
MACHINE NOISE		
KEYBOARD STROKES		
OTHER		

10

Decisions to evacuate are made by the building owner/tenant in conjunction with the Police and Fire Departments. Owners/tenants are often asked to assist with the search for the bomb. This is because the police are not familiar with the workplace and management and employees will be more able to easily identify something out of place or suspicious.

Elevators

Elevators are one of the safest modes of transportation there is. However, from time to time they may malfunction. Since there are many varieties of elevators, management needs to be familiar with their specific make, model, and owner's manual of operation. Management should design a plan regarding procedures in the case of an elevator malfunction, and these procedures should include the following information for anyone trapped within:

Elevator
malfunction

- Remain calm.
- Use the phone in the elevator car to call for help.
- Make noise if there is not a phone available.
- Do not attempt to crawl out of the elevator cab when the doors are open between floors. Remain in the cab or serious injury may result.
- Do not try to force open an elevator door.

The Fire Department will secure the elevator and safely remove the trapped individual(s) as soon as they are able.

Emergency phones should be in all elevator cars. During fires, the elevators will be recalled to the primary or secondary landing zones. In the event of a fire, do not attempt to use the elevators. They will be out of service to prevent them from being called to the fire floor. Firefighters will be able to take control of the elevators for firefighting operations.

Demonstrations, Property Crimes, Crimes against Persons, and Active Shooter situations

Civil instability

Management should make preparations in advance. Should civil instability erupt, everyone may need to leave the area. Management should establish an emergency plan that includes where everyone can go, including a secondary location in case someone is unable to get to the first location. Make sure all members of staff know the plan. Everyone must know the locations of police stations and hospitals in the area. Individual employees should keep a backpack filled with emergency rations and supplies, as well as a small amount of non-perishable food and bottled water. It should be easily carried, thus not be too heavy. Everyone should have an emergency credit or payment card and a small supply of cash readily available.

Demonstrations
- If a demonstration reaches a point where there is potential for danger, or possible law violations are occurring, contact the Police Department or call the emergency number:
  - Notify dispatch of the location of the demonstration
  - Indicate the estimated number of people involved in the demonstration
  - Indicate whether individuals are violent or threatening anyone
  - Indicate whether any weapons are involved
  - Follow directions of emergency personnel

10

- If you are unable to safely leave, lock yourself in a safe area until emergency personnel can respond. Make sure all doors and windows are locked. If possible, have a cell phone for communication with emergency personnel.
- Remain calm. Do not attempt to intervene or confront any individuals involved in the disturbance. Avoid engaging in discussions or attempting to negotiate with individuals engaged in a civil disturbance. Wait calmly until emergency personnel arrives.

Crimes against persons/property
- Contact the Police Department or call the emergency number.
- Obtains and provide a good description of the suspect(s).
- Do not intervene, especially if the suspect or suspects are armed.
- Be a good witness.
- Stay safe.

Overall, when in an emergency situation, individuals should make sure they have a supply of the following:

Individuals

- Water
- Necessary prescription medications
- Food that does not require cooking
- First aid supplies
- Lighting (in the event of a power outage)
- Sanitation supplies (in the event that the municipal water system is unusable), including cleaning supplies and toilet supplies
- A way to stay warm in severe cold or harsh winter conditions
- Over-the-counter medications and/or herbal remedies to treat illnesses at home
- Survival and first aid manuals (hard copies in case the internet and power grid are down)
- Alternative communications devices (such as a hand-crank radio) to stay up to date on current events
- Off-grid entertainment: arts and craft supplies, puzzles, games, books, crossword or word search puzzles, needlework, journals

Active shooter
In the event that an active shooter enters the property, all employees should consider the following options: Run, Hide, or Fight. Each employee should do what they believe will offer the best chance of safety for themselves and others. There are many online video tutorials on the Run/Hide/Fight strategy available.

Run, Hide, or Fight

10

Severe weather
Natural disasters such as severe weather (e.g. thunderstorms, tornadoes, cyclones or hurricanes) are a potential threat in many areas of the world. The following suggested areas of responsibility are designed to provide safety, minimise the loss of assets, and reduce the disruption of normal operations. The various weather services will report the movement of severe weather that may present a threat to a particular area; if the Security Department feels that guests or employees are in danger of harm, they should contact the floors and implement pre-set emergency procedures. Even though it may cause some inconvenience, occupants should always comply. The safety plan should contain the following instructions:

Comply

Actions to be taken:
- If time permits, take the stairwell to the basement level for shelter.
  - This is generally the safest location
  - Do not go to the 1st floor/lobby or outside of the building.
- If imminent danger exists, move to the centre of the building and seek cover under a heavy piece of furniture, e.g. a desk or table.
  - The centre of the building may include stairways, restrooms (toilets), or rooms without any windows.
- Keep your radio or television tuned to a local broadcasting station for information.
- Above all, remain calm and assist those who need guidance.

The Security Department should also monitor the weather's progression and give the 'All Clear' to occupants when the threat of severe weather has passed.

Earthquakes

An earthquake will cause some alarm; it is imperative that everyone reacts in a calm fashion if one should occur. The quake itself will only last a few moments; the damage may be extensive and devastating, however. In those areas of the world prone to earthquakes, the safety plan of the hospitality property should include instructions on what to do in the event of an earthquake and how to react afterwards (i.e. do's and don'ts). There should also be a list of required contents for an earthquake kit, and the safety plan should contain the following instructions:

- Actions to be taken during the earthquake
  - Remain calm and assist others.
  - Do not use elevators.
  - Do not exit the building.
  - Take cover under a sturdy object or move to the centre of the building.
  - If you are outdoors, try to get into an open area away from power lines and buildings.
- Actions to be taken after the earthquake
  - Remain calm and assist others.
  - Check for fire; if possible, extinguish any fires found.
  - Do not use matches or lighters as natural gas may be present.
  - Know where your earthquake kit is and retrieve it.
  - Check for damage to utilities and appliances. Shut them off if possible. Everyone should be aware of power lines, leaking natural gas, spilled chemicals, flooding water.
  - Use caution when moving about. The building may have structural weaknesses, or may have (partially) collapsed. Aftershocks may occur. These may further weaken the integrity of the structure.

There are no set rules which will fully eliminate danger. However, danger and injury can be reduced by following the guidelines above. The property and its management should be prepared to be self-sufficient for 48 to 72 hours following the earthquake. The Fire Department may not be able to respond, and help may be delayed due to circumstances.

Hazardous materials

Incidents involving hazardous materials can occur anywhere and at any time. Whether large or small, an incident involving hazardous materials can

Extensive and devastating

cause serious problems if not handled quickly and properly. Hazardous materials are not necessarily confined to chemicals used in industrial applications, and not all buildings have hazardous materials located on site. But those that do, need a plan of action before any problem arises. The safety plan of the property should contain the following instructions in addition to any manufacturers' recommendations tailored to the particular chemicals: *Chemicals*

- Close off the exposed area and leave immediately.
- Have an inventory list of all on-site chemicals.
- Know what to do you have been in contact with any potentially hazardous chemicals under uncontrolled circumstances.
- Notify the Fire Department and make sure you have the list of on-site chemicals and material safety data sheets (MSDS).   *Material safety data sheets*
- Keep in mind that it may be harmful to help persons who have come in contact with the chemical or chemicals concerned. Hazardous material incidents must be handled by trained Hazardous Materials Response personnel using specialised equipment.
- Have a designated person or deputy remain at the front of the building to provide the Fire Department with the inventory lists and number of exposed victims.

Under occupational safety and health regulations, management is required to maintain, on-site, a full list of MSDSs for all hazardous substances used, stored, or produced in the facility, and these MSDSs must be accessible to all the employees.

Employees with disabilities during emergencies

Taken with permission from the Disability Alliance BC's Workplace emergency planning for workers with disabilities: A handbook for employers and workers (2008), the following information provides insights into an employer's responsibility to provide a safe place for all employees, including those employees with disabilities. A workplace presents many potential hazards   *Hazards* for workers with disabilities during an emergency or disaster. It is important that all workers and employers are aware of these hazards and know what to do to prevent injury or death. Planning for alternative communication, inclusive evacuation, and recovery procedures is of critical importance to employee safety in hazardous situations. Knowledge, planning, and practice will protect workers with disabilities and save lives.

There are many examples of how disabilities impact emergency planning.   *Examples* The deaf or hard of hearing may not have the ability to hear or react to auditory emergency warning systems or aural instructions. Visual disabilities af-   *Visual* fect a person's ability to visually identify escape routes, directional information, instructions, objects or hazards. This will increase their evacuation time. Mobility disabilities may affect a person's ability to independently   *Mobility* leave the worksite, use stairs, or open doors. Respiratory disabilities may   *Respiratory* affect a person's ability to walk long distances and perform tasks that require excessive physical activity, such as evacuating a building. These limitations may be exacerbated by smoke, dust, fumes or chemicals. Speech   *Speech* disabilities, such as difficulties with articulation, voice strength, language expression or total loss of speech, will affect a person's ability for spoken communication during an emergency. Cognitive disabilities may affect a per-   *Cognitive* son's ability to respond to emergencies by causing memory loss, problems with orientation, distractibility, difficulty with perception, and difficulty with

10

Mental

thinking logically. Mental illness or mental disorders are health conditions that are characterised by alterations in thinking, mood or behaviour, which may be exacerbated in an emergency situation.

Determining staff/volunteer needs and personnel resources starts with assessing staff and volunteer needs during an emergency. This should be done by establishing a process within the emergency planning consisting of:

- Requiring self-assessment and self-disclosure of workers and volunteers with disabilities, and obtaining information on their needs during emergencies.
- Enabling workers to notify management of changes in their (dis)ability, or the development of temporary disabilities, such as recent injuries or surgeries.
- Maintaining a list for emergency personnel of the workers who need assistance during emergencies and their location in the building.
- Ensuring that the collection of personal information concerning an employee's disability for the purposes of the workplace emergency plan is in compliance with applicable Privacy Acts.
- Determining accommodation options for emergency notification and evacuation. Asking employees who need accommodation for their suggestions, working together and planning for changes in the employee's condition.

The aforementioned recommendations should be followed by identifying staff and volunteers to assist workers with disabilities during an emergency. This is done by establishing a network of co-workers who can assist persons with disabilities during emergencies. When identifying this network, the following should be considered:

- Network members should be physically and mentally capable of performing the task.
- Network members do not need assistance themselves.
- Network members should work the same hours and in the same area as the person they will be assisting.
- Disabled employees should be involved in selecting those who will be trained to assist them during an emergency (a minimum of two assisting individuals is recommended).

10

Everybody says I look
just like my mom!

It is important to carry out an assessment of non-structural hazards and barriers in the workplace by:

Non-structural hazards

- Doing a walk-through of the facility with disabled employees and identify barriers to successful evacuation.
- Looking for objects in the workplace that may fall and injure employees, as well as any objects that may obstruct passages or could hinder disabled individuals from safely exiting the building.

Address any identified worksite hazards and barriers for workers with disabilities by:
- Establishing a party responsible for addressing any identified hazards and barriers
- Establishing a process for how any hazards are to be addressed
- Monitoring existing hazards
- Establishing a system for reporting new (potential) hazards

The ability to communicate quickly with all employees in the building is critical during an emergency. Management should consider:

Communicate quickly

- Ensuring that all employees and visitors – including those who are deaf, hard of hearing, or suffering from visual impairments – have access to the same information in a detailed, appropriate, and timely manner.
- Putting multiple methods in place to notify individuals of emergency plans and procedures; providing alternative formats appropriate to the workforce.
- During emergency training sessions and meetings, providing sign language interpreters, assistive listening devices or other aids to enable effective communication with .
- Installing visual alarms/lighted fire strobes for employees who are deaf or hard of hearing.
- Providing tactile/Braille signage and maps and/or audible directional signage to assist workers with visual disabilities who may need to navigate smoke-filled exit routes.
- Providing colour coded fire doors and exit ways for workers with cognitive disabilities.
- Providing a picture book of drill procedures for workers with cognitive disabilities.

If evacuations are required, it is the responsibility of management to ensure the same level of safety for all employees during the evacuation. Management should also include the safe evacuation of personnel during non-business hours – shift workers and building cleaners – in their emergency plans. Notwithstanding management's responsibilities, employees with disabilities also have responsibilities in such instances. Disabled employees should:

Non-business hours

Responsibilities

- Be familiar with the building and the evacuation options – exits, stairwells, ramps, and areas of refuge.
- Know the workplace emergency evacuation plan.
- Work with management to select co-workers able to assist them in case of an emergency.
- Participate in emergency drills.
- Be aware of emergency notification systems at the workplace.
- Alert security personnel when entering the building after non-business hours, informing them of where they will be located and the assistance they might need.

10

During an emergency, staff may be required to be interacting with people with various types of disabilities for any number of reasons. The following is a list of ways to interact with people, sorted by individual disabilities:

- Visual disabilities
  - Announce your presence.
  - Address the individual naturally and directly.
  - Ask the individual what kind of assistance they need.
  - Describe the action needed to be taken in advance.
  - Describe any obstacles in the path.
  - Let the individual take your arm for guidance; do not grab them unannounced.
  - After evacuating an individual with a visual disability to a place of safety, do not leave them unassisted.
  - If the individual has a service animal, ensure the animal is evacuated with that person.
  - Do not pet or feed service animals on duty.
- Deaf or hard of hearing
  - Flick the lights when entering the work areas of a person who is deaf or hard of hearing to get their attention.
  - Use pen and paper; write slowly and let the individual read along as you write.
  - Make sure the individual has understood the urgency of the message.
  - Be patient.
  - Face the individual directly and speak naturally for those who can lip-read.
  - Provide the individual with a flashlight for signalling their location if separated from the group while evacuating, and to facilitate lip-reading in the dark.
- People with cognitive and learning disabilities
  - Always accompany an individual with a cognitive or learning disability because they may be confused by emergency instructions and signs for evacuation.
  - Use simple directions and instructions.
  - Be patient – the more severe the disability, the greater the expected response time.
  - Be prepared to bodily remove the individual from danger if they are unable to respond to instructions.
  - Communicate with them in a calm manner.
- People with mobility disabilities
  - Always ask the individual about the best way to assist them.
  - Do not hold onto a person's wheelchair if not prompted, as it is part of their personal space.

10.3.3   Handling other security issues in hotels

Threats to guests' privacy

It is the duty of management to protect the privacy of their guests, and perhaps particularly those in the public eye. Steps must be taken to ensure that information about guests is not disclosed to third parties.

Threats to guests' property

In the interest of protecting the reputation of the hotel, it is also important that management ensures the safety of guests' property from forces both

Public eye

internal as well as external. If, for example, the hotel is located in a relatively unsafe geographical area, guests should be made aware of the situation, especially if they intend to go out at night.

Rising demand for dangerous activities

A new issue is the demand by guests and groups to be allowed to experience high-risk or dangerous activities as a part of their overall experience. The need to be competitive with other hotels and services is driving hotels to offer or allow guests to partake in unusual and risky pursuits. Some examples of activities being allowed or even offered are wild or exotic animals for special events, bungee-jumping, water activities such as parasailing and jet skiing, extreme sports, fireworks displays, and fire walking. In these situations, the Security Department's role should be to ensure activities are either performed in the safest manner possible or outsourced to a professional company that possesses the appropriate skills and levels of insurance coverage to handle such matters.

Unusual and risky pursuits

Threats to asset security and theft

Safe lodging and a hotel's reputation for safety are critical if not paramount to ensure success. Management must properly provide for the protection and maintenance of their assets, whether human, physical or intangible. A hotel's reputation and standard conduct of business is based on the protection afforded to guests, employees, visitors, contractors, and the physical structure of the premises and anything pertinent to the property contained therein. Some special characteristics of the hospitality industry make it more vulnerable to theft. These can be summarised as follows:

Reputation

- Despite the expansion of electronic means of settling transactions using credit and debit cards and the use of charge accounts, many transactions are still carried out using cash, especially in hotel bars and restaurants. Some of these outlets also operate all day and night, which requires many shift changes. These revenue departments do accumulate lots of cash over the course of a day, making more cash available for theft.

Cash

- Items found in hospitality inventory are generally of a variety that employees and guests would employ for their private use. Additionally, some of these items are of high value relative to their size or weight, and can be easily consumed on the spot or hidden to be taken away later. Products such as quality wines, seafood, steak, and expensive containers of food products are valuable to dishonest employees who may remove them for personal use or for sale to third parties.

Hospitality inventory

Private use

10

It is also unfortunate that some employees, but especially guests, have a propensity to pilfer items of hotel inventory as 'souvenirs'. Guests have been known to leave their hotels with a variety of items – virtually anything not securely fastened down, including paintings, valuable decorations, towels, mats, sheets, blankets, coat hangers and lamps. Other guests may simply leave the property without paying their bills, and such guests, called walk-outs, skippers or runners, have been divided into the following three groups by Abbott and Lewry (1999, p. 72):

Souvenirs

Walk-outs

- 'Accidentals' are those guests who simply forget to pay. They may be confused over who was due to settle an account, or may genuinely forget an 'extras' bill. Forgetfulness is a real possibility, so hotel management

Accidentals

should always be tactful when contacting a walk-out. Genuine 'accidentals' are normally highly embarrassed and pay up immediately.

Opportunists
- 'Opportunists' are those who had every intention of paying their bills when they first checked in, but who subsequently realised that they could get away without doing so. Hotels whose design allows guests to reach the car park without passing by the reception desk have found a number of their guests yielding to this kind of temptation.

Premeditators
- 'Premeditators' are those guests who never had any intention of paying in the first place, and who sometimes go to considerable lengths in order to avoid doing so. These guests generally stay for short periods and move to other hotels as soon as payment is demanded. Experienced hotel staff can often detect premeditated walkouts.

Strict internal control
To prevent employee theft and embezzlement, management has to establish strict internal control methods and procedures for employees at all levels to follow. These methods and procedures ensure that employees keep to management policies, operate efficiently, and also protect the organisation's assets from waste, theft, and embezzlement. In addition to the various internal control proposals previously indicated in Chapter 8, such methods and procedures should be based on the following principles:
- Instituting management leadership and supervision in which a management board should establish the policies at the highest level, which should then be communicated and enforced at all levels. Employees are **Honest** generally honest but may yield to temptations in the absence of good internal control systems. Management's involvement in the internal control process leads the way for employees to follow. It should be about 'doing what we do' and not only doing 'what we tell you to do'.
- Establishing preventative instead of reactive control procedures, which is based on Benjamin Franklin's adage that 'An ounce of prevention is worth a pound of cure', and that it is thus preferable to eliminate the opportunity for theft and embezzlement than to play detective after the crime. In **Prevention** the long run, prevention is more cost effective and productive, and with proper preventative procedures, nothing will be left to detective actions.

Effective monitoring
- Enabling effective monitoring of the control system in which all existing control systems must be constantly monitored to ensure that they still provide the needed output, and are also flexible enough to be modified if need be. Having employees spend time and energy filling in forms that are not checked is both expensive and discouraging. If a reporting form needs to be changed or is redundant, then it should be modified, or replaced entirely with a more adequate version.

Records
- Maintaining adequate records should be an important consideration for effective internal control. These forms, reports and records include such forms as registration cards, time cards, folios, guest cheques, payroll cheques, purchase orders and receiving reports. These documents should be designed in such a way as to allow all their users to easily understand them. To make the control process easier, these documents should be pre-numbered, and should be only prepared at the time of the transaction to reduce the possibility of errors. When pre-numbered documents are issued, employees receiving the documents should be required to sign for them to establish responsibility and accountability. The accounting department should oversee all documents, even though they are actually used by employees in other departments. Using good forms, reports and records causes employees to be more careful, reducing theft

and fraud to a minimum. The types of forms, reports, and other records used in the internal control system depend entirely on the size and type of establishment.

- Establishing written procedure manuals. Every job or activity within the hospitality industry can be described in written form in what is called the procedure manual. This manual should list the details of each position, describing how and when to carry out each activity. This informs employees of what the policy and procedures are. These written procedures are particularly important in the hospitality industry, where employee turnover is relatively high, and continuous employee training to support the system of internal control is necessary. Procedure manuals help maintain consistent job performance especially as new employees are concerned, as well as in cases where employees are called to temporarily fill in for absent colleagues.

  Procedure manual

- Designing organisational charts. In very small operations, one owner/ manager can effectively supervise all employees; most operations, however, are divided into various functional areas, such as general management, human resources, sales and marketing, production, finance and accounting, and property operations and maintenance. The organisational chart displays the organisational structure of the operation indicating the relationships and relative ranks of its parts and positions or jobs. Employees must know the organisational chart and respect the chain of command, except in exceptional situations like management fraud where employees may be required to skip some of the links in the chain. For more information on organisational charts, refer to Chapter 2.

  Organisational chart

- Attributing responsibility. Responsibility for a specific task or activity should always be given to a single individual who is then fully informed of their duties and obligations. This attribution of responsibility lets management know exactly where to start investigations in case of problems. However, this principle should also be viewed from the employee's perspective. Since employees are responsible for their actions, any conditions must allow them to carry their responsibilities effectively; no one should be allowed to interfere in another's actions except after proper delegation of the duties.

  Responsibility

- Establishing proper authorisation procedures and creating audit trails. All business transactions must be properly authorised by supervisory persons. Management's authorisation can be given in two forms: general or specific. General authorisation is provided to employees for the normal performance of their duties, such as selling items on the menus at listed prices. Specific authorisation is needed in case there are to be deviations from the general authorisation, such as putting a limit on the amount of fixed assets that can be purchased; if that limit is to be passed, the CEO must approve by a written authorisation. The audit trail documents each transaction from the time it was initiated to its final recording in the operation's general ledger. A good audit trail ensures the possibility of tracking transactions from start to finish.

  Authorisation procedures

  10

- Maintaining a division of duties which is also referred to as a 'separation of duties' or 'segregation of duties'. This principle means that no one involved in any transaction should have complete control of that transaction. This is done by separating the custody of assets from the record-keeping or accountability of those assets. This segregation of duties prevents theft and fraud while at the same time detecting theft and fraud. This principle can only be thwarted in cases of collusion whereby

  Division of duties

two or more employees decide to defraud the establishment by acting together.

Splitting responsibilities

- Separating responsibility for related transactions, so that the work of one employee is verified by the work of another. This keeps one person from having too much control over assets and may prevent theft. Splitting responsibilities in related transactions does not mean there are unnecessary and costly duplication of work, but instead means there are two tasks that must be carried out by two separate employees for purposes of control. The additional costs of the second person's time conducting the verification are normally more than mitigated by the increased net income resulting from a reduction of losses due to undetected errors.

Selection, training and supervision

- Establishing careful selection, training and supervision procedures for employees. In the hospitality industry, it is very important to have competent, trustworthy and well-trained employees to ensure sustainable and profitable operations. This means that hospitality establishments should have good systems in place for pre-employment screening of job applicants, selecting employees, providing adequate employee orientation, on-the-job training, and periodic evaluation. Personnel at all levels must be trained properly for them to be able to accomplish the activities required of them. Employees must know what those activities entail and also how to carry them out. Employees should be able to recognise the importance of their particular activities and jobs in the overall objectives of the establishment. Supervisory personnel should have the skills necessary to maintain the standards of the establishment and motivate personnel under their supervision. The hotel operation should also offer adequate reward policies for its employees, with clearly defined future possibilities in case of continued employment.

- Limiting the number of employees with access to assets such as cash and inventory. The greater the number of employees with access to cash or inventory, the greater the risk of losses – whether by theft or through simple mismanagement. Responsibility for an asset cannot be fixed to a single employee if all other employees have unlimited and uncontrolled access to that asset. Additionally, the quantities of such assets should be maintained at the barest minimum. Limiting access and maintaining low quantities may lead to some operational conflicts, however. Hotel operations are required to perform a balancing act of ensuring there is always enough quantity to prevent running out of stock; the limitation of access to assets should not be so cumbersome as to severely restrict efficient operations. `Access to assets`

- Wherever feasible, employees (especially those in accounting, cash-handling and other clerical positions) should be rotated. Employees who know they are not going to be doing the same job for a long time are less likely to be dishonest; job rotation also prevents employees from becoming bored from constantly carrying out the same tasks. Rotation provides flexibility for job assignments and gives employees a better understanding of how jobs relate to each other. Scheduling mandatory vacations for all employees should be part of management's human resources' policies. Employees may be discouraged from theft or fraud if they know that, during their vacation, some other individual will control the assets they are currently managing and that, if theft or fraud has occurred, it may be discovered during their a vacation. In situations where theft or fraud has not yet occurred, the new individual may discover weaknesses in the control system not previously reported or apparent. This may lead to the creation of new preventative internal control measures. `Rotation`

- Performing surprise checks by other employees as well as carrying out independent performance checks. Random but expected checks of cash, merchandise and inventories should be frequently carried out by independent employees. Such checks should be frequent but not routine or systematic. Top management should occasionally get involved in the process. In most hospitality operations, independent performance checks are carried out by internal auditors. An internal audit is the appraisal of the operating and accounting controls of an organisation to ensure that internal control procedures are being followed and assets are adequately safeguarded. Internal auditors are responsible for appraising the effectiveness of operating and accounting controls, and for verifying the reliability of forms, records, reports, and other supporting documentation to ensure that internal control policies and procedures are being followed and assets are adequately safeguarded. All companies should undergo periodic external audits carried out by independent external auditors. External auditors do not only verify financial statements, but also study and test the internal accounting control system. The stronger the internal accounting control system, the more it can be relied upon; all other things being equal, a strong internal control system requires less external auditing. `Surprise checks` `Internal audit`

- Establishing forms, budgets and internal reports. Properly evaluating results requires forms and reports providing information about all aspects `Information`

10

of the business. These forms and reports provide management with the information needed to determine if standards are respected or if standards can be improved, and to take corrective actions in case of. Budgets help ensure that management goals are attained. Examples of internal reports include daily operations' reports, weekly forecasts, future bookings' reports and the annual budgets, some of which are already covered in Chapter 8.

Physical controls • Setting up physical controls and using machines. Physical controls include security devices and measures for safeguarding the assets of the property, such as CCTV cameras, safes, locked storerooms, and locked storage compartments, as well as mechanical and electronic equipment used in executing and recording transactions. Machines vastly reduce the possibilities of theft or fraud and should be set up wherever possible. Installing machines where employees are no longer required to perform a task manually also has the advantage of reducing labour costs and improving efficiency. Common machines include the front office billing and audit equipment, bar and restaurant cash registers, point-of-sale systems (POS), and mechanical or electronic drink-dispensing bar equipment.

• Employees with access to cash, records, or stores as well as top management should be bonded through an insurance policy called the fidelity bond. The fidelity bond protects the operation from losses incurred by employee dishonesty, because the establishment is reimbursed for up to the face value of the insurance policy for the loss suffered.

Summary

▶ Hotels face the dilemma of having to keep their assets as secure as possible while at the same time keeping their properties open and welcoming.

▶ Managing safety and security is vital to delivering hospitality.

▶ A safety and security manager establishes plans related such topics as bomb threats, emergency communication and evacuation, employee safety training, fire safety systems, guest and employee safety, and room key security.

▶ There are rules and regulations to ensure that hospitality operations practices and procedures are done in such a way that the environment in which guests are received and employees work is a safe one.

▶ While large hotel chains have very elaborate safety and security procedures, management in small hospitality operations should endeavour to:
- control hazards and develop a safety plan
- continually inspect the workplace
- investigate incidents
- maintain adequate records
- make safety a fundamental part of the business
- regularly talk with employees
- train employees

▶ With increased industry focus on safety and security issues, there are many security systems designed to prevent, detect, respond to, and recover from serious security incidents. Some of these systems are:
- Fire alarms
- Panic alarms
- Intrusion or burglar alarms
- Monitoring devices
- Access control systems
- Key control systems and dispensers
- CCTV
- Documentation and reporting software
- Tracking systems
- Lost and found management systems
- Employee lockers

10

▶ As accidents and emergencies can occur unexpectedly and at any time, it is imperative that hospitality operations have adequate arrangements, knowledge and procedures to handle them. Any hotel should have a safety plan consisting of:
- a fire evacuation plan
- a fire safety plan
- an emergency operations plan

10

Questions and assignments for reflection

1   Hotels are caught in the dilemma of keeping their assets as secure as possible while keeping their properties open and welcoming. How should they organise and ensure a safe and secure environment for guests and staff?

2   Consider the safety programmes established by hotels. How elaborate do you think safety and security programmes should be? Which parts would you omit and why?

3   Why is it important for management to include employees when developing safety programmes?

4   What importance do you see in formulating a fire evacuation plan for a hospitality operation?

5   Review the emergency operations plan presented in this chapter. What do you consider to be its most important feature(s)? Explain your choice(s).

10

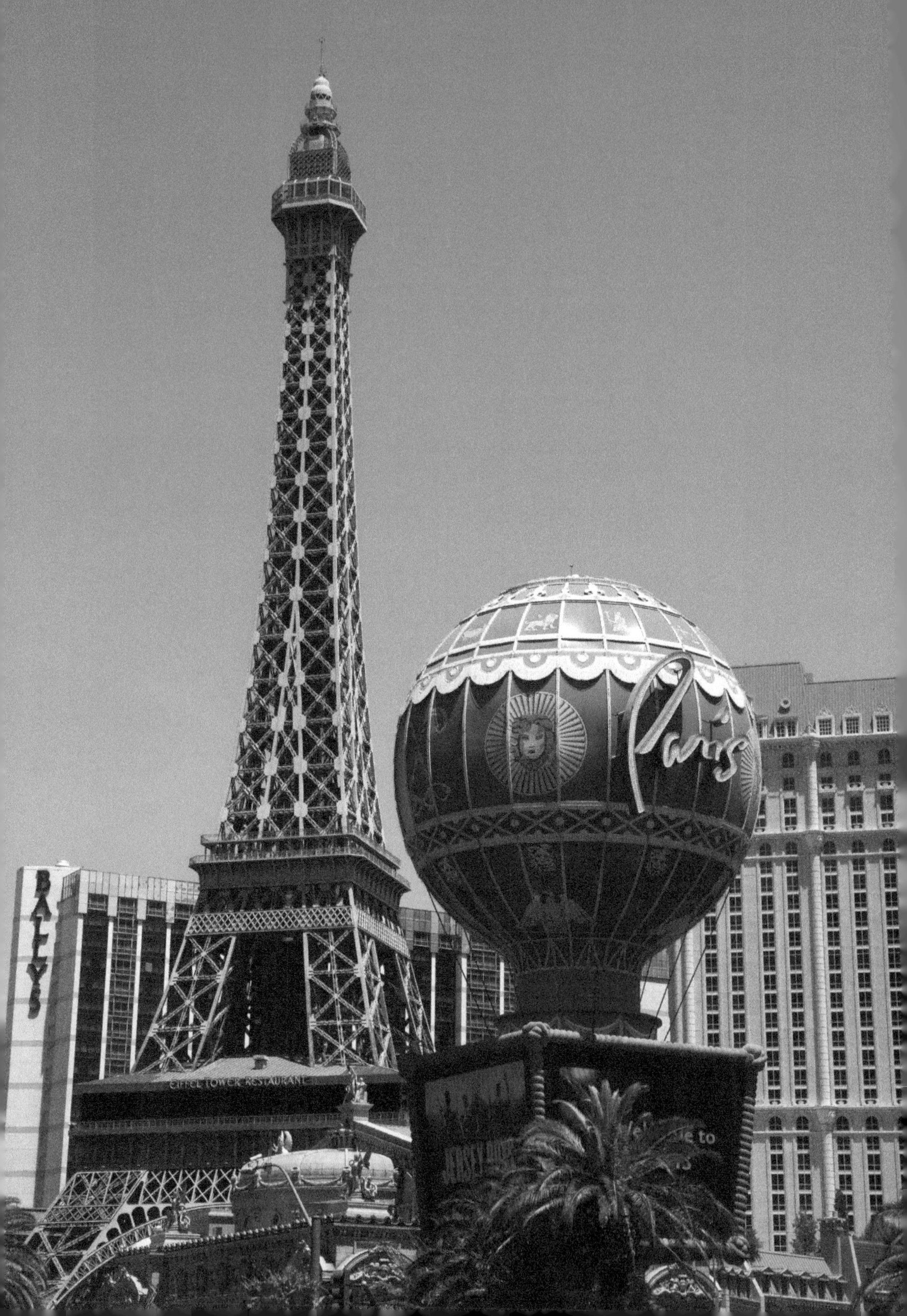
BALLYS
EIFFEL TOWER RESTAURANT
Paris

11

Managing Hospitality Services

Prof. C. Lashley

11.1 Introduction

The management of service experiences to consumers presents all organisations with difficulties. The nature of the service encounter is such that it is perishable, and involves face-to-face interactions between service providers and consumers; and standardising techniques like those employed in manufacturing cannot easily be adopted. Service interactions are also intangible, and represent unique encounters between the service provider and the served. This chapter explores these issue and shows how service firms have attempted to overcome the difficulties inherent in service transactions. Branding and consequent operational standards aim to help shape customer expectations and experiences of being served in the brand. This chapter first discusses services in general and some of the service aspects that have been influential in shaping different service offers, and thereby in helping to define hotel brands and market segmentation. The chapter also considers some of the problems associated with hotel service delivery and management of multi-unit brands. Finally, the chapter briefly discusses variations in hotel service qualities which subsequently inform brand identities.

11.2 About services

Hospitality involves the supply of food and/or drink and/or accommodation in a service context. That said, the nature of the food, drink and accommodation supplied varies, in intensity and price. Clearly, luxury hotels, three-star, and budget accommodations, represent different service experiences for the customer, and require different service performance from service personnel. While the type and quality of products on offer to customers is important, the key feature for hospitality managers to understand is the precise nature of the service experience being supplied, and what customers are expecting of each specific service encounter. Customer expectations are best understood by building a picture of the key features of service. This

Service experiences

Service performance

Service encounter

11

United States of America, Las Vegas: Eiffel Tower at Paris Hotel and Casino shows how different brands offer different bundles of service experiences to customers. That is, there are service experiences that are of different types, over and above the nature of the food, drink or accommodation offered.

Almost all services, including hotel services, can be said to have four features that make them different from manufactured products. Two of these features are of lesser importance in shaping service types, though they are important in service management. The other two features are key factors in building an understanding of the variations in hospitality services.

11.2.1   Minor factors

Time

Instant interaction

In most cases, a service involves an instant interaction between a customer and an employee. The instance of service is over and gone the moment it has occurred. It cannot be produced in advance, nor can it be taken back and reworked if a problem occurs. A receptionist's smile cannot be re-enacted if it strikes a customer as mechanical, or as less than genuine. Clearly,

Perishable

this perishable feature of the service encounter means that hotel firms have to get it right first go. Service operation systems, communications and staff training are essential in assisting in the delivery of consistent service quality which gets it right every time.

Face-to-face

In most hospitality situations, the service received by customers involves face-to-face interactions. Customers and staff can see each other, and customers evaluate the performance of an employee through a whole range of

Conscious and subconscious cues

conscious and subconscious cues. Thus body language, tone of voice, words used, appearance and personal hygiene help build a picture of an employee that establishes the customer's impression of the organisation and its service. This means that employees should be well trained in the various techniques used to develop the appropriate feelings of welcome and the importance of customers as individuals. In addition, employee satisfaction and dissatisfaction become crucial. JW Marriott is quoted as saying: '*It*

Customer loyalty

takes happy workers to make happy customers'. Customer loyalty is likely to be most successfully built on the basis of contacts with staff that make them feel welcome and cared for, and with sentiments that appear to be genuinely felt by the person or persons concerned.

11.2.2   Major factors

The product-service dimension

All hotel services involve the customer being supplied with a combination of physical products, and service based on contact with customers. In a hotel, physical elements obviously involve room design – *en-suite* facilities, food and drink – as well as public area décor and other features of physical amenities. In addition, customers are supplied services by staff – the friendliness with which they are approached – the speed of service – an on-going relationship with service staff. These tangible and intangible aspects of the services cover a wide range of issues that can be presented in a list according to the extent that each is tangible and measurable, or intangible and difficult to measure. Room size is a tangible and measurable aspect of the customer's hotel experience. Operating systems and manuals can specify size, consistency of room décor, bed comfort, cleanliness, etc., supplied to customers. However, the décor of a property may involve a physical assessment of the state of repair and cleanliness, but also involve a psychological dimension in its impact on customer mood and impression difficult to measure.

Physical elements

Intangible aspects

Psychological dimension

Similarly, the intangible service aspect of the customer's experience involves some factors that are clearly difficult to measure. The impact of an employee's smile, the body language of staff behind the reception desk; these create an impression, but are difficult to define and measure. That said, role models, best practice incidents and core values dissemination can be shared through training. Without dismissing the problems, some aspects of intangible service elements are measurable. The time it takes for a customer to receive the starter after having placed an order in a restaurant, or the time it takes to be acknowledged while waiting at the reception desk, for example, can be identified and measured against a standard. These aspects contribute to a customer's evaluation of service quality, and can be subject to specific targets and measures in time.

Training

Standard

Figure 11.1 provides an example of some of these tangible product and intangible service aspects of the customer's experience at a hotel. While all hospitality services involve combinations of these product and service aspects in their offer to customers, not all are valued equally. In some cases, the tangible product aspects are more important sources of customer satisfaction. In other cases, the intangible service factors become more important.

Customer satisfaction

11

FIGURE 11.1 Tangible and intangible elements of customer service at a hotel

Relatively easy to measure

PRODUCT		SERVICE
Physical facilities - bed comfort, bathroom etc.	Tangible elements	Time waiting for service
Range and choice of items		Speed of service
Ancillary goods - leisure facilities, etc.		Reliability
Dining facilities, menu, wines, etc.		Competence of staff
Ambience - music etc.		Communication skills
Cleanliness		Willingness to help
Appearance of staff		Responsiveness
Image	Intangible elements	Responsibility for customer care
		Hospitality and hospitableness

Relatively difficult to measure

In hospitality service contexts, the same brand may represent a different cluster of benefits, depending on the means by which customers are supplied with products and services. The activities listed in Figure 11.2 provide an example of the different levels of service intensity in three different hotel departments. A restaurant operation involves traditional service interactions between customer and staff. A bar service requires limited interactions but needs to build a relationship with customers. Issues to do with acknowledgement of the customer, waiting time and service speed, as well as product quality, are important. Reception desk personnel have relatively simple and brief interactions with customers, but are fundamental in establishing guest welcome and hospitableness.

Service intensity

As indicated above, the range and complexity of hospitality services does vary. The source of customer satisfaction also varies. In some cases, satisfaction is largely product-derived, such as through taste, variety, size, temperature, etc. In other cases, these factors, while important, are supplemented by the range and quality of contact with service. It follows that employee management varies according to the complexity and predictability of service needs.

FIGURE 11.2 Example of customer interactions in a hotel context

Restaurant	Bar service	Hotel reception
1. Greet & seat customers, give out menus 2. Take drinks order 3. Serve drinks 4. Take food order 5. Serve first course 6. Check back - starter OK? 7. Clear starter plates 8. Serve main course 9. Check back - main course OK? 10. Clear main course plates 11. Offer sweet menu 12. Take order for sweets 13. Check back - sweets OK? 14. Offer coffee 15. Serve coffee 16. Offer refill 17. Present bill 18. Payment 19. Provide receipt 20. Salutation	1. Acknowledge/greet customer 2. Take order 3. Supply order and request payment 4. Accept payment 5. Receipt 6. Salutation 7. Talk with customer when not serving 8. Clear empty glasses, etc 9. Serve drinks, take money etc., as requested	1. Acknowledge/greet waiting customer 2. Accept booking 3. Allocate room 4. Tell customer of charge 5. Accept payment 6. Salutation

11

The predictable-personal dimension

Given the personal nature of the service interaction, customers are faced with a difficulty in predicting the quality of the service they expect to receive. For reasons already outlined earlier in this chapter, customers cannot judge the quality of an experience until they've taken part in it. This issue partly explains the success of branded standardised service businesses in hotel markets. These hotel brands attempt to make it clear to each customer what to expect, and spend lots of time and energy attempting to ensure that customer expectations are met.

Branded standardised service

© Noordhoff Uitgevers bv

11.3 Hospitality service types

Not all services can be standardised; some services have to be tailored to the needs of the individual. Professional services, like dental and medical services, are the most obvious examples. In hospitality services, there are clearly limits to the degree to which services can be fully customised, because operating systems and standardised offers which attract customers to the brand also limit the possibilities for giving each customer a totally individual service. In many ways, it is possible to personalise the nature of a customer's experiences. It is possible to provide service that either allows a wide choice through which service is personalised or, through service interaction, it is possible to encourage a customer to feel important as an individual. Traditional pubs are able to create a sense of customer uniqueness because of high levels of repeat visits that are associated with the 'local', and the use of personalised glasses, or standing locations at a bar, etc.

Customised

Personalised

It is possible to detect a services continuum that ranks different types of service experience in the way they offer a customer fairly predictable service, and variations in the degree to which different services personalise customer experience. Most services involve some elements of personalisation because of contacts with service personnel, but the degree to which predictability or personalisation are important varies between services.

Services continuum

The tangibility-intangibility continuum and customisation-standardisation continuum interact to create four ideal service types. These ideal service types are useful because they show that not all service firms are making the same offers to customers. The extent to which services are standardised or customised for individual customers, and the importance of the tangible and intangible aspects of service, vary between services. Figure 11.3 is a representation of these major influences, identifying the four service types that shape both the nature of service being supplied and staff performance required to deliver that service experience. While it may be true that few hotel brands represent any one of these types, each represents a position closer to one or another of the ideal types; the model is helpful in establishing the essential features of customer offer and service experiences.

Ideal service types

FIGURE 11.3 Ideal service types

	Tangible	Intangible
Customised	Operations - service shop Marketing - choice dependent Human resources - consultation approach	Operations – professional services Marketing - customisation dependent Human resources – professional approach
Standardised	Operations - service factory Marketing - uniformity dependent Human resources - production line approach	Operations - mass service Marketing - relationship dependent Human resources - participative approach

11.3.1 Professional services

Professional services represent a service offer both intangible and customised to the individual customer service need. In these circumstances, customer needs are hard to predict and rely on service delivery personnel assessing client needs, and then providing the performance that meets

11

these needs. The most appropriate management style therefore relies on developing service providers with a wide array of service skills. They exercise professional judgement to first assess, and then deliver, the service needed. Within the hospitality sector, catering consultants, sector lawyers, accountants, human resource personnel and educators may be considered examples of these professional roles.

Professional judgement

11.3.2   Service factory services

Service factory services (uniformity dependent) are services that have major tangible features and are also standardised for all users. Most service customers are given the same service, and there are few opportunities to make personal choices about the service received. McDonald's restaurants provide the most famous example, with these types of service being referred to as McDonaldised services. Services delivered are subject to the same principles as mass production of manufactured products. Service standards define not just products, but also many of the intangible aspects of a service encounter. Service manuals set down maximum waiting times, product production times, and in many cases, script the words service staff are to use when dealing with customers. From the customer's perspective, the attraction is that standard procedures reduce uncertainty about products and service encounters experienced. Clearly, the fast food companies exemplify this approach, but these models are also being adopted in the budget hotel sector.

McDonaldised services

11.3.3   Mass services

Mass services (relationship dependent) are highly standardised in the tangible dimensions of the service offered, but aim to develop relationships with customers through the delivery of intangibles. Brands adopting this model have standardised menus, portion sizes, prices, room sizes and décor, etc. A customer has the security of knowing what to expect, but the service encounter aims to be more personal. Employees are therefore encouraged to develop personal relationships with customers, remembering service preferences, being empowered to deal with unusual requests, and correcting mistakes without having to refer to a more senior colleague, etc. Customers have the security of knowing what to expect in the tangibles, but also that intangibles are delivered in a way that is sensitive to their needs and experiences. The more up-market hotels and restaurants are examples of this service type.

Personal relationships

11.3.4   Service shop (choice dependent) services

The offer is dominantly tangible, though some element of choice is built into the customer offer. By offering a wide selection of pre-planned options, an organisation is not giving complete freedom of choice, but the service performance is amended to meet the needs of pre-defined customer occasions, creating the appearance of services meeting individual customer needs. These mass customised services are similar to popular manufactured brands that allow customers to choose the model that best suits their needs. The car manufacture sector is the most obvious product market where basic models can be amended to meet perceived needs of identified market segments. Service personnel are required to amend their service performance according to the needs of the customer occasions – anniversary – wedding party – stag/hen do, etc. In the restaurant sector, TGI Fridays is an example, as are boutique hotels.

Pre-planned options

11

© Noordhoff Uitgevers bv

FIGURE 11.4 Hospitality service types

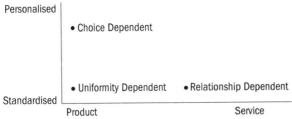

Figure 11.4 shows three ideal types of hospitality service depending on the nature of the offer on these dimensions. As demonstrated, while most hospitality services supply customers with a set of service elements that are simultaneously standard and shaped to the customers' needs, they also offer service benefits which supply physical products served to customers. By bringing these two sets of factors together, a number of ideal service types are revealed; three of these have particular relevance to hospitality customer service occasions as indicated earlier in this section.

11.4 Managing the service experience

Hotel organisations provide food and/or drink and/or accommodation in a service context. Each of these terms needs close consideration so as to understand the nature of the business at both corporate and unit level. Large hotel organisations provide these services in a way that is:

- Branded: usually sold under a brand name through a chain of hotels incorporating bars, restaurants and accommodations services. The brand represents a cluster of attributes or benefits to customers who have a pretty good idea of what to expect before entering the premises; *Brand*
- Customer focussed: a consequence of branding is to shape the nature of the products and services that make up the brand to particular customer types and needs and experiences. Issues to do with age, gender, social class, income, region, consumption patterns and service needs help hoteliers consider the nature of the brand and the messages required by customers; *Customer types*
- Standardised: though it does vary according to the nature of the brand and business, standardisation follows from the requirement of customers for consistency and predictability. Typically, the menu of items, prices charged, décor and building layout are standardised across all hotels in the brand; *Consistency and predictability*
- Consistent in quality: management of a hospitality experience has to be concerned with ensuring customers get the experience they expect. That is, not only the physical products but also the type of service from staff must be consistent and in line with customer expectations. Management of service quality, staff training and performance appraisal therefore become important tools; *Consistent*
- Managed via operating systems: consistency and standardisation across dozens or hundreds of hotels usually require that all hotels operate according to a centrally designed system which guides the way products and services are purchased, assembled and delivered to guests. In many *Centrally designed system*

11

cases, these systems also set down how training, recruitment and other staff management issues are to be handled;

Communication

- Sales driven: using techniques from the retail goods sector, hospitality businesses are concerned to ensure that communication with customers is clear. The nature of products and services on offer is stated in a way that allows minimal confusion or misunderstanding. Point of sale materials and staff training in 'up-selling' techniques, together with an array of other techniques, attempt to maximise sales to each customer;

Advertising

- Mass marketed: to generate customer identification and to shape clear communications with customers, hospitality retailing organisations frequently use mass advertising through television and newspapers, as well as other promotional techniques to inform customers about the brand and services on offer;

Characteristics

- Location defined: these managed properties have a defined set of location characteristics that define them – typical size, high street, suburban or trunk road locations, property types, age characteristics, parking facilities, or proximity to transport links are some of such characteristics.

Over the past few decades, branded hospitality services have taken an increasing share of hotel business in many countries. The consistency of service, lower costs through the scale of their operations and appeal of a variety of brands to target markets have ensured wide success.

Managers working in these branded hospitality businesses need to understand the nature of the brand in which they are working; that is, what is it that customers are connecting to? Using this understanding, managers are able to focus on what customers expect and what has to be done to ensure that customer expectations are met. Most importantly, managers in branded hotel businesses need to understand, and work within, the disciplines of the brand. Customers who experience different types or levels of service, price, or quality in different establishments in the same brand become confused about what the brand represents. Their expectations become less clear and more uncertain. A likely consequence is that they will seek out competitors that appear more consistent.

11.5 Downsides

Difficult issues

While branded hospitality services have been very successful in capturing a significant share of the hotel business, they face some difficult issues to manage. Many of the features of these operations which have brought about their success also lead to problems, which are discussed below.

11.5.1   Management skills

In the past, successful management in smaller hotels and accommodations was often defined as being 'a nice couple that like having people around'.

Host

In other words, the need to be a welcoming and friendly host for customers, and to maintain good product quality standards, were deemed key contributors to success. Nowadays, the high volume businesses directly managed in brand formats require different skills. A tightly defined brand supported with operating systems, quality management techniques and policies derived at Head Office can lead organisations to adopt a command and control

Command and control

style which allows little scope for individual manager or employee initiative.

Managers at unit level are expected to work according to the 'one best way'. As will be shown, for some businesses, this is consistent with the offer to customers, but sometimes creates unnecessary difficulties because managers feel stifled or discouraged from being creative in their work.

11.5.2   Employee dissatisfaction

The operating systems, tight product specifications and 'one best way' job designs allow little scope for individual flair and creativity. Employees experience jobs that are tightly controlled, routine and monotonous. On top of this, the uneven pace of work in many hospitality services, together with difficulties inherent in serving customers, adds additional stress to hotel work. Consequently, many hotel operations face high labour turnover. It is not unusual for hotels to experience average labour turnover of over 150% per year across the whole brand, with some jobs and units recording labour turnover of over 500% per year. Apart from the direct costs of replacing staff – which can be a considerable added cost in itself – managers face difficulties through the sheer volume of recruitment, selection, and training they need to undertake.

Labour turnover

11.5.3   Service inconsistencies

Problems occur for several reasons. Firstly, the very scale of these organisations means they are attempting to deliver consistent customer experiences through a very large number of units. Hundreds of unit management personnel and thousands of staff members must all share an understanding of the brand and be prepared to work within the rigidities of operating procedures. With so many people involved, there are clearly many opportunities for things to go wrong.

Scale

The second problem relates to the labour turnover difficulty. When labour turnover occurs at high levels, a constant stream of new employees is joining the organisation because many are leaving. In these circumstances, it is difficult to communicate and train employees to the desired standards.

The very nature of service contact means that both employees and customers may react inconsistently with each other. Customer perceptions of different employees shape the way they evaluate the service and employees as people. It may be unrealistic to expect employees to always act with good grace or a desire to delight the customer; tiredness, boredom, and frustration with management can occasionally cause service problems.

11.5.4   Customer service needs

While customers are attracted to the certainties of branded service operations, they often dislike being treated as faceless numbers. Customer expectations vary for different brands. In some cases, the individual may want more consistency and standardisation, yet in other cases expect the service to be more personal and custom tailored. The same individual may want different experiences from the same hospitality operation depending on their mood, the time of day, and the occasion. Furthermore, customer service needs are dynamic. As more people experience hospitality services, their expectations move and shift. Hospitality service organisations have to constantly review and audit customer expectations. They can never sit back and assume they know what customers want.

Different experiences

Review and audit

11

© Noordhoff Uitgevers bv

11.5.5   Local and regional tastes

National branded hospitality services may come across tension in their need to maintain a standardised national brand through which customers learn to know what to expect when encountering local or regional tastes that cut across the standard brand. That is, customers may expect to be able to order certain drinks or products in a local restaurant or pub, yet find that the brand does not normally stock these items; managers have been instructed not to provide services 'out of brand', potentially leaving some of the customers dissatisfied.

11.5.6   The big-is-ugly syndrome

Slow to change

As we have seen, the scale and coverage of large hotel operations brings advantages through cost reduction and standardisation, but can be unwieldy and slow to change. In fast moving consumer markets, such as in the hotel sector, much standardised operating systems and centralised controls can be a disadvantage. The narrow span of control and tall hierarchies that help the organisation manage consistency over a lot of units makes for long lines of communication and slow decision-making processes. It is, therefore, very easy for such organisations to miss changes in consumer taste and be unresponsive to variations in the customer base; a situation made more complex by the impact of the immediate local market competition for each hotel.

11.6 Hotel types and examples

Unusual requests

Hotel service brands encompass elements of the issues discussed above. The more luxury brands tend to include high levels of tangible provision through the design of the accommodation, in-room facilities, and guest services provided to individual customers. Public areas are designed to communicate high standards, à la carte restaurant(s), cocktail bars, and leisure clubs, etc. The intangible services are also at a high level, and in most cases, services meet unusual requests as they occur – though most expected service requests are predicted in advance. Within the framework of hospitality services suggested above, these are essentially relationship dependent services.

Predictability

The more budget end accommodation brands tend to focus on limited services but at high degree of predictability in both tangibles and intangibles. They meet guest predictability and safety needs in a highly standardised format. In-room provision includes private rooms and *en-suite* facilities, with few other in-room services. Most have in-room tea and coffee making facilities. Contact with staff is minimal, and the offer is highly tangible and standardised. Increasingly, budget hotel operators are introducing self-check-in and self-check-out services and drinks vending machines. These represent a uniformity dependent brand, employing the ideal types shown above.

Short-term rental

A variant of this uniformity dependent offer reduces the service interaction further. Many larger hotel operators are introducing properties based on a short-term rental model. Here, customers rent accommodations for a short period, similar to the traditional hotel, but with cooking and dining facilities provided within the accommodation. The average floor space is greater than in a hotel, and lounge, kitchen/dining facilities are typically added to the hotel room facilities. The key feature is that the service offer is highly tangible oriented, service interactions are minimal, and uniformity is more easily delivered; it is not dependent on service staff interactions.

11

The following identifies a widely accepted framework of categories of hotels according to the quality of the tangible facilities and levels of service provided to guests – some of which have been introduced in Chapter 2 from an operation's perspective.

11.6.1   Historic inns and boutique hotels

These are typically smaller and intimate properties that create a sense of hospitableness, personalised to guests because of the smaller scale of operations. Often independently owned, though in some cases the properties may be owned by a large company, and operated in the form of a franchise. The key to this model is the intimacy offered, and the perceived sincerity of the hospitality provided.

Smaller and intimate

11

11.6.2   Full-scale luxury

These offer the highest quality levels of facilities and guest services. There are one or more restaurants including at least one restaurant featuring an à la carte menu. The service is personalised to guests and, in some more luxury-end cases, a maid/valet is allocated to each room. These hotels offer high quality leisure facilities. Luxury hotels are classified as being five stars or five diamonds, depending on the country in which the individual property is located. While the facilities offered communicate luxury, the defining characteristic of this category of hotel is in the service level offered by service personnel. There is typically a high proportion of staff to guests.

Highest quality

Defining characteristic

11.6.3   Full-service

These offer high quality physical amenities. Luxurious décor and in-room design, as well as high quality public areas. There are high quality restaurant(s) and bar facilities together with on-site leisure facilities including pool(s), gyms and health clubs, together with conference facilities and arrays of meeting rooms, car-parks, etc.

11.6.4   Focussed or selected service hotels

These are smaller, or medium-sized hotels that offer limited services, and cater to identified market segments, such as business travellers – most guests are single travellers away from home for work-related activities. These hotels are likely to offer serviced accommodation but are unlikely to provide leisure facilities or full service restaurants. Locations are typically close to popular business destinations, or close to major transport routes.

Serviced accommodation

11.6.5   Economy and limited service

Basic

Small to medium-sized hotels offering minimal facilities. They offer basic accommodations with little additional service such as bars or restaurants. They are focussed on a particular demographic profile that wants accommodation at a 'budget price'. These economy and limited service properties may offer restaurant or bar services through another local establishment, and perhaps a basic continental breakfast.

11.6.6   Extended stay

Preferential rates

These are small to medium hotels offering accommodation in hotels that provide preferential rates for those staying for (several) weeks or months. Customers may be those who need accommodation because of temporary relocation requirements. On-site service may be limited to breakfast provision, with few other facilities such as restaurants, bars and leisure clubs, provided.

11.6.7   Timeshare

Semi-serviced

Timeshares provide joint ownership by purchasing the rights to use a property at a pre-determined time of year. Typically, these properties are individual accommodations located alongside luxury hotels or leisure facilities. The accommodation is semi-serviced in that it is cleaned and serviced weekly, though optionally more frequently at an additional charge. Guests have the choice of living self-sufficiently in the accommodation, or using the facilities and grounds of the hotel.

11.6.8   Motel

Direct access

Motels were initially popular in the 1950s and 1960s, where they met the need for budget accommodation to respond to the increasing volume of work-related travelling. Usually, they are low-rise properties with direct access to rooms and car-parking facilities close to major towns or transport routes. In more recent years, budget hotel brands have been fulfilling these market needs.

Summary

▶ This chapter outlines some of the principles associated with all service transactions. Service organisations, such as hotel companies, have attempted to meet customer service uncertainties by the use of hotel branding and standard operating procedures.

▶ Hotel brands define both the physical qualities and facilities that each property delivers, and the level of service intensity a customer can expect.

▶ Standard operating procedures help organisations define what it is they are attempting to deliver and also assist in service quality management.

▶ While there have been substantial benefits to customers and hospitality service organisations, these organisations are not without difficulties. Highly standardised service offers can be restrictive, inflexible and slow to change in response to customer tastes.

▶ Many hospitality service organisations experience high labour turnover of employees who find the restricted operations monotonous and boring. High levels of labour turnover create problems for delivering service quality, increasing costs and putting pressure on managers who have to spend a high proportion of their time recruiting replacement staff.

▶ While all hotels provide some form of accommodation and/or food and/or beverages to clients, the physical décor, direct hospitality facilities, as well as added services provided vary and provide defining features of the brand; essentially that which attracts customers.

▶ Although there are some common features of hospitality service organisations, not all services are the same. Apart from obvious differences in physical food, drinks and accommodations offered in different businesses, the nature of the service experience also varies. In particular, the product-services and the standardised-customised dimensions interact to create three service types which apply to hospitality services organisations.

▶ Customers who buy uniformity oriented services are buying services that are highly standardised and predictable and more product dependent. Choice dependent services allow customers a wide choice through which to build their own service experience. In these cases, customers are attracted to services which are product dependent, but which are also capable of being adapted to personal needs. Relationship dependent services involve services which are standardised but require more

11

significant service interactions. Customer satisfaction is most influenced by the nature of the service experience received.

▶ The internal design features of the brand are also supported by a number of star or diamond rating systems that provide potential guests with pre-purchase information about what to expect, thereby assisting in hotel search activities when planning to visit a new destination.

▶ To varying degrees, each type of hospitality service faces problems of customer loyalty and the need to build a loyal customer base. A common feature is that customers, who may be referred to as guests, are well aware of the commercial relationship with the hospitality service supplier. Hospitality services need to carefully consider the human activity of hospitality and the qualities which define hospitable behaviour

▶ Sorted by quality of tangible facilities and levels of service provided to guests, a widely accepted framework of categories of hotels includes: full-scale luxury; full-service; historic inns and boutique hotels; focussed or selected service hotels; economy and limited service; extended stays; timeshares; and motels.

11

Questions and assignments for reflection

1   Critically discuss the phrase, 'It takes happy workers to make happy customers'.

2   Evaluate the similarities and differences between budget and high-end hotel service providers.

3   Discuss the key benefits of hotel brands from a customer's perspective.

4   Analyse the key difficulties faced by large branded hotel chains.

5   Describe the steps that hotel chains can take to avoid the 'big-is-ugly' syndrome'.

11

12
Conceiving Hospitality Processes

M. N. Chibili

12.1 Introduction

Chapter 11 introduced the management of services within the hospitality industry, which will be expanded on in this chapter – here, the creation of various hospitality processes, process characteristics, performance objectives, and service concepts is further explained and illustrated. Students should realise that, in order to better understand some of these concepts and processes, in some instances examples from the manufacturing world have been used; this is not dissimilar from certain areas of the hospitality industry, such as in the kitchen where products (food items) are prepared and produced.

12.2 Process characteristics and performance objectives

The operations system of an organisation is the part that produces the organisation's products. In hospitality organisations, the product is primarily a service accompanied at times with some form of physical goods (a drink or a meal, for example). All organisations have a conversion process transforming input into output. When goods and services are produced, these are converted into cash in order to acquire more resources to keep the conversion process active. A conversion process defined by manufacture (or production) yields a tangible output: a product. On the other hand, a conversion process defined by service yields an intangible output: an activity, an action, a performance, or an effort. Generally, the following characteristics are used to differentiate between manufacturing and service operations:

Operations system

Conversion process

- Consumption of output
- Customer participation in conversion
- Degree of customer contact
- Measurement of performance
- Nature of work (jobs)
- Tangible and intangible nature of output

12

French Polynesia:, Bora Bora: The Four Seasons Resort

The basic distinction between goods and services is most easily illustrated as shown in Figure 12.1.

FIGURE 12.1 Basic difference between goods and services

Basic difference between goods and services

Goods	Services
Physical commodity	Process or Activity
Tangible	Intangible
Homogenous	Heterogenous
Production and Distribution separate from Consumption	Production, Distribution, and Consumption are simultaneous
Can be stockpiled	Cannot be stockpiled
Transfer of Ownership is possible	Transfer of Ownership impossible

Tangible products

The manufacturing sector is characterised by tangible products; output that customers consume over time; jobs that use less labour and more equipment; little customer contact; no customer participation in the conversion process (in production), and sophisticated methods for measuring production activities and resource consumption as products are made.

Intangible outputs

The service sector to which the hospitality industry belongs, on the other hand, is characterised by intangible outputs; outputs that customers consume immediately; jobs that use more labour and less equipment; direct customer contact; frequent customer participation in the conversion process, and basic methods for measuring conversion activities and resource consumption.

12.2.1   Inputs, outputs and the models

Process

A process is defined as a sequence of actions performed in order to achieve a result, a series of changes that happens naturally, or a method of producing goods and services by converting inputs into outputs. In this book, this last definition has been adopted; the conversion of input into output is based on the performance objectives of the organisation. For all operations, the goal is to create some kind of added value, so that the output is worth more to the consumers than just the sum of the individual input.

Performance objectives

Based on Mullins (2005, 1993), organisations can be viewed as open systems as illustrated in the open systems model of which a hospitality example is shown in Figure 12.2. In this model, organisations take input from the environment (output from other systems) and through a series of activities transform or convert this input into output (input to other systems) to achieve some objective. In terms of this open systems model, a business organisation takes in resources such as people, finance, raw materials and information from its environment, transforms or converts these, and returns them to the environment in various forms of output such as goods produced, services provided, completed processes or procedures. It does so in order to achieve certain goals such as profit, market standing, and level of sales or consumer satisfaction.

Open systems

FIGURE 12.2 The hotel as an open system (adapted from Mullins, 1993)

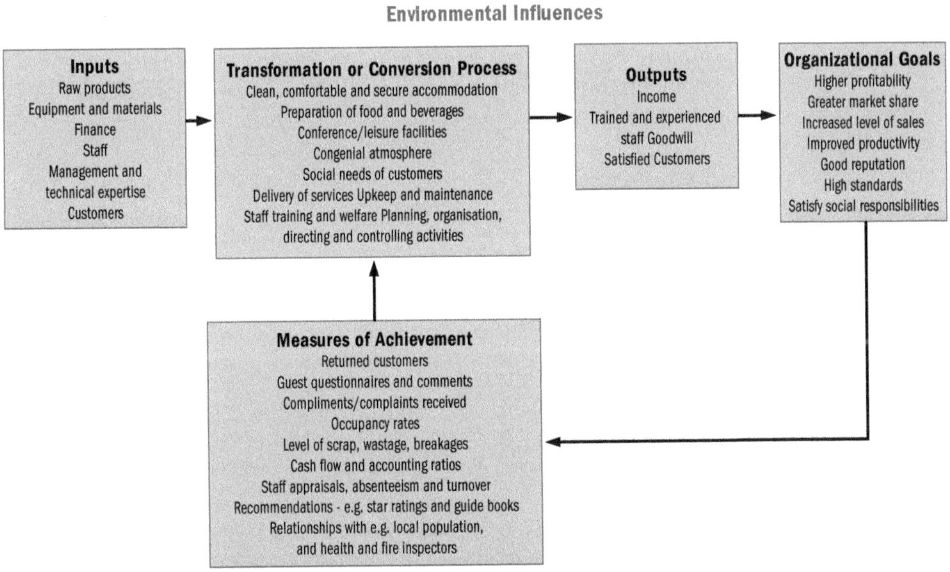

Environmental Influences

Inputs
Raw products
Equipment and materials
Finance
Staff
Management and technical expertise
Customers

Transformation or Conversion Process
Clean, comfortable and secure accommodation
Preparation of food and beverages
Conference/leisure facilities
Congenial atmosphere
Social needs of customers
Delivery of services Upkeep and maintenance
Staff training and welfare Planning, organisation, directing and controlling activities

Outputs
Income
Trained and experienced staff Goodwill
Satisfied Customers

Organizational Goals
Higher profitability
Greater market share
Increased level of sales
Improved productivity
Good reputation
High standards
Satisfy social responsibilities

Measures of Achievement
Returned customers
Guest questionnaires and comments
Compliments/complaints received
Occupancy rates
Level of scrap, wastage, breakages
Cash flow and accounting ratios
Staff appraisals, absenteeism and turnover
Recommendations - e.g. star ratings and guide books
Relationships with e.g. local population, and health and fire inspectors

The hotel is in continuous interaction with the external environment of which it is a part. In order to be effective and maintain its survival and development, a hotel must respond to the opportunities and challenges and risks and limitations presented by the changing circumstances. The open systems approach establishes a hotel within its total environment and emphasises the importance of multiple channels of interaction. The increasing rate of change (technical, economic, social and governmental) has highlighted the need to study the hotel as a total organisation and to adopt a systems approach. In addition to these major areas of change, hotels face a multitude of constantly changing environmental factors which affect operations and performances but are beyond the control of hotel management.

Multiple channels of interaction

12

Mullins (1993) provides the following examples of possible external environmental influences on the operations and performance of organisations:
- government actions on the rate of VAT, transport policies, health and safety regulations, drink-driving laws;
- inflation, interest rates, levels of unemployment;
- international situations and foreign exchange rates;
- technological advances;
- activities of competitors;
- local business trade, or tourism or leisure attractions;
- major trends towards eating organically-grown produce;
- increased leisure time for wider ranges of the population;
- bankruptcy of, or a major strike at, an important supplier;
- large increases in trade union activities and membership;
- the opening or closing of a local catering college;
- long spells of particularly good or poor weather.

Without explicitly including the external environment, the second model, shown in Figure 12.3 and called the input-transformation-output model, demonstrates that all operations produce products and services by changing input into output using an 'input-transformation-output' process. Basi-
Resources   cally, operations are processes that take in a set of input resources which are used to transform something, or are transformed themselves, into output of products and services. Although all operations conform to this general input-transformation-output model, they differ in the nature of their specific input and output.

FIGURE 12.3 The input-transformation-output model

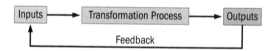

Based on the model in Figure 12.3, some input is used up in the process of creating goods or services; other input plays a part in the creation process but is not used up. These types of input are usually classified into two subgroups:
Transformed
resources   • Transformed resources, which are those that are transformed in some way by the operation to produce the goods or services that are its outputs. Examples include materials consisting of physical input to the process, information that is treated or used in the process, and customers who are transformed in one way or another;
Transforming
resources   • Transforming resources, which are those used to perform the transformation process. Examples include the staff made up of people directly involved in or supporting the transformation process (sometimes called labour), and facilities composed of the plant, property and equipment (sometimes called capital). Organisations vary in their mix of labour and capital in their input, with highly automated activities being more capital intensive.

The transformation process is any activity or group of activities that takes one or more forms of input, transforms and adds value to them, and thereby providing output destined for internal or external customers. In cases where the input is raw materials, it is somewhat easy to identify the trans-

12

formation involved, such as when various ingredients are combined into a dish. However, in cases where the input is information or people, identifying the transformation may be more difficult; such as when a restaurant transforms two different customers after serving to them the same dish resulting into two different outcomes – one satisfied, the other dissatisfied. In general, the transformation process leads to:

- changes in the positioning of materials, information or customers;
- changes in the ownership of materials or information;
- changes in the physical characteristics of materials or customers;
- changes in the physiological or psychological state of customers;
- changes in the purpose or form of information;
- storage or accommodation of materials, information or customers.

Frequently, all three types of input – materials, information and customers – are transformed by the same organisation. One useful way of categorising different types of transformation is:

- manufacture – physical creation of products (for example bottles of gin);
- transport – movement of materials or customers (for example a shuttle service);
- supply – change in ownership of goods (for example in gift shops);
- service – handling customers or storing materials (for example restaurants or parking lots).

The input-transformation-output model can also be identified within organisations themselves, where there are several units or departments which act as smaller units of the overall organisation. As several different transformations are typically required to produce a good or service, the overall transformation can be described as the macro operation, whereas the more detailed transformations within the macro operation can be described as the micro operations. If, for example, the macro operation in a brewery is making beer, each of the milling, mashing, lautering, boiling, whirl pooling, cooling, fermenting, maturing, filtering, packaging and distribution components, as indicated in Figure 12.4, are independent micro operations receiving input from the previous level, and producing output for the next level in the macro operation until the final product is made ready for the consumer.

Within organisations

Macro operation

Micro operations

FIGURE 12.4 Micro operations in beer making (Source: www.ibdasiapac.com.au)

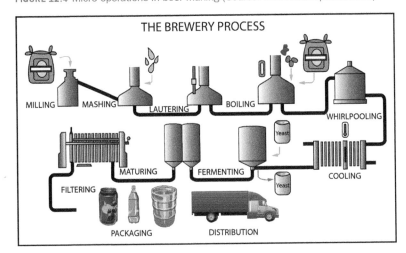

THE BREWERY PROCESS

MILLING · MASHING · LAUTERING · BOILING · WHIRLPOOLING · Yeast · COOLING · MATURING · FERMENTING · Yeast · FILTERING · PACKAGING · DISTRIBUTION

12

12.2.2   Process dimensions

All operations processes have one thing in common – they all take their input and transform it into output. In order to better understand the different types of operations, they have been categorised into four principal dimensions, commonly called the Four Vs of Operations – volume, variety, variation in demand, and visibility (Slack, Brandon-Jones & Johnston, 2013). These dimensions try to answer the following basic questions:

Four Vs of Operations

- Volume – how many products or services are made by the operation?
- Variety – how many different types of products or services are made by the operation?
- Variation in demand – how much does the level of demand for the products and services of the operation change over time?
- Visibility – how much of the operation's internal functioning is exposed to its customers in the course of the creation of their products and services?

In most industries, one can find examples at either end of each dimension. In the transportation industry, for example, a taxi service is low volume while a bus service or mass rapid transit service is high volume. In accounting, corporate tax advising is high variety because all large corporations have different needs, while financial auditing, carried out to comply with legislation, is relatively standardised. In food manufacture, the demand for ice-cream varies considerably depending on the weather, while the demand for bread is much more stable and more predictable. In dental care, dentists perform high visibility operations but rely on dental technicians in factory-type laboratories to produce dentures and other required tools and materials.

These dimensions are most useful in predicting how easy it is for an operation to operate at low cost. Based on Slack et al. (2013), Figure 12.5 is an adaptation which shows a typology of operations indicating the dimensions and their implications on the cost of creating products or services.

FIGURE 12.5 Typology of operations indicating dimensions and their implications

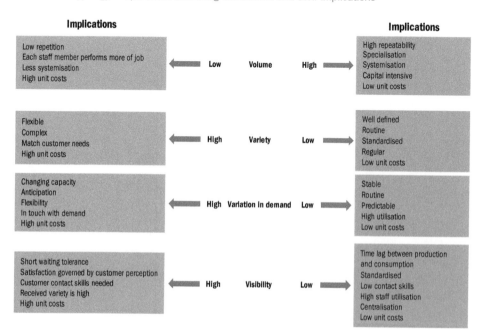

© Noordhoff Uitgevers bv

The volume dimension

A good example of the volume dimension is the McDonald's Corporation, which is a well-known example of high volume, low cost fast food production. The volume of their operation is key to how their business is organised. Essential to their operation is the repeatability of the tasks their workers perform, as well as the systemisation of the work where standards and procedures drive the way in which each part of the job is carried out. This combination ensures lower unit costs. In contrast, a local café has a much lower volume of output, less labour, less systemisation, and each worker completes a wider variety of tasks which results in higher unit costs.

Repeatability

It is important to distinguish between actual and maximum volumes an operation (such as a restaurant) can cope with by establishing its capacity, defined as the maximum level of value added activity a process can achieve over a period of time. In general, capacity is fixed, such as hotels having a fixed number of rooms or restaurants with a fixed number of seats. Since demand varies over time, this creates an imbalance between capacity and demand. The degree to which capacity is used (utilisation) is measured by dividing the actual output by the available capacity.

Capacity

Demand

The volume dimension has different implications depending on whether it is at high or low level. In the case of low volume levels, a company's operations have such characteristics as low repetition in everyday procedures, and individual staff member possibly being called on to perform more than one job. In other words, employees are multifunctional, there is less systemisation, and there are high unit costs. When volume levels are high, a company's operations have such characteristics as high repeatability in everyday procedures, more specialisation and more systemisation. Such operations are much more capital intensive, leading to lower unit costs.

Systemisation

The variety dimension

A common example used to describe the variety dimension is the contrast between a taxi service and a bus service. Both offer passengers hired transportation services, but a taxi service has a much higher variety dimension as they pick up and drop off their passengers basically whenever and wherever required. A bus, on the other hand, normally operates on a predetermined scheduled route and time. Despite the fact that both transport customers, the variety and flexibility is high for the taxi service and low for the bus service.

Flexibility

In the field of restaurants, there are two important aspects to be considered when assessing or measuring variety. The first is the range of different foods that a restaurant serves, which can be easily identified by counting the number of different items on its menu list. The second aspect is considering whether a restaurant can customise its food according to customer preferences; whether it can serve steaks from very rare to overdone; whether customers can select the fillings for their sandwiches. The variety dimension also has its own implications depending on whether it is high or low. The high side of the scale has more flexibility in the procedure, more complexity, an increased attempt to match customer needs, and generally higher unit costs. On the other hand, when a company is on the lower side of the scale, the procedures are well defined, there is more routine and standardisation, and unit costs are lower.

Range

Customise

12

The variation in demand dimension

To illustrate the variation in demand dimension, Slack et al. (2013) used the demand pattern for a successful summer holiday resort hotel and indicated that, unsurprisingly, more customers want to stay there during summer vacation times than in the middle of winter. At the height of 'the season' the hotel could be up to full capacity. Off-season demand, however, could be a small fraction of its capacity. Such a marked variation in demand means that an operation must change its capacity in some way, for example, by hiring extra staff for the summer. The hotel must try to predict the likely level of demand. If it predicts wrongly, this could result in too much or too little capacity. Additionally, recruitment costs, overtime costs and underutilisation of rooms all have the effect of increasing a hotel's costs of operation compared to a hotel of a similar standard with level demand. A hotel with relatively level demand can plan its activities well in advance. Staff can be scheduled, food can be bought, and rooms can be cleaned in a routine and predictable manner. This results in a high utilisation of resources, and unit costs which are likely to be lower than those in hotels with a highly variable demand pattern.

Off-season

In using a restaurant to illustrate the variation in demand dimension, perhaps the easiest way to measure variation in demand is by comparing the ratio of peak demand on a certain day or during a certain week to the lowest demand during that day or week. If, for example, the restaurant was operating at full capacity during the busiest period compared to at merely around 20% during its lowest period, then the peak to trough ratio is 5:1.

Peak to trough ratio

The variation in demand has many implications that can be seen from a company's characteristics. If there is a high variation in demand, a company is constantly changing its capacity; there is more necessity to try and anticipate customers' needs and more need to try and be more flexible, there are more requirements to match changes in demand, and unit costs are higher. If, on the other hand, there is a low variation in demand, a company has a stable and more predictable demand; its operations are more routine; but there is a higher utilisation of resources, and unit costs are lower as well.

The visibility dimension

This last dimension refers to how much of an operation's activities its customers experience, or to what extent an operation is exposed to its customers. Generally, customer-processing operations are more exposed to customers than material- or information-processing operations. But even customer-processing operations have some choice as to how visible they wish their operations to be. Examples of a high visibility dimension would be a courier company, where package delivery status can be checked online, or a retail store goods can be personally selected and paid for at the check-out counter. An example of a low visibility dimension would be a web design company that takes an order for creating or modifying of a website, subsequently advising that the new website will be ready sometime in the future. Visibility is a slightly more difficult dimension of operations to envisage, and it is made additionally harder by the fact that some operations, such as hotels, have both high- and low-visibility processes as demarcated by the differences between the activities that take place at front-of-house and those handled at back-of-house.

Returning to the restaurant example, visibility can be assessed by, for example, asking the customers a simple question: 'How much of the preparation of the food did you witness?' Though it is unusual to see every aspect of the food preparation process (such as the preparation of all components), it is possible to partake in the preparation process as is common in certain Asian style restaurants where customers select the ingredients and watch the chef finalise the cooking process.

The implications of the visibility dimension also depend on whether there is high or low visibility. If visibility is high, customers will have a relatively short waiting tolerance, and may walk out if not served in a reasonable time. Customers' perceptions, rather than objective criteria, are also important, requiring staff with good customer contact skills. It is difficult for high-visibility operations to achieve high productivity of resources, so these tend to be relatively high-cost operations. On the other hand, if visibility is low, there is a time difference between production and consumption, processes are more standardised and employees are very much involved but do not require extensive customer contact skills. In such instances, there is the possibility for a relatively easy centralisation of activities that enables low unit costs.

12.2.3 Performance objectives

Performance objectives are the goals an organisation must achieve, selected based on the strategy of the organisation, and influenced by its relevant stakeholders. As such, management of the operation has an impact on the broad categories of stakeholders who could have an interest in, or are affected by, the operation. Figure 12.6 indicates some major stakeholders and some of their main concerns in relation to any organisation.

Exposed

Difficult

Waiting tolerance

Contact skills

Goals

12

FIGURE 12.6 Major stakeholders and some of their concerns

Stakeholders	Concerns
Community	jobs, involvement, environmental protection, shares, truthful communication.
Creditors	credit score, new contracts, liquidity and solvency.
Customers	value, quality, customer care, ethical products.
Employees	rates of pay, job security, compensation, respect, truthful communication.
Government	taxation, VAT, legislation, employment, truthful reporting, diversity, legalities, externalities.
Investors	return on investment, income, solvency.
Management	plan, control, organize, coordinate, perform, succeed, sustain, survive
Owner(s)	profitability, longevity, market share, market standing, succession planning, raising capital, growth, social goals.
Suppliers	liquidity, contract terms, equitable business opportunities.
Trade Unions	quality, worker protection, jobs.

Having defined its corporate strategy, an organisation subsequently identifies the operational performance objectives it must meet to achieve its strategy. This is followed by defining the measurements it aims to use to determine if the performance objectives have been met. The organisation then configures its operating environment to accomplish one or more of the operational performance objectives. Slack et al. (2013), as well as many other authors, have identified five basic 'performance objectives' which are applicable to all types of operations.

Quality

Without errors

The ability to produce in accordance with specifications and without errors. By 'doing things right', operations seek to influence the quality of a company's goods and services. Externally, quality is an important aspect of customer satisfaction or dissatisfaction. Internally, enhanced quality helps both to reduce costs and to increase dependability.

Speed

Quickly

The ability to do things quickly in response to customer demands, thereby offering shorter lead times between when a customer orders a product or service and when said order is received. By 'doing things fast', operations seek to influence the speed with which goods and services are delivered. Externally, speed is an important aspect of customer service. Internally, speed reduces inventory by decreasing internal throughput times as well as reducing risks by delaying the commitment of resources.

Dependability

Promises made

The ability to deliver products and services in accordance with promises made to customers. By 'doing things on time', operations seek to influence the dependability of the delivery of goods and services. Externally, dependability is an important aspect of customer service. Internally, dependability within operations increases operational reliability, thus saving time and money that would otherwise be used in solving reliability problems and giving stability to the operation.

Flexibility

Change

The ability to change operations. By 'changing what they do', operations seek to influence the flexibility with which the company produces goods and services. Externally, flexibility can be viewed from four perspectives: prod-

© Noordhoff Uitgevers bv

uct/service flexibility; mix flexibility; volume flexibility; and delivery flexibility. Internally, flexibility can help speed up response times, save time wasted in changeovers, and maintain dependability.

Cost

The ability to produce at low costs (as cost-effective as possible). By 'doing things cheaply', operations seek to influence the cost of the company's goods and services. Externally, low costs allow organisations to reduce their prices in order to increase volumes or, alternatively, increase profitability on existing volume levels. Internally, cost performance is helped by good performances in the other performance objectives.

Cheaply

Excelling at one or more of these operation performance objectives can allow an organisation to pursue a business strategy based on a corresponding competitive factor. It is important to note, however, that the success of any particular business strategy depends not only on the ability of operations to achieve excellence in the appropriate performance objectives, but also very much hinges on whether customers appreciate the chosen competitive factors on which the business strategy is based.

To adequately illustrate these performance objectives in the hospitality context, the following case study, entitled 'Operations objectives at the Penang Mutiara', taken from Slack et al. (2013, pp 64-65), has been included as Text 12.1. Though illustrative, it should be noted that some of the practices in the real-life hotel may have changed since the case study was conducted.

TEXT 12.1

Operations objectives at the Penang Mutiara

There are many luxurious hotels in the South-East Asia region but few can compare with the Penang Mutiara, a 440-room top-of-the-market hotel which nestles in the lush greenery of Malaysia's Indian Ocean Coast. Owned by Pernas–OUE of Malaysia and managed by Singapore Mandarin International Hotels, the hotel's General Manager is under no illusions about the importance of running an effective operation. *'Managing a hotel of this size is an immensely complicated task', he says. 'Our customers have every right to be demanding. They expect first-class service and that's what we have to give them. If we have any problems with managing this operation, the customer sees them immediately and that's the biggest incentive for us to take operations performance seriously. Our quality of service just has to be impeccable. This means dealing with the basics. For example, our staff must be courteous at all times and yet also friendly towards our guests. And of course they must have the knowledge to be able to answer guests' questions. The building and equipment – in fact all the hardware of the operation – must support the luxury atmosphere which we have created in the hotel. Stylish design and top-class materials not only create the right impression but, if we choose them carefully, are also durable so the hotel still looks good over the years. Most of all, though, quality is about anticipating our guests' needs, thinking ahead so you can identify what will delight or irritate a guest.'*

The hotel tries to anticipate guests' needs in a number of ways. For example, if guests have been to the hotel before, staff avoid their having to repeat the information they gave on the previous visit. Reception staff simply check to see if guests have stayed before, retrieve the information and take them straight to their room without irritating delays. Quality of service also means hel-

12

ping sort out their own problems. If the airline loses a guest's luggage en route to the hotel, for example, he or she will arrive at the hotel understandably irritated. *'The fact that it is not us who have irritated them is not really the issue. It is our job to make them feel better.'*

Speed, in terms of fast response to customers' requests is something else that is important. *'A guest just should not be kept waiting. If a guest has a request, he or she has that request now so it needs to be sorted out now. This is not always easy but we do our best. For example, if every guest in the hotel tonight decided to call room service and request a meal instead of going to the restaurants, our room service department would obviously be grossly overloaded and customers would have to wait an unacceptably long time before the meals were brought up to their rooms. We cope with this by keeping a close watch on how demand for room service is building up. If we think it's going to get above the level where response time to customers would become unacceptably long, we will call in staff from other restaurants in the hotel. Of course, to do this we have to make sure that our staff are multi-skilled. In fact we have a policy of making sure that restaurant staff can always do more than one job. It's this kind of flexibility which allows us to maintain fast response to the customer.'*

Dependability is also a fundamental principle of a well-managed hotel. *'We must always keep our promises. For example, rooms must be ready on time and accounts must be ready for presentation when a guest departs; the guests expect a dependable service and anything less than full dependability is a legitimate cause for dissatisfaction.'*

It is on the grand occasions, however, when dependability is particularly important in the hotel. When staging a banquet, for example, everything has to be on time. Drinks, food, entertainment have to be available exactly as planned. Any deviation from the plan will very soon be noticed by customers. *'It is largely a matter of planning the details and anticipating what could go wrong. Once we've*

done the planning we can anticipate possible problems and plan how to cope with them, or better still, prevent them from occurring in the first place.'

Flexibility means a number of things to the hotel. First of all it means that they should be able to meet a guest's requests. *'We never like to say NO!. For example, if a guest asks for some Camembert cheese and we don't have it in stock, we will make sure that someone goes to the supermarket and tries to get it. If, in spite of our best efforts, we can't get any we will negotiate an alternative solution with the guest. This has an important side-effect – it greatly helps us to maintain the motivation of our staff. We are constantly being asked to do the seemingly impossible – yet we do it, and our staff think it's great. We all like to be part of an organisation which is capable of achieving the very difficult, if not the impossible.'*

Flexibility in the hotel also means the ability to cope with the seasonal fluctuations in demand. They achieve this partly by using temporary part-time staff. In the back-office parts of the hotel this isn't a major problem. In the laundry, for example, it is relatively easy to put on an extra shift in busy periods by increasing staffing levels. However, this is more of a problem in the parts of the hotel that have direct contact with the customer. *'New temporary staff can't be expected to have the same customer contact skills as our more regular staff. Our solution to this is to keep the temporary staff as far in the background as we possibly can and make sure that our skilled, well-trained staff are the ones who usually interact with the customer. So, for example, a waiter who would normally take orders, service the food, and take away the dirty plates would in peak times restrict his or her activities to taking orders and serving the food. The less skilled part of the job, taking away the plates, could be left to temporary staff.'*

As far as cost is concerned, around 60 per cent of the hotel's total operating expenses go on food and beverages, so one obvious way of keeping costs down is by making sure that food is not wasted. Energy costs, at 6 per cent of total operating costs, are also a potential source of saving. However, although cost savings are welcome, the hotel is very careful never to compromise the quality of its service in order to cut costs. *'It is impeccable customer service which gives us our competitive advantage, not price. Good service means that our guests return again and again. At times, around half our* *guests are people who have been before. The more guests we have, the higher is our utilization of rooms and restaurants, and this is what really keeps cost per guest down and profitability reasonable. So in the end we've come full circle: it's the quality of our service which keeps our volumes high and our costs low.'*

It is uncertain whether an organisation can perform in all five performance objectives very well simultaneously. Trying to do so is likely to lead to confusion if managers pursue different objectives at different times. This confusion may lead to sub-standard performance and the inability to excel in any one of the performance objectives. Thus, depending on the type of operation or process involved, an organisation has to prioritise and make choices regarding which performance objectives should be focussed on. This may result in having to 'trade-off' less than excellent performance in one aspect of the operations in order to achieve excellence in another. This concept of trade-off in operations objectives was introduced by Skinner (1969), who argued that operations could not be 'all things to all people'. What was needed was to identify a single goal or 'task' for operations; a clear set of competitive priorities to act as the objective. This task would then act as the benchmark against which all decisions and actions in operations could be judged.

Confusion

Trade-off

In the manufacturing domain, it is worth noting that some scholars reject the concept of the trade-off. They indicate that some organisations have the ability to outperform their competitors on multiple dimensions. These organisations appear to produce better quality, and offer a greater dependability and a faster response to changing market conditions and lower costs. Ferdows and de Meyer (1990) argue that certain operational capabilities enhance one another, allowing excellence to be built-up in a cumulative fashion, such as in a sand cone. Using the model shown in Figure 12.7, Ferdows and de Meyer (1990) indicate that there is an ideal sequence in which operational capabilities should be developed.

Outperform

Cumulative

FIGURE 12.7 Sand cone model of operational excellence

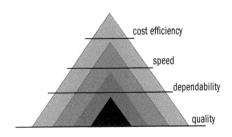

cost efficiency

speed

dependability

quality

12

Their argument (1990, p. 174) was that:

'A precondition to all lasting improvements in manufacturing capabilities is improvements in the quality performance of the company. Once the efforts in improvements in quality get underway and some results are obtained, while the efforts to improve the quality continue to expand, some efforts should be focused on making the production process more dependable. Next, improvement of speed should be added to these efforts-again, while the activities aimed at improving the quality and dependability are further enhanced and expanded. (Speed of response in manufacturing is essentially the way manufacturing flexibility can be gauged - i.e., how fast production can react to new customer requirements, changing production volumes, introduction of new product, etc.) Improvements in speed should be built cumulatively upon the foundations of quality and dependability. It is after these efforts are put in place that the company should start programmes which are aimed directly at cost efficiency improvements, and again, do that while all the previous efforts continue to expand at increasingly higher rates. Cost improvements which result from this pattern of allocation of management attention and resources will be more lasting, and ultimately the company will be able to enjoy improved performance in quality, dependability, flexibility, and cost efficiency simultaneously.'

'We have sometimes depicted this cumulative model as a sand cone with different layers. The sand is, in this case, a stand-in for management effort and resources. To obtain a sand cone, one has to create first a stable foundation of quality improvements. Pouring more sand, one enlarges the quality foundation while starting also tackling the dependability of the production system. To build a taller sand cone, an increasing amount of sand needs to be poured, thereby while enhancing the quality and dependability layers, building the foundation for improving the speed of response of manufacturing. By pouring still more sand, and enhancing the foundation layers of quality, dependability, and speed still further, one can start building stable and well-founded cost improvement programmes.'

'This analogy helps us explain an important characteristic of our model: that moving up each step in the path towards development of lasting manufacturing capabilities requires exponentially more efforts to go for the earlier steps. For example, to improve the cost efficiency by 10% it will be necessary to improve the speed by a larger percentage, say 15, dependability by yet a larger percentage, say 25, and quality by still larger, say 40%. Once again, we should clarify that we are not saying that this is the only way to reduce costs; what we are saying is that even when there are no slacks in the system, costs can be reduced at no expense in terms of other capabilities - in fact by enhancing the other capabilities. Moreover, improvements obtained in this manner, being essentially due to deeper penetration of good manufacturing management practices in the organisation, would be more stable and likely to last.'

© Noordhoff Uitgevers bv

12

12.2.4   Process choices and service operation relationships

Chapter 11 introduced hospitality service types based on the interactions between the tangibility-intangibility continuum and the customisation-standardisation continuum. The focus now shifts to add process types viewed from the
manufacturing perspective, since a kitchen of a hotel can also be considered
to be a manufacturing unit. In general, manufacturing operations are characterised as indicated in the product-process matrix shown in Figure 12.8,
mainly adapted and explained in the subsections that follow from a process
management document available at www.ohio.edu/people/cutright/process-
management.doc.

Project process

A project is a temporary endeavour designed to produce a unique product,   *Temporary*
service or result with a defined beginning and end, undertaken to meet
unique goals and objectives, and typically brings about beneficial change or
added value. As such, project processes deal with separate, usually highly
customised products. A project process is characterised by a high degree of
job customisation, a large scope, and a release of resources once the project is completed. A project process lies at the high-customisation, low-vol-
ume end of the product-process matrix. The sequence of operations and
processes involved in each project is unique, creating one-of-a-kind products
or services tailored specifically to customer orders. Although some projects
may look similar, each is unique. Firms with project processes sell them-   *Unique*
selves on the basis of their capabilities, rather than on that of specific products or services. Some projects tend to be large, complex, and take a long
time. Many interrelated tasks must be completed, which requires close coordination. Resources needed for a project are assembled and then released
for further use once the project is finished. Projects typically make heavy
use of certain skills and resources at particular stages and then have little
use for them for the remainder of the process. A project process is based

FIGURE 12.8 Manufacturing product-process matrix

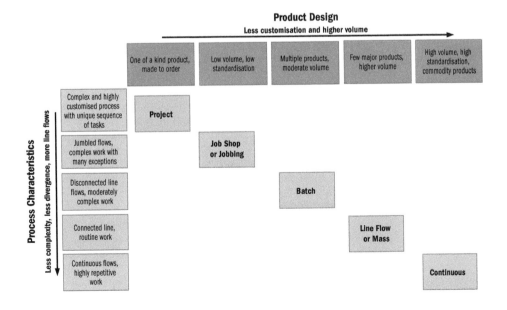

on a flexible flow strategy, with work flows redefined for each new project. Some general examples of project processes are building a new ship for a cruise company, running a political campaign, performing management consulting work, or developing new technology or new product. Some hospitality-specific examples of project processes are building a new resort hotel, baking a special wedding cake, planning a major banqueting event, or installing a new PMS at a hotel.

Job shop (jobbing) process

Small batches

A job shop or jobbing process is one in which small batches of a variety of custom products are made. In the job shop process flow, most of the created products require a unique set-up and sequence of process steps. Such processes deal with very high variety and low volumes and the operation's has to divide resources between the products. The resources of the operation are processed in a series of products but, although all products require the same level of attention, each differs in its exact needs. While its degree of repetition is low, the job shop process does enable the flexibility needed to produce a variety of products or services in significant quantities. Customisation is relatively high and the volume for any one product or service is low. The work force and equipment are flexible and handle various tasks.

Made to order

Typically, products are made to order, and are not produced ahead of time. The specific needs of the next customer are unknown, and the timing of repeat orders from the same customer is unpredictable. Each new order is handled as a single unit – as a job. A job shop process primarily involves the use of flexible flow strategy, with resources organised around the process. Most jobs have a different sequence of processing steps. General examples include custom metal processing shops, hospital emergency rooms, printing presses, or customised furniture makers. Within the hospitality industry, some activities in the hotel kitchen could be classified as jobbing processes, as some special food items are made in low volumes by skilled chefs.

Batch flow process

Batch production is a technique in which the object in question is created

Stage by stage

stage by stage over a series of workstations, producing different batches of products. A batch flow process differs from the job shop process with respect to volume, variety, and quantity. A major difference is that volumes are higher because the same or similar products or services are provided recurrently. Another difference is that a narrower range of products or services is provided. Here, variety is achieved more through an assemble-to-order strategy than following a job shop's make-to-order strategy, and some of the components for the final product or service may be produced in advance.

Larger quantities

Furthermore, production lots or customer groups are handled in larger quantities (or batches) than they are with job shop processes. If the size of the batch is as small as about two or three, however, the batch process differs little from the job shop, especially if each batch is a totally new product. If the batches are large, on the other hand, batch processes can be fairly repetitive. A batch of one product or customer group is processed, and then production is switched to the next. Eventually, the first product or service is produced once again. Batch flow processes have average or moderate volumes, but variety is still too great to warrant dedicating substantial resources to each product or service. In the batch flow process, the flow pattern is jumbled, with no standard sequence of operations throughout the produc-

© Noordhoff Uitgevers bv

tion facility. More dominant paths do emerge than at a job shop, however, and some segments of the process do have a linear flow. Some examples of batch flow processes are found in scheduling air travel, many types of manufacturing (clothes, furniture, equipment etc.), and processing bank loans. Within the hospitality industry, examples abound in the kitchen where food is prepared in batches with each batch going through the standard preparation, cooking, and storage, but each batch composed as a dish on a different plate.

Dominant paths

Line flow (or mass) process

Line flow or mass process is an arrangement of machines, tools, and workers in which a product is assembled by having each of these perform a specific, successive operation on an incomplete unit as it passes in a series of stages organised in a direct line. This involves a continuous movement of items through the production process. When one task is finished, the next task must start immediately until the final product is finished or the customer is served. A line flow process lies between the batch process and the continuous process; its volumes are high, and the products or services are standardised. This allows resources to be organised around a product or service. Materials move linearly from one operation to the next according to a fixed sequence, with little inventory held between operations. Each operation performs the same process over and over, with little variability in products or services provided. Production orders are not directly linked to customer orders, as is the case with project process or job process.

Manufacturers with line flow processes often follow a 'make-to-stock' strategy, with standard products held in inventory so that they are available once a customer places an order. However, apart from the 'assemble-to-order' strategy and mass customisation, there are other possibilities associated with line flow processes. Product variety is possible by carefully managing the addition of standard options to the main product or service. Alternatives of a product may be produced in a mass process, such as on an assembly line, but the process itself is not affected. The equipment used at each stage of the process can be designed to handle several different types of components loaded into the assembly equipment. This means that, provided the sequence of components in the equipment is synchronised with the sequence of models moving through the process, the process seems to be almost entirely repetitive. The most common examples of line flow processes are found in assembly lines used in the production of automobiles, home appliances, and packaged food items. Hospitality industry examples include fast-food restaurants and cafeterias.

Series of stages

Fixed sequence

Make-to-stock

Continuous flow process

Continuous production is a flow production method used to manufacture, produce, or process materials in a non-stop manner. Continuous production is called a continuous process or a continuous flow process because the materials, such as liquids, gasses, wood fibres, or powders being processed, are continuously in motion, undergo chemical reactions or are subject to mechanical or heat treatment. This means operating 24 hours per day, seven days per week to maximise utilisation and to avoid expensive shutdowns and re-starts on top of occasional semi-annual or annual maintenance shutdowns. Some chemical plants can operate for more than one or two years without shutting down. Blast furnaces can run over four to ten years without stopping. A continuous process is the extreme end of high-

Non-stop

Maximise utilisation

12

volume, low variety, standardised production, with rigid line flows, tightly linked process segments, and high capital intensity. For the continuous process, although products may be stored during the process, the principal characteristic is a smooth flow from one part of the process to another. Examples are petroleum refineries, chemical plants, breweries, blast furnaces, and processed food production plants. An electricity generating plant represents one of few continuous processes found in the service sector; thinking of the hospitality industry specifically, it is very difficult to identify a purely continuous process.

Using a design like the one used for manufacturing industries (the product-process matrix), the service-process matrix has been designed for the services industry; here, services have been classified into the four categories of professional service, service shop, mass service, and service factory. These types have already been explained in Chapter 11 based on the tangibility-intangibility continuum and the customisation-standardisation continu-

Labour intensity

um. Based on customer involvement and degree of labour intensity, the service-process matrix is illustrated in Figure 12.9; on the other hand, the service process matrix based on the customer involvement and degree of

Capital intensity

capital intensity is as illustrated in Figure 12.10. Notably, the degree of labour intensity is determined by the relationship between amounts of labour used in a process compared to the capital required. The degree of labour intensity is typically measured in proportion to the amount of capital required to produce a good or service, in which the higher the proportion of labour costs required, the more labour intensive the business is considered to be. A business is considered more capital intensive if, on the other hand, the ratio of capital required to the amount of labour required is much higher. Customer involvement is the extent to which customers interact with a process. The amount of customer involvement may range from self-service, through customisation of the product, to deciding the time and place a service is to be provided.

FIGURE 12.9 Service-process matrix based on customer involvement and degree of labour intensity

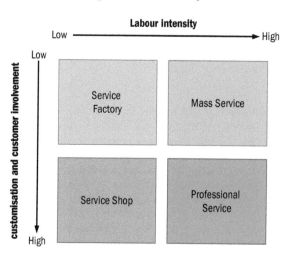

FIGURE 12.10 Service-process matrix based on customer involvement and degree of capital intensity

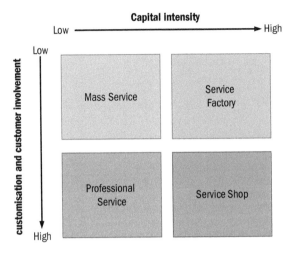

In addition to the examples offered in Chapter 11, professional services are high contact organisations where customers spend a considerable time in the service process; such services have high levels of customisation while their capital intensity is low, resulting in high labour intensity. For service shops, the work force and customers also interact frequently; capital intensity tends to be high and thus labour intensity low, but customisation remains high. Mass service processes are quite different from the first two processes, because customised customer involvement is low, with tightly controlled service specifications; capital intensity is low because automation is difficult to achieve, so labour intensity is high. The service factory involves the bare minimum of customised customer involvement, where what little contact between employees and customers exists is reserved for standardised services. If a customer is involved in the process, it is only in some form of self-service; within service factories, capital intensity is high.

12.3 Service concepts

A hospitality organisation is able to deliver its products and services once it has integrated its assets, employees, materials and processes. As noted in Chapter 11, service experiences are of different types over and above the nature of the food, drinks or accommodations offered. The combination of employee skills, materials and processes within the hospitality organisation must be appropriately integrated to result in a 'planned' or 'designed' service experience for customers.

Service experiences

12

Johnston, Clark and Shulver (2012) indicate that the service concept is an important way of capturing the nature of a service so that customers know what to expect, and staff understand what to provide. They define the service concept as a:

Shared and articulated understanding of the nature of the service provided and received, which should capture information about:
- The organising idea – the essence of the service bought, or used, by the customer
- The service provided – the service process and its outputs which have been designed, created and enacted by the operation using its input resources, including the customer
- The service received:
  - The customer experience – the customer's direct and personal interpretation of, and response to, their interaction with and participation in the service process, and its outputs, involving a journey through a series of touch points/steps.
  - The service outcomes – the results for the customer of the service process and their experience including 'products', benefits, emotions, judgements, and intentions. (2012, p. 48)

To illustrate the various aspects of the service concept, Johnston et al. (2012, p. 49) used the Alton Towers entertainment park as indicated in Figure 12.11.

FIGURE 12.11 Service concept of Alton Towers

Organisation	**Alton Towers**	
Organising idea	**A great day out at a theme park**	
Service concept (summary)	A great day out with friends or family at a UK theme park that provides an inclusive package of over 100 rides and attractions to suit all ages and tastes with thrills, fun, fantasy, fast food and magnificent gardens.	
Service provided	• Car parking • Transport to entrance • Ticketing • Security • Clean and tidy park • Uniformed and helpful staff • Fair queuing systems	• White knuckle rides • Shows and attractions • Children's rides • Well-kept gardens • Food outlets • Toilets • Street entertainers
Service received	**Customer experience:** • Easy parking • Good signage • Exhilarating rides • Enjoyable attractions • Full day out • Fun time • Never a dull moment • Lots of rides • Lots of food available • Helpful staff • Clean toilets	**Outcomes:** • Good food • 18 rides used • 3 attractions experienced • Fun day out with the family • Thrills • Terrifying rides • Exhausting • Car parking is extra • Good value for money • Want to go again • Will recommend to friends

12

The value of the service concept is in bringing together the various ele- **Value**
ments of the service – operational elements, marketing emphasis and customer requirements – to produce a meaningful all-encompassing definition
of service, which should be sufficiently detailed to provide a working service
specification. Notably, the service concept must not be confused with other
notions such as the service promise, the business proposition, the 8 Ps,
the business model, the vision, the mission, the value, an idea, or the
brand, most of which indicate what and how the organisation provides in
terms of services, without integrating the major component of the customer
experience and service outcomes.

12.3.1   Designing a service concept

There is no standard formula for designing successful service concepts.
Since the nature of services varies greatly, so does the variety in service
concepts. In all cases, it is necessary that all stakeholders have a common **Stakeholders**
understanding of what the service concept is, and why it should be so. A
major difficulty in designing a new service is making the intangibility of the
service idea tangible to stakeholders. Consequently, all parties involved in
designing a service concept need a shared understanding of the planned **Shared**
service in order to ensure a smooth transition from the idea to its design, **understanding**
implementation and delivery, ensuring the service will meet the needs of
customers who are also part of the service delivery.

Service design methods are inspired by various disciplines, such as anthropology, social studies, ethnography, information and management science,
and interaction design. Their purpose is to design back and front of house **Purpose**
definitions of services according to customer needs and service provider
competences and capabilities. This is expected to lead to a service that is
user-friendly, competitive and relevant for customers, while at the same time
sustainable for service providers. Service design concepts and ideas are
typically portrayed visually, using different representation techniques according to the culture, skills and level of understanding of stakeholders involved
in the service processes. While products are created and exist before being
purchased and used, services are created at the same moment they are
provided and used. Though a designer can propose the exact configurations
of a new product, a designer therefore cannot suggest the result of the interaction between customers and service providers in the same way, nor
can a designer prescribe the form and characteristics of any emotional value created by the service.

Along with the most traditional methods used for product design, service design also requires methods and tools to manage new elements of the design process, such as the time and interaction between actors. An overview
of the approaches for designing services was proposed by Morelli (2006), **Approaches**
who suggested three main directions:
- Identification of actors involved in the definition of the service, using appropriate analytical tools;
- Definition of possible service scenarios, verifying use cases, sequences
  of actions and actors' role, in order to define the requirements for the
  service and its logical and organisational structure;
- Representation of the service, using techniques that illustrate all components of the service, including physical elements, interactions, logical
  links and temporal sequences.

Tools

Analytical tools refer to anthropology, social studies, ethnography and social construction of technology, cultural probes, and video-ethnography and different observational techniques that are used to gather data about user behaviour. Design tools aim at producing a blueprint of the service, which describes the nature and characteristics of the interaction occurring in the service. Design tools include service scenarios (which describe the interaction), and use cases (which illustrate in detail the temporal sequences in a service encounter). Used in service design, these tools have been adequately adapted in order to include more information concerning material and immaterial components of a service, temporal sequences, and physical flows. Other techniques, such as JIT and TQM, are used to produce function-

Functional models

al models of the service system and to control its processes (see Chapters 14 and 16). Such tools, though, may prove too rigid to describe services because of the high level of uncertainty related to customer behaviour. Representation techniques are critical in service design because of the need to communicate inner mechanisms of services to actors, such as final users, who are not supposed to be familiar with technical language or representational techniques. For this reason, the interaction on the front office is often illustrated using storyboards. Other representational techniques, such as video sketching, have been used to explicate the system of interactions or a platform in a service. Video sketching is notable for being a quick and effective tool to stimulate customer participation in the development of the service and their involvement in the value production process.

Lovelock and Wirtz (2011) underline the need of service marketers to maintain a holistic view of the entire performance they want their customers to experience; they indicate that the value proposition must integrate three es-

Essential components

sential components – the core product, the supplementary services, and the delivery processes:

Core product

- The core product – the central component that supplies the principal, problem-solving benefits that customers seek, such as a hotel satisfying the need of a safe place to sleep for the night;

Supplementary services

- The supplementary services – services that augment the core product, facilitating its use and enhancing its value and appealing to the customer's overall experience, such as room service or valet parking;

Delivery processes

- The delivery processes – the processes used to deliver both the core product and the supplementary services. These must address the following issues:
  - The manner in which different service components are delivered to the customer.
  - The nature of the customer's role in those processes.
  - The duration of the delivery.
  - The prescribed level and style of the service to be offered.

Figure 12.12, taken from Lovelock and Wirtz (2011, p. 107), depicts the service offering for an overnight stay.

Figure 12.12 illustrates that the core product (overnight rental of bedroom) is defined by service level, scheduling, process nature, and customer role.

12

FIGURE 12.12 A service offering for an overnight hotel stay

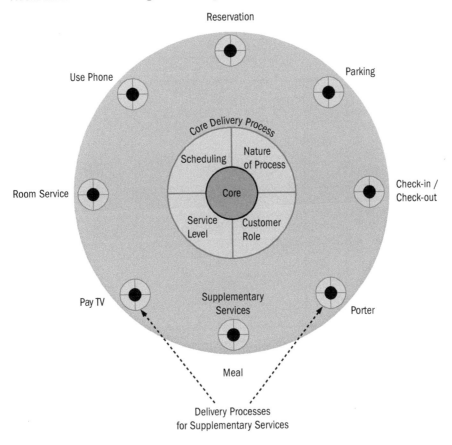

Around the core product are some supplementary services, such as meals, parking or room service, for which delivery processes must be specified individually.

To illustrate their point further, Lovelock and Wirtz (2011, p. 108) indicate that there are 'two kinds of supplementary services: facilitating supplementary services, which are either needed for service delivery or help in the use of the core product; and enhancing supplementary services, which add extra value for customers'. Lovelock and Wirtz have classified these different supplementary services into eight clusters, portrayed by petals surrounding the centre of a flower which they have termed the 'flower of service'. The petals are ordered in a clockwise sequence depending on how likely they are to be encountered by customers. However, the sequence may sometimes vary. Payment may have to be made before the service is delivered rather than afterwards, for instance. In a well-designed and well-managed service organisation, the petals and centre are fresh and well-formed. A service that is badly designed or poorly delivered is like a flower with missing or dried petals, and even if the centre is still perfect, the flower will look unattractive. Figures 12.13 and 12.14 show the distribution of supplementary services between facilitating services and enhancing services, and the 'flower of service' respectively, followed by brief definitions and explanations.

Facilitating

Enhancing

12

FIGURE 12.13 Distribution of supplementary services

Facilitating Services	Enhancing Services
Information	Consultation
Order-taking	Hospitality
Billing	Safekeeping
Payment	Exceptions

FIGURE 12.14 The flower of service

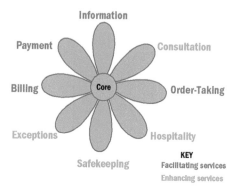

Information

Timely and accurate

To obtain full value from any goods or services, existing and prospective customers need relevant, timely and accurate information. Such information may sometimes be required by law, such as with the conditions of sale and use, warnings, reminders, and notifications of changes. Customers do appreciate advice on how to get the most value from a service and how to avoid problems, as well as necessary documentation such as reservation confirmation, receipts or account activity summaries. Traditionally, information is provided to customers via front-line employees, printed notices, brochures, and instruction book(let)s. Nowadays, information is also provided through videos or software-driven tutorials, touchscreen video displays, or company web sites.

Consultation

Dialogue

Counselling

Advice

This involves a dialogue with customer, used to probe customer requirements and subsequently develop a solution suited to a customer's needs. Effective consultation requires an understanding of each customer's current situation before suggesting a suitable course of action. Good customer records can be a great help in this respect, particularly if relevant data can easily be retrieved from a remote terminal. Counselling is another type of consultation; less direct than consultation, it involves helping customers understand their situations better so that they can come up with their 'own' solutions and action programmes. Lastly, another form of consultation is advice; this can also be offered through tutorials, group training programmes, and public demonstrations.

Order-taking

Once customers are ready to buy, a company can start accepting applications, orders, reservations, appointments, and check-ins. It is necessary for

© Noordhoff Uitgevers bv

this process to be polite, fast and accurate, so that customers do not waste time or endure unnecessary mental or physical effort. Orders can be received via sales personnel, phone lines, e-mails or online facilities.

Hospitality

Ideally, hospitality-related services should reflect a genuine pleasure at meeting new customers and greeting old ones when they return. Just as all hospitality industry operations consider their customers to be guests, well-managed businesses try, at least in small ways, to ensure their employees treat their customers in a similar fashion. As such, courtesy and consideration for customer needs should be taken into account in both face-to-face encounters as well as in telephone interactions. If, for example, customers have to wait outdoors before service can be provided, then a thoughtful service provider will offer weather protection. If, on the other hand, customers have to wait indoors, a waiting area with seating or even entertainment should be provided, with service providers ensuring they recruit employees who are naturally warm, welcoming, and considerate.

Courtesy and consideration

Safekeeping

When visiting service sites, customers regularly ask for their personal belongings to be well looked after; some guests may avoid certain locations simply because they do not have safekeeping services such as safes or convenient car parks. On-site safekeeping services include cloakrooms, luggage transport, handling and storage, safekeeping of valuables, and child care or pet care.

Exceptions

Exceptions involve supplementary services that fall outside normal service delivery and include special requests in advance of service delivery, covering special communications, problem solving, and restitutions. Companies should anticipate exceptions and develop back-up plans and guidelines so employees do not appear helpless or surprised when customers ask for special assistance. Managers need to keep an eye on the level of exceptional requests. Too many of such requests may indicate that existing procedures need to be changed. A flexible approach to exceptions is generally a good idea, because it reflects responsiveness to customer needs; on the other hand, too many exceptions may have a negative impact on other customers who may become envious, and may also overburden employees.

Special requests

Billing

Unless a service is free, billing is to be expected. Customers usually expect bills to be timely, clear, informative, and properly itemised. Providing inaccurate, illegible, or incomplete bills risks disappointing customers who may, up until that point, have been quite satisfied with their experience. If customers are already dissatisfied, a billing mistake may make them even more so. Busy customers dislike being kept waiting for a bill to be prepared. There are different ways in which bills can be presented to customers more swiftly. Hotels now have express check-outs, and many others push requested bills showing charges to date under guestroom doors on the morning of departure, or offer guests the choice of having their bills displayed on the TV monitors in their rooms beforehand.

Properly itemised

12

Payment

In most cases, a bill requires a customer to take action on payment. This can be done via self-service payment systems, direct-to-payee or intermediary systems, or automatic deductions from financial deposits. Customers essentially expect easy and convenient means of transferring payment, be it in their home countries or while travelling abroad. For self-service payment systems, payments may be made by inserting coins, banknotes, tokens or cards into machines. Good maintenance of the equipment is important.

Not every core product is surrounded by supplementary services from all eight petals. Industries such as the hotel industry tend to have more supplementary services, since they involve close (and, at times, extended) interactions with guests. As such, if customers do not visit service points, the need for hospitality may be more limited. The nature of the core product thus helps determine which supplementary services are be required to add value for both the organisation and the customer.

12.3.2   Service operations concept

Hospitality services are exposed to different levels of customer contact, some of which may be very brief (low contact) – a prospective guest making a call for reservation purposes and not following up with an eventual visit to the hotel. On the other hand, this customer contact may extend over a longer time frame (high contact) and involve multiple interactions of varying degrees of complexity – a business guest attending a conference at a hotel over the course of a working week. In low customer contact situations, there is very little, if any, face-to-face contact between customers and service organisations. There is a growing tendency for low customer contact nowadays; contributing factors are technological developments and perceived convenience. Hotels support their guests in this tendency by, for example, offering multiple avenues for check-in, such as through apps, self-service kiosks or at the reception desk. In high customer contact situations, guests and service organisations are in constant contact during the service delivery. Here, the customer is exposed to many physical clues

Easy and convenient

Add value

Low contact

High contact

Technological developments

12

© Noordhoff Uitgevers bv

about the organisation, which include the interior and exterior of its buildings, its fixtures, furnishings and equipment, the appearance and behaviour of its employees, as well as, at times, the appearance and behaviour of other customers.

As customers interact with a hospitality operation, its employees or even other guests, it should be noted that these interactions may add or remove value (friendly and competent employees, or drunk and rowdy patrons at the bar, respectively). Consequently, hospitality operations have to coordinate all interactions to make sure that customers get the service experience they came for. One way of assuring this is to have a well-established service operations concept, in which visible components of the service can be divided into those relating to employees, and those relating to physical facilities and equipment. Customers show less involvement in factors beyond their direct sphere of contact or control, such as back-of-house operations. The service operations concept stipulates its geographical scope, its scheduling of operations, a description of the facility's design and layout, an indication of how and when operating assets should be deployed to perform specific tasks, and clarifies which tasks are assigned to front of house operations and which to back of house operations.

Value

The geographical scope represents the area the hospitality operation has to deal with. As such, an international hotel chain that has hotels across five continents has to keep in contact with, and search for data regarding, associated markets. On the other hand, a local restaurant in a city that receives lots of guests from a neighbouring country would do well to find a lot of information about that neighbouring country's market and the preferences of associated guests.

Geographical scope

Though seemingly obvious, scheduling and opening times of hospitality operations have an important role in overall customer satisfaction. Depending on the type of hospitality operation, schedules may be established on the basis of hours (e.g. in cafés for temporary workers), days (e.g. full-time employees at a hotel) or even seasons (e.g. on cruise ships or at seasonal resorts). A hospitality operation should be aware of the relation between its opening times and its different target groups. If children are among the target groups, a hospitality operation may have to open its doors at other times than if its target groups are composed of adults only.

Scheduling

The design and layout of an operation is basically about the physical location of its transforming resources. Design and layout are concerned with deciding where to put an operation's facilities, machines, equipment and staff, and have a major influence in determining the way in which transformed resources – materials, information and customers – flow through the operation. These factors are very important for guests of hospitality operations, since the factors define the guests' stay, what they eat and drink, or how they sleep.

Layout

12

The deployment of operating assets relates to the set of repeatable, quantifiable and measurable activities performed within the hospitality organisation in order to successfully prepare and deliver products and services for eventual consumption by, and interaction with, the customers. Operating assets mainly concern the presence, availability, volume and manner of use of

Operating assets

different facilities found within the organisation. Flexible use of different room spaces is becoming very important in the running of a hotel or a restaurant, for example.

Competitive edge

Companies that invest in their employees' professional and personal development gain a competitive edge over their rivals and have a more committed workforce (see Chapter 6). This is especially true within the hospitality industry that experiences high employee turnover. How employees are treated and how much they value the hospitality organisation they work for therefore has an impact on how that hospitality organisation performs. Diversity, health and safety, workplace conditions, personal development, work/life balance and remuneration are issues that hospitality industry employers need to address to ensure a happy, motivated workforce. For this to be smoothly carried out and appreciated by the stakeholders, however, employees need to know their roles and positions within the organisation, be they at the front office or in any of the back office positions. It is therefore important that every employee knows what to do when guests visit the organisation, which is reflected in the organisational chart as discussed and illustrated in Chapters 2, 4 and 5.

Roles and positions

12.3.3   Service delivery process

Define

Service delivery is basically the act of providing a service to customers. It is concerned with where, when and how a service is delivered to guests. Throughout the service delivery process, service providers aim to clearly define the content of services to be provided, clearly define the roles and responsibilities of participants (customers as well as service providers), and set service quality expectations as well as availability and timeliness. Within the service delivery process, there is a distinction between the sequencing of steps, the extent of delegation, the nature of contact, the nature of processes, the allocation of limited capacity, and imagery and atmosphere. The service delivery system also includes the visible parts of the service operations system – buildings, fixtures, furnishings and equipment, and, at times, the appearance and behaviour of other customers.

Sequencing

The sequencing of the service delivery steps is concerned with where and when the steps of the service delivery process should take place; these are very easily illustrated using flowcharts which provide insight and clarity into the different phases of the service delivery process (see Chapter 13). Flowcharts make clear what has to be done in front-of-house, but also what elements are necessary at back-of-house.

Delegation

Outsourced

Delegation is the practice of turning over work-related tasks and/or authority to employees, subordinates, or other third parties. The extent to which delegation is required is connected to the size and range of, and parties responsible for, the service delivery processes that have to be carried out. With technological developments (especially those related to the digital age), delegation has become very important. The extent of delegation determines the elements of the service delivery that the organisation performs on its own, as well as those that can be outsourced. Since almost all services can be outsourced these days, it is not strange to notice that, in a more traditional hotel, perhaps only the laundry and security are outsourced; but in most recently opened hotels, even such activities as general management, personnel or finance administration are outsourced.

12

The nature of contact within the service delivery process is much more concerned with the different ways that customers come into contact with the organisation providing the service. It determines whether customers are received on the premises of the service provider, or whether the service provider goes to its customers. Contact between parties at a distance is another possibility. The nature of contact probably starts with elements of written communication like a travel guide, a website or a brochure. It is also possible that contact starts through a telephone call, a fax or an e-mail. One of the most characteristic features of contact in the hospitality industry is that, in most cases, guests have to come to the service provider. This means that guests have to incur some manner of costs (financial, temporal, and psychological) to obtain the service.

Nature of contact

The nature of the process is much more concerned with how customers are served: individual service, batch service or self-service. Guests may be served individually at a table or in a room. Batch service may occur if guests are part of a group using larger tables. Guest self-service may take place at banquets or through other self-service modes.

Nature of the process

The protocol for allocating limited capacity is much more concerned with reservation and queueing procedures. Much attention has to be paid to the ways guests can make reservations; with technologies continually developing and improving, these procedures are changing as well. For queues, this is about predicting their lengths and perceived durations. The analysis of queues is important, because the results are often used when making business decisions about resources needed to provide a service (see Chapter 13). In the protocol for allocating limited capacity, attention also has to be paid to yield management whatever the size of the hospitality organisation; all organisations benefit from proper yield management strategies.

Capacity

Queues

Within the service delivery system, attention must also be paid to the imagery and the atmosphere. The service operation system design and layout are much more about the hardware of the organisation (building, size of rooms, routing, kinds of tables, chairs etc.); but the service delivery system regards imagery and atmosphere quite differently. Important factors here are background music, seasonal variations in décor and images summer, Christmas), perceived front-of-house interaction between employees, perceived handling of possible conflicts between different guest groups (small children, youngsters, and the elderly).

Atmosphere

12

Summary

► An organisation's operations system generates its products; for hospitality organisations, this is primarily a service accompanied at times with some manner of physical goods. All organisations have a conversion process transforming input into output. A conversion process that includes manufacturing (or production) yields a tangible output, while a conversion process that includes service yields an intangible output. The following characteristics are used to differentiate between manufacturing and service operations:
  • Consumption of output
  • Customer participation in conversion
  • Degree of customer contact
  • Measurement of performance
  • Nature of work (jobs)
  • Tangible and intangible nature of output

► A process is a sequence of actions performed in order to achieve a result, a series of changes that happens naturally, or a method of producing goods and services by converting input into output.

► Mullins regards organisations as open systems as described in the open systems model; organisations take input from the environment and, through a series of activities, transform or convert this input into output.

► The input-transformation-output model shows that all operations generate products and services by changing input into output using an 'input-transformation-output' process; here, operations are processes that take in a set of input resources which are used to transform, or are transformed into, something to generate output of products and services.

► Operations are categorised into four principal dimensions – volume, variety, variation in demand, and visibility.

► Performance objectives are the goals that an organisation must achieve, selected based on its strategy, and influenced by its relevant stakeholders. There are five main such objectives: quality; speed; dependability; flexibility; and cost.

► Due to the uncertainty of organisations being able to excel in all five performance objectives, the concept of 'trade-off' was introduced by Skinner, who argued that operations could not be 'all things to all people'. This requires operations to identify a single goal or 'task'; a clear set of competitive priorities to act as an objective. Countering Skinner's trade-off argument, Ferdows and de Meyer argued that certain operational capabilities enhance one another, enabling excellence to be built up in a cumulative fashion across the objectives, as illustrated in their sand cone model.

► Manufacturing operations can be arranged in a product-process matrix, in which process characteristics and product design are plotted along different axes to generate five types of processes: project; job shop; batch flow; line flow; and continuous flow.

► The service-process matrix has been designed for the services industry, with services classified into four categories: professional service; service shop; mass service; and service factory.

► The service concept is a shared and articulated understanding of the nature of the service provided and received; it should capture information about the organising idea, the service provided, and the service received. The service concept is an important way of capturing the nature of a service, informing customers of what to expect, and staff of what to provide.

► As the nature of services varies tremendously, there is no standard formula for designing service processes. As such, in designing service processes, it is necessary for all stakeholders to have a common understanding of what definition of and reasons for the particular service concept.

► Morelli suggests three main directions in service design, including: the identification of actors involved in the definition of the service; the definition of possible service scenarios; and the representation of the service, using techniques that illustrate all service components.

► Lovelock and Wirtz underline the need for service marketers to maintain a holistic view of the entire performance they want their customers to experience; they indicate that the value proposition must integrate three essential components:
  • core product – the central component that supplies the principal, problem-solving benefits that customers are after;
  • supplementary services – services that augment core products, facilitate their use and enhance the value and appeal of customers' overall experience;
  • delivery processes – the processes used to deliver both core products and the supplementary services.

► Lovelock and Wirtz have classified supplementary services into eight clusters portrayed by petals surrounding the centre of a flower. Termed the 'flower of service', its petals are arranged in a clockwise sequence by the likelihood with which they can be expected to be encountered by customers. The petals are: information, consultation, order-taking, hospitality, safekeeping, exceptions, billing, and payment. Some of these are facilitating services, whereas the other are enhancing services.

12

▶ Hospitality services are exposed to different levels of customer contact; some low, some high. The service operations concept stipulates:
- Geographical scope;
- Scheduling operations;
- A description of the facility's design and layout;
- An indication of asset deployment;
- A distinction between front-of-house tasks and back-of-house tasks.

© Noordhoff Uitgevers bv

Questions and assignments for reflection

1   This chapter discussed process characteristics. Compare and contrast Mullin's views of organisations (such as hotels) as open systems to the input-transformation-output model?

2   Figure 12.5 illustrates the typology of operations indicating the various process dimensions and their cost implications. Using an example from the hospitality industry, illustrate costs and other implications of the four process dimensions.

3   The Penang Mutiara case in Text 12.1 describes how quality, speed, dependability, flexibility and cost impact a hotel's external customers. Explain how each of these performance objectives may have internal benefits.

4   To what extent do degrees of labour intensity and capital intensity interact with customisation and customer involvement to determine the various types of services in the service-process matrix?

5   Figure 12.12 depicts the service offering for an overnight stay. Explain how the core product, supplementary services, and delivery processes are integrated in the context of the overnight hotel stay.

12

13
Designing Hospitality Processes

M. N. Chibili

13.1 Introduction

Designing hospitality processes is about making the services we employ usable, easy and desirable. As has been indicated in many of the previous chapters, service happens over time and consists of touchpoints – either people, information, products or spaces that we encounter. A menu, a chair or a waitress, for example, are all touchpoints that make up a restaurant service. Designing hospitality processes is about creating these touchpoints and defining how they interact both with each other and with the user. An important part of designing great service is determining who the users of that service will be – guests, employees or suppliers. The use of design tools and methods can deliver an in-depth understanding of user behaviours, likes and needs, which allows new solutions to be developed. These solutions can be used to redesign an existing service and improving its usability, or it can be used to create an entirely new service.

13.2 Configuring the processes

Once the general design of a process has been conceived, its separate activities must be configured. Slack et al. (2013, p. 109) state that:

> 'This detailed design of a process involves identifying all the individual activities that are needed to meet the objectives of the process, and deciding on the sequence in which these activities are to be performed and who is going to do them. There will, of course, be some constraints to this. Some activities must be carried out before others and some activities can only be done by certain people or equipment. Nevertheless, for a process of any reasonable size, the number of alternative process designs is usually large. Because of this, process design is often done using some simple visual approach such as process mapping.'

Individual activities

Sequence

United States of America, New Jersey, Atlantic City: The Revel

13

13.2.1 Process mapping and service blueprinting

Workflow
diagram

Purpose

Process mapping, also called process analysis, is the practice of using a workflow diagram to promote a clearer understanding of a process or series of parallel processes. It allows one to describe how activities (information, materials, or people) within a process are linked. The purpose of process mapping is to use diagrams to better understand processes currently in use and to identify possible improvements in order to provide better customer focus and satisfaction. Process mapping helps to identify the best and most suitable practices, and to find appropriate benchmarks that can be used to measure how services can be better presented to the customers. HTC

FIGURE 13.1 Some common process mapping symbols

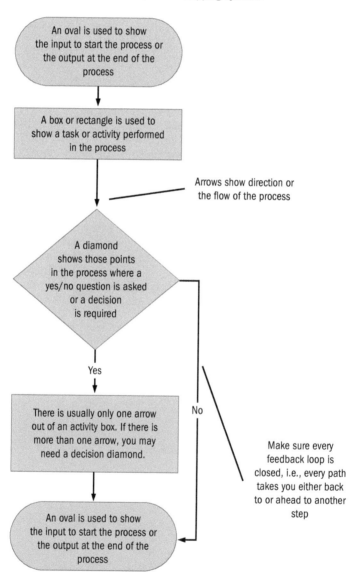

Consulting (www.htc-consult.com) indicates that process mapping itself 'should be led by the process owner but should also include input from their team and indeed consultation with other parties across the business. It is critical that the maps accurately depict how a current process actually works in practice'. In developing these maps, major activities must be identified first; subsequently, sub-tasks must be defined within each of the broader areas of activity. In order to design process maps (also called flowcharts), some common symbols have been adopted over time – however, there is no universally used or accepted set of symbols for specific types of processes. Some common process mapping symbols, accompanied by their meanings, are illustrated in Figure 13.1.

Flowcharts

Creating flowcharts in Microsoft Word, for example, is fairly straightforward. In the Insert – Shapes menu option, there is a palette of 28 shapes termed 'flowchart' (Word 2013); placing the cursor over these symbols displays their titles. The names of the symbols are shown in Figure 13.2; from left to right (FLTR), and from top to bottom.

FIGURE 13.2 Flowchart symbols from Microsoft Office Word 2013

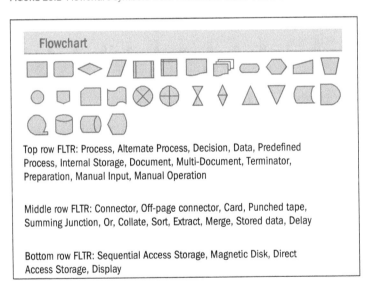

Flowchart

Top row FLTR: Process, Alternate Process, Decision, Data, Predefined Process, Internal Storage, Document, Multi-Document, Terminator, Preparation, Manual Input, Manual Operation

Middle row FLTR: Connector, Off-page connector, Card, Punched tape, Summing Junction, Or, Collate, Sort, Extract, Merge, Stored data, Delay

Bottom row FLTR: Sequential Access Storage, Magnetic Disk, Direct Access Storage, Display

In order to create process maps, the following easy steps can be used (adapted from the Iowa State University of Science and Technology, www.fpm.iastate.edu):

Step 1: Determine the boundaries
    1 Where does a process begin?
    2 Where does a process end?

Step 2: List the steps
    1 Use a verb to start the task description.
    2 Use a flowchart to either provide (the minimum amount of) information required to understand the general process flow or to describe every finite action and decision point in greater detail.

Step 3: Sequence the steps
1   Use post-it notes so tasks can be moved around.
2   Do not draw arrows until later.

Step 4: Draw appropriate symbols
Start with the basic symbols:
1   Ovals indicate input used to start the process or output gained at the end of the process.
2   Boxes or rectangles indicate tasks or activities performed in the process.
3   Arrows indicate process direction flow.
4   Diamonds indicate points in the process where yes/no questions are asked or where decisions are required.
5   There is usually only one arrow leading from an activity box. If there is more than one arrow, the addition of a decision diamond may be required.
6   If there are feedback arrows, make sure the feedback loop is closed; i.e. it should lead back to the input box.

Step 5: System model
1   Draw charts using the system model approach.
2   Input – use information based on people, machines, materials, methods, and environments.
3   Process – use sequential or parallel subsets of processes.
4   Output – use outcomes or desired results.
5   Control – use best in class business rules.
6   Feedback – use information gained from surveys or feedback.

Step 6: Check for completeness
Include pertinent chart information, using title and date for easy reference.

Step 7: Finalise the flowchart
1   Consider if this process is being run the way it should.
2   Establish whether people are following the process as charted.
3   Establish whether consensus has been reached.
4   Remove what is redundant; add what is missing.

Blueprint

While flowcharts describe existing processes, a blueprint shows how a service process is constructed in detail; it also shows details of what is visible to customers and identifies possible bottlenecks in a service process. Wilson, Zeithaml, Bitner, and Gremler (2012, p. 181) define service blueprinting as 'a tool for simultaneously depicting the service process, the points of customer contact, and the evidence of the service from the customer's point of view'. A service blueprint can be regarded as a two-dimensional representation of a service as shown in Figure 13.3: the horizontal axis represents the time line of an individual process step, which can be taken care of either by the service provider or by the customer; the vertical axis represents the individual stages of interaction between the provider and the customer.

Interaction

© Noordhoff Uitgevers bv

FIGURE 13.3 The components of a service blueprint

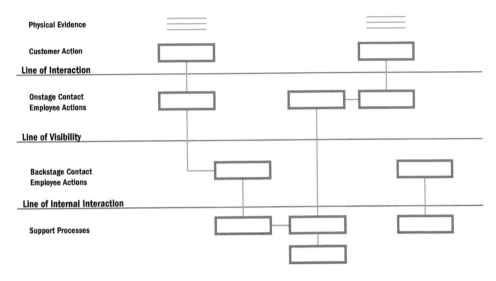

1 The customer action layer, representing the service that the customer is actually provided with when the service marketing concept is put into practice.
2 The onstage contact employee actions layer, indicating all actions performed by staff members in contact with the customers.
3 The backstage contact employee layer, indicating all actions the contact employee needs to able to perform to support the customer steps which do not require onstage activities.
4 The support processes layer, indicating all other processes needed to retain the processes in the first three layers which are not carried out by a contact employee.
5 Lastly, at the top, the physical evidence, representing the physical evidence that the customer came into contact with the organisation.

These layers are connected by the lines of interaction, visibility and internal interaction. The line of interaction separates customer actions from provider actions, and represents direct interactions or joint activities. The line of visibility differentiates between activities visible or not visible to the customer. The line of internal interaction separates front office from back office (inter) actions.

Adapted from Lovelock and Wirtz (2011), the basic steps in developing a service blueprint are as follows:
1 Identify the key activities involved in a service offering
2 Define the value chain before drilling down to process level
3 Distinguish between 'front stage' and 'back stage' activities
4 Clarify front stage activities between customers and employees, and back stage support and systems
5 Identify potential bottlenecks
   a Take preventative measures
   b Prepare contingencies

13

6 Develop standards for execution of each activity
 a Time for task completion
 b Maximum waiting time
 c Scripts used to guide interaction between employees and customers

Active process

Bottlenecks

Developing a service blueprint is an active process that can be used to bring teams together and to visually develop and communicate the service delivery process or service innovation. It is also a useful mechanism for identifying bottlenecks and for solving service delivery problems. Figure 13.4 is a sample of a service blueprint for an overnight stay at a hotel shown on a board using post-its.

The design of service blueprints is always top-down; this has the advantage that any action performed in the organisation actually supports the product or service the organisation wants to deliver to its customers.

Some advantages of service blueprinting
Service blueprinting facilitates the service design and required service improvement processes used to:

Service failures

- Identify potential service bottlenecks – the service designers can design the service in such a way as to avoid identified possible service failures; this can improve the quality of the service and the customer experience.
- Identify possible supplementary services – a visual representation helps service designers in identifying possible supplementary services required for each core service offering. Integrating more supplementary

Supplementary services

services with the core services will improve service offerings directed at customers; at the same time, it will streamline the organisation's processes and eventually all organisational units.

Ideal and efficient

- Optimise service co-creation processes – the service designers can design a service blueprint for an ideal and efficient service process for the different areas of service offering and then compare them to existing service process drawings. Using this approach, service designers can identify the overheads for the customer and the organisation in the current service co-creation process and propose necessary improvements.
- Improve service delivery process times for better efficiency and productivity – since modern-day customers are very time sensitive, service delivery

Delivery time

time is one of the key aspects for quality of service and competitive positioning. Analytical approaches can help service designers in designing efficient steps at the various customer contact points to help improve both customer and employee satisfaction and productivity.
- Identify the points of possible rule-breaking and theft in the service process – this will allow service designers to plan possible preventative ac-

Preventative actions

tions as solutions at the identified points.

13.2.2   Facility layout and design

Basic objective

The facility layout is an important component of a business's overall operations, both in terms of maximising the effectiveness of the production process and in terms of meeting the needs of employees. The basic objective of layout is to ensure a smooth flow of work, materials, and information through a system. The basic definition of a 'facility' is the space in which a business's activities take place. The layout and design of that space greatly impact how the work is done – the flow of work, materials, and information through the system. Layout is often the first thing people will notice on en-

© Noordhoff Uitgevers bv

FIGURE 13.4 Sample service blueprint – overnight hotel stay (Source: www.phonakpro.com)

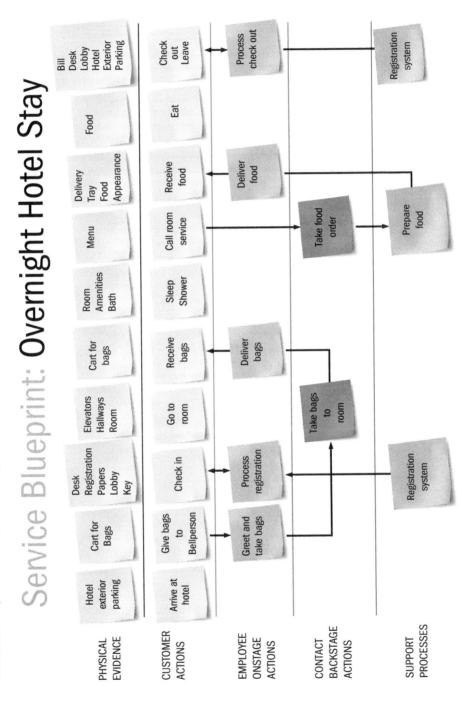

Service Blueprint: Overnight Hotel Stay

tering an operation because it influences its appearance. The key to good facility layout and design is the integration of the needs of people (personnel and customers), materials (raw, finished, and in-process), and machinery in such a way as to create a single, well-functioning system.

Factors in determining layout and design

There are many operational criteria to consider when building or renovating a facility for maximum layout effectiveness, including:

- Ease of communication and support – facilities should be laid out so that communication within various areas of the business and interactions with vendors and customers can be done in an easy and effective manner. Similarly, support areas should be stationed in areas that allow them to serve operating areas.
- Ease of future expansion or change – facilities should be designed so that they can be easily expanded or adjusted to meet changing production requirements.
- Flow of movement – facility design should reflect a recognition of the importance of smooth process flow.
- Impact on employee morale and job satisfaction – since countless studies have indicated that employee morale has a major impact on productivity, owners and managers should be mindful of this factor when considering facility design alternatives.
- Handling materials – facility layout should make it possible to handle materials (products, equipment, containers, etc.) in an orderly and efficient manner.
- Output needs – the facility should be laid out in a way that is conducive to helping the business meet its production needs.
- Promotional value – if a business commonly receives visitors in the form of customers, vendors, investors, etc., the owner may want to make sure that the facility layout is an attractive one that further cements or polishes the company's reputation. Design factors that can influence the degree of attractiveness of a facility are not limited to the design of the production area itself; other important aspects include, for instance, the ease of performing maintenance/cleaning tasks.
- Safety – facility layout should enable a business to operate effectively and in accordance with Occupational Safety and Health Administration guidelines and other legal restrictions.
- Shipping and receiving – a business should leave ample room for this aspect of operations.
- Space utilisation – this aspect of facility design includes everything from making sure that traffic lanes are wide enough to making certain that inventory storage warehouses or rooms utilise as much vertical space as possible.

Easy and effective

Employee morale

Reputation

Traffic

Some of the goals in designing the facility are to ensure a minimum amount of handling of materials, to avoid bottlenecks, to minimise machine interference, to ensure high employee morale and safety, and to ensure flexibility.

Layout requirements can also differ dramatically by industry. The needs of service-oriented businesses, for instance, often depend on whether customers receive the service at the physical location of the business (such as at a restaurant) or whether the business goes to the customer's home or place of business to provide the service (as with caterers). In the case of the latter, these businesses will likely have facility layouts that emphasise storage space for their equipment, rather than spacious customer seating areas. Slack et al. (2013) indicate that there are four basic layout types and that these layout types are closely related to the process types (see Chapter 12). As shown in Figure 13.5, they are: fixed position layout; functional layout; cellular layout; and product (line) layout, including their main process types, performance objectives and common hospitality examples.

FIGURE 13.5 The relationship between basic layout types, process types and performance objectives

Basic layout type	Main process type	Main performance objectives	Commonly found in
Cellular	Mass services	Speed and cost	Buffet
Fixed position	Service shops, with aspects of professional services	Quality and flexibility	À la carte restaurant
Functional	Service shops	Dependability and quality	Kitchen
Product (Line)	Mass services	Speed and cost	Cafeteria

Layout types

The major layout types contained in Figure 13.5 are explained below.

Cellular layout

A cellular layout is one where the transformed resources entering the operation are pre-selected (or pre-select themselves) to move to one part of the operation (or cell) in which all transforming resources are located, thereby meeting their immediate processing needs. After being processed in one cell, the transformed resources may go on to another cell (for more information on transforming versus transformed resources, see Chapter 12). A common example in the field of hospitality is the breakfast buffet where similar products are grouped together in their own areas. Possible advantages of cellular layout are the ability for a good compromise between costs and flexibility for relatively high-variety operations; fast throughput; group work, which can result in good motivation. However, its disadvantages include potentially requiring costly redesign of an existing layout; potentially requiring more space and equipment; potential for under-utilisation of existing facilities.

Breakfast buffet

Fixed position layout

A fixed-position layout is appropriate for a product that is too large or too heavy to move. Battleships, for example, are not produced on an assembly line. For services, other reasons may dictate the fixed position (e.g., an à la carte restaurant service as discussed in Chapter 5). Other fixed-position layout examples include construction (e.g., buildings, dams, and electric or nuclear power plants), shipbuilding, aircraft, aerospace, farming, oil drilling, home repair, and automated car washes. As such, the recipient of the process is stationary, and the equipment, machinery, facility and people who do the processing move as needed. Its advantages include very high product flexibility; products or customers are not moved or disturbed; a high variety of tasks for staff. Its disadvantages include very high unit costs; potential difficulties in scheduling space and; frequent potential movement of plant and staff.

À la carte restaurant

13

Functional layout

The functional layout (also called process layout in some literature) conforms to the needs and convenience of the functions performed by the transforming resources within the processes. In functional layout, similar resources or processes are located together. Motivations can include that it is convenient to group them together, or that the utilisation of transforming resources is hereby improved. Functional layout means that when materials, information or customers flow through the operation, their route is determined according to their needs. Different products or customers will have different needs and therefore take different routes. The separation of different activities in a kitchen is an example of this layout. Its advantages include: high product flexibility; relative robustness in dealing with disruptions; relative ease of supervision of equipment or facilities. Some of its disadvantages are under-utilisation of facilities; potentially very high work-in-progress or customer queuing; potential difficulties in controlling the complex flow.

Product (line) layout

Product layouts are found in mass services with repetitive assembly, and in process or continuous flow industries. Product layout involves locating transforming resources entirely for the convenience of transformed resources. In a product layout, resources are arranged sequentially, based on the routing of the products. In theory, this sequential layout allows the entire process to be laid out in a straight line, which at times may be totally dedicated to the production of only one product or product version. The flow of the line can then be subdivided so that labour and equipment are utilised smoothly throughout the operation. An example of product layout in the field of hospitality would be a cafeteria. Some of its advantages include low unit costs for high volume; possible opportunities for specialisation of equipment; materials or customer movement is convenient. Its disadvantages include potentially decreased flexibility; less robustness in case of disruption; potentially very repetitive.

Figure 13.6 is an example of a restaurant complex borrowed from Slack et al. (2013, p. 200); it shows a combination of all the layout types grouped together.

FIGURE 13.6 A restaurant complex with all four basic layout types

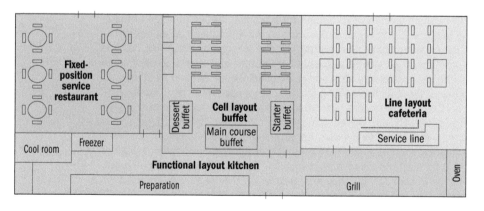

13.2.3   Job design

Job design is the way in which a company structures the content and environment of individual staff member's jobs within the workplace, and the interface with the technology or facilities that they use. The theories of Maslow and Herzberg (see Chapter 6) suggest that there is more to successful work practices than simply requiring people to unthinkingly repeat simple tasks: stimulation, variety, initiative, recognition and team-work are all seen as valuable contributors to motivation and productivity. There are situations, however, where traditional production lines in which each person does only one simple repetitive task, do minimise marginal costs of production. However, these calculations do not take into account:

Work practices

- Employee indifference with regard to improving production methods;
- Poor product or service quality resulting from employees not identifying with what they are producing;
- Costs of recruitment and training caused by high staff turnover likely to result from employees disliking their jobs;
- Costs of staff shortages.

Designing for health and safety – ergonomics

Ergonomics is a science-based discipline that brings together knowledge from other subjects, such as anatomy, physiology, psychology, engineering and statistics, employed to ensure that designs complement the strengths and abilities of individual people and minimise the effects of their limitations (www.ergonomics.org.uk). Rather than expecting employees to adapt to a design that forces them to work in an uncomfortable, stressful or dangerous way, ergonomists and human factors specialists seek to understand how a product, workplace or system can be (re)designed to suit the people who need to use it. They take into account such factors as age, size, strength, cognitive ability, prior experience, cultural expectations and goals.

Suit the people

13

FIGURE 13.7 Some hospitality health and safety issues for ergonomic designers

Manual Handling	Any activity requiring a person to use force to lift, lower, push, pull, carry or otherwise move or restrain an object. For example: • lifting heavy objects (plates, trays, stocking bar supplies) • repetitive or forceful movements • work carried out in awkward postures.
The Work Environment	The characteristics of the area where you work. Elements include floors and other surfaces, noise, lighting, temperature, ventilation, accessibility and housekeeping. The most common causes of injury arising from the work environment in the food industry are slips, trips and falls, and heat stress.
Plant	The term 'plant' refers to both powered and non-powered equipment. Caterers, chefs and kitchen staff use many items (slicers, mincers, knives, mixers, etc.) which have the potential to cause injury. • guarding moving parts • the power source (e.g. electricity) • the risk of fire or explosion • noise • vibration • radiation • stability (how well the plant is mounted or secured) • the use of pressure vessels (e.g. espresso machines).
Heat	Burns are very common in the hospitality industry. Many operations involve contact with hot food, equipment, surfaces and liquids. Heat is a risk when: • cooking food • taking food from ovens, bain-maries etc. • making beverages using hot equipment or steam
Electricity	Electrical equipment is widely used in the hospitality industry. Because of frequent use and cleaning, its electrical safety may be compromised, exposing workers to the risk of shock, burns, or fatal injury. Electrical accidents are usually caused by: • using faulty equipment • working with damaged leads • unsafe work practices, or • a combination of the above.

Figure 13.7 shows some of the health and safety issues related to the hospitality industry that ergonomics designers take into account.

Designing for efficiency – scientific management
One of the earliest approaches to job design was laid out by Taylor (1911). Taylor's premise behind scientific management was that for any given job, there is an optimal or best way to structure that job to maximise performance. He also developed two principles allowing managers structure their jobs appropriately. The first is job simplification, which means deconstructing work into the simplest individual components. Just like everything around us is made up of atoms and molecules, Taylor's theory states that every piece of work has tiny individual components. For example, see Section 5.4.1 in Chapter 5 which has all the phases and related tasks applicable to a fine-dining restaurant. The second principle, job specialisation, is related to the first. Once 'simple tasks' have been determined, employees should be tasked to perform specific tasks and focus on them exclusively – hence specialisation, like the specialist chefs indicated in Section 5.4.3 in Chapter 5.

Simplification

Specialisation

Determining the best way to perform each task is not easy, but can be done using time and motion studies, which analyse body movements to determine the fastest or most efficient ways employees can perform a given task. Based on the results, managers can set realistic expectations and performance goals for employees. One of the flaws of scientific management is that it only focuses on extrinsic motivation – that is, it only uses factors like pay and compensation to motivate employees to perform. Employees who are only there for a pay check are less likely to be loyal than employees who actually enjoy their work.

Flaws

While the scientific management method can be beneficial in assembly-line settings like factories or fast food restaurants, it has its drawbacks. Creativity is important in any business setting, and the scientific management approach deemphasizes creativity. By its nature, it requires employees to follow strict protocols and engage in the exact same behaviours day in and day out; therefore, it does not motivate employees to come up with new ways to solve problems and increase efficiency, and often precludes them from doing so. In fact, the rigidity can become demoralising to employees if they start to feel like drones or machines.

Drawbacks

Designing for motivation – behavioural approaches

This approach stresses the importance of the human factor in increasing productivity. According to behavioural studies, there is a positive correlation between improved workplace conditions and employee performance. Behavioural studies kick-started the modern human resource management practices that have resulted in much improved employee treatment. In the 1960s and 1970s these considerations gave rise to the job redesign movement which attempted to improve jobs (and employee performance) by deliberately designing better jobs. A useful way to consider a job's design elements is the job characteristic model (Hackman, Oldham, Janson and Purdy, (1975) where five core job characteristics are identified:

Human factor

Redesign movement

- Skill variety: Does the job require various activities which, in turn, require employees to develop a variety of skills and talents?
- Task identity: Does the job allow employees to identify with the work in hand (the finished item or service)?
- Task significance: Does the job have an impact on other people's lives, either in society in general, or in (a sub-group within) the company or firm?
- Autonomy (responsibility): Does the job provide the employee with significant freedom, independence, and discretion in scheduling the work and in determining the procedures to be used in carrying it out?
- Feedback (understanding of the results of work): Is the employee provided with feedback on effectiveness and performance?

The first three of these characteristics contribute to the meaningfulness of the work or job. Hackman et al. (1975) suggest that these characteristics produce the following outcomes:

- High intrinsic motivation, leading to high productivity
- High job performance (quality)
- High employee satisfaction
- Low absenteeism
- Low employee turnover

13

There are three basic types of practices for the deliberate improvement in a job's characteristics: job enlargement, job rotation and job enrichment. Job

Enlargement

enlargement means allowing an employee to take on more tasks, while still functioning at the same level. The job cycle time is increased; there is some more variety and therefore less boredom. Job rotation moves employees

Rotation

around from one simple task to another, possibly on a daily basis. This introduces the employee to some additional skills (though all at the same level), thereby reducing boredom, and perhaps providing initial insight into task

Enrichment

identity. Job enrichment is a vertical change because it gives an employee some responsibility, discretion and authority that would previously have been exercised by supervisors and managers. Not only does this increase task significance but it adds to autonomy. Feedback can also become more comprehensive.

Empowerment

Other behavioural approaches include: empowerment, which is a term used in job design to indicate an increase in authority given to people to make

Multi-skilling

decisions within their job or changes to the job itself; multi-skilling which is about increasing the range of skills of individuals in order to increase their

Flexible working

motivation and/or improve their flexibility; flexible working, which increases the possibility for individuals to vary the times at which they work, which

Teleworking

can be on a short-term or an annual basis; and teleworking, which is the ability to work from home using telecommunications and/or computer technology.

13.3 Capacity

Fixed

A central issue in the management of hospitality organisations is the fact that capacity is usually constrained: a hotel has a fixed number of rooms, a restaurant has a more or less fixed number of tables. However, customer

Demand

demand can vary widely over time. The objective of managing hospitality operations is to obtain maximum revenue from this fixed capacity. While Slack et al. (2013, p. 324) define capacity as 'the maximum level of value-added activity over a period of time that the process can achieve under normal operating conditions,' Lovelock and Wirtz (2011) indicate that productive capacity can take several forms:

Facilities

1 Physical facilities designed to contain customers and used for people-processing services or mental stimulus processing services, e.g. beds, rooms, or seats.

2 Physical facilities designed for storing or processing goods that either belong to customers or are being offered to them for sale, e.g. safes and parking lots.

Equipment

3 Physical equipment used to process people, possessions, or information, e.g. PMS equipment.

Staffing levels

4 Labour as part of productive capacity in all high-contact services and many low contact ones. If staffing levels are not high enough, customers may be kept waiting and service may become rushed.

Infrastructure

5 Infrastructure. Many organisations depend on access to sufficient capacity in the public or private infrastructure to be able to deliver quality service to their own customers. Examples of this infrastructure are roads or airports.

Mövenpick Hotel Amsterdam City Centre

13.3.1   Planning capacity

Planning capacity involves long-term, short-term and medium-term considerations. Long-term strategic considerations relate to the overall level of capacity, while short-term and medium-term considerations relate to variations in capacity requirements due to seasonal, random, and irregular fluctuations in demand. An important component of planning capacity is to find a balance between long term supply and capabilities of the organisation and the predicted level of long term demand. Organisations also have to plan for actual changes in capacity, changes in consumer wants and demands, technology and even the environment. When evaluating alternatives in planning capacity, managers have to consider both qualitative and quantitative aspects of the business. These aspects involve economic factors, public opinions, and personal preferences of managers. As such, capacity planning is a key factor in designing systems.

Fluctuations

Lovelock and Wirtz (2011) indicate that, at any given moment, a fixed-capacity service may face one of four conditions:

Conditions

- Excess demand – the level of demand exceeds maximum available capacity; as a result, some customers are denied service and business is lost.
- Demand exceeds desired capacity – no one is actually turned away, but conditions are crowded; service quality seems lower and customers feel dissatisfied.
- Demand and supply are well balanced at the level of desired capacity – staff and facilities are busy without being overworked; customers receive good service without delays.
- Excess capacity – demand is below desired capacity and resources are not used fully, resulting in low productivity. There is a risk that customers may find the experience disappointing or have doubts about whether the firm can survive.

13

For the hospitality industry, there are two basic ways to overcoming the prob-lem of varying demand. One is to adjust the level of capacity to meet the changes in demand, and the second approach is to manage the level of de-mand using marketing strategies (Lovelock & Wirtz, 2011).

Managing levels of capacity

Adjusting the level of capacity can be done using the following methods (Lovelock & Wirtz, 2011):

Stretching or shrinking
- Stretching or shrinking capacity levels – while nothing is done to the ac-tual level of capacity, it serves more people with the same level of capac-ity. Examples include extending opening times, serving meals round the clock, reducing the average amount of time that customers spend in the process through faster service of menus and bills, or offering simpler menus during busy hours.

Downtime
- Scheduling downtime during periods of low demand – all repairs and ren-ovations are to be done when demand is expected to be low; employee holidays are also to be taken during such periods, for example.

Cross-trained
- Cross-training employees – if employees can be cross-trained to perform a variety of tasks, they can be shifted around when needed. This increas-es the capacity of the total system.

- Using part-time employees – examples include using additional hotel em-ployees during holiday periods and major conferences.

Self-service
- Inviting customers to perform self-service – capacity can be increased by involving customers in the co-production of certain tasks, such as install-ing self-service technologies for check-in and check-out activities.

Share
- Asking customers to share – capacity can be stretched by asking custom-ers to share, for example in using a hotel shuttle service.

Flexible
- Creating flexible capacity – capacity is designed so that it can be recon-figured. For example, tables in a restaurant can all be two-seaters; when necessary, two tables can be combined to seat four, or three tables com-bined to seat six.

Extra
- Renting or sharing extra facilities and equipment – to reduce spending on fixed assets, a service business may be able to rent extra space or ma-chines at peak times.

Managing levels of demand

Lovelock and Wirtz (2011) also indicate that there are five basic ways to manage demand:
- Take no action, and leave demand to settle.
- Reduce demand during peak periods.
- Increase demand during low periods.
- Inventory demand using waiting lines and queuing systems.
- Inventory demand using reservation systems.

Figure 13.8 is adapted from Lovelock and Wirtz (2011, p. 256), and shows the links between these five methods and the situations of excess demand and excess capacity. Many hospitality businesses face both situations at different points in the cycle of demand, and should consider using the strat-egies described.

FIGURE 13.8 Alternative demand management situations

	Capacity Situation	
Approaches To Manage Demand	**Insufficient Capacity** *(Excess Demand)*	**Excess Capacity** *(Insufficient Demand)*
Take no action	Unorganised queuing results (may irritate customers and discourage future use)	Capacity is wasted (customers may have a disappointing experience for services such as theater)
Reduce demand	Higher prices will increase profits Communication can encourage use in other time slots (can this effort be focussed on less profitable and desirable segments?)	Take no action (but see preceding)
Increase demand	Take no action unless opportunities exist to stimulate (and give priority to) more profitable segments	Lower prices selectively (try to avoid cannibalising existing business; ensure that all relevant costs are covered) Use communications and variation in products and distribution (but recognise extra costs, if any, and make sure that appropriate trade-offs are made between profitability and use levels)
Inventory demand by formalised wait and queuing system	Match appropriate queue configuration to service process Consider priority system for most desirable segments and make other customers shift to off-peak periods Consider separate queues based on urgency, duration, and premium pricing of service Shorten customers' perceptions of waiting time and make their waits more comfortable	Not applicable
Inventory demand by reservation system	Focus on yield and reserve capacity for less price-sensitive customers Consider a priority system for important segments Make other customers shift to off-peak periods	Clarify that capacity is available and let customers make reservation at their preferred time slot

13.3.2 Measuring capacity

Capacity planners try to answer the following three basic questions:

1 What kind of capacity will be required?
2 How much of available capacity will be required?
3 When will said capacity be required?

To be able to answer these questions, planners are required to have good forecasting knowledge, and to make use of adequate forecasting tools. Without an estimate of future demand, it is impossible to effectively plan for future events. Chapter 13 of Chibili (2016 – Basic Management Accounting for the Hospitality Industry, 2nd edition) provides a detailed analysis on forecasting approaches and selections, and how forecasting is done in the hospitality industry. Measuring capacity is not as straightforward as may be assumed because, though hotels have a fixed number of rooms and restaurants have a fixed number of seats, the challenge for hospitality managers is to find the best fit between the varying demand and this capacity. The service delivery system should therefore be broken down into its component parts. The

Forecasting

Best fit

13

current capacity of each component and a reasonable estimate of its potential should be calculated to arrive at the demand forecast. Each plan or option a manager considers can be budgeted, and the best fit for each particular service selected. When selecting a measure of capacity, it is best to choose one that will not need updating. When dealing with more than one product, it is best to measure capacity in terms of each individual product – capacity measures need to be tailored to specific situations.

Individual product

13.3.3   Waiting line management (queuing)

Waiting line (or queue) management is critical in the hospitality industry. It concerns how customers are managed in such a way as to reduce waiting times and improve quality of service. Queue management deals with cases where customer arrival is random; therefore, service rendered is also random. A hospitality organisation can enhance its efficiency and improve its profitability through implementing an efficient queue management system. Waiting customers are associated with costs, and there are also costs associated with adding increased capacity to reduce service time. Having to wait to be served is a common occurrence in hotels and restaurants; hospitality managers therefore need to work on ways and means to reduce waiting times and create satisfied customers without incurring any additional costs. Generally, queue management problems are trade-off situations between the costs of the time spent in waiting as opposed to the costs of acquiring additional capacity.

Random

Trade-off

In waiting line analyses, there is the theory of a finite population of customers as well as that of an infinite population of customers. The finite population scenario considers a fixed or limited number of customers visiting the service counter within the same period, and it also assumes that once a customer is served, that customer will leave the line thus reducing the overall number of queuing customers. But there is also the chance that a customer, having once been served, re-visits the service counter for additional service, which leads to an increase in the finite population. The infinite population theory, on the other hand, looks at scenarios where any reductions or additions regarding the number of customers do not impact the overall workability of the service delivery process.

Finite population

Infinite population

A typical queueing system has the following components:
*   Arrival process – the different components of customer arrival. Customer arrival can be single, batch or bulk, as distribution of time, in finite population, or in infinite population.
*   Service mechanism – the available resources for customer service, queue structure to provide the service and pre-emption of service. The underlining assumption here is that customer service time is independent of their arrival in the queue.
*   Queue characteristics – the selection of customers from the queue for service. Generally, customer selection occurs using a principle of first come first served, random, or last in first out. As a result, customers leave if the queue is long, customer leave if they have waited too long or switch to a perceived faster serving queue.

Components

There are different ways in which queues can be configured; Figure 13.9 is a self-explanatory representation taken from Lovelock and Wirtz (2011, p. 263) showing some of these configurations.

© Noordhoff Uitgevers bv

FIGURE 13.9 Alternative queue configurations

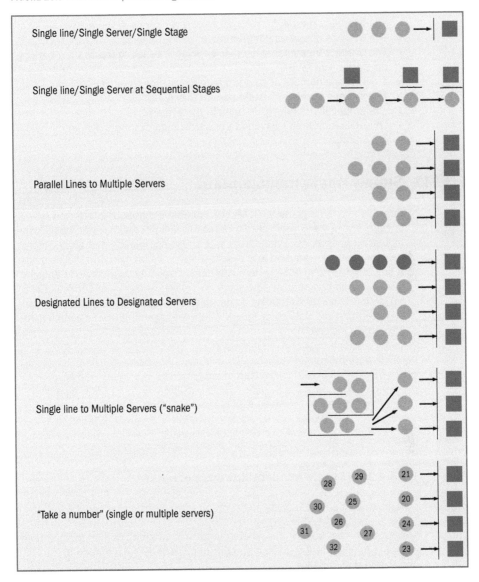

There are multiple models used to determine various components of a queuing system depending on whether the source is finite or infinite; it lies beyond the scope of this book to go into their details in full. However, in general, service systems are classified in terms of their number of channels (number of servers), and number of phases (number of required service stops). Most models determine:

Channels

Phases

- A population from which customers originate
- An arrival rate
- A form of queue
- A service rate
- An exit

13

In the queuing analysis for a hospitality operation, the following aspects of its waiting-line system can be defined:

- The average time each customer or object spends in the queue
- The average queue length (in number of customers)
- The average time each customer or object spends in the system (waiting time + service time)
- The average number of customers in the system (queue + at Front Desk)
- The average number of customers in the queue
- The probability of having no units in the system
- The utilisation factor, which is the percentage of time a system is operational

13.4 Supply chain management

Interlinked processes

Supply chain management (SCM) encompasses a host of interlinked processes, but in the context of this chapter it is limited to how the hospitality industry manages its relationships with those companies that supply materials, equipment, and food and beverage items consumed on a daily basis. A smoothly running SCM system can help hospitality organisations acquire a sustainable competitive advantage, improving product and service quality while simultaneously reducing costs. Before proceeding, it should however be noted that the Council of Supply Chain Management Professionals (CSCMP, 2015) indicate that:

> Supply chain management encompasses the planning and management of all activities involved in sourcing and procurement, conversion, and all logistics management activities. Importantly, it also includes coordination and collaboration with channel partners, which can be suppliers, intermediaries, third party service providers, and customers. In essence, supply chain management integrates supply and demand management within and across companies.

13.4.1   Supply relationships and networks

An efficient SCM system is able to positively enhance the five performance objectives of any hospitality organisation (discussed in Section 12.2.3) in the following ways (Slack et al., 2013):

- Quality – the quality of a product or service when it reaches the customer is a function of the qualitative performance of every operation in the chain that supplied it;
- Speed – a two-fold definition in this context. The first is how quickly customers can be served – an important element in any business's ability to compete. An alternative definition of speed is the time it takes for goods and services to move through the chain;
- Dependability – reduces uncertainty within the chain. This is why delivery dependability is often measured as 'on time, in full' in supply chains;
- Flexibility – the chain's ability to cope with changes and disturbances;
- Cost – costs derived from each operation in a chain doing business with each other.

Flows

Essentially, SCM flows can be divided into three main flows:

1 Flow of products;
2 Flow of information;
3 Financial flow.

The flow of the products includes the movements of goods from a supplier to a customer, as well as customer returns or additional service requirements. The flow of information involves transmitting the orders between parties and updating the delivery status of products. The financial flow consists of credit terms, e-payments, payment schedules, discount information, and the consignment and title ownership arrangements of the products. The basic supply chain network for a hotel, for example, should look like Figure 13.10.

FIGURE 13.10 Basic supply chain of a hotel

⟶ flow of products   ◄ ► financial and information flows

All participants in the supply chain are interconnected through the product, financial and information flows. Products flow comprises the movement and storage of all goods and materials; this flow represents the most prominent part of the supply chain. In addition, the two-way flow of information is very important in order to keep all participants in the supply chain informed of the flow of the goods and services in both directions. This allows a timely detection of possible problems and flow management. The financial flow is also important considering that all participants in the supply chain want to be paid for their products and services in time or as soon as possible.

Prominent

Johnston et al. (2012) indicate that a supply chain is the set of links, or network, which joins together internal and external suppliers with internal and external consumers; SCM is usually viewed from the perspective of one of the major organisations within the network. Many supply networks are much more complex than indicated in Figure 13.10, and involve second- or even third-tier suppliers as well as second-tier customers in those cases where customers are not the end-users of a product. Internal service supply networks can also be found within hotels, with examples being procurement, kitchen, front office, customer services, and accounting providing each other with internal services. A procurement department, for example, is responsible for handling and providing pricing guidelines related to all orders made by other departments in the hotel, while the accounting department is responsible for providing financial control data and purchase orders, and cross-checking them against delivery notes from the departments concerned.

External

Internal

The aim of any hotel organisation is to try and co-ordinate the set of activities and interrelationships while often having very little power or leverage to do so, despite being the party generally responsible for paying for services. Effectiveness, then, is dependent on the co-ordination between various organisations in the network. The key requirement for organisations involved in such networks is collaboration with each other and with customers. Effective supply chains are those that work in close collaboration. Having the right information in the appropriate format understood by all nodes in the supply chain allows individual organisations to better manage their operations and minimise costs.

Power

Collaboration

13

SCM is concerned with reducing inventory through providing better information, and with management of the flow of materials (logistics) through the supply network. The difficulty is that inventory is often partly used up to enable high levels of service. Organisations need to manage their inventories very carefully, because there are significant cost savings to be made. A local seafood restaurant wanting to develop reliable and frequent supplying sources of fresh fish to serve to its customers should realise that sitting on their stock for too long will affect either wastage costs or customer health (Johnston et al., 2012).

13.4.2   Managing supply networks

Johnston et al. (2012) indicate multiple methods of managing supply networks. Together with other information necessary for understanding and managing supplier relationships, these methods have been summarised as follows.

Managing via intermediaries

Some supply chains or networks involve 'middlemen': distributors, agents or dealers who take responsibility for managing a section of the supply chain, thus making management of the chain easier for the service provider or customer. Travel agents, for example, act as intermediaries between customers and tour operators and see their role as helping customers choose an appropriate holiday and providing information about a wide range of holidays and information and access to a range of related services, such as providing transport to an airport or providing currency services. Some advantages of using intermediaries include customer proximity, local knowledge, focussed expertise, lower service margins, and lower required capacity. A major issue in dealing with intermediaries is that their objectives may not always coincide with those of the main organisation or, indeed, those of the customer. Figure 13.11 represents the military model borrowed from Johnston et al. (2012, p. 140), which suggests that intermediaries may be compared to mercenaries, fighting for a cause primarily because they are being paid. The key dimension in the model is that of in-house control. The trade-off for a service organisation adopting the intermediary approach is between potential costs of poor quality of service and lost customers, and the cost of forming and maintaining a distributed network of service units.

Travel agents

FIGURE 13.11 The military model

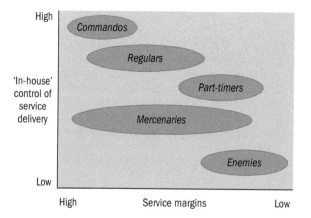

Johnston et al. (2012) indicate that the primary reasons for maintaining high in-house control of service include (p. 141):
- Increasing depth and breadth of customer relationships
- Ensuring that customer complaints are effectively dealt with and that rapid feedback for process improvement is facilitated
- Retaining control of innovative products and services for which there are limited resources.

The *Commandos* are highly trained service personnel, often used as 'hit squads', able to tackle most problems on their own with little or no management direction. The *Regulars* are less comprehensively skilled than the *Commandos* and are less able to work without direction. The *Part-timers* are the customers themselves, trained by the parent organisation to carry out service tasks for themselves. The *Mercenaries* are not part of the parent organisation, and their main reason for fighting on the side of the main organisation is that they are being paid to do so. They may switch sides if there is sufficient incentive, and do not share the culture of the parent organisation. The *Enemies* are on an opposing side. It may be that the parent organisation has decided not to provide service in all circumstances, particularly if the profit margins are small.

Switch sides

It is important to provide intermediaries with sufficient financial incentive while developing the customer service values required to generate customer loyalty, for example by offering financial incentives, punishments, expertise, training and information systems and technology. Recruitment and training of intermediaries is critical, particularly for those organisations choosing to operate through franchises. The criteria used for selecting intermediaries should be at least as rigorous as those used for selecting suppliers.

Franchises

Disintermediation
This is the removal of some intermediaries, an approach that may lead to such benefits as reduced costs and greater responsiveness, but may also increase management task for the person or organisation requiring the service. A poignant illustration of disintermediation, related to the holiday industry, is found in Figure 13.12 (Johnston et al., 2012, p. 142).

FIGURE 13.12 Holiday supply chains and disintermediation

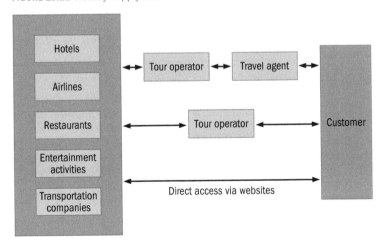

13

Travel agents traditionally sell holidays to customers through shops in town centres or shopping malls. Customers may be individuals or group travellers. Travel agents sell a range of 'products', or packages, offered by a number of tour operators. These tour operators each independently negotiate with a range of hotels, airlines, restaurants, entertainment activities and venues, and transportation companies, for example, to create a package holiday aimed at a particular market. Given the size of their operations, they are often able to achieve substantial discounts and can hold services for many months (often on a call-off or 'as required' basis) while the travel agents sell the packages.

Cutting out

Over the past few years, tour operators have been cutting out travel agents and selling directly to the public, although they have had to incur additional costs in the form of call centres or websites used to sell and service their products. Even greater disintermediation is visible with hotels, airlines, and car rental companies etc. having made their services available and bookable directly through websites, thus cutting out both tour operators and travel agents. The advantages may be greater control and sometimes lower costs for consumers, but certainly at the expense of considerably greater supplier efforts in order to co-ordinate multiple supply networks.

Outsourcing and off-shoring

Affects

Outsourcing, and the related off-shoring, is moving responsibility for part of an operation to a specialist company. It usually affects a peripheral activity but, occasionally, a core activity may be split off. Organisations using outsourcing believe that there are financial and strategic benefits to be had from letting a specialist supplier manage what used to be in-house tasks. A key reason for the effectiveness of outsourcers is that they can offer benefits of economies of scale and investment in information systems that provide opportunities for operational effectiveness (for more information on outsourcing, see Chapters 4 and 8).

Developing supply partnerships

As the pace of competition quickens, it has become increasingly common for organisations to enter into partnerships and alliances for a number of strategic reasons:
- Entering a new geographic region, where a partner may have a stronger market presence
- Providing a package of products and services that require the joint expertise of partners to deliver
- Developing new expertise in association with others, sharing resources in order to gain joint benefits.

The function of purchasing or procurement

Important activity

The area traditionally responsible for managing the supply chain is the purchasing and supply or procurement department. This is an important activity found in all organisations, potentially responsible for a large amount of spending. Procurement is traditionally an internal service provided by a dedicated team of professionals. It typically operates at the interface between the organisation's external supplier marketplace and the organisation's operational processes. Procurement has many of the characteristics of the marketing function, although it faces the other direction in the supply chain.

13

© Noordhoff Uitgevers bv

Procurement is usually responsible for the identification of (internal) customer needs, translation of those needs into specifications, management of the delivery of products and services, and an assessment of (internal) customer satisfaction with those products and services. Other elements of the process involve communication with suppliers – sourcing, requests for tenders, price negotiation, ordering, receipt and invoicing. Electronic procurement systems are a form of disintermediation. In essence, e-procurement systems mirror the procurement process through the provision of two distinct, but connected, infrastructures – internal processing (via, for example, corporate intranet) and external communication with the supply base (via, for example, internet-based platforms). Such systems allow individual employees to search for items, check availability, place and track orders and initiate payment on delivery. Research has found that e-procurement provides three key benefits compared to traditional procurement: greater customer satisfaction; greater reliability; and significant savings in the cost of purchasing (Johnston et al., 2012).

Elements

E-procurement

Supplier selection
A key decision in SCM is the selection of suppliers; apart from cost and quality, some important selection criteria are:
- Commercial awareness
- Financial standing
- Focus on continuous improvement activities
- People management skills, including training and industrial relations record
- Productivity
- Quality management approach
- Shared values.

Johnston et al. (2012, p. 150) offer an excerpt illustrating supplier selection criteria according to Danny Meyer, an American entrepreneur:

> 'Most businesses ordinarily just go with the best supplier that offers the best price. Of course pricing for us is an important calculation; but for us, excellence, hospitality, and shared values must also be prominent factors in the selection process. It's hard for me to imagine deriving so much pleasure from the restaurant business were it not for the important and enjoyable relationships we've had with our suppliers. And the range of those relationships is broad; greenmarket farmers, wine producers, cheesemongers, printers, graphic designers. The enthusiasm with which we approach each day is infused with a deep respect for how well we represent those people who have supplied us with the tools to succeed.'

A major consideration is the extent to which a buyer's requirements comprise a significant amount of the supplier's business. A supplier totally dedicated to one buyer may seem like a good idea at first, but may lead to complacency in the relationship. Many buying organisations set targets that limit the proportion of business to be conducted with any one supplier. This has the particular benefit of retaining a viable supplier base, even if that one buyer's business should decline.

Complacency

13

Measuring performance – service-level agreements

Contracts

Service-level agreements (SLAs) are forms of contracts agreed between service suppliers and service purchasers or users. These contracts are usually found in a business-to-business context, often between internal suppliers and customers where a traditional contract is not felt to be appropriate. They are an important means of managing the relationship between partners in a supply chain. Whether for internal or external use, an SLA goes beyond the traditional remit of a contract, i.e. a statement of a service specification and its associated cost or price (Johnston et al., 2012). There are three key features of an SLA:

Key features

- Setting a service specification (agreeing on key dimensions of performance, agreeing on how each dimension is to be measured, setting mutually agreed targets for each dimension, and defining where the responsibility for the measurement of each dimension lies);
- Dealing with day-to-day, routine issues (providing a mechanism for reporting performance against standards at agreed intervals, and setting out the procedures to be invoked if a failure against the standard should occur);
- Developing the relationship between the supplier and the customer in the long-term.

Understanding the barriers to supply chain management

Barriers

Although SCM makes sense to organisations in many ways, there are a number of barriers to successful implementation, which need to be addressed and overcome:

- Lack of systems capability
- Complacency if organisations do not see the need for SCM, potentially ignoring it until a new entrant operates in a different mode.
- Information being used for a variety of conflicting purposes.
- Mistrust if previous, over-inflated estimates of demand led to suppliers reducing capacity allocations to levels below those required.
- Power games where a reorganisation along supply chain lines is potentially resisted by individuals whose power base is diminished as a result of the reorganisation.

Efficient SCM helps reduce costs by developing and implementing contracts and agreements with suppliers of hospitality products and services, secure competitive prices for hotel requirements, and enhance the quality of the products and services.

© Noordhoff Uitgevers bv

Summary

▶ The detailed design of a process involves identifying all individual activities that are needed to meet the objectives of the process, deciding who is going to perform these activities, and in which sequence they are to be performed.

▶ Process design is often done using some simple visual approach. A good example is process mapping, which creates a workflow diagram used to provide insight into a process or a series of parallel processes. It employs diagrams to illustrate the processes currently in use, and to identify possible improvements allowing for better customer focus and satisfaction.

▶ Process maps are also called flowcharts; there are commonly, but not universally, accepted symbols used in designing them, as well as steps used in creating them.

▶ Blueprints detail how a service process is built-up, what is visible to customers, and where there are possible bottlenecks in the service process. In blueprints, the time line of the single process steps is plotted horizontally, and the different stages of interaction between the provider and the customer are separately indicated vertically. Stages of interaction differentiate between lines of interaction, visibility, and internal interaction that intersperse the various stages of interaction.

▶ Facility layout is an important component of a business's overall operations, and its basic objective is to ensure a smooth flow of work, materials, and information through the system. Layout is often the first thing visitors notice on entering an operation because it influences appearance.

▶ The main operational criteria in determining layout and design include:
  • Ease of communication and support
  • Ease of future expansion or change
  • Flow of movement
  • Impact on employee morale and job satisfaction
  • Handling of materials
  • Output needs
  • Promotional value
  • Safety
  • Shipping and receiving
  • Utilisation of space

13

▶ Layout requirements differ by industry and there are four basic layout types: fixed position layout; functional layout; cellular layout; and product (line) layout.

▶ Job design is the way in which a company structures the content and environment of individual staff members' jobs within the workplace, and the interface with the technology or facilities they use. There are three main approaches to job designing:
- Designing for health and safety – ergonomics
- Designing for efficiency – scientific management
- Designing for motivation – behavioural approaches

▶ Hospitality organisations are faced with issues of fixed capacity as demand varies widely over time. As such, managing capacity is vital. Capacity is the maximum level of value-added activity over a period of time that a process can achieve under normal operating conditions. Productive capacity can take several forms – physical facilities, physical equipment, labour, and infrastructure.

▶ Capacity should be properly planned through the management of levels of capacity and demand. It should also be properly measured.

▶ Waiting line or queue management is concerned with treating customers in such a way as to reduce waiting times and improve quality of service. Since waiting for service is a common occurrence in hotels and restaurants, hospitality managers need to work on ways and means to reduce waiting times and ensure satisfied customers without incurring additional costs.

▶ A typical queue system has the following components: arrival process; service mechanism; and queue characteristics. There are various models of queuing systems but they are generally able to determine multiple required critical areas for hospitality operations. These critical areas can include the average time each customer or object spends in the queue, the average number of customers in the queue and in the system, the average time each customer or object spends in the system, and the utilisation factor.

▶ Supply chain management encompasses the planning and managing of all activities involved in sourcing, procurement, conversion, and logistics management. More importantly, it also includes coordination and collaboration with channel partners, whether suppliers, intermediaries, third party service providers, or customers. Essentially, supply chain management integrates supply and demand management within and across companies.

▶ Supply networks can be managed through intermediaries, disintermediation, outsourcing, off-shoring and partnerships.

▶ Service-level agreements are an important means of managing the relationship between partners in a supply chain; these agreements are contracts agreed upon between service suppliers and service purchasers or users.

13

Questions and assignments for reflection

1   Based on the information in this chapter, how should the processes of a hospitality operation be designed in detail? Which of the various tools do you prefer, and why?

2   Discuss the relationship between the basic layout types using your knowledge of the main performance objectives. Indicate how these types relate to each other for hospitality operations such as restaurants.

3   Compare and contrast the various job design approaches as discussed in this chapter. Which would be the most suitable for you if you were the HR manager of a hotel chain?

4   Why is waiting line management a critical hospitality management issue? How should queues be managed within the hospitality industry?

5   Indicate the similarities and differences between the three main ways of managing supply networks as discussed in this chapter. Which would you prefer for your ideal organisation, and why?

13

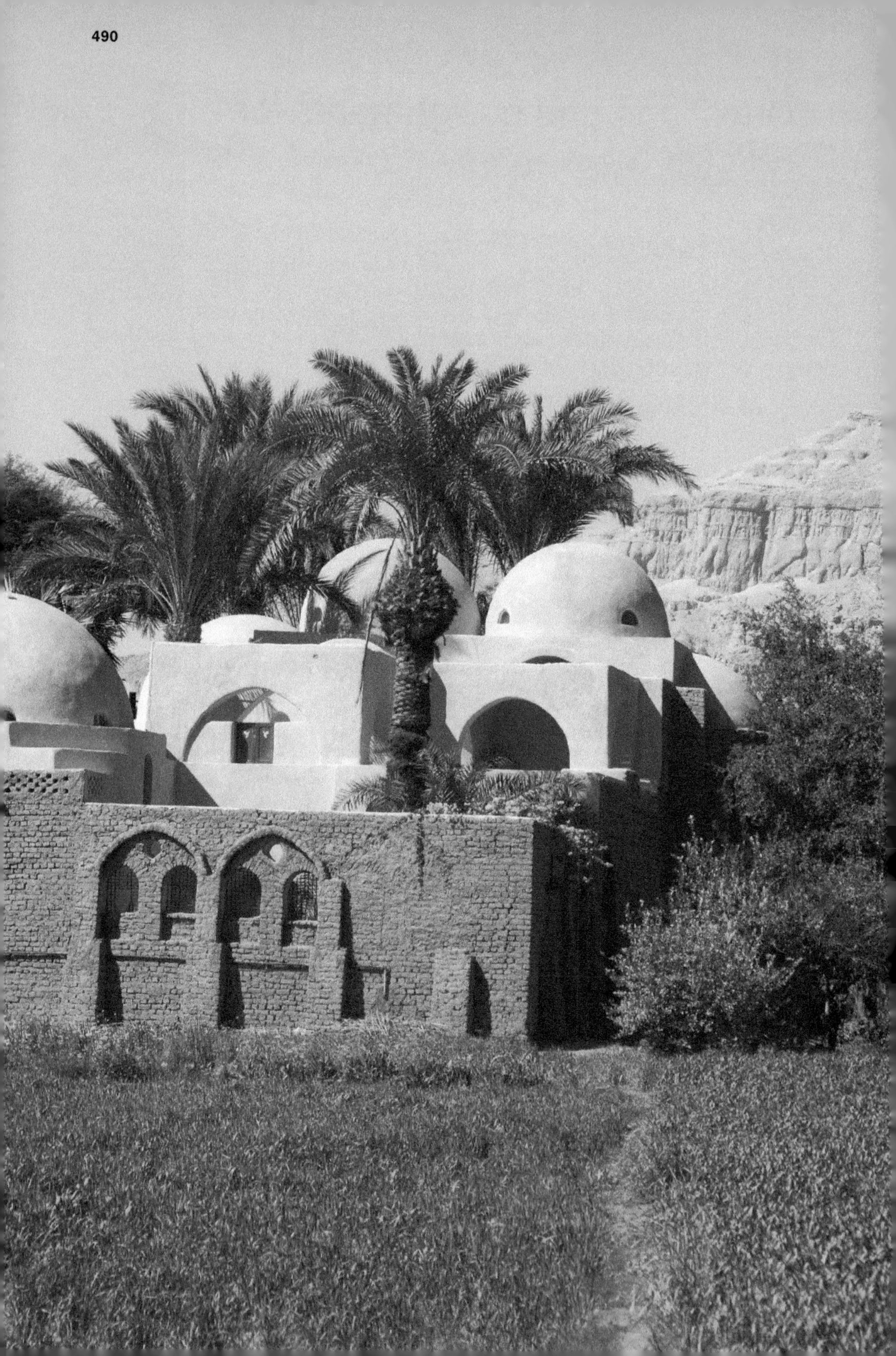

14
Delivering Hospitality Services

Prof. C. Lashley

14.1 Introduction

A major concern for hotel managers is in ensuring that visitor experiences at least meet expectations. Customer dissatisfaction occurs when customers feel they are not getting what they expect – equipment that does not work, facilities looking shabby, or staff not serving them in a hospitable or friendly way. Customer retention and the attraction of new customers depends on ensuring that customers have a clear idea of what to expect from a hotel operator, and ensuring that their expectations are lived up to. The key issue for hotel management is to deliver what they have said they will deliver. Tangible products and services and employee performance are fundamental elements of successful hotel service delivery.

14.2 Same pool of customers

Too many hotel companies have, in the past, paid too little attention to guest experiences beyond sale. Yet all hotels are in competition for customers. They need to:

Competition

- Retain existing guests and minimise guest visits to competitors in the same area; or
- Attract guests from competitor destinations; and
- Maximise hotel traffic.

Maximising weekly traffic ensures more spending towards the hotel's accommodations, restaurants, bars or other leisure services. Fixed costs remain the same; whatever the number of visitors, maximising spending on any one week produces higher profits. Creating customer dissatisfaction produces the reverse effect; fewer guests visit the site, which reduces traffic profits. In effect, the same levels of fixed costs are recouped over lower sales volumes: profits fall.

Dissatisfaction

Egypt, Oasis of Siwa: Shali Resort

© Noordhoff Uitgevers bv

14

14.3 Satisfiers and dissatisfiers

Motivational states

Herzberg et al. (1957) provide a useful model for understanding customer responses to service experiences. Figure 14.1 lists potential dissatisfiers and satisfiers in hotel services. Essentially, they suggest three motivational states. Dissatisfiers are those aspects of service that cause dissatisfaction – if they are not as expected, or are defective.

If hotel visitors find dissatisfiers to be as expected, or even better than expected, they do not cause satisfaction; only an absence of dissatisfaction. Satisfaction only comes from the satisfier list of emotional experiences, largely dependent on frontline staff. Satisfied customers are the most likely to (want to) return to the destination.

FIGURE 14.1 Herzberg et al.'s satisfiers and dissatisfiers applied to hotel operations

Dissatisfiers	Satisfiers
Own room or suite décor	Quality of guest/host transactions
Décor of the hotel	Hospitableness of hosts
Quality of equipment in accommodation	Emotional responses to service
Quality of leisure equipment	Treatment exceeds guest expectations
Landscaping of grounds	Frontline staff performance
Parking facilities	Empathy
Range of leisure facilities	Feeling at home away from home
Restaurant and bar choices	
Alternative destination attractions	

Hospitable and friendly

Hotel managers therefore have to ensure that the tangible aspects of the offer meet customer expectations to avoid dissatisfaction, but also have to ensure that the service interactions with staff are always hospitable and friendly, and produce a favourable emotional experience for visitors.

The matrix in Figure 14.2 is not an exhaustive list of product and service tangibles and intangibles for hotel experiences. It does, however, show some aspects of hospitality operations as being more measurable and capable of being monitored than others. The significance of different features varies between different types of service operations, and the nature of how characteristics are defined varies as well. Speed is one of the tangible aspects of the service provided, for example. Most service operational standards set down maximum target waiting times for guests at the reception desk or while waiting to be served meals or drinks.

Measurable

Operational standards

FIGURE 14.2 Quality characteristics matrix for a hospitality operation

	Tangible	Intangible
Nature of product	Hotel buildings and facilities Room and facilities The food and drink products offered in the hotel Serving goods (plates, glasses, cutlery, linen, etc.) Information (menu) Process (e.g. credit cards)	Atmosphere Décor and furnishings Feeling Comfort Perceived quality
The service contact	Actions Accuracy of communication prior to visit Accommodation preparedness Process Speed Script Corrective action	Warmth Feeling at home away from home Feeling valued as guests Friendliness Care Complaint handling Fault correction Hospitableness

14.4 Characteristics of the experience

Service requirements vary according to the service being purchased; in essence, it is important to communicate an expectation and then ensure that these planned customer expectations are met during the service experiences. Guest expectations of service quality become an important defining feature of service quality when compared to experiences of the service. Guests have a base level of expectations of any service – their minimum expectancy. They have a level of expectation of what a service should be like versus what they are looking for.

Expectations

Guests also predict the expected quality. Visitors may vary in their expectations; and customers with more experience with a service may well have higher expectations than those with less experience of it. Hotel operators have a role in shaping expectations, and may influence consumer expectations through advertising and other promotional activities. It is important that the service delivered in a hotel matches these expectations it has engendered in its audience.

14

14.5 Service quality management systems

Given the difficulties inherent in service delivery, quality management systems have been developed for the quality management of services. These service quality management systems have been used extensively in hospitality operations. They aim to be more responsive to the intangible elements of service but are often unable to capture key transactions between guests and hosts that differentiated hospitality services from other types of services. A few of these systems are introduced and discussed in this chapter, and expanded on in Chapter 16.

14.5.1   SERVQUAL

This is a contraction of service and quality – it is a quality management framework developed by Zeithaml, Parasuraman and Berry (1990) to measure quality in the service sector. It has been widely used by hotel companies
to compare customer expectations to customer experiences, thereby indicating where the strengths and weaknesses of service delivery may be found. The performance of different competitors can be compared to the service organisation's own performance. A defining characteristic is that it
reveals 'five service gaps' where there may be a mismatch between the expectation of the service level and the perception of the service delivered. Figure 14.3 highlights the five dimensions identified based on the SERVQUAL system of quality evaluation.

Compare

Service gaps

The model defines the five dimensions of service, and suggests that these provide a framework for understanding where service quality management problems are occurring. There are some physical elements included with the tangibles, but most of the items included in the SERVQUAL list relate to employee performance. Frontline staff recruitment, induction, training and development, motivation, rewards and performance monitoring are therefore crucial elements of management of service quality. Employee performance around customers is a key determinant of service quality delivery and of customer satisfaction.

La Verne York, Jan Bossema and Victoria Snouck Hurgronje from Stenden Hotel, Leeuwarden, The Netherlands

14

Service gaps focus on the points where a mismatch between expectations of service requirements by management, set standards set, achieved standards achieved, or service standards communicated to customers produce a situation where customer perception of the service delivered do not correspond to that of the expected service.

Responsiveness, assurance and empathy are elements of this model; these underscore the importance of employee performance in a service encounter. Given the nature of services, it is often difficult to predict what employees should say or do in given service encounters.

FIGURE 14.3 The five dimensions of service

Dimension	Definition
Reliability	The ability to perform the promised service dependably and accurately
Tangibles	The appearance of physical facilities, equipment, personnel and communication materials
Responsiveness	The willingness to help customers and provide prompt service
Assurance	The knowledge and courtesy of employees and their ability to convey trust and confidence
Empathy	The caring individualised attention paid to the customer

Given the obvious importance of employee performance, some writers look to critical incidents in which employee responses can be shown to either save a situation and create customer satisfaction, or fail a situation (which may already be a bad one) and thereby create dissatisfaction (Zeithaml, Bitner & Gremler, 2009). Their findings suggest three broad groups of incidents illustrated in Figure 14.4:

Critical incidents

- Employee reactions to service delivery system failures;
- Employee reactions to customer needs or requests;
- Unprompted or unsolicited employee actions.

Each group represented a cluster of incidents in which employee behaviour could result in either customer satisfaction or customer dissatisfaction.

Employee reactions to service delivery system failures can be critical, because customers are more likely to pardon a service failure if the fault is acknowledged and quickly corrected. Any problem not corrected at hotel level may result in complaints to head office and, moreover, lead to a customer lost. Taking into account that word of mouth travels fast, a lost customer may end up costing far more than a replaced meal or free bottle of wine that might have corrected the initial situation.

System failures

Similarly, employee reactions to customer needs and requests are important in all service situations; there are bound to be occasions where customers want something not normally sold by the operation, or where they make a mistake and want some assistance in correcting their error. Customers are much more likely to respond positively if they are treated with flexibility and if service employees make every effort to meet customer needs.

© Noordhoff Uitgevers bv

14

FIGURE 14.4 Positive and negative response to critical service incidents in hotels

Critical incident	Customer satisfaction	Customer dissatisfaction
Employee responses to service delivery failure	Could be turned into incidents that employees use to their advantage and generate customer satisfaction. If an employee reacts quickly to service failure by responding sensitively to customer experiences – say by compensating the customer or upgrading a customer to a higher status service.	Staff responses are likely to be a source of a dissatisfaction – where the employee fails to provide an apology, an adequate explanation, or argues with the customer and denies the problem.
Employee responses to customer needs and requests	Employee responsiveness, flexibility and confidence that they can match whatever the customer requests are important sources of a positive customer response.	Similarly, employee intransigence, inflexibility, and perceived incompetence are all likely sources of customer dissatisfaction.
Unprompted and unsolicited employee actions	This might involve employee behaviours that made the customer feel special, or where an act of unexpected generosity took the customer by surprise.	Customer dissatisfaction could be the result of a failure to give the customer the level of attention expected, or inadequate information, or might involve inappropriate behaviour such as the use of bad language, scruffy appearance, or surly behaviour etc.

Unprompted and unsolicited employee actions incorporate actions outside of customer expectations of the service encounter. If employee performance is beyond customer expectation of the service, the incident may produce satisfaction – exceeding customer expectations may involve certain details of employee performance. Employees of TGI Fridays, for example, are encouraged to perform in a way that further establishes the brand's identity of humour and a 'fun' atmosphere offered to customers. This often involves providing balloons or singing songs at birthday celebrations.

Costs

The issue of employee performance and customer satisfaction takes on added urgency if a firm shifts its focus to the costs of lost business and the benefits of generating customer loyalty.

14

14.5.2   Quality management and hotel operations

The earliest developments in quality stem from the manufacturing industry; many hotel organisations have unquestioningly adopted and adapted these different approaches, though manufacturing systems do not always match the needs of a service organisation. Hotel organisations need to adapt sys- *Adapt* tems to match the service offer to their customers. The following is a brief overview of different systems and terms used:

- Quality inspection
  Actual output of a product or service is checked against standard specifications. Defective (pre-)products are then reworked or scrapped. While quality inspection is undertaken via line managers – quality inspectors or mystery customers – the approach is frequently limited by the nature of *Limited* hotel products and services. It is not always possible to retroactively fix a faulty greeting or service. Nor is the cause of the fault always readily identifiable.
  Nevertheless, this system is widely used by hotel developers when completing the construction of physical buildings and facilities.
- Quality control
  Quality is designed into the specifications of the production of rooms, meals, drinks and services through detailed standards. Quality checks are introduced throughout the various stages of the process, for example between departments. At its heart, the approach is still concerned with detecting and correcting faults. It will not improve quality, but does show *Detecting and* where defined standards have not been met. *correcting*
  The use of mystery customers has widely been used in hotel operation management. Mystery customers act as customers and file a report of their experience to management.
  As before, the quality control process of verification and fault detection is built into the process used by many hotel companies.
- Quality assurance
  Rather than waiting for faults to occur, the focus on quality is designed into the process in a way as to prevent faults altogether. If faults do occur, they are corrected as they happen. This approach involves developing a documented and planned quality system. Quality assurance re- *Planned* quires total organisational commitment and involvement of all employees in the process. A key problem is that, although quality assurance may deliver consistent faultless products and services, it may not be what customers want.
- Total quality management (TQM)
  The focus is on customers and the satisfaction of customer needs. This *Focus* system is fully aimed at customer satisfaction and the removal of any barriers to delivering same. People in the organisation are key to successfully achieving customer satisfaction – employee training, motivation and empowerment are crucial. As before, successful implementation requires total cultural commitment; this can be difficult, because it is often hard to change an organisation's culture. This system provides a potentially valuable model for successful service quality delivery in hotel management.

The approaches listed are not in and of themselves mutually exclusive; one approach may build on another and effective quality programmes often incorporate aspects of all approaches mentioned. Systems based on TQM

14

therefore still need to involve quality inspection and quality control, though the number of faults and problems should be greatly reduced.

14.5.3   Total quality hotel management

Useful model

Hotel managers may work within an organisation that employs one or more of the systems discussed, but in some cases there may not be a formal system for defining, managing or monitoring service quality in the hotel. In other cases, quality systems are in place, but are not adequately managed. TQM, provides a useful model that can be used across the breadth of an organisation, or in the limited space of individual properties. Hotel organisations require quality systems that are holistic enough to allow for the characteristics of services and the varied perceptions of customers. TQM appears to offer service organisations the system required.

Even though there are several forms of TQM, Figure 14.5 contains a list of 16 principles covering several broad features of TQM found in most descriptions of the concept. At its heart, TQM defines a commitment to quality services as a core organisational concern. The commitment of senior management is crucial and the approach has to permeate every aspect of an organisation (or hotel).

FIGURE 14.5 Principles of TQM

1	Highest priority given to quality throughout the organisation
2	Quality is defined in terms of customer satisfaction
3	Customers are defined as those who have both internal and external relationships with the organisation - includes employees, shareholders, and the wider community
4	Customer satisfaction and the building of long term relationships are at the core of the organisation
5	The organisation's aims will be clearly stated and accessible to all
6	The principles, beliefs, values and quality is communicated throughout the organisation
7	Total Quality Management creates an ethos which pervades all aspects of the organisation's activities
8	Core values of honesty, integrity, trust and openness are essential ingredients of Total Quality Management
9	The Total Quality organisation is intended to be mutually beneficial to all concerned and operates in a climate of mutual respect for all stakeholders
10	The health and safety of all organisation members and customers are given priority
11	The Total Quality organisation offers individuals the chance to participate and feel ownership of the success of the enterprise
12	Commitment is generated in individuals and teams through leadership from senior management
13	Total Quality Management results in an organisation-wide commitment to continuous improvement
14	Performance measurement, assessment and auditing of the organisation's activities is a common feature of Total Quality Management
15	Total Quality Management aims to use resources more effectively and members are encouraged to be considering ways of using resources more effectively
16	Total Quality Management requires appropriate investment to ensure that planned activities occur

Cultural environment

The approach is particularly attractive to hospitality operations, because it aims to create a cultural environment in which employees, operating independently, are guided by a commitment to delighting customers because they have internalised the service objectives and values. These internalised

14

values, beliefs and objectives ensure employees aspire to customer satisfaction and quality improvement, without managerial rewards or punishments.

The similarities between TQM and empowerment are not accidental, because many of those writing about the benefits of TQM as an approach for managing service organisations also advocate the need to empower frontline staff with authority to correct defects, and respond to service failures as they occur (Kaufmann, Lashley, & Schreier, 2009). Furthermore, employee empowerment is important for employees to respond to unusual customer requests, or use their experience and creativity to look for ways of delighting customers. These aspirations for TQM and empowerment are relevant to the three critical incidents illustrated in Figure 14.4, which could either create or damage customer satisfaction. These are all occasions where employee behaviour impacts either positively or negatively on customer satisfaction and perceptions of service quality. TQM provides an organisational setting in which empowered employees, through a heightened sense of their own personal efficacy, will respond in the desired way.

Similarities

14.5.4   Empowering employees

Changes in working arrangements that claim to be empowering for employees cover a diverse set of arrangements that represent a variety of levels and forms of employee engagement. At one level, empowerment, as rhetoric, provides a convenient device for naming a range of changes that suggests a win-win situation, without critically examining the experiences of the empowered. Some of these different forms are listed in Figure 14.6. The effectiveness of a particular initiative in producing the necessary changes in work performance are largely dependent on the 'state of empowerment' experiences by an employee. That is, the extent to which any one initiative generates feelings of personal effectiveness and control over situations where employees can make a difference.

Rhetoric

FIGURE 14.6 Some forms of employee involvement in service operations

Initiatives
Quality Circles
Total Quality Management
Suggestion Schemes
Autonomous Work Groups
Whatever it Takes Training
Team Briefings
Delayering

It is possible to generate an analytical framework used to describe initiatives in the degree, form, level, range and power involved for employees, irrespective of whether the initiative was termed 'involvement', 'participation', 'democracy' or 'empowerment'. The nature of a service encounter may require employees to exercise varying degrees of discretion. In turn, these in-

Discretion

14

Managerial
intentions

tentions shape the form which empowerment takes. Figure 14.7 provides an overview of managerial intentions for employee engagement, and suggests appropriate forms for empowerment to take.

FIGURE 14.7 Forms of employee engagement

Forms of engagement	Initiatives used
Engagement Through Participation	Autonomous Work Groups
	Whatever it Takes Training
	Job Enrichment
Engagement Through Consultation	Quality Circles
	Team Briefings
	Suggestion Schemes
Engagement Through Commitment	Employee Share Ownership
	Profit Sharing and Bonus Schemes
	Quality of Working Life Programs – job rotation – job enlargement
Engagement Through Delayering	Job Re-design
	Re-training
	Autonomous Work Groups
	Job Enrichment
	Profit Sharing and Bonus Schemes

Engagement through participation

Delegates

This is where an organisation delegates to employees some of the decision-making which, in a traditional organisation, would be the domain of management. This may be referred to as empowering through participation, and involves participant styles of management and employees in making decisions jointly with management, or having some decisions delegated to them. Employees participate in identifying and satisfying customer needs, as in the case of Marriott Hotels, make decisions about work planning, organising, or scheduling, as in the case of Harvester Restaurants, or joint planning.

In continental Europe particularly, employees may participate in decision-making at non-operational levels. Here, the use of a Works Council, or Worker Directors, may involve representatives of the workforce in decisions that are more concerned with matters of business policy and strategy. In this situation, European participants make decisions at strategic levels, and initiatives are often motivated by democratic or pluralistic motives; motives that recognise that democracy in the workplace is an extension of the democratic society, or where decisions are more effective if they reflect worker insights.

Engagement through consultation

Experiences

If managerial concern is to reap the benefits of employee experiences, ideas and suggestions, it may be their intention to engage employees for consultation by providing feedback, sharing information and making suggestions. Frontline service employees are in a unique position to contribute to problem resolution, communicate trends in customer service needs, and identify the impact of company policies on service delivery.

14

The use of 'quality circles' in the Accor Group, or 'team briefings' in Hilton Hotels, are techniques that attempt to include the ideas and experiences of employees in the managerial decision-making process. Suggestions may refer to anything from immediate tasks, involving both tangibles and intangibles, through business strategy and employment policy issues. Importantly, managers continue to make the decisions. Employees who choose to participate are directly involved, but participation in these programmes is typically voluntary. The intention is that organisational effectiveness is improved through better communication with frontline employees; employees feel empowered through being involved in consultation and problem-solving processes and, it is hoped, are thus more committed to organisational objectives and service quality improvement.

Engagement through commitment

By empowering employees through greater commitment to the organisation's goals, employees take more responsibility for their own performance and improvement. The skills and talents of employees are realised and put to work for the benefit of the organisation. This produces more satisfied customers and greater profits. Employees are likely to be more adaptable to change, and perhaps even accepting of organisational downsizing and redundancies. Unlike participation and consultation, this form of employee engagement takes place in traditional command and control organisational structures. Securing employee commitment is a key concern of employee recruitment, induction, training and development, reward and evaluation schemes. Fundamentally, there is recognition of the importance of employee performance in building competitive advantage and loyal customers.

Responsibility

14

Attempts to achieve greater employee commitment overlap and inter-relate with engagement through both employee participation and employee consultation. However, some initiatives are quite specifically aimed at greater employee commitment. In these cases, it is hoped that greater commitment will result in the development of attitudes positive to the organisation, employee performance more closely matched to organisational and customer needs, and more stability among the workforce.

Other forms of empowerment are intended to gain greater employee commitment through improvements in job satisfaction and feelings of value to the organisation. Thus, changes in job design through increased job rotation, together with techniques mentioned earlier under both employee participation and employee involvement are intended to change attitudes and reduce feelings of 'Them and (or even *against*) Us'.

Engagement through delayering

Levels

As a consequence of organisational growth many firms are concerned with structures that increase the levels of managers between frontline and senior executives; there has been increasing interest in reducing the number of tiers of management in organisational structures. Excellent companies are said to be 'flatter' and 'close to the customer'. Hotel operators, like their counterparts in manufacturing, have been keen to explore the possibilities of delayering their organisations. The benefits of delayering an organisation come both from in cutting overheads via the reduction of administrative costs, and by locating the organisation closer to customers. Quality gains and greater responsiveness to environmental changes are said to be the result (Lashley, 2011).

Span of control

The multi-unit nature of hotel companies, located close to specific destinations, have added particular problems for hotel firms. If they retain a reasonable span of control across hundreds or thousands of hotels, they inevitably involve large numbers of management tiers. On the other hand, increasing the span of control by making middle and senior managers responsible for more hotels reduces potential control of each individual business. This may result in problems for a branded hotel business selling consistency to its customers. Allowing lower levels of organisational management to make decisions formerly made at senior levels has appeared to be an answer to this dilemma for many hotel companies (Lashley, 2011).

The intentions of managers, and their perceptions of the nature of the customer offer, is likely to shape the form of employee engagement introduced. That said, managerial intentions may not always be singly motivated or consistent. The previous discussion, suggesting a framework of meanings, does not exclude the possibility that managers may have intentions covering one or all of the motives (participation, consultation, commitment and delayering). As a consequence, initiatives may incorporate a variety of forms. Secondly, it is important to remember that management decision-making does involve a degree of choice, and selected formats need not always be based on a 'rational fit'. The ideology, prior training, managerial vision, together with the internal political processes, culture and history of the organisation may be powerful determinants in selections made by managers as to the form of employee engagement introduced.

14

14.6 Hospitableness

Traditional service quality literature suggests that employee performance is a key determinant of service quality and, thereby, customer satisfaction (Kaufmann et al., 2009). In particular, the intangible aspects of services and the need to provide unique service experiences to customers, together with the perishability of services, mean that frontline employees have a fundamental role to play. That said, hotel experiences are fundamentally about hospitality and acts of hospitableness.

Fundamental role

This section argues that traditional service management techniques fail to recognise the potentially unique relationship between guests and hosts in hotel operations. This is not to say that the more conventional and rational approaches do not have their place, but there is a need to recognise that hospitality and tourism experiences have important emotional dimensions that traditional marketing approaches tend to downplay. By understanding the hospitality transaction between guests and hosts, hotel marketing and commercial operators can deliver customer experiences which build up customer loyalty. While general service literature is helpful, it fails to establish the essential role of providing hospitable experiences for guests.

Emotional dimensions

As indicated in Chapter 1, extending hospitality to strangers is an ancient tradition stretching back thousands of years. The duty of accepting strangers on their own terms has been a feature of human societies across the globe and through time. Many contemporary industrialised societies seem to have lost touch with the obligation to be hospitable. But hotel companies should take note of these traditions of hospitality and hospitableness to better understand guest needs, and to build a genuinely competitive advantage. To better understand the commercial applications of hospitality it is necessary to explore hospitality in its widest sense.

Lost touch

In times past, hospitality and the need to be hospitable were highly valued in all communities, even those where these obligations are no longer central to the culture and the behaviour of hosts to guests. Being genuinely hospitable to travellers and less fortunate members of the community was seen as a good thing and was highly valued. In modern societies, hospitality and the expectation of hospitableness are not afforded anywhere near the same cultural and religious status they enjoyed in the past. Importantly, being hospitable in a private setting involves a host being responsible for their guest's happiness. There is a special link between both parties; guest and host are part of a mutual pact. The host may become the guest and the guest may become the host on other occasions. In private domestic settings, hospitality:

Modern societies

Mutual pact

- is a process involving mutual give and take (obligation);
- is generous;
- is unselfish;
- is open-handed;
- is welcoming; and
- is warm.

14

Motives

Most importantly hospitality is based on appropriate motives, and is about more than merely hosting. A good host may be effective at keeping glasses full, food on the table and the room temperature comfortable, but may be acting with ulterior motives – personal gain or vanity. Good hospitality requires the right motives:

- a desire for a guest's company;
- a pleasure taken in entertaining;
- a desire to please others;
- a concern for the needs of others; and
- a duty to be hospitable.

Hospitable people are those who possess one or more of these motives for entertaining. This raises difficulties for many hotel organisations. The commercial rationale by which they operate often distorts the relationship with their guests. The commercial rationale sells hotel-based hospitality as a commodity. Guests become customers, and both host and guest develop a reduced sense of mutual obligation. As a consequence, many hotel organisations report difficulties in retaining customers, and in encouraging more repeat visits by existing customers.

Commercial
rationale

Clearly, individual hotel operators cannot change society's sense of hospitality, nor run their operations as though they were private domestic hosts; but they might be better able to build a community of customers more robustly loyal if they better understood hospitality in these contexts. Genu-

14

ine hospitality is closely linked to values of generosity, beneficence and mutual obligations, for example. While not suggesting that profit-driven organisations give away their products, a consideration of how regular customers can be rewarded with extra benefits which celebrate their importance and uniqueness as individuals could be successful. The key here is to make these 'gifts' appear to be acts of genuine generosity, rather than the formulaic 'giveaways' typical of many branded hospitality businesses.

Hospitality retailers need to consider recruiting, selecting and training hosts capable of being hospitable, and displaying characteristics of hospitableness. The implication is that the recruitment of people who genuinely trained in, reflecting on, and working to the values of hospitableness, is important for building loyal customers.

Summary

▶ This chapter shows that customer service quality management is an important, possibly vital, aspect of hotel management. The retention of existing customers and the ability to attract new customers to the property are essential for sales growth.

▶ The loss of regular customers has a material impact on sales revenues and profits. In addition, dissatisfied customers rarely keep their experiences to themselves; by the time they tell their friends and acquaintances, the amount of business lost can be exceedingly costly.

▶ Service quality management is difficult because customer satisfaction is associated with customer expectations. Not all customers use a hotel for the same occasions, and their expectations and assessment of incidents critical to service success vary. In addition, employee assessments of customer needs may not match customer expectations either.

▶ The nature of service encounters is difficult to determine because of the intangible aspects of service and the difficulties caused by the perishable nature of hospitality and hotel services. It is not possible to retroactively repair a smile or a false greeting.

▶ Total Quality Management provides a useful model for hospitality operations. Different types of service offers require different TQM approaches, but all offers depend on a cultural commitment to delivering high quality service. Additionally, employee skills and performance are essential to successfully meeting customer expectations.

▶ Traditional service management techniques fail to recognise the potentially unique relationship between guests and hosts in hotel operations. By understanding the hospitality transaction between guests and hosts, hotel marketing and commercial operators can deliver customer experiences which build up customer loyalty

▶ Individual hotel operators cannot change society's sense of hospitality nor run their operations as though they were private domestic hosts, but they might be better able to build a community of customers more robustly loyal if they better understood hospitality in these contexts. Genuine hospitality is closely linked to values of generosity, beneficence and mutual obligations.

14

Questions and assignments for reflection

1   Discuss the service types and how they fit with employee performance.

2   Critically discuss quality control and quality assurance.

3   Critically discuss TQM as a policy for hotel operators.

4   What are the benefits of engagement through participation?

5   Describe what is meant by hospitableness.

15

Managing Change in the Hospitality Industry

L. Benhadda and M. N. Chibili

15.1 Introduction

The hospitality industry is an ever-metamorphosing industry in which change is a constant reality and innovation is the key to survival – in the hospitality industry, almost every property, brand or segment is undergoing change. This is noticeable in the industry's constant adaptation to the wishes of its customers, and adaptations imposed by technological evolution. Furthermore, the hospitality industry is based on services partly created during interaction, with customers having different needs and expectations. Adapting to these needs and expectations is crucial for success in the industry. Apart from globalisation, cultural pluralism, knowledge capital and technologies place the industry in an era of discontinuity where relentless change is inevitable. This chapter discusses the theoretical foundations of managing change in the hospitality industry by reviewing its drivers, the relationships between change and organisational culture, models of change process, resistance to change, and HR management within a changing environment.

15.1.1 The drivers of change

In times of uncertainty, hospitality industry managers wonder which changes have the greatest impact on their businesses in the future. For them to be able to have an insight into these changes and their possible impacts, they first need to assess the drivers instigating the change.

A change driver is considered to be a strategic and very often unavoidable cause for change, and can be both external and internal to the organisation. Major factors that will likely have significant impact across the hospitality industry include the main drivers as indicated in Figure 15.1.

Unavoidable cause

Macro and micro environmental factors

In today's business environment, everything is changing. Customer tastes and preferences, competition, prices, policies, people and employees, and

India, Rajasthan (Bagar): Piramal Haveli Heritage Hotel

15

FIGURE 15.1 The drivers of change

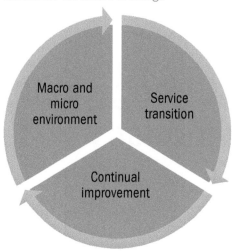

External

products can change overnight. Keeping customers and other stakeholders loyal to a hospitality company is a difficult task, as it is impacted by external influences.

Hospitality businesses have to respond to external and internal environmental factors in order to maintain or improve their performances. External factors include political, economic, social, and technological events or circumstances, which have an influence on the operating environment within which a hospitality business functions. These factors can be considered at both macro and micro levels, in which they affect the sector as a whole, or its

Examples

sub-sections or specific organisations. Some examples are the impact of regional conflicts, regional or global recession, demographic changes, movements in property prices, increased leisure buying power, increasing globalisation, the emergence of new markets and new business centres in newly industrialised countries, and the increasing use of the Internet by both busi-

Internal

nesses and individuals. Internal factors are illustrated in the changes in ownership due to mergers and acquisitions, the procedural or policy changes in order to reinforce brand differentiation or customer focus, and restructuring in order to achieve greater job flexibility, expansion or downsizing, for example. The key to successful change management lies not only in being able to respond to these drivers of change, but also to anticipate them.

In order to cope with ongoing change in customers' demands or needs, many hotels have even adopted new names and brands. Figure 15.2 is a news article about such a rebranding move by the Shangri-La Hotels and Resorts in 2014, which clearly shows the major factors that prompted the need for the change.

TEXT 15.1

Rebranding within the Shangri-La Hotels and Resorts

Shangri-La rebrands Traders Hotels as Hotel Jen, Clement Huang, 15/09/2014

Shangri-La Hotels and Resorts is rebranding its Traders Hotels properties as Hotel Jen.

The change will be rolled-out quickly, a process that started today in Singapore with the opening of Hotel Jen Orchard Gateway, a property that had originally been earmarked as a Traders property.

Switchover: Hotel Jen Orchard Gateway in Singapore had been earmarked as a Traders property

Shangri-La plans for there to be ten Hotel Jen properties in the Asia-Pacific region by March 2015. The existing Traders Hotels to be rebranded will be those in Hong Kong, Brisbane, Penang, Johor Bahru, Manila, Maldives, Beijing, Shenyan and Singapore.

The brand aims to provide guests with 'efficiency and care', particularly through the use of technology, which will include free Wi-Fi and mobile charging stations.

The dining concept offered by Hotel Jen will place an emphasis on local produce, and free coffee and grab-and-go kiosks will be available.

Greg Dogan, president and CEO of Shangri-La Hotels and Resorts, said: 'The Traders brand has had a 25-year history of suc-

cess in generating solid business, carving out a niche amidst a highly competitive industry and building a loyal base of customers.

'However, we are looking to the future and – based on extensive consumer research and insight into the way our target market lives and travels, including talking and listening to our customers – we are recognising and responding to the global travel trends and particular needs of this new generation traveller.

'This will keep us relevant and competitive for the next 20 years to come.'

(Source: www.businesstraveller.com)

15

Food and
beverage

Within the hospitality industry, the food and beverage sector in particular bears the brunt of this continuous change because of the constant alterations of customer preferences and eating habits, supply market fluctuations, health awareness, and intense competition.

Service transition

Technological
developments

Service transition is the introduction of new capabilities and skills to smoothen the transfer of new services to customers. The interaction between employees and customers has become very complex due to technological developments and the digital age. Customers nowadays expect more from frontline and other hotel staff members, especially in terms of their knowledge of a hotel's offerings, and their displayed attitude and cultural knowledge. This affects the human resource department's tasks in recruiting new staff members and training existing ones, taking into consideration that the hospitality industry is known to be an industry characterised by low-skilled, low-paid, and highly diversified staff in terms of nationalities and behaviour (see Chapter 6).

Continual improvement

Value for
customers

Continual improvement is derived from the concept of organisational development and learning. In the hospitality industry, organisations strive to create and maintain value for customers through the improvement of the design, introduction, and operation of their services. Constant measurements as to the effectiveness of the services offered through customer surveys is one of the methods to find out points for improvement. If an organisation follows a bottom-up approach, employees could be another source of information.

Quality

The key requirement for continual improvement is to design and implement a defined improvement plan that specifies the activities required to improve the quality of certain services. Text 15.2 is an article by Elliott Mest in Hotelmanagement (2015, pp 35-36) that highlights how technology and segmentation have been influencing change within the hospitality industry.

TEXT 15.2

Technology and segmentation influencing change in the hospitality industry.

Technology, segmentation speed hotel operations evolution

By C. Elliott Mest

During his journey from cleaning pools and cutting grass to becoming president and CEO of Hospitality Ventures Management Group, Robert Cole was able to watch the hospitality industry evolve from the ground up. 'I literally grew up in the hotel business,' Cole said, as he recalled the days when franchisors would have two to four brands under their umbrella. 'Now the big guys have 10 to 13 on average.'

The biggest change in industry operations, according to Cole, was learning who the industry's true customer transformed into over the past decade. 'Ten years ago, less than 3 percent of our reservations were made online, now they are somewhere between 30 [percent] and 40 percent,' Cole said. 'Four and five years ago I would ask GMs who our No. 1 customer is. The correct answer was and is: the Internet.'

Beds and dinner

Mike Marshall, president & CEO of Marshall Hotels & Resorts, said that the biggest operations change on the guestroom side came in the form of beds. 'I remember buying the cheapest beds I could buy until the Westin Heavenly Bed came along,' Marshall said. 'You just didn't think about it.'

According to Marshall, the industry shifted from a focus on walk-in business to reservations based, from a hospitality business to a service business. Another change is the amenity creep that has slowly cast itself over guestrooms, beginning with premium TV channels and ending in flat-screen TVs. 'I've seen a lot of amenity creep become expected, even in lower-end hotels,' Marshall said. 'Everyone expects decent bathroom products; you don't win points for that anymore. And if you don't have a flat-screen, high-definition TV, your room just feels old.'

'From my perspective, [food-and beverage] has changed the most,' said Gerry Chase, president and COO of New Castle Hotels & Resorts. 'In the 1970s, hotels would have 3,000-square-foot bars with live entertainment, 10-piece bands earning $ 2 million in revenue every year through the early 1980s.'

This was a period where the hotel restaurant was the restaurant of choice in a local area, but then the baby-boomer generation began to enter a new period in their lives. 'The baby boomers grew up, they had children and were no longer at the bars,' Chase said. 'Those 'action lounges' as we called them are almost all junior ballrooms and meeting space now.'

A new customer

Murray L. Dow, president of the Dow Hotel Company, said the biggest shift he has seen is the evolution of customer preferences and how hotels have adapted to them.

'In the '70s, the high end was controlled by Westin and the low end was controlled by Holiday Inn – pretty clear cut,' Dow said. 'At that time we thought there were two segments, high and low, but Marriott and Hilton shook things up and now there is so much differentiation, from lifestyle and boutique to luxury and low end.'

Since then, segmentation has taken off. Dow said that the majority of the new brands and soft brands being created to corner all available niche markets have been successful because they are part of a larger umbrella. 'Guests are still searching for their individual needs and wants,' Dow said. 'Guests are attracted to independents because they offer different services and atmospheres.'

'Guests now want an experiential stay; they want their stay to be different,' Chase said. 'It's travel with a mission rather than travel for travel's sake. Even in our Internet-dominated environment, people want the personal touch.'

Micromanagement

Away from the big picture, small-scale hotel operations also have changed a great deal over the years, and while computers have streamlined processes such as check-in and property management, they introduced new concerns that conflicted with the hospitality side of the business.

'When we first installed computers, all you saw were the front-desk agents' heads as they looked down to type. We lost the banter between staff and guests,' Marshall said. 'This improved with better programs and more tech-savvy employees, but revenue management is more important than ever before and has grown too complicated for many properties.'

Marshall said that for a hotel to maximize its revenue management, it needs to understand its market and how external factors such as weather and special occasions affect rates, adapting at a moment's notice. 'Unfortunately, today we have unsophisticated hoteliers, many owner/operators with one or two hotels that don't understand the business as well as they should,' Marshall said. 'Revenue-management concepts from the big brands have helped them, but it has been a hindrance for a long time, and continues to be.'

'With the current state of the Internet, with [online travel agencies] and the market segmented as it is, big flags have automated systems and sell times,' Chase said. 'In the past, pricing was scheduled seasonally. Today, pricing happens day-by-day, and sometimes hourly. It has become automated, sophisticated and effective if you are monitoring it.'

15.1.2   Five ways of thinking about change

Assumptions

To explore the contrasting approaches to change, it is crucial to find out the underlying assumptions which define the attributes of process of change. Caluwé and Vermaak (2003) introduced five colours to reflect those underlying assumptions for change. Figure 15.2 is a summary of the five colours and their meanings. For Caluwé and Vermaak, thinking in colours provides an appropriate framework to communicate change according to one's own and others' paradigms. Each colour paradigm is associated with certain beliefs, characteristics, ideals and pitfalls when applied to a particular situation.

Yellow-print thinking

Colour of power

Yellow-print thinking is based on socio-political concepts relating to organisations, in which interest, conflict, and power play important roles. It is called 'yellow-print thinking' because, in the philosophy of Caluwé and Vermaak, yellow is the colour of power (e.g. symbols like the sun, fire) and of the type of process ('brooding and coalition formation around a fire'). Yellow-print thinking assumes that people change their viewpoints if their interests are fulfilled or if they are convinced by a certain idea for change. This type of change advocates forming coalitions or power blocks as change is considered a power game or negotiation exercise needed to solve internal or external challenges. This way of thinking is appropriate for a process of change which involves different parties having to work with each other to achieve complex goals. The success and failure of change depends on the ability to get all (or the most important) key players on board. The most often used interventions in this type of change are communicating, lobbying, negotiating and resolving conflicts through third parties. It is therefore difficult to predict change results, since these depend on the influence, mindset changes, and agreements among important players.

Blue-print thinking

Rational design

Blue-print thinking is based on the rational design and implementation of change, like in project work and scientific management. A blueprint is the (architectural) design or plan drawn up beforehand, and guarantees the actual outcome. Blue-print thinking explains that organisations and people change when clear goals and structures are set to define tasks, clarify positions, and establish timeframes. Since change is considered a rational process, it is important to manage and continuously monitor this process based on pre-determined indicators to reach desired results. The methods

© Noordhoff Uitgevers bv

FIGURE 15.2 Five ways of thinking about change – Caluwé and Vermaak (2003)

	Yellow print	Blue print	Red print	Green print	White print
Something changes when you	bring common interests together	think first and then act according to a plan	stimulate people in the right way	create settings for collective learning	create space for spontaneous evolution
in a/an	power game	rational process	exchange exercises	learning process	dynamic process
and create	a feasible solution, a win-win situation	the best solution, a brave new world	a motivating solution the best fit	a solution that people develop themselves	a solution that releases energy
The result is...	forming coalitions changing top structures	project management strategic analysis	assessment & reward, social gatherings	training and coaching, open systems planning	open space meetings self-steering teams
by a/an...	facilitator who uses his own power base	expert in the field	HRM expert	facilitator who supports people	someone who uses his being as instrument
aimed at...	positions and context	knowledge and results	procedures and working climate	the setting and communication	patterns and meanings
Result is...	partly unknown and shifting	described and guaranteed	outlined but not guaranteed	envisaged but not guaranteed	unpredictable
Safeguarded by...	decision documents and power balances	benchmarking and iso systems	HRM systems	a learning organisation	self-management
The pitfalls lie in...	dreaming and lose-lose	ignoring external and irrational aspects	ignoring power and smothering brilliance	excluding no-one and lack of action	superficial understanding and laissez faire

15

used to analyse the situation in blue-print thinking are SWOT, benchmarking, total quality management, and balanced scorecards, for example. The blue-print thinking change process may be short compared to other ways of thinking, because it is based on defined plans and a timeframe. Room for mistakes is reduced, as the motto is to 'think first and act second'. Thinking and doing occur in sequence. Agents of change are experts in the contents of change and are responsible for the implementation and control of the change process. They should therefore be results-oriented, decisive, accurate, and dedicated.

Timeframe

Red-print thinking

Red-print thinking is rooted in human resource management with the focus of this way of thinking being people. The red colour refers to the colour of human blood. The human being must be influenced, tempted, seduced, and stimulated. Changing the behaviour of people is reached by stimulating and motivating them. The concept of barter is critical to the motivation of people. People are motivated to do something if they (expect to) receive something back for their efforts and development. Incentives, personal care, and personal and professional development are among the rewards that can stimulate people to develop their competences and get the best out of them. The purpose is to bridge a possible gap between the needs of individuals and those of the organisation. Aside from rewards, other relevant interventions for such a way of thinking about change are management's persuasive style of reasons for change, employee wellness programmes, social activities, and team building activities. The red-print thinking change process takes time. Results of a change can be planned in advance but are influenced by the reactions of people. The agents of change can change plans based on those reactions. Agents are supposed to motivate, coach and facilitate people to accept change by being inspiring, careful, and loyal. In the red-print thinking change process, the human factor is central, and people will implement change if they are guided in the right direction.

People

Purpose

Green-print thinking

Green-print thinking has its roots in the concept of organisational development. Changing and learning are closely linked and can be exchangeable in meaning and usage. People change when they learn. The colour green refers both green lighting people's ideas and learning, and to growth (as in nature). Green-print thinking is devoted to learning and the development of people and organisations. To develop an organisation capable of change, continuous learning and development are needed. The purpose is to reinforce individual learning abilities and create a learning environment where people are motivated to discover the limits of their competences and engage in learning situations. The process of change takes place when people and organisations learn by setting up learning situations and giving and receiving feedback.

Learning

Green-print thinking allows people to take ownership of their learning; required interventions are mainly coaching, stimulation, feedback, and leadership trainings. The green-print thinking change process takes time as learning cannot be forced. Outcomes are difficult to predict. It depends on the

Takes time

willingness and ability to learn and the extent and effectiveness of learning. Agents of change facilitate and do not control people. They design learning situations, give feedback, support experimenting with new behaviour, structure communication, and support people in their objective to learn with each other and from each other in order to establish continuous learning and collective settings. Their attributes are empathy, creativity, and openness.

White-print thinking
White-print thinking, also called chaos thinking, focusses on inspiration and flow since people and organisations change in dynamic situations and in an atmosphere where creativity and spontaneity are fostered. The colour white reflects all colours. It illustrates openness and allows room for self-organisation and evolution. The outcome of change remains mostly a surprise. In white-print thinking, the dominant idea is that everything is in motion and changes autonomously. Complexity is preferred and seen as a source of enrichment. White-print thinking considers change to be understanding the opportunities, renewal and creativity more than managing or directing change. Making sense is crucial in the white-print thinking change process. Interventions needed to remove obstacles and increase peoples' energy are, for example, open space meetings, appreciative enquiry, dialogue, search conferences, and self-steering teams. The role of the agents of change is secondary, and restricted to coaching, supporting, and empowering. Inner desires and strengths of people, both individually and as groups, are the decisive factors.

Chaos thinking

Surprise

15.1.3   Types of change
Organisations change because they want different business results, motivated by ambition as well as by aversion. An organisation may seek to move to a new state of affairs because management wants to spend less money, make more money, or some combination of the two. Change is almost never easy. People rarely do things the way they do because they want to do a bad job. Current ways of working within most organisations are the result of historical precedent, habits, and reactions to past challenges, the influence of technology, and directions from senior management. Adopting a new way of working means leaving the world of the proven and familiar behind, and entering a new world that, at first, may seem strange. Organisational change is defined as the process by which alterations occur to the structure and functions of a social construct. Organisational change is management's attempt to have employees think, behave and perform differently. Some members embrace and engage in initiatives for change readily, while others fight the change to the death and deny its necessity.

Alterations

Change is considered a natural phenomenon dictated by various internal and external forces, but the perspectives on and terminologies of change differ drastically. Van de Ven and Poole (1995) suggest four basic theories to explain why and how organisations change, with each presenting differing conceptual motors driving change:
- Life-cycle theory to achieve long-term growth;
- Teleological theory to focus on a common goal;
- Dialectical theory to react to different tensions and contradictions; and finally
- Evolution theory to react sustainably to changing regulations.

Natural phenomenon

15

Areas of concern   Several scholars have emphasised two areas of concern related to organisational change (Kotter & Schlesinger, 1979; Beer & Nohria, 2000). The first area is directed at ways of convincing employees of the need for change, while the second emphasises employee attitudes and behaviour towards change. Change is a multi-level phenomenon that happens at the organisational, departmental, or individual levels. The individual level concerns the attitudes and behaviours of employees towards organisational change. Moreover, organisational change can also be categorised as either episodic/planned or continuous/emergent:

Planned   • Episodic or planned change is a deliberate and purposeful change which asks for transformational or revolutionary changes. Such a change needs a step by step sequence and the 'push' approach. The transformational change is a controlled or top-down change, which means that top management decides a change needs to be made, and creates a step-by-step plan of implementation that employees follow in order to minimise risks. An example of such change is the change of an organisation's culture. Change

Episodic   managers believe that episodic change helps to overcome problems and creates positive reactions from employees as the procedure is clear. However, the top-down and push character of this approach to change is responsible for creating affective, cognitive and behavioural problems.

Emergent   • Continuous or emergent change, on the other hand, is an evolutionary change where a bundle of incremental adjustments or improvements takes place in one part of a system and follows a pull-driven approach. Emergent change is adaptive and initiated at different levels of the organisation; it empowers employees at the operational level to influence change by giving feedback and suggestions.

Organisational change is a deeply-rooted change in which assumptions once taken-for-granted are questioned and subject to change. This change is sensitive and asks for careful introduction and implementation as there is a high

Classified   chance that employees will resist it. Therefore, change can be classified by

FIGURE 15.3 Classifications of change

	Extent of change	
	Transformation	**Realignment**
Incremental	**Evolution:** Transformational change implemented gradually through inter-related initivities; likely to be proactive change undertaken in participation of the need for future change.	**Adaptation:** Change undertaken to realign the way in which the organisation operates; implemented in a series of steps
Big Bang	**Revolution:** Transformational change that occurs via simultaneous initiatives on many fronts: • more likely to be forced and reactive because of the changing competitive conditions that the organisation is facing	**Reconstruction:** Change undertaken to realign the way in which the organisation operates with many iniatives implemented simultaneously: • often forced and reactive because of a changing competitive context

Speed of change (left margin label for rows)

the extent to which it is needed and the speed required to achieve it, as suggested by Hope Hailey and Balogun (2002), and illustrated in Figure 15.3.

Transformation entails fundamental changes which revolutionise an organisation's existing values and paradigms. Transformation requires changing an organisation's culture. It is a fundamental change that cannot be handled within the existing organisational paradigm.

Transformation

Realignment involves a change which is in line with the current assumptions and values, and is introduced step by step. Realignment does not involve a fundamental reappraisal of the central assumptions and beliefs held within the organisation.

Realignment

Incremental change reflects a long-term change; if implemented successfully, it can result in transformational changes. Incremental change can take a long period of time, but results in a fundamentally different organisation once completed.

Incremental

Big Bang means an unexpected and forced change due to crisis situations. Big Bang change is likely to be a reactive transformation using simultaneous initiatives on many fronts, often in a relatively short space of time.

Big Bang

15.1.4 Change context and design

Hope Hailey and Balogun (2002) similarly developed a framework called the 'change kaleidoscope', here shown in Figure 15.4. This framework was designed in order to make contextual aspects and design options easily

Change kaleidoscope

FIGURE 15.4 Change kaleidoscope – Hope Hailey & Balogun (2002)

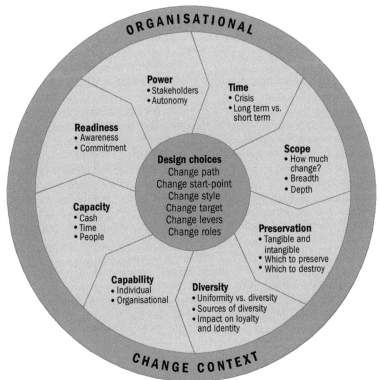

15

accessible to its practitioners; it draws on a wide array of different implementation options open to those designing change within organisations.

Diagnostic tool

This framework forms a diagnostic tool for managers, and encourages:
- a rigorous contextual analysis;
- a consideration of a range of implementation options;
- an awareness of one's own preferences about change and how these limit the options considered; and
- a development of the evaluation of change.

The outer ring relates to the wider strategic context of change. The middle
ring relates to specific contextual factors that need to be considered when
formulating a change plan. The inner circle gives a menu of choices and interventions (design choices) available to change agents.

The contextual factors of change

Features

The context demonstrates the features that shape change and gives indications to managers and agents of change on how to lead and proceed with
change. Each feature can be evaluated as positive, negative or neutral in
the context of change; such an evaluation indicates either resistance or
commitment to change. The main contextual factors of change are:
- Time – it is very important to define the duration of change to determine
whether change should last longer and is meant for long-term strategic
development, or if it is a quick reaction to a crisis or a need.
- Scope – changing an entire organisation differs from changing parts of
an organisation. While the organisation itself may need a transformational change, parts of it might only require a realignment type of change, for
example.
- Preservation – the type of change dictates what is to be retained or removed, such as culture, competences and people.
- Diversity – different departments have different sub-cultures, and people – this diversity may be based on, for example, nationality, different
orientations, or gender.
- Capability – when defining change, the capabilities to cope with and implement change need to be verified at the individual, managerial and organisational levels.
- Capacity – the existing physical and human resources available to deal
with the change process, such as the amount of money available for it.
- Readiness – employees have to be ready for the change by being aware
of the necessity of change, and show commitment to change.
- Power – which party is to take the decisions to proceed and implement
change? Change can be a top-down process; alternatively, employees may
be empowered to take decisions during the formulation or implementation of
change (e.g. complete involvement). Such decisions concerning power are
related to the leadership style, which is either transformational or directive.

The design choices

*Implementation
options*

There are also six main implementation options available to agents of
change, and the key factors are:
- Change path – specifying types of change in terms of timescales, extent
of change, and desired outcomes.
- Change start-point – choosing how change is initiated – top-down or bottom-up.
- Change style – choosing the management style to be adopted to lead the
change – directive, coercive, participative, or supportive.

- Change target – changing people's output, their behaviour, or attitudes and values.
- Change interventions – identifying the range of levers and mechanisms to be deployed across the different technical, political and cultural sub-systems within an organisation, as well as the array of inter-personal interventions, such as education, communication, training and personal development
- Change roles – assigning roles and responsibilities – leadership, use of consultants, and role of change taskforces.

Hope Hailey and Balogun (2002) recognised that, despite the strength of the change kaleidoscope in its recognition of the complexity of change and the need for change designs to be context-sensitive, the change kaleidoscope needs to be used in combination with other frameworks, such as the cultural web (discussed in Section 15.2.3). The change kaleidoscope is primarily a mechanism for dealing with planned change, and it is most appropriate when there is a particular end goal that needs to be achieved.

15.1.5   Change approaches

Managers and change agents apply different approaches to organisational change. It is beyond the scope of this work to review all the various perspectives from which approaches to organisational change have been studied. As such, in this section, three approaches to organisational change implementation are discussed and explained: action research, appreciative research inquiry, and parallel learning structures.

Action research approach
Lewin (1951), who devised the force field analysis model (see Section 15.3.1) is often regarded as the inventor of action research. The action research approach stipulates that change is a combination of action orientation, like changing attitudes and behaviours, and research orientation, such as testing theory. Action orientation entails diagnosing problems, creating and applying interventions to solve those problems. Research orientation, on the other hand, includes applying conceptual models, collecting data to diagnose the problems effectively, and evaluating if a theory works in practical situations step-by-step (McShane & Von Glinow, 2010).

Combination

The action research approach adopts the open system, and agents of change are required to anticipate the expected and unexpected consequences of change interventions. Moreover, this approach calls for a high participation of staff members in terms of knowledge and commitment in both the research and interventions phases. The action research process starts with diagnosing the need for change by collecting and analysing data, and deciding on objectives. The second step in the process is introducing the intervention by implementing the desired change. The last step is evaluating and stabilising change by determining the change effectiveness and making it part of the daily routines.

Phases

The action research approach has dominated organisational change thinking for many years, but some experts have complained that the problem-oriented nature of action research focusses on the negative dynamics of the group or system rather than the positive opportunities and potential they offer (McShane & Von Glinow, 2010).

15

Positive
orientation

Appreciative inquiry approach

The appreciative inquiry approach tries to break the traditional problem-solving mentality and introduces a new approach based on focussing on establishing and improving positive qualities and traits within individuals and organisations. It stresses the strengths of an organisation more than eliminating or reducing its weaknesses. The positive orientation of this approach helps individuals and groups within an organisation to overcome their negative perceptions of certain situations and establish a more positive perspective of existing possibilities. The appreciative inquiry process is based on the 'Four-D' model shown in Figure 15.5, adopted from McShane and Von Glinow (2010, p. 459).

FIGURE 15.5 Four-D model of appreciative inquiry approach

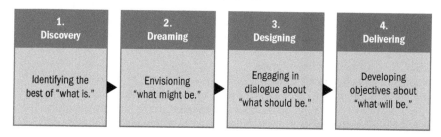

The model starts with discovery, which means identifying the positive aspects of the situation by interviewing staff members or collecting data using guest surveys. This is followed by dreaming, which entails envisioning what may be possible in ideal situations. This makes employees feel safer and volunteer their hopes and aspirations. The third step is designing, which involves engaging in dialogue about what the situation ought to be. All staff members are invited to take part in the dialogue. The final stage is delivering, in which staff members establish specific objectives and directions for their own organisation on the basis of their model outcome.

Less structured

It should be noted that, despite its successes in implementing change within organisations, McShane and Von Glinow (2010) indicate that appreciative inquiry is not always the best approach to changing teams or organisations, and, indeed, it has not always been successful. Appreciative inquiry requires participants who are willing to let go of the problem-oriented approach and leaders who are willing to accept an appreciative inquiry's less structured process. Another concern is that research has not yet examined the contingencies of this approach. In other words, we do not yet know under what conditions appreciative inquiry is a useful approach to organisational change and under what conditions it is less effective. Overall, appreciative inquiry has much to offer the organisational change process, but understand its potential and limitations is just in its early stages (McShane & Von Glinow, 2010).

Parallel learning structures approach

Participative
coalitions

Parallel learning structures approach is based on participative coalitions of staff members at all levels. The coalitions follow an action research approach to achieve a successful change. The purpose of creating such social structures is to increase an organisation's capacity for learning. An example of this approach is that of Royal Dutch Shell, which used parallel learning structures to improve and emphasise its customer focus all over the world. Executives had meetings (retail boot camps) with six country teams of front-line staff members. The staff members learned about competitive trends and marketing tools and, once back home, used that information to study their markets and develop improvement plans (McShane & Von Glinow, 2010).

15.2 Change and organisational culture

Changing an organisation's culture is one of the most difficult challenges in governance and administration. This is because an organisation's culture involves interconnecting sets of goals, roles, processes, values, communications practices, attitudes and assumptions. These elements fit together as a mutually reinforcing system and combine to prevent any attempt to change the culture. That is why single-fix solutions may appear to make progress for a while, but eventually the interconnecting elements of organisational culture take over and change is inevitably overcome by the previously existing organisational culture. Changing a culture is a large-scale undertaking, and eventually all organisational tools for changing minds will need to be put into play. However, the order in which they are deployed has a critical impact on the likelihood of success.

Large-scale

15.2.1   Defining organisational culture
Schein (2010, p. 18) defined culture as:

> 'A pattern of shared basic assumptions that was learned by a group as it solved its problems of external adaptation and internal integration that has worked well enough to be considered valid and, therefore, to be taught to new members as the correct way to perceive, think, and feel in relation to those problems.'

However, he earlier indicated that, for the purpose of defining organisational culture, 'it is important to recognise that a fragmented or differentiated organisational culture usually reflects a multiplicity of subcultures, and within those subcultures there are shared assumptions' (2004, p. 21). Organisational culture reflects 'how we do things here'. It influences the working behaviour as it sets rules for what is accepted. In addition, organisational culture arises from a combination of founding figures and turnaround leaders, a distinctive company history, and stages of development. Furthermore, the nature of the market, product characteristics, industry and national context also play a role in forming organisational cultures. Hospitality organisations are impacted by the hospitality industry characteristics epitomised by instability, uncertainty, and continuous change. Organisational culture is made up of three elements: artefacts, espoused beliefs and values, and basic underlying assumptions, as explained here:

Elements

- Artefacts – the observable parts of an organisation such as its logo, building, staff dress code, colours, employee behaviour, names, language, and so on.

Artefacts

- Espoused beliefs and values – the evaluative beliefs that determine employee behaviour and unite them in achieving a common vision. Many hospitality organisations have established their shared values (see Chapter 2,

15

Espoused values

Texts 2.11 and 2.12). Values are a combination of espoused values and enacted values. Espoused values are the principles, standards, and goals established by the founder or leader of an organisation. These espoused values represent the core, purpose and goals (mission and vision) of the company philosophy, and are reflected in its strategies. Espoused values also determine the right-wrong/good-bad behaviour of all stakeholders in an organisation. Enacted values, on the other hand, are the values and norms held by individual employees and reflected in their behaviour, such as punctuality, communication, and pro-activeness.

Enacted values

Assumptions

• Basic underlying assumptions – all that is taken for granted. Values become assumptions if they occur unconsciously, such as Front Office employees greeting guests with a smile.

15.2.2   Strong versus adaptive organisational cultures

Homogeneous

A strong organisational culture refers to a homogeneous culture, meaning that all members of one organisational culture have the same or similar opinions on their culture. In contrast, a weak organisational culture indicates heterogeneity with lesser bonding among members in regard to certain values and assumptions. Moreover, a strong organisational culture is difficult to imitate, and members' commitment, motivation, solidarity, sense of identity and performance are high. Those organisations with strong organisational cultures operate better in stable and predictable environments. Therefore, they have difficulty with adapting to changing environments, and members respond to stimulus because of their alignment to organisational values. A weak organisational culture, on the other hand, has better chances of succeeding in an unstable environment, since values are rather superficial and people are ready to adapt to change more easily because of a lack of a sense of belonging. In summary, strong organisational cultures facilitate internal integration, control and coordination, but are a barrier in adapting to change. A strong organisational culture becomes weak when shared values, beliefs and attitudes interfere with the needs of business, strategy, and stakeholders.

15.2.3   The cultural web and change

Corporate culture often becomes the focus of attention during periods of organisational change – for example when companies merge and their cultures clash, or when growth and other strategic change mean that the existing culture becomes inappropriate, and hinders rather than supports progress. In more static environments, cultural issues may be responsible for low morale, absenteeism or high staff turnover, with all of the adverse effects these issues can have on productivity. So, for all its elusiveness, corporate culture can have a huge impact on an organisation's work environment and output. Fortunately, while corporate culture can be elusive, ap-

Assess

proaches have been developed to help assess it. Such is the cultural web (Figure 15.6), developed by Johnson (1992), which provides an approach to looking at and changing an organisation's culture. The cultural web enables organisations to identify the main determinants of their cultures. It is also considered a tool for identifying and changing organisational culture. A strong organisational culture establishes a clear picture for every employee

Seven elements

concerning the interrelated seven elements of the cultural web.

FIGURE 15.6 The cultural web of an organisation

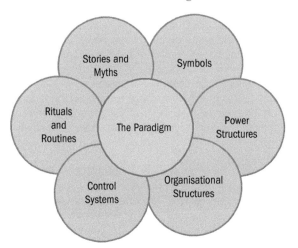

The elements of the cultural web are explained as follows:
- Paradigm – the core of a common set of assumptions that is taken for   *Core*
  granted; it can be related to Schein's (2010) layer of basic assumptions
  and is difficult to change. Environmental forces and organisational capabilities undoubtedly affect the performance of an organisation but do not
  in and of themselves create organisational strategy: people create strategy, and the mechanism by which this occurs at the cognitive, cultural
  level is the paradigm.
- Rituals and routines – routines are described as the way employees inter-   *Interact*
  act with each other, also linking different departments. They describe
  how things should happen and are often taken for granted, hence hard to
  change. Rituals strengthen routines, by signalling what is especially valued by a company. This can be done formally (training programmes, periodic assessment) or informally (Christmas parties, Saturday night
  drinks).
- Stories and myths – these provide an insight into an organisation's his-   *Insight*
  tory, important events, heroes, and villains. They are communicated
  among employees and to the external environment (customers, suppli-
  ers, others). An example of stories is the case of Walmart's 10-foot rule.   *10-Foot rule*
  Sam Walton, founder of Walmart, spent his life practicing what he called
  'the ten-foot rule'. The rule is simple: if you come within 10 feet (about 3
  metres) of a customer, look them in the eye, smile and ask if you can
  help. While on store visits, Walton would encourage his sales associates
  to take the 'ten-foot rule pledge'. And in Walmart's headquarters in Ben-
  tonville, it was *de rigueur* to flash one's pearly whites when within smiling
  distance of anyone. That smile became part of the Walmart culture.
- Symbols – these are logos, offices, cars, language terminology and titles,
  which become a short-hand representation of the nature of the organisation. Symbols represent the organisation to the outside world.
- Power structures – this is identified by a group of people or an individual
  who hold the power in an organisation due to their expertise or status.   *Expertise or*
  The bigger a group or the greater the power of an individual, the more in-   *status*
  fluence they are able to exercise on the organisation. Empowerment is

15

15

Monitor

an example of a power structure in which employees may make their own decisions.
- Organisational structures – these reflect the power structure by showing the relationships between the elements of control and power, and among various power groups or individuals – top-down or bottom-up communication.
- Control systems – these outline which systems an organisation uses to monitor and manage the organisation's performance; these systems indicate what is important to an organisation. Control systems may govern finances, rewards, and measurements to determine an organisation's effectiveness and efficiency.

The cultural web explains why certain organisations fail to adapt quickly and effectively to the changing environment. Such organisations find it difficult to break the paradigm and related elements to respond to adjustments which ask for fundamental or cultural changes. Furthermore, organisations find that some elements of the cultural web are easier to change than others. It may be easier, for example, to change the formal organisational structure than it is to change long established routines and habits.

15.2.4 Organisational culture types and change – the Cameron and Quinn competing values framework

Effective organisations

Major dimensions

The competing values framework was initially developed from research conducted on the major indicators of effective organisations. Key questions of the investigation were related to the main criteria for determining an organisation's effectiveness, key factors that define organisational effectiveness, and indicators people use to judge an organisation's effectiveness. Campbell, Brownas, Peterson, and Dunnette (1974) created a list of thirty-nine indicators which represent a full set of all possible measurements of organisational effectiveness. The dataset was analysed by Quinn and Rohrbaugh (1983) to determine whether patterns or clusters of key factors of effectiveness could be identified. They identified two major dimensions that organise the indicators into four main clusters. One dimension differentiates effectiveness criteria that emphasise flexibility, discretion, and dynamism from criteria that emphasise stability, order, and control. This continuum range from organisational versatility and pliability on one end to organisational steadiness and durability on the other end. The second dimension differentiates effectiveness criteria that emphasise an internal orientation, integration, and unity from criteria that emphasise an external orientation, differentiation, and rivalry. This continuum range from organisational cohesion and consonance on the one end to organisational separation and independence on the other. Together, these two dimensions form four quadrants, each representing a distinct set of organisational effectiveness indicators.

Four clusters

Figure 15.7 illustrates the relationships between these two dimensions. These indicators of effectiveness represent what people value about an organisation's performance. They define what is seen as good and right and appropriate. The four clusters of criteria define the core values of perceptions of organisations. Cameron and Quinn (2006) indicate these four core values notably represent opposite or competing assumptions, with each continuum highlighting a core value opposite from the corresponding value at the other end.

FIGURE 15.7 The competing values framework

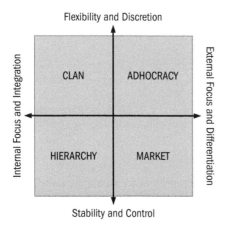

Each quadrant represents basic assumptions, orientations, and values which are the elements that comprise an organisational culture. The organisational culture assessment instrument (OCAI), developed by Cameron and Quinn (2006), shown in Appendix F is the instrument that permits an organisation to diagnose its dominant orientation based on these core culture types, and also assists in diagnosing an organisation's cultural strength, type, and congruence. The competing values framework makes clear that achieving valued outcomes in each of the quadrants is crucial for organisational effectiveness in the long term. While pursuing value creation strategies, leaders should consider multiple outcomes in each of the quadrants. Narrowly defining value to include only financial outcomes, for example, often ends up producing only short-term results while compromising long-term creation of value. The development of a well-rounded portfolio of outcomes guided by the competing values framework is an important prerequisite for ensuring long-term success and value enhancement.

Diagnose

Clan culture
This working environment is a friendly one. People have a lot in common, similar to a large family. The leaders or executives are seen as mentors or maybe even father or mother figures. Organisational cohesion is ensured by loyalty and tradition. There is great involvement. The organisation emphasises long-term Human Resource development and moral bonding. Success is defined within the framework of addressing the needs of clients and caring for people. The organisation promotes teamwork, participation, and consensus. Its main characteristics are:

Loyalty and tradition

- Leader type: facilitator, mentor, team builder
- Value drivers: commitment, communication, development
- Theory of effectiveness: Human Resource development and participation are effective
- Quality improvement strategy: empowering, team building, involving employees, developing Human Resources, communicating openly

Adhocracy culture
This is a dynamic and creative working environment. Employees take risks. Leaders are seen as innovators and risk takers. Experiments and innovation

Risk takers

are a source of common ground within the organisation. Prominence is emphasised. The long-term goal is to grow and create new resources. The availability of new products or services is seen as success. This organisation promotes individual initiative and freedom. Its main characteristics are:

- Leader type: innovator, entrepreneur, visionary
- Value drivers: innovative output, transformation, agility
- Theory of effectiveness: innovativeness, vision and new resources are effective
- Quality improvement strategy: surprising and delighting, creating new standards, anticipating needs, improving continuously, finding creative solutions

Market culture

Competitive

This is a results-based organisation that emphasises finishing jobs and getting things done. People are competitive and focussed on goals. Leaders are hard drivers, producers, and rivals at the same time. They are tough and have high expectations. The emphasis on winning keeps the organisation together. Reputation and success are the most important. Long-term focus is on rival activities and reaching goals. Market penetration and stock are the definitions of success. Competitive prices and market leadership are important. The organisational style is based on competition. Its main characteristics are:

- Leader type: hard driver, competitor, producer
- Value drivers: market share, goal achievement, profitability
- Theory of effectiveness: aggressively competing and focussing on customers is effective
- Quality improvement strategy: measuring client preferences, improving productivity, creating external partnerships, enhancing competiveness, involving customers and suppliers

Hierarchy culture

Formal rules

This is a formalised and structured working environment. Procedures dictate what people do. Leaders are proud of their efficiency-based coordination and organisation. Keeping the organisation functioning smoothly is paramount. Formal rules and policy keep the organisation together. Long-term goals are stability and results, paired with efficient and smooth execution of tasks. Dependable delivery, smooth planning, and low costs define success. Personnel management has to guarantee work and predictability. Its main characteristics are:

- Leader type: coordinator, monitor, organiser
- Value drivers: efficiency, timeliness, consistency, and uniformity
- Theory of effectiveness: control and efficiency with capable processes are effective
- Quality improvement strategy: detecting errors, benchmarking, controlling processes, solving problems systematically, using quality tools

The organisational culture assessment instrument (OCAI)

This instrument is in the form of a questionnaire (see Appendix F) that requires individuals within an organisation to respond to six items based on a series of four alternatives each. It is used to predict an organisation's culture and organisational performance. It helps identify the organisation's current culture (the Now column), and also helps to identify the culture individuals within the organisation think should be developed to match future demands of the environment and opportunities to be faced by the organisation in five years' time (the Preferred column).

The OCAI consists of six items, each with four alternatives. A total of 100 points is awarded among these four alternatives, depending on the extent to which each alternative is similar to ones own organisation. A higher number of points is given to the alternative most similar to that used in one's organisation, but the total should always be 100 points for each of the six items. The columns are filled one at a time, with the preferred column filled in about five minutes after completing the now column. The OCAI is scored by simple arithmetic calculations. The first step is to look for the average of, for example, all the A responses [(1A +2A + 3A + 4A + 5A + 6A) divided by 6] in the 'Now' column. These same is also done for the B, C and D responses. The second step is to do the same, but now for the 'Preferred' column. To determine an organisation's cultural profile, the scores are plotted in graphs that indicate the cultural profile. The mechanics of constructing and plotting the cultural profiles can be found in Chapter 4 of Cameron and Quinn (2006); and in the current section of this work, only a representation of such a culture profile is shown. Figure 15.8 is the profile of an organisation's current and preferred cultures (Cameron & Quinn, 2006, p. 86).

FIGURE 15.8 Profile of an organisation's current and preferred cultures.

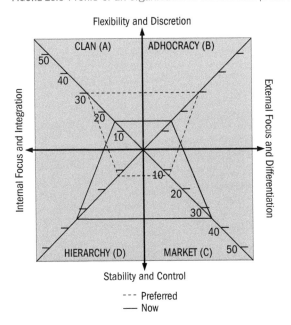

In a study of hotels in Turkey, Ergün and Tasgit (2013) showed that there is a significant relationship between an organisation's cultural features and innovation performance. The innovation performance of hotels, which had characteristics of adhocracy culture and market culture, was more positive than in those hotels with clan culture and hierarchy culture characteristics.

🔢 Models of change process

There are numerous models available that address the change process at both the individual level and those that offer guidance and structure to organisations that intend to carry out innovation activities. In this section, three models are discussed: Lewin's force field analysis model; Lewin's 3 steps model of change; and Kotter's 8-step process of change model.

15.3.1   Lewin's force field analysis model

Lewin (1951) introduced the force field analysis model to help managers understand how the change process works. The model, shown in Figure 15.9, illustrates that change situations should be considered in terms of driving forces and restraining forces. The driving forces are factors that push an organisation to move to a new state by making employees aware of the necessity of change. For the hospitality industry, those driving forces are, for example, the constant changing needs of customers, technological advancements, globalisation, changing workforce, and internal factors such as changes in culture due to a merger or acquisition. The restraining forces, on the other hand, are factors that hinder the change to occur; for instance sticking to a status quo and resisting change. To accept change, an equilibrium between the driving and restraining forces is needed. This means that the agents of change have to strengthen the driving forces and weaken the restraining forces.

Driving forces

Restraining forces

FIGURE 15.9 Lewin's force field analysis model

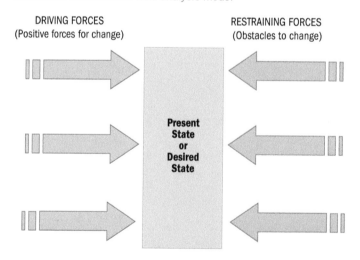

DRIVING FORCES
(Positive forces for change)

RESTRAINING FORCES
(Obstacles to change)

**Present
State
or
Desired
State**

15.3.2   Lewin's 3 steps model of change

Lewin (1951) similarly developed a change model involving three steps: unfreezing, changing and refreezing, which combine into a very simple and practical model for understanding the change process. The process of change entails creating the perception that a change is needed, then moving toward the new, desired level of behaviour and, finally, solidifying that new behaviour as the norm. The model is still widely used and serves as the basis for many modern change models. Figure 15.10 shows the 3 steps in the change process.

Simple and practical

© Noordhoff Uitgevers bv

FIGURE 15.10 Lewin's 3 steps model of change

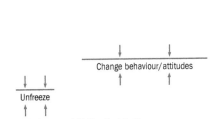

Step 1 – Unfreezing

Before a change can be implemented, it must go through the initial step of unfreezing. The goal during the unfreezing stage is to create an awareness of how the status quo, or current level of acceptability, is hindering the organisation. Old behaviours, ways of thinking, processes, people and organisational structures must all be carefully examined to show employees how necessary a change is for the organisation to create or maintain a competitive advantage in the marketplace. Communication is especially important during the unfreezing stage, so that employees can become informed about the imminent change, the logic behind it and how it will benefit individual employees. This is based on the idea that the more employees know about a change and the more they feel it is necessary and urgent, the more motivated they will be to accept the change.

Awareness

Communication

Step 2 – Changing

Now that the employees are 'unfrozen', they can begin to move. Lewin (1951) recognised that change is a process whereby the organisation must transition or move into a new state of being. This changing step, also referred to as 'transitioning' or 'moving,' is marked by the implementation of the change. This is when the change becomes real. It is also, consequently, the time that most people struggle with the new reality. It is a time marked by uncertainty and fear, making it the hardest step to overcome. During the changing step, employees begin to learn new behaviours, processes and ways of thinking. The more prepared they are for this step, the easier it is to complete. For this reason, education, communication, support and time are critical for employees as they become familiar with the change.

Implementation

Hardest step

Step 3 – Refreezing

Lewin (1951) initially called the final step of his change model 'freezing', but many refer to it as 'refreezing' to symbolise the act of reinforcing, stabilising and solidifying the new state after the change. The changes made to organisational processes, goals, structure, offerings or people are accepted and refrozen as the new norm or status quo. He found the refreezing step to be especially important to ensure that employees do not return to their old ways of thinking or doing before the implementation of the change. Efforts must be made to guarantee change is not lost; it needs to be cemented into the organisation's culture and maintained as the acceptable way of thinking or doing. Positive rewards and acknowledgment of individualised

Accepted and refrozen

15

15

efforts are often used to reinforce the new state because it is believed that positively reinforced behaviour will likely be repeated. The refreezing step is seemingly outdated in contemporary business due to the continuous need for change. It seems unnecessary to spend time freezing a new state when chances are it will need to be re-evaluated and possibly changed again in the immediate future. However, without the refreezing step, there is a high chance that people will return to the old ways.

Okumus and Hemmington (1998) carried out a study related to the change process within hotels at the unit level and found there were no indications in any of the cases investigated that Lewin's 3 steps model of change was used or applicable; while the hotel managers rarely sought to refreeze a new position, it was nevertheless evident that after every change some fine tuning took place, and almost every hotel had plans to implement further change. They concluded that Lewin's unfreezing and refreezing steps do not appear relevant to current hotel organisational practices.

15.3.3   Kotter's 8-step change process model

Kotter introduced the 8-step change process in 1996, and in 2014 carried out some adjustments, while indicating that both versions are still relevant and effective today, and that they are designed to serve different contexts and objectives, as shown in Figure 15.11.

FIGURE 15.11 Differences between the versions of Kotter's 8-Step process of change

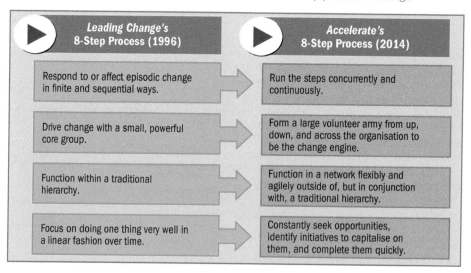

© Noordhoff Uitgevers bv

Taking into account the differences in context and objectives, only the stages of the new and enhanced 8-Step process shown in Figure 15.12 are adapted and explained in this section (Kotter, 2014).

Create a sense of urgency around a single big opportunity

This is absolutely critical to heightening the organisation's awareness that it needs continual strategic adjustments and that these should always be

aligned with the biggest opportunity in sight. Urgency starts at the top of the

FIGURE 15.12 Kotter's enhanced 8-Step process of change

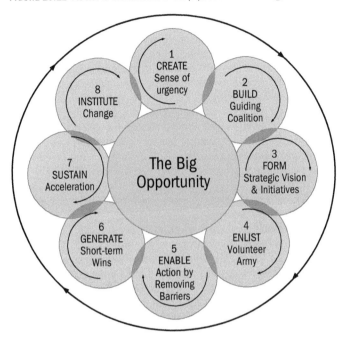

hierarchy, and it is important that executives keep acknowledging and reinforcing it so that employees wake up every morning determined to find some action they can take to move toward that opportunity during their day. Sufficient urgency around a strategically rational and emotionally exciting opportunity is the bedrock upon which all else is built, and ongoing urgency provides a strong competitive advantage. It can galvanize a volunteer army and keep a dual operating system in good working order. It moves managers to focus on opportunities and allows the network to grow for the benefit of the organisation. Without an abiding sense of urgency, no chance of creating a grander business can survive.

Build and maintain a guiding coalition
The core of a strategy network is the guiding coalition, which is made up of volunteers from throughout the organisation. The guiding coalition is selected to represent each of the hierarchy's departments and levels, with a broad range of skills. It must be made up of people whom leadership trusts, and must include at least a few outstanding leaders and managers. This ensures that the guiding coalition can gather and process information as no hierarchy ever could. All members of the guiding coalition are equal – no internal hierarchy can slow down the transfer of information. The coalition can see inside and outside the enterprise, knows the details and the big picture, and uses this information to make good enterprise-wide decisions about which strategic initiatives to launch and how best to do so. The social dynamics of the guiding coalition may be uncomfortable at first, but once a team learns how to operate well, most members seem to love being part of it.

Volunteers

Equal

15

Feasible and easy

Formulate a strategic vision and develop change initiatives designed to capitalise on the big opportunity

The vision serves as a strategic true north for a dual operating system. A well-formulated vision is focussed on taking advantage of a big make-or-break opportunity. The right vision is feasible and easy to communicate. It is emotionally appealing as well as strategically smart. And it gives a guiding coalition a picture of success and enough information and direction to make consequential decisions on the fly, without having to seek permission at every turn. To keep the two parts of a dual operating system connected and aligned, the guiding coalition must show drafts of the vision and initiatives to the organisation's executive committee for comments. A well-functioning guiding coalition treats the committee's comments as highly valuable input but does not automatically accept them as commands.

Communicate the vision and strategy to create buy-in and attract a growing volunteer army

Viral

Vital

A vividly formulated, high-stakes vision and strategy, promulgated by a guiding coalition in ways both memorable and authentic, prompts people to discuss these without the cynicism often encountered by messages cascading down the hierarchy. Done right and/or creatively, such communications can go viral, attracting employees who buy in to the ambition of the message and begin to share a commitment to it. Members of a volunteer army also help in optimising the daily business of the organisation – they are not a separate group of consultants, new hires, or task force appointees. They have organisational knowledge, relationships, credibility, and influence. They understand the need for change – they are often the first to see threats or opportunities – and have the zeal to implement it. It is vital that this army is made up of individuals who bring energy, commitment, and genuine enthusiasm. In military terms, they are not grunts carrying out orders from the brass. Rather, they are change leaders. Whereas hierarchies require management to maintain an efficient status quo, networks demand leadership from within every individual.

Accelerate movement toward the vision and opportunity by ensuring that the network removes barriers

Quickly and efficiently

A hypothetical situation: say a sales representative has received customer complaints about bureaucratic hang-ups and does not know how to fix the problem nor have the time to think about it. Someone in the network gets wind of this, writes up a description, sends it out to the volunteer army, and five people immediately step forward. They set up a call to trace why this is happening, figure out how to remove the barrier, and design a solution – a better CRM system, perhaps. Such a team probably includes someone from IT who has technical expertise and can help identify where the money for the new system should come from. The team works with additional volunteers who have relevant information – from whatever area may be germane – to act quickly and efficiently. The time between the first call and an initial suggested solution may be as little as two weeks – a model of accelerated action. The network team settles on a practical solution that properly supports the sales team. Then, its members take their observations and suggestions to the Chief Information Officer, who gives feedback and may free up a budget and resources. Design and implementation occur in the network and are instituted within the hierarchy. If the network is truly operating hand-in-glove with the hierarchy, the people in the hierarchy should be chomping at the bit to install a new CRM system.

Celebrate visible, significant short-term wins

A strategy network's credibility does not last long without confirmation that its decisions and actions are actually benefiting the organisation. Sceptics erect obstacles unless they see proof that a dual operating system is creating real results. People have only so much patience, so proof must come *Proof* quickly. To ensure success, the best short-term wins should be obvious, unambiguous, and clearly related to the vision. Celebrating those wins rallies the volunteer army and prompts more employees to buy in. Success breeds success. If wins are not forthcoming, that in itself is useful feedback: something is wrong. A committed guiding coalition, with many eyes and ears to take in the reality of the situation and with no status or territory to protect, can quickly tweak either the decisions it has made or the methods used for implementing those decisions.

Never let up. Keep learning from experience. Don't declare victory too soon

Organisations must continue to carry through on strategic initiatives and create new ones, to adapt to shifting business environments, and thus en- *Adapt* hance their competitive positions. As soon as an organisation takes its foot off the gas, cultural and political resistance arise. This, again, is why urgency is so central to the strategic part of the dual operating system. It keeps people going. If it is weak to begin with, or neglected in the course of events, the volunteer army's determination will sag, and the temptation to slow down or stop becomes irresistible. Volunteers will start focussing on their work in the hierarchy, and the hierarchy will dominate once more.

Institutionalise strategic changes in the culture

No strategic initiative, big or small, is complete until it has been incorporated *Incorporated* into day-to-day activities. A new direction or method must sink into the very fabric of the culture of the enterprise – it will do so if the initiative produces visible results and sends the organisation into a strategically better future.

15.4 Resistance to change

Smollan (2006) indicate that resistance is often seen as refusal to engage in the change or subverting it, but can also be conceptualised as reluctance or inertia. Resistance is here defined as any attitude or behaviour that reflects a person's unwillingness to make or support a desired change as it is perceived as a threat. Resistance to change hinders the change process, slows down *Threat* implementation, and increases costs. There are three types of resistance:

1 Blind resistance – employees' fear and refusal of any change; employees displaying defensive attitudes;
2 Political resistance – employees' loss of valuable possessions such as position or personal benefits; and
3 Ideological resistance – employees' conviction of the uselessness of the need for change.

15

15

Resistance to change may be expressed in various forms: withdrawal, resignation, retirement, absenteeism, lateness, intention to quit, cynicism, and voluntary turnover.

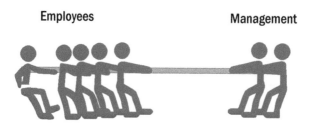

Commitment to change is considered to be the opposite of resistance to change. Commitment to change is positively correlated to a positive attitude and behaviour towards organisational change. Employees committed to change display a supportive attitude to the change process and implementation. Meyer and Allen (1997) indicate in their three-component model that employees' commitment during organisational change is split into three components:

Three-component model

1 Affective commitment – employees perform tasks at a high quality, perform additional little extras, and appear passionate about a job during the change period.
2 Continuance commitment – employees stay on in the company and perform well in their obligations due to earlier obtained benefits.
3 Normative commitment – employees fulfil their duties to avoid costs and do a bit more than required to maintain employment.

Committed employees

Impact on performance

Commitment implies an intention to persist in a course of action. Therefore, organisations often try to foster commitment in their employees to achieve stability and reduce costly turnover. It is commonly believed that committed employees also work harder and are more likely to 'go the extra mile' to achieve organisational objectives (Meyer & Allen, 2004). Research has consistently demonstrated that commitment does indeed contribute to a reduction in turnover. But there are limits to the assumption regarding its impact on performance. Research conducted to test the three-component model of commitment demonstrated that commitment can be characterised by different mind-sets – desire, obligation, and cost (Meyer & Allen, 2004). Employees with a strong affective commitment scores (high ACS) stay because they want to; those with strong normative commitment scores (high NCS) stay because they feel they ought to; and those with strong continuance commitment scores (high CCS) stay because they have to. Research consistently shows that employees who want to stay (high ACS) tend to perform at a higher level than those who do not (low ACS). Employees who remain out of obligation (high NCS) also tend to out-perform those who feel no such obligation (low NCS), but the effect on performance is not as strong as that observed for desire. Lastly, employees who have to stay primarily to avoid losing something of value (e.g. benefits or seniority) often have little incentive to do anything more than is required to retain their positions (see also Allen & Meyer, 1996, 2000; Meyer, Stanley, Herscovitch, & Topolnytsky, 2002).

15.4.1   Resistance factors

Resistance or commitment to an organisational change is triggered by a variety of variables which define the attitude towards change. One of the most inexplicable problems business executives face is that of employee resistance to change. Such resistance may take a number of forms: persistent reduction in output, an increase in the number of resignations and requests for transfer, chronic quarrels, and hostility, wildcat or slowdown strikes, and, of course, the expression of a lot of pseudo-logical reasons why the change will not work. Even the more petty forms of this resistance can be troublesome. Text 15.3 illustrates this issue of resistance to change and some of the reasons behind it.

Forms

15

TEXT 15.3

Overcome The 5 Main Reasons People Resist Change

Overcome The 5 Main Reasons People Resist Change, Lisa Quast, 11/26/2012, Forbeswoman

A career coaching client, newly promoted into a management position, called me to discuss a situation at work. *'We had to reduce expenses within the company so I made some changes in the organizational structure of the department by consolidating a few positions, putting several projects on hold, cancelling one project, and letting a few people go,'* she explained. *'I didn't think it would be any big deal, but some employees in the department are acting like I'm as ruthless as Attila the Hun. Several are avoiding me and a few have become downright hostile in their attitude towards me. I don't understand why they're acting this way.'*

Leadership is about leading, but it's also about implementing change, as my client found out. While many people like to joke that the only constant in business is change, change has an interesting way of affecting people that can often result in resistance. This resistance can range from fairly subtle, such as avoidance or passive aggressive behavior, all the way to outright defiance, hostility, and sabotage. The best way to avoid resistance to change? Seek to uncover potential resistance *prior* to implementing change.

What my client didn't realize is that she wasn't just a manager, she was also an implementer of change within the department. According to Rosabeth Moss Kanter, Professor of Business Administration at Harvard Business School, 'The best tool for leaders of change is to understand the predictable, universal sources of resistance in each situation and then strategize around them.'

Prior to making changes that will affect others, it's important for managers to carefully think through: 1) what the specific changes include, 2) who the changes will impact, 3) how it will impact them, and 4) how they might react (understanding reasons why people might resist the changes). Knowing this information makes it easier to create a plan of action for a smooth implementation of the changes.

Let's look at my client's situation using this process:
- **What the specific changes include:** In this case, the changes involved re-structuring the department, consolidating numerous positions, laying off several employees, cancelling one project, and putting several other projects on hold. No small changes, indeed!
- **Who the changes will impact:** Mainly all of the department employees, but the changes could also impact other stakeholder groups, such as if any of the projects cancelled or put on hold include cross-functional team members from other departments.
- **How the changes will impact them:** The

15

biggest impact is to the employees being laid off, as there will be both emotional and financial impact. Employees whose jobs will change could also have emotional and financial implications, although to a lesser extent. Employees' job tasks will change for those whose projects were put on hold or cancelled. Finally, there will be an emotional impact to everyone in the department, whether or not they are directly affected by the changes.

After analyzing this information, the next step is to look at what I've found are the 5 main reasons why people resist change:

- **Fear of the unknown/surprise:** This type of resistance occurs mainly when change is implemented without warning the affected stakeholders before the change occurs. When change (especially what is perceived as negative change) is pushed onto people without giving them adequate warning and without helping them through the process of understanding what the change will include and how their jobs/work will be affected, it can cause people to push back against the change due to their fear of the unknown.
- **Mistrust:** If the individuals in a department highly respect their manager because the manager has built up trust over a period of time, the team will be more accepting of any changes. If the manager is new and has not yet earned the trust of their employees (like my client), then mistrust can manifest itself into resistance to change.
- **Loss of job security/control:** This type of resistance often occurs when companies announce they will be restructuring or downsizing. This causes fear among employees that they will lose their jobs or be moved into other positions without their input.

- **Bad timing:** As the old saying goes, 'Timing is everything'. Heaping too much change on employees over a short period of time can cause resistance. If change is not implemented at the right time or with the right level of tact or empathy, it usually won't work.
- **An individual's predisposition toward change:** Differences exist in people's overall tolerance for change. Some people enjoy change because it provides them with an opportunity to learn new things and grow personally and professionally. Others abhor change because they prefer a set routine – these are usually the people who become suspicious of change and are more likely to resist.

Bottom Line: Take the time to understand 1) what the specific changes include, 2) who the changes will impact, 3) how it will impact them, and 4) why they might resist the changes.

Being aware of the reasons people resist change will help you implement change with fewer issues. Eliminate fear of the unknown by letting affected groups know there will be changes coming. Avoid mistrust and the feeling of loss of control by getting others involved in the changes before they occur and asking them to offer input and feedback. Prevent bad timing by providing a clear vision and reason for the changes along with a timetable or schedule of what to expect and when to expect it.

Implementing change is never painless, but it can be a lot less painful for everyone when it is done with empathy and compassion after thorough analysis, planning, and strategizing.

(Source: www.forbes.com)

Factors

As shown in Text 15.3, there are many variables or factors that have an influence on employees resistance to change; according to Smollan (2006), these include their readiness to change, perceived outcomes of change, perceived justification of change, perceived scale, frequency, speed, and timing of change, personality traits, previous personal experience with change, and leadership and management support.

Readiness to change

Readiness is an important factor that influences employee support of change initiatives. Several models and theories identify readiness as a crucial construct during change process because it enables leaders to align employee beliefs and cognitions with those of the leaders and goals of the organisation (Holt, Armenakis, Feild, & Harris, 2007). Readiness can be viewed in terms of the change process, the change content, and the change context. It should be noted that:

Crucial construct

1 Organisational change process is about the extent of employee participation during the steps of implementation.
2 Organisational change content refers to the administrative, procedural, technological, or structural aspects of the organisation.
3 Organisational change context includes the environment and conditions in which employees function.

Perceived outcomes of change

Generally speaking, employee perception of the outcomes for themselves, other colleagues and the organisation has a crucial impact on their reactions to any organisational change. This means that positive outcomes produce positive emotions, such as joy, pride and relief, and negative outcomes generate negative emotions, like resentment, fear of losing one's job or position, or being tasked with a high workload. If employees are not able to predict the outcomes, however, their response remains neutral or 'ambivalent' until a clear explanation is provided. Uncertainty of outcomes and long waiting periods may cause frustration and anxiety.

Crucial impact

Smollan (2006) suggest that autonomy and empowerment as an outcome of change may be appreciated by employees and create a positive reaction to change. However, employees may equally resist change based on empowerment, as they fear the negative outcomes such as increased responsibility and high workload. Uncertainty and fear of failure to perform and adapt to a new situation may lead to employees developing a negative attitude to change.

Outcomes are divided into intrinsic and extrinsic. Intrinsic outcomes are communication, managerial support, responsibility and meaningful work; extrinsic outcomes are salary and benefits. The intrinsic outcomes are more appreciated by employees than extrinsic ones (Smollan, 2006).

Intrinsic and extrinsic

There are differences between employees declared 'at risk' or perceiving themselves 'at risk', and employees who are 'safe'. The ones 'at risk' may experience more negative emotional reactions than others. The outcomes for employees themselves produce a higher degree of emotional intensity than those for other colleagues or the company itself, since focussing on own personal benefits is a natural concern.

Perceived justice of change

Perception of fairness during a change process is best understood from the perspective of organisational justice. There are four types of justice:

Types of justice

1 Distributive justice, related to the extent that benefits are equally distributed among stakeholders.
2 Procedural justice, linked to the perceptions of how decisions are made. Employees perceive a decision to change as fair if they are given relevant information and the opportunity to voice their contribution in the decision-making process.

15

3 Interactional justice, concerning how managers communicate procedures and outcomes to employees; sub-divided into interpersonal justice (politeness, respect, and dignity when interacting with people), and informational justice (accuracy and timing of information given).

4 Systemic justice, refers to the perceived fairness of certain practices within the organisation; is linked to organisational culture.

Subjective

The perceptions of justice are considered to be subjective, and evaluations of justice are based on employees individual experience, values and personality. Individuals compare their outcomes with others to evaluate the extent of fairness for themselves. Psychological contracts dictate the non-written mutual obligations between employees and the organisation, and produce strong emotional reactions if violated. Employees perceive such violations as unfair, leading to intentions to quit and a decrease in organisational citizenship behaviour (OCB). OCB has undergone definitional revisions since the late 1980s. OCB refers to anything that employees choose to do, spontaneously and of their own accord, which often lies outside of their specified contractual obligations. In other words, it is discretionary. OCB may not always be directly and formally recognised or rewarded by the company, through salary increments or promotions for example, though of course OCB may be reflected in favourable supervisor and co-worker ratings, or better performance appraisals. In this way it can facilitate future reward gain indirectly. Finally, and critically, OCB must promote the effective functioning of the organisation (Organ, Podsakoff, & MacKenzie, 2006).

Perceived scale, frequency, speed, and timing of change
These are explained as follows:

More efforts

- **Scale of change** – impacts employee perception of change. Large scale change asks for more efforts and competencies, and employees find it difficult to cope with all the changes. This may lead to negative psychological effects, such as burnouts. Large-scale change also causes anxiety, and employees develop different defensive mechanisms to protect themselves. Managers, on the other hand, show a high commitment to large-scale change through the expression of 'pleasant high activation emotions' such as excitement and optimism. However, after some time, negative 'low activation emotions' appear due to fatigue and disappointment.

Negative emotions

- **Frequency of change** – since change is an on-going process and part of organisational development, companies change constantly. Such frequency of change arouses negative emotions, because it demands extras from the recipients of change in terms of physical and mental skills, and causes stress and exhaustion. Moreover, the frequency of change provokes employee cynicism, and negative emotions linked to personal status, security, working conditions and management trust. Low job satisfaction and high turnover are strongly correlated to frequency of change.

Barrier

- **Speed of change** – refers to how employees perceive the speed of change as a barrier towards their participation and quality of work. They are stressed out if no time is given for investigation, information seeking and consultation. Directive leadership is the most used style of leadership in a fast-paced change situation.

Initiate

- **Timing of change** – refers to the right time to initiate change and the timing of stages of a change process. Timing is related to frequency and speed of change since employees need some time (re)energise and intersperse major change initiatives among carefully paced periods of smaller, organic change.

Personality traits

Several scholars investigated the common personality traits (Goleman, 1998; Van der Zee & Wabeke, 2004). However, the Big Five Factor model (O.C.E.A.N) was said to be the most reliable and used model to explore patterns of behaviour and test their impact on individuals' reactions to change (Vakola, Tsaousis, & Nikolaou, 2004; Moon, Kamdar, Mayar & Takeuchi, 2008). The O.C.E.A.N. is explained as follows:

- The first personality trait is **openness** to experience change, which shows readiness to adapt to change. The main characteristics of this personality trait are: imagination, insight, feelings, ideas, actions, values, interests, and aesthetics.   Openness
- The second trait is **conscientiousness**, which is high performance to achieve success. The common features of this trait are: high level of thoughtfulness, control, goal-oriented behaviour, competence, order, mindfulness to details, self-discipline, dutifulness, and striving for achievement.   Conscientiousness
- The third trait is **extraversion**, which enables individuals to express their opinions and influence decisions. This trait is defined by the following features: excitability, sociability, talkativeness, assertiveness, positive emotions, warmth, and emotional expressiveness.   Extraversion
- The fourth trait is **agreeableness**, which indicates a positive and optimistic view to accept change. Its attributes are: trust, altruism, kindness, affection, socialisation, modesty, compliance, and tender-mindedness.   Agreeableness
- The fifth and last trait is **neuroticism**, which may cause individuals to experience anxiety and stress due to change. Individuals governed by this trait may experience the following: moodiness, irritability, emotional instability, anxiety, depression, vulnerability, sadness, and angry hostility.   Neuroticism

Judge, Thoresen, Pucik and Welbourne (1999) found seven personality factors predicting reactions to change and clustered them into two categories:

- Positive concept, which entails locus of control, self-efficacy, self-esteem, and positive affectivity   Positive concept
- Risk tolerance, which involves openness, tolerance of ambiguity, and risk aversion.   Risk tolerance

Based on multiple studies (Smollan, 2006; Judge et al., 1999), it can be said that different personality traits impact employees' cognitive, affective, and behavioural reactions to change. The most influential personality traits that facilitate acceptance to change are a mixture of some factors of the big five factors and Judge et al.'s (1999) seven personality traits, but personality can be equally influenced by environmental factors, such as previous experience of change.

Previous experience of change

Previous experience of change impacts the attitude to change and produces two reactions toward new change, since it was used as a frame of reference to assess new change. Positive experience of previously undergone change creates a feeling of ease and acceptance or even enthusiasm toward change, while a negative experience leads to fear, cynicism, pessimism, and resistance to change. The same research also indicates that despite past failures, employees may accept new change if the environment was supportive in terms of clear communication and good relationship with change leaders. However, frequent change may trigger negative reactions even if previous change experiences were successful. In short, previous ex-

15

perience of change may produce negative or positive reactions to change; a supportive environment, especially management support, may further reduce the influences of negative experiences (Kiefer, 2005; Smolan, 2006; Self, Armenakis, & Schraeder, 2007).

Leadership and management support

Transformational

There is a common consensus among researchers that the perception of employees of change leaders/managers is based on leader abilities, emotional intelligence, and trustworthiness (Smollan, 2006). Transformational leadership and charismatic leadership are strongly linked to organisational change as research shows that there was a positive correlation between those two leadership styles and adaptation to organisational change. Transformational leaders persuade their followers through inspirational motivation, intellectual stimulation, and individualised consideration. Employees perceive management support in a positive way if they feel that their ideas are taken seriously, change goals are clearly explained, feedback is given, and autonomy is provided (Szabla, 2007).

Empathy

Change leaders need to cope with different emotions during the change process. Emotional intelligence skills enable change leaders/managers to recognise, understand and manage their own emotions, such as fear, anger and frustration, recognised and understand employee emotional reactions, and provide necessary support. Empathy is considered crucial in managing emotions, resolving conflicts during an organisational change process, and building trust by influencing employees' cognitive and affective aspects. Employee perception of the trustworthiness of change leaders/managers impact employee reactions to change.

15.4.2 Strategies to deal with resistance to change

Six approaches

In order to limit resistance to change, Kotter and Schlesinger (1979) established six approaches as listed in Figure 15.13, followed by an explanation.

FIGURE 15.13 Approaches to overcoming resistance to change

Approach	Commonly used in situations	Advantages	Drawbacks
Education + communication	Where there is a lack of information or inaccurate information and analysis.	Once persuaded, people will often help with the implementation of the change.	Can be very time consuming if lots of people are involved.
Participation + involvement	Where the initiators do not have all the information they need to design the change, and where others have considerable power to resist.	People who participate will be committed to implementing change, and any relevant information they have will be integrated into the change plan.	Can be very time consuming if participators design an inappropriate change.
Facilitation + support	Where people are resisting because of adjustment problems.	No other approach works as well with adjustment problems.	Can be time consuming, expensive, and still fail.
Negotiation + agreement	Where someone or some group will clearly lose out in a change, and where that group has considerable power to resist.	Sometimes it is a relatively easy way to avoid major resistance.	Can be too expensive in many cases if it alerts others to negotiate for compliance.
Manipulation + co-optation	Where other tactics will not work or are too expensive.	It can be a relatively quick and inexpensive solution to resistance problems.	Can lead to future problems if people feel manipulated.
Explicit + implicit coercion	Where speed is essential, and the change initiators possess considerable power.	It is speedy and can overcome any kind of resistance.	Can be risky if it leaves people mad at the initiators.

15

Education and communication

One of the most common ways to overcome resistance to change is to educate people about said change beforehand. Communication of ideas helps people see the need for and the logic behind a change. The education process can involve one-on-one discussions, presentations to groups, or memos and reports. This can be ideal when resistance is based on inadequate or inaccurate information and analysis, especially if the initiators need the resisters' help in implementing change. But some managers overlook the fact that a programme of this sort requires a good relationship between initiators and resisters, or if the latter do not believe what they are told. It also requires time and effort, particularly if many people are involved.

Beforehand

Participation and involvement

If the initiators involve potential resisters in some aspect of the design and implementation of change, they can often forestall resistance. With a participative change effort, initiators listen to people potentially affected by change involves and use their advice. Many managers have quite strong feelings about participation – sometimes positive and sometimes negative. That is, some managers feel there should always be participation during change efforts, while others feel this is virtually always a mistake. Both attitudes can create problems for a manager, because neither is very realistic. If change initiators believe they do not have the information they need to design and implement a change, or if they need the wholehearted commitment of others to do so, involving others makes very good sense. In general, participation leads to commitment, not merely compliance, and in some instances, commitment is needed for change to be successful. However, the participation process can not only lead to a poor solution if the process is not carefully managed, but can also be enormously time consuming. If a change must be made immediately, it may simply take too long to involve others.

Forestall

Time consuming

Facilitation and support

Another way that managers can deal with potential resistance to change is by being supportive. This process may include providing training, giving employees time off after a demanding period, or simply listening and providing emotional support. Facilitation and support are most helpful when fear and anxiety lie at the heart of resistance. Seasoned, tough managers often overlook or ignore this kind of resistance, as well as the efficacy of facilitative ways of dealing with it. The basic drawback of this approach is that it can be time consuming and expensive and still fail. If time, money, and patience are not available, then using supportive methods is not very practical.

Helpful

Expensive

Negotiation and agreement

Another way to deal with resistance is to offer incentives to active or potential resisters. For instance, management may consider higher union wage rates in return for a work rule change, increase an individual's pension benefits in return for an early retirement. Negotiation is particularly appropriate if it is clear that someone is going to lose out as a result of change, and yet their power to resist is significant. Negotiated agreements can be a relatively easy way to avoid major resistance, though, like some other processes, they may become expensive. Once a manager makes it clear that negotiation is the option open to avoid major resistance, this may also increase the possibilities of blackmail.

Incentives

Easy way

Manipulation and co-optation

Covert attempts

In some situations, managers also resort to covert attempts to influence others. Manipulation, in this context, normally involves a very selective use of information and a conscious structuring of events. One common form of manipulation is co-optation. Co-opting an individual usually involves giving them a desirable role in the design or implementation of change. Co-opting a group involves giving one of its leaders, or someone management respects, a key role in the design or implementation of change. This is not a form of participation, however, because the initiators do not want the advice of the co-opted party, merely their endorsement. Under certain circumstanc-

Inexpensive

es, co-optation can be a relatively inexpensive and easy way to gain an individual's or a group's support (cheaper, for example, than negotiation, and

Drawbacks

quicker than participation). Nevertheless, it has its drawbacks. If people feel they are being tricked into not resisting, are not being treated equally, or are being lied to, they may respond very negatively. Other forms of manipulation have drawbacks too, sometimes to an even greater extent. Most people are likely to greet what they perceive as covert treatment or lies with a negative response. However, people do manipulate others successfully – particularly if other tactics are not feasible or have failed. Having no other alternative, and not enough time to educate, involve, or support people, and without the power or other resources to negotiate, coerce, or co-opt them, managers have resorted to manipulating information channels in order to scare people into thinking there is a crisis coming that they can avoid only by changing.

Explicit and implicit coercion

Lastly, managers often deal with resistance coercively. Here, they essentially

Force

force people to accept change by explicitly or implicitly threatening them (with the loss of jobs, promotion possibilities, and so forth) or by actually

Risky

firing or transferring them. As with manipulation, using coercion is a risky process, because inevitably people strongly resent forced change. But in situations where speed is essential and where changes will not be popular, regardless of how they are introduced, coercion may be a manager's only option.

Successful organisational change efforts are always characterised by the skilful application of a number of these approaches, often in very different combinations. However, successful efforts share two characteristics – managers employ approaches with a sensitivity to their strengths and limita-

Common mistake

tions, and appraise the situation realistically. The most common mistake managers make is to use only one approach or a limited set regardless of the situation. A second common mistake that managers make is to approach change in a disjointed and incremental way that is not a part of a clearly considered strategy.

15.5 Managing the people side of change

Organisations today face unprecedented levels of organisational change, and it is no wonder that many leaders are uncertain as to how to manage it all. Hiatt and Creasey (2003, p. 3) found that managers fell short when managing the people side of change, and encountered:

© Noordhoff Uitgevers bv

1 Managers who were unwilling to assign needed resources to a project or would not allow representative(s) adequate time to participate;
2 Managers who filtered out important messages or started negative conversations about change;
3 Employees who became distracted and lost interest in their current work responsibilities, thereby impacting overall productivity and customers experience;
4 Valued employees who left the organisation;
5 More people taking sick leave or not showing up for work;
6 Unforeseen obstacles to change that seemingly appeared from nowhere; and
7 A lack of funding for change

In other words, things did not go exactly as planned. The unexpected happened. Not managing the people side of change impacted managers' success and introduced risk into their projects. Leaders have the potential to not only manage resistance once it appears, but to prevent it in the first place. Unfortunately, many business leaders and project teams do not appreciate their role in managing the people side of change until after resistance impacts their success. This section focusses on how leaders may approach managing change from the people side to create engagement in and adoption of change across the organisation from the two perspectives of the strategic management level, from that of the middle managers as change agents, and using other valuable leadership skills.

Unexpected

15.5.1   Strategic leadership

Although many people use the terms interchangeably, management and leadership are not the same thing. Employers in the hospitality industry, in particular, hire candidates with the training, experience and education necessary to master leadership challenges specific to the industry. Hospitality managers must be fully prepared to apply strong leadership skills to the various challenges of the industry in order to help keep their associates and guests happy. There are many definitions of leadership: Rost (1991) for example counted 221 definitions, and Yukl (1989) pointed out that some commentators argue that leaders are able to influence people by means other than the traditional carrot and stick or reward and punishment approaches. Leaders are able to influence people by instilling or creating empathy for work goals, appealing to people's higher-order social and self-esteem needs – leaders do not coerce their colleagues or subordinates into action, but they inspire. The skills required to be a strategic leader are as diverse as the definitions of leadership. In this section, those definitions explained by Schoemaker, Krupp and Howland (2013, pp. 131-134) are adopted and adapted. Schoemaker et al. identified the six skills shown in Figure 15.14. When mastered and used in concert, these six skills allow leaders to think strategically and navigate the unknown effectively. They indicate that each of these skills has received attention in leadership literature, but usually in isolation and seldom in the special context of the high stakes and deep uncertainty that can make or break both companies and careers.

Many definitions

Six skills

15

© Noordhoff Uitgevers bv

FIGURE 15.14 6 strategic leadership skills

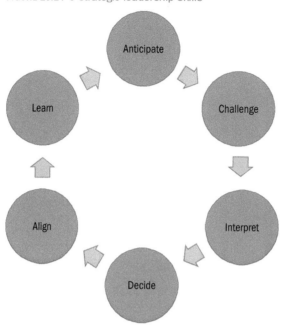

Anticipate

Most organisations and leaders are poor at detecting ambiguous threats and opportunities on the periphery of their business. Coors' executives, famously, were late seeing the trend toward low-carb beers. Lego's management missed the electronic revolution in toys and gaming. Strategic leaders, in contrast, are constantly vigilant, honing their ability to anticipate their circumstances by scanning the environment for signals of change. To improve the ability to anticipate, leaders should:

Constantly vigilant

- Talk to their customers, suppliers, and other partners to understand their challenges.
- Conduct market research and business simulations to understand competitors' perspectives, gauge likely reactions to new initiatives or products, and predict potential disruptive offerings.
- Use scenario planning to imagine various futures and prepare for the unexpected.
- Look at a fast-growing rival and examine perceived puzzling actions it has taken.
- List customers they have recently lost and try to figure out why.
- Attend conferences and events in other industries or functions.

Challenge

Strategic thinkers question the status quo. They challenge their own and others' assumptions and encourage divergent points of view. Only after careful reflection and examination of a problem through many lenses do they take decisive action. This requires patience, courage, and an open mind. To improve their ability to challenge, leaders should:

Careful reflection

- Focus on the root causes of a problem rather than the symptoms, and apply the '5 Whys?' of Sakichi Toyoda, Toyota's founder.

- List long-standing assumptions of an aspect of the business, and ask a diverse group if these assumptions hold true.
- Encourage debate by holding 'safe zone' meetings where open dialogue and conflict are expected and welcomed.
- Create a rotating position for the express purpose of questioning the status quo.
- Include naysayers in a decision process to signal challenges early.
- Capture input from people not directly affected by a decision, who may have a good perspective on the repercussions.

Interpret

Leaders who challenge in the right way invariably elicit complex and conflicting information. That is why the best leaders are also able to interpret. Instead of reflexively seeing or hearing what they expect, they should synthesise all available input. They need to recognise patterns, push through ambiguity, and look for new insights. Finland's former president, J. K. Paasikivi, was fond of saying that wisdom begins by recognising the facts and then 're-cognising,' or rethinking, them to expose their hidden implications. To improve their ability to interpret, leaders should:

Synthesise

- List at least three possible explanations for what they are observing when analysing ambiguous data, and invite perspectives from diverse stakeholders.
- Force themselves to zoom in to see the details and out to see the big picture.
- Actively look for missing information and evidence that disconfirms their hypotheses.
- Supplement observation with quantitative analysis.
- Step away – go for a walk, look at art, put on non-traditional music, play Ping-Pong – to promote an open mind.

Decide

In uncertain times, decision makers may have to make tough calls with incomplete information, and must often do so quickly. Strategic thinkers, however, insist on multiple options at the outset and do not get prematurely locked into simplistic go/no-go choices. They do not shoot from the hip but follow a disciplined process that balances rigor with speed, considers trade-offs involved, and takes both short- and long-term goals into account. In the end, strategic leaders must have the courage of their convictions – informed by a robust decision process. To improve their ability to decide, leaders should:

Disciplined process

- Reframe binary decisions by explicitly asking their teams, 'What other options do we have?'
- Divide big decisions into pieces to understand component parts and better see unintended consequences.
- Tailor their decision criteria to long-term versus short-term projects.
- Let others know where they are in their decision process. Are they still seeking divergent ideas and debate, or are they moving toward a final selection?
- Determine who needs to be directly involved and who can influence the success of their decision.
- Consider pilots or experiments instead of big bets, and make staged commitments.

15

Align

Strategic leaders must be adept at finding common ground and achieving buy-in among stakeholders who have disparate views and agendas. This requires active outreach. Success depends on proactive communication, trust building, and frequent engagement. To improve their ability to align, leaders should:

Active outreach

- Communicate early and often to combat the two most common complaints in organisations: 'No one ever asked me' and 'No one ever told me.'
- Identify key internal and external stakeholders, mapping their positions on the leader's initiative and pinpointing any misalignment of interests, and look for hidden agendas and coalitions.
- Use structured and facilitated conversations to expose areas of misunderstanding or resistance.
- Reach out to resisters directly to understand their concerns and then address them.
- Be vigilant in monitoring stakeholders' positions during the rollout of the leader's initiative or strategy.
- Recognise and otherwise reward colleagues who support team alignment.

Learn

Strategic leaders are the focal point for organisational learning. They promote a culture of inquiry, and search for the lessons in both successful and unsuccessful outcomes. They study failures – their own and their teams' – in an open, constructive way to find hidden lessons. To improve their ability to learn, leaders should:

Study failures

- Institute after-action reviews, document lessons learned from major decisions or milestones (including the termination of a failing project), and broadly communicate the resulting insights.
- Reward managers who try something laudable but fail in terms of outcomes.
- Conduct annual learning audits to see where decisions and team interactions may have fallen short.
- Identify initiatives that are not producing as expected and examine the root causes.
- Create a culture in which inquiry is valued and mistakes are viewed as learning opportunities.

Becoming a strategic leader means identifying weaknesses in the six skills discussed above and correcting them. Schoemaker et al. (2013) concluded that strength in one skill cannot easily compensate for a deficit in another, so it is important to methodically optimise all six abilities. Strategic leaders are individuals upon whom strategy development and change within the organisation are seen to be dependent. To conclude, strategic leaders are:

Optimise all six

- Individuals personally identified with, and central to, the strategy of their organisations.
- Individuals whose personality or reputation may result in others willingly deferring to them and seeing strategy development as their domain.
- Individuals within some organisations who may be central because they are the owners or founders, as is often the case in small businesses.

© Noordhoff Uitgevers bv

15.5.2   The roles of the middle managers as change agents

The middle managers are considered to be those managers who occupy all positions between the top strategic managers and the first-level supervisors, and form the linking pin between senior management teams and the rest of the organisation. Burgess (2013), studying the role of middle managers in corporate entrepreneurship (defined as a type of proactive behaviour that can stimulate desired innovation), concluded that (pp. 199-200):

Linking pin

> Middle managers in hotels, as in other industries, are expected to convert senior management's ideas into practise, motivating and encouraging their staff to find new ways to make money within the difficult environment currently affecting hotels. To be effective, innovation and risk-taking are encouraged and facilitated, middle managers within the unit supporting and advising each other and adopting a team approach to identifying issues and finding innovative solutions.

Within the context of change as exemplified in corporate entrepreneurship, middle managers have the roles illustrated in Figure 15.15. This information is taken from and explained using Burgess (2013, p. 195).

FIGURE 15.15 Roles of middle managers within corporate entrepreneurship

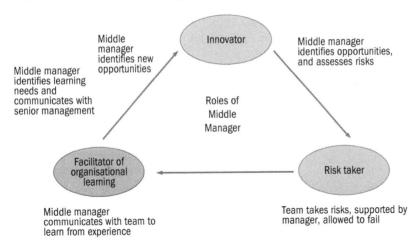

As an innovator, the middle manager is able to identify and introduce both formal and informal innovative processes, which relies on both the organisation's and the individual manager's encouraging ideas. The middle manager is motivated by innovation as it can then lead to power, the ability to instigate change, potential rewards and recognition. Middle managers need expert knowledge of their area, often of a specialist nature, in order to be able to identify innovative opportunities as well as the resources required for implementing new practises. Middle managers promote their ideas to senior management, highlighting the importance of appropriate structures and communication.

Identify and introduce

15

Trial-and-error

As a risk taker, this attitude is critical to a positive approach to the change process, with trial-and-error being essential to learning, but depends on both senior and middle management providing an appropriate encouraging environment or culture. Organisations must show that failure is tolerated possibility, so that middle managers can feel empowered to take risks. If they are afraid of the consequences of failure for themselves and their team, lacking support from senior management and with fears about job security, resistance and stress can ensue – with potential longer term effects on the change process.

Promote learning

As a facilitator of organisational learning, learning from experience is a critical element in the change process. Organisations in which there are strong, open cultures that recognise the multilevel nature of learning perform more effectively. As a channel between senior management and operational levels, it is important that middle managers learn from others and promote learning for both themselves and their reporting staff. A positive approach to learning, therefore, impacts managers' ability to contribute effectively towards innovation, the efficiency of the organisation, and ultimately optimises profits for stakeholders.

15.5.3   Other valuable leadership skills – social intelligence, cultural intelligence and emotional intelligence

More art than science

This section concludes with a review of some very important skills needed by contemporary hospitality leaders and managers, especially considering the diverse environments in which they have to operate, as well as the diversity of the workforce found in basically every single hospitality organisation. It is not unusual to read stories of some highly intelligent, highly skilled executives promoted into leadership positions only to fail; at the same time, others with solid – but not extraordinary – intellectual abilities and technical skills promoted into similar positions, succeeded. This supports the belief that identifying individuals with the 'right stuff' to be leaders is more art than science. After all, the personal styles of superb leaders vary: some leaders are subdued and analytical while others shout their manifestos from on high. These differences raise the question of what really makes a great leader, and the answer may lie in the understanding of social intelligence, cultural intelligence and emotional intelligence.

Social intelligence

Defined

Social intelligence is considered to be the human capacity – due to their large brains – of effectively negotiating complex social relationships and environments, and is an aggregated measure of self- and social-awareness, evolved social beliefs and attitudes, and a capacity and appetite to manage complex social change. It was originally defined by Thorndike (1920, p. 228) as 'the ability to understand and manage men and women, boys and girls, to act wisely in human relations'. The team at the Social Intelligence Lab believe a person with a high social intelligence quotient (SQ) is no better or worse than someone with a low SQ; they just have different attitudes, hopes, interests and desires.

The SQ is a statistical abstraction similar to the standard score approach used in intelligence quotient (IQ) tests, with a mean of 100. Unlike the standard IQ test, the SQ is not a fixed model, however. It leans more towards the theory that intelligence is not a fixed attribute, but a complex hierarchy of information-processing skills underlying an adaptive equilibrium between the individual and the environment. Individuals can therefore change their SQ by altering their attitudes and behaviour in response to their complex social environment. The social intelligence hypothesis asserts that complex socialisation – politics, romance, family relationships, quarrels, making-up, collaboration, reciprocity, altruism: in short, social intelligence – was the driving force in developing the size of human brains, and that social intelligence provides humans with the ability to use their large brains in complex social circumstances to this day. The demands of living together drove the human need for intelligence. Social intelligence was therefore a critical factor in the expansion of human brain size. It is believed that social intelligence or the richness of human qualitative life, rather than human quantitative intelligence, truly make humans what they are. Goleman (2006) has drawn on social neuroscience research to propose that social intelligence is made up of social awareness (including empathy, attunement, empathetic accuracy, and social cognition) and social facility (including synchrony, self-presentation, influence, and concern), as indicated in Figure 15.16 (Goleman, 2006, p. 84):

Hypothesis

15

FIGURE 15.16 Components of social intelligence

Social Awareness

Social awareness refers to a spectrum that runs from instantaneously sensing another's inner state, to understanding her feelings and thoughts, to 'getting' complicated social situations.
It includes:
- *Primal empathy:* Feeling with other; sensing nonverbal emotional signals.
- *Attunement:* Listening with full receptivity; attuning to a person.
- *Empathetic accuracy:* Understanding another person's thoughts, feelings and intentions.
- *Social cognition:* Knowing how the social world works.

Social Facility

Simply sensing how another feels, or knowing what they think or intend, does not guarantee fruitful interactions. Social facility builds on social awareness to allow smooth, effective interactions. The spectrum of social facility includes:
- *Synchrony:* Interacting smoothly at the nonverbal level.
- *Self-presentation:* Presenting ourselves effectively.
- *Influence:* Shaping the outcome of social interactions.
- *Concern:* Caring about other's needs and acting accordingly.

The ingredients of social intelligence are organised into two broad categories: social awareness, a sense of others – and social facility, or how that awareness is made use of. Social awareness refers to a spectrum that runs from primal empathy (instantaneously sensing another's inner state) through empathetic accuracy (understanding their feelings and thoughts) to social cognition ('getting' complicated social situations). Yet simply sensing how another feels, or knowing what they think or intend, does not guarantee

15

fruitful interactions. Social facility builds on social awareness to allow smooth, effective interactions. The spectrum of social facility includes self-presentation, influence, concern, and synchrony (interacting smoothly at the non-verbal level).

Range

Both the social awareness and social facility domains range from basic, 'low-road' capacities, to more complex 'high-road' articulations. By 'low-road,' Goleman (2006) means the neural circuitry that operates beneath human awareness, automatically and effortlessly, with immense speed, so that, when captivated by an attractive face, such attractions are due to the low road. The 'high road', on the other hand, runs through neural systems that work more methodically and step by step, with deliberate effort. Humans are aware of the high road, and it allows at least some control over their inner lives, denied by the low road. Pondering how to move from the initial attraction to an active approach is when the neural systems move from the low road to the high road. Conventional ideas of social intelligence have too often focussed on high-road talents like social knowledge, or the capacity for extracting rules, protocols, and norms that guide appropriate behaviour in a given social setting. Although this cognitive approach has served well in linguistics and in artificial intelligence, it is of limited use when applied to human relationships. It neglects essential non-cognitive abilities like primal empathy and synchrony, and ignores capacities like concern.

Direct link

Insight and behaviour

Unlike Goleman, who links social intelligence to advances in social neuroscience, Albrecht (2006) assumes a more practical, consultant-oriented approach, and defines social intelligence as 'the ability to get along well with others and get them to co-operate with you' (p. iii). His approach visualises a direct link between social intelligence and management. The following is adapted from Morris Brown's review of Albrecht's 2006 work. Social intelligence can be characterised as a basic understanding of people (i.e., a kind of strategic social awareness) and a set of component skills for interacting successfully with others. Social intelligence thus consists of both insight and behaviour. The extremes of social intelligence can be thought of as either 'toxic' or 'nourishing.' Whereas toxic behaviours are those that cause others to feel devalued, inadequate, intimidated, angry, frustrated, or guilty, nourishing behaviours cause others to feel valued, capable, loved, respected, and appreciated. People with high social intelligence (those who are socially aware and basically nourishing) are magnetic – thus the expression 'magnetic personality.' Social intelligence can reduce conflicts, create collaboration . . . and mobilise people toward common goals. Albrecht believes that the biggest single cause of low social intelligence is simply a lack of insight. Toxic people are often so preoccupied with their own personal struggles that they do not understand their impact on others; thus, they need help in seeing themselves as others do. The S.P.A.C.E. model shown in Figure 15.17 is Albrecht's model for describing, assessing, and developing social intelligence, used as a means of helping individuals obtain this critical insight.

FIGURE 15.17 The S.P.A.C.E. model

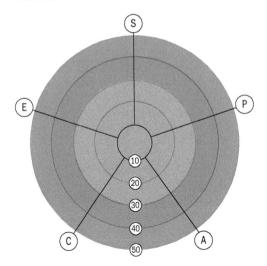

The 'S' factor represents a person's situational awareness (or situational 'radar') – the ability to understand and empathise with people in different situations, sense their feelings and possible intentions, and 'read' situations based on a practical knowledge of human nature. It includes a knowledge of cultural 'holograms' – unspoken background patterns, paradigms, and social rules that govern various situations. It means having an appreciation for the various viewpoints of others and a practical sense of the ways people react to stress, conflict, and uncertainty. Individuals who are self-centred, preoccupied with their own feelings, needs, and interests, probably have difficulties in getting acceptance and co-operation from others. Having a good situational radar means having a respectful interest in other people, which they tend to return. Albrecht notes that much of social dumbness comes from missing clues, both verbalised and unspoken. Situational awareness thus involves knowing when to speak and when to hold one's tongue. It is the ability to size up a situation rather quickly, and provide the best response based on one's intuitive radar and real-time intelligence.

Situational awareness

Practical knowledge

Social dumbness

The 'P' factor represents presence – the way a person affects individuals or groups through physical appearance, mood, demeanour, and body language, and how they occupy space in a room. It is a bearing – a physicality that gives and begets respect and attention. It involves listening with skill, and creates and provides a quality of self-assurance and effectiveness that allows a person to connect with others. And, though looks count, the primary element of a positive presence is an inviting demeanour. People therefore need to pay attention to whether they are conveying confidence, professionalism, kindness, and friendliness, or whether they are communicating shyness, insecurity, animosity, or indifference.

Presence

Bearing

Inviting demeanour

The 'A' factor represents authenticity – a dimension that reveals how honest and sincere individuals are with themselves and others. Albrecht believes that, when people respect themselves, have faith in their personal values and beliefs, and are 'straight' with others, they are likely to behave in ways that others perceive as authentic. If people consciously or unconsciously

Authenticity

feel that others do not accept, respect, love or co-operate with them, i.e. if people act according to their own needs and priorities, they are likely to behave in ways that others perceive as inauthentic. However, in the context of social intelligence, authenticity involves more than simply being oneself, and

Connect genuinely

includes the ability to connect genuinely with other people – which demands empathy and compassion. What some psychotherapists call narcissism (i.e. malignant self-love), Albrecht sees as another variant of inauthentic behaviour, which can become pathological if it renders an individual incapable of engaging in two-way relationships of mutuality, sharing, and support. It is therefore possible to have well-developed 'people skills' and yet lack the emotional depth to be considered truly socially intelligent.

Clarity

The 'C' factor represents clarity – the ability to express one's thoughts, opinions, ideas, and intentions clearly; to understand the power of language as

Language

a medium of thought and expression; and to use language as a strategic asset. Albrecht notes, for example, that those with high social intelligence clarity have mastered the ability to move from a 'sky-high' level of abstract communication to a ground- or concrete-level. In other words, they can pilot a 'verbal helicopter,' choosing terms, figures of speech, expression, analogies, and metaphors that position the listener's thinking process at the desired altitude. They are thereby capable of taking their listeners down to the lowest level of detail or up to the highest level of generality. People who lack this skill cannot seem to control the throttle or the stick, moving too fast from the concrete to the abstract or spending too much time at one level or the other. Individuals with high social intelligence clarity have also mastered

Elevator speech

the 'elevator speech' – a brief, compelling distillation of an important idea or a proposed course of action, issue, or point of view that can be conveyed in the time it takes to ride an elevator with someone. As more and more situations challenge people to home in on the essential elements of a message, and to express them in a compact and effective way, composing elevator speeches becomes an increasingly useful skill – especially for business

Monitor

professionals. Another critical clarity skill is the ability to monitor one's own language patterns and the language patterns of others, so as to avoid certain verbal pathologies that can cause both individual and collective misunderstandings, conflicts, or even psychological maladjustments. Albrecht re-

Dirty language

fers to these corrupted linguistic forms as dirty language that can intimidate, offend, anger, alienate or confuse others, and thus muddy com-

Clean language

munications. By contrast, clean language uses more neutral verbal patterns and word choices that invite empathy, open-mindedness, and the free exchange of ideas.

Empathy

The 'E' factor represents empathy – a dimension that invites individuals to look at how truly aware and considerate they are of the feelings of others and how capable they are of tuning in to other people as unique individuals. In its usual connotation, being empathetic means identifying with another person and appreciating and/or sharing their feelings. However, in the con-

Connectedness

text of social intelligence, there is also a sense of connectedness, which inspires people to co-operate. Thus, Albrecht defines empathy as 'a state of positive feeling between two people, commonly referred to as a condition of rapport.' Gaining the personal and practical benefits that come with building empathy and maintaining quality relationships requires that individuals avoid or abandon such toxic behaviours as: withholding positive strokes, throwing verbal barbs, being patronising, seeking approval excessively, being insincerely flattering, playing games, speaking dogmatically, violating confidences and breaking promises, complaining excessively, criticising, ridiculing, inducing guilt, and giving unwanted advice. Killing other people's ideas by saying such things as, 'It won't work here,' 'We have tried it before,' or 'It costs too much' is particularly toxic, especially in business situations. However, using certain key 'idea-selling' statements (e.g., 'May I ask a question?', 'Before we make our final decision, let's review our options', 'Maybe you'd like to reconsider your opinion, since ...') can often get people to listen and respond with greater receptiveness. The next step in building empathy involves adopting or increasing the use of nourishing behaviours, which requires more than just avoiding toxicity. Empathy requires a long-term investment, not an episodic application of charm. Without a proactive commitment to add value as other people perceive it, eliminating toxic behaviour only produces apathy. Albrecht believes there are two opportunities to build empathy. With the first – the moment-to-moment experience of connecting with people – one can usually establish a strong empathetic connection by being attentive, being appreciative, and offering affirmation. With the second – the 'maintenance' process – one keeps a relationship healthy over time, and lives by the Platinum Rule: 'Do unto others as others prefer to be done unto.'

Nourishing behaviours

Cultural intelligence

Earley and Ang (2003) introduced the concept of cultural intelligence. Since then, they and other researchers have come up with multiple definitions of cultural intelligence as seen in Figure 15.18.

Definitions

FIGURE 15.18 Some definitions of cultural intelligence

Some definitions of cultural intelligence		
2003	Earley & Ang	A person's ability to adapt effectively to new cultural contexts.
2004	Earley & Mosakowski	Seemingly natural ability to interpret someone's unfamiliar and ambiguous gestures in just the way that person's compatriots and colleagues would, even to mirror them.
2006	Brislin, Worthley, & MacNab	People's success (or lack thereof) when adjusting to another culture, for example, on an overseas business assignment.
2006	Johnson, Lenartowicz, & Apud	An individual's effectiveness in drawing upon a set of knowledge, skills, and personal attributes in order to work successfully with people from different national cultural backgrounds at home or abroad.
2006	Ng & Earley	Capability to be effective across cultural settings.

The analysis of cultural intelligence in this section is based on Earley and Mosakowski (2004), in which they indicate that it should come as no surprise that human actions, gestures, and speech patterns a person encounters in a foreign business setting are subject to an even wider range of interpretations, including ones that can make misunderstandings likely and co-operation impossible. Occasionally, however, an outsider has a seemingly natural ability to interpret someone's unfamiliar and ambiguous gestures in just the way that person's compatriots and colleagues would, and even mirror them. They term this cultural intelligence, or CQ. In a world where crossing boundaries is routine, CQ becomes a vitally important aptitude and skill, and not just for international bankers and borrowers. Companies, too, have

Natural ability

Cultural code

cultures, often very distinctive; anyone who joins a new company spends the first few weeks deciphering its cultural code. Within any large company, there are sparring subcultures as well. Departments, divisions, professions, geographical regions – each has a constellation of manners, meanings, histories, and values that confuse an interloper and cause them to stumble. Unless, that is, they have a high CQ. A person with high cultural intelligence can somehow tease out of a person's or group's behaviour those features true of all people and all groups, those peculiar to one person or group, and those neither universal nor idiosyncratic. People who are socially the most successful among their peers often have the greatest difficulty making sense of, and then being accepted by, cultural strangers. Those who fully embody the habits and norms of their native culture may be the most alien when they enter a culture not their own. Sometimes, people who are somewhat detached from their own culture can more easily adopt the mores and even body language of an unfamiliar host. They are used to being observers and making a conscious effort to fit in.

Although some aspects of cultural intelligence are innate, anyone reasonably alert, motivated, and poised can attain an acceptable level of cultural intelligence (Earley & Mosakowski, 2004). Given the number of cross-functional assignments, job transfers, new employers, and distant postings most corporate managers are likely to experience in the course of a career, low CQ can turn out to be an inherent disadvantage.

Three components

Earley and Mosakowski (2004) identify three components of cultural intelligence: the cognitive; the physical; and the emotional/motivational. Cultural intelligence resides in the body and the heart as well as the head. Although most managers are not equally strong in all three areas, each faculty is seriously hampered without the other two.

Head

Rote learning about the beliefs, customs, and taboos of foreign cultures, the approach corporate training programmes tend to favour, never prepares a person for every situation that arises, nor does it prevent terrible gaffes. However, inquiring about the meaning of some custom often proves unavailing because natives may be reticent about explaining themselves to strangers, or may have had little practice looking at their own culture analytically.

Devise learning strategies

Instead, a newcomer needs to devise learning strategies. Although most people find it difficult to discover a point of entry into alien cultures, whose very coherence can make them seem like separate, parallel worlds, an individual with high cognitive CQ notices clues as to a culture's shared understandings. These can appear in any form and any context but somehow indicate a line of interpretation worth pursuing.

Body

Must prove

Foreign hosts, guests, or colleagues are not disarmed by simply showing an understanding of their culture; a person's actions and demeanour must prove they have to some extent already entered that other world. Whether in giving a handshake or ordering a coffee, evidence of an ability to mirror the customs and gestures of the people around proves that a person esteems them well enough to want to be like them. By adopting people's habits and mannerisms, a person eventually comes to understand what it is like to be like those others in the most elemental way. They, in turn, become more trusting and open.

Heart

Adapting to a new culture involves overcoming obstacles and setbacks. People can do that only if they believe in their own efficacy. If they persevered in the face of challenging situations in the past, their confidence grew. Confidence is always rooted in the mastery of a particular task or set of circumstances. People who do not believe themselves capable of understanding people from unfamiliar cultures often give up after their efforts are met with hostility or incomprehension. By contrast, those with high motivation, upon confronting obstacles, setbacks, or even failure, reengage with greater vigour. To stay motivated, highly efficacious people do not depend on obtaining rewards which may be unconventional or long delayed.

Believe

Diagnosing cultural intelligence

Figure 15.19 – 'Diagnosing your cultural intelligence' allows people to assess the three facets of their own cultural intelligence, and learn where their relative strengths and weaknesses lie. Attaining a high absolute score is not the objective.

The statements in Figure 15.19 reflect different facets of cultural intelligence; for each set, the scores are added up and averaged by dividing by 4. For purposes of personal development, it is advised that scores are compared to those of other colleagues. An average score of 3 indicates an area that needs improvement, whereas an average greater than 4.5 reflects a true cultural intelligence strength. Answering the questions in Figure 15.19 allows people to determine which cultural intelligence profile best describes them. The profiles are:

Cultural intelligence profile

- The provincial – can be quite effective when working with people of similar background but runs into trouble when venturing farther afield.
- The analyst – methodically deciphers a foreign culture's rules and expectations by resorting to a variety of elaborate learning strategies.
- The natural – relies entirely on intuition rather than a systematic learning style, and is rarely steered wrong by first impressions.
- The ambassador – like many political appointees, may not know much about a new culture, but convincingly communicates certainty of belonging there.
- The mimic – has a high degree of control over actions and behaviour, if not a great deal of insight into the significance of cultural cues picked up on. Mimicry definitely puts hosts and guests at ease, facilitates communication, and builds trust. Mimicry is not, however, the same as pure imitation, which can be interpreted as mocking.
- The chameleon – possesses high levels of all three CQ components and is a very uncommon managerial type. They may even be mistaken for a native of the country. More importantly, chameleons do not generate any of the ripples that unassimilated foreigners inevitably do. Some are able to achieve results that natives cannot, due to their insider's skills and outsider's perspective.

Many managers are a hybrid of two or more of these types. Earley and Mosakowski (2004) discovered that even more prevalent than the ambassador was a hybrid of that type and the analyst, and indicated that, unlike other aspects of personality, cultural intelligence can be developed in psychologically healthy and professionally competent people through the following six steps:

Hybrid

Can be developed

15

FIGURE 15.19 Diagnosing your cultural intelligence (Source: Harvard Business Review, October 2004, 4)

Rate the extent to which you agree with each statement, using the scale:
1 = strongly disagree, 2 = disagree, 3 = neutral, 4 = agree, 5 = strongly agree.

_____ Before I interact with people from a new culture, I ask myself what I hope to achieve.

_____ If I encouter something unexpected while working in a new culture, I use this experience to figure out new ways to approach other cultures in the future.

_____ I plan how I'm going to relate to people from a different culture before I meet them.

+ _____ When I come into a new cultural situation, I can immediately sense whether something is going well or something is wrong.

Total _____ : 4 = [ ] Cognitive CQ

_____ It is easy for me to change my body language (for example, eye contact or posture) to suit people from a different culture.

_____ I can alter my expression when a cultural encounter requires it.

_____ I modify my speech style (for example, accent or tone) to suit people from a different culture.

+ _____ I easily change the way I act when a cross-cultural encounter seems to require it.

Total _____ : 4 = [ ] Physical CQ

_____ I have confidence that I can deal well with people from a different culture.

_____ I am certain that I can befriend people whose cultural backgrounds are different from mine.

_____ I can adapt to the lifestyle of a different culture with relative ease.

+ _____ I am confident that I can deal with a cultural situation that's unfamiliar.

Total _____ : 4 = [ ] Emotional/ motivational CQ

Step 1 – examine current CQ strengths and weaknesses in order to establish a starting point for subsequent development efforts;

Step 2 – select an adequate training that focusses on the weaknesses. For example, someone lacking physical CQ may enrol in acting classes. Someone lacking cognitive CQ may work on developing analogical and inductive reasoning;

Step 3 – apply the general training;

Step 4 – organise personal resources to support the chosen approach;

Step 5 – move into the cultural setting that needs to be mastered; and

Step 6 – re-evaluate the newly developed skills and how effective they have
been in the new setting (perhaps after collecting 360-degree feedback from individual colleagues or eavesdropping on a casual focus group formed to discuss an individual's progress).

According to Livermore (2011), cultural intelligence consists of four components summarised as follows:
1 Drive – being motivated to learn about a new culture or setting;
2 Knowledge – studying how culture shapes people's behaviours, values,
   and beliefs;
3 Strategy – being able to factor culture into longer-term planning; and
4 Action – behaving in a culturally sensitive way – including being able to
   'think on one's feet' in difficult situations.

Since cultural intelligence is not innate, each of these components can be
developed. It should be noted that people with high cultural intelligence are
not experts in every culture; rather, they use observation, empathy, and intelligence to read people and situations, and make informed decisions
about why others are acting as they are. They also use cultural intelligence
to monitor their own actions. Instead of making quick judgments or relying
on stereotypes, they observe what is happening and adapt their own behaviour accordingly.

Emotional intelligence
In simple terms, emotional intelligence is the ability to understand and man-   Understand and
age one's own emotions, and those of other people around. People with a   manage
high degree of emotional intelligence know what they are feeling, what their
emotions mean, and how these emotions can affect other people. For leaders, having emotional intelligence is essential for success. Goleman (1995)
showed the factors at work when people of high IQ flounder and those of
modest IQ do surprisingly well. These factors add up to a different way of

15

15

Nurtured and
strengthened

being smart: 'emotional intelligence'. This includes self-awareness and im-
pulse control, persistence, zeal and self-motivation, empathy and social
deftness. These are the qualities that mark people who excel in real life:
those whose intimate relationships flourish, those who are stars in the
workplace. These are also the hallmarks of character and self-discipline, of
altruism and compassion. Emotional intelligence is not fixed at birth and it
can be nurtured and strengthened. Mayer and Salovey (1997, p. 10) defined
emotional intelligence as follows:

> Emotional intelligence involves the ability to accurately perceive, ap-
> praise, and express emotion; the ability to access and/or generate
> feelings when they facilitate thought; the ability to understand emo-
> tion and emotional knowledge; and the ability to regulate emotions
> to promote emotional and intellectual growth.

Components

Goleman (1998) later introduced five components of emotional intelligence
at work that allow individuals to recognise, connect with, and learn from
their own and other people's mental states as indicated in Figure 15.20,
and followed by a brief explanation.

FIGURE 15.20 Five components of emotional intelligence at work

	Definition	**Hallmarks**
Self-Awareness	The ability to recognise and under-stand your moods, emotions, and drives, as well as their effects on others	Self-confidence Realistic self-assessment Self-deprecating sense of humour
Self-Regulation	The ability to control or redirect im-pulses and moods The propensity to suspend judgment and think before acting	Trustworthiness and integrity Comfort with ambiguity Openness to change
Motivation	A passion to work for reasons that go beyond money or status A propensity to pursue goals with energy and persistence	Strong drive to achieve Optimism, even in the face of failure Organisational commitment
Empathy	The ability to understand the emo-tional makeup of other people Skill in treating people according to their emotional reactions	Expertise in building and retaining talent Cross-cultural sensitivity Service to clients and customers
Social Skill	Proficiency in managing relation-ships and building networks An ability to find common ground and build rapport	Effectiveness in leading change Persuasiveness Expertise in building and leading teams

1 Self-awareness – people with high emotional intelligence are usually very
self-aware. They understand their emotions and, because of this, they do
not let their feelings rule them. They are confident because they trust
their intuition and do not let their emotions get out of control. They are
also willing to take an honest look at themselves. They know their
strengths and weaknesses, and they work on these areas so they can
perform better. Many people believe that self-awareness is the most
important part of emotional intelligence.

2 Self-regulation – the ability to control emotions and impulses. People who self-regulate typically do not allow themselves to become too angry or jealous, and they do not make impulsive, careless decisions. They think before they act. Characteristics of self-regulation are thoughtfulness, comfort with change, integrity, and the ability to say no.

3 Motivation – people with a high degree of emotional intelligence are usually motivated. They are willing to defer immediate results for long-term success. They are highly productive, love a challenge, and are very effective in whatever they do.

4 Empathy – this is perhaps the second-most important element of emotional intelligence. Empathy is the ability to identify with and understand the wants, needs, and viewpoints of others. Empathetic people are good at recognising the feelings of others, even when those feelings are not obvious. As a result, empathetic people are usually excellent at managing relationships, listening, and relating to others. They avoid stereotyping and judging too quickly, and live their lives in a very open, honest way.

5 Social skills – it is usually easy to talk to and enjoy the company of people with good social skills, which are another sign of high emotional intelligence. Those with strong social skills are typically team players. Rather than focus on their own success first, they help others develop and shine. They can manage disputes, are excellent communicators, and are masters at building and maintaining relationships.

An understanding of what exactly constitutes emotional intelligence is important not only because the capacity is so central to leadership but also because people strong in some of its elements can be utterly lacking in others – sometimes to disastrous effect. Since emotional intelligence can be learned and developed, there are multiple ways that this can be done by using strategies such as these, courtesy of Mindtools: `Important`

`Strategies`

- Observe how you react to people. Do you rush to judgment before you know all of the facts? Do you stereotype? Look honestly at how you think and interact with other people. Try to put yourself in their place, and be more open and accepting of their perspectives and needs.
- Look at your work environment. Do you seek attention for your accomplishments? Humility can be a wonderful quality, and it does not mean that you are shy or lack self-confidence. When you practice humility, you say that you know what you did, and you can be quietly confident about it. Give others a chance to shine – put the focus on them, and do not worry too much about getting praise for yourself.
- Do a self-evaluation. What are your weaknesses? Are you willing to accept that you are not perfect and that you could work on some areas to make yourself a better person? Have the courage to look at yourself honestly – it can change your life.
- Examine how you react to stressful situations. Do you become upset every time there is a delay or something does not happen the way you want? Do you blame others or become angry at them, even when it is not their fault? The ability to stay calm and in control in difficult situations is highly valued – in the business world and outside it. Keep your emotions under control when things go wrong.
- Take responsibility for your actions. If you hurt someone's feelings, apologize directly – do not ignore what you did or avoid the person. People are usually more willing to forgive and forget if you make an honest attempt to make things right.

15

15

- Examine how your actions will affect others – before you take those actions. If your decision will impact others, put yourself in their place. How will they feel if you do this? Would you want that experience? If you must take the action, how can you help others deal with the effects?
  Source: www.mindtools.com

Although regular intelligence is important to success in life, emotional intelligence is key to relating well to others and achieving one's own goals. Many people believe that emotional intelligence is at least as important as regular intelligence, and many companies now use emotional intelligence testing when hiring new staff (Mindtools).

Summary

▶ The hospitality industry is based on services which are co-created during the interaction with customers having different needs and expectations. As globalisation, cultural pluralism, knowledge capital and technologies place the industry in an era of discontinuity where relentless change is inevitable, adapting to the needs and expectations of customers is crucial for success within the hospitality industry.

▶ Change drivers are considered to be the strategic and very often unavoidable causes for change, and can be both external and internal to the organisation. The major drivers for change are macro and micro environmental factors, service transition, and the need for continual improvement.

▶ The underlying assumptions that define the attributes of the change process are defined using five colours.

▶ Yellow-print thinking is based on socio-political concepts relating to organisations, in which interest, conflict, and power play important roles.

▶ Blue-print thinking is based on the rational design and implementation of change, like in project work and scientific management.

▶ Red-print thinking is rooted in human resources management with the focus of this way of thinking being people.

▶ Green-print thinking has its roots in the concept of organisational development. Changing and learning are closely linked and can be exchangeable in meaning and usage. People change when they learn.

▶ White-print thinking, also called chaos thinking, focusses on inspiration and flow since people and organisations change in dynamic situations and in an atmosphere where creativity and spontaneity are fostered.

▶ While change can be either episodic or continuous, it can also be classified by the extent of change needed and the speed required to achieve it, leading to the different change types such as transformation, realignment, incremental and the big bang.

▶ The change kaleidoscope, primarily a mechanism for dealing with planned change, makes it easy for organisational change designers to assess contextual aspects (time scope, preservation, diversity, capability, capacity, readiness, and power) and design options (change path, change start point, change style, change target, change interventions

15

and change roles) from the very wide array of different implementation options available.

▶ There are many different approaches to organisational change implementation; action research, appreciative research inquiry, and parallel learning structures are some of them.

▶ While the organisational culture reflects how things are done within the organisation, it is made up of three groups of elements – artefacts, espoused beliefs and values, and basic underlying assumptions.

▶ The cultural web provides an approach to looking at and changing an organisation's culture; its elements are the paradigm, rituals and routines, stories and myths, symbols, power structures, organisational structures, and control systems.

▶ Based on the Competing Values Framework and by using the Organizational Culture Assessment Instrument, an organisation can determine its dominant culture among the four quadrants found in the framework. These quadrants, namely clan culture, adhocracy culture, market culture, and hierarchy culture, each represent a distinct set of organisational effectiveness indicators.

▶ There are many models that both address the change process at the individual level and offer guidance and structure to organisations that intend to carry out innovation activities. Among these are Lewin's force field analysis model, Lewin's 3 steps model of change, and Kotter's 8-step process of change model.

▶ Accepting change within organisations is not always an easy matter, and there are multiple reasons for resisting change. There are also well tested strategies to overcome resistance to change, however. These include education and communication, participation and involvement, facilitation and support, negotiation and agreement, manipulation and co-optation, and explicit and implicit coercion.

▶ Though used interchangeably, management and leadership are not the same thing. Despite the multiplicity of leadership definitions, hospitality managers must be fully prepared to apply strong leadership skills to the various challenges of the industry in order to help keep their associates and guests happy. The industry should look for leaders who are able to inspire, and possess other skills such as social intelligence, cultural intelligence and emotional intelligence.

Questions and assignments for reflection

1   Critically discuss the drivers of change and show how the underlying assumptions of change are reflected in the ways of thinking about change.

2   There are numerous models available that address the change process at both the individual and organisational levels. Three models are discussed: Lewin's force field analysis model; Lewin's 3 steps model of change; and Kotter's 8-step process of change model. Compare and contrast the change process of the three models. Which of the models will you consider implementing? Why?

3   The competing values framework was developed to assess the effectiveness of organisations. How would you evaluate the role of the different types of culture – clan, adhocracy, hierarchy, and market – to achieve such an effectiveness?

4   Define the factors that trigger a positive or negative attitude towards change and explain the main strategies change agents establish to cope with resistance to change.

5   Discuss how diverse environments and workforce diversity urge managers and leaders to acquire new leadership skills, such as social, cultural and emotional intelligence.

© Noordhoff Uitgevers bv

16

Managing Quality in the Hospitality Industry

M. N. Chibili

16.1 Introduction

Quality assurance is any methodical process of checking whether a product or service being developed meets specified requirements. A quality assurance system promotes increased customer confidence and a company's credibility, improves work processes and efficiency, and enables a company to better compete with others. In this chapter, quality management systems and models and the seven basic tools used for the continuous improvement of quality are discussed.

16.2 Quality management systems and models

A quality management system (QMS) is a collection of business processes focussed on achieving quality policy and quality objectives to meet customer requirements. It is defined as the organisational structure, policies, procedures, processes and resources needed to implement quality management. Adapted from a United Kingdom Department of Trade and Industry's (UKDTI) document on quality management systems, an organisation benefits from establishing an effective QMS. The cornerstone of any quality organisation is the concept of the customer and service provider working together for their mutual benefit. For this collaboration to become effective, the customer – service provider interfaces must extend into, and outside of, the organisation, and beyond immediate customers and suppliers. A QMS can be defined as a set of co-ordinated activities to direct and manage an organisation in order to continually improve the effectiveness and efficiency of its performance. These activities interact, and are affected by being in, the system, so the isolation and study of each one in detail does not necessarily lead to an understanding of the system as a whole. The main thrust of a QMS is in defining the processes, which result in producing quality products and services, rather than detecting defective products or services after they have been produced (UKDTI).

QMS

Cornerstone

Main thrust

China, Nanjing: The Zifeng Tower

The UKDTI indicate that a fully documented QMS ensures two important requirements are met:

Customers' requirements

- The customers' requirements – confidence in the ability of the organisation to deliver the desired product and service, meeting customer needs and expectations consistently;

Organisation's requirements

- The organisation's requirements – both internally and externally, and at an optimum cost with efficient use of available resources – materials, human, technology and information.

These requirements can only be truly met if objective evidence to support the system activities is provided in the form of information and data, from the ultimate supplier to the ultimate customer.

A QMS enables an organisation to achieve the goals and objectives set out in its policy and strategy. It provides consistency and satisfaction in terms of methods, materials, equipment, etc., and interacts with all activities of the organisation, beginning with the identification of customer requirements and ending with their satisfaction, at every transaction interface. The UKDTI indicate that a good QMS can be considered a wedge that stops an organisation from slipping down from its good practices, shown in Figure 16.1.

FIGURE 16.1 QMS as a wedge supporting organisational progress (UKDTI)

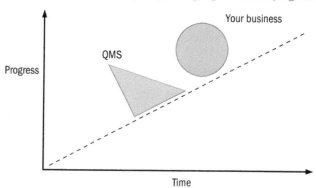

Before elaborating on some of the various systems and models in existence related to assessing quality within organisations, the immediate focus will briefly turn to the notion of quality as it relates to service industries or, more specifically, the hospitality industry. In simple terms, and as explained in Chapter 14, service quality is an assessment of how well a delivered service conforms to a customer's expectations. Hospitality organisations often assess the service quality provided to their customers in order to improve their services, to quickly identify problems, and to better assess client satisfaction. One of the best known group of studies related to service quality was initiated by Zeithaml, Parasuraman, and Berry, who initially identified ten dimensions used by consumers to evaluate service quality. This initial set of

Notion of quality

Service quality
Dimensions

ten dimensions was later fine-tuned to the following five: tangibles (appearance of physical elements); reliability (dependable and accurate performance); responsiveness (promptness and helpfulness); assurance (credibility, competence, courtesy and security); and empathy (good communications, customer understanding and easy access). These were earlier discussed in Chapter 14 of this work.

Early QMS emphasised predictable outcomes of an industrial product production line, using simple statistics and random sampling. By the 20th century, labour input was typically the most costly input in most industrialised societies; as a result, focus shifted to team co-operation and dynamics, especially the early signalling of problems via a continuous improvement cycle. In the 21st century, QMS has tended to converge with sustainability and transparency initiatives, as both investor and customer satisfaction and perceived quality are increasingly tied to these factors (www.alpha-concepts. com). Some of these systems (SERVQUAL and TQM) were discussed in Chapter 14.

Predictable outcomes

16

Converge

16.2.1   ISO

The International Organisation for Standardisation (ISO) develops and publishes international standards covering many domains, but the ISO 9000 group addresses various aspects of quality management and contains some of ISO's best known standards. These standards provide guidance and tools for companies and organisations who want to ensure that their products and services consistently meet customer requirements, and that quality is consistently improved. The standards in the ISO 9000 family include:
- ISO 9001:2008 – establishes the requirements of a quality management system;
- ISO 9000:2005 – covers the basic concepts and language;
- ISO 9004:2009 – focusses on how to make a quality management system more efficient and effective;
- ISO 19011:2011 – provides guidance on internal and external audits of quality management systems.

ISO

Standards

The ISO website (www.iso.org) offers a wealth of information, but it should suffice to note here that the ISO 9001:2008 establishes the criteria for a quality management system and it is the only standard in the family of ISO standards according to which certification can be provided. It can be used by any organisation, large or small, regardless of its field of activity. In fact, ISO 9001:2008 is implemented by over one million companies and organisations in over 170 countries.

Many hospitality organisations have obtained the certification as shown in the excerpt in Text 16.1, taken with permission from HotelierMiddleEast. com on 13/08/2015.

TEXT 16.1

Best Practice: A hotel's quest for quality

David Edgcumbe, *April 22nd, 2013*

Every hotel wants to ensure that its services are up to scratch, but which systems are in place to guarantee they are fit for purpose? Consultants and hoteliers explain why they are beginning to embrace international standards, despite the extra paperwork that comes with them.

Every day, throughout the Middle East, hoteliers and service staff work tirelessly to operate their hotels to the high standards expected from one of the most luxurious and exciting destinations in the world.

The Ramada Hotel & Suites Ajman, United Arab Emirates

However, for a growing number of hotels hard work is no longer enough and with more competition entering the market, increasing numbers are turning to ISO certificates to guide quality assurance processes.

Who or what is ISO?

ISO, or the International Organisation for Standardisation, is one of the world's largest developers of voluntary International Standards and has published more than 19,500 covering almost all aspects of technology and business from food safety to computers, agriculture to healthcare.

However, keen eyed hoteliers who have noticed the word voluntary above may be surprised to know that while ISO develops and publishes International Standards, they don't actively enforce them, instead partnering with worldwide accreditation bodies who in turn license local and regional certification bodies to perform audits on participating businesses. Confused? You will be.

Vilhelm Paus Hedberg is the Middle East managing director of QMS Global FZE, one of the certification bodies that works with Middle Eastern companies to prepare, audit and award ISO certifications. As a certification body it is QMS Global's responsibility to audit companies that have applied for ISO certifications and pass or fail them depending on their results.

However, it is also QMS Global which advises each company on the work they must do in order to be successful, with gap analyses and pre-audits all part of a process that can take years to complete. So why would a hotel want to put itself through such an ordeal?

'Of the hotels that come to us for certification, while some are trying to abide by local law or regulations, most simply only want to have a quality system embedded into their operations,' says Hedberg.

Hedberg thankfully goes onto to clarify that while there may be thousands of separate International Standards, only a few are commonly used and popular with the hotel industry. The first and most common is ISO 9001:2008 - quality management, while others focus on food safety, the environment and health and safety.

'Most hotels and companies will have these processes in place already, and ISO 9001:2008 essentially boils down to pretty standard good business practices,' admits Hedburg. 'However, most of our clients don't actually realise they have these processes in place and end up benefitting from the auditing process that forces them to document all of their processes and procedures.

'For example, for a hotel the auditing process will require them to conduct customer surveys as well as an organised back office system with reference keeping and documentation control. Furthermore, hotels will also have to perform internal process reviews of their own systems as well as management reviews to ensure that everything is being monitored and measured correctly,' explains Hedburg.

'Hotels can benefit from these programmes with an increase to their bottom line as they cut down on wasted work, as wasted resources are found and isolated and mistakes are tracked.

'Other benefits for hotels include communicating a positive message to its staff and customers that the hotel is pursuing a sense of quality management. It also identifies and encourages more efficient and time saving processes while highlighting deficiencies within the organisation, reducing costs and delivering an improved quality of service,' concludes Hedburg.

Intelligent ISO

Another expert on the use of ISO certifications for the quality assurance process for Middle Eastern hotels is Sterling International Consulting FZE senior manager Kaushal Sutaria, who offers advice and guidance for companies considering taking on the challenge.

'We provide ISO consultancy services to a host of companies across the Middle East, but hotels are a rapidly growing part of our business and are receiving more enquiries from hotels all the time,' admits Sutaria.

One trend that Sutaria identifies is that as the hospitality market in the Middle East continues to heat up, hotels will increasingly see ISO certification as a vital way of standing out from the competition.

However, hotels wanting to begin the process of accreditation won't necessarily have the knowledge to navigate the world of quality management systems and pre-audits, which is where a third party consultant such as Sutaria comes in.

'A lot of our clients come to us because they need more information, or help understanding how they can implement or begin the process. They also have to understand the importance of the hotel management communicating this information to their staff and that these processes are essential to the efficient running of their hotel,' states Sutaria.

Seal of Quality

One hotelier that understands the importance of quality assurance is Al Bustan Rotana Dubai & Al Murooj Rotana Dubai cluster general manager Hussein Hachem, who describes a process that 'is highly important in any business particularly for the hospitality industry as it ensures the viability of our hotels'.

'Without a quality assurance system,' he continues, 'a hotel may survive but it will not be able to reach its maximum potential. Quality assurance covers a very broad spectrum; it's not only focused solely on the quality of

16

The Jumeirah Emirates Hotel Tower in Dubai, UAE

products and services in the hotel, but also on the quality of practices and processes.

Effectively implemented, our quality assurance procedures obviously help us increase our loyal customers, further strengthen our reputation, pushes for growth and development among our colleagues as well as ensuring value for money throughout our operations and for our guests,' details Hachem.

He goes on to explain that the Al Bustan and Al Murooj Rotana is assessed through a variety of methods including set processes in training and development (off job, on job, work instructions, etc.), spot checks, quizzes, internal audits, customer audits and mystery visits. The resultant reports are then carefully analysed and suggested corrections are then strictly implemented.

'Our QA process has been created to lead us to getting more repeat guests through consistency in our operation while continuous improvement is the key to increasing our customer's satisfaction.

'Obviously, all these are directly linked to the increases in our business, revenue and profit,' concludes Hachem.

Certified results
One of the hotels that has really embraced the ISO process is Atlantis The Palm, Dubai with the director projects and quality Alan Lim particularly enthusiastic about the impact of the process so far.

'Transparency is one of the main benefits of ISO because now all your guidelines are transparent and you know exactly what is expected of you. The dos and don'ts that have to be fulfilled are clearly specified on paper,' says Lim.

'For example, one main focus of this system is that you need to set your targets. They must be measurable targets and smart targets and based on outcomes, but we have the ability to decide how we go about getting the necessary tasks done.'

While he admits that ISO can seem initially daunting for most companies with no obvious benefits at the end of it, Lim believes that the only real danger for hotels is if they simply go through the motions of the process, collect their certification but never really understand exactly how these processes can benefit them.

'Our whole ISO certification process took around two years, and we ended up going into every department and process mapping every aspect of what we do. There is no checklist provided for this, there is a standards manual but it is only 15-20 pages long.

The most popular ISO certifications are by their very nature generic because they can be applied to companies from very different industries, whether with one employee or 1000, as long as you have a customer, a legal framework and organisation,' explains Lim.

'But what this allowed us to do is create a PDCA system, which stands for plan, do, check and act; which for us at Atlantis

© Noordhoff Uitgevers bv

means that we plan before we do, we do what we plan, we check what we've done and then take action so it becomes a continuously improving system.

So you set your targets, you get it done, you've done your measurement and reviewed it and determined what needs to be learned and improved, taken action and then you set another higher target for yourself next year,' enthuses Lim.

Quality Coffee
To explain his point, Lim uses the example of the Atlantis' lobby coffee house: Plato's. Every day, before opening, Plato's staff complete an extensive checklist of tasks that ensures the venue complies with the necessary standards. This list may include such simple items as ensuring all surfaces are clean or that all of the necessary machines are turned on.

This list is checked by a manager each day who can then be certain that the correct procedures are being followed by their staff.

'Even though some items on this checklist may come naturally to our staff, it helps them because the guidelines are now more transparent. They no longer have to assume what tasks they have to perform and know exactly what is expected of them,' says Lim.

'Of course I understand it may take our staff more time to complete a checklist of tasks every morning, rather than simply completing each task as a part of their normal routine.

However, this system is a way to assure the team that they have done their job properly, while the manager now does not have to check every little detail throughout the day to make sure nothing has been forgotten, but can instead simply check the list has been completed at the end of the day,' explains Lim.

According to Lim, the system at Plato's is one example of a procedure that is carried out hundreds of times throughout the resort every day.

By using ISO accreditation as a way to challenge and improve its existing quality assurance practices, Atlantis has created a way of accurately mapping the everyday tasks of its employees. Once an operation has been broken down into its basic processes, it is then much easier to measure and compare your property's performance with the competition, Lim explains.

'We carry out around 250 mystery shops throughout the resort, carried out by professional third parties that measure whether we are meeting our own standards and following our procedures.

The measurements taken by these assessments then allow us to compare ourselves with our competition. Because if we can equate our level of performance with a given number, then we compare that number with the performance of our competitors and see where we are doing well or where we will need to improved,' admits Lim.

'While there are no laws forcing us to do this, I believe the hotel industry would benefit from more regulation as that would ensure that the standard of hotels in this region becomes more standardised and there will be more consistency in the way that hotels operate,' concludes Lim.

CASE STUDY 1
THE HOTEL: Kempinski Nile Hotel, Cairo
THE LEADER: Marten Schwass, GM

Objective
The QA process of the Kempinski Nile Hotel is not only critical but crucial. If you don't have a constant and regular check on your standards, you are not able to recognise flaws and mistakes as they appear. It is a tool that we take seriously and it is the essence of developing our team and management. Our objective is to make sure that we remain the number one luxury property in Cairo in terms of quality of service, which is something that is clearly reflected in our rankings on review sites and through guest feedback.

16

Strategy

We are signed with Leading Quality Assurance (LQA), an independent quality assurance auditor, which means that a mystery shopper visits our property twice a year. We also have a daily quality assurance spot check conducted by our training department. Based on their feedback the hotel's management team then develops a training plan to ensure that we meet and exceed the standards set by LQA. As the hotel's general manager I am personally involved in the process of creating, conducting and monitoring this plan.

Results

I take pride in having achieved an 89% rating with LQA, which is the highest ranking in Cairo. This is also clearly reflected in our positioning as the number one-rated Cairo hotel on Tripadvisor, a position we have been proud to hold since 2010.

CASE STUDY 2
THE HOTEL: Ramada Hotel & Suites Ajman
THE LEADER: Iftikhar Hamdani, general manager

Objective

Quality Assurance is a key factor in the successful operation of any hotel. It is essential for any quality hotel to certify and process check all operational systems and procedures.

Strategy

Working under the umbrella of Wyndham Hotel Group we have mystery guests that visit to check that the set corporate guidelines and standards are in place. This audit is carried out by an external audit company and it is always very helpful to see the rating of the hotel. If any hotel fails continually three times, their contract can be cancelled. At Ramada Ajman, we have a Quality Assurance Committee as well as monthly self-assessments prior to any Wyndham audit to make sure that our standards are maintained in all areas.

Results

We maintain communication between our Quality Assurance Committee and our operation team to ensure we avoid failing any of the hotel's stringent guest standards. This helps us boost the ratings/reviews from our guests and to increase overall business, which encourages repeat clients and word of mouth sales. That is the reason why for the last two years we are one of the leading hotels in the northern emirates in terms of hotel occupancy. We sold 100,000 room nights in 2011 and 105,000 room nights in 2012. We are confident that we will top that again this year too.

CASE STUDY 3
THE HOTEL: Tilal Liwa Hotel
THE LEADER: Ayman Ashor, general manager

Objective

Tilal Liwa Hotel's aim is to be one of the finest hotel destinations in UAE and for that we have to give a first-class service to all our guests. Quality is one of the most significant ingredients that affects the level of our success and we ensure to have a standard operation procedure on board in each and every department, particularly in food and beverage. Using the HACCP (Hazard Analysis and Critical Control Points) implementation procedure helps us improve our service through consistency without failing to serve our guests safe, high quality food.

Strategy

HACCP is a control process system, so we have difference kinds of monitoring procedures such as accurate food temperature readings and high quality food production standards. Additionally we ensure that our employees pass essential food hygiene training programmes required by the Abu Dhabi Government.

Results

Ever since we have implemented our stringent quality assurance processes we have noticed many improvements, the most important of which is a satisfied, happy and returning guest.

(Source: www.hotelier.middleeast.com)

© Noordhoff Uitgevers bv

As illustrated in Text 16.1, the ISO 9001:2008 is based on a number of quality management principles, including strong customer focus, motivation and implication of top management, process approach, and continual improvement. The complete list of principles is:

Principles

- Principle 1 – Customer focus;
- Principle 2 – Leadership;
- Principle 3 – Involvement of people;
- Principle 4 – Process approach;
- Principle 5 – System approach to management;
- Principle 6 – Continual improvement;
- Principle 7 – Factual approach to decision making;
- Principle 8 – Mutually beneficial supplier relationships.

Using ISO 9001:2008 helps ensure that customers get consistent, good quality products and services, which in turn brings many business benefits. Checking whether a system works is a vital part of ISO 9001:2008. An organisation must perform internal audits to check how its quality management system is working. An organisation may decide to invite an independent certification body to verify that a QMS is in conformity with the standard, but this is not required. Alternatively, ISO may invite its clients to audit the quality system themselves.

The ISO certification process is carried out by external certification bodies; a company or organisation cannot be certified by ISO directly. ISO's Committee on Conformity Assessment (CASCO) has produced a number of standards related to the certification process, which are used by certification bodies. When choosing a certification body, ISO advises as follows:

Certification bodies

- Evaluate several certification bodies;
- Check whether the certification body uses the relevant CASCO standards;
- Check whether the preferred body is accredited. Accreditation is not compulsory, and non-accreditation does not necessarily mean a body is not reputable, but accreditation does provide independent confirmation of competence. To find an accredited certification body, organisations are advised to contact their national accreditation body or visit the International Accreditation Forum.

16.2.2   The EFQM excellence model

The EFQM (European Foundation for Quality Management) excellence model provides a holistic tool for assessing how effective an organisation is in developing and delivering a stakeholder focussed strategy. In its 2013 revision, the EFQM excellence model allows people to understand the cause and effect relationships between what their organisation does and what results it achieves. All the information in this section is taken and adapted from the EFQM website: www.efqm.org. The EFQM excellence model consists of a set of three integrated components:

Stakeholder focussed

Integrated components

- The fundamental concepts, which define the underlying principles that form the foundation for achieving sustainable excellence in any organisation;
- The criteria, which provide a framework to help organisations put fundamental concepts and RADAR (see Figure 16.4) thinking into practice;
- RADAR, which is a simple but powerful tool used as a driving force for systematic improvement in all areas of an organisation.

The EFQM excellence model can be applied to any organisation, regardless of size, sector or level of maturity. It is non-prescriptive, and takes into ac-

Organisation

count a number of different concepts. It provides a common language that enables organisations to effectively share their knowledge and experience, both inside and outside their own organisation. There are 8 fundamental concepts as shown in Figure 16.2, and followed by a brief explanation.

Fundamental concepts

FIGURE 16.2 The 8 fundamental concepts of the EFQM excellence model

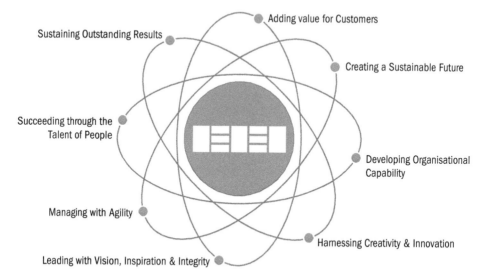

Adding value for Customers

Sustaining Outstanding Results

Creating a Sustainable Future

Succeeding through the Talent of People

Developing Organisational Capability

Managing with Agility

Harnessing Creativity & Innovation

Leading with Vision, Inspiration & Integrity

Adding value for customers – excellent organisations consistently add value for customers by understanding, anticipating and fulfilling needs, expectations and opportunities.

Creating a sustainable future – excellent organisations have a positive impact on the world around them by enhancing their performance while simultaneously advancing the economic, environmental and social conditions within the communities they touch.

Developing organisational capability – excellent organisations enhance their capabilities by effectively managing change within and beyond organisational boundaries.

Harnessing creativity & innovation – excellent organisations generate increased value and levels of performance through continual improvement and systematic innovation by harnessing the creativity of their stakeholders.

Leading with vision, inspiration & integrity – excellent organisations have leaders who shape the future and make it happen, acting as role models of values and ethics.

Managing with agility – excellent organisations are widely recognised for their ability to identify and respond effectively and efficiently to opportunities and threats.

Succeeding through the talent of people – excellent organisations value their people and create a culture of empowerment for the achievement of both organisational and personal goals.

Sustaining outstanding results – excellent organisations achieve sustained outstanding results that meet both short and long term needs of all their stakeholders, within the context of their operating environment.

The criteria
The EFQM excellence model, as shown in Figure 16.3, allows people to understand the cause and effect relationships between an organisation's activities, the Enablers, and the Results it achieves.

16

FIGURE 16.3 The EFQM excellence model criteria

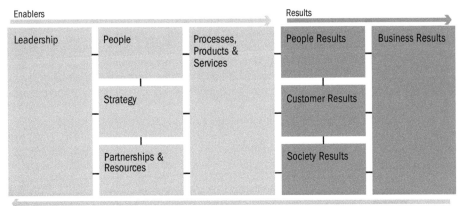

© EFQM 2012

To achieve sustained success, an organisation needs strong leadership and clear strategic direction. It needs to develop and improve people, partnerships and processes to deliver value-adding products and services to their customers. If the right approaches are effectively implemented, they will achieve the results they and their stakeholders expect.

Enabler criterion – there are 5 enablers, pictured on the left-hand side of the EFQM excellence model. These are things an organisation needs to do in order to develop and implement its strategy.

Enabler criterion

1 Leadership – excellent organisations have leaders who shape the future and make it happen, acting as role models of values and ethics and inspiring trust at all times. They are flexible, enabling the organisation to anticipate and react in a timely manner to ensure the on-going success of the organisation;

Leadership

2 Strategy – excellent organisations implement their mission and vision by developing and deploying a stakeholder-focussed strategy. Policies, plans, objectives and processes are developed and deployed to deliver that strategy;

Strategy

3 People – excellent organisations value their people and create a culture that allows the mutually beneficial achievement of organisational and personal goals. They develop the capabilities of their people and promote fairness and equality. They care for, communicate, reward and recognise, in a way that motivates people, builds commitment and enables them to use their skills and knowledge for the benefit of the organisation;

People

16

Partnerships & resources

4 Partnerships & resources – excellent organisations plan and manage external partnerships, suppliers and internal resources in order to support strategy and policies and the effective operation of processes;

Processes

5 Processes, products & services – excellent organisations design, manage and improve processes to generate increasing value for customers and other stakeholders.

Results criterion

Results criterion – there are also four result areas, shown on the right-hand side of the EFQM excellence model. These are the results an organisation achieves, in line with its strategic goals. In all the four results areas, excellent organisations:

- develop a set of key performance indicators and related outcomes to determine the successful deployment of their strategy, based on the needs and expectations of the relevant stakeholder groups;
- set clear targets for key results, based on the needs and expectations of their business stakeholders, in line with their chosen strategy;
- segment results to understand the performance of specific areas of the organisation, and the experience, needs and expectations of their stakeholders;
- demonstrate positive or sustained good business results over at least 3 years;
- clearly understand the underlying reasons and drivers of observed trends and the impact these results will have on other performance indicators and related outcomes;
- have confidence in their future performance and results based on their understanding of the cause and effect relationships established;
- understand how their key results compare to similar organisations and use this data, where relevant, for target setting.

Customer

1 Customer results – excellent organisations achieve and sustain outstanding results that meet or exceed the needs and expectations of their customers;

People

2 People results – excellent organisations achieve and sustain outstanding results that meet or exceed the needs and expectations of their people;

3 Society results – excellent organisations achieve and sustain outstanding results that meet or exceed the needs and expectations of relevant stakeholders within society;

Business

4 Business results – excellent organisations achieve and sustain outstanding results that meet or exceed the needs and expectations of their business stakeholders.

RADAR

RADAR

The RADAR logic is an assessment framework and management tool that provides a structured approach to questioning the performance of an organisation and it is illustrated in Figure 16.4.

At the highest level, RADAR logic states an organisation should:
- Determine the **Results** it is aiming to achieve as part of its strategy;
- Plan and develop an integrated set of sound **Approaches** to deliver the required results both now and in the future;
- **Deploy** the approaches in a systematic way to ensure implementation;
- **Assess** and **Refine** the deployed approaches based on monitoring and analysis of the results achieved and on-going learning activities.

FIGURE 16.4 The EFQM excellence model's RADAR

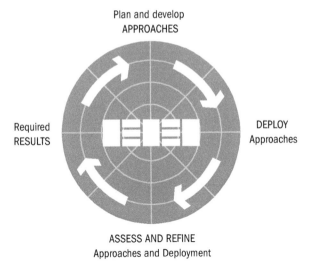

Plan and develop
APPROACHES

Required
RESULTS

DEPLOY
Approaches

ASSESS AND REFINE
Approaches and Deployment

The EFQM excellence model can be used to assess an organisation's current capabilities. The output of an assessment is normally a number of strengths and opportunities to improve future performance. Identifying an organisation's strengths is important not only so it continues doing the things it does well, but also because these strengths may help in addressing the issues identified. The Foundation indicates that, by definition, complying with a defined standard is not excellence. Excellence is about going beyond what is expected. Unlike auditing against a standard, an assessment gives the management team a number of opportunities – options. The points an organisation chooses to address, and how it chooses to address them, depends on its own strategic priorities.

In a study based on assessing the EFQM excellence model in the Croatian hospitality industry, Alfirevic, Peronja, and Plazibat (2013, p. 663) concluded that:

> 'All high-quality hotels have significantly better scores than the medium-quality ones, except for the EFQM criteria of providing resources and partnerships, as well as achieving results for employees. These two criteria of business excellence should be the targets for better implementation in all Croatian hotels, with high-quality (4* and 5*) ones being aware that their leadership in quality can be endangered by excessive cutting of costs (which is shown by inefficient allocation of financial resources). Another group of problems could be related to putting their partnerships with suppliers and distributions in danger by not paying their financial obligations on time, or using other inappropriate approaches.'

Text 16.2 is an illustration of one hotel's pride in being awarded the EFQM excellence award Level 4.

16

TEXT 16.2

Clontarf Castle Hotel wins EFQM Award for special recognition, (09 Feb 2010)

Clontarf Castle Hotel was among a group of twenty tourism establishments honoured at the Failte Ireland Optimus Awards. The hotel received the top level award (European Foundation for Quality Management Award Level 4) for special recognition for its ongoing commitment to continuous improvement and business excellence.

The Optimus programme, developed by Failte Ireland, aims to help tourism establishments – including hotels, restaurants and visitor centres – achieve excellence in every aspect of their business by providing a practical approach to improving the quality, value and delight that visitors experience during their stay in Ireland.

Clontarf Castle Hotel, Dublin

Speaking at the event, Chairman of Failte Ireland, Redmond O' Donoghue congratulated the award winners. 'This year we have twenty winners who are receiving recognition for their commitment to quality through the Optimus programme. Today's recipients are located throughout the country, representing twelve countries in all, and reflect well on the tourism industry's willingness to embrace change and innovation towards self-improvement. I would like to commend your willingness to take on Optimus at a challenging time for tourism. This demonstrates your ability to embrace challenges and deal with them proactively. For our part, we in Failte Ireland are committed to working with you and others in the industry to overcome the challenges posed by the current economic climate. Indeed, 2010 will see us enhancing our level of practical business support offered to tourism enterprises.'

He continued: 'The EFQM Recognised for Excellence Level 4 award is synonymous with the highest standards of quality management. The evident drive, commitment and achievement of the team at Clontarf Castle Hotel are very clearly demonstrated by this award. They deserve to be proud of the results they have delivered in raising the profile of quality management within the Irish tourism industry.'

The 'Optimus' programme is a national quality standard and business improvement tool for the Irish tourism industry with an emphasis on business improvement. The programme helps enterprises understand their performance and then assists them in establishing priorities around making continuous improvement.

Tony Lenehan, Head of Food, Hospitality and Standards at Failte Ireland stressed the importance of Optimus in the current trading conditions 'll would like to congratulate all twenty businesses on their achievement. Not just on the accolade that they have received today but on their business acumen which has seen them embrace a management framework that brings tangible business benefits.

These twenty achievers have undergone a full assessment based on the Optimus framework. This assessment confirms the performance of these organisations and their ability to embed the principles of continuous improvement across their business while transforming these principles into tangible results.'

Further information on the Optimus Awards and programmes is available online from www.optimus.ie

16.2.3 Lean Thinking (just-in-time)

Lean Thinking, also known as 'just-in-time' (JIT) or simply 'lean' (or other variants like 'lean synchronisation' and 'lean integration'), originated in Japan. The concept of Lean Thinking was developed in the automotive sector in the 1950s through pioneering work at Toyota. Lean Thinking can be described as the pursuit of perfection by constantly eliminating waste through problem solving. To identify its relevance for the food and drinks service sector, Lean Thinking is defined by Oakdene Hollins Research & Consulting (2013, p. 1) as:

Lean Thinking

> A way of focusing on what the customer values and is willing to pay for; any activity that does not add to value, as perceived by the end customer, is waste. This waste includes any use of resources – cost, time, movement, material, energy, water, and labour.

In short, Lean Thinking aims to instantly meet demand with perfect quality and zero waste. Put differently, it means that the flow of products and services should always deliver exactly what customers want (perfect quality), in the exact quantities (neither too much nor too little), exactly where required (not to the wrong location), exactly when needed (not too early or too late), and at the lowest possible cost. It results in items flowing rapidly and smoothly through processes, operations and supply networks. Slack et al. (2013, p. 590) indicate that the key elements of Lean Thinking, when used as an improvement approach, are:

Zero waste

- customer-centricity;
- internal customer – supplier relationships;
- perfection is the goal;
- synchronised flow;
- reduce variation;
- include all people;
- waste elimination.

One of the success factors of Lean Thinking is that it can be applied to any type and size of organisation – it is highly adaptable. Some organisations view waste elimination as the most important of all the elements of Lean Thinking (James, 2011). In fact, they sometimes see Lean as consisting almost exclusively of waste elimination but fail to realise that effective waste elimination is only best achieved through changes in behaviour.

The key drivers for implementing Lean in an organisation are identified by Oakdene Hollins Research & Consulting (2013, p. 45) as:

Key drivers

- cost reduction;
- quality improvement;
- development of efficient processes;
- variation reduction.

Implementing Lean can have significant quantitative impact for an organisation, including an increase in operating efficiency and a reduction of throughput times and inventories. Productivity also increases as reduction of the Lean wastes allows the organisation to run at capacity, reducing costs and defect rates. Ultimately, this reduces the number of errors reaching customers. These benefits are relatively easily seen, but there are a number of broader benefits of Lean implementation including:

Benefits

16

16

- decrease of work in progress and associated costs;
- increased customer satisfaction due to timely delivery of services or goods and more consistent levels of service;
- consolidation of product service lines and department resulting in more standard processes and reduced variability.

All of these benefits are tangible and can be measured, allowing organisations to identify specific, measurable improvements that have been made through Lean implementation. Metrics may include financial savings, reduced lead times or reduced inventory. Lean implementation can also have qualitative impacts involving 'human elements' and, most importantly, can result in a new culture of continuous improvement embedded into daily operations. Text 16.3 illustrates a case of a hotel implementing the Lean approach in Japan.

TEXT 16.3

Offering excellent value at low cost

Yukai Resort in the famous Gero Onsen Hot spring area of Japan is part of a traditional Japanese hotel chain which performs lean hotel operations in order to offer great value to their customers, reduce cost and remain competitive in the fierce hospitality industry.

The standard hotel rate in the Gero Onsen Hot spring area is 15,000 yen or approximately US $180.00 per person/per night which includes dinner, breakfast and entrance to the hot spring.

At Yukai Resort, the price for the same offering is 7,500 yen (US $91.00) – every day of the year; regardless of high/low season. You may be surprised to hear that Yukai Resort is of high quality, they offer delicious international and Japanese meals and the surrounds are beautiful.

What's their secret?
Lean management and the multi-function worker
Put simply, all resort duties are shared by all personnel. This has allowed the resort to

operate with minimal staff and reduce costs overall while maintaining high quality.

For instance: The receptionists, in their free time will go to areas needing assistance; perhaps the kitchen or laundry.

Dinner and breakfast are buffet style, which reduces staffing requirements.

Staff are also active in lean management or lean kaizen efforts. The manager leads Kaizen circles weekly and monthly.

Employee engagement is key. This style of operation is extremely advantageous to both management and personnel. Cost minimization is an obvious benefit. For staff, this system allows them to gain experience in all aspects of hotel operations and gives them an opportunity to have direct input in improvement activities. It's not only empowering and motivating but also excellent in terms of career development.

(Source: www.process-improvement-japan.com)

Oakdene Hollins Research & Consulting (2013, p. 254) also indicate that, as concerns smaller players in the food-service chain, for Lean Thinking to be a success, staff need to be trained effectively: 'People don't want to read a manual, they respond better when they are shown Lean approaches in an easily understandable way'. Given the importance of changing cultures

and engaging staff at all levels, the following are seen as key factors facili-   Key factors
tating the success of Lean Thinking approaches:
- Providing teams with confidence to innovate;
- Confirming, documenting and distributing actions, responsibilities and deadlines;
- Identifying and addressing individuals' concerns;
- Capitalising on individuals' positive feelings;
- Committing teams to reporting deadlines;
- Co-ordinating and cross fertilising among teams;
- Scrutinising and constructively criticising progress to other teams;
- Capturing business results and teachings;
- Sharing success stories/tools with other categories.

The extensive study of the application of Lean Thinking within the UK food and drinks sector by Oakdene Hollins Research & Consulting (2013, p. 256) ended on the following observation:

> 'In terms of root causes, much of the waste (in the sense of subop-
> timal resource use) in the UK retail, wholesale and distribution sub-
> sectors seemingly arises from the coincidence of a growing custom-
> er demand for an ever-changing selection of 'fresh', short shelf-life
> food products and the stochasticity of that demand, the latter exac-
> erbated by unpredictable weather and other events. Given the dog-
> ma that empty shelves and lost sales are 'worse' than waste due to
> overproduction, demand amplification is the typical result. Such fac-
> tors may underlie the waste arising in other sections of the supply
> chain, especially in manufacture and filling.'

Six Sigma, the following model to be discussed, is closely linked to Lean Thinking. It should be noted that, in some cases, the two have been linked together in what is termed Lean Six Sigma.

16.2.4   Six Sigma
This section is designed based on excerpts from the website of the ASQ
(American Society for Quality – www.asq.org), Six Sigma is a set of techniques   Six Sigma
and tools for process improvement developed by Motorola in 1986 when they
were trying to deal with increasing warranty claims. Its success caused it to
be adopted and championed by Jack Welch, who made it a central component
of his business strategy at General Electric Corporation in 1995.

Six Sigma aims to improve the quality output of any process by identifying
and removing the causes of defects (errors) and minimising the variability in   Defects
manufacturing and business processes. It uses a set of quality management methods, mainly empirical statistical methods, and creates a special
infrastructure of people within the organisation ('Champions', 'Black Belts',   Infrastructure of people
'Green Belts', 'Yellow Belts', etc.) who are experts in these methods. Each
Six Sigma project carried out within an organisation follows a defined sequence of steps and has quantified value targets, for example to reduce
process cycle time, reduce pollution, reduce costs, increase customer satisfaction, or increase profits.

Though Six Sigma originated as a set of practices designed to improve manufacturing processes and eliminate defects, its application has now been
extended to other types of business processes. The word 'sigma' is a

© Noordhoff Uitgevers bv

Central idea

statistical term that measures how far a given process deviates from per-fection. The central idea behind Six Sigma is that if the number of defects in a process can be measured, it becomes possible to systematically figure out how to eliminate them and get as close to zero defects as possible. In

DPMO

Six Sigma, a defect is defined as any process output that does not meet customer specifications, or that could lead to creating an output that does not meet customer specifications. An opportunity is defined as a chance for non-conformance, or not meeting the required specifications. In essence, Six Sigma focusses on reducing variance in processes, and its target is 3.4 DPMO (defects per million opportunities), or one in which 99.99966% (the yield) of all opportunities to produce some feature of a part are statistically expected to be free of defects. A comparison of the defect rates and yields at different sigma levels is shown in Figure 16.5.

FIGURE 16.5 Comparative process sigma table

PROCESS SIGMA TABLE

SIGMA LEVEL	DEFECT RATE	YIELD
2σ	308,770 dpmo	69.10000%
3σ	66,811 dpmo	93.33000%
4σ	6,210 dpmo	99.38000%
5σ	233 dpmo	99.97700%
6σ	3.44 dpmo	99.99966%

Depending on the type of business process it is used in, Six Sigma has two methodologies composed of five phases each. For business projects aimed at improving an existing business process, DMAIC; for business projects aimed at creating a new product or process design, DMADV or DFSS. The application of these methodologies is generally rolled out over the course of many months or even years. The end result is a product or service that is fully aligned with customer expectations, wants and needs.

DMAIC project methodology

DMAIC

The roadmap of DMAIC is shown in Figure 16.6.
The standard five phases related to DMAIC project methodology are defined as follows:

Define

Define
The main objective of this stage is to outline the borders of the project.
- Stakeholders agree on the parameters that are to define the project.
- Scope and budgetary items, as well as customer needs, are aligned with project goals.
- Team development takes place as the project begins to take shape.

Measure

Measure
The main objective is to collect data pertinent to the scope of the project.
- Leaders collect reliable baseline data to compare to future results.
- Teams create a detailed map of all interrelated business processes to elucidate areas of possible performance enhancement.

FIGURE 16.6 The roadmap of DMAIC

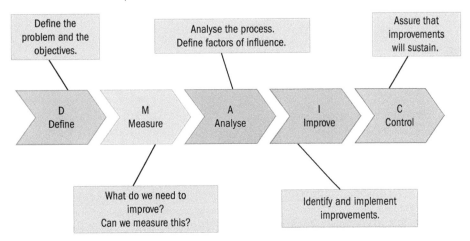

16

Analyse   Analyse
The main objective is to reveal the root cause of business inefficiencies.
• Analysis of data reveals areas where the implementation of change can
  provide the most effective results.
• Groups discuss ways the data highlights areas ripe for improvement.

Improve   Improve
The main objective at the end of this stage is to complete a test run of a
change that is to be widely implemented.
• Teams and stakeholders devise methods to address the process deficiencies uncovered during the data analysis process.
• Groups finalise and test a change aimed at mitigating the ineffective process.
• Improvements are ongoing and include feedback analysis and stakeholder participation.

Control   Control
The objective of the last stage of the methodology is to develop metrics that
help leaders monitor and document continued success.
• Six Sigma strategies are adaptive and on-going.
• Adjustments can be made and new changes may be implemented as a
  result of the completion of this first cycle of the process.

At the end of the cycle, either additional processes are addressed or the initial project is completed. It should be noted that some organisations have
added a Recognise phase at the beginning, which means being able to recognise the right problem to work on, leading to an RDMAIC project methodology.

DMADV project methodology   DMADV
The roadmap of DMADV, also known as DFSS (Design For Six Sigma), is   DFSS
shown in Figure 16.7.

FIGURE 16.7 The roadmap of DMADV

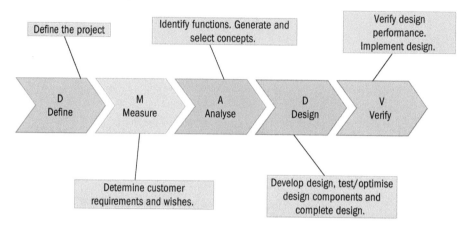

The five phases of DMADV project methodology are defined as follows:

Define

Define
Project leaders identify wants and needs believed to be considered most important to customers. Wants and needs are identified through historical information, customer feedback, and other information sources.
- Teams are assembled to drive the process.
- Metrics and other tests are developed in alignment with customer information.

Measure

Measure
The second part of the process is to use the defined metrics to collect data
and record specifications in a way that can be utilised to help drive the rest
of the process.
- All processes needed to successfully manufacture the product or service
  are assigned metrics for later evaluation.
- Technology teams test the metrics and then apply them.

Analyse

Analyse
The result of the manufacturing process (i.e. finished product or service) is
tested by internal teams to create a baseline for improvement.
- Leaders use data to identify areas of adjustment within the processes
  that will deliver improvement to either the quality or manufacturing process of a finished product or service.
- Teams set final processes in place and make adjustments as needed.

Design

Design
The results of internal tests are compared to customer wants and needs.
Any additional adjustments needed are made.
- The improved manufacturing process is tested and test groups of cus-
  tomers provide feedback before the final product or service is widely re-
  leased.

Verify

Verify
The last stage in the methodology is continuous. While the product or service is being released and customer reviews are coming in, the processes
may be adjusted.

- Metrics are further developed to keep track of continuous customer feedback on the product or service.
- New data may lead to other changes that need to be addressed, so the initial process may lead to new applications of DMADV in subsequent areas.

The distinctions of DMAIC and DMADV are aimed at viewing different sectors of a business simultaneously, but addressing them separately. Despite their unique distinctions, the methodologies overlap during the examination process and share the same end goal –the enhancement of the business processes.

Many hotels have well established Six Sigma professional programmes for their associates and offer specialist courses in the Six Sigma domain as illustrated in Text 16.4, taken from Starwood Hotels and Resorts.

16

TEXT 16.4

Six Sigma at the Starwood Hotels and Resorts

Six Sigma is an internationally recognized approach that helps associates develop innovative, customer-focused solutions and quickly disseminate those innovations across the entire organisation.

The Six Sigma program at Starwood Hotels & Resorts Worldwide, Inc. is unique to the hospitality industry. Six Sigma has helped increase our financial performance by improving the quality and consistency of our guests' experiences as well as those of our internal customers. It provides the framework and tools we need to create and maintain superior standards at all properties while dramatically improving the bottom line. The Six Sigma organisation reports to divisional leadership and is aligned with the division's goals and priorities.

Six Sigma candidates are tasked with achieving innovative process improvements in their area of responsibility through the Six Sigma, Lean and Kaizen methodologies. These improvements must result in measurable financial and/or customer loyalty gains. Specialized training teaches Six Sigma associates to be project leaders who can mobilize their team members as well as others in the organisation to accomplish the aggressive goals specified in the Project Charter.

Ideal candidates for this discipline have the ability to embrace and implement change,

break down cultural barriers, and lead major initiatives across multiple departments. Six Sigma professionals possess excellent analytical and diagnostic skills and are enthusiastic and passionate about what they do.

Here are the various levels of opportunity that exist in Six Sigma:
- Green Belts (GBs) have full-time positions with a portion of their time dedicated to being the Six Sigma point person and project champion and manager.
- Black Belts (BBs) are full-time resources who typically work on new projects. They are a resource to GBs and members of the property's Executive Committee.
- Master Black Belts are a full-time resource dedicated to creating and managing a portfolio of Six Sigma projects in a given division, area or region. They are a resource to BBs, GBs and Six Sigma Council members in their area.

(Source: www.starwoodhotels.com)

16.2.5   The Plan-Do-Check- Act (PDCA) Cycle

PDCA cycle

The PDCA cycle, (also known as the 'Deming circle/cycle/wheel', 'Shewhart cycle', or 'control circle/cycle') is a continuous quality improvement model consisting of a logical sequence of four repetitive steps for the continuous improvement of processes and products, and learning. It was made popular by Deming, who referred to it as the 'Shewhart cycle'. Its origin can be traced to Shewhart who, in the 1920's, introduced the concept of PLAN, DO and SEE. Later on, Deming modified the PDCA cycle to the 'Plan, Do, Study, Act' (PDSA) cycle, because he felt that 'check' emphasised inspection over analysis (Moen & Norman, 2009). A fundamental principle of the PDCA cycle is repetition – once a hypothesis is confirmed (or debunked), executing the cycle again will extend knowledge further. Repeating the PDCA cycle can lead an organisation closer to its goal, which is usually perfect operation and output. The PDSA cycle is illustrated in Figure 16.8.

PDSA cycle

FIGURE 16.8 The PDSA cycle

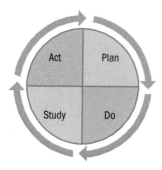

The four phases of the Plan-Do-Study-Act Cycle involve:

Plan
- Plan: This involves identifying a goal or purpose, formulating a theory, defining success metrics and putting a plan into action. It useful to employ tools like cause and effect diagrams and the 5 Whys to help get to the root of any problem; it may be appropriate to map what process is at the root of the problem. This phase ends with gathering all information required to draft solutions.

Do
- Do: Here, the components of the plan, such as making a product, are implemented. This phase involves several activities, such as:
  - generating possible solutions
  - selecting the best of these solutions using appropriate analysis tools (such as impact analysis);
  - implementing a pilot project on a small scale basis, with a small group, or in a limited geographical area, or using some other trial design appropriate to the nature of the problem, product or initiative.
    It is very important to note that 'Do' here means 'try' or 'test'. It does not mean 'implement fully', because full implementation occurs during the 'Act' phase.

Study
- Study: Here, the outcomes are monitored to test the validity of the plan to signal signs of progress and success, or problems and areas for improvement. In this phase, an organisation measures how effective a pilot solution has been, and gathers any resulting teachings that could make it even better. Depending on the success of a pilot, the number of areas for improvement that have been identified, and the scope of the whole

initiative, an organisation may decide to repeat the 'Do' and 'Study' phases, incorporating the additional improvements. Once an organisation is finally satisfied that the costs of repeating the Do-Study sub-cycle would outweigh the benefits, they can move on to the final phase.

- Act: Here, the cycle is closed, integrating the teachings generated by the entire process, which can be used to adjust goals, change methods or even reformulate theories altogether.

Act

16

These four steps are repeated over and over as part of a never-ending cycle of continual improvement. There can be any number of iterations of the 'Do' and 'Study' phases, as the solution is refined, retested, re-refined and re-tested again.

The PDSA cycle provides a useful, controlled problem solving process. It is most effective in:

Effective In

- Avoiding the large scale wastage of resources that comes with the full scale implementation of a mediocre or poor solution;
- Exploring a range of possible new solutions to problems, and trying them out and improving them in a controlled way before selecting one for full implementation;
- Helping to implement continuous improvement approaches, such as the Kaizen approach (see 16.2.9), as the cycle is repeated again and again as new areas for improvement are sought and solved;
- Identifying new solutions and improvement to processes that are repeated frequently. In this situation, there will be benefits from extra improvements built in to the process many times over once it is implemented.

It should be noted that the use of the PDSA cycle is slower and more measured than a straightforward implementation, and is surely not appropriate in actual emergency situations.

In studies about hotel service quality improvement based on the PDCA cycle, Sun (2013) concludes that using the PDCA cycle comes with some associated problems as it is used in accordance with a predetermined framework that may lead to inertial thinking, a lack of inspiration and a lack of innovation with some managers. Therefore, in the process of using the cycle, managers should foster its strengths and avoid its weaknesses, using new ideas and ways to uncover solutions to identified quality problems so that quality continuously improves. In addition, Borkar and Koranne (2014, p. 24) indicate that:

> 'Continuous improvement programs add value to the organisations in many ways. Hotel business being capital intensive and which requires long wait for returns on investment requires improving continuously as per the changing patterns of guest requirements and perception of quality. New processes are designed; tested and then the staff is trained to practice it.'

16.2.6   Business process re-engineering (BPR)

BPR involves the radical redesign of core business processes to achieve dramatic improvements in productivity, cycle times and quality. Hammer and Champy (1993, p. 32) defined BPR as 'the fundamental rethinking and radical redesign of business processes to achieve dramatic improvements in critical contemporary modern measures of performance, such as cost,

BPR

16

Rethink

quality, service, and speed.' In BPR, companies start with a blank sheet of paper and rethink existing processes to deliver more value to their customers, typically by adopting a new value system that places increased emphasis on customer needs. The companies reduce organisational layers and eliminate unproductive activities in two key areas. Firstly, by redesigning functional organisations into cross-functional teams, and secondly by using technology to improve data dissemination and decision making. It is believed that information technology had the potential to enable the fundamental redesign of the processes, which acted as the catalyst in bringing ideas together. The principles of BPR can be summarised as:

Principles

1 Organise around outcomes, not tasks;
2 Identify all of an organisation's processes and prioritise them in order of the redesign urgency;
3 Integrate information processing work into the real work that produces the information
4 Treat geographically dispersed resources as though they were centralised;
5 Link parallel activities in the workflow instead of just integrating results;
6 Put the decision point where the work is performed, and build controls into the process;
7 Capture information once and at its source.

Key actions

In order to implement BPR within an organisation, the following key actions need to be taken (Zigiaris, 2000):

- Selection of the strategic (added-value) processes for redesign;
- Simplify new processes – minimise steps – optimise efficiency by modelling;
- Organise a team of employees for each process and assign a role for the process coordinator;
- Organise the workflow – document transfer and control;
- Assign responsibilities and roles for each process;
- Automate processes using IT (Intranets, Extranets, Workflow Management);
- Train the process team to efficiently manage and operate the new process;
- Introduce the redesigned process into the business organisational structure.

Most re-engineering methodologies share common elements, but simple differences can have a significant impact on the success or failure of a project. After a project area has been identified, the methodologies for re-engineering business processes may be used. In order for a company aiming to apply BPR to select the best methodology, sequence processes, and implement the appropriate BPR plan, it has to create an effective and actionable vision. There are four basic requirements to creating an effective vision:

Vision

- The right combination of individuals come together to form an optimistic and energised team;
- Clear objectives exist and the scope for the project is well defined and understood;
- The team is able to anticipate future results and look back, rather than stand in the present and look forward; and
- The vision is rooted in a set of guiding principles.

All BPR methodologies may be divided into general 'model' stages (Zigiaris, 2000):

- The Envision stage: the company reviews the existing strategy and business processes – based on that review, business processes for improvement are targeted and IT opportunities are identified;
- The Initiation stage: project teams are assigned. Performance goals, project planning and employee notification are set;
- The Diagnosis stage: documentation of processes and sub-processes takes place in terms of process attributes (activities, resources, communication, roles, IT and costs);
- The Redesign stage: new process design is developed by devising process design alternatives and using brainstorming and creativity techniques;
- The Reconstruction stage: management technique changes occur to ensure smooth migration to the new process responsibilities and human resource roles;
- The Evaluation stage: the new process is monitored to examine total quality programmes and to determine if goals are met.

Stages

Envision

Initiation

Diagnosis

Redesign

Reconstruction

Evaluation

BPR has aroused considerable controversy, mainly because BPR sometimes only looks at work activities rather than the people performing the work. Because of this, people become 'cogs in a machine'. There certainly is evidence that BPR is often accompanied by a significant reduction in staff. Studies conducted at the time BPR was at its peak often revealed that the majority of BPR projects could reduce staff levels by over 20% (Davenport, 1995). BPR was often viewed simply as an excuse for getting rid of staff. Companies that wished to 'downsize' used BPR as the pretext, putting short-term interests of shareholders of the company above either longer-term interests or the interests of the company's employees. Moreover, a combination of radical redesign together with downsizing could mean that the essential core of experience was lost from the organisation. This leaves an organisation vulnerable to market turbulences since it no longer possesses the knowledge and experience of how to cope with unexpected changes (Slack et al., 2013).

Controversy

Downsize

16.2.7 Hazard analysis and critical control points (HACCP)

Adapted from the US Food and Drug Administration's HACCP Principles & Application Guidelines (www.fda.gov), HACCP is a management system in which food safety is addressed through the analysis and control of biological, chemical, and physical hazards. The system covers all stages from raw material production, procurement and handling, to manufacturing, distribution and consumption of the finished product. The HACCP concept was pioneered in the 1960s by the Pillsbury Company, the United States Army, and the United States National Aeronautics and Space Administration (NASA) as a collaborative development for the production of safe foods for the United States space programme. NASA wanted a 'zero defects' programme to guarantee the safety of the foods astronauts were to consume in space. Pillsbury therefore introduced and adopted HACCP as the system that could provide the greatest safety while reducing dependence on end-product inspection and testing. HACCP emphasises control of the process as far upstream in the processing system as possible by utilising operator control and/or continuous monitoring techniques at critical control points. Pillsbury presented the HACCP concept publicly at a conference for food protection in 1971. The use of HACCP principles in the promulgation of regulations for

HACCP

Hazards

Zero defects

low-acid canned food was completed in 1974 by the United States' Food and Drug Administration (FDA). In the early 1980s, the HACCP approach was adopted by other major food companies. The United States' National Academy of Science recommended in 1985 that the HACCP approach be adopted in food processing establishments to ensure food safety. More recently, numerous groups, including, for example, the International Commission on Microbiological Specifications for Foods (ICMSF) and the International Association of Milk, Food and Environmental Sanitarians (IAMFES), have recommended the broad application of HACCP to food safety. Food safety should never be compromised, as this could have very serious consequences on consumers. Text 16.5 illustrates the need for a critical approach to food safety.

TEXT 16.5

Salmonella incidents prompt new food safety guidelines

Increases in the number of salmonella cases in Australia have been recorded even as the overall number of food poisoning cases has dropped from 4.3 to 4.1 million, between 2000 and 2010. The findings have prompted the Food Produce Safety Centre for Australia and New Zealand to issue new guidelines to industry. 'Our aim was to reinvigorate the safety, to give it greater focus, make information available to industry,' said FPSC-ANZ Technology Manager, Richard Bennett. 'Industry put this as their Number One priority for what we actually needed.'

The guidelines have been issued less than a month after a salmonella outbreak affected more than 35 people who attended high tea at a five star Melbourne hotel, The Langham. Instances of salmonella in Victoria increased by half since 2012, while in Queensland the number of cases had doubled in the last year, according to the respective Department of Health websites.

'Salmonella is a bacteria that can be found in the guts of infected humans, warm blooded animals, birds and reptiles and it's also present in the environment,' says Martin Stone, a director with HACCP Australia, a food technology organisation specializing in food safety and its application in production and manufacturing. 'Animal hosts shed potentially millions of bacteria, and salmonella survives quite well outside of the host, it's a robust bacteria.'

Where food producers and manufacturers must take care is in managing the complex supply chain for ready to eat foods, according to Mr Stone. 'From the environment, salmonella can be transferred into raw produce through the soil and water supply. So plants such as lettuce, bean sprouts, and almonds have been affected by this route.' 'Other routes of infection include cross-contamination from raw foods into cooked and ready to eat foods through direct contact from a source or through an insect pest', Mr Stone adds.

It is important to consider water sources, water reuse and practices, as well as getting rid of known contaminants such as rodents and food waste, and maintaining strict hygiene practices, according to Mr Stone. 'Food industry workers certainly should not overlook cleaning and sanitation in pack sheds, and consider what the end use of a product is,' he said. 'There is a water problem in some parts of Australia, in terms of availability, and I'm not saying that recycled water can't be made safe, but I would be very cautious before using it that anywhere on a product like lettuce, for example.'

Even companies using run off water, collected on roofs, should take care, Mr Stone cautioned, because there could be contaminants such as bird droppings present on the rooftop that could introduce bacteria like salmonella into the water.

(Source: www.freshplaza.com)

Managing restaurant food safety requires adhering to the principles of HACCP at all levels and combining these with an active managerial control. Regulators play an important role in maintaining a food safety system in all retail food establishments. The regulators and the industry can work together to understand establishments' perspectives on the variety of food preparation and service needs encountered in each – from a facility with minimal food service to a very complex operation that serves hundreds to thousands of meals daily. The HACCP, which is science based and systematic, identifies specific hazards and measures the degree to which these hazards are controlled to ensure the safety of food. HACCP is a tool used to assess hazards and establish control systems that focus on prevention, rather than relying mainly on end-product testing. Any HACCP system is capable of accommodating change, such as advances in equipment design, processing procedures, or technological developments.

Regulators

Systematic

HACCP can be applied throughout the food chain from primary production to final consumption; its implementation should be guided by scientific evidence of risks to human health. As well as enhancing food safety, the implementation of HACCP can provide other significant benefits. In addition, the application of HACCP systems can benefit inspection by regulatory authorities, and promote international trade by increasing confidence in food safety (The Food and Agricultural Organisation, 2015).

The successful application of HACCP requires the full commitment and involvement of management and the work force. It also requires a multidisciplinary approach – this multidisciplinary approach should include, where appropriate to that particular study, expertise in agronomy, veterinary health, production, microbiology, medicine, public health, food technology, environmental health, chemistry and engineering. The application of HACCP is compatible with the implementation of quality management systems, such as the ISO 9000 series, and is the system of choice in the management of food safety within such systems.

Multidisciplinary

The HACCP system consists of the following seven principles:
- Principle 1 – conduct a hazard analysis;
- Principle 2 – determine critical control points (CCPs);
- Principle 3 – establish critical limits;
- Principle 4 – establish a system to monitor control of the CCP;
- Principle 5 – establish corrective action to be taken when monitoring indicates that a particular CCP is not under control;
- Principle 6 – establish procedures for verification to confirm the HACCP system is working effectively;
- Principle 7 – establish documentation concerning all procedures and records appropriate to these principles and their application.

Principles

The seven HACCP principles are included in the international standard ISO 22000:2005 (www.iso.org). This standard is a complete food safety and quality management system incorporating the elements of prerequisite programmes, HACCP, and the quality management system, which together form an organisation's TQM system. ISO 22000:2005 specifies requirements for food safety management systems where an organisation in the food chain needs to demonstrate its ability to control food safety hazards in order to ensure food is safe at the time of human consumption. It is applicable to all

ISO 22000:2005

16

organisations, regardless of size, which are involved in any aspect of the food chain and want to implement systems that consistently provide safe products. Meeting one or more requirements of ISO 22000:2005 can be accomplished through the use of internal and/or external resources. ISO 22000:2005 specifies requirements for an organisation to:

- plan, implement, operate, maintain and update a food safety management system aimed at providing products that, according to their intended use, are safe for the consumer;
- demonstrate compliance with applicable statutory and regulatory food safety requirements;
- evaluate and assess customer requirements and demonstrate conformity with those mutually agreed customer requirements that relate to food safety, in order to enhance customer satisfaction;
- effectively communicate food safety issues to their suppliers, customers and relevant interested parties in the food chain;
- ensure that the organisation conforms to its stated food safety policy;
- demonstrate such conformity to relevant interested parties; and
- obtain certification or registration of its food safety management system by an external organisation, or make a self-assessment or self-declaration of conformity to ISO 22000:2005.

Guidelines for the application of the HACCP system

Prior to application of HACCP to any sector of the food chain, that sector should be operating according to the Codex General Principles of Food Hygiene, the appropriate Codex Codes of Practice, and appropriate food safety legislation. It should be noted that the Codex Alimentarius (Latin for 'Book of Food') is a collection of internationally recognised standards, codes of practice, guidelines and other recommendations relating to foods, food production and food safety. The texts of the Codex Alimentarius are developed and maintained by the Codex Alimentarius Commission that was established in 1961 by the Food and Agriculture Organisation of the United Nations (FAO), and was joined by the World Health Organisation (WHO) in 1962. The Commission's main goals are to protect the health of consumers and ensure fair practices in the international food trade. The Codex Alimentarius is recognised by the World Trade Organisation as an international reference point for the resolution of disputes concerning food safety and consumer protection. As of 2015, there were 187 members of the Codex Alimentarius Commission – 186 member countries and 1 member organization, the European Union (EU). (Source: http://www.fao.org/fao-who-codexalimentarius/codex-home/en/)

Codex Alimentarius

Commitment

Management commitment is necessary for implementation of an effective HACCP system. During hazard identification, evaluation, and subsequent operations in designing and applying HACCP systems, management should also consider the impact of raw materials, ingredients, food manufacturing practices, roles of manufacturing processes to control hazards, likely end-uses of the products, categories of consumers of concern, and epidemiological evidence relative to food safety. The intent of the HACCP system is to focus control at CCPs. Redesigning the operation should be considered if a hazard which must be controlled is identified but no CCPs are found. HACCP should be applied to each specific operation separately. CCPs identified in any given example of a Codex Code of Hygienic Practice may not be the only ones identified for a specific application or may be of a different

CCPs

nature. The HACCP application should be reviewed; necessary changes should be made if a modification is made to any product, process, or step. When applying HACCP it is important to be flexible where appropriate given the context of the application, taking into account the nature and the size of the operation.

The application of HACCP principles consists of the following tasks as identified in these 12 steps adapted from FAO documentation:

12 Steps

Step 1 – Assemble an HACCP team

HACCP team

The food operation should assure that appropriate product specific knowledge and expertise is available for the development of an effective HACCP plan. Optimally, this may be accomplished by assembling a multidisciplinary team. Where such expertise is not available on site, expert advice should be obtained from other sources. The scope of the HACCP plan should be identified. The scope should describe which segment of the food chain is involved and the general classes of hazards to be addressed (e.g. does the HACCP plan cover all classes of hazards or only selected classes).

Step 2 – Describe the product

Describe

A full description of the product should be drafted to include relevant safety information, such as composition, physical/chemical structure (including A_w, pH, etc.), fungal/static treatments (heat-treatment, freezing, brining, smoking, etc.), packaging, durability, storage conditions, and method of distribution.

Step 3 – Identify the product's intended use

Intended use

The intended use should be based on the expected uses of the product by end users or consumers. In specific cases, vulnerable groups of the population, e.g. institutional feeding, may have to be considered.

Step 4 – Construct the flow diagram

Flow diagram

The flow diagram should be constructed by the HACCP team. The flow diagram should cover all steps in the operation. When applying HACCP to a given operation, consideration should be given to the steps preceding and following the specified operation.

Step 5 – Carry out an on-site confirmation of flow diagram

Confirmation

The HACCP team should confirm processing operations against the flow diagram during all stages and hours of operation, and amend the flow diagram where appropriate.

Step 6 – List all potential hazards associated with each step, conduct a hazard analysis, and consider any measures to control identified hazards (Principle 1)

Hazard analysis

The HACCP team should list all hazards that may be reasonably expected to occur at every step from primary production, processing, manufacture, and distribution to the point of consumption. The HACCP team should next conduct a hazard analysis for the HACCP plan to identify which hazards are of such a nature that their elimination or reduction to acceptable levels is essential to the production of a safe food.

16

In conducting the hazard analysis, the following information should be included wherever possible:

- the likelihood of occurrence of hazards and severity of their adverse health effects;
- the qualitative and/or quantitative evaluation of the presence of hazards;
- survival or multiplication of microorganisms of concern;
- production or persistence of toxins, chemicals or physical agents in foods; and,
- conditions leading to the above.

The HACCP team must then consider what control measures, if any, exist and can be applied for each hazard. More than one control measure may be required to control specific hazards; conversely, more than one hazard may be controlled by a specified control measure.

Critical control points

Step 7 – Determine the critical control points (Principle 2)
There may be more than one CCP at which control is applied to address the same hazard. The determination of a CCP in the HACCP system can be facilitated by the application of a decision tree (such as shown in Figure 16.9), which indicates a logical reasoning approach.

Application of a decision tree should be flexible, whether the operation is for production, slaughter, processing, storage, distribution, or other. It should be used for guidance when determining CCPs. This example of a decision tree may not be applicable to all situations. Other approaches may be used or even required. Training in the application of the decision tree is recommended. If a hazard has been identified at a step where control is necessary for safety, and no control measure exists at that step or any other, then the product or process should be modified at that step or at any earlier or later stage to include a control measure.

Critical limits

Step 8 – Establish critical limits for each CCP (Principle 3)
Critical limits must be specified and validated for each CCP if possible. In some cases, more than one critical limit may be elaborated upon at a particular step. Criteria often used include measurements of temperature, time, moisture level, pH, A_w, available chlorine, and sensory parameters such as visual appearance or texture.

Monitoring system

Step 9 – Establish a monitoring system for each CCP (Principle 4)
Monitoring is the scheduled measuring or observing of a CCP relative to its critical limits. TM monitoring procedures must be able to detect loss of control at the CCP. Additionally, monitoring should ideally provide this information in time, allowing for timely adjustments to ensure control of the process to prevent violating critical limits. Where possible, process adjustments should be made when monitoring results indicate a trend towards loss of control at a CCP. Adjustments should be taken before a deviation occurs. Data derived from monitoring must be evaluated by a designated person with the required knowledge and authority to carry out corrective actions when indicated. If monitoring is not continuous, the amount or frequency of monitoring must be sufficient to guarantee the CCP is in control. Most monitoring procedures for CCPs need to be done rapidly because they relate to on-line processes where there is not enough time for lengthy analytical testing. Physical and chemical measurements are often preferred to microbio-

FIGURE 16.9 Example of a decision tree to identify CCPs (answer the questions in sequence)

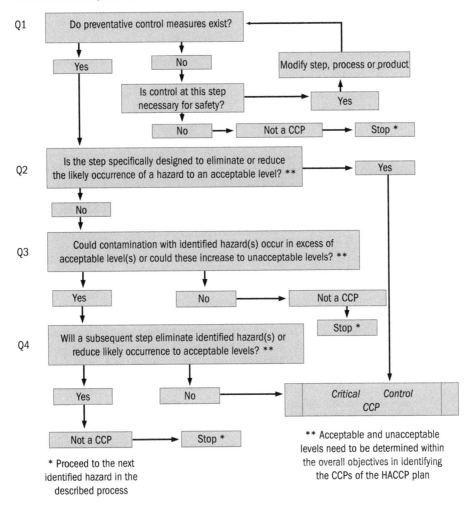

logical testing because they may be done rapidly and can often indicate microbiological control of the product. All records and documents associated with monitoring CCPs must be signed by the persons doing the monitoring and by responsible reviewing officials of the organisation.

Step 10 – Establish corrective actions (Principle 5)
Specific corrective actions must be developed for each CCP in the HACCP system in order to deal with deviations when they occur. The actions must ensure that the CCP is brought under control. Actions taken must also include proper disposition of the affected product. Deviation and product disposition procedures must be documented in the HACCP record keeping.

Corrective actions

Step 11 – Establish verification procedures (Principle 6)
Establish procedures for verification. Verification and auditing methods, procedures, and tests, including random sampling and analysis, can be used to determine if the HACCP system is working correctly. The frequency

Verification

© Noordhoff Uitgevers bv

of verification should be sufficient to confirm that the HACCP system is working effectively. Examples of verification activities include:

- Review of the HACCP system and its records;
- Review of deviations and product dispositions;
- Confirmation that CCPs are kept under control.

Where possible, validation activities should include actions to confirm the efficacy of all elements of the HACCP plan.

Documentation

Step 12 – Establish documentation and record keeping (Principle 7)
Efficient and accurate record keeping is essential to the application of an HACCP system. HACCP procedures should be documented. Documentation and record keeping should be appropriate to the nature and size of the operation. Documentation examples are:

- Hazard analysis;
- CCP determination;
- Critical limit determination.

Record examples are:

- CCP monitoring activities;
- Deviations and associated corrective actions;
- Modifications to the HACCP system.

The training of personnel in industry, government and academia in HACCP principles and applications, and the increasing awareness of consumers are essential elements for the effective implementation of HACCP. As an aid in developing specific training to support an HACCP plan, working instructions and procedures should be developed to define the tasks of the operating personnel to be stationed at each CCP. A good co-operation between primary producer, industry, trade groups, consumer organisations, and responsible authorities is of vital importance. Opportunities should be provided for joint training of industry and control authorities to encourage and maintain a continuous dialogue and create a climate of understanding in the practical application of HACCP.

16.2.8   The Gaps model of service quality

Gaps model

The Gaps model of service quality, was developed by Zeithaml, Berry and Parasuraman (1990) with five gaps; this section discusses the version described in Zeithaml, Bitner and Gremler (2009). The gaps, which may be roughly defined as the differences between the perceptions and expectations of users, are divided among the very important customer gap, and four different service provider gaps designed to help in closing the customer gap. These gaps are shown in Figure 16.10.

The customer gap

Customer gap

The customer gap is the difference between customer expectations and customer perceptions. Customer expectations are what a customer expects based on available resources; they are influenced by cultural background, family lifestyle, personality, demographics, advertising, experience with similar products and information available online. Customer perception is totally subjective and is based on a customer's interaction with a product or service. Perception is derived from a customer's satisfaction of a specific product or service and the quality of service delivery. The customer gap is the

FIGURE 16.10 The Gaps model of service quality (Zeithaml et al., 2009, p. 43)

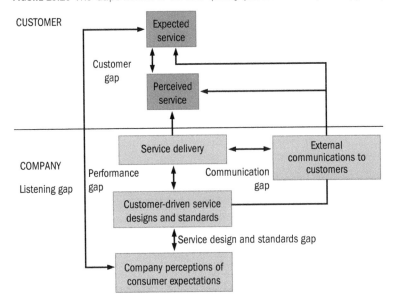

16

most important gap; in an ideal world, a customer's expectation would be almost identical to their perception. In a customer oriented strategy, delivering quality service for a specific product should be based on a clear understanding of the target market. Understanding customer needs and knowing customer expectations may be the best way to close the gap.

Given the importance of understanding customer expectations in order to deliver service quality, it is important to understand how such expectations are formed. Customer expectations are formed or influenced as a result of many factors. These factors include personal needs, previous experience, word of mouth communication, and explicit and implicit business communications.

Personal needs – any customer has what they regard as a set of key personal needs they expect a service to address. Clearly, these vary from service to service and from customer to customer. An inadequate understanding of these personal needs by the service provider makes it difficult to design and deliver appropriate service.

Previous experience – repeat customers have already had earlier experience with a product or service. This previous experience as a customer partly influences their expectations of future service. One customer, for example, may have low expectations because of poor previous service. Another may have high expectations because service quality last time was high. Customers may even refer to previous experience with other organisations in this context.

Word of mouth communications – customer expectations are shaped in part by word-of-mouth communication about the service and its provider. Effectively, this relates to communication from sources other than the service provider itself. Friends, family, colleagues are obvious sources in this context. Various

Expectation

Personal needs

Previous experience

Word of mouth

© Noordhoff Uitgevers bv

media may similarly be a source of such communication, as may other organisations such as inspection and audit agencies or central governments. An important question for a service provider to answer is whether they know what others are saying about their service.

Business communications
Explicit business communications – some communications about an organisation may relate to statements about the organisation made by the organisation itself. Such statements may come from employees or in the form of leaflets, publicity, or marketing materials.

Implicit business communications – customers may infer certain information about an organisation from possibly unrelated actions taken by that organisation. A newly renovated restaurant may lead a customer to assume that other aspects of service quality will be high. Similarly, a motel that is visibly in need of redecoration may lead to inferences about service quality gaps in other dimensions.

The provider gaps
Provider gaps
The four different service provider gaps are the listening gap, the service design and standards gap, the service performance gap, and the communication gap. These gaps are called provider gaps because they occur within an organisation.

Listening gap
* Provider gap 1 – the listening gap
  This is the difference between customer expectations of service and a provider understanding those expectations. The key factors leading to the listening gap are shown in Figure 16.11 (Zeithaml et al., 2009, p. 34).

FIGURE 16.11 Key factors leading to the listening gap (provider gap 1)

Customer expectations

Gap 1

* *Inadequate marketing research orientation*
  Insufficient marketing research
  Research not focused on service quality
  Inadequate use of market research
* *Lack of upward communication*
  Lack of interaction between management and customers
  Insufficient communication between contact employees and managers
  Too many layers between contact personnel and top management
* *Insufficient relationship focus*
  Lack of market segmentation
  Focus on transactions rather than relationships
  Focus on new customers rather than relationship customers
* *Inadequate service recovery*
  Lack of encouragement to listen to customer complaints
  Failure to make amends when things go wrong
  No appropriate recovery mechanisms in place for service failures

Company perceptions of customer expectations

- Provider gap 2 – the service design and standards gap
  This is the difference between an organisation's understanding of customer expectations and the development of customer-driven service design and standards. The key factors leading to the service design and
  standards gap are shown in Figure 16.12 (Zeithaml et al., 2009, p. 37).

Standards gap

FIGURE 16.12 Key factors leading to the service design and standards gap
(provider gap 2)

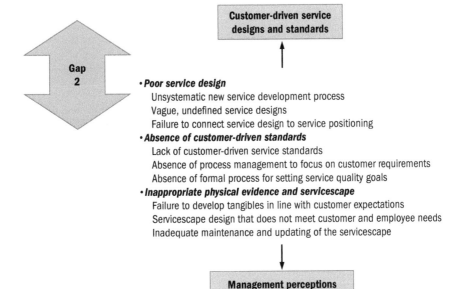

- Provider gap 3 – the service performance gap
  This is the difference between the development of customer-driven service standards and the actual service performance by an organisation's
  employees. The key factors leading to the service performance gap are
  shown in Figure 16.13 (Zeithaml et al., 2009, p. 39).

Service performance gap

- Provider gap 4 – the communication gap
  This is the difference between an organisation's external communication
  and what it actually delivers to customers. The key factors leading to the
  communication gap are shown in Figure 16.14 (Zeithaml et al., 2009, p. 42).

Communication gap

As noted in the key factors leading to the various gaps, gap analysis in-
volves internal and external analysis. Externally, an organisation must com-
municate with customers. Internally, it must determine service delivery and
service design. For a successful implementation of gap analysis, the follow-
ing steps can be used:
- Identification of customer expectations;
- Identification of customer experiences;
- Identification of management perceptions;
- Evaluation of service standards;
- Evaluation of customer communications.

16

FIGURE 16.13 Key factors leading to the service performance gap (provider gap 3)

| Customer-driven service designs and standards |

- *Deficiencies in human resource policies*
    Ineffective recruitment
    Role ambiguity and role conflict
    Poor employee–technology job fit
    Inappropriate evaluation and compensation systems
    Lack of empowerment, perceived control, and teamwork
- *Failure to match supply and demand*
    Failure to smooth peaks and valleys of demand
    Inappropriate customer mix
    Over-reliance on price to smooth demand
- *Customers not fulfilling roles*
    Customers lack knowledge of their roles and responsibilities
    Customers negatively impact each other
- *Problems with service intermediaries*
    Channel conflict over objectives and performance
    Channel conflict over costs and rewards
    Difficulty controlling quality and consistency
    Tension between empowerment and control

| Service delivery |

Focus-group

The identification of customer expectations and experiences may begin with focus-group interviews. Groups of customers, typically numbering seven to twelve per group, are invited to discuss their satisfaction with services or products. During this process, expectations and experiences are recorded. This process is usually successful in identifying those service and product attributes that are most important to customer satisfaction. After focus-group interviews are completed, expectations and experiences can be measured using more formal, quantitative methods. The expectations, experiences and perceptions may then be measured using Likert-scales. The gaps can then simply be calculated as the arithmetic difference between the measurements for each of the attributes. A team can then be assigned the duty of evaluating manager perceptions, service standards, and communications to pinpoint discrepancies. Once gaps are identified, management must take appropriate steps to fill or narrow these gaps (Zeithaml et al., 2009).

Likert-scales

Team

The main reason gap analysis is important to organisations is the fact that gaps between customer expectations and customer experiences lead to customer dissatisfaction. Consequently, measuring gaps is the first step in enhancing customer satisfaction. Additional competitive advantages can be achieved by exceeding customer expectations. Customer satisfaction leads to repeat purchases, and repeat purchases lead to loyal customers. In turn,

FIGURE 16.14 The key factors leading to the communication gap (provider gap 4)

Gap 4

Service delivery

• *Lack of integrated services marketing communications*
  Tendency to view each external communication as independent
  Not including interactive marketing in communications plan
  Absence of strong internal marketing program
• *Ineffective management of customer expectations*
  Not managing customer expectation through all forms of communcation
  Not adequately educating customers
• *Overpromising*
  Overpromising in advertising
  Overpromising in personal selling
  Overpromising through physical evidence cues
• *Inadequate horizontal communications*
  Insufficient communication between sales and operations
  Insufficient communication between advertising and operations
  Differences in policies and procedures across branches or units
• *Inappropriate pricing*
  High prices that raise customer expectations
  Prices that are not tied to customer perceptions of value

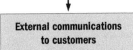

External communications
to customers

16

customer loyalty leads to enhanced brand equity and higher profits. Consequently, understanding customer perceptions is important to an organisation's performance. As such, gap analysis is used as a tool to narrow the gap between perceptions and reality, thus enhancing customer satisfaction (Zeithaml et al., 2009).

16.2.9 Kaizen
Kaizen is a very simple concept, formed of the two Japanese characters 'kai', meaning 'change', and 'zen', meaning 'good'. Therefore, in the business sense 'kaizen' means, 'change for the better', or 'improvement'. The most important proponent of the concept of Kaizen was Deming (see 16.2.5). Kaizen is based on analysing every part of a process down to its smallest detail, seeing how every part of the process can be improved, looking at how employees' actions, equipment, and materials can be improved, and looking at ways of saving time and reducing waste. Kaizen is grounded on the belief that the people doing a particular job often know how that job can be improved better than everyone else, including their

KAI = CHANGE

Kaizen

ZEN = GOOD

Detail

"CHANGE FOR THE BETTER"
Kaizen = Continuous Improvement
by Everybody! Everyday! Everywhere!

superiors; and that they should be given the responsibility for making those improvements. The emphasis in the Kaizen approach is on many small improvements, rather than on quantum leaps (www.michailolidis.gr).

Text 16.6 illustrates some of the little improvements linked to the Kaizen method of quality improvement within the hospitality industry.

TEXT 16.6

The Day Other Countries Teach Japan about Kaizen

How top hotels are slashing costs and boosting customer satisfaction

May 28, 2012 Satoshi Kawashima

Kaizen, or continuous quality improvement, may be treading water in its motherland, but its star is on the rise outside Japan. With decidedly mixed feelings, JBpress Editor in Chief Satoshi Kawashima reports on how ultra-luxury hotel operator Fairmont Raffles Hotels International is using Kaizen to stay best in class.

28% rise in profit

If you've ever been to San Francisco, chances are you've visited the historic Fairmont Hotel with its panoramic hilltop view. If you've been to the Canadian Rockies, you can't have missed the Banff Springs Hotel and the Chateau Lake Louise Hotel.

The Plaza Hotel in New York

One of the unique pleasures of visiting Singapore is to sip a Singapore Sling at the famous Raffles Hotel, and while in London you can't beat chatting over cocktails at the Savoy.

New York wouldn't be the same without the Plaza Hotel, location of the Plaza Accord of 1985, another Japanese surrender, in that it set in course a chain of events that led to Japan's disastrous asset price bubble.

But this isn't a travel article and I haven't chosen those hotels at random. All of them are now run by the same group, Fairmont Raffles Hotels International.

And they all have one other thing in common: they're passionately using Japanese Kaizen techniques with great success.

Never mind cheap hotels whose selling point is cost performance, you can now hear Japanese quality improvement terminology like kaizen and muri, mura and muda (three types of waste) being used even at ultra-luxury overseas hotels.

Business improvement methods invented in Japan may be waning here, but they're on the rise globally. I have mixed feelings: on one hand I'm happy to see Kaizen adopted around the world, but I'm also saddened that Japan's decreased use of it might portend this country's decline.

Since this hotel group began using Kaizen two years ago profits have apparently increased 28%.

They increased efficiency by reducing time spent in meetings and writing e-mails, which led to a sharp reduction in overtime.

They set up a system whereby all staff can do one another's jobs – housekeeping staff can work at front desk, front desk staff can serve as bellboys, and so on. This enables staff to help one another out in peak times for any job type. By standardizing work processes it also leads to improved efficiency and better customer service.

Employees coming up with ideas for improvements are given rewards of 5 to 100 dollars, depending on the idea's effectiveness.

Not surprisingly, staff have come up with many good Kaizen ideas.

Successfully used overseas in other industries too.

Here's a case in point: a housekeeping staff member suggested leaving a reminder to save energy on the key card slots for the electricity, as many guests were leaving one of their key cards in the slot when they went out.

This little tweak dramatically reduced electricity costs.

Another example? Quite a few guests' key cards had stopped working because of exposure to magnets, so the group solved the problem by introducing new key cards with the very latest technologies.

Guests who had to go back down to front desk because their card didn't work were understandably annoyed. This improvement reduced costs and also improved customer service.

This example was announced at the recent 2nd Annual Asian Lean Six Sigma and Process Excellence Summit in Singapore.

Other examples were also presented, such as the global hearing-aid maker that reduced costs and improved its products by introducing Kaizen, and numerous cases of use of Kaizen in hospital management.

Kaizen, it would seem, has spread exceptionally far since its birth in Japan. One summit participant, Kazutoshi Maki, who has written on quality improvement for JBpress before, says Asian people are increasingly interested in Kaizen and product quality initiatives.

As all these examples of Kaizen outside Japan suggest, Japan may soon have to relinquish its position as master to its innovative former apprentices.

(Source: jbpress.ismedia.jp)

16.3 Analytical tools for continuous improvement

There are seven basic tools of quality, first emphasized by Kaoru Ishikawa, a professor of engineering at Tokyo University; they are cause-and-effect diagrams; check sheets; control charts; histograms; Pareto charts; scatter diagrams; and flowcharts. The first six are discussed in this section based on adaptations from Tague (2005); flowcharts have earlier been discussed in Section 13.2.1.

Tools of quality

16.3.1 Cause-and-effect diagram (also called Ishikawa or fishbone diagram)

The cause-and-effect diagram identifies many possible causes of an effect or problem. It can be used to structure a brainstorming session as it helps to immediately sort ideas into useful categories. In designing a cause-and-effect diagram, Tague suggests the following steps and materials:
1 Provide a flipchart or whiteboard and marking pens;

Cause-and-effect

2 Agree on a problem statement (effect). Write it at the centre right of the flipchart or whiteboard. Draw a box around it and draw a horizontal arrow running to it;

3 Brainstorm the major categories of causes of the problem. If this is difficult, use generic headings. For services, the major acceptable clusters are the four Ps (People – management, employees, personnel, customers, suppliers etc., Procedures – methods, Policies – measurements, and Plant – location, technology, materials used and equipment). Note that there are other variations, such as the six Ms (manpower, materials, measurements, Mother Nature – environment, methods and machines) or the four Ss (surroundings, suppliers, systems and skills);
Write the categories of causes as branches of the main arrow;

4 Brainstorm to expose the possible causes of the problem. Ask: 'Why does this happen?' As each idea is given, the facilitator writes it as a branch from the appropriate category. Causes can be written in several places if they relate to several categories;

5 Restate the question 'Why does this happen?' for each cause. Branch sub–causes off from the causes. Continue to ask 'Why?' to generate deeper levels of causes. Layers of branches indicate causal relationships;

6 When the group runs out of initial ideas, focus attention to places on the chart where ideas are few;

7 Lastly, evaluate the outcomes of the cause-and-effect diagram after all participants agree on its content.

Figure 16.15 is a basic example of a cause-and-effect diagram based on the six Ms (manpower, materials, measurements, Mother Nature, method and machines).

FIGURE 16.15 Basic example of a cause-and-effect diagram – six Ms

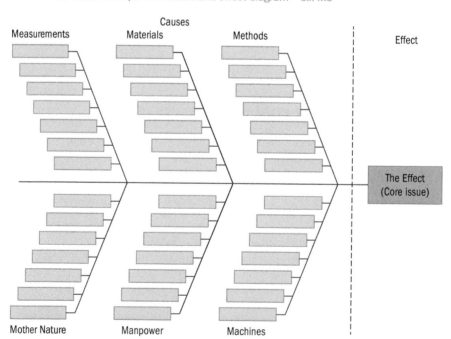

© Noordhoff Uitgevers bv

16.3.2   Check sheet

The check sheet, also called a defect concentration diagram, is a struc-   *Check sheet*
tured, prepared form for collecting and analysing data. It is a generic tool
that can be adapted to a wide variety of purposes, such as when observing
and collecting data repeatedly by employing the same person or using the
same location; when collecting data on the frequency or patterns of events,
problems, defects, defect location, defect causes, etc.; or when collecting
data from a production process. In using check sheets, the following proce-   *Procedure*
dure is suggested:

1 Decide on the event or problem to be observed. Develop operational definitions;
2 Decide when and for how long to collect data;
3 Design the form. Set it up so that data can be recorded by simply ticking
   boxes or using similar methodology so that data does not have to be re-
   copied for analysis;
4 Label all spaces on the form;
5 Test the check sheet for a short trial period to be sure it collects the appropriate data and is easy to use;
6 Record data on the check sheet each time the targeted event or problem
   occurs.

Figure 16.16 is an example of a blank check sheet allowing the user to tick
marks recording the frequency of occurrence of observed events over a certain period of time.

FIGURE 16.16 Blank check sheet sample

Project Name: _____
Name of Data Recorder: _____
Location: _____
Data Collection Dates: _____

Events to be observed	Days							TOTAL
	Sunday	Monday	Tuesday	Wednesday	Thursday	Friday	Saturday	
Event 1								
Event 2								
Event 3								
Event 4								
Event 5								
Event 6								
TOTAL								

16.3.3   Control chart

The control chart, also called the statistical process control chart, is a   *Control chart*
graph that is used to study how a process changes over time, with data
plotted chronologically. A control chart always has a central line for the average value, an upper line for the upper control limit, and a lower line for the
lower control limit. These lines will have been previously determined from
historical data. By comparing current data to these established lines, con-

clusions can be drawn about whether a process variation is consistent ('in control') or is unpredictable ('out of control', affected by special causes of variation). Control charts for variable data are used in pairs, with the top chart monitoring the average value of the distribution of data from the process, and the bottom chart monitoring the range of the distribution. Control charts for attributing data are used singly. Control charts are used:

- When controlling ongoing processes by finding and correcting problems as they occur;
- When predicting the expected range of outcomes from a process;
- When determining whether a process is stable (in statistical control);
- When analysing patterns of process variation from special causes (non-routine events) or common causes (built into the process);
- When determining whether the quality improvement project should aim to prevent specific problems or to make fundamental changes to the process.

A control chart consists of:

- Points representing a statistic (e.g., averages, ranges, proportions) of the measurements of a quality characteristic in samples taken from the process at different times (i.e., the data);
- The mean of this statistic is calculated using the samples;
- A centre line is drawn at the value of the mean of the statistic;
- The standard error (σ) of the statistic is also calculated using the samples;
- The upper control limit (UCL) and the lower control limit (LCL), both of which are sometimes called the 'natural process limits', that indicate the threshold at which the process output is considered statistically unlikely, are drawn typically at 3 standard errors from the centre line.

Basic procedure

In using control charts, the following basic procedure is suggested:

1 Choose the appropriate control chart for the data;
2 Determine the appropriate time period for collecting and plotting data;
3 Collect the data, construct the chart and analyse the data;
4 Look for 'out of control' signals on the control chart. If one is identified, mark it on the chart and investigate the cause. Document how it was investigated, what caused it, how it was corrected, and what was learned. 'Out of control' signals are defined as follows:

Control limits

   - A single point outside the control limits. In Figure 16.17, point 16 is above the UCL.
   - Two out of three successive points are on the same side of the centre line and further away than 2 σ away. In Figure 16.17, point 4 matches that definition.
   - Four out of five successive points are on the same side of the centre line and further away than 1 σ.
   - A run of eight points in a row is on the same side of the centre line. For larger samples, this is 10 out of 11, 12 out of 14, or 16 out of 20. In Figure 16.17, point 21 is eighth in a row above the centre line.
   - Obvious consistent or persistent patterns that suggest something unusual about the data or process.

5 Continue to plot data as it is generated. As each new data point is plotted, check for new 'out of control' signals;
6 When a new control chart is begun, the process may already be out of control. If so, the control limits calculated from the first 20 points are now considered conditional limits. If there are at least 20 sequential

FIGURE 16.17 'Out of control' signals in a control chart

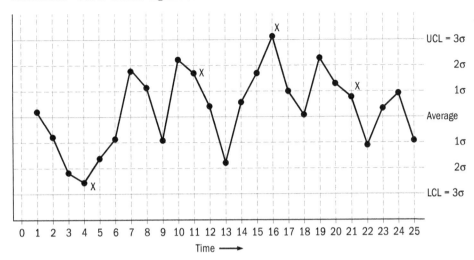

16

points from a period when the process is operating in control, recalculate the control limits.

16.3.4 Histogram

The histogram is a frequency distribution that shows how often each differ-   **Histogram**
ent value occurs in a set of data. A histogram is the most commonly used
graph to show frequency distributions. It looks very much like a bar chart,
but there are important differences between the two. A histogram is to be
used:

- When encountering numerical data;
- When having to visualise the shape of the data's distribution, especially
  when determining whether the output of a process is approximately nor-
  mally distributed;
- When analysing whether a process can meet a customer's requirements;
- When analysing what the output of a supplier's process looks like;
- When seeing whether a process change has occurred from one time pe-
  riod to another;
- When determining whether the output of two or more processes is differ-
  ent;
- When needing to communicate the distribution of the data quickly and
  easily to others.

Typical histogram shapes and their meanings
Normal – this is a common pattern: a bell–
shaped curve known as the 'normal distribution.'
In a normal distribution, points are as likely to occur on one side of the average as on the other,
but it should be noted that there are other distributions that look similar to the normal distribution. Statistical calculations must be used to
prove a normal distribution.

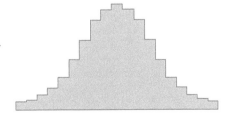

16

Skewed

Skewed – this is an asymmetrical distribution because of a natural limit preventing outcomes on one side. The distribution's peak is off centre towards the limit, and a tail stretches away from it. These distributions are called right– or left–skewed according to the direction of the tail. The sample picture is of a right-skewed distribution.

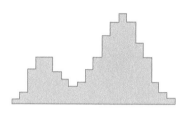

Bimodal

Double-peaked or bimodal – this distribution has two 'humps', similar to a Bactrian camel. The outcomes of two processes with different distributions are combined in one set of data. A distribution of production data from a two-shift operation might be bimodal, for example, if each shift produces a different distribution of results.

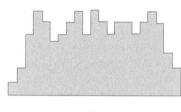

Multimodal

Plateau – this can also be called a multimodal distribution, in which several processes with normal distributions are combined. Because there are many peaks close together, the top of the distribution resembles a plateau.

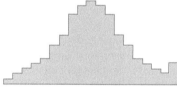

Edge peak

Edge peak – this distribution looks like the normal distribution, except that it has a large peak at one tail. This peak is usually caused by faulty construction of the histogram, with data lumped together into a group labelled 'greater than…'

Comb

Comb – in this distribution, the bars are alternatively tall or short. This distribution often results from rounded-off data and/or an incorrectly constructed histogram. Temperature data rounded off to the nearest 0.2 degrees would show a comb shape, for example, if the bar width for the histogram were 0.1 degree.

Heart-cut

Truncated or heart-cut – this looks like a normal distribution with the tails cut off. In a supply relationship, for example, the supplier may be producing a normal distribution of materials and then relying on inspection to separate what is within specification limits from what is outside of specification limits. The resulting shipments to the customer from inside the specifications limits results in a heart-cut distribution.

© Noordhoff Uitgevers bv

Dog food – this is when results near the average are missing. If a customer receives this kind of distribution, someone else receives a heart cut, and the customer is left with 'dog food,' a dog's dinner of odds and ends left over after its master's meal. Even though what a customer receives is within specifications, the product falls into two clusters: one near the upper specification limit and one near the lower specification limit. This variation often causes problems in the customer process.

Dog food

16

Constructing a histogram

Many basic software programmes can construct a histogram. The following are the steps such a programme uses to construct a histogram. The first step is find the highest and lowest data value in the set of data. From these numbers, the range can be computed by subtracting the minimum value from the maximum value. There is no set rule but, as a rough guide, the range should be divided by five for small sets of data and 20 for larger sets. The results give a class width or bin width, which may have to be rounded up. Once the class width is determined, a class should be selected to include the minimum data value. The class width should be used to produce subsequent classes, stopping when a class that includes the maximum data value is produced.

Construct

After determining the classes, the next step is drafting a table of frequencies. The first column should list the classes in increasing order. The next column should have a tally for each of the classes. The third column is for the count or frequency of data in each class. The final column is for the relative frequency of each class, and indicates what proportion of the data is in that particular class.

The construction of the histogram is now completed by taking the following steps:

Steps

1 Drawing a horizontal line. This is where the classes are denoted;
2 Placing evenly spaced marks along this line that correspond to the classes;
3 Labelling the marks so that the scale is clear, and naming the horizontal axis;
4 Drawing a vertical line just to the left of the lowest class;
5 Choosing a scale for the vertical axis to accommodate the class with the highest frequency;
6 Labelling the marks so that the scale is clear, and naming the vertical axis;
7 Entering bars for each class. The height of each bar should correspond to the frequency of the class at the base of the bar.

It should be noted that, before drawing any conclusions from a histogram related to any process, the process must be carefully verified to establish it was operating normally during the time period studied. If any unusual events affected the process during the time period of the histogram, the analysis of the histogram shape probably cannot be generalised to all time periods.

16.3.5   Pareto chart

A Pareto chart, named after Vilfredo Pareto (1848–1923), is a type of chart that contains both bars and a line graph, where individual values are represented in descending order by bars, and the cumulative total is represented

Pareto chart

16

by the line. In the Pareto chart, the left vertical axis is the frequency of occurrence, but can alternatively represent cost or other important units of measurement. The right vertical axis is the cumulative percentage of the total number of occurrences, total cost, or total of the particular unit of measure. Because the reasons are in decreasing order, the cumulative function is a concave one. The purpose of the Pareto chart is to highlight the most important among a (typically large) set of factors. In quality control, it is often used to represent the most common sources of defects, the highest occurring types of defect, or the most frequent reasons for customer complaints, and so on. The Pareto chart should be used:

Purpose

- When analysing data about the frequency of problems or causes in a process;
- When encountering many problems or causes, and having a need to focus on the most significant;
- When analysing broad causes by looking at their specific components;
- When communicating with others about data.

Steps

The steps in the Pareto chart procedure are:

Step 1 Deciding what categories are to be used to group items;

Step 2 Deciding what measurement is appropriate. Common measurements are frequency, quantity, cost and time;

Step 3 Deciding what period of time the Pareto chart is to cover (one work cycle – one full day – a week or otherwise);

Step 4 Collecting the data, recording the category each time (or assembling data that already exists);

Step 5 Subtotalling the measurements for each category;

Step 6 Determining the appropriate scale for the measurements that have been collected – the maximum value is the largest subtotal from step 5. (If optional steps 8 and 9 below are carried out, the maximum value is the sum of all subtotals in step 5). Mark the scale on the left side of the chart;

Step 7 Constructing and labelling bars for each category – place the tallest at the far left, then the next tallest to its right and so on. If there are many categories with small measurements, they can be grouped as 'other';

(Steps 8 and 9 are optional but are useful for analysis and communication).

Step 8 Calculating the percentage for each category: the subtotal for that category divided by the total for all categories – draw a right vertical axis and label it with percentages, making sure the two scales match: For example, the left measurement that corresponds to one-half should be exactly opposite 50% on the right scale;

Step 9 Calculating and drawing cumulative sums – add the subtotals for the first and second categories, place a dot above the second bar indicating that sum. To that sum, add the subtotal for the third category, and place a dot above the third bar for that new sum. Continue the process for all bars, connecting the dots starting at the top of the first bar. The last dot should reach 100 percent on the right scale.

Pareto chart examples

Figure 16.18 shows how many customer complaints were received in each of five categories during a specific period of time. This is followed by Figure 16.19, which takes the largest category, 'documents', from Figure 16.18, breaks it down into six categories of document-related complaints, and shows the cumulative values. If all complaints cause equal distress to the customer, working on eliminating document-related complaints has the most impact; of those, working on quality certificates would be most fruitful.

FIGURE 16.18 Types of customer complaints in a period

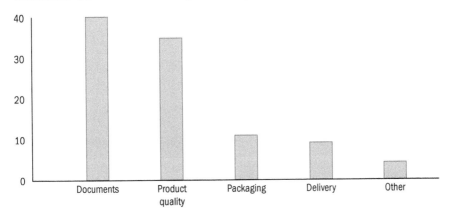

FIGURE 16.19 Types of document complaints for a period

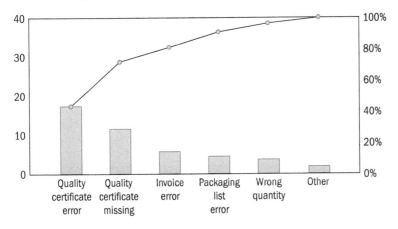

16.3.6   Scatter plot

The scatter plot, also called the 'scatter diagram' or the 'X–Y graph', plots pairs of numerical data, with one variable on each axis, to look for a relationship between them. If the variables are correlated, the points fall along a line or a curve. The better the correlation, the tighter the points hug the line. The scatter plot should be used:

Scatter plot

- When paired numerical data is available;
- When dependent variables may have multiple values for each value of the independent variable; or
- When trying to determine whether two variables are related, such as...
  - when trying to identify potential root causes of problems;
  - after brainstorming causes and effects using a fishbone diagram, to determine
  - objectively whether a particular cause and effect are related;
  - when determining whether two effects that appear to be related both occur with the same cause;
  - when testing for autocorrelation before constructing a control chart.

In designing a scatter diagram, the procedure is:

Step 1 Collecting data – gather 50 to 100 paired samples of data that show a possible relationship;

Step 2 Drawing the diagram – draw roughly equal horizontal and vertical axes of the diagram, creating a square plotting area. Label the axes in convenient multiples (1, 2, 5, etc.) increasing on the horizontal axes from left to right and on the vertical axis from bottom to top. Label both axes;

Step 3 Plotting paired data – plot the data on the chart, using concentric circles to indicate repeated data points;

Step 4 Titling and labelling the diagram;

Step 5 Interpreting data.

Correlations

Scatter diagrams generally show one of six possible correlations between variables:

- Strong positive correlation, in which the value of Y clearly increases as the value of X increases;
- Strong negative correlation, in which the value of Y clearly decreases as the value of X increases;
- Weak positive correlation, in which the value of Y increases slightly as the value of X increases;
- Weak negative correlation, in which the value of Y decreases slightly as the value of X increases;
- Complex correlation, in which the value of Y seems to be related to the value of X, but the relationship is not easily determined;
- No correlation, in which there is no demonstrated connection between the two variables.

It should be noted that, while the diagram shows relationships, it does not by itself prove that the value of one variable has an influence on the other. In addition to possible cause-and-effect relationships, a scatter diagram can show that two variables are from an unknown common cause, or that one variable can be used as a surrogate for the other. Figure 16.20 illustrates various examples of the six possible relationships in scatter diagrams.

FIGURE 16.20 Scatter diagram relationships examples

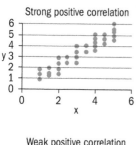

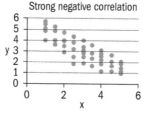

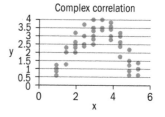

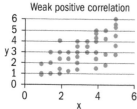

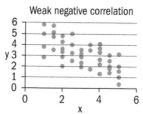

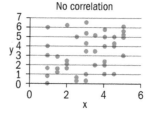

Summary

▶ A quality management system (QMS) is a set of co-ordinated activities for directing and managing an organisation in order to continually improve the effectiveness and efficiency of its performance, ensuring that the requirements of both customers and the organisation are met.

▶ A good QMS should be able to prevent an organisation from slipping down from its own best practices.

▶ Service quality as defined by Zeithaml, Parasuraman, and Berry identifies five service quality dimensions used by consumers to evaluate organisations; these dimensions are tangibles, reliability, responsiveness, assurance, and empathy.

▶ The ISO 9000 group of standards addresses various aspects of quality management and contains some of ISO's best known standards. The standards provide guidance and tools for companies and organisations who want to ensure that products and services consistently meet customer requirements, and that quality is consistently improved. The standards in the ISO 9000 family include ISO 9001:2008, ISO 9000:2005, ISO 9004:2009, and ISO 19011:2011.

▶ The EFQM Excellence Model provides a holistic tool for assessing how effective an organisation is in developing and delivering a stakeholder focussed strategy. Its 2013 revision allows an insight into the cause and effect relationships between what an organisation does and the results it achieves. It consists of fundamental concepts, criteria, and RADAR.

▶ Lean Thinking is a way of focussing on what a customer values and is willing to pay for; any activity that does not add to value as perceived by an end customer is considered waste. This waste includes any use of resources – cost, time, movement, material, energy, water, and labour. Key elements of Lean Thinking include customer-centricity, internal customer–supplier relationships, perfection is the goal, synchronised flow, reduce variation, include all people, and waste elimination. Key drivers for implementing Lean in an organisation are cost reduction, quality improvement, development of efficient processes, and variation reduction.

▶ Six Sigma aims to improve the quality output of any process by identifying and removing causes of any defects (errors) and minimising variability in manufacturing and business processes. It uses a set of quality management methods, mainly empirical statistical methods, and creates a special infrastructure of people within an organisation who are experts in these methods. The projects follow defined sequences of steps and have quantified value targets. Its central idea is that if the number of defects in a process can be measured, it becomes possible to systematically figure out how to eliminate them and get as close to zero defects as possible. There are two methodologies, generally rolled out over the course of many months or even years, each composed of five phases each, the DMAIC, and the DMADV or DFSS.

▶ The PDCA cycle is a continuous quality improvement model made up of a logical sequence of four repetitive steps. It is aimed at the continuous improvement of processes and products, and learning. The PDCA cycle has been modified into the PDSA cycle, the fundamental principle of which is repetition.

▶ BPR involves a radical redesign of core business processes to achieve dramatic improvements in productivity, cycle times and quality. Using BPR, companies start with a blank sheet of paper and rethink existing processes to deliver more value to their customers by typically adopting a new value system that places increased emphasis on customer needs. BPR is controversial because it sometimes only looks at work activities rather than the people performing the work.

▶ HACCP is a management system in which food safety is addressed through the analysis and control of biological, chemical, and physical hazards. The system involves all processes from raw material production, procurement and handling, to manufacturing, distribution and consumption of the finished product. It can be applied throughout the food chain from primary production to final consumption, and its implementation should be guided by scientific evidence of risks to human health. The system has seven principles which are included in the international standard ISO 22000:2005.

▶ The Gaps model of service quality addresses the issues which arise from the very important customer gap and four different service provider gaps. The Gaps model is designed to help in closing customer gaps, which are the listening gap, the service design and standards gap, the service performance gap, and the communication gap. Gap analysis is important to organisations because any gaps between customer expectations and customer experiences lead to customer dissatisfaction.

▶ Kaizen means change for the better, or continuous improvement. It is based on analysing every part of a process down to the smallest detail, seeing how each part of the process can be improved, looking at how employees' actions, equipment, and materials can be improved and, lastly, looking at ways of saving time and reducing waste. It is based on the belief that the people doing a particular job often know better than everyone else, including their superiors, how that job can be improved; and that those people should be given the responsibility for making improvements.

▶ There are seven basic analytical tools for the continuous improvement of quality. They are cause-and-effect diagrams, check sheets, control charts, histograms, Pareto charts, scatter diagrams, and flowcharts.

© Noordhoff Uitgevers bv

Questions and assignments for reflection

1   Discuss why it is necessary for an assessment of quality to be carried out by hospitality organisations, and why a good QMS can be considered as a wedge within organisations.

2   Assess the relevance of the application of ISO standards within hospitality settings based on the cases contained in Text 16.1.

3   What should excellent organisations do in order to be able to satisfy all four results areas of the EFQM excellence model?

4   Compare and contrast Lean Thinking, Six Sigma and BPR. Determine which is best suited for assessing the quality of the services provided by the major departments of a hospitality operation.

5   Why do you think the seven principles of the HAACP have been included in the international standard ISO 22000:2005?

Appendices
Appendix A

Sample SOP for dusting hotel rooms

Housekeeping Department Sample Standard Operating Procedure Dusting of the Hotel Rooms
Dusting doors and windows: • From your caddy basket take a duster. • Fold duster into four folds. • Sprinkle with dusting solution and dust inside and outside of each door, frame and wooden window frames. • For areas which cannot be reached, use a feather duster and remove the dust and cobwebs.
Dusting mirrors and fixtures: • If the mirrors have wooden panels, then dust them. • Wipe the mirrors with a damp cloth or sponge. • Wipe the mirrors again with a clean dry cloth from top downwards • Dust the picture frames with the dusting cloth, and wipe them again with a cloth sprayed with surface cleaner in order to provide a polished finish.
Dusting dressing table and night stands: • Wipe the side, front, edges and top using dusting cloth. • Open the drawer and wipe inside in case the guest has checked-out. • Polish all surfaces using a cloth sprayed with surface cleaner solution.
Wipe and disinfect the telephone: • Pick up the receiver and listen for the dial tone. • Report any issues found on the telephone to the Facility Engineering and Maintenance Department. • Spray disinfectant on the wiping cloth, and wipe the mouthpiece and earphone. • Repeat the same steps on any other room and/or bathroom telephones.
Dusting other furniture: • Remove any items on the table. • Wipe the table surface with a wiping cloth sprayed with surface cleaner. • Start cleaning from the top and work towards the base and legs of the table. • Dust and wipe all the chairs. • Dust all lamp shades, and other fittings.
Dusting LCD TV, I-Pod Dock, and Alarm clock: • Turn off the TV, as it is easier to spot the dirt on the black surface. • For cleaning the LCD screen use, use a soft, clean, lint-free, dry cloth or a microfiber cloth. • Never use cleaning fluids, wax, or chemicals to clean the LCD screen. • Wipe the frames of the TV with the same cloth. • Use a microfiber cloth to clean other electronic gadgets in the room.
General Dusting Tips: • Wipe gently removing dusts and fingerprints. • High dusting that cannot be reached with cloth should be done with a feather brush. • Dusting is done with the A/C on, and main door open for aeration of room. • All areas are dusted with a duster or a feather brush whichever is more appropriate.

Appendix B

- -

Sample hotel room inspection checklist

Room Number			Date	
Room Type				
Housekeeping Spot Checklist	Weight		Room Score	Remarks
Entrance/Hall				
1 Door (locked) and clean/spot free, no kick marks, no cobwebs	1			
2 Electricity in the whole room/light plan	5			
3 'Please do not disturb sign' in right position + red / Emergency plan in hallway	1			
4 Closet and five coat hangers (same direction) + laundry list/bag in the right position	1			
5 Smell in the room	5			
Room				
6 Mirrors, clean and spotless, no dust, no cobwebs	5			
7 Dust in the room, working table, bed head/under the beds, nightstands, lights	4			
8 Desk - 4 Nespresso cups (2 orange & 2 purple), 2 coffee cups, saucers, similar spoons, 4 packets of sugar, 4 packets of sweetener, 4 packets of milk, 3 different kinds of tea. The water boiler, and the Nespresso machine are both dry and clean	5			
9 Chair at the desk, clean	3			
10 Waste basket + lid placed under the table (knot of the bag turned back)	2			
11 Mini bar turned off, information card in the mini bar,	4			
12 Information folder clean and neat, welcome letter/guest ABC/room service card/city map	1			
13 Safe door must be open, and in the safe the safety information on top	3			

14	Curtains in the right position (cover the wall, straight and all hooks intact). Clean window ledge and closed window	2		
15	Heating in room set at Level 2 (September - May), air-conditioning off (18° C), with remote control and information on top of TV	5		
16	Side table: chairs set symmetrically, seat cushions, 2 blue glasses, 2 bottles (still & sparkling) filled to the same level, 1 white tray, nuts and apricots (not too full and covered separately), 3 differently flavored chocolate bars	3		
17	Electric cords out of sight in the whole room (as much as possible)	3		
18	Bed: bedspreads have to be symmetrical, not touching the floor, duvet till top in cover	5		
19	Nightstand lamps are placed symmetrically against beds, seam to the back, telephone notebook and pen (logo is up), alarm clock, (right time and no alarm set). No dust on light bulbs and under glass plate	3		
	Bathroom			
20	No hairs in the bathroom, floor, sink, bath and toilet.	5		
21	No spots in bathroom, shower, bathtub, sink, showerhead, taps. Make sure everything is dry	5		
22	Toilet brush: clean and dry. Toilet: flushed down and clean inside, air freshened	5		
23	Mirrors and shower door, clean and spotless, no dust, no cobwebs	5		
24	Guest supplies: 1 shampoo, 1 shower gel, 1 body lotion, 1 conditioner and 1 soap placed neatly on tray. 1 paper cup next to sink. Guest supplies will be adjusted to the number of guests in the hotel room. 1 Bath crystals in SC rooms and 2 for 2 guests.	5		
25	Towels - 1 small with facecloth, 1 big, 1 bath mat, open side not visible to the guest, folded right. Shower timer placed next to shower. Towels are adjusted to number of guests in the room	5		
26	In SC rooms, the bathrobes are adjusted to the amount of guests in the room	2		
27	Showerhead not full of water	2		
28	Hairdryer is working	4		
29	Heating in bathroom placed on asterisk (*)	1		
	Total	**100**		
	Deduction			
	Final Room Percentage			

Inspected By —————————————————   **Signature** —————————————

Appendix C

Legal alcohol drinking and purchasing ages – Europe (2015)

Country/region	De jure (by law)	
ABV = Alcohol by volume	**Drinking age**	**Purchase age**
Albania	None	18
Armenia	None	18
Austria	16 for beer and wine and 18 for distilled beverages	
Azerbaijan	18	
Belarus	18	
Belgium	None	16 for beer and wine
		18 for spirits
Bosnia and Herzegovina	None	18
Bulgaria	None	18
Croatia	None	18
Cyprus	17	
Czech Republic	None	18
Denmark	None	16 to buy alcohol <16.5% ABV, 18 to buy alcohol >16.5% ABV, 18 to be served in restaurants, bars, discos etc.
Estonia	18	
Finland	18 for possession and purchase of 1.2–22% ABV, 20 for possession and purchase of 23–80% ABV, 18 for all in bars, clubs and restaurants	
France	None	18
Georgia	None	16
Germany	De jure, none but de facto 16 for beer and wine, and 18 for spirits	16 for beer and wine and 18 for spirits
Gibraltar	None	18 or 16 if the alcoholic beverage is beer, wine or cider below 15% ABV, or the alcoholic beverage is served in a bottle, or a pre-packaged container below 5.5% ABV.

Country/region	De jure (by law)	
Greece	18	None
Hungary	18	
Iceland	None	20
Ireland	18	
Italy	None	18
Kosovo	None	18
Latvia	None	18
Liechtenstein	16 for wine, beer and cider, and 18 for spirits and spirit-based beverages.	
Lithuania	18	
Luxembourg	None	16
Macedonia	18	
Malta	17	
Moldova	None	16
Montenegro	None	18
Netherlands	None	18
Norway	None	18 (<22%), 20 (≥22% ABV)
Poland	None	18
Portugal	None	18
Romania	18	
Russia	None	18
Serbia	18	
Slovakia	None	18
Slovenia	None	18
Spain	None	18 overall but 16 in Asturias
Sweden	None (drinking supervised in private 'in moderation')	None (less than 2.25% ABV), 18 (bars and restaurants), 18 (2.25%-3.5% ABV in food shops), and 20 (Systembolaget shops.
Switzerland	None	16 for fermented alcoholic drinks with less than 15% ABV and natural wines with less than 18% ABV; and 18 for spirits.
Turkey	18	
Ukraine	18	
United Kingdom	18	18

Appendix D

Routine Maintenance Checklist
Day 1 of 5 – Routine Maintenance Checklist (HP Hotels)

Day 1 of 5 Routine Maintenance Checklist (HP Hotels)		
Perform these Day One activities, making an entry as each task has been completed		
Tasks	Initials	Date
GROUNDS		
Canopy – Wash down. Check for stains, leaks, and fallen patches.		
Exterior Windows/Railings – Clean. Check condition.		
Exterior Lights – Remove bugs. Check and replace bulbs.		
Exterior Signs Clean. Check condition, attachments.		
Exterior Trash Cans – Check condition, cleanliness.		
Dumpsters – Secure gate. Check cleanliness.		
Satellite Dish – Remove leaves, dirt, etc.		
Parking Lot – Check striping, drains. Perform any sealing, painting.		
Landscaping – Check condition.		
Sprinklers – Turn on and test heads.		
Fencing – Check condition.		
Flag/Flagpole – Check flag, replace flag if tattered or torn.		
ROOF		
General Area – Remove trash, debris.		
General Equipment – Check for leaks, peeling insulation, unwrapped lines.		
Drains – Clear debris. Check for standing water.		
Exhaust Fans/Timer – Check for smooth, quiet operation.		
AC Units – Clean and replace filters.		
Satellite Equipment – Remove debris. Check attachments.		
Exterior Lights – Check for obstructed photocells.		
Mansard Roof Panels – Check condition, attachments, repair as needed.		
Flashing – Check for damage, repair as needed.		

Day 2 of 5 – Routine Maintenance Checklist (HP Hotels)

Day 2 of 5 Routine Maintenance Checklist (HP Hotels)		
Perform these Day Two activities, making an entry as each task has been completed		
Tasks	Initials	Date
HALLWAYS, WALKWAYS, STAIRWELLS		
Begin on top floor and work your way down.		
Stairwell Doors – Check closing, security, condition.		
Stairwell – Check handrails, cleanliness, condition.		
Emergency/Exit Lights – Dust and clean. Operate in test mode. Check bulbs, attachment.		
Sprinklers – Check for leaks, insects, other hazards.		
Fire Extinguishers – Check cabinet for chips, cleanliness. Check charge, annual inspection date.		
Hallway Signs – Check placement and attachments.		
Lights/Light Covers – Remove bugs, debris. Check and replace bulbs and covers.		
Ceilings – Check for chips and marks (possible leaks), cleanliness.		
Walls – Check for chipped paint, torn vinyl, nicks.		
Electrical Outlets/Switch plates – Check for cracks, looseness.		
Doors/Frames – Check for smooth operation. Check for chipped paint, tarnished or loose doorknobs.		
Baseboards – Check for stains, damage, wear.		
Carpet – Check for loose threads, worn seams, burns, stains.		
Vending Area – Check floors, cleanliness, condition. Remove any lime deposits.		
Vending Machines – Check operation. Call vendor if repairs necessary.		
Ice Machines – Check water connections, drains, ice production, cleanliness. Remove any lime deposits.		
SWIMMING POOL AND SPA		
Fencing, Decking and Pool Cover – Check condition, cleanliness.		
Door – Inspect security, verify self-closing and catching correctly.		
Telephone – Verify automatic ring to switchboard.		
Chemicals, Filtration and Draining – Check operation (in season), verify daily records.		
Furniture – Check cleanliness, condition.		
Life Safety Equipment, Signage – Verify condition, cleanliness.		

© Noordhoff Uitgevers bv

Day 3 of 5 – Routine Maintenance Checklist (HP Hotels)

Day 3 of 5 Routine Maintenance Checklist (HP Hotels)		
Perform these Day Three activities, making an entry as each task has been completed		
Tasks	**Initials**	**Date**
STORAGE AREAS		
Walls – Check for chips, marks.		
Floors – Check cleanliness, wax condition. Remove obstructions.		
Electrical Panel – Check for security, accurate labeling, and lockout/tag out materials.		
Ozone Machines – Check filter cleanliness, condition.		
HOUSEKEEPING DEPARTMENT		
Doors, Walls and Floors – Check cleanliness, condition.		
Dryers – Remove any lint. Clean outside vent cover. Check cleanliness behind dryers. Check for sufficient combustion air and make up air. If you see red flames, shut down dryers.		
Washers – Check behind washer for drain debris, water leaks. Check chemicals. Check supply lines for detergent flow.		
Linen Chute – Check door attachment, floor chutes for locks.		
Fire Extinguisher – Check charge, annual inspection date.		
First Aid Kit – Check and replace supply levels, expiration dates. Replace out of date supplies.		
Hall/Sidewalk – Wash down area.		
ELEVATOR		
Call Panels – Check lights, operation.		
Doors – Check for scratches.		
Telephone – Check for operation. Verify automatic ring to switchboard.		
Lights – Clean covers. Check for operation, replace bulbs if necessary.		
Elevator Tracks – Check cleanliness.		
EMPLOYEE BREAKROOM		
Restrooms – Check condition, cleanliness supplies, operation of all facilities.		
Flooring – Check condition, cleanliness, repair as needed.		
Furnishings – Check condition, cleanliness, repair as needed		

Day 4 of 5 – Routine Maintenance Checklist (HP Hotels)

Day 4 of 5 Routine Maintenance Checklist (HP Hotels)		
Perform these Day Four activities, making an entry as each task has been completed		
Tasks	**Initials**	**Date**
PUMP ROOM		
Pressure Gauges – Check system pressure, suction pressure gauges on water pressure devices set at manufacturer recommendations.		
ELECTRICAL ROOMS		
Entire Room – Keep clear, clean and free of debris.		
Breakers – Check for heat. If any, notify electrician. Check for tripped breakers. Investigate any that are tripped.		
BOILER ROOM		
Boiler – Check operation. Verify temperatures to manufacturer specifications.		
Exhaust Fans/Vents – Check operation.		
Heater – Check operation in winter.		
Circulating Pump – Check operation.		
MAINTENANCE SHOP		
Floor/Counters – Check neatness, organization.		
Flammables – Check for proper storage.		
Fire Extinguisher – Check charge, annual inspection date.		
Spare Room Keys – Check security.		
HOTEL VAN		
Interior – Check cleanliness, condition.		
Exterior – Check cleanliness, condition.		
General Maintenance – Ensure oil changes and tune-ups have been conducted on a regular basis. Check tire tread, air conditioning and belts. Make sure state inspection and license tag is up-to-date.		

Day 5 of 5 – Routine maintenance checklist (HP Hotels)

Day 5 of 5 Routine Maintenance Checklist (HP Hotels)		
Perform these Day Five activities, making an entry as each task has been completed. Use the Day One Maintenance Checklist next time.		
Tasks	**Initials**	**Date**
LOBBY		
Ceilings – Check for chips and marks (possible leaks), cleanliness.		
Lights – Check and replace bulbs. Check condition, cleanliness.		
Emergency Lights – Check operation, attachment.		
Ceiling Fans – Clean. Check operation.		
Walls – Check for chipped paint, torn vinyl, nicks, condition of wood.		
Door Handles/Railings – Check condition, attachment.		
Brass Fixtures – Check condition, shine.		
Draperies – Check for sun stains, loose hooks.		
Furniture – Check for tears, stains, wear.		
Laminates – Check attachment, condition.		
Luggage Carts – Check operation, condition.		
Telephones – Check dial tone on pay and house phones.		
Public Restrooms – Check cleanliness, fixture operation, condition, supplies.		
Water Fountain – Check water flow, condition. Clear drain. Remove any lime deposits.		
Air Conditioner Filters – Check condition. Clean.		
Carpet – Check for stains, burns, loose threads, worn seams.		
Tiles – Check grout, condition, cleanliness. Repair/replace any loose, chipped.		
Rugs – Check condition, cleanliness.		
PANTRY		
Cabinets – Check for loose hinges, marks, chips.		
Refrigerator/Freezer – Check cleanliness, temperature level.		
Sink – Check operation, cleanliness. Remove any lime deposits.		

Day 5 of 5 Routine Maintenance Checklist (HP Hotels)		
OFFICE		
Electrical Panels – Check for tripped breakers. Investigate any that are tripped.		
Air Conditioning – Check operation to protect computer equipment.		
Laminates – Check condition, attachment.		
Carpets – Check for cleanliness, loose threads, worn seams.		
EXERCISE ROOM		
Doors, Walls and Floors – Check cleanliness, condition.		
Lights – Check, replace bulbs, condition, cleanliness.		
Shelving – Check condition, cleanliness.		
Equipment – Check condition, operation.		
Telephone – Test functionality, automatic ring to switchboard.		
Television/Remote – Check condition, operations.		
EXECUTIVE CENTER		
Door, Walls and Floors – Check cleanliness, condition.		
Furnishings – Check cleanliness, condition.		
Office Equipment – Check cleanliness, condition.		
GUEST LAUNDRY		
Doors, Walls and Floors – Check cleanliness, condition.		
Dryer – Remove any lint, clean outside vent cover, check combustion behind dryers, and check for sufficient combustion air and make-up air.		
Washer – Check behind washer for drain debris, water leaks.		
Folding Table – Check for condition, cleanliness.		
FRONT DESK		
Furnishings – Check cleanliness, condition.		
Computer Equipment – Check cleanliness, connections.		
Wall Covering – Check for condition, cleanliness.		
Telephone – Check for cleanliness, functionality.		
Key Card Machine – Functionality.		
Safe Deposit Boxes – Make sure all keys accounted for, guard key in good condition.		

Appendix E

Principal hotel-specific laws in some European countries related to health and safety.

Principal Hotel-specific Laws in Europe related to Health and Safety	
Austria	Requisite permits under the Austrian Industrial Codes and the building permit impose specific conditions on health and safety. Additionally local fire & safety laws apply. Operators have to comply with these rules.
Belgium	Each region has its own hotel fire and safety regulations which require the production of a safety certificate prior to opening a hotel. Precise security norms have to be respected regarding fire protection, lift, electricity, gas, means of access and exit, etc. The certificate is only valid for 5 years. The local municipality is responsible for the issue and control of the certificate. A licence to operate a hotel is not granted without a valid safety certificate. Other rules apply to swimming pools and spas.
Bulgaria	There are detailed rules and regulations promulgated by the Bulgarian State Agency of Tourism and the Ministry of Regional Development & Public Works applicable to all hotels. Rules must be complied with both as to the construction and the subsequent operation of the hotel. Health and safety conditions must meet the special needs of people with disabilities in compliance with statute, which requires non-discrimination against people with disabilities including through the provision of a barrier-free living environment and easy access.
Croatia	Detailed rules and regulations regarding health and safety (fire protection, health standards, heating, noise protection, etc.) apply under the laws and byelaws for tourism and construction. Rules must be complied with both as to the construction and subsequent operation of the hotel. Pursuant to Croatian byelaws, all new buildings categorised as hotels have to be designed for guests with special needs (i.e. entrances, communications, sanitary arrangements). Entrances and elevators have to be marked with braille signs.
Czech Republic	Hotels are required to have an operational plan stipulating rules for the prevention of infection and other diseases, the manner of working with linen and cleaning processes. The plan must be approved by the health authority. Hotels adjacent to lakes used for swimming are obliged to check quality of water by a certified person and report the findings to the relevant health authority. Approximately 1% of a hotel's rooms (with a minimum of 1) must be designed for use by disabled persons. The same disabled access construction rules apply to hotels as to other buildings open to the public.
France	The employer must ensure that the work place is clean and sanitary, and in compliance with specific regulations as to heat, lighting, noise, sanitation and meals etc. There are generally applicable health and safety obligations. Additional health and safety measures are imposed on certain types of businesses to ensure employees' protection (in particular for employees lodged by the company in staff accommodation). Specific internal rules and regulations comprising health and safety measures must be drafted by the employer if it employs more than 20 individuals. A Health and Safety Committee is mandatory in any establishment where 50 persons have been employed during a continuous or discontinuous period of 12 months over the previous 3 years. Non-compliance with the health and safety regulations may trigger the personal liability of the employer and since 1 January 2006, the criminal liability of any company employer i.e. the corporate entity (*personne morale*). General fire protection and safety provisions for establishments accessible by the pubic are applicable to hotels which are classified under type O in the Construction and Housing Code. Regulations are applicable to the construction and refurbishment as well as the subsequent operation of hotels.
Germany	Fire & safety law applies. Operating companies must comply with these rules as to the construction, refurbishment and operation of the hotel.

Principal Hotel-specific Laws in Europe related to Health and Safety	
Hungary	No specific rules are applicable to hotels.
Italy	Hotel management must exercise reasonable care in the health and safety aspects of the hotel premises for the benefit of their guests. Management must ensure the cleanliness of premises and rooms. It must ensure fire safety for the protection of lodging guests. In particular, careful and regular evaluation of the fire alarm, sprinkler, and extinguishing systems, fire prevention and containment, safe and adequate egress, electrical safety and employee training in fire safety must all be undertaken. Maintenance and inspections of heating and air-conditioning systems must also be carried out regularly so as to ensure appropriate indoor air quality. Hotels are also required to identify and evaluate safety and health hazards so as to implement mitigation remedies and programmes. Pursuant to public places anti-smoking legislation, hotel common areas (e.g. lobby, restaurant, convention hall, etc.) must be smoke-free. Smoking is only allowed in special sealed-off areas fitted with smoke extractors and inside hotel suites reserved for smoking guests. Hotels are also required to ensure good disabled access facilities and to remove any physical barriers making it difficult for disabled users to access hotel premises and services.
Netherlands	General fire & safety laws apply. These general regulations must be complied with on the construction, refurbishment and operation of a hotel. There are no specific rules as to disabled access (which are covered by the general rules).
Poland	The Ministry of Economics and Labour has issued detailed rules applicable to all hotels. Rules must be complied with both during the construction and subsequent operation of a hotel. Hotel operators may, for the purpose of ensuring order and the safety of guests and their property, issue regulations binding on all persons. There are detailed rules applicable to all hotels with respect to adaptation of the buildings to the needs of the disabled.
Romania	General fire protection provisions are applicable to hotels. A fire prevention authorisation is part of the documentation filed by the hotel in order to obtain the classification certificate.
Russia	General fire & safety rules apply to hotels with certain specific features. For instance hotel rooms may not accommodate any facilities intended for using or storing explosive or inflammable substances or materials; and fire escape plans must be posted in hotel rooms. Certain additional health requirements are imposed on hotels. For example, hotel personnel must undergo initial and subsequent regular medical examinations.
Slovakia	Health and safety laws provide for connection to cold and hot potable water, room area requirements, room clearance requirements, room equipment, personal hygiene equipment, ventilation arrangements, installation of fire alarm, corridor width, etc. Disabled access: Existing buildings must have at least one entrance without steps and a slope from street to hotel level. For new buildings the main entrance must comply with this requirement.
Spain	There are detailed rules and regulations approved by the Ministry of Industry and by Regional Authorities applicable to hotels. There are rules governing certain items such as the size on the rooms and the supply of specific services by hotels, depending of their category. There are specific rules as to disabled access in relation to installations to existing buildings and governing the construction of new buildings for public use. Hotels must adapt their structures to accord to the fire and escape plans published by Regional Tourism Authorities.
Switzerland	Fire and safety laws apply. Certain Cantons have requirements for non-smoking areas. In most Cantons there are price regulations for beverages (e.g. at least 3 non-alcoholic beverages have to be offered at a lower price than the cheapest alcoholic beverage). The construction and renewal of publicly accessible buildings such as hotels and restaurants must meet the requirement of disabled access to the building and the facilities within (e.g., toilets, lifts, etc.).
United Kingdom	The hotel should carry out a fire risk assessment for the purpose of identifying fire precautions that it needs to take to comply with the Fire Regulations. From July 2007, smoking was banned in all enclosed public areas, including all public areas in hotels. Rooms are excluded from 'public areas' and may be designated as smoking rooms, but only if they do not share a ventilation system with non-smoking rooms. Where the hotel draws water from a private water supply, it must ensure that the water meets certain minimum qualitative standards and register the supply with the local authority.
	Adapted from the CMS Guide to Principal Hotel-Specific Laws in Europe, 2007

Appendix F

Organisational culture assessment instrument (OCAI)

		The Organisational Culture Assessment Instrument - Current Profile	Now	Preferred
		1. Dominant Characteristics		
1A		The organisation is a very personal place. It is like an extended family. People seem to share a lot of themselves.		
1B		The organisation is a very dynamic and entrepreneurial place. People are willing to stick their necks out and take risks.		
1C		The organisation is very results-oriented. A major concern is with getting the job done. People are vey competitive and achievement-oriented.		
1D		The organisation is a very controlled and structured place. Formal procedures generally govern what people do.		
		Total	100	100
		2. Organisational Leadership		
2A		The leadership in the organisation is generally considered to exemplify mentoring, facilitating, or nurturing.		
2B		The leadership in the organisation is generally considered to exemplify entrepreneurship, innovation, or risk taking.		
2C		The leadership in the organisation is generally considered to exemplify a no-nonsense, aggressive, results-oriented focus.		
2D		The leadership in the organisation is generally considered to exemplify coordinating, organising, or smooth-running efficiency.		
		Total	100	100
		3. Management of Employees		
3A		The management style in the organisation is characterised by teamwork, consensus, and participation.		
3B		The management style in the organisation is characterised by individual risk taking, innovation, freedom, and uniqueness.		
3C		The management style in the organisation is characterised by hard-driving competitiveness, high demands, and achievement.		
3D		The management style in the organisation is characterised by security of employment, conformity, predictability, and stability in relationships.		
		Total	100	100

Organisational culture assessment instrument (OCAI) (*continued*)

	The Organisational Culture Assessment Instrument - Current Profile	Now	Preferred
	4. Organisation Glue		
4A	The glue that holds the organisation together is loyalty and mutual trust. Commitment to this organisation runs high.		
4B	The glue that holds the organisation together is commitment to innovation and development. There is an emphasis on being on the cutting edge.		
4C	The glue that holds the organisation together is the emphasis on achievement and goal accomplishment.		
4D	The glue that holds the organisation together is formal rules and policies. Maintaing a smooth-running organisation is important.		
	Total	**100**	**100**
	5. Strategic Emphases		
5A	The organisation emphasises human development. High trust, openness, and participation persist.		
5B	The organisation emphasises aquiring new resources and creating new challenges. Trying new things and prospecting for opportunities are valued.		
5C	The organisation emphasises competitive actions and achievement. Hitting stretch targets and winning in the marketplace are dominant.		
5D	The organisation emphasises permanence and stability. Efficiency, control, and smooth operations are important.		
	Total	**100**	**100**
	6. Criteria of Success		
6A	The organisation defines success on the basis of the development of human resources, teamwork, employee commitment, and concern for people.		
6B	The organisation defines success on the basis of having the most unique or newest products. It is a product leader and innovator.		
6C	The organisation defines success on the basis of winning in the marketplace and outpacing the competition. Competitive market leadership is key.		
6D	The organisation defines success on the basis of efficiency. Dependable delivery, smooth scheduling, and low-cost production are critical.		
	Total	**100**	**100**

About the editor and authors

The following authors have contributed to this book edited by M. N. Chibili.

Michael N. Chibili is a senior lecturer at the Stenden Hotel Management School – Stenden University of Applied Sciences, Leeuwarden, the Netherlands. He holds a BSc and an MSc in Economics from the University of Yaoundé, Cameroon, and also an MA in International Service Management from CHN/London Metropolitan University. He is equally a researcher at the Academy of International Hospitality Research – Stenden University of Applied Sciences, Leeuwarden, the Netherlands.

Professor **Conrad Lashley** is a research fellow at the Academy of International Hospitality Research – Stenden University of Applied Sciences, Leeuwarden, the Netherlands. He is Editor for Taylor and Francis' *Hospitality, Leisure and Tourism* series of books, Editor Emeritus for the *Hospitality & Society* Journal, as well as co-editor for *Research in Hospitality Management*. He is the author or editor of sixteen books, including *In Search of Hospitality: theoretical perspectives and debates*, and *Hospitality: a social lens*.

Dr **Bill Rowson** is a senior lecturer at the Stenden Hotel Management School – Stenden University of Applied Sciences, Leeuwarden, the Netherlands. He holds a BA (Hons) in Business Studies from the University of Wolverhampton and a Ph.D. in Employee Relations – Impact of NMW on Small Independent Hotels, from Manchester Metropolitan University. He is equally a researcher at the Academy of International Hospitality Research – Stenden University of Applied Sciences, Leeuwarden, the Netherlands.

Saskia M. Penninga is a lecturer at the Stenden Hotel Management School – Stenden University of Applied Sciences, Leeuwarden, the Netherlands. She holds a Bachelor in Hotel Management from CHN University, Leeuwarden, the Netherlands, and an MA in International Service Management from Stenden University of Applied Sciences/London Metropolitan University. Before commencing her teaching career, she worked and held management positions in the hotel industry, mainly in the Rooms Department, for several years.

Shane de Bruyn is a practical instructor at the service departments of Stenden Hotel, which is part of the Stenden Hotel Management School – Stenden University of Applied Sciences, Leeuwarden, the Netherlands. He holds a Bachelor in Hotel Management from CHN University, Leeuwarden, the Netherlands. He is a wine connoisseur and has worked in different Food and Beverage management positions in various hotels and restaurants.

Latifa Benhadda is a lecturer at the Stenden Hotel Management School –
Stenden University of Applied Sciences, Leeuwarden, the Netherlands. She
has a BA in English Studies from the University of Moulay Ismail, Morocco, a
BBA in International Hospitality Management from CHN University, as well
as an MA in International Service Management from Stenden University of
Applied Sciences/London Metropolitan University.

References

Abbott, P. & Lewry, S. (1999). *Front office: Procedures, social skills, yield and management* (2nd ed.). Oxford: Butterworth-Heinemann.

AHMA-FMC (1997). *Hotel Internal Control Guide*, Educational Institute – American Hotel and Motel Association, Lansing, Michigan.

Agyemang-Duah, P., Aikins, I., Asibey, O. & Broni, A. O. (2014). Evaluating the impact of outsourcing of non-core functions in the hotel industry, *European Journal of Business Innovation Research*, 2(3), 25-45.

Albrecht, K. (2006). *Social intelligence: The new science of success*. San Francisco: Jossey-Bass.

Alfirevic, A. M., Peronja, I. & Plazibat, I. (2013). Business excellence in Croatian hotel industry: Results of empirical research, Chapter 38 in DAAAM International Scientific Book 2013, pp. 655-664, B. Katalinic & Z. Tekic (Eds.), Published by DAAAM International, ISBN 978-3-901509-94-0, ISSN 1726-9687, Vienna, Austria. DOI:10.2507/daaam.scibook.2013.38.

Allen, N. J. & Meyer, J. P. (1996). Affective, continuance, and normative commitment to the organization: an examination of construct validity. *Journal of Vocational Behavior, 49*, 252-276.

Allen, N. J. & Meyer, J. P. (2000). Construct validation in organizational behavior research: The case of organizational commitment. In R. D. Goffin & E. Helmes (Eds.), *Problems and solutions in human assessment: Honouring Douglas N. Jackson at seventy*, 285-314. Norwell, MA, Kluwer.

Anderson, V. (2007). *The value of learning: From return on investment to return on expectation*. London: Chartered Institute of Personnel and Development.

Armstrong, M. (2006). *Performance management: Key strategies and practical guidelines*. 3rd ed. London: Kogan Page.

Armstrong, M. (2012). *Handbook of reward management practice: Improving performance through reward*. London: Kogan Page.

Baker, S., Huyton, J. & Bradley, P. (2000). *Principles of hotel front office operations* (2nd ed.). London: Cengage Learning EMEA.

Ball, S., Rimmington, M. & Rowson, B. (2007). Independent restaurants in Sheffield: Current practices and trends in food procurement. A report for EAT Sheffield, published by the Centre for International Hospitality Management Research: Sheffield Hallam University. June 2007.

Bardi, J. A. (2011). *Hotel front office management* (5th ed.). Hoboken: John Wiley & Sons, Inc.

Beer, M. & Nohria, N. (Eds.). (2000). *Breaking the code of change*. Boston: Harvard Business School Press.

Berry, L. L. (1999). *Discovering the soul of service: The nine drivers of sustainable business success*. New York: The Free Press.

Borkar, S. & Koranne, S. (2014). Study of service quality management in hotel industry. *Pacific Business Review International, 6*(9) 21-25.

Brislin, R., Worthley, R. & MacNab, B. (2006). Cultural intelligence: Understanding behaviors that serve people's goals. *Group and Organization Management, 31*(1), 40-55.

636

Brymer, R. A. & Johanson, M. M. (2011). Hospitality: An introduction. Dubuque: Kendall Hunt Publishing Company.

Burgess, C. (2013). Factors influencing middle managers' ability to contribute to corporate entrepreneurship. *International Journal of Hospitality Management, 32,* 193–201. *Business Review International, 6*(9) 21-25.

Callan, R. J. & Fearon, R. (1997). Townhouse hotels: An emerging sector, *International Journal of Contemporary Hospitality Management, 9*(4), 168-175.

Caluwé, L. de & Vermaak, H. (2003). *Learning to change. A guide for organizational change agents.* Thousand Oaks: Sage Publications, Inc.

Cameron, K. S. & Quinn, R. E. (2006). *Diagnosing and changing organizational culture: Based on the competing values framework,* (Revised ed.). San Francisco: Jossey-Bass.

Campbell, J. P., Brownas, E. A., Peterson, N. G. & Dunnette, M. D. (1974). *The measurement of organizational effectiveness: A review of relevant research and opinion.* Minneapolis: Navy Personnel Research and Development Center, Personnel Decisions.

Cannell, M. (1997). Practice makes perfect. *People Management, 6* March: 26-33.

Casado, M. (2012). *Housekeeping management* (2nd ed.). Hoboken: John Wiley & Sons, Inc.

Chibili, M. N. (2016). *Basic Management Accounting for the Hospitality Industry* (2nd ed.). Groningen/Houten: Noordhoff Uitgevers.

Chung-Herrera, B., Enz, C. & Lankau, M. (2003). Grooming future hospitality leaders: A competencies model, *Cornell Hotel and Restaurant Administration Quarterly, 44*(3), 17-25.

CIPD (2011). *Learning and talent development report.* London: Chartered Institute of Personnel and Development.

CIPD (2015). *Learning to work survey, March, 2015,* London: Chartered Institute of Personnel and Development.

Clifton, D. (2012). Hospitality security: *Managing, security in today's hotel, lodging, entertainment, and tourism environment.* Boca Raton: CRC Press.

Connolly, D. & Haley, M. G. (2008). Information technology strategy in the hospitality industry. In B. Brotherton & R. C. Wood (Eds.), *The Sage Handbook of Hospitality Management.* London: Sage Publications.

Council of Supply Chain Management Professionals (2015). *CSCMP's Definition of Supply Chain Management.* Available at: http://cscmp.org/about-us/supply-chain-management-definitions (accessed 11/08/2015).

Davenport, T. (1995) Reengineering – the fad that forgot people, *Fast Company.* Available at: http://www.fastcompany.com/26310/fad-forgot-people (accessed 14/08/2015).

Dessler, G. (2013). *Human resource management* (13th ed.). Boston: Pearson.

Development Economics (2015). The value of soft skills to the UK economy: A report prepared for McDonalds UK. January. London: Development Economics.

Diehl, T. M. (1973). Computers in hotels – 1973. *Cornell Hotel and Restaurant Administration Quarterly, 1973, 13*(4), 2-23.

Earley, P. C. & Ang, S. (2003). *Cultural intelligence: Individual interactions across cultures.* Stanford: Stanford University Press.

Earley, P. C. & Mosakowski, E. (2004). Cultural Intelligence, *Harvard Business Review,* October, 1-8.

Edelenbos, J. & van Buuren, R. (2005). The learning evaluation: A theoretical and empirical exploration. *Evaluation Review, 29:* 591-612.

Elliott Mest, C. (2015). Technology, segmentation speed hotel operations evolution, *Hotel Management, 230*(9), 35-36.

Ergün, E. & Tasgit, Y. E. (2013). Cultures of adhocracy, clan, hierarchy and market and innovation performance: a case of hotels in Turkey, *Journal of Travel and Tourism Research (Online), 13*(1/2).

Ferdows, K. & de Meyer, A. (1990). Lasting improvement in manufacturing: in search of a new theory. *Journal of Operations Management 9*(2): 168–184.

Forgacs, G. (2010). *Revenue management: Maximizing revenue in hospitality operations.* Lansing: American Hotel & Lodging Educational Institute.

Ganaie, M. Y. & Mudasir, H. (2015). A study of social intelligence and academic achievement of college students of District Srinagar, J & K, India, *Journal of American Science, 11* (3), 23-27.

Gilmore, S. & Williams, S. (2013). *Human resource management* (2nd ed.). Oxford: OUP

Goleman, D. (1995). Emotional intelligence: Why it can matter more than IQ. New York: Bantam Books Inc.

Goleman, D. (1998). What makes a leader? *Harvard Business Review, 76*(6), 93-102.

Goleman, D. (2006). *Social intelligence: the new science of human relationships.* New York: Bantam Books Inc.

Guerci, M. & Vinante, M. (2011). Training evaluation: An analysis of the stakeholders' evaluation needs'. *Journal of European Industrial Training, 35*(4): 385-410.

Gunnarsson, J. & Blohm, O. (2003) *Hostmanship: The art of making people feel welcome.* Stockholm: Dialogos Förlag.

Hackman, J. R., Oldham, G., Janson, R. & Purdy, K. (1975). A new strategy for job enrichment. *California Management Review, 17*(4) 57-71.

Hammer, M. & Champy, J. A. (1993). *Reengineering the corporation: A manifesto for business revolution.* New York: Harper Business Books.

Harvard Business Review Staff (2004). Leading by feel, *Harvard Business Review, 82*(1) 27.

Hayes, D. K. & Miller, A. A. (2011). *Revenue management for the hospitality industry.* Hoboken: John Wiley & Sons Inc.

Hayes, D. K. & Ninemeier, J. D. (2005), *Hotel operations management.* Upper Saddle River: Pearson Education Limited.

Hayes, D. K. & Ninemeier, J. D. (2007), *Hotel operations management* (2nd ed.). Upper Saddle River: Pearson Prentice Hall.

Hensens, W. (2001). *Classifying the Melati hotels: A study of the classification of the Melati hotels in Yogyakarta, Indonesia.* (Unpublished Master of Arts Dissertation, University of North London).

Hensens, W., Struwig, M. & Dayan, O. (2011). Do social media display correct conventional hotel ratings? *Research in Hospitality Management 2011, 1*(1): 9–17. DOI: 10.2989/ RHM.2011.1.1.4.1094.

Herzberg, F., Mausner, B., Peterson, R. O. & Capwell, D. F. (1957). *Job attitudes: Review of research and opinion.* Pittsburgh, PA: Psychological Service of Pittsburgh.

Hiatt, J. M. & Creasey, T. J. (2003). *Change management: The people side of change.* Loveland: Prosci Learning Center Publications.

Holt, D. T., Armenakis, A. A., Feild, H. S. & Harris, S. G. (2007). Readiness for organizational change: The systematic development of a scale. *The Journal of applied behavioral science, 43*(2), 232-255.

Hope Hailey, V. & Balogun, J. (2002). Devising context sensitive approaches to change: The example of Glaxo Wellcome, *Long Range Planning 35*(2), 153–178.

Hotel Association of New York City, Inc. (2014). *Uniform system of accounts for the lodging industry* (11th ed.). Lansing: American Hotel and Lodging Educational Institute.

Hotel Energy Solutions (2011). Analysis on energy use by European hotels: Online survey and desk research. Hotel Energy Solutions project publications.

Hotel Proprietors Ordinance (1997). To amend the law relating to inns and innkeepers, Cap. 158, Hong Kong.

Incomes Data Service (2011). Performance management. *IDS HR Studies, 936.*

Ielacqua, L. & Smith, T. (2012). Hotel contracts: To lease or not to lease. London: *HVS.*

Industrial Relations Services (2009). Using corporate websites for recruitment: the 2009 survey, *IRS Review.*

James, T. (2011). *Operations strategy.* Bookboon.com.

Jansen, A. M. (2008). *Rooms division management.* Meppel: Edu'Actief.

Johnson, G. (1992). Managing strategic change: strategy, culture and action, *Long Range Planning, 25*(1), 28-36.

Johnson, J. P., Lenartowicz, T. & Apud, S. (2006). Cross-cultural competence in international business: Toward a definition and a model. *Journal of International Business Studies, 37* (4) 525-543.

Johnston, R., Clark, G. & Shulver, M. (2012*). Service operations management: Improving service delivery* (4th ed.). Harlow: Pearson Education Limited.

Judge, T. A., Thoresen, C. J., Pucik, V. & Welbourne, T. M. (1999). Managerial coping with organizational change, *Journal of Applied Psychology, 84*(1), 107-122.

Kapiki, S. (2011). Energy management in hospitality: A study of the Thessaloniki1 Hotels. *Institute of Organization and Management in Industry* (ORGMASZ).

Kaplan, R. & Norton, D. (1996). *The balanced scorecard: Translating strategy into action,* Boston, MA: Harvard Business School Press.

Kasavana, M. L. & Brooks, R. M. (2009). *Managing front office operations* (8th ed.). Lansing: American Hotel & Lodging Educational Institute.

Kasper, H., Helsdingen, P. & Gabbot, M. (2006). *Services Marketing Management, (*2nd ed.). Chichester: John Wiley and Sons Ltd.

Kaufmann, T. J., Lashley, C. & Schreier, L. A. (2009). *Timeshare management: The key issues of hospitality managers*. Oxford, UK: Butterworth-Heinemann.

Kennerly, M. & Bourne, M (2003). *Assessing and maximizing the impact of measuring business performance.* Cranfield: Centre for Business Performance, Cranfield School of Management.

Kiefer, T. (2005). Feeling bad: Antecedents and consequences of negative emotions in ongoing change. *Journal of Organizational Behavior, 26*(8), 875-897.

Klosse, P. (2004). *The concept of flavour styles to classify flavor*. Hoog Soeren, Netherlands: Academie voor Gastronomie.

Kotler, P. & Armstrong, G. (2013). *Principles of Marketing* (14th ed.). Boston: Pearson Prentice Hall.

Kotter, J. P. (1982). The general managers. *Harvard Business Review, 60*(6), 156-67.

Kotter, J. P. (2014). *Accelerate: Building strategic agility for a faster-moving world*. Boston: HBR Press.

Kotter, J. P. & Schlesinger, L. A. (1979). Choosing strategies for change, *Harvard Business Review*, February–March, 106–114.

Lam, T. & Ham, M. X. J. (2005). A study of outsourcing strategy: a case involving the hotel industry in Shanghai, China, *International Journal of Hospitality Management, 24* (1), 41-56.

Lashley, C. (2011). *Hospitality retail management: A unit manager's guide*. Abingdon, UK: Routledge.

Lashley, C. & Rowson, B. (2002). A Franchise by any other name? Tenancy arrangements in the pub sector. *International Journal of Hospitality Management, 21*(4), 353-369.

Lashley, C. & Rowson, B. (2004). *The benefits of training pub retailers: Building the skills base of franchisees in the Punch Pub Company*. CAUTHE Conference proceedings. Darwin: Charles Darwin University.

Lewin, K. (1951). *Field theory in social science: Selected theoretical papers*. New York: Harper & Row.

Livermore, D. A. (2011). *The cultural intelligence difference: Master the one skill you can't do without in today's global economy*. New York: American Management Association.

Lockyer, C. & Scholarios, D. (2005). Selecting hotel staff: Why best practice does not always work. *International Journal of Contemporary Hospitality Management, 16*(2), 121–135.

Lovelock, C. & Wirtz, J. (2011). *Services marketing: People, technology, strategy* (7th ed.). Harlow: Pearson Education Limited.

Luthans, F. (1988). Successful vs. effective real managers, *The Academy of Management Executive, 11*(2), 127–32.

Martin, R. J. (1998). *Professional management of housekeeping operations* (3rd ed.). New York: John Wiley & Sons Inc.

Maslow, A. (1954). *Motivation and Personality.* New York: Harper and Row.

Mayer, J. D. & Salovey, P. (1997). What is emotional intelligence? In P. Salovey & D. Sluyter, (Eds.). *Emotional development and emotional intelligence: Educational implications* (pp 3-31). New York: Basic Books.

McShane, S. L. & Von Glinow, M. A. Y. (2010). *Organizational behavior: Emerging knowledge and practice for the real world* (5th ed.). Boston: McGraw-Hill/Irwin.

Meyer, J. P. & Allen, N. J. (1997). *Commitment in the workplace: Theory, research, and application.* Thousand Oaks: Sage Publications.

Meyer, J. P. & Allen, N. J. (2004). TCM employee commitment survey: Academic users Guide 2004. University of Western Ontario.

Meyer, J. P. Stanley, D. J., Herscovitch, L. & Topolnytsky, L. (2002). Affective, continuance and normative commitment to the organization: A meta-analysis of antecedents, correlates and consequences, *Journal of Vocational Behavior, 61*(1), 20-52.

Mintel (2004). Hotel Grading Schemes – Europe, *Travel & Tourism Analyst*, April.

Moen, R. & Norman, C. (2009). Evolution of the PDCA Cycle Proceedings of the 7th ANQ Congress Tokyo 2009, September 17, 2009 (PDF). Retrieved 28 July 2015.

Moon, H., Kamdar, D., Mayar, D. M. & Takeuchi, R. (2008). Me or we. The role of personality and justice as other centered antecedents to taking charge within organizations. *Journal of Applied Psychology, 93*(1), 84-94.

Morelli, N. (2006). Developing new PSS, methodologies and operational tools. *Journal of Cleaner Production 14*(17): 1495–1501.

Morris Brown L. (2006). Social intelligence: the new science of success, *Business Book Review™ 23* (1). Retrieved July 4 2015 from https://www.karlalbrecht.com/downloads/SocialIntelligence-BBR.pdf.

Mounts, G. B. & Meinzer, O. (2011). The hotel engineering function: Organization, people and issues in the modern era. In M. J. O'Fallon & D. G. Rutherford (Eds.), *Hotel management and operations*, 5th ed. (pp. 189-199). Hoboken: John Wiley & Sons, Inc.

Mullins, L. J. (1993). The hotel and the open systems model of organisational analysis. *The Service Industries Journal, 13* (1): 1-16.

Mullins, L. J. (2005). *Management and organisational behaviour.* Harlow: Pearson Education Limited.

Nebel, E. C. & Ghei, A. (2011). A conceptual framework of the hotel general manager's job. In M. J. O'Fallon & D. G. Rutherford (Eds.), *Hotel Management and Operations* (5th ed.) (pp. 91-100). Hoboken: John Wiley & Sons, Inc.

Ng, K.-Y. & Earley, P. C. (2006). Culture + intelligence: Old constructs, new frontiers. *Group and Organization Management, 31*(1), 4-19.

Ninemeier, J. D. & Perdue, J. (2005). *Hospitality operations: Careers in the world's greatest Industry*. Upper Saddle River: Pearson Education, Inc.

Nitschke, A. A. & Frye, W. D. (2008). *Managing housekeeping operations.* Lansing: American Hotel & Lodging Educational Institute.

O'Fallon, M. J. & Rutherford, D. G. (Ed.) (2011). *Hotel management and operations* (5th ed.). Hoboken: John Wiley & Sons, Inc.

Oakdene Hollins Research & Consulting (2013). The role of Lean thinking in increasing resource efficiency in the UK food and drink supply chain. DEFRA- UK.

Office for National Statistics (2014). Labour Force Survey.

Okumus, F. & Hemmington, N. (1998). Management of the change process in hotel companies: A new way to evaluate your strategy, *International Journal of Hospitality Management 17* (4), 363-374.

Organ, D. W., Podsakoff, P. M. & MacKenzie S. P. (2006). *Organizational citizenship behavior: Its nature, antecedents, and consequences.* London: Sage Publications.

People 1st (2014). *Return on investment of training.* London: People 1st.

Price, L. (1994). Poor personnel practice in the hotel and catering industry – does it matter? *Human Resource Management Journal, 4(4)*, 44–62.

Quinn, R. E. & Rohrbaugh, J. (1983). A spatial model of effectiveness criteria: Towards a competing values approach to organizational analysis. *Management Science, 29* (3), 363–377.

Reviere, R., Berkowitz, S., Carter, C. C. & Gergusan, C. G. (Eds.). (1996). *Needs assessment: A creative and practical guide for social scientists.* Washington: Taylor and Francis.

Rost, J. C. (1991). Leadership for the twenty-first century. West Port: Praeger Publishers.

Rowson, B. & Lashley, C. (2007). Measuring the benefits of bespoke training: The balanced scorecard approach. The 16th Annual CHME Conference, Oxford Brookes University 9th -11th May 2007.

Rushmore, S. (1993).The rise and fall of trophy hotels. *Lodging Hospitality, 49(6)*, 16.

Ryan, R. (1998). Rooms for improvement, *The Sunday Times*, 13 September.

Schein, E. H. (2004). Organizational culture and leadership, (3rd ed.). San Francisco: Jossey-Bass.

Schein, E. H. (2010). Organizational culture and leadership, (4th ed.). San Francisco: Jossey-Bass.

Schoemaker, P. J. H., Krupp, S. & Howland, S (2013). Strategic leadership: the essential skills, *Harvard Business Review*, January-February, 131-134.

Self, D. R., Armenakis, A. A. & Schraeder, M. (2007). Organizational change content , process, and context: A simultaneous analysis of employee reactions. *Journal of Change Management, 7(2)*, 211-229.

Skinner, W. (1969). Manufacturing: The missing link in corporate strategy. *Harvard Business Review 47(3)*: 136–145.

Slack N., Brandon-Jones A. & Johnston R. (2013). *Operations management* (7th ed.). Harlow: Pearson Education Limited.

Smollan, R. K. (2006). Minds, hearts and deeds: Cognitive, affective and behavioural responses to change, *Journal of Change Management, 6(2)*, 143–158.

Sun, G. (2013). A study on the continuous improvement of hotel service quality based on the PDCA cycle. In E. Qi, J. Shen, & R. Dou (Eds.), *The 19th international conference on industrial engineering and engineering management: Engineering economics management* (pp. 1151-1161). Berlin: Springer-Verlag.

Szabla, D. (2007). A multidimensional view of resistance to organizational change: across perceived change leadership strategies. *Human Resource Development Quarterly, 18(4)*, 525-558.

Tague, N. R. (2005) *The Quality Toolbox* (2nd ed.). Milwaukee: ASQ Quality Press.

Taylor, F. W. (1911). *The Principles of Scientific Management.* New York: Harper and Brothers Publishers.

Thorndike, E. L. (1920). Intelligence and its use, *Harper's Monthly Magazine, 140*, 227-235.

Tranter, K. A., Stuart-Hill, T. & Parker, J. (2009). *An introduction to revenue management for the hospitality industry: Principles and practices for the real world.* Upper Saddle River: Pearson Prentice Hall.

Tuppen, H. (2013). Water management and responsibility in hotels, www.greenhotelier.org.

UKCES (2014). Employer skills survey 2013: UK results. London: UK Commission for Employment and Skills.

Vakola, M., Tsaousis, I. & Nikolaou, I. (2004). The role of emotional intelligence and personality variables on attitudes toward organizational change. *Journal of Managerial Psychology, 19*, 88-110.

Vallen, G. K. & Vallen, J. J. (2013), *Check-in check-out: Managing hotel operations* (9th ed.). Upper Saddle River: Prentice Hall.

Van de Ven, A. H. & Poole, M. S. (1995). Explaining development and change in organizations, *Academy of Management Review, 20(3)*, 510–540.

Van der Zee, K. & Wabeke, R. (2004). Is trait emotional intelligence simply or more than just a trait? *European Journal of Personality, 18*, 243-263.

Wheelen T. L. & Hunger, J. D. (2008). *Strategic Management and Business Policy – Concepts and Cases,* (11th ed.). Upper Saddle River: Prentice Hall.

Wilson, A., Zeithaml, V. A., Bitner, M. J. & Gremler, D. D. (2012). *Service marketing: Integrating customer focus across the firm* (2nd European ed.). Maidenhead: McGraw-Hill Education.

Witkin, B. R. & Altschuld, J. W. (1995). *Planning and conducting needs assessments: A practical guide*. Thousand Oaks: Sage Publications.

Yukl, G. (1989). Managerial leadership: A review of theory and research, *Journal of Management, 15*(2), 251-289.

Zeithaml, V. A., Bitner, M. J. & Gremler, D. D. (2009). *Service marketing: Integrating customer focus across the firm* (5th ed.). New York: McGraw-Hill/Irwin.

Zeithaml, V. A., Parasuraman, A. & Berry, L. L. (1990). *Delivering quality service: Balancing customer perceptions and expectations*. New York: The Free Press.

Zigiaris, S. (2000). Innoregio: *Dissemination of innovation and knowledge management techniques*, [Report] BPR Hellas SA.

Websites

Text 1.13: www.hotelmanagement.net
Text 1.14: www.unwto.org
Text 2.1: www.travel.michelin.co.uk
Text 2.2: www.hotelstars.eu
Texts 2.3 & 2.4: www.worldhotelrating.com
Text 2.12: www.ft.com
Text 2.13: www.hotelstars.eu
Text 2.14: www.null-stern-hotel.ch
Text 2.15: www.icehotel.com
Text 2.16: www.guardian.co.uk
Text 2.17: www.aecom.com
Text 2.18: www.christianfoundationgrants.com
Text 2.19: www.managementhelp.org
Text 2.20: www.hiltonworldwide.com
Text 2.21: www.accor.com
Text 2.25: www.sleeping-around.com
Text 3.2: www.hotelmule.com
Text 3.3: www.exec2exec.com
Text 3.7: lifeofarevenuemanager.wordpress.com
Text 4.4: www.metasearchmanager.com
Text 4.13: www.lesclefsdor.org
Text 4.16: www.hotelnewsnow.com
Text 4.17: www.hotelmanagement.net
Text 4.20: www.sprinklr.com
Text 4.27: www.blycolin.com/nl
Text 4.29: www.hotelnewsnow.com
Text 5.1: www.hospitalityinstitute.nl
Text 5.4: www.kingoffruit.com.au
Texts 6.6 & 6.7: www.investorsinpeople.co.uk
Text 6.8: www.love2reward.co.uk
Text 6.10: www.reed.co.uk
Text 7.9: www.mplans.com
Text 7.11: www.guestcentric.com
Text 8.2: www.forbes.com
Text 9.8: www.hospitalitynet.org

Text 9.9: www.hawthornehotelblog.com
Text 9.10: www.hotelmanagement.net
Text 9.12: www.greenhotelier.org
Text 10.3: www.hmi-online.com
Text 10.5: www.hoteladvisor.cc
Text 12.4: www.ibdasiapac.com.au
Text 13.2: www.fpm.iastate.edu
Text 13.4: www.phonakpro.com
Text 15.2: www.businesstraveller.com
Text 15.3: www.hotelmanagement.net
Text 15.16: www.forbes.com
Text 15.17: www.mindtools.com
Text 16.2: www.hoteliermiddleeast.com
Text 16.6: www.clontarfcastle.ie
Text 16.7: www.process-improvement-japan.com
Text 16.11: www.starwoodhotels.com
Text 16.13: www.freshplaza.com
Text 16.20: jbpress.ismedia.jp

Register

© Noordhoff Uitgevers bv

Illustration acknowledgements

Picture Research: Daliz, Den Haag; Pieter de Blok, Zwolle; Editekst, Een

Photo's:
Shutterstock, New York: p. 8, 16, 19 b, 25, 27, 35, 39, 40, 48, 64, 92, 108, 149, 168 b, 169 o, 172, 173, 174, 175, 176, 177, 178, 179, 180 o, 181, 182, 184, 185, 232, 234, 240, 244, 268, 279, 334, 369, 379, 380, 404, 410, 426, 434, 452, 460, 471, 566, 572, 604
Henni van Beek / Rijksmuseum, Amsterdam: p. 18
Bernard Gagnon / Wikipedia: p. 19 o
WJ. Bennit / Boston Beheld, Boston: p. 22
Club Med, Parijs: p. 30
Shangri-La Hotel, Singapore: p. 33
Pudi Boutique Hotel in Shanghai, China: p. 34
Archief Noordhoff Uitgevers / Corel Collection: p. 38, 142, 260, 291, 356, 559
Mövenpick Hotel, Amsterdam City Centre: p. 42, 122, 128, 152, 154, 158, 224, 228, 229, 314, 337, 343, 475, 492, 504
Tourist Hotel Complex IZMAILOVO ('Gamma', 'Delta'), Moscow: p. 57
Stenden Hotel / La Verne York / Marijke de Beer / Victoria Snouck Hurgronje / Jan Bossema, Leeuwarden: p. 66, 86, 97, 120, 130, 139, 186 o, 217, 227, 350, 428, 494, 496, 501
www.icehotel.com: p. 71
Flickr / Secret Cinema, San Francisco: p. 72
Restaurant Wannee, Stenden Hotel Leeuwarden: p. 78, 196, 203, 208, 250, 272, 277, 391, 412
Thulani Xhali, Leeuwarden: p. 100
Joke Talsma & Roelien Bos, Leeuwarden: p. 106
Protel Air: p. 112, 113, 114, 115
iStockphoto, Calgery: p. 118, 164, 298, 319, 353, 367, 421, 490, 508
Daliz Ontwerp, Den Haag: p. 123
Maurice Janssen, Amsterdam: p. 132
IHG / Crown Plaza Hotel, Amsterdam: p. 133
123RF, San Fransisco: p. 135, 222
www.sprinklr.com: p. 145
blycolin, Zaltbommel: p. 154
Brenda de Zwaan, Leeuwarden: p. 168 o
Royal Collection Trust / © Her Majesty Queen Elizabeth II: p. 169 b
Photobucket, New York: p. 180 b
Ernest Lefebvre, Amsterdam: p. 183
Erik van Loo, Restaurant Parkheuvel, Rotterdam: p. 186 b
Bert Spiertz / Hollandse Hoogte, Den Haag: p. 189
HMS Host, Amsterdam: p. 190
Albert Kooy, Leeuwarden: p. 195
Maartje Nelissen, Leeuwarden: p. 197, 198, 199

NH Hotels: p. 219
Hawthorne Hotel, Salem: p. 352
Len Collection/ Alamy Stock Photo/ Image Select, Wassenaar: p. 360
Ariadne Van Zandbergen/ Hollandse Hoogte, Den Haag: p. 376
The Rezidor Hotel Group, Brussel: p. 381
Safepak Corporation: p. 386
Geoff Pugh/ REX/ Hollandse Hoogte, Den Haag: p. 388
Jen Orchard Gateway Hotel, Japan: p. 511
Ramada Hotel And Suites Ajman, United Arab Emirates: p. 570
Clontarf Castle Hotel, Dublin: p. 580

Technical drawings:
ISS Integra, Chennai, India

© Noordhoff Uitgevers bv